Hugh Johnson's
Encyclopedia of
TREES

Hugh Johnson's Encyclopedia of

TREES

Second Edition of the original International Book of Trees

Completely Revised and Expanded to include a Newly Illustrated A-Z Index of Tree Species

GALLERY BOOKS
An imprint of W. H. Smith Publishers Inc.
112 Madison Avenue
New York, New York 10016

Poplars
by Gwen Raverat

Hugh Johnson's Encyclopedia of Trees was edited and
designed by Mitchell Beazley International Limited

Editor   **Dian Taylor**
Designer   **Ruth Levy**
Editorial Assistants   **Sue McKinstry
Alison Hancock, Charles Mitchell**

Hugh Johnson's Encyclopedia of Trees
© Mitchell Beazley Publishers 1973 and 1984
Text © Hugh Johnson 1973 and 1984
Additional illustrations © Mitchell Beazley 1980 and 1984
Botanical captions in The A-Z Index of Tree Species
are based on the captions in *Trees*, a Mitchell Beazley
Nature Handbook, by Keith Rushforth,
© Mitchell Beazley Publishers 1980 and 1984

First published as *The International Book of Trees* 1973

Published in USA 1984 by
Gallery Books
An imprint of W. H. Smith Publishers Inc.
112 Madison Avenue
New York, New York 10016

ISBN 0 8317—4817—6

Printed and bound in Spain by
Printer Industria Grafica, S.A.,
Sant Vicenc dels Horts, Barcelona
D.L.B. 16759 — 1984

Contents

Foreword 7
Introduction 8

The World of Trees

How a Tree Grows 10
The Leaves 12
The Flowers 14
The Fruit 16
How a Tree Works 18
The History in a Tree 20
Roots and the Soil 22
How Trees are Named 24
Trees and the Weather 26
The Advance of Spring 28
Zones of Tree Hardiness
   in North America and Europe 30
Man and the Forest 32
The Forest Encroaches 34
Poison in the Air 36
The Ice Ages 38
The Old World 40
The New World 42
The World Expands 44
Giants and Gentility 46
Explorers in the East 48
Collectors and Creators 50

Tree Planting and Care
The Modern Nursery 52
Using Trees in Garden and Landscape:
   Choosing the Species 54
Planning for Planting 56
Trees for Shade,
   Shelter and Seclusion 58
Planting Trees 60
Maintenance 62
Pruning and other Arts 64

Guide to the World's Trees

The Conifers
Introduction 66
The Ginkgo or Maidenhair Tree 68
The Pines of North America 70
The Pines of Asia 74
The Pines of Europe 76
The Silver Firs of North America 78
The Silver Firs of Europe and Asia 80
The Douglas Fir 82
The Spruces of North America 84
The Spruces of Europe and Asia 86
The Hemlocks 88

The True Cedars 90
The Larches 92
The True Cypresses 94
The False Cypresses 98
False Cypresses
   and Leyland Cypress 100
The Thujas or Arborvitae 102
The Incense Cedars 104
The Junipers 105
The Yews 108
The Plum Yews and Podocarps 110
Swamp Cypresses
   and Dawn Redwoods 112
Giant Sequoias
   and Coast Redwoods 114
The Pacific 'Cedars' and 'Pines' 116
The Dwarf Conifers 118
The Palms 120

The Broadleaves
Introduction 124
The Tulip Tree and the Magnolias 126
The Magnolias 128
The Bays and Laurels 130
Witch Hazels, Sweetgums
   and Parrotias 132
The Planes 134
The Elms 136
The Elms of Europe and America 138
The Zelkovas and Hackberries 140
The Figs and Mulberries 142
The Walnuts 144
Hickories and Wingnuts 146
The Beeches 148
The Southern Beeches 152
The Oaks 154
The Oaks of Europe and Asia 156
The Oaks of North America 158
The Chestnuts 162
The Birches 164
The Alders 168
The Hornbeams and Hazels 170
The Trees of the Tea Family 172
Limes, Lindens or Basswoods 174
The Willows 176
Poplars, Cottonwoods and Aspens 180
Heather and Strawberry Trees 184
The Rhododendrons 186
Persimmons, Silverbells
   and Snowbells 188
Roses, Shadblows, Mespilus and
   Cotoneaster 190
The Hawthorns 192

Quinces, Medlars
   and Crab-Apples 194
The Crab-Apples 196
The Flowering Cherries of Japan 198
The Flowering Cherries 200
Peaches, Plums
   and Cherry Laurels 202
Pear Trees, Whitebeams and
   Mountain Ashes 204
Locusts and False Acacias 208
Laburnum, Redbuds
   and the Silk Tree 210
The Eucalypts or Gum Trees 212
Eucalypts, Silk Oak, Fire-bush and
   Oleasters 214
The Dogwoods 216
Dove Trees and Black Gums 218
The Hollies 220
Holly and Box 222
Horse Chestnuts and Buckeyes 224
The Maples of North America 226
The Maples of the East 230
The Maples of Europe 232
Cashews and Sumachs 234
The Citrus Trees 236
The Ashes of North America
   and Europe 238
Olives and Fringe-Trees 240
The Tree of Heaven
   and the Cedrelas 242
Empress Trees and Indian Beans 244
The Elders 246

Reference Section

Illustrated A-Z Index
   of Tree Species 247
Urban, Pastoral,
   Classical, Romantic 312
Natural Forest Vegetation 314
A Twelve-Month Succession of
   Ornamental Flowers, Fruit
   and Foliage 316
A Chart of Tree Discoveries 318
Tree Pests and Diseases 320
Rates of Tree Growth 322
A Guide to Choosing Trees 326
The Meanings of Botanical Names 328
General Index 332
Acknowledgments 336

Foreword

to original edition
by Sir George Taylor
D.Sc., F.R.S., Ll.D., F.R.S.E., V.M.H.,
Former Director of the Royal Botanic Gardens, Kew

People are planting more trees, and care more about trees, than ever before. The spread of urban blight and ugliness and the new ecological awareness have prompted many of us to see in trees the best and surest living antidote to the despoliation of our towns, and there is a growing appreciation of the countryside to which we all endeavour to escape.

But how to find out more about trees? During my 15 years as Director of the Royal Botanic Gardens at Kew I realized that there was a significant gap in the popular literature about them. There are scientific books and papers and a plethora of works for the specialist, particularly the aboriculturist and the gardener; very rewarding but in many cases not always easy in their application. And there is the sentimental approach; sympathetic but somewhat unhelpful. Everyman's tree book, which did justice to this complex and enthralling subject, didn't seem to exist.

This is why I feel that Hugh Johnson's timely book is likely to become a familiar and much-consulted work for many, many readers throughout the temperate regions of the world. It is just what is needed: the work of a talented writer well-versed in the subject without being fully immersed; one who can see it from an outsider's point of view. I have been impressed by its comprehensiveness, pleased to find it so full of accurate information, and truly delighted to see a subject which has preoccupied much of my life made so fresh and such fun.

Hugh Johnson has travelled widely and delved deeply in quest of trees and tree lore and he writes without prejudice or inhibition, eager to share his vivid enjoyment and remarkable understanding. If you start reading his book with a feeling for trees I don't see how you can finish it without loving them.

George Taylor

Introduction

A traveller should be a botanist, for in all views plants form the chief embellishment –

Charles Darwin

I remember a before-and-after sequence of two photographs in *Time* magazine. Before: main street in some New England town; all harmony; comely cream clapboard dappled with light from the crowns of an avenue of tremendous elms. After: the elms gone; comeliness has become nakedness. What was all proportion and peace is desolate.

Darwin could have been more specific. Not of all landscapes, but of most, he could have said 'trees form the chief embellishment'. Of all plants they are the most prominent and the most permanent, the ones that set the scene and dictate the atmosphere.

This is the aspect of trees that I have written a book about. I have not harped on the value of trees as creators of the air we breathe, or as our most versatile and universal raw material. Nobody is in any doubt today about the necessity of trees to keep our planet in being.

My aim in this book is to bring trees into focus for everybody like myself, who was aware of trees, loved trees, but in a way so vague that it now seems to me quite shameful. It is a personal account. I am not a botanist, nor a forester, nor even (except in my own garden) a gardener, but a writer who has found in trees a new point of contact with creation, a source of wonder and satisfaction which has the inestimable advantage of growing almost everywhere.

What I hope this book does is to make vivid through words and pictures the essential differences between the great groups of trees, to tell their story, and then go on to enjoy the pleasures of their subtly, elaborately, almost endlessly varying designs – the

species and varieties of familiar families from all over the temperate world.

A theme with countless variations is a never-ending source of pleasure. It is true of wine: it is even more true of trees. The theme is simply a plant with a trunk, branches, twigs, leaves. Yet think of a giant elm, and think of a cherry, stooping with soft flowers – and think of a resiny old fir crusted with lichen. Can anything make a more fascinating collection? For once possession is not the point. Trees are wonderfully public property. Wherever you go you are enjoying somebody's trees: and not a penny changes hands.

I have tried not to be pedantic about what is or isn't a tree. There is a classic definition. It calls for a woody plant (capable of) growing 20 feet high and tending to a single stem (though it may have more). What do you do, though, if the thing is single-stemmed as can be, palpably tree-like and permanent, but has never grown over ten feet? Or what do you do if it is 30 feet high but hopelessly and incurably bushy?

My answer has tended to be inclusive rather than exclusive. It is one of the wonders of the subject that the first cousin of a 200-foot mammoth can be a two-foot pigmy. And the relationship adds enormously to the pleasure of growing the pigmy – which is all most people have room for.

Lionel de Rothschild, one of the world's greatest growers of rhododendrons, was once lecturing a city gardening club. 'Gentlemen', he began, 'no garden, however small, should be without its two acres of rough woodland.' For most of the human race those must be two acres of the mind. But what pleasure there is, and how much to be learned about our place in God's universe, in going about them observantly, equipped with even a little knowledge.

I could not possibly have written this book without the extraordinary generosity and enthusiasm of the lifelong professional

plantsmen who have been at my elbow to answer my questions and curb my too sweeping conclusions. Sir George Taylor I must thank first, for giving me the confidence to get started. Alan Mitchell of the Forestry Commission has not spared himself nor his incredible store of information. Ken Beckett, former Technical Editor of the Gardener's Chronicle, Roy Lancaster, the curator of Hillier's arboretum in Hampshire, and Oscar Traczewitz, head forester of the International Paper Company, have answered innumerable questions and put me right countless times. Dame Sylvia Crowe, past President of the Institute of Landscape Architects, was good enough to read my chapters on the use of trees in the garden and landscape and make valuable suggestions. The Librarians of the Royal Botanic Gardens at Kew, the Royal Horticultural Society and the Cambridge University Library have been exceptionally helpful. Well over a hundred photographers have been involved. Among them all I must single out one of the world's remarkable amateurs, Dick van Hoey Smith; himself the owner of a famous arboretum, Trompenburg, in Rotterdam. Nearly 150 of the pictures of rarer trees in this book are his.

This second edition, enlarged by 48 pages, has enabled us to illustrate the Index of Tree Species with more than 150 paintings, including details invaluable for recognition, and to add particulars of an extra 100 species and varieties of trees of notable interest to gardeners. For compiling the up-to-date and realistic list of trees that are truly scarce in cultivation, I am deeply grateful to Michael Lear of the National Trust, who has surveyed the tree collections of the National Trust in Britain.

Opposite
Hugh Johnson in his garden in Essex.

How a Tree Grows

It is winter—the time of drought and dormancy in the plant world. The herbs have taken refuge beneath the soil. Grass and the daisies and violets crouch low, hoping for a covering of snow to protect them from the drying wind. Yet far above the trees sail in the scudding clouds; invulnerable; asleep.

What distinguishes a tree from all other plants is the wooden structure it raises above the ground. By annual additions it builds a tall scaffold on which to hang its leaves, its flowers and its fruit. Each new year's growth is no more than a crop of twigs. Yet those twigs contain in essence the identity of the tree: in time they become branches; eventually perhaps huge limbs. In the winter tower of tracery you can still detect the way the buds formed along the first frail shoots.

Each year's shoot springs from a bud, and ends by forming new buds. The buds are the resting stage common to most trees of the temperate world, where day-length and temperature sharply differentiate the seasons. Each contains in miniature a whole new shoot—either of twig and leaves or of flowers. Even before the shoot of the current year has reached its final size the next year's buds are brewing. By June or July they are complete—even though the embryo growth they hold will not appear until the following March or April. So it was last year's spring that determined the extent of this year's growth.

One bud on each shoot is different from the rest. It is the bud farthest from the tree's roots—the last on the limb: the leader. The nearer this bud is to a vertical position over the centre of the tree the more marked its dominance will be. The force of gravity, you might say, is its authority. It is able to assert its dominance through the agency of hormones. It forms the hormone auxin in its growing tip; gravity distributes it to the buds lying behind. Auxin has the effect of moderating vigour—leaving more of the available sap for the leader to use in in-creasing its lead, and in forming the biggest of the buds, the one that will be dominant next year.

This is the plan for a tree with the simplest construction—for example a spruce. In a broadleaf tree the same chemistry applies—but soon to a number of leaders as the tree's crown widens out.

Meanwhile what of the other buds, the ones that are being deprived? The shoots they produce are shorter, with a different function. They are the leaf and flower bearers. Their role is to fill out the canopy of the tree to take advantage of all the light, or to carry the flowers and fruit.

Take away the leader, however, and the auxin-making function is inherited by the next shoot down: one that would otherwise have remained in subjection; perhaps a spur with a few leaves. A new leader is born.

The buds are many, but they are not formed at random. They stick to the characteristic pattern of the species, which is the

Below *Part of a ginkgo twig with a short (or spur) shoot, which grows only a millimetre a year, enough to form new buds for leaves and flowers.*

Left *A section of a trunk showing how even 'suppressed' buds which are held in reserve in case the leader is lost grow outwards each year just enough to keep pace with the annual growth-ring. The lower left bud on the trunk is totally suppressed. The one above it has formed a short shoot like the ginkgo's (above). On the right a mature branch has been lost but a* *suppressed bud from when it was much younger has kept up with the thickening of the trunk round it and will probably break to make a new shoot.*

Below *Some of the buds formed two years ago in the angles of the leaves are still suppressed. The horse-shoe scar under the bud, where the leaf stood, still shows rings where its veins were attached.*

A three-year-old twig of horse chestnut shows three annual growth-rings. Its centre is still pith, which disappears with age.

Above *Two years ago the big sticky terminal bud was here—scales from the scars are still visible. The leader's hormones deprived the side-buds of vigour. They have grown only slightly in two years; in time they will probably be shaded out and drop off.*

Right *There are three possible budding and branching patterns: alternate (one bud at a time: left) opposite (two at a time: centre) and whorled (three or more: right).*

Above *Where a leading shoot with its power of dominating and suppressing the lower branches is broken its function is inherited by the stronger side-shoot just behind it. The process is easiest to watch in conifers like the spruce* *above. As soon as a side-branch takes over to grow upright it changes its own budding and branching pattern. Instead of producing only side-shoots in one plane it starts branching all round in whorls.*

A cross-section of a bud (far left) shows the shoot and all its leaves ready formed. They are complete by mid-summer of the year before they appear. Beside it is the flower bud of the same plant, the common lilac. Here the whole flower-structure with scores of little flowers, also ready formed, is packed within scales that are modified leaves.

Logically you would expect the final tree to consist of all its annual increments: to be able to count all the annual shoots since it was a seedling. Up to a certain age most conifers (which make a single whorl or tier of branches every year) allow you to do this. Some poplars and alders do the same. But with most broadleaf trees the scent quickly gets cold.

One thing that simplifies it is the death-rate among twigs. Most of the older side-shoots are disposed of in this way. In ten years, if a branch produced and kept only two side-shoots a year, the total number would be 19,683. In fact the count on a ten-year-old birch was 238. As the tree moves on beyond them, casting them into shade, they simply drop off.

What complicates it are the external influences forcing or persuading the tree to take up a certain attitude. Of these gravity, light and wind are the most important.

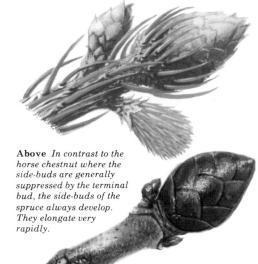

Above In contrast to the horse chestnut where the side-buds are generally suppressed by the terminal bud, the side-buds of the spruce always develop. They elongate very rapidly.

same as the arrangement of its leaves. Each bud forms in the angle which a leaf makes with the twig.

The tree's ultimate aim is to form a head which will give it the maximum exposure to the light. In the forest all the light is overhead: side-branches are shaded out and die: nothing but a narrow crown of up-reared branches can reach the light amid the press of other trees. But in the open field a tree builds up its head in its own characteristic way. There is no mistaking the tall fan of the elm or the oak's zigzag rhythm.

The two-year-old section of the twig (below) lies between two rings of old bud-scars. One of the buds has developed into the one-year-old side-shoot; the other remains suppressed.

Last year's growth started at the bud-scars (left). Each succeeding pair of leaves and side-buds is at right angles to the one before.

There are no side-shoots yet on the one-year-old twig, but buds are ready just above where the old leaves fell. One or both of the buds above left will shoot and bear leaves this year. The surface of the twig is marked with breathing pores ('lenticels') to supplement the activity of the leaves.

Above The sticky bud which contains the coming year's new shoot, enclosed in scales which are themselves a form of leaf and covered with protective resin (more common in conifers than broadleaves). Unless the main shoot is destroyed its side-buds will probably get no farther than the little shoots on the far left.

The tree's mature shape is characteristic of the way it has branched all its life, subject to its habit of shedding unnecessary branches and to the effects of the elements.

An oak (above) starts with a distinct main stem, but by the age of 20 it is already hard to say which is the leading shoot. Dominance is shared by all the main branches that can reach the light. The crown soon becomes and

remains rounded to expose the maximum leaf-area. Most oaks grow on from a side bud. Hence their restless zig-zag pattern of branches.

A pine at 12 years (small tree above) is a pyramid of almost-regular whorls of branches: one whorl for each year of its life. As it grows it gradually shades out and kills its own lower branches. Much later in life than the oak it starts to spread:

the leader loses dominance and the upper branches compete, making a broad crown.

A willow is a prolific producer and shedder of twigs all its (comparatively short) life. Every new twig is at an acute angle

to its parent and hence reaches as far into the light and competes strongly with it. It is easy to see the big tree as an extended version of the little one, and both as an extended much-twigged branch.

The Leaves

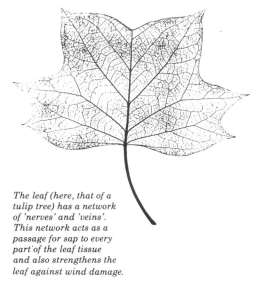

The leaf (here, that of a tulip tree) has a network of 'nerves' and 'veins'. This network acts as a passage for sap to every part of the leaf tissue and also strengthens the leaf against wind damage.

The permanent wooden structure is peculiar to trees. The temporary organs that clothe it—the leaves, the flowers and fruit—are not. Their functions are the same as in every other plant.

The leaf has the task of collecting food. Ninety per cent of the solid matter that makes up the trunk, the branches and the roots themselves is carbohydrates plucked, as it were, out of the sky by the feeding leaves. A leaf becomes self-supporting remarkably quickly. Before it is even half-grown it has started exporting nourishment to the rest of the tree.

Leaves get nourishment out of both the air and the ground. They do the first by photosynthesis: they hold up to the sunlight delicate vessels impregnated with chlorophyll and filled with water. The chlorophyll causes an exchange of hydrogen (from the water) with carbon and oxygen (from the carbon dioxide in the atmosphere). Carbon is the tree's chief food: from it it can make

the sugars and starches it needs.

The leaves are extremely effective evaporating plants; very nearly as efficient as an open water surface like a pond. Their turnover of water is far greater than photosynthesis demands. It is responsible for the whole circulation of sap round the tree. As the leaves lose water to the air they draw it up through the twigs, the branches and the trunk out of the roots, and ultimately out of the soil, below them. With the water, which can be as much as two or three hundred gallons a day in summer, they draw dissolved minerals from the soil. This is the tree's secondary source of solid supplies—and also of course its whole system of getting the supplies to where they are needed.

Leaves have a short life—perhaps six months on the average. The longest any leaf hangs on a tree is seven or eight years (on certain firs). But most leaves, even of 'evergreen' trees, fall and are replaced every year. Evergreen leaves can simply be defined as leaves that are adapted to survive the winter. The adaptation consists of a more miserly evaporation system: a thicker skin, generally a simpler shape (since the longer the margin of any surface in relation to its area the more water vapour will 'flow off' it), and very often a coating of wax, giving the leaves a bluish cast, into the bargain.

The only thing that can be said about leaf shape is that in itself it can't be very important: so many variants arise from tree to tree of the same species, and even from branch to branch and twig to twig. Most broadleaf trees have produced versions with 'cut' leaves—leaves with jagged, deeply embayed margins. Many conifers (see pages 118–9) have congested or otherwise eccentric varieties. They seem to make no difference to the tree's functioning.

Leaf colours can vary within species almost as much. A red pigment overlaying the green of the chlorophyll gives a 'copper' effect. Sometimes a low level of chlorophyll makes the leaves yellow or golden. But lack

of chlorophyll means less photosynthesis and hence less food: yellow trees are slower-growing.

The last act for many leaves is the most colourful. It is their function, before they die, to convert starch into sugar which the tree can store as reserve supplies. But cold nights prevent them passing on to the tree the sugar they have made, so it builds up in the leaf tissue. In many leaves the result is a red pigment. As the chlorophyll is decomposing at the same time, whatever pigment the leaf contains (in such cases red, but usually yellow) is no longer masked by green: its chrysanthemum colours emerge.

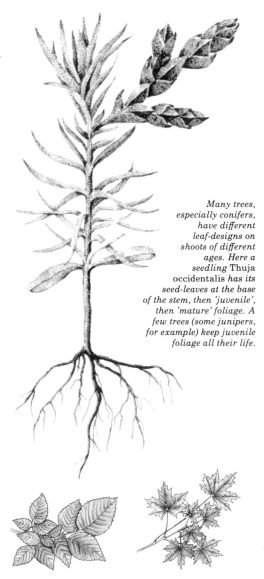

Many trees, especially conifers, have different leaf-designs on shoots of different ages. Here a seedling Thuja occidentalis has its seed-leaves at the base of the stem, then 'juvenile', then 'mature' foliage. A few trees (some junipers, for example) keep juvenile foliage all their life.

Leaves tightly packed in the bud begin to expand with the arrival of spring. Once expanded the leaves draw the sap up the trunk of the tree. The force which makes the sap rise to swell the leaves remains a mystery.

Here the swelling of the leaves of a horse chestnut forces the enfolding bud-scales (themselves a modified form of leaf) to hinge back. Once clear of the bud-scales the leaves, already fully formed, unfold (see pages 224–5).

It takes infinite subtle adjustments of shoot- and stalk-length and -angle (and also of leaf-size) to make the best use of the light (and thereby ensure the maximum photosynthesis). Beech (above left) is particularly

effective at making an almost unbroken mosaic of leaves which casts deep shade. Some maple leaves (above right) have to grow stalks as long as themselves to manoeuvre into the light.

Deciduous leaves are either 'simple'–i.e. the blade is in one piece–or 'compound'–i.e. composed of a number of separate leaflets.

The leaf is the tree's feeding and breathing organ. Below right are the deciduous (i.e. one-season only) leaf of an oak and the evergreen leaves or needles of a pine. Evergreen leaves, designed to survive a winter when water is more or less unobtainable, usually have a much smaller area than deciduous leaves. The total leaf area of a typical conifer is one quarter that of a broadleaf tree the same size. A big oak has some 250,000 leaves. The stalk gives them mobility, which helps them survive gales. Points and lobes make rain-water run off quickly. The upper side of the leaf has a waxy cuticle to prevent excessive transpiration. The lower side has minute hairs to keep water from coating the surface. Water prevents the proper function of the breathing pores and encourages fungal infection.

The elm's is an example of a simple leaf with a serrated edge.

Most conifers have needle leaves (though many such as Thuja and cypress have tiny 'scale' leaves).

Maple leaves are described as 'palmate', from the palm of a hand.

Horse chestnut has 'compound' leaves in a 'palmate' pattern.

The commonest compound leaf-form is 'pinnate', from the Latin for feather.

Below left *The magnified cross-section of a leaf shows its cell-structure. On the upper surface the cuticle; then a clear layer of epidermis cells; then a layer of 'palisade' cells full of chlorophyll, through which run the veins; then a spongy layer in which a further set of cells containing chlorophyll float in contact with the carbon dioxide imbibed through the breathing pores in the lower epidermis. Each pore is closed by a ring of two guard-cells; this becomes flaccid when sap is in short supply, but stiffens like an inflatable lifebuoy and opens the hole when water is available.*

Open breathing pore

Hydrogen 6.2%	Carbon 43.5%
Nitrogen 1.5%	Oxygen 44.4%
Potassium 0.9%	Other minerals 3.5%

Deciduous leaves fall when cells break down in the area known as the 'abscission layer' between leafstalk and twig. Later a layer of cork forms over the wound producing a leaf-scar. Some leaves (e.g. of young beech) fail to form such a layer. They die but cannot break off, so they hang dead on the tree until new leaves push them off in spring.

Cold autumn nights prevent the passage of sugar from the leaves to other parts of the tree. The resulting build-up of sugar leads to brilliant colours.

Evergreen conifer needles (those of a 'five-needled' pine, above) have a harder cuticle and often a thicker layer of wax to slow down their transpiration– essential in winter in northern zones because of the lack of water. Their breathing pores are concentrated in lines, often white with ac-cumulated wax, usually on the underside (or inner side where needles are bunched together).

Above *Between 80 and 90 per cent of the bulk of a living tree is water drawn from the ground by the roots. Of the remaining 10 to 20 per cent no less than 91 per cent is derived from the atmosphere by the leaves, which are thus the tree's main* feeding organs, collecting all the carbon and oxygen the tree needs. Apart from water, with its all important supply of hydro-gen, the roots provide nitrogen, potassium, calcium, phosphorus sulphur, iron and magnesium.

13

The Flowers

It is always hard not to fall into the trap of anthropomorphism – in other words of attributing to inanimate objects our own feelings and motives. It is specially hard when you come to talk about sex. Why, we are bound to ask, do plants have to go through the whole risky business of sexual reproduction, entrusting their seed to the elements, or to insects, when it can give them no pleasure and must enormously reduce the chances of successfully reproducing at all?

Most plants, after all, can reproduce themselves by other means: either by sending out suckers from the root, or forming new roots on a side branch in contact with the ground, or just detaching a piece to start a new life on its own. A few depend on such means: their sexual system has broken down and their seeds are never fertile. Yet all plants have some arrangements for mixing their own characteristics with others of their kind. It is a prerequisite of evolution: a genetic lottery where a new combination may make a superior product.

And strange to say (anthropomorphism creeping in again) it is when they feel their life in danger, either through old age or because nutrition is lacking, that they make the most efforts at reproduction and produce the most flowers. Richly-manured orchards bear little fruit. Big flower (and fruit) years follow sunny and dry summers, when nutrients (except carbohydrates from the sun) are in short supply.

Flowers are the plant's sex organs. They exist to exchange genes (and hence characteristics) with neighbours of the same species. Chancy as it obviously is to try to establish physical contact between a speck of dust on one tree and a minute egg on another, this is what they have to achieve.

There are as many forms of flowers as there are plants. Indeed our system of classifying and naming plants is largely based on flower designs. There is such a thing as a 'perfect' flower. In it both sexes are present, which should make things much

Above *Pollen grains of Korean fir magnified 40 times, showing the two balloon-like compartments that help them float on air.*

Left *Pollen designs. From left to right: holly magnified 800 times, birch and ash both magnified 1,200 times.*

Above *Flowers of the Kanzan cherry are 'perfect', having both male and female parts, although they are 'semi-double' (i.e. with several rings of petals). Many 'double' flowers sacrifice their sexual parts for petals.*

Below *Conifers strictly speaking don't have flowers, though the function of their 'strobili' is the same. At the shoot-tip on the left are female strobili of lodgepole pine and clustering on the right are male ones. The females eventually develop into cones.*

The diagram below shows how the characters of the parents of a hybrid, though blended in the first generation of the cross (e.g. red and white flowers producing a pink offspring) are still retained as possibilities in the hybrid's genetic makeup. The first cross (F1) gets half its chromosomes from each parent. But it can *make red- or white-flower pollen and ovules. These have four possibilities for recombination (F2); two of them pink, two like the original parents. The offspring of the second cross (F3) will be white, pink and red. The white and red have reverted to the parental colour; only the pink shows its hybrid parentage.*

The two main agencies of pollination (i.e. of conveying pollen from one tree to another) are insects like the bee (top) which are attracted to the flower by nectar created for the purpose, and the *wind; in the lower picture pollen is being dispersed by the wind from the male 'flowers' of a Scots pine. The 'flowers' or strobili are usually crowded on shoots near the bottom of the tree.*

Catkins are a common form of tree-flower. The alder, shown here, has separate male long catkins and female short ones on the same tree. The latter are strangely analogous in appearance to those of a conifer.

easier. However (in the words of C. C. Sprengel, who in 1793 discovered the relationship between flowers and insects) 'Nature wishes crossing to occur'. All sorts of checks and barriers are built in to see that a flower does not fertilize itself. The pollen ripens at a different time from the ovule. Often the pollen is incompatible with its own tree's ovules. Or if by any chance they do couple the self-fertilized flower often falls off the tree before it can become a fruit.

What the flower hopes for (so to speak) is a fine breezy day for the pollen to be carried away in a golden shower to the next tree. And for the tree to windward to oblige with a similar gilding.

Wind pollination tends to be the rule for forest trees. Their flowers, in consequence, are nothing much to look at and have no smell. Trees that need to attract insects to carry their pollen (which are often the trees of the open ground at the forest edge) go in for more elaborate designs. They are the cherries, the magnolias, the willows, and all the chief ornaments of our gardens.

Most forest trees, in fact, have separate flowers for each sex (some for pollen, others for ovules) but have both types of flower on every tree. This is true, too, of all the conifers except the yew and its allies, *Araucaria*, and juniper which have separate

all-male and all-female trees. But most ornamental trees have both sexes in each flower.

To speak of conifers in terms of flowers is not strictly correct. Their female organs are called strobili. They tend to be on the upper branches, while their pollen organs are on the lower: a simple precaution against the pollen falling too easily on to the ovules of the same tree.

Flowers enable the forester or the nurseryman to combine characteristics he likes in two different trees by making a hybrid. The trees have to be genetically very close. He can no more cross a willow and an oak than a dog and a cat. But if he sees, say, two beautiful pines, one taller and the other straighter than all the rest, he can ensure the pollination of one by the other. He puts a bag over the branch-end carrying the female strobili before they are mature, and injects into the bag pollen from the other tree. With luck the pine trees from the resulting seeds will be both tall and straight.

In the nursery business crossing has given us many of our most useful garden trees. There remain, I should perhaps add, gardeners who believe no hybrid can have the grace and perfection of a natural species. It is too late to introduce them to C. C. Sprengel.

Left *An example of a hybrid camellia in which the sexual parts have been converted into more petals. Cuttings are the only way of propagating sterile forms like this.*

Left *The 'perfect' flower of Magnolia × soulangiana. The primitive race of magnolias all have 'perfect' flowers containing the organs of both sexes.*

P   Sporophytic cells

F1   Possible sexual cells of the hybrid

F2

F3

The Fruit

The fruit of a broadleaf tree (or any flowering plant) is the female part of the flower – the ovary, with the ovule inside – fertilized and grown to ripeness. The ovule becomes the seed; the ovary the seed's covering. Taking the peach as an example, the ovule is the kernel of the stone, the ovary is its shell. Round it is a fleshy covering which is a development not of the flower itself, but of the stem just below it.

Conifers are technically quite different. Their ovules never have ovaries; the kernel has no shell. They may, however, (as juniper berries do) have a fleshy covering; again derived, like the peach's flesh, from their former stalks.

Fruit always has one simple purpose: to put as much distance as possible between itself and its parent tree. Some of nature's most inventive adaptations come into play to persuade the birds, the beasts and the elements to cooperate.

When a tree clothes its seed in a substantial parcel of sweet flesh, as plums for example do, it is sacrificing a great deal of hard-won starch to make sure of interesting the birds. Come to that the flowers alone, put out to attract insects, use a fair quantity. Someone calculated that the 200,000 flowers on one cherry tree used 25 pounds of starch.

Almost all fruit serves simply to feed animals. Yet so big and so long-lived are the forest-trees that if one in a hundred of the acorns produced escapes being eaten, and one in a hundred of these germinates, and one in a hundred of the seedlings survives to make a mature acorn-bearing oak, the oak population will remain the same.

Most seed ripens in the autumn – conifer seed in the second autumn after its fertilization. It is designed to spend the winter dormant either on the tree or on the ground; then to germinate the following spring. Winter cold is actually necessary to activate it and break its dormancy: a precaution against it germinating as soon as it falls only to be killed by the ensuing cold weather. When the gardener exposes his seed to cold and damp he calls it 'stratifying'. Seeds have been known to stay dormant for 1,000 years.

In the ripe seed there are the beginnings of a little root and a tiny shoot, with one or more seed-leaves which act as storage organs for food and usually as the first operating leaves of the new plant. These are the cotyledons, whose rather obscure influence pervades the whole world of plant classification. Trees with two or more cotyledons produce wood in concentric rings: the classic tree pattern. Trees with only one grow as a cluster of fibrous bundles that gets longer but not fatter. The great 'Monocot' is the palm.

This engraving of the common mountain ash of Europe, or rowan, with its heavy trusses of scarlet berries, was made in Venice in 1565 by Petrus Andreas Mathiolus. His superb illustrations were re-used time and again in early herbals.

Above *Alders in nature are waterside trees: their seeds (released from fruit very like cones) are equipped with tiny bladders full of air which float them off downstream to a damp place to germinate.*

Below *The 'keys' of the maple family rely on aerodynamics to make them flutter and spin far enough from the parent tree to make propagation possible.*

Below *Thousands of broadleaf species have their seeds distributed by birds who feed on their berries: it is an unusual adaptation for conifers. The thrush (shown here) feeds on yew berries for their fleshy coating; the poisonous seed passes through the digestive system unaffected.*

Above *In hoarding acorns for winter feed, squirrels inevitably lose some in the ground so that they are effectually planted. Jays— particularly greedy and forgetful—are also one of the oak's best friends.*

Above *Poplars and willows produce very light seeds with a little sail of cottony fluff which catches the wind and can carry them for miles. This is probably the most effective of all means of distribution.*

Below *A few species like the witch hazel have contrived a spring mechanism to catapult their seeds into open ground, often as much as 40 feet away from the parent tree.*

Below *Four stages in germination—the progress from seed to seedling. First, usually in the spring after the seed has been sown, the root-tip splits the outer covering of the seed. The tiny seed-leaves (or*

cotyledons) are fully developed at this stage, but remain in the seed husk.

There is enough fuel stored in the seed to power the rootlet until, guided by gravity, it has turned downwards and

buried its tip in the earth. From that moment it can supplement the seed's supplies and provide energy for the seed-leaves to swell up and emerge.

The final stage in germination is reached when the stem of the

seedling straightens and the seed-leaves fan out and start the process of photosynthesis. Now the tiny bud in their midst will swell to produce the stem and first true leaves of the new tree.

How a Tree Works

The heart of a tree is dead. All its life goes on just under the surface, in a band of cells no thicker than a film that separates the bark from the wood. If you scratch through the bark of any living twig you will find a thin green layer. Immediately within this lies the cambium (from the Latin for 'exchange'). Only the cambium has the power of making new wood. If you destroy a band of it round the trunk the tree dies.

It is the remarkable power of the cambium layer to make three different kinds of new cells at once. Every year it deposits new wood cells on its inner side, thickening the trunk of the tree. So it has to grow itself, to surround the increased bulk. It also has to keep adding 'phloem', or inner bark, to keep up with the expanding circumference.

Within this narrow zone of bark, cambium and the new outer ring of wood, the tree's whole circulation system functions. The sap goes up in the new wood, and comes down in the phloem. So much has been known for centuries through the simple experiment of girdling. If you strip a ring of bark off a tree (leaving the cambium intact) the top continues to get its water supply: what suffers is the roots. The water coming down from the leaves with its store of carbohydrates, the product of photosynthesis, fails

to reach them. They lose their ability to grow and exploit new ground: eventually the whole tree lacks its ration of minerals and nitrogen from the soil, and dies.

It is still a matter for wonder how frail leaves, transpiring as much as 300 feet or even more above the ground, can have the power to pull a column of water up that distance to supply themselves. It used to be thought that the roots pushed it up – which is, of course, equally mysterious. Now it is known that the roots have some pushing power in spring, before there are leaves to pull, but that leaves are perfectly capable of this feat of suction. What makes it possible is the cellular structure of the wood, which takes the fullest advantage of the principle of surface-tension. Water particles are highly mobile, but they are reluctant to part company with each other. It is almost as hard to tear them apart as it is to compress them. So if you pull one end of a long thin stream, the rest has the strength to hang on and follow.

A wood structure with longer cells that made the passage of sap more efficient was one of the evolutionary improvements on the ancient conifers that the newer broadleaves made. There is a simple experiment you can do to compare the two. If you strip a small vertical piece of bark off a tree and

stab the bare wood across the fibres with a penknife, a white mark above and below the cut shows where the air has filled the cells. On a broadleaf tree the mark is much longer than it is on a conifer.

The price for having bigger cells, though, is the danger of air bubbles in the sapstream breaking the flow. Ice creates the problem. When water freezes (as sap obviously does in trees in a very cold winter) air dissolved in it forms bubbles. In small cells (as in conifers) they simply disappear when the sap thaws. But what happens in bigger ones? The water columns, once ruptured, might never be restored.

What has only recently been discovered is that most of the sap in broadleaves rises in the ring of wood made that very year. The sap need not rely even on the previous year's wood to give it a passage upwards, so efficient is the cambium at making new wood in the spring before the leaves have started drawing the sap up. 'This fabulous efficiency'–I quote Zimmermann and Brown's *Trees: Structure and Function*– 'takes place at the expense of safety.' It was the downfall of the American chestnut and may well be of the elm: the fungi that kill both do so by blocking the current year's wood cells, and with them the main stream of sap.

Girdling→

The circulation of sap (that is, water containing food) is shown in the diagram left. The red lines and arrows indicate water (drawn from the ground by the roots) moving upwards in the outermost layers of wood to the leaves. Most of this water is lost to the air by evaporation from the leaves. The blue lines and arrows are the sap on its downward journey in the inner layer of the bark, outside the cambium (see opposite). This pattern of circulation was discovered by removing the bark or 'girdling' and finding that it was the roots that were thus deprived of nourishment, not the tree above.

A magnified section of an annual ring of wood shows the long vertical cells in which the sap moves up the trunk, crossed at right angles in places by 'rays' of shorter cells. 'Rays' are used for conveying reserve supplies across the tree

to where they are needed. Where the vertical cells appear to be interrupted they are simply hidden by ray-cells. The only breaks in the tubes are the perforated cell ends, which help to support unbroken a column of water sometimes over 300 feet high. A

comparison between 'early wood', which the tree makes in spring, and 'late wood', which it makes in summer, would show that early wood tube-cells are much bigger, having much more water to carry to the developing leaves, shoots and flowers. The difference in cell size gives the characteristic lighter and darker shading of annual rings.

The texture of the bark is largely decided by the bark or cork cambium. In many trees it grows in shallow overlapping arcs; the bark eventually (left) cracks at their edges as the trunk swells. In others (right, eucalyptus) it forms a thin peeling sheath near the surface, which is constantly renewed.

This cross-section of a tree trunk breaks it down into five principal concentric layers: bark, inner bark or phloem, cambium, sapwood and heartwood.

The bark (1) is a protective layer, sometimes (as on birches) a mere skin but on some trees (redwoods, for example) as much as a foot thick. This outer bark is continually being produced by its own specialised cambium. The photographs (above) show how the position of this cambium determines whether the bark peels or cracks.

The inner bark or phloem (2) is a spongy layer providing an easy downward passage for the sap. The sap carries sugar from the leaves to feed new wood cells and supply the roots with energy.

If the cambium layer (3) could be detached (as here) from the bark and wood it would be practically invisible, being only one cell thick. Yet the power of the tree to live and grow is contained in this infinitesimal film. The cambium is continually producing on its inner side wood (xylem) cells and on its outer phloem cells.

Sapwood (4) is all the wood that still functions; it carries sap up the tree, stores nutrients, or transports them from one part of the tree to another. Most sap flows in the new ring of wood made in the current year (see next page for a discussion of annual rings). If this is blocked, as it is by such fungus infections as Dutch elm disease, the tree may die; the older rings cannot keep it alive on their own.

The heartwood (5) is dead. It is a receptacle for the tree's waste matter, which makes it toxic to most organisms that might feed on it (and also darkens it). Yet if air reaches the dead heart of a tree it soon decays and leaves the tree hollow. The only function of heartwood is to give the tree strength and rigidity. It has not been explained how a tree can bend its dead heartwood in order to reach out to the light.

The History in a Tree

Every year the growing tree buries its past in another ring of functioning wood. The oldest part of the tree, the middle, having died, grows harder in death and provides the tree with its backbone. So long as it is sealed off from the air by living tissue on the outside it is virtually incorruptible. Each year's new ring remains just as it was when it was added: a faithful record of one year of the tree's history. Count them, and you know the tree's age.

The size of the new shoot the tree makes each year is decided by the weather of the previous summer when the bud was formed. Not so the annual ring. What affects its width seems to be (subject of course to such outside influences as fertilizers) the weather while it is actually forming. The rainfall of the previous winter is important, since it provides the ground-water of the spring—the sap which will flood up the new ring as it forms. Even more decisive, because more variable, are the sun and rain of the current spring and summer. Growth-rings, therefore, are an immediate record of the weather of the growing season.

But rings are rarely perfect. Trees are not so often round as oval, or fluted, or just plain lop-sided in cross-section.

A forest tree, sheltered on all sides and striving upwards for the light, is likely to be the nearest to a perfect cylinder. The more open-grown and wind-buffeted a tree is the more it will taper, broadening at the base where the leverage of the top applies the greatest strain.

Conifers and broadleaves react in different ways to the strains of wind; conifers putting on extra growth on the leeward side, broadleaves on the windward. The same applies to the strain of gravity on horizontal branches; conifers build up the branch on its underside, broadleaves on its upper. Both result in an oval cross-section, longer in the axis of gravity or prevailing wind.

The annual growth rings of a tree record more than just the fat and lean years when it grew quickly or scarcely at all. The right is a complete record of typical events in the life of a tree.

The tree was felled when 47 years old. A rough guide to the age of most normal trees is to allow one year for each inch of the girth at shoulder-height: e.g. a tree ten feet round is about 120 years old.

1 At five years old the slender tree, growing straight, was knocked sideways by the fall of a neighbour. It reacted by growing twice as strongly on the lower side in an attempt to correct its slant. Five years later it was upright again.

2 When the tree was 14 years old a ground-fire swept through the forest. The bark and cambium on the windward side were destroyed. In subsequent years they grew over the wound by degrees: it took six years to close it completely.

3 Other trees growing around gradually deprived the tree of light and robbed it of moisture. When it was 27 years old 'thinning' of the woods suddenly brought it into the open. There was a great leap in growth-rate, still visible in the rings.

4 Six years of rapid growth followed. Then came a drought; its effects on the tree are visible for six rings. Very serious drought can damage the roots enough to slow down growth even for years after normal rainfall returns.

This bristlecone pine in the White Mountains of California may be 3,000 years old. More than half the tree is dead: the live part grows infinitesimally slowly. Dead wood does not rot in the desert atmosphere.

Shipping a gigantic slab of a 3,000-year-old redwood over to England in 1851 was a piece of pure showmanship. Europe has no prehistoric trees: everyone was awed that anything should live so long.

Since the 1950s there has been much more constructive activity in the far west, based on the discovery of pines far older (though far smaller) than the redwoods. It is not their age alone, however, that makes them so exceptionally interesting. It is the strange conditions under which they grow, 10,000 feet up in the White Mountains of California, in a state of chronic drought. Where redwoods grow it rains without fail: every year they add a ring of wood about the same size. But where the bristlecone pine grows there is so little rain that the tree is a super-sensitive rain gauge. Every annual ring is different: and the story they tell goes back (so far) no less than 8,200 years.

There is no tree that old still alive. The oldest living specimen is 4,900. But a special department of the University of Arizona has developed a technique for matching samples of wood from living and dead trees—even from broken-off bits lying on the desert floor —to build up a continuous series of rings.

The rings are microscopically narrow. On one sample there are 1,100 rings in the space of five inches. But the sequence of relative widths never repeats for more than a year or two. Any substantial sample has enough rings either to be unique or to overlap with another. A computer soon finds out which and puts it in its place.

The University expects eventually to push the records back to 10,000 years of weather — back in fact to the centuries when the last ice age was in retreat. The value of the work to weathermen is obvious. But in 1969 another startling issue came to light.

Wood whose age was exactly known was tested by the Carbon-14 method, the accepted means of dating prehistoric sites. But the answer came out wrong. The pines revealed that the basic assumption of C-14 dating, that the carbon in the atmosphere is at a constant level, holds good only for the last 3,500 years. Before that time the errors mount up rapidly: there was a 700-year error within the millennium before 1500 B.C.

As a result the presumed dates of some of the most important early structures have had to be changed. Stonehenge has been back-dated 1,000 years – upsetting the notion that technology was inherited by western Europe from the East. The implications of all this have yet to be gone into fully. But the fact remains that a Californian desert tree is able to bear witness to events long before history began.

Bristlecone pines have been growing for 8,200 years on desert land too dry for any other vegetation. This 'forest' at 10,000 feet, annual rainfall 12 inches, was discovered in 1955.

Right *Timber from a 17th-century Mexican mission is examined for data of prehistoric weather.*

Above *The University of Arizona prefers whole sections of trees for dating, but can take a 'core' sample of a living tree without harming it. The core is extracted by hand with a fine auger.*

1910-27

1910-49

1920-68

Dendrochronology is historical research through tree-rings. The rain-sensitive bristlecone pine keeps a faithful record of the year's rainfall with thicker or thinner growth-rings. No log sequence is remotely likely to be repeated: a computer, therefore, can match any sample 'core' of wood (like those illustrated here) with others that overlap it in date, pushing the series farther and farther back into prehistory as more samples are analysed. Rings vary in absolute width between specimens, but the relative widths of every year are reliably the same.

Roots and the Soil

There is a discipline about the top-hamper of a tree. It obeys its own specific rules of growth. In contrast the roots are opportunists; they go wherever they find the feeding best. E. H. Wilson told the story of a particularly happy-looking ivy on the walls of Magdalen College, Oxford, which turned out to have got into the cellar and drunk a whole barrel of port.

We know much less about the roots of trees than about their branches, simply because they are out of sight. Very rarely has a tree been excavated *in toto*, like the example on the opposite page.

The roots have three jobs to do. They anchor the tree in the ground; they are the tree's chief source of water; and they have to forage for the elements from the soil that are a small but vital part of every cell.

The first root every tree (and every plant) puts out from its germinating seed is a tap-root. Its course is directed by gravity. All the seed knows is that the ground is downwards. The tap-root is a sort of emergency action to plug into the supplies as quickly as possible. Thereafter most trees soon concentrate on exploiting the top-soil, normally the richest in organic matter. Most feeding roots of most trees are found within six inches of the surface.

Spruces, beeches and poplars are examples of trees which rarely root deep, even when young. Firs, most oaks and many pines on the other hand go on with a tap-root for several years, which makes them much harder trees to transplant. What happens then depends on the soil. The deepest a tree root has been followed into the ground was 21 feet; that was a pine on sand – the most permeable of soils. Far more commonly the tap-root withers away and side-roots take over.

Roots go where it is easy to go. If they can they will follow old worm-tunnels or spaces where previous roots have died and rotted. They have to be wary only of the water-table; the level below which the soil is permanently wet. Their policy here is brinkmanship: they need the water, but they need oxygen too. They like to keep a toe in, but if they are submerged for long the roots of most trees drown. On the whole a fluctuating water-table is not such a safe bet as the rain permeating from above.

As the crown of the tree spreads, the roots extend to keep up with it. They are at their most active under the drip-line, where the rain falling on the crown runs off round the circumference. Trees like Lombardy poplars with upright branches that encourage the rain to run down their trunks have more roots close in where it falls.

Root growth is almost constant, stopping

The shape of a tree's root system depends less on the type of tree than the type of soil. Certain trees predominate on certain soil-types, but where their roots go is a question of tapping the supply of nutrients, water and oxygen with the least physical obstruction in the way. On these two pages four typical forest soil-types are depicted.

On this page are some of the roots of an oak in 'brown earth'; the typical soil of deciduous woodlands in areas of relatively low rainfall, slightly acid but rich in bacteria which quickly break down into humus the surface layer of vegetable litter. Flowers and fungi typical of such woodlands (known as 'dry oakwood') are

1 *Wood meadow-grass*
2 *Bilberry*
3 Lactarius quietus
4 *Pignut*
5 *Boletus pulverulentus*
6 *Inkcap*
7 *Stinkhorn*
8 *Woodsorrel*
9 *Foxglove*

The soil is about five feet deep, free-draining, loose-textured and fertile. Most of the tree's feeding roots are in the top 12 inches, the 'topsoil' layer with the most humus. There are no definite 'horizons', or layers of different material. Topsoil fades off into subsoil; 'sinker' roots find matter to exploit right down to the bedrock. The upper sub-soil gets its rich rust colour from iron which oxidises readily in well-aerated conditions and is the most visible of all minerals in the soil. In more acid soils the iron oxides dissolve and are 'leached' into lower layers, as opposite. Here they remain evenly distributed on all levels, as do the other essential minerals (phosphorus, potassium, nitrogen, sulphur, calcium and magnesium).

Above *Some of the creatures of the brown earth forest floor. The woodlouse, which loves damp ground, lives on decaying plants and rotting wood. The snail, commonest where the herb* layer is lush, loves nettlebeds. The earth-worm, valuable for aerating the soil with his tunnels, pulls fallen leaves underground for food with remarkable strength. The centipede *lives under stone or bark: its front legs are poison-claws for killing larvae for food. The grey slug, commonest on beech trunks in wet weather, hides under the bark in dry weather.*

A root elongates in the area behind the tip. The function of the cap is to produce a constant supply of new cells to be sloughed off as the tip advances. These discarded cells lubricate the root's passage through the soil.

The function of the root-hairs is to increase the absorbing capacity of the root. Water and mineral salts pass through the cortex into the xylem; the start of the transpiration stream which ends with evaporation from the leaves.

Left *Fungi have the secret of making tree-roots more efficient. Trees in forests usually rely on their characteristic mycorrhizae. They supplant the tree's own root-hairs, feeding on the tree's carbohydrates but in exchange giving the roots increased access to the nutrients in the soil.*

Left *The roots of a pine are growing in a 'podsol', a common soil-type in regions of high rainfall where the net water movement in the soil is downward (because little dry weather draws subsoil water to the surface by evaporation). The calcium in the surface layers is dissolved and washed ('leached') to lower levels, leaving the topsoil very acid. Bacteria cannot flourish in such acidity, so leaves and other organic matter are broken down into humus very slowly. Earthworms are also absent, so the soil lacks their air-tunnels and has relatively little oxygen. Typical surface plants on such soil are*

1 *Male fern*
2 *Boletus badius*
3 *Boletus luterus*
4 *Twin-flower*
5 *Winter green*
6 *Lactarius deliciosus*
7 *Bilberry*
8 *Boletus granulatus*
9 *Bell heather*

Iron and aluminium in the soil dissolve under acid conditions. With so much water passing downward they too are carried to lower levels, leaving a pale 'horizon' without minerals below the topsoil. Under this, just above the bedrock, is the 'deposition layer' where the leached goodness ends up. The pine as a young tree struck out with a taproot, which found rich nourishment when it reached the deposition layer. Later 'sinker' roots, made by the growing tree looking for anchorage against the wind, also penetrated the leached layer with little branching, but proliferated with rootlets when they reached the buried minerals. Meanwhile most of the feeding roots occupy the same top 12 inches as those of the oak, where they can benefit not only from the humus but also from the help of mycorrhizae (see above).

Above *The coniferous forest floor is the home of* wood ants; *their hills, built of needles, can house 100,000. The* black slug, *an omnivorous beast, dies in hard frost, but its eggs survive.*

Left *The total root spread of a tree can be far wider than its crown. This 26-year-old apple tree was unearthed complete by the East Malling Research Station in Kent, the pioneers of 'dwarfing' rootstocks.*

Woodland known as 'damp oakwood' has a 'gley' soil. Gley occurs where drainage is bad, the soil has little oxygen and iron cannot oxidise. Often an impermeable layer of clay keeps the water level high. Airless, water-logged soil below is seen as a dark grey 'horizon'. Oak, ash and hazel grow well but root shallow. Herbs include wild angelica, bramble, woundwort, herb robert, tufted vetch, vernal grass.

Typical chalk-land soil ('rendzina') is a very shallow layer of fertile topsoil with good humus breakdown and efficient drainage. Below is nothing but chalk or limestone. The surface can (through 'leaching') be acidic even a few inches above pure calcium. Beech and ash are typical rendzina trees, most conifers are unhappy. Herbs include dog's mercury, ramsons, fescue, bugle, avena, wood sanicle.

only in freezing weather. It is only new and growing roots that function actively in collecting supplies. In the area where the action is, just behind the root-tip, root, root-hairs and soil are intimately knit together.

Not only are cells from the root-tip constantly being sloughed off to lubricate its passage, but drops of acids (chiefly carbonic) are exuded from the growing cells to dissolve the elements they need. The root's relation with the soil is as much chemical as physical: if the free water in the soil has all gone it can even tap water which is chemically part of the soil.

Many roots have allies: fungal friends or mycorrhizae with which they form a close association and which are characteristic of the tree (as truffles are of certain oaks). The fungi act as go-betweens. The roots supply them with sugars; they supply the roots with minerals from the soil. The reason why alkaline soil is fatal to many trees is that it kills these essential partners.

The acidity or alkalinity of soil is expressed as its 'pH'. The rating is based on the concentration of hydrogen ions in solution: the higher the concentration the more acid the soil. A neutral solution has a hydrogen ion concentration of one in 10 million (i.e. $1:10,000,000$, or $\frac{1}{10^7}$ or 10^{-7} (ten to the power of minus seven). The figure seven is the pH. A lower pH number therefore means a higher concentration of acidic ions. A pH of 6 is ten times more acid than a pH of 7.

How Trees are Named

When we talk about a species we mean a group of similar plants, which grow together in nature, breed together, and produce offspring like themselves.

When we talk about a genus we mean a group of such species, consistently different in detail, not normally inter-breeding, but usually linked in a fairly obvious way. The English settlers arriving in New England recognized the oaks as oaks, even though the species they knew back home was not among them. From ancient times these two broad categories of natural objects have been instinctively acknowledged.

But a more searching scrutiny of the natural world has also suggested (to Aristotle in the first place) that there are broader groups and deeper relationships to be found. It is easy to think up ways of classifying anything. You could make lists of trees with yellow flowers, or peeling bark, and have a system of a sort. But it would prove nothing because it would be limited to the characteristic you happened to choose. You could neither deduce nor predict anything from it. Aristotle guessed that there is a natural order of relationships where everything has a place. There was no clue, though, as to where to look for it.

Even Linnaeus, who is known as the father of modern taxonomy (the science of classifying natural objects), was in the dark about the 'natural order'. He classified plants by their sexual characteristics: number of stamens, ovaries and so forth. His instinct was right, yet he admitted his system was artificial and would be superseded when the key came to light.

What natural links he did see he incorporated in a 'fragment of a natural system'. So far as it goes it still holds good. Taxonomists who followed him built on it until by the middle of the last century most of the genera of flowering plants had been assigned to 'families'.

Yet still the key, the link (if any) between genus and genus, between family and family, was unguessed at. It was left to Charles Darwin to supply it: plants are alike because they have common ancestors.

Darwin said: 'All true classification is genealogical . . . community of descent is the hidden bond which naturalists have unconsciously been seeking.'

Since Darwin's day taxonomy and phylogeny (the science of the ancestry of things) have marched side by side—without, it must be admitted, getting very much further. Proof of ancestral links 100 million years ago are not easy to find. Fossil evidence has hardly ever helped: largely because the taxonomically significant bits—flower parts—rarely make legible fossils.

Evolutionary history has been likened to a tree. Only the most recent shoots are visible, but breaks in the canopy show that two or three of the shoots come from one branchlet, or maybe that two or three branchlets come from one branch. The main bulk of the tree, the trunk and limbs which are the early stages of evolution, is invisible. The taxonomist's job is to reconstruct it from what he can see; the plants of today.

He gets most help in discovering links from flower structure. Flowers reflect the chances of mutation, the way the genetic dice fell. They have been less influenced by environment than, say, leaves or buds.

The daisy family, the *Compositae*, is an example of how far apart ecological adaptation can take related plants. It includes trees, shrubs, vines, herbs, even succulents —in every climate, on every soil, using every method of pollination and distribut-

Taxodiaceae (swamp cypress family; sequoia illustrated): narrow leaves arranged in a spiral. Roundish cones with spiralling leathery or woody scales.

Cupressaceae *(cypress family): tiny scale-like leaves pressed close to the twigs. Small roundish cones start fleshy and ripen woody. Male 'flowers' are at branch tips.*

Taxaceae *(yew family): typical conifers in leaves and habit, unusual in being either male or female. Single-ovule female 'flowers' develop into open-ended berry-like 'cones'.*

Ginkgoaceae *(ginkgo family): has the oldest genus of tree still living, alone in its family, unaltered for 100 million years. The ginkgo's naked seeds relate it to the conifers; it has catkins for male flowers.*

Cyatheaceae *(tree ferns): reproduction like that of all ferns in two stages: the spores under the leaves have no sex. They drop off and grow into little flat plants (right). These have sexual spores which create another tree fern.*

Theophrastus (died 287 B.C.), a pupil of Aristotle, the first man to classify plants as 'woody' or 'herbaceous', though better known for his classification of the 'characters' of men.

Pinaceae *(pine family): narrow leaves in spirals, though sometimes in rows or tufts. Woody cones have two seeds per scale: bracts of flowers often remain visible in cone (as here in Abies koreana).*

Magnoliaceae *(magnolia family): bisexual flowers with stamens and petals attached below protruding female organs, which develop into a cone-like mass of seeds with a substantial food-store or endosperm.*

The evolution of trees can only be diagrammatically represented in the most tentative way. The symbolic tree here branches through concentric rings of 60 million years each. The green areas among its branches are suggestions as to the origins of the plant divisions, widest at the period of their greatest importance. The Angiosperm division (for example) came into prominence between 60 and 120 million years ago. Round the margin and described in the captions above are examples of important tree families deriving from the evolutionary groups, with the principal characteristics (largely of their flowers) by which they are classified.

[Diagram labels: Magnoliaceae, Pinaceae, Taxodiaceae, Cupressaceae, Taxaceae, Ginkgoaceae, Cyatheaceae, Fa..., Gymnospermae, Pinaceae, Cupressaceae, Taxodiaceae, Araucariaceae, Taxaceae, Podocarpaceae, Ginkgoales, Cordait..., Pteridophyta, 0 60 120 180 240 300]

Carl Linné (Linnaeus) (1707–78), the great Swedish naturalist, is considered to be the founder of modern botany. The binomial system for naming plants was established by his work.

Fagaceae *(beech family): male and female flowers on same tree, male flowers tassel-like. Fruit surrounded by a woody cup. Seed has no endosperm.*

Salicaceae *(willow family): sexes on different trees, male and female flowers both catkins. Fruit a capsule of many hairy seeds without endosperm. Leaves alternate and simple.*

Charles de Lécluse (Clusius)(1526–1609) from Flanders made the first real botanical (as opposed to medicine-herb) garden at Leiden in Holland.

Rosaceae *(rose family): bisexual flowers usually with parts in fives. Fruit depends on development of 'receptacle' and number of ovules (Prunus, here, has one). Leaves have tiny leaflets at base.*

ing seeds. Yet a common flower-design, of a group of tiny florets making a composite flower, is the clear link between all the family's members.

On the other hand there is an appeal open to common sense. The maples could, on the strength of their flowers alone, be chopped up into several different genera. Yet maples all have such similar fruit, all have the opposite branching pattern, and most of them have such obviously related leaves that to split them up would be pedantry.

The microscope has given us new aspects of plants to examine. Wood structure and the design of pollen grains are two of the most important. They have frequently confirmed what had already been deduced from the flowers.

The species is the basic category of plant, but it is not the smallest. Within the species there may be several varieties;

often local forms with an ecological reason (extreme exposure, for example) for being the way they are. It is a matter of botanical judgement what constitutes a species and what a variety. As Arthur Cronquist of the New York Botanic Garden says: 'Custom, in such matters, is merely the sum of a series of individual opinions, plus inertia.'

Custom has been given teeth, however, by an international rule of nomenclature that says that the first person to have given an accurate description of a species from a specimen and named it in print (and of course in Latin) was right. To prevent any confusion the 'author's' name–in a shortened form (e.g. L. for Linnaeus)–becomes part of the full name of the plant in botanical works (but not in this). About a quarter of a million flowering plants now have such names. On pages 328-31 is a list of tree-names and their exact meanings.

Leguminosae *(pea family; laburnum illustrated): most flowers irregular with five petals. Fruit a pod with two or more seeds, no endosperm. Leaves usually compound.*

Aceraceae *(maple family): opposite leaves and 'keys' for fruit consisting of two winged nutlets joined at their bases. Flowers have five petals, five sepals but eight stamens.*

Myrtaceae *(myrtle family; eucalyptus illustrated): bisexual flowers in clusters; the many stamens often have coloured stems. Fruit a berry, drupe or capsule. Leaves leathery and opposite.*

Oleaceae *(olive family): opposite leaves and bisexual flowers, usually with four petals and two stamens. Fruits vary: olive has drupes; ash, winged nuts.*

Palmaceae *(palms; coconut illustrated): unbranched stems of uniform thickness with terminal spiral of divided frond-like leaves. Flowers small, usually uni-sexual. Three ovules; one matures into seed with massive endosperm.*

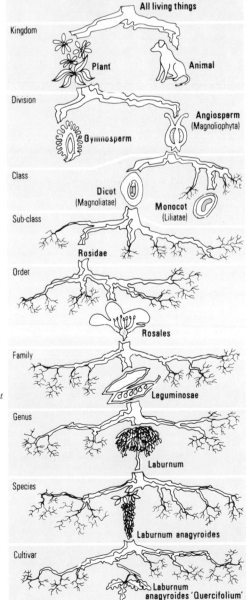

Right *The classification of a garden plant starts (at the bottom) with the smallest division: cultivar. It works up in bigger and bigger groupings. Laburnum is a member of the pea family, the Rosales order, the Rosidae sub-class, Dicotyledon class, Angiosperm Division of the Plant Kingdom.*

Trees and the Weather

Climate is the crucial factor in deciding what trees grow where. Its broadest movements in geological time have governed the evolution of tree species. Relatively recent climate changes have settled the present natural distribution of these species round the globe.

The ancestors of all our trees were tropical plants. In the tropics the seasons are only vaguely marked by temperature changes: what alters most from one time of year to another is rainfall. Most tropical plants are evergreen, and can grow either constantly or intermittently whenever there is enough moisture, without fear of damage by cold.

Trees that adapted to life in the temperate zones, with marked winters, did so by learning to live with the seasons. A temperate-zone tree in its own habitat is precisely adapted to the exact weather pattern its parents and grandparents have undergone. It is what we call 'hardy', because it has learnt to do the right thing at the right time and not risk exposing its vulnerable stages of growth to weather that can harm them.

It has developed a clock that tells it when, judging by past experience, it is safe to get started in the spring, and when it had better pull in its horns for the winter.

The most graphic illustration of how trees find (literally) their own climatic level is seen along the course of a mountain range that runs from north to south. At the top of this page is a diagram of the western ranges of the United States and Canada. The tapering pattern of each tree's range from south to north tells the story. In the Sierras it finds its ecological niche at considerable altitudes. In the Cascades (and farther north still, in the Coast Range) the same basic climatic conditions, the length of time the snow lies, the number of days above 40°F. in which it can grow and ripen new wood, force it right down to sea-level.

As soon as a tree is moved (or its seed is planted) out of its accustomed zone it is in potential danger. It seems odd that a larch from Siberia (for example) would be anything but delighted to be moved to a softer climate. You would expect it to luxuriate in the longer growing season, while still being totally 'hardy'; whereas what happens in practice is that it is lured out of its safe dormancy by higher temperatures than it expects too early in the spring. It starts growth, only to be cut back by late spring frosts. This happens repeatedly, and it dies.

The converse happens when a southern tree is moved north. It is relatively safe in the spring: it waits for warmer weather. But it keeps growing too late in the summer

and its new wood is still soft and green when the first autumn frosts strike. Again, lack of hardiness really means being programmed for the wrong climate.

Perhaps more surprising is the difficulty trees experience in moving from the west coast to the east of North America—or from the East to Europe. The difference between a continental climate and an oceanic one can be more upsetting to the rhythm than a simple move from north to south. Western conifers are as unhappy in New England as oaks from Ohio are in Britain or France.

The most extreme example is a cold-climate tree which is moved to the subtropics. What can happen here is that its buds may fail to open at all. Built into its schedule is the need for a cold spell (the winter) to break their dormancy. If there is perpetual warmth it is stuck: in all probability it will die.

In forestry the question of provenance (i.e. exactly where the seed comes from) is clearly of the greatest importance. The forester's object is to extend the growth period of his trees as far as he can without putting them in danger of frost damage. He has little room for manoeuvre, but if he can even add a week to the growing season by getting seed from 100 miles farther south without the trees suffering he has added (say) a whole year's growth in 20 years, or five per cent. In practice much better results, even up to 30 per cent, are achieved.

Where winter damage, as opposed to damage by late or early frost, is concerned, trees from different zones are on a more equal footing. Many, if not most, temperate-

Above *Snow can be a vital protection to trees; especially to evergreens in dry mountain sunshine and intense cold. Here firs are completely shrouded in snow in the mountains of Hokkaido, northern Japan.*
Right *More damage is done to trees by untimely spring frost than by winter cold. A typical spring frost merely makes these alder leaves wilt. Less hardy trees can lose their new leaves.*

A prevailing wind can deform trees by preventing them shooting on the windward side. New shoots can grow only in the shelter of old ones; the tree trails over to leeward.

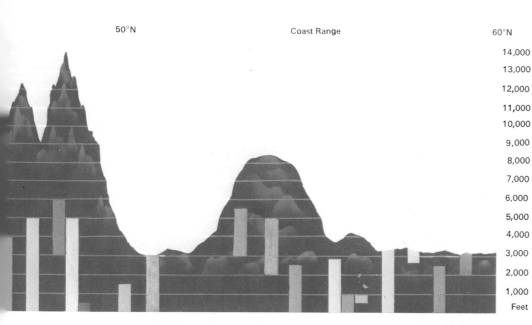

50°N   Coast Range   60°N

14,000
13,000
12,000
11,000
10,000
9,000
8,000
7,000
6,000
5,000
4,000
3,000
2,000
1,000
Feet

Alpine fir *Abies lasiocarpa*	Mountain hemlock *Tsuga mertensiana*
Bigleaf maple *Acer macrophyllum*	Ponderosa pine *Pinus ponderosa*
Black cottonwood *Populus trichocarpa*	Sugar pine *Pinus lambertiana*
Douglas fir *Pseudotsuga menziesii*	Western juniper *Juniperus occidentalis*
Engelmann spruce *Picea engelmanii*	Western red cedar *Thuja plicata*
Grand fir *Abies grandis*	Western white pine *Pinus monticola*

zone trees can stand being frozen solid while they are dormant (although some are more used to it than others, and none like it to happen suddenly). What more often hurts, and can kill, is winter drought.

While the ground is frozen in winter there is no water available to the roots. But high winds and often low humidity keep on evaporating water from the branches. Even the twigs of leafless trees transpire to some extent in these conditions. So the tree begins to dry out. On evergreens it shows in the browning of the leaves by the end of even a normal winter. A longer period of intense cold with clear skies and a high wind can easily prove fatal.

The Arnold Arboretum at Boston has perhaps (of all scholarly institutions) the most experience of testing temperate trees in hard winters. It argues that if one statistic is to be used to try to map plant hardiness zones it should be minimum temperature. Rainfall is important; soil has its influence; microclimates (see illustrations on right) are vital. But on a broad front it is the lowest regular winter temperatures that decide whether a tree will survive or not.

On pages 30 and 31 the hardiness zone map developed by Dr. Alfred Rehder at the Arnold Arboretum for the whole of North America is matched by a similar map on the same principles done (for the first time) for Europe. On pages 314 and 315 maps show the natural forest vegetation of the same areas, so that it is possible to follow the apparent effects of minimum temperatures on the selection of species to be found in the wild.

Local frost: cause and effect

Above *Where either clouds or a tree canopy insulate the layer of warm air above ground from the open sky, heat (red) cannot escape; frost is unlikely. On a night without cloud, heat is free to leave the ground, until (above right) soil temperature falls below air temperature. Then soil takes heat (yellow arrow) from air near to the ground, causing 'radiation' frost.*

Below left *Cold air created in a thin layer at ground level will flow downhill and collect like water in hollows and valleys, which thus become 'frost pockets'. The height to which this hollow fills with frost is marked by the dead lower branches of the trees.*

Below right *The house and its garden are protected from frost. Trees uphill prevent it flowing down the hill, the slope below lets it run off. But the valley floor is unprotected: cold air comes in from the left foreground hill.*

The Advance of Spring

The ripple of bursting buds, of woods growing amber with catkins, white with dogwood, tender green with the opening leaf, moves inexorably northward in the spring. Even in the dead of the year there are stirrings of swelling buds, early catkins on willows, eccentric bushes with winter flowers. But it is when the last frosts of spring pass that the full flush transforms the woods. In Florida and Naples this is as early as the first week of March. In New England not until about eight weeks later, about the first of May. At Edinburgh it is the last week of April.

The rising temperature is the prime mover in releasing leaves and flowers from their protecting buds. Spring moves north at a predictable pace in flat and open country. But local factors can cause wide variations on the same latitude. Latitude clearly bears little relation to the relative timing of spring in Europe and eastern North America.

Altitude is important. The temperature drops 1°F. for every 300 feet you climb. The practical effect of this on tree growth depends on other local conditions, but 300 feet extra altitude has been observed to shorten the total growing season in the eastern States by five days, in the Alps by six and in Scotland by twelve.

Cities have the reverse effect. With the warmth and shelter they provide they can greatly advance the spring. London has pear blossom three weeks before a country garden only 50 miles away. Even a sheltering house wall can bring a tree into blossom a week or two ahead of its neighbour standing unprotected in the open.

Daylength is the other deciding factor. However unseasonably warm it may be at the end of winter, or however miserably cold in the spring, trees are governed in the cycle by the photoperiod: the number of hours of darkness.

In the tropics daylength varies no more than do the seasons: day and night are always about equal; trees grow year-round. As far north as Oslo, however, there is a bare seven hours of daylight in January, compared with 17 in June. At the March equinox the north catches up with and overtakes the south in daylight hours. Thereafter its plants can begin to make up for their shorter growing season by using the extra light.

The tables on these pages show the hours of daylight at different latitudes in Europe and America from January to June, together with the actual blooming and leafing dates of nine species of trees. The dates are averages worked out over some 20 years.

The interaction of temperature, daylength and local factors gives some surprising results. For example a magnolia which blooms in London in mid-March waits until mid-May in Fribourg in Switzerland, five degrees of latitude to the south but in the northern foothills of the Alps. The same magnolia flowers in late March in both Seattle and Washington D.C. (8° to the south)—but here it is the continental climate of the east which holds it back. It is interesting to speculate on the relevant influences using

Day-length	EARLY	MID.	LATE	
18h 50m				60°N
17h 35m				56°N
16h 43m				52°N
15h 55m				47°N
15h 29m				44°N
15h 1m				40°N

June

Day length	Early	Mid.	Late		May
17h 4m				60°N	
16h 15m				56°N	
15h 37m				52°N	
14h 55m				47°N	
14h 44m				44°N	
14h 21m				40°N	

Day length	Early	Mid.	Late		April	
14h 28m				60°N	Oslo
14h 6m				56°N	Edinburgh
13h 50m				52°N	London
13h 32m				47°N	Fribourg
13h 22m				44°N	Montpellier
13h 13m				40°N	Coimbra

Day-length	EARLY	MID.	LATE		March
11h 44m				60°N	
11h 47m				56°N	
11h 49m				52°N	
11h 52m				47°N	
11h 53m				44°N	
11h 55m				40°N	

Day-length	EARLY	MID.	LATE		February
9h 17m				60°N	
9h 42m				56°N	
10h 1m				52°N	
10h 21m				47°N	
10h 33m				44°N	
10h 4 5m				40°N	

Day-length	EARLY	MID.	LATE		January
6h 40m				60°N	
7h 33m				56°N	
8h 14m				52°N	
8h 53m				47°N	
9h 14m				44°N	
9h 37m				40°N	

Europe

- Oslo
- Edinburgh
- London
- Fribourg
- Montpellier
- Coimbra

these tables in conjunction with the hardiness zone maps overleaf.

Seasonal variation–the phenomenon of an 'early' or a 'late' spring is totally unpredictable. When a cold spell holds up flowering for an unnaturally long time it can result in trees that normally flower one after the other coming out together.

In most years, however, the one thing that is predictable is the order of flowering and coming into leaf. This is the really essential information for any planter. With it he can dispose his trees either to give him one short season of glory when he will be the envy of the neighbourhood with every tree aglow; or a calculated series of detonations so that for months on end there is always one tree flowering somewhere in the picture. Or a sequence of set pieces, of groups of complementary colour and form, which must be the object of every gardener who has the facilities and the space. The year-long sequence of special features (flowers, foliage and fruit) of 100 species is given on pages 316-17 in the Reference Section.

Common laburnum — *Laburnum anagyroides*
Cornelian cherry — *Cornus mas*
English oak — *Quercus robur*
European pussy willow — *Salix caprea*
Hawthorn — *Crataegus monogyna*
Japanese or oriental cherry — *Prunus serrulata*
Magnolia — *Magnolia × soulangiana*
Norway maple — *Acer platanoides*
Shadblow — *Amelanchier grandiflora*

Zones of Tree Hardiness in North America and Europe

Whether a tree will live and grow in any region, given suitable soil and adequate moisture, depends on the lowest temperatures it will encounter (see pages 26–27). On this page we reproduce the map of the hardiness zones of North America compiled by the Arnold Arboretum on the basis of average annual minimum temperatures – a map that has long been taken as a guide by the horticultural industry. Opposite is a map of Europe on the same basis.

As an example of how they work the phrase 'zone 9' in the text (and in the notes in the A-Z Index of Tree Species) identifies a tree that will survive in temperature zone 9 – as marked on the maps – or south of it, but only in exceptional circumstances in the next zone northwards, zone 8. Such broad generalizations of course have many exceptions: altitude lowers the temperature locally; big lakes have the opposite effect.

The North American map is dominated by the influence of the great land- (and ice-) mass to the north. You can picture the situation as cold radiating from somewhere in Manitoba. Only the mountain ranges (and to some extent the warm Gulf of Mexico) distort this continental influence. Otherwise minimum temperatures rise in concentric bands to the subtropical fringes of southern California and Florida.

The rainfall map (top of the page opposite) shows that most of the major centres of population in North America fall in zones of adequate average rainfall for most trees (over 30 inches a year) – though this does not mean that trees will not benefit from deep watering in dry spells. The annual figures do not show, for example, that California's rain comes mainly in winter, making watering very necessary in summer. In most of the United States more rain falls between May and October than between November and April.

The overwhelming influences on Europe

Zone 1	below −50°	Zone 4	−20° to −10°	Zone 7	5° to 10°	Zone 10	30° to 40°
Zone 2	−50° to −35°	Zone 5	−10° to −5°	Zone 8	10° to 20°		
Zone 3	−35° to −20°	Zone 6	−5° to 5°	Zone 9	20° to 30°	Highlands and Mountain Ranges	

are the Atlantic Ocean, the cold land-mass of Asia, and the warm-air-mass over the Sahara. The ocean with its warm Gulf Stream is so effective in keeping winter temperatures up that, mountains apart, the hardiness zones of Britain and most of northern Europe run west-east rather than north-south. Where the Atlantic and Saharan influences coincide in southern Spain, winter temperatures are as high as in Florida, ten degrees of latitude or 700 miles farther south.

Rainfall also follows a mainly west-east pattern, but as in America annual levels are adequate in most populated regions.

Inches	Inches
Above 60	20 to 30
40 to 60	10 to 20
30 to 40	below 10

Man and the Forest

Old-fashioned forestry, in the days when it seemed inconceivable that the supply of trees would ever run out, consisted of choosing the biggest and best, chopping them down and sawing them up.

Modern forestry works differently. The great virgin woods of Europe were exhausted centuries ago. In America they would be exhausted by now had conservationists not begun lobbying in the early years of this century for control of what was cut where. Instead of cutting and moving on, the modern forester has to assume that the trees will have to go on coming off the same land for ever.

Modern forestry means planting as many trees as you cut, or more; protecting the stock from disease, animals, people, fire; and cutting it on a rotation basis. It also means sowing only seed that is perfectly suited to the soil and climate, and only the seed of really good fault-free trees. The climate question is discussed on pages 26–27. The basic principles of tree-breeding are shown on pages 14–15.

The process of making the forester's dream, the fast and flawless tree, is a recent one. Since the 18th century landowners have realized that it makes sense to leave one or two of the biggest trees, rather than unusable runts, to reseed and restock land they have cut over. But juggling with chromosomes is very much a 20th-century idea.

In practice it means running seed orchards, where the fertilizing of trees can be done under supervision and the results controlled. A typical seed orchard would be a few acres of young pine trees, too young to bear seed themselves. On them are grafted the upper, seed-bearing branches of the best of the older trees. To collect such branches the forester takes his gun into the woods. When he sees a tree taller and straighter than all the rest he shoots off branch-tips where the flowers will be.

A 'stand' of larch, halfway to maturity, is being 'thinned' – having the less successful trees cut for pulp to allow the best to develop for timber. The logs are sawn to eight-foot lengths and debarked by this machine. In some very modern forests a chipping machine reduces the whole tree to pulpable chips on the spot. In this way even the branches can be used and transport is made much easier.

Extraction of timber from the woods is often a problem. On flat ground special tractors can drag or carry it to collection points for trucks on forest roads.

Trees hide tents. Forests can absorb more holiday-makers than any other landscape. The possibilities for pleasure in productive forests have long been exploited in North America: in Europe the idea is relatively new.

Left *This 18th-century copper engraving shows the workings of an early American saw-mill. The incoming logs are sawn up into planks of varying length. Today the logs would be debarked before being sawn up.*

Right *The percentage of the land area under forest in 15 countries, and the proportions of the forest which are (in the main) coniferous and deciduous, are shown in the diagrams.*

In the orchard the flowers are within reach. It is easy to protect them from random pollination and fertilize them only with pollen from another chosen tree. Then in due course it is easy to collect the cones and know just what seed you are sowing.

Along with care of the stock goes care of the land. Most forest is in unfarmable country; often on precipitous terrain. The difficulty here is in getting the wood out without irreparably damaging the soil, which is often held in place only by the trees. Road-building in the mountains is so expensive that helicopters and even balloons have been used to airlift timber.

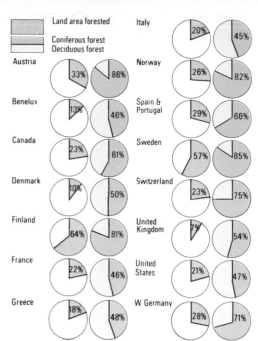

Land area forested
Coniferous forest
Deciduous forest

Austria 33% 86%
Benelux 13% 46%
Canada 23% 61%
Denmark 10% 50%
Finland 64% 81%
France 22% 46%
Greece 18% 48%
Italy 20% 45%
Norway 26% 82%
Spain & Portugal 29% 66%
Sweden 57% 85%
Switzerland 23% 75%
United Kingdom 7% 54%
United States 21% 47%
W. Germany 28% 71%

On land that has been cut over a few of the best trees are sometimes left to sow their (superior) seed. Seed is also sown by aeroplane today, and experiments in dropping seedlings in tiny 'bombs' of soil are being carried out.

One means of combating forest fires is the hilltop fire-tower, set on stilts. In summer the towers are manned for 24 hours a day.

Logging on steep watershed areas brings problems – the soil is easily disturbed; timber may have to be lifted by helicopter and sometimes balloon.

The forester's ideal tree is one with the longest possible straight trunk without branches. Close planting ensures bottom branches will die in the shade and drop off, leaving knot-free timber.

By leaving appropriate indigenous trees in special situations (willow or alder by waterside, for example) the forester can help overcome the perils of monoculture, offering a habitat to a much wider range of wildlife. An old oak is the most valuable wildlife tree of all: hundreds of different insect species are found on oak – particularly on dead branches.

The Forest Encroaches

A sand dune is very poor in wildlife. A forest is immensely rich. The more different kinds of trees a forest contains the richer its wildlife will be.

The shores of Lake Michigan provide an opportunity (in the Indiana Dunes National Park, for example) to see the process of enrichment in action. The lake has retreated, leaving ponds interspersed with sand dunes. The plant communities on the dunes are stages between sand and forest.

Those nearest the lake have only a sketchy covering of marram grass, sandreed and *Artemisia*. Eventually, they begin to bind the sand with their roots and enrich it with their litter. Insects diversify enormously. The pond starts to silt up.

At the second stage there is enough soil (sand plus humus from herbs) to support shrubs and pioneer trees: willow, cottonwood, sand cherry and wild plum. Insects increase and attract birds. The margins of the pond contract with flourishing vegetation. Bass give way to catfish. Beavers carry wood into the water.

The pond has become marshy ground by the fourth stage. On the dune there are pines and junipers, even a few young oaks. Water insects reach and pass their climax, to be succeeded by bees, flies, ants, beetles.

Squirrels and ruffed grouse arrive.

Soil builds up in the old pond hollow and changes chemically. Earthworms and snails appear. At first the forest is fairly open with oak and hickory as the big trees above a dense scrub of blackberry, hazel, redbud, cherries, roses and blueberry. The range of insects grows and with it the range of birds. Mammals of all kinds appear.

The final stage of dense beech and maple forest can succeed the oak and hickory. But both types also coexist on dunes of the same age. Owls, woodpeckers and hawks join the birds. Deer are fairly common and black bear put in an appearance.

Below *The illustrations show the progress of the dunes from bare beach to high forest, the chart the successive increase of the different populations.*

The Grass Stage
The pond below has black bass, the dunes grass and termites.

The Scrub Stage
Grasses give way to scrub and pioneer trees. The pond grows a rushy edge and starts to silt up, helped by the work of the beaver. Pollen-gathering and wood-boring insects and mosquitoes attract birds. Amphibian life reaches a peak; at the end of this stage reptiles emerge.

The Pine Stage
The pond is now marsh, fish vanish, aquatic insects reach a climax. Conifers are dominant: jack pine and juniper on the dunes, larch (tamarack) on the marsh-land. New kinds of insects and fruit bring more birds. Mammals begin with the squirrel.

The Oak/Hickory Stage
Oak and hickory dominate a mature community with a rich undergrowth. Plenty of light allows innumerable species of plants. Insect, bird, reptile (snakes) and mammal life continues to diversify with white-tailed deer among the higher mammals.

The Beech/Maple Stage
A denser forest of beech and maple may finally take over. Undergrowth diminishes but all forms of life continue to proliferate. The black bear symbolizes a rich and mature wildlife population.

Stage One *Grassy Dunes*   **Stage Two** *Shrubs*   **Stage Three** *Pine Forest*   **Stage Four** *Oak and Hickory Forest*   **Stage Five** *Beech and Maple Forest*

Plants

Insects

Birds

Mammals

DUNES

Plants

Fish/Aquatic insects

Amphibians and Reptiles

PONDS

Lake Michigan (top) is an
example of how forest
encroaches. The section
(above) of the dunes area
illustrates the recession of
the lake and gradual
emergence of vegetation.
In the Indiana Dunes
National Park (right), the
lake has retreated, leaving
ponds interspersed with
sand dunes.

Poison in the Air

The process of establishing forest described on the previous pages is all too easily reversible. As a lake can retreat, so it can also encroach. All ecosystems are fragile. But most of the surviving forest of industrialized countries is particularly so because it occupies the least naturally fertile land—sometimes a mere shallow deposit of accumulated organic matter over impermeable rock. If the trees are cut or die, erosion will soon wash the granite bare again. Anything that threatens the trees threatens the soil, and vice versa.

Just how fragile forests are, and how little we really know about the checks and balances that keep them in being, has become tragically clear in the past decade. The phenomenon known as 'acid rain', though it is much more complex than the name implies, has taken a terrible toll of some of Europe's proudest forests, and is causing deep concern in the United States.

Acid rain was described and named by a Swedish scientist, Svante Odèn, in 1967. As the term is used now, it refers to the deposition, whether in liquid form as rain, or in solid or gaseous form, of sulphuric and nitric compounds derived, in the main, from the burning of fossil fuels—coal, gas and oil. Something in the order of 100 million tons of sulphur dioxide alone is pumped into the atmosphere every year by the factories, power plants and vehicles of Europe and North America. Oxides of nitrogen, at least half of them from automobile exhausts, are in the same order of magnitude.

The chemicals can fall back to earth locally in dust form, but tall chimneys are designed to carry them into the cloud layer, where with moisture and sunshine they form other compounds, often being carried by weather systems hundreds or even thousands of miles before being precipitated in rain or snow as sulphuric and nitric acid.

The problem has therefore no national boundaries but applies unequally wherever the weather wills. Its effects are most severely felt in areas where the soil is already acid. Alkaline soils (such as most of the farmland of Europe) have a 'buffering' effect, reacting with the acids to neutralize them—even to turn them into fertilizing compounds. But where no limestone, calcium or magnesium is present in the soil its acidity steadily rises. Lakes receiving the run-off become so acid that their fish die, and even their plankton: they become unnaturally clear, blue and lifeless—a condition now seen in south-west Norway, parts of northern Britain and certain lakes in the north-eastern United States. Trees on shallow acid forest soils are poisoned, both through their roots (aluminium mobilized by acids may be the main culprit) and through their leaves.

Above *The obvious emissions of smoke from tall chimneys and cooling towers do not tell the whole story. These high structures were constructed to vent the sulphur dioxide and nitrogen dioxides away from the immediate environs of power station and factory high into the cloud layer. We now know that once in the atmosphere these gases are transformed into acidic chemicals and toxic heavy metal particles which can be carried by weather systems over vast distances before being deposited back on earth in mist, rain and snow in what is today called acid rain.*

Above *A clear sign of the effects of atmospheric pollution is the unnatural yellowing leading to eventual loss of needles on evergreen conifers — the first of the great forest trees to suffer.*

The conifers, with their evergreen needles, suffer first. The most serious damage has been reported from the central forests of West Germany, including the Black Forest, particularly at high altitudes where another culprit, ozone, a derivative of the nitric oxides, is held responsible. It seems that ozone at high levels in summer, when the sun's radiation is intense and there may well be drought at the roots, damages needles which then, in winter, succumb easily to attack from acidic rain, and particularly acidic mists.

There are other particular factors that may account for the more rapid recent decline of trees growing above about 1,600 feet (500 metres). Many of them are old; soils at this height tend to be more fragile — and 1976 was a year of acute drought which may have had long-term stress effects. Certainly the most recent (1984) figures are tragic. A third of all forests in West Germany have now been affected. In Bavaria almost half the magnificent forest beeches, with their shallow root systems, are sick and the figure for fir trees is 80 per cent. One-third of all the mature spruces in the state of Hesse are affected. Czechoslovakia and East Germany may possibly be in an even worse state; the pines of eastern Holland are suffering; while across the Atlantic the Adirondack mountains are particularly badly hit; and eastern Canada and even California are reporting damage they ascribe to acid rain.

This is not to mention the known and unknown effects the same pollution is having on human and animal health (it is known to be associated with chronic bronchitis and asthma; it also liberates heavy metals into the water supply), or on buildings and other structures, where it corrodes metals and stonework.

A pollution problem of this magnitude transcends all sectional, and even national, interests. Unfortunately it does not dictate any remedial action that we can be sure will have the required effect. Scientists, while becoming more and more convinced that they know the mechanisms — or at least some of the mechanisms — of destruction, cannot yet pinpoint which particular sources of pollution are most culpable. At present the only answer seems to be a universal tightening of regulations on exhaust emissions; an enormous task which would take at least a decade to become effective, however much money is spent. Whether it can ever be justified on simply economic grounds is very doubtful. How do you value the amenity of the Black Forest?

The best cause for hope is the experience of Japan, which made strict rules on air pollution in 1968. During the following seven years, while energy consumption doubled, sulphur emissions were halved. Whether Europe and the United States can follow Japan's example is a harsh test of political will.

Above *Trees in exposed sites are the first to go. Poor soil and abnormal climatic changes, such as long periods of drought or high winds, reduce resistance to pollutants which will weaken and eventually kill the trees completely.*

Right *Modern foresters are experimenting with many new techniques for measuring the levels and effects of pollution. Plastic collar loops around tree trunks collect the trickling rain water which will be tainted with toxic chemicals that have been deposited on the bark and foliage.*

The Ice Ages

We should glance back a moment at the origins of the forest. When the club-mosses reared up from the swamp and ferns formed the first trees—perhaps some 400 million years ago—they existed in a blanket of carbon dioxide. There was no living creature; there was no breathable air. But there was photosynthesis.

The coal in the ground is the carbon from that unbreathable sky. Tens of millions of years of forest, building trees with carbon and leaving oxygen as the by-product, was the origin of our world. Life on earth was made possible by trees.

We must leap unknowable millennia of evolution to reach the relatively recent past. The period known as the Tertiary, from (perhaps) 38 million to (perhaps) 12 million years ago, was furnished with trees shaped just as we know them. What was different was their numbers. The forest was boundless; it reached from pole to pole. And it was homogeneous; the same species, from a range far wider than we know today, might occur anywhere in that great sea of trees.

In early Tertiary times the climate was distinctly warmer than today: the vegetation of Europe was like that of modern Southeast Asia. By the Pliocene (i.e. late Tertiary) era gradual cooling had killed off the subtropical components of the northern temperate forest or caused them to become mere herbs, leaving a rich mixture of all the families found round the world today at these latitudes. Asia, America and Europe alike had swamp cypress, magnolia, sequoia, sweet gum, ginkgo, incense cedar, umbrella pine, as well as oak, beech and the other common trees we know.

This was the situation about a million years ago when the climate began to change for the worse, and went on changing till the sea froze at the poles, and trees died, and their offspring too, unless they could find a place unoccupied by other trees where the ice had not yet reached.

There was not one ice age, but four: Gunz, Mindel, Riss and Würm (or such are the comic-opera names science has given them). They were leisurely affairs. Between Gunz and Mindel (which was the coldest, and saw the ice reach its maximum dimensions) there was a temperate period of something like 60,000 years, when conditions may have been similar to our time. Come to that, we are quite probably merely enjoying an interglacial period ourselves.

Vast numbers of species perished for ever as the arctic cold came south. Geography was the decisive factor. Where there was a line of retreat, a continuous land-mass, species could fall back in tolerably good order. America and eastern Asia provided these conditions. Where there was a high east-west mountain range, or a sea with no way round, vegetation had its back to the wall. Between them the Alps, the Pyrenees and the Mediterranean cut off the last hope of most of the species of Europe (which up to that time had been as rich in trees as the rest of the world). Only about 36 genera, and very few species of these, survive as European 'natives'; whereas in China there are only six of the whole temperate world's genera missing.

The southern hemisphere, particularly Africa, suffered earlier than the north; a great glacier over South Africa advanced into the Tropics some 250 million years ago; retreat to the north was prevented by an ocean where the Sahara now lies. Tropical Africa today has nothing like the richness of flora of South America or Southeast Asia.

There were special conditions which sometimes allowed survival from the ice. One was extreme drought: in a place where rain (or snow) rarely fell, in the lee of a great mountain range, the ice may never have built up. Some botanists believe that such refuges were numerous, particularly at high altitudes, and account for many of today's local species. On the other hand there were conditions which extinguished a race even where the ice was miles away: there is no harder barrier for a plant to cross than a closed community of other plants, taking up all the available space. This may well have been the case in, say, the south of France, which was never frozen but which failed to provide a refuge for many plants from the north.

The total effect of the ice ages was an enormous acceleration of evolution. Without them the world would still be in the age of reptiles. The effect of refugee plants streaming across the continents was to stimulate genetic crossing, to favour what would previously have been unsuitable mutations. Nor is the process by any means at a standstill today. We can watch the pines for example still in full cry, reconquering the hills.

Fourteen thousand years ago the ice retreated for the last time (so far). The variations in climate since that time have been relatively slight, but enough to favour different trees at different times. What flourished when is known to us primarily by the analysis of the pollen grains found in recent lake sediments in the strata of peat.

In the immediately post-glacial 'subarctic' period, the areas where the ice had been were still raw mineral soil and an unchecked wind allowed only the toughest trees—dwarf birches and willows—to make the first colonizing moves.

Bottom *One million years ago, just before the first ice age, typical European forest vegetation included the present oaks, birch, spruce etc. but also scores of trees we think of as American or Asiatic: magnolias, redwoods, hickories, white pines, incense cedars, umbrella pines, plum yews, ginkgos.*

Extent of glacier ice
▽▽▽ Extent of sea ice

Left *The last ice age reached its fullest extent of glaciation 20,000 years ago, covering most of North America, all of Scandinavia and north-western Asia, some of northern Europe and all the northern oceans. The ice-sheet built up chiefly where westerly winds brought rain. Siberia, mostly low-lying and* completely sheltered from the west by the Asiatic land-mass, largely escaped glaciation; no solid front of ice descended into China as it did into America and Europe. The whole of China was therefore a refuge for such trees as could stand the cold. In America trees retreated south; in Europe most of them perished.

Left *Since the last ice age ended in about 10,000 B.C. the world's climate has not been static. The temperature rose irregularly through the 'Boreal' periods to a maximum in the 'Atlantic' period about 4,000 B.C. Since then, again irregularly, it has cooled. This chart records the effect of these changes on the tree populations of Europe and the United States. The leafier the stem (on the chart) the more the trees in question flourished. 'Pollen counts' in datable strata (usually in peat) provide the evidence. Overall there appears to be a certain symmetry in the pattern, pivoting approximately round the 'Atlantic' period. To this extent it bears out the theory that we are living between two ice ages.*

The maps, right and below, illustrate the effects of the ice ages and other climatic changes on the distribution of two important groups of trees, the sequoias and the magnolias. Sequoia remains have been found in fossils over most of the northern hemisphere—even in Greenland. Yet today, as a result of climate and competition, the two members of the genus are confined to tiny separate areas of California (inset).

A B Redwood:
Present area of distribution:
A Coastal Redwood (Sequoia sempervirens)
B Sierra Redwood or 'big tree' (Sequoiadendron giganteum)
● Fossil localities

Right *Fossil remains of magnolias show that before the ice ages they were well distributed round the northern hemisphere; certainly more so than the present evidence (on the map) proves. But they belonged to one of the families that the ice ages wiped out entirely in Europe. The combination of the Mediterranean and the Alps left them no route southward. All our magnolias today come from Asia and America.*

Magnolia:
● Fossil localities
🟩 Present area of distribution

Since then, starting some 11,000 years ago, there was a build-up through a cool, then a more continental and extreme climate to a climax of relative warmth and wetness–the 'Atlantic' period of between 7,500 and 5,000 years ago, the era when some of the bristlecone pines still alive today were seedlings.

Their lifetime has seen a reversal of the previous trends; another dry, continental and extreme period followed by about 1,500 years of lower temperatures and more rain, the era (in human terms) of the classical civilizations and the Dark Ages. About 1000 (A.D.) another trend becomes discernible–now with plenty of still-living trees to give evidence: the relatively warm and dry period in which we live.

To speak in terms of broad trends is the best anyone can do, reviewing such a span of time. What is worth remembering, however, is that the answer to any particular question need not lie in the great averages of history. Cataclysms and catastrophes are as much a part of evolutionary history as the gradual attrition of the ages. Whether or where a species exists can be decided by one great frost; one plague of locusts; one unaccountable wave of natural competition. The movements of nature can take millennia –or they can happen in a flash.

Left *The theory of continental drift holds that one huge land-mass broke up and has been drifting apart since, taking plants with it. But geologists say the rift (if any) was at least 200 million years ago: too early for modern plant distribution.*

Chart labels (left side, top to bottom):

EUROPE | UNITED STATES

2,000 AD
1,000 AD
Sub-Atlantic
0
1,000 BC
Sub-Boreal
2,000 BC
3,000 BC
4,000 BC
Atlantic
5,000 BC
Boreal
6,000 BC
7,000 BC
Pre-Boreal
8,000 BC
9,000 BC
10,000 BC
Late-Glacial
11,000 BC
12,000 BC

Europe annotations: Wetter / Climate deteriorates; Cooler & drier; Warm & wet climatic optimum; English Channel forms; Drier Rapid warming; Sub-arctic gradual warming; Arctic conditions Tundra

United States annotations: Cool & wet; Oldest sequoia germinates; Becoming cooler and wetter Oldest bristlecone germinates; Peak of warmth; Warm, dry; Extensive prairie; Becoming drier; Gradual warming; Arctic conditions Tundra

Europe species: Juniper | Birch | Pine | Hazel | Oak | Beech
United States species: Spruce | Pine | Oak | Hickory | Hemlock | Chestnut

The Old World

Tree distribution since the last ice age has been the slow setting to rights of what the ice disjointed. At first the process was infinitely gradual, through colonization and evolution. But later, since the dawn of civilization when man began moving plants about, redistribution has happened at a faster and faster pace–so that today, in countries which the ice overran and which have since seen a succession of civilizations, the question of what tree is native has little meaning.

Native when? When the ice advanced? Or retreated? Before man set about destroying the forest? In the earliest written account?

We know little of the early years. We know that the peach tree and the mulberry came from the Orient, the walnut from the Caucasus, the fig from Persia.

But what trees the Romans brought, or what plants they moved from one part of their empire to another, are questions we can no longer answer.

Plants of usefulness are cultivated and transported before plants of ornament. If the Romans took the sweet chestnut and the walnut with them to France and Britain it was for their fruit.

But the Romans were rose-lovers as well as gourmands and fanatical ablutionists.

The walnut from Persia was one of the useful trees introduced into cultivation in classical times. Engraving from a 16th-century Swiss herbal.

Diggings at Chichester (their port of Regnum) have uncovered a palace garden made exactly to Pliny's instructions–to the very size and depth and spacing of the flower-beds. It would be surprising if the nurserymen of Rome did not export to officers abroad the plants they loved at home.

The systematic study of plants had been initiated by the Greeks. It was continued by the Romans. Then in the Middle Ages it lapsed into a mixture of carpenter's know-how, herbalist's mumbo-jumbo and poetical symbolism. Chaucer made a catalogue of trees, which is a fair sample:

The bilder ook, and eek the hardy asshe;
The piler elm, the coffre unto careyne;
The boxtree piper; holm to whippes lasshe;
The sayling firr; the cipres, deth to pleyne;
The shooter ew, the asp for shaftes pleyne;
The olive of pees, and eek the drunken vyne,
The victor palm, the laurer to devyne.

The Renaissance brought the classical systems to light again. Learned apothecaries in the north of Europe found that the plants of ancient Greece failed to tally with the local flora. Modern botany began with their 'herbals'.

The gardens of the Villa Lante, north of Rome, were begun by Vignola in 1566. In such Renaissance gardens trees were treated as architectural elements.

Albertus Magnus (1193–1280), a German Dominican monk, was the greatest exponent of Aristotle's botanical work in the Middle Ages. He taught at Cologne and Paris.

John Gerard (1545–1612) was author of the famous Herball or Generall Historie of Plantes, published in 1597. It is vivid writing, but still largely concerned with medicine.

John Parkinson (1567–1650), early plant collector, and author of Paradisus in sole Paradisus terrestris, or a garden of all sorts of pleasant flowers which our English ayre will permitt to be noursed up . . .

John Tradescant (died 1637?) was gardener to King Charles I, travelled to Russia and Algiers and made a collection of plants at Lambeth. His son John followed in his footsteps, sailing to Virginia.

Europe's earliest botanic garden at Leiden, Holland, was made in 1594 by the

The cedar of Lebanon was introduced to Britain from Turkey in 1638.

This engraving is from an early 17th-century French herbal.

The first herbal in English was William Turner's, published in 1546. Gerard's popular and readable *Herball*, largely plagiarized from the work of the Dutchman Dodoens, appeared in 1597; John Parkinson's *Paradisus in Sole* in 1629. Parkinson was an ardent collector and may himself have introduced new species into cultivation.

At the same time, what had seemed an inexhaustible supply of timber began to look disturbingly thin. By the beginning of the 16th century Royal Statutes were enjoining replanting. The Great Wood of Scotland (the Caledonian Forest) is described as 'utterly destroyed'. Books of husbandry (the first, Fitzherbert's, in 1523) began to give instructions for planting trees.

The first botanical expeditions (in the same period) covered the ancient world, most of it then in the Turkish empire. One might say that consolidation and realization of the trees of the Old World, including the world of the Bible, took up to the middle of the 17th century. About 1600 Europe received the horse chestnut from Asia Minor; by mid-century she had the cedar of Lebanon.

There is a great stock-taking in John Evelyn's *Sylva* of 1662. The monarchy had been restored to an England worse off than ever for timber–particularly for oak, without which there could be no navy. National security literally depended on oak trees–as France realized in the following century. Evelyn was commissioned by the Royal Society to discourse on growing trees. He did it with such gusto (and apparent knowledge) that his discourse was still being printed a century later.

While England was worrying about warships, France was getting on with the serious business of planting avenues. The same year as *Sylva* saw the culmination of the French style of landscaping: Le Nôtre's design for the park of Vaux-le-Vicomte.

Landscape design had advanced hand in hand with baroque building. Concern was entirely with form: plants were treated as far as possible as lifeless absolutes: an avenue and a colonnade came to the same thing; so did a hedge and a wall. Handled by masters, trees did what they were told.

As Kip's engravings of English country houses of the period show, however, there were fewer masters than gardens. A banal formality was the general rule. The first botanic gardens were not much advanced in design from the knot gardens of the Tudors.

This engraving of Vaux-le-Vicomte shows how the vast formal gardens of France were conceived as settings for self-satisfied people in huge numbers. Trees were mere building materials.

great botanist Clusius. His original plan has been reconstructed recently.

John Ray of Essex (1627–1705) originated the division of plants into monocotyledons and dicotyledons. His Historia Plantarum *was published in 1686–1704 and included the first printed account of American trees.*

The Swiss Jean Bauhin c. 1541–1613 established a botanic garden at Lyon, France. His Historia Plantarum Universalis, *not published till 1650, set new standards in accurate and concise plant description.*

André Le Nôtre (1613–1700) was the chief practitioner of the majestic French style of landscaping of the 'Grand Siècle'; he designed the parks of Versailles and Vaux-le-Vicomte. Vanbrugh in England was influenced by him.

John Evelyn (1620–1706), diarist, dilettante and friend of Charles II, published his great Sylva, *a Discourse on Forest Trees in 1662.*

The New World

John Bartram *(1699–1777), the first native American botanist, was responsible, through his* correspondence with Collinson, for introducing many American trees to Europe.

Henry Compton *(1632–1713) was the first great patron of botany in North* America, sending botanically-trained missionaries to the Indians.

Peter Collinson, *London merchant and Quaker, formed a famous* friendship with the American botanist John Bartram.

A strong current had started to run by the time of England's Civil War. King Charles I's gardener went to Russia (whence he may have introduced the larch to England) and Spain and North Africa. His son, the second John Tradescant, sailed for Virginia. With the Tradescants begins the introduction of the trees of the New World.

Whether it was actually the younger Tradescant–who went three times to Virginia–or correspondents of his father, or other returning colonists who brought them, we shall never know. But by 1656 the plantlist of the 'museum' the Tradescants kept in their Lambeth garden included many of the biggest and most striking of the trees of the American east coast: the black locust or false acacia, named *Robinia* after Tradescant's friend Jean Robin, curator of the Paris Jardin dés Plantes; the tulip tree; the swamp cypress; the eastern red cedar.

Evelyn mentions the tulip tree (which he calls the Virginia poplar) and the *Thuja.* He speaks of 'great opportunities ... we have of every day improving our stores with so many useful trees from the American plantations'.

The man who seized the opportunities was the Bishop of London, Henry Compton, a nobleman and former mercenary. From his palace at Fulham he directed the spiritual affairs of the colonies, sending missionaries among the Indians, and choosing for his men such as could spot an unknown plant and, spotting it, get it safely home.

His palace garden became an important centre for the plants of America. Among the trees introduced there (by his missionary John Bannister) was the first magnolia grown in Europe, the swamp-bay, *Magnolia virginiana*. The black walnut, the box elder, the balsam poplar, the balsam fir, the scarlet oak, the flowering dogwood were others.

The first home-grown American botanist was John Bartram, the son of a Quaker settler at Philadelphia, who farmed the banks of the Schuylkill River. By a happy chance he was put in touch with a London linen-draper named Peter Collinson, another Quaker, who had a passion for plants, particularly for trees, and (not being in a position to send out missionaries) was looking for an American to collect plants and seeds for him. Their correspondence began in 1732 and continued until Collinson died a third of a century later. By then Linnaeus was ready to describe Bartram as 'the greatest living botanist in the world'.

His discoveries numbered some 200 species. He found them by wandering about alone in Indian country, from the Great Lakes down to Georgia. Courage has always been as important as eyesight to people who seek new plants.

The list of Bartram's trees is awe-inspiring. It includes the sugar and silver maples; the American ash, elm and lime; the black, red and white oaks; *Magnolia grandiflora*; the river birch; the long-leaf and the short-leaf pines. Nor was it entirely a one-way traffic. The cedar of Lebanon (in 1746) and the horse chestnut (in 1753) were two of the

Bishop Compton's Fulham Palace *on the river Thames had the first garden in Europe to boast such trees as magnolia, flowering dogwood, white pine and scarlet oak.*

Right *The 18th century saw the making of England's great 'natural' landscape gardens. Capability Brown's Stowe, shown here, is typical. But the great influx of new trees was virtually ignored.*

John Stuart, *3rd Earl of Bute (1713–92), was a great amateur botanist,* *first effective Director of Kew and later a deplorable Prime Minister.*

William Aiton, *the first Superintendent of Kew (from 1759 to 1793).* Philip Miller *of Chelsea Physick Garden, father of horticultural journalism.*

André Michaux *introduced such trees as the ginkgo to America at his* *Charleston nursery and wrote the first study of American oaks.*

trees Collinson sent Bartram for his own collection, America's first botanic garden.

What started as a private arrangement became almost a public institution as the results began to be seen. Collinson shared the costs with subscribers: at first the young Lord Petre, whose estate was at Ingatestone in Essex; then the Dukes of Richmond, of Bedford, of Norfolk; then Frederick, Prince of Wales, father of King George III, who with his wife, Princess Augusta, lived at Kew House by the Thames, just west of London.

The story of Kew, the greatest of the world's botanic gardens, begins here. The Prince and Princess provided a nucleus for the mushrooming interest in new plants. They employed the great William Kent (and later Capability Brown) to landscape their grounds. They asked the Earl of Bute, a Scot and (one might almost say therefore) no

mean botanist, to supervise their planting. The Prince died in 1751, but Princess Augusta pressed on. In 1759 she appointed William Aiton the first Curator of the Royal Botanic Garden. He was another Scot, trained at the already famous Chelsea Physick Garden by its celebrated curator, Philip Miller, the author of *The Gardener's Dictionary*. Between them Aiton and his son were at Kew for no less than 82 years.

What perhaps has more to do with trees is the interest some of the great landowners began to take in the new introductions. The Duchess of Beaufort at Badminton, the Duke of Argyll at Hounslow and the Duke of Atholl in Perthshire became passionate tree-planters. Lord Weymouth at Longleat planted so many of the new white pines from New England that they became known by his name. Records begin here for the growth of many trees that are still alive today, with

every biographical detail known.

What was strange and disappointing, however, was the ignorance of all this by the great landscapers. England was at that very moment going through the greatest redecoration she has ever had. The old parks and gardens were being rooted up wholesale, to be replaced by the placid quasi-natural landscape favoured first by Bridgeman and Kent, then by the all-powerful Brown.

As Humphrey Repton, their more sophisticated successor, remarked: 'Their trees are of one general kind, while the variety of nature's productions is endless, and ought to be duly studied'.

The Royal Botanic Garden at Kew, *originally a private royal collection, now the world's greatest botanical institution, is dominated by its pagoda.*

André Michaux's *greatest work was his* Flora of North America *of 1803 from which this painting of leaf and flower of the tulip tree is taken.*

The World Expands

China is the mother of gardens. The Chinese emperors loved and collected plants for almost 5,000 years. Large parts of China have been cultivated for so long that the notion of a wild plant is laughable: everything desirable is cultivated; everything else extinct. Species of the most prized plants – paeonies, chrysanthemums, camellias – have been improved and treasured for century after century.

But China had no intention of letting the barbarians in. After Marco Polo's 13th-century visitation there was a pause of more than 300 years before another contact was allowed, under the pressure of a western world curious and hungry for trade. It was the 18th century before any westerner got even a toehold to look for plants.

The toehold was one of the East India Company's 'factories' on the coast; the westerner was James Cunningham, a surgeon with the company, who visited Amoy in the Formosa strait in 1698 and Chusan, an island south of Shanghai, in 1700. He was forbidden to ramble outside the port, but he procured paintings of Chinese plants and specimens of what the nurseries had to sell.

The French were more subtle – and more successful. They had no trading rights but gained entry to the country by sending missionaries trained in skills the Chinese lacked: glass-blowing; clock-making; engineering. By this means Father Pierre d'Incarville reached Peking in 1742 and stayed for 15 years. He had the commission of France's greatest botanist, Bernard de Jussieu, to collect for the Royal gardens and the Jardin des Plantes in Paris. He also had London correspondents – among them the insatiable Collinson. The fruits of his labours included the tree of heaven, the silk tree (*Albizia julibrissin*), the *Cedrela*, the *Sophora*, the Chinese *Thuja*, the Chinese juniper and the golden-rain tree (*Koelreuteria paniculata*).

All connections with China, however,

Right Alexander von Humboldt *(1769–1859) visited Mexico and Peru on one of the greatest of all scientific journeys. Botany was only one of his many interests: the Humboldt current bears his name. The first major tree-collection in temperate South America was made by William Lobb in Chile in the 1840s for Veitch's nursery.*

Above left Duhamel du Monceau *(1700–82) was a distinguished French engineer and agriculturist. The* Nouveau Duhamel, *a posthumous edition of his work on trees, was superbly illustrated by Redouté.*

Left Engelbert Kaempfer *(1651–1715), a doctor to the Dutch Company in Japan, took part in diplomatic missions to Tokyo in the spring of 1690 and 1691 and brought the West its first Japanese flowering cherries, and also magnolias. He discovered the ginkgo.*

Right Carl Peter Thunberg *(1743–1828), a pupil of Linnaeus at Uppsala in Sweden, held the same post as Kaempfer 85 years later. He ran a nursery on Deshima, the Dutch island in Nagasaki harbour, and collected maples, oaks, cherries and conifers amongst other plants. He published in 1784 the first* Flora Japonica.

Below Philipp Franz von Siebold *(1791–1866), held the same physician's post as Kaempfer and Thunberg from 1826 to 1830, when he was expelled from Japan for spying. He introduced azaleas, camellias, hydrangeas and other garden plants during this stay, and later* Paulownia *and Japanese crab.*

were subject to the imperial whim. D'Incarville had been lucky; after him the doors closed again. But a glimpse had been enough: *chinoiserie* was all the rage in Europe – in furnishing, in decoration; even, for a while, in gardening (witness the pagoda built in 1761 at Kew).

With Japan the story was much the same: a tantalizing glimpse, followed by drawn blinds.

The earliest confrontation between the Japanese and the Europeans had not been a happy one. The Europeans were kept effectively at arm's length; only the Dutch were allowed any trade at all, and they were confined to an island in Nagasaki harbour, except for annual envoys permitted to bring presents to the Emperor at Yedo – as Tokyo was then called.

Engelbert Kaempfer, a German doctor and botanist in the employ of the Dutch East India Company, made the journey to Yedo twice, in 1690 and 1691, and gave the first report of Japanese trees. The ginkgo (a Chinese tree, but imported to Japan, like the art of gardening itself, at a very early period) was his most important discovery; he also sent back to Holland maples and flowering cherries. He was the last European botanist to visit Japan for more than 80 years.

By the time his successor, Carl Thunberg, a pupil of Linnaeus, reached Yedo in 1776 there was a new spirit abroad in Europe. Captain Cook had visited Australia; Francis Masson (the first professional plant-collector) had returned from the Cape; the botanist William Roxburgh had left for Calcutta. The French were heading for Peru.

The new spirit was summed up in the person of Sir Joseph Banks, Lord Bute's successor at Kew and one of the most knowledgeable and enthusiastic (and richest) patrons that exploration has ever had. He himself had sailed with Cook. Now he saw to it that every expedition was equipped with a competent young botanist. And incidentally, that the loot should come to swell the great collection he was making at Kew.

The chart of tree-introductions on pages 318-19 illustrates perfectly the situation at the end of the 18th century. Introductions from the Mediterranean had come in a steady flow for centuries. A colossal flood from eastern North America had steadied to a stream, largely from the work in the southeast of another emissary of Kew, John Fraser. But the rest – the Far East, the American west and the whole of the southern hemisphere – were about to be ransacked for the undreamt-of wealth of trees that was to treble the number known to the western world within the next century.

Left *The Orient became a rage in 18th-century Europe. English gardens were decked out in fanciful 'Chinese' style.*

Above left Captain James Cook *proclaimed New South Wales a British possession at Botany Bay in 1770. Sir Joseph Banks was on the expedition.*

Above Bernard de Jussieu *(1699–1777) foreshadowed the 'natural system' of botanical classification, ran the Jardin des Plantes in Paris and started a botanical garden at the Trianon, Versailles, for Louis XV.*

Giants and Gentility

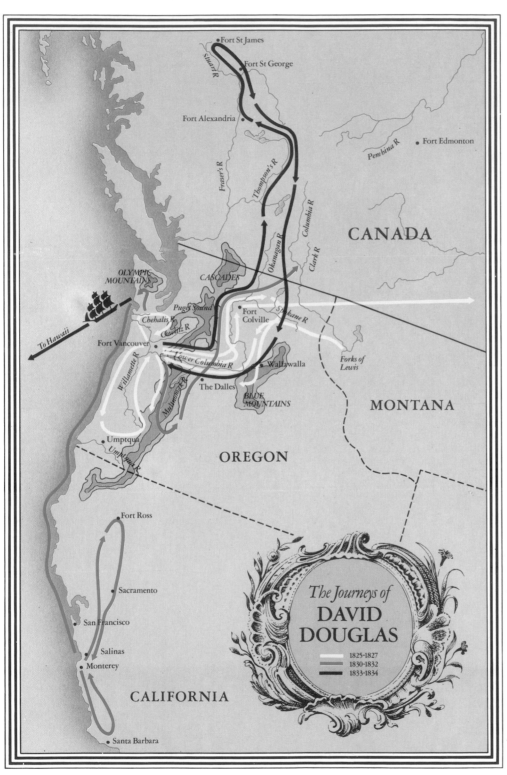

The Journeys of David Douglas

The first news that the Pacific coast of America held something quite exceptional for the botanist came from Captain Vancouver's voyage of 1792. His botanist–I almost said his Scotsman–was Archibald Menzies. With justifiable excitement Menzies reported the Douglas fir, the Alaska cedar (or Nootka cypress), the Sitka spruce and the coast redwood: all trees twice as high as anything he had seen before.

John Bartram had dreamed of an expedition to the west many years before. His scheme eventually took place, 37 years after his death, when Thomas Jefferson organized the 40-strong Lewis and Clark expedition. But it lacked Bartram, or even a lesser botanist. The expedition returned from the coast (having spent two and a half years on the way) with a very modest collection of seeds, without apparently having even seen Menzies' great trees.

When in 1824 London got round to sending a collector Sir Joseph Banks was dead, and Kew (temporarily, for political reasons) out of favour and short of funds. It was the Horticultural Society (founded in the year Lewis and Clark set out from St Louis) which commissioned the trip. At the recommendation of the great William Jackson Hooker, then at Glasgow but later to be the most illustrious director Kew has ever had, the man chosen was David Douglas, son of a stonemason from Scone in Perthshire, a self-taught botanist who had impressed Hooker as having unusual qualities.

Courage is common currency among plant-collectors. The stories of their exploits, and not infrequently of their uncomfortable ends, has made many a good book. But by any standards Douglas was special. He was a Highlander with an obsession. He addressed himself to the northwestern wilderness with the energy of a fanatic. The Indians learnt to treat this strange 'grass-man' (as they called him) with the utmost respect.

In a Stewart tartan coat, and with tea (of which he drank gallons) as his only comfort, he travelled thousands of miles of trackless country, very often quite alone, carrying on his back (and above his head through icy torrents) a prodigious load of specimens, seeds, cones–even, at one time, two living eagles. To be wet through, to be wounded, to be starving apparently meant nothing to him if he scented a new tree farther on.

His first expedition to the Columbia River (not counting the eight and a half month voyage out, of which no less than six weeks was spent waiting to cross the dangerous sand-bar at the river-mouth) lasted from April 1825 to March 1827, when he left for home overland by the Hudson's Bay Com-

Archibald Menzies *(1754–1842), naval surgeon and botanist, sailed on Vancouver's 'Discovery' on its voyage of exploration to the Northwest in the 1790s. He was the first botanist to see the colossal conifers of the Pacific coast. The Latin name of the Douglas fir (Pseudotsuga menziesii) commemorates him.*

Thomas Nuttall *(1786–1859), from Liverpool, tried several times to cross North America and finally succeeded at the age of 50 after a gruelling journey over the mountains. From 1822 to 1834 he was Curator of the Harvard Botanic Garden.*

John Claudius Loudon *(1783–1843), journalist and encyclopedist, made the first complete record of hardy trees then known and their implications for horticulture in his* astonishing Arboretum et Fructicetum Britannicum, *shortened to 1,200 pages in 1842 as* Trees and Shrubs of Great Britain. *He coined the 'gardenesque' style.*

A. J. Downing *was the Loudon of North America, publishing his* The fruits and fruit trees of America *in 1845. He was also the leading American landscape designer of his day, pioneering the creation of urban parks for recreation.*

Frederick Law Olmsted *was inspired by Sir Joseph Paxton's design of Birkenhead Park, Liverpool, to compete in designing Central Park, New York (1858). Having won the competition he went on to become the father of the U.S. National Parks.*

pany's 'express'. His haul from this journey, in trees alone (and there was much else besides) included the Douglas fir, the Sitka spruce, the noble and lovely firs, the bigleaf maple, the ponderosa, the bigcone, the sugar and the western white pines. He wrote to Hooker 'you will begin to think that I manufacture pines at my pleasure'.

He reached the Columbia river on his second expedition in 1830. This time he also went to California and made Monterey his base. All the time he was sending home not packets but chests of seeds. His job was not just to discover but to introduce, which he did so effectively that his finds were able to go immediately into circulation to scores of collections. His trees were becoming well known while he was still camping in the wilderness.

St Petersburg's famous botanical garden was among his clients. He was invited by the Czar to make the appalling journey homewards through Alaska and Siberia. In 1832, full of enthusiasm, he set off from Fort Vancouver. But this expedition came to grief in the wilds of British Columbia. He had to return, canoe-wrecked and dispirited, now blind in one eye.

Douglas met his end in Hawaii 18 months later. He fell into a bull-pit and was killed by a wild bull. He was only thirty-five.

For 20 years after Douglas's death the West was alive with botanists and the world agog to see what they found. Thomas Nuttall arrived by the Hudson Bay route the following year (and found the dogwood of the west, *Cornus nuttallii*, which Douglas must have been very unlucky to miss). Theodor Hartweg, sponsored by the Horticultural Society, sent home seed of the redwood, the Monterey cypress and the chinkapin. A group of Scots landowners formed themselves into the Oregon Association and sent John Jeffrey (who found the Jeffrey pine and the western hemlock and introduced Douglas's grand fir). Veitch's famous nursery at Exeter sent William Lobb, who had pioneered exploration in Chile. He brought back, among new trees, the giant sequoia, the western red cedar (*Thuja plicata*), the white fir and the lovely Santa Lucia fir. That was in 1853: the gold-rush was on; there were hotels in the west.

If there is a contemporary of Douglas's to compare with him in prodigious output, though in a different field, it is John Claudius Loudon. Douglas delved; Loudon (you might say) span. Loudon was the author of the seven volumes of the *Arboretum et Fructicetum Britannicum*, the first attempt to describe, from both the botanist's and the gardener's point of view, the vast range of trees then available; most of them new. He was also the editor of his own magazine and author of (among other thick books) an *Encyclopedia of Cottage, Farm and Villa Architecture* and *The Suburban Gardener and Villa Companion*.

The last gives all too clear a picture of the world to which these glorious trees were being introduced. This is Loudon on plant-introduction: 'It is the beautiful work of civilization, of patriotism, and of adventure, first to collect these all into our country, and, next, to distribute them to others.'

Loudon divided all gardens into four classes – from first-rate to fourth-rate. Most modern gardens would make him rush to add an eighth- and ninth-rate. He is full of good practical information and advice. But whereas the 'natural' landscapers and their school had swept all garden fussiness aside, ignored new trees and dealt only in 'prospects', Loudon preached a more dangerous creed: 'When it is once properly understood that no residence in the modern style can have a claim to be considered as laid out in good taste, in which all the trees and shrubs employed are not either foreign ones, or improved varieties of indigenous ones, the grounds of every country seat, from the cottage to the mansion, will become an arboretum.'

The first crossing of North America to the Pacific was made in 1804–06 by Captains Lewis and Clark. For botany it had more symbolic than practical significance.

Loudon's Suburban Gardener and Villa Companion *(1838) set the scene to which the discoveries of the dauntless botanists were introduced. Gardening reached a low ebb at the very moment when it received its greatest opportunity.*

Explorers in the East

Botanists were running hither and thither like ants as the 19th century opened. The only places where they still met more than physical difficulties were in the Far East. Work there was by maddeningly remote control: East India Company factories on the coast of China were the only point of contact. Plant-hungry collectors (of whom there were more and more) resorted to commissioning the masters of East Indiamen to visit the nurseries of Macao and Canton on their behalf. They got beautiful cultivated flowers, but still no idea of the trees and shrubs of the unknown interior.

The enterprise of a Bavarian eye-doctor, Philipp von Siebold, was richly rewarded when he managed (on the strength of his ability to cure cataract) to steal into Japan and take a first proper survey of her flora. That was in 1823. But the frustrations continued until China was finally bullied into opening her frontiers in 1844, and until Commodore Perry and his warships made it plain to the Japanese (in 1853) that what America was not given willingly she was quite prepared to take.

The story of who went where in that amazing hunting ground, and what they found, is told in the accompanying map and illustrations. There was (and is) a lot to absorb in a single sustained draught–which is more or less the way it happened. We have still hardly taken stock of the superb flora of western China–particularly of the south-western reaches of the Himalayas. One thing which has clearly emerged, though, is the close relations between the species of China and North America. Their similar ice-age history continually crops up in parallel survivals.

The same period saw the exploration of Sikkim and the hugely fertile middle heights of the central Himalayas, initially by Joseph Hooker, son of the director of Kew (who was later to take his turn in that august chair). The great English craze for rhododendrons starts here.

Father Jean Marie Delavay, *the first European botanist in western China (1838–95), discovered scores of good garden plants in Yunnan. A magnolia and silver fir bear his name.* 3C

Jean André Soulié *(1858–1905) discovered the butterfly-bush buddleia and several rhododendrons in Szechwan.* 3C

Father Paul Perny *(1818 –1907) discovered the holly which bears his name.* 3D

Paul Guillaume Farges *(1844–1912) sent seeds to Vilmorin, including the first Davidia. He discovered many rhododendrons and the splendid silver fir that bears his name.* 2D

▲ **Above Father Armand David** *(1826–1900) was a distinguished French zoologist and botanist. Apart from Davidia, he discovered numerous species called* davidii *and* armandii. 1 *and* 3C

SZECHWAN **Province**

Chengku **Centre of botanical interest**

Fortune 1860 **Botanist with main date of visit (where known)**

Thomas Lobb *(1809–63) collected for the London nursery firm of Veitch (who also sent William Lobb to Chile and California). A Cryptomeria bears his name.* 3B

◄ **Left Sir Joseph Hooker** *(1817–1911), later Director of Kew Gardens, returned from the Himalayas in 1850 with magnificent rhododendrons. He introduced the Himalayan birch and reported, amongst other trees, the biggest of all magnolias,* Magnolia campbellii. 3A *and* B

Henry John Elwes *(1846– 1922), co-author of a great book on trees (see page 50), visited Sikkim in 1870.* 3B

Victor Jacquemont *(1801–32) reported the deodar cedar. Several plants are named after him.* 2A

Nathaniel Wallich *(1786 –1854), a Danish surgeon, 30 years Director of the Calcutta Botanic Garden, introduced* Rhododendron arboreum, Himalayan white pine, *and* Cotoneaster frigidus; *he also discovered many garden plants.* 2A, 3 *and* 4B

Frank Ludlow *and* **George Sherriff** *made the most famous of recent Tibetan expeditions, finding mainly rhododendrons and primulas.* 3B

Engelbert Kaempfer *(see pages 44/5).* 2F

Right Frank Kingdon-Ward *(1885–1958) from Manchester explored and collected for over 40 years between Tibet and Burma. Plants named* wardii *(including a rhododendron, camellia, holly and cherry) are his introductions.* 3B, 4B *and* C. ▶

Right Robert Fortune
(1812–80) was the first collector in China to have relative freedom. He was sent by the Horticultural Society in 1843 and introduced many essential garden plants. His trees included the false larch, the Chinese plum yew, the umbrella pine and the Cryptomeria. *2 and 3D, 3 and 4E, 2F*

James Cunningham, *the first botanist to introduce Chinese plants (in 1698), is commemorated by the Chinese 'fir',* Cunninghamia. *4D, 3E*
Carl Peter Thunberg *(see page 45). 2E*

Pierre d'Incarville
(1706–57), a Jesuit priest, whose introductions, from Peking, included the tree of heaven, pagoda tree and goldenrain tree. 2D
Philipp von Siebold *(see page 45). 3E, 2F*

Right Carl Maximowicz
(1827–91) of the St. Petersburg Botanic Garden became the greatest living authority on the plants of Manchuria and Japan in the 1860s. He introduced magnolias, Stewartia pseudo-camellia, oaks, firs, pines, maples. The monarch birch, later introduced by Sargent, bears his name. 2D, 1 and 3E, 1 and 2F

Dr. Clarke Abel *(1780–1826) visited Peking in a diplomatic mission, reported the Chinese elm, and introduced the ornamental apricot and the shrub* Abelia. *2 and 4D*

Right Ernest Henry 'Chinese' Wilson
(1876–1930), first for Veitch's nursery, then for the Arnold Arboretum made the greatest individual collection of Chinese trees in four journeys. His trees include the paperbark maple, giant dogwood and Magnolia wilsonii. 3C, 3 and 4D, 2F

William Kerr *(died 1814) was sent from Kew to China by Sir Joseph Banks and lived there eight years. The Chinese juniper is the most important tree he introduced. 4D*

Grigori Nicolaevich Potanin *(1835–1920) explored 'Tebbuland' (plants from here are called 'tangutica'). The Chinese larch bears his name. 2C and D*

Left John Gould Veitch *of the famous Chelsea nursery family visited Japan in 1860. He collected Magnolia stellata and 17 new conifers, including the Japanese larch and Japanese fir, Veitch's fir from Fuji, and the Yezo, Hondo and tiger-tail spruces. His son J. H. Veitch did much to popularize Japanese flowering cherries. 1 and 2F*

Below George Forrest *(1873–1932) was the greatest of all collectors of rhododendrons, introducing hundreds of species including R. giganteum and R. sinograde to the Edinburgh Botanic Garden. He also specialised in primulas. He introduced a beautiful silver fir and a snakebark maple, both called forrestii. 4C*

Alexander von Bunge *(1803–90) collected in north China for St. Petersburg; discovered Pinus bungeana. 1D*

Richard Oldham *(1838–64), the last official collector for Kew, introduced the Japanese snowbell tree. 2 and 3E*

Charles Maries *(1851–1902), sent by Veitch's nursery, pioneered in far-northern Japan, finding 'Maries' fir'. He had a less successful visit to China. 3D, 1F*

Frank Meyer *was sent to China by the U.S. Department of Agriculture in 1905. He drowned in the Yangtze in 1918. He imported millet, rice and Acer ginnala, Chinese horse chestnut and Juniperus squamata 'Meyeri'. 1, 2 and 3E*

Reginald Farrer *(1880–1920) and Euan Cox, botanical writers, visited Yunnan in 1919 and introduced the coffin-tree juniper, J. coxii. 1, 2 and 3C*

Augustine Henry *(1857–1930), an Irish doctor, began to botanize out of boredom at Ichang. His huge haul from central China included ten new maples, cherries, elms, Chinese honey-locust and coffee-tree, Tilia henryi and T. oliveri. In retirement he joined Elwes in writing* The Trees of Great Britain and Ireland. *4C, 3 and 4D*

Charles Sprague Sargent *(1841–1927) founder of the Arnold Arboretum (see page 50) collected the superb Sargent's cherry and crab in Japan. 1 and 2F*

Collingwood Ingram *has been since 1927 the greatest collector and exponent of Japanese flowering cherries (see page 198). 2 and 3F*

Right Joseph Rock, *born in Vienna, collected for the Arnold Arboretum in 'Tebbuland', which he described as 'a garden of Eden' with an enormous variety of plants. A beautiful mountain ash bears his name. 2 and 4C*

Left Lady Amherst, *wife of the Governor-General of India, seen here tree-viewing from an elephant, is the only woman in this story. She introduced Clematis montana, and splendid pheasants– but no temperate trees. 2A*

Collectors and Creators

What happened to the fruits of all these expeditions? Who were the collectors, and do their collections still survive? Did they take Loudon's advice and ban everything not imported or improved from their grounds? Did a school of gardening emerge that could keep up with such a wealth of wonderful new material?

The answer to the last question is yes–eventually. To the second last it is no–thank goodness. The collections made in the last century do still exist, many of them: but they have reached full maturity; often over-maturity.

Perhaps the most important tree collection to be founded in the last century was the Arnold Arboretum, attached to Harvard University. It occupies part of the Boston park system, which was magnificently landscaped by Frederick Olmsted in the 1860s. It depended, as Kew had done, on a giant to get it going. The giant was Charles Sprague Sargent, a patrician Bostonian whose name crops up everywhere in this or any book on trees. Sargent himself introduced a number of species of flowering cherries and crab apples from Japan. But most important he created the study of native American trees, particularly eastern ones, and their suitability for ordinary gardens. Today, despite Boston's hard climate, the Arboretum is one of the world's greatest collections, particularly strong in flowering trees; crabs and cherries and hawthorns.

After Sargent's death Ernest Wilson, two of whose Chinese journeys had been for the Arboretum, took charge. But he was killed in a car accident in 1930. Among the important books to emerge from the Arnold Arboretum are Sargent's own great 14-volume *Silva of North America*; Alfred Rehder's *Manual of Cultivated Trees and Shrubs*; several very enjoyable and rather lushly-written books by Wilson; and Donald Wyman's *Trees for American Gardens*.

What is now the National Arboretum of France was founded about the same time. The name Vilmorin is another that constantly arises in tree-talk. Maurice de Vilmorin was one of a family that had patronized botanical collection (and run a nursery) since the 18th century. At les Barres, near Montargis in the Loiret, he received seeds from all over the world and made a great collection of trees. When he died in 1918 it was given to the state. But its somewhat remote situation is against it. It is a fascinating (rather than a beautiful) place to visit today. Its only importance is as a school for foresters.

In England the great private achievement of the last century was the Holford family's arboretum at Westonbirt in Gloucester-shire. Two generations of Holfords concentrated for 96 years on their superb collection, which is now virtually the British national arboretum, run by the Forestry Commission. In this century the National Pinetum at Bedgebury in Kent has been added to the country's virtual reference-library of living trees of the temperate world.

Britain has never been in danger of losing the lead as the greatest tree-collecting nation. Perhaps because of the poverty of her natural flora, certainly because of her mild and gently rainy climate, the number of considerable collections of exotic trees is immense. In Scotland it is staggering. Perhaps the same combination of national characteristics and climatic conditions have made the British collect trees and lay down their famous cellars of wine.

The literature of trees kept pace with the collections. The first decade of this century saw the publication of the two greatest reference books on arboriculture. The first, which was privately published for subscribers, was the seven volumes of Elwes and Henry's *Trees of Great Britain and Ireland*. As a piece of scholarship it is unlikely ever to be repeated. Both the authors were immensely travelled (Henry was an early collector in China) and they knew between them where every tree grew and to what size. They had no difficulty in citing specimens in Ecuador or Edinburgh, illustrating many of them with those inimitable full-plate platinum photographs of the period.

The second book was W. J. Bean's *Trees and Shrubs Hardy in the British Isles*, which is still the standard reference work on the subject (and not just in Britain). The revised edition in four volumes is being published by stages at the moment.

That turn-of-the-century period was vitally important in questions of taste as well as scholarship. The gruff, opinionated William Robinson joined forces with the shrewd and sensitive Gertrude Jekyll. Both wrote extraordinarily influential books and both made gardens along quite new lines. Perhaps we should throw into the pot the influence of Josiah Conder, whose book on the landscape gardening of Japan showed the West for the first time what the great oriental tradition of gardening was really like–in photographs.

Robinson's approach is easy to illustrate with a quotation: 'The idea that every choice tree in our pleasure grounds should be set out by itself like an electric lamp-post is deeply impressed on the gardening mind.'

What he and Gertrude Jekyll advocated was a form of gardening exactly opposite to the laborious formalities of the Victorian age. It needed much more knowledge of plants and far greater sensitivity and observation. It looked easy, but in fact was far harder than bedding out in rows. What they wanted was to use the thrilling new exotics in a context of natural (or natural-looking) woodland so that both they and the humdrum natives came to life in a new way.

It is hard to know where to begin or where to end in a list of the great gardens that benefited by their ideas. Certainly English wealth was never more effectively used to create beauty than by men like Leonard Messel at Nymans in Sussex, Lord Aberconway at Bodnant in Wales, or Sir Eric Savill in Windsor Great Park. The influence of these practical examples of constructing the earthly paradise by really knowing the plants of other countries and blending them with one's own has been felt all over the world.

As Repton had said, 'the variety of nature's productions is endless, and ought to be duly studied'.

Charles Sprague Sargent (1841–1927) was America's greatest dendrologist. He was the first Director of the Arnold Arboretum, travelled in the East, employed 'Chinese' Wilson, and perhaps most important set America to studying her rich ornamental tree-resources.

1 Gertrude Jekyll's Wood & Garden of 1898 had an enormous influence on the English (and hence on the world's) attitude to gardens. She saw beauty in natural effects, as here in her illustration of Scots pines broken by a snowstorm.

2 William Robinson's The English Flower Garden of 1883 was reprinted almost annually for over 25 years, while a whole generation of gardeners imbibed his outspoken rejection of Victorian fussiness and formality.

3 Josiah Conder's Landscape Gardening in Japan of 1893 showed the western world the gardens of the East for the first time. It was illustrated with excellent photographs and explanatory diagrams.

4 The seven volumes of Elwes and Henry's book, privately published in 1906–13, publicly for the first time only in 1969, are one of the greatest compilations of tree-data and descriptions. This epic work celebrates the last golden age of tree-scholarship and arboretum-making.

5 W. J. Bean's still-standard reference book, Trees and Shrubs Hardy in the British Isles, has swollen from two volumes to four in 60 years as knowledge and experience has been amassed. Bean was curator of Kew Gardens. In 1914 when his book was first published many of the Chinese species mentioned were so recently discovered that they had never flowered in cultivation.

1

2

3

4

5

The Modern Nursery

Nursery cultivars or
varieties of trees which
will not 'come true' from
seed must be propagated
by cuttings; and if
cuttings will not root,
by grafting on to related
but easier 'stocks'.
Grafting and preparing
cuttings is done in a
special 'house' next to the
'mist house'.

A big open barn holds
tractors and implements.

The mist house has
benches fitted with spray
bars which maintain a
heavy mist in the air
around boxes of cuttings:
ideal conditions for the
cuttings to root.
Temperature in the house
is kept at about 70°F.

While explorers have brought thousands of new species into cultivation from the wilds, nurserymen have contributed almost as many to the huge range of trees for gardens through the less dramatic processes of breeding and selection.

An explorer brings home a new species, or a new variety of a known species. A nurseryman crosses one species with another to give us a hybrid with better garden performance–faster growth or more flaunting flowers–than either parent. Also, he watches his seed-beds like a hawk for any interesting deviant that nature may send his way. Many of the most-planted trees today are man-made, or at least man-maintained. Some 'cultivars' (varieties selected for desirable qualities) reproduce themselves faithfully through seed. But a great number can only be kept in being through the arts of propagation that by-pass the sexual system: rooting cuttings or grafting. Otherwise the special qualities of these 'clones' will go back into the genetic melting pot.

The names of many of the famous nurseries of the past are preserved in the names of the plants they bred or selected: Lucombe of Exeter, Späth of Berlin, Vilmorin of Paris, Veitch of Chelsea. These names are as familiar to the gardener as the great names of today: Hillier, Treseder of Truro, Hesse of Bremen, Germany, Gulf Stream of Virginia or Wayside Gardens of Mentor, Ohio.

The bread and butter work of a nursery, however, is simply a production system for a wide range of plants. The modern trend inevitably is to narrow the range to what the public regularly calls for. We have modelled the nursery on this page after one that determinedly does the opposite. It is a very reduced version of the workings of Hillier of Winchester, England. Hillier's *Manual of Trees and Shrubs*, which was formerly their catalogue, is a descriptive list of almost 8,000 species of trees and shrubs that at one time their nursery could supply. No other nursery in the world has attempted such a range: to be, in fact, a commercial botanic garden. Where trees in this book prove hard to find—as alas a number of them will—Hilliers is still a good place to start the hunt.

Terence Dalley.

Where seed of popular
trees is available in
quantity it is sown in a
field by a tractor like any
crop. An operator on the
back controls the flow
of seed.

Seed in bulk and cuttings
waiting for handling are
kept in a cool store at
about 38°F. Cuttings can
usually be kept in good
condition for months.
They have survived after
being carried across the
world with their ends
stuck in a potato.

'Tunnel-houses' covered
with polythene are a
common form of money-
saving greenhouse for
nurturing young plants
just struck from cuttings.
Cuttings need to have a
weaning period in a
humid atmosphere.

Container-grown trees are
stored in container beds
full of damp sand and
peat. These trees, and the
bigger ones in pots or cans
in front of the mist-house,
are ready for sale at any
time of the year.

Certain trees such as maples and flowering cherries and crabs are 'lined out' in the open ground until ready for sale. They are 'lifted' by hand and despatched either bare-rooted or 'balled' in burlap or sacking.

A tractor with a spray-bar can spray several lines of seedlings at once with insecticides, or selective weed killer, from nozzles designed to spray over or between the rows.

It is essential to keep the young trees' roots compact and densely fibrous. The technique used is to 'undercut' them with a sharp blade pulled by a tractor. Any tendency for the tree to make an unmovable tap-root is thus thwarted.

Small quantities of seed are sown by hand in beds with irrigation pipes permanently fixed. Behind, low 'tunnel-cloches' have 'mist' pipes for striking cuttings (of, for example, Leyland cypress) in summer.

One area is permanently planted with the stock trees from which cuttings (and sometimes seeds) are taken. Short side shoots are generally needed for propagating most broadleaf species.

Modern potting is done by a machine. Rooted plants are taken from the mist house or lifted from frames and potted up by the hundred in the potting-shed. In the corner is a heap of potting compost.

In this production nursery the sales centre is separate. The vast range of species for sale at different sizes to thousands of customers can necessitate the use of a computer for accounting.

The chemical armoury of a modern nursery is formidable. Insecticides and other chemicals are kept in a locked store and their use strictly regulated. Fertilizers are stored in a separate room.

53

Choosing the Species

Trees are the most telling plants in any landscape. In a garden they are decisive. They control more than its character: its sense of scale; its sense of privacy. If trees are used boldly they can create powerful effects with an almost incredible economy of means.

The various functional uses to which trees are put in gardens and streets and parks are discussed on the following pages. But the first essential is to choose a tree; to know what forms and colours and textures have what other characteristics; to be able to weigh up the various siren-voices (like speed of growth, colour, flowers).

Consider the position of the man with room for one tree outside his house—my dilemma when I lived in London. I wanted it to do everything a tree can. I thought bright gold or silver foliage would be nice, so long as it had brilliant autumn colour. But then of course I wanted it to be evergreen, to get full value from it in winter. I knew there were trees with lovely pink and peeling bark, so I wanted that. And the flowers were to be amazingly double, persistent, and fill the house with scent—and of course lead with hardly a pause to large scarlet fruit which the birds found bitter (but I, of course, found sweet).

(I planted a plane.)

Every tree-lover with a garden goes through the stage of picking the most different trees: the ice-blue spires; the bright-yellow turbans; the leaves like dinner-plates. There is a special bed in my vegetable garden for them while I make up my mind where they will go. The answer very often should be nowhere.

For there is a link, even in the suburbs, between the garden and the land. And the clue is to find it, and exploit it, and push the contrast further and further, yet still keep it in control: never to start by fighting it with the most different tree you can find.

Almost everywhere there is a dominant tree, or trees; even in the suburbs. America's lovely style of having undifferentiated private areas (the very opposite of Europe's tight fencing and hedging) in a common sward, often with big trees in common, or apparently so, sets the scene perfectly.

Where suburbs have gone over—as so often in England—to Nowhere trees like the dreary purple-leafed plum they need bringing back to the dominance of something real. It will be to everybody's relief when a big forest tree starts asserting itself. It could even (to be in keeping) flower, if it—let us say—were a tulip tree or a big wild cherry.

Let us consider the feeling that a tree is only really there if it is covered with flowers; a common feeling among gardeners, especially with small gardens. First, it is true that the frothy mass of blossom gives the sense of spring in a way nothing else can. But even if you pretend that the two weeks of blossom is really two months—the whole spring—that leaves ten. Not many flowering trees earn their keep in a small space on this basis. Nearest to it are the few cherries that colour well in autumn, or perhaps the crabs that bear fruit long after their leaves have gone.

The same frantic feeling of wanting more than just a tree is expressed in the need for coloured leaves. A single red-leaved, silver-grey or gold-variegated tree, among green ones, can have the effect of enhancing and setting off both itself and its surroundings. By the streetful, on the other hand, red or yellow trees have the very opposite effect, like a whole meal of soup or sweet.

Does the same thing apply to odd-shaped trees? Should we prefer the standard big-head in standard green?

The answer lies in the surroundings. Does your neighbour 20 yards away have a weeping willow? One is enough. If there is none in the street, and you have 50 feet each way to spare, there are few more rewarding trees to grow: among the earliest in spring with their golden young leaves; among the latest to fall, still fresh and green in October.

Is an evergreen really better value? Func-

Forming prospects, shifting hills, planting clumps, damming and diverting streams all have an 18th-century flavour today. Yet today far more landscaping is being done than in the 18th century.

Earth-moving is now much cheaper and easier. And we have a wider knowledge and choice of trees than did Repton (at work here, from his Observations . . . on Landscape Gardening, 1803).

tion aside (if you need it to hide the power-station, there is no argument) the seasons emphatically expressed by a deciduous tree are much more satisfying. It didn't take me long to love the winter sketch of my plane tree against the sky as much as its fat buds bursting, its big leaves forming, its new shoots lengthening and all the rest of its miraculous performance.

Forms, Patterns and Textures

As far as the army is concerned a tree is either a Christmas tree or a bushy-topped tree. But as soon as a civilian starts analysing the range of tree characters it is amazing how many clear categories appear. To take form (in the sense of overall shape) alone: I can think of trees that are tower-like, cloud-like, vase-like, tiered, weeping, multi-trunked (like huge shrubs), columnar, globular, pyramidal (or more strictly speaking conic), mound-like, and just plain irregular and picturesque, like an old Scots pine.

Humphrey Repton (whose late 18th-century writings on landscape design are still the great textbook) points out how—to go no further than army distinctions—the jagged lines of Christmas trees produce a sense of drama (he calls it harshness); whereas the cloud-like outlines of bushy-topped trees give an air of serenity. He went on to urge the association of each with the most unlike architecture: B.T.T.'s with Gothic (which is vertical in emphasis and C.T.'s with Grecian (which is horizontal).

The more open and characterful forms belong in the foreground of the picture. It is easy to see that a silver birch, an olive or a Lebanon cedar (or a tight column like an

1 Vase-like: Zelkova
2 Multi-trunked: Amelanchier
3 Picturesque: Pine
4 Columnar: Cypress
5 Tower-like: English elm
6 Cloud-like: Ash
7 Conic: Spruce
8 Weeping: Willow

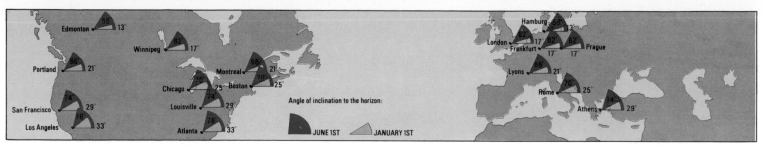

Trees near a house can provide shade just where it is needed, or they can make it gloomy all the year round. The angle of the sun is the decisive factor. In winter it rises to only about a quarter of its summer height. The chart above shows its January and June height at mid-day at different latitudes.

The sun's path through the sky is also very much shorter in winter. The diagrams (right) show the course of the sun in January and June in two places, Boston (or Provence) and Miami. In summer it travels round about two-thirds of the compass, rising in the northeast, climbing high at noon (in Miami almost to the zenith) and setting in the northwest; in winter only about one-third, rising in the south-east, and setting in the southwest. The smaller diagrams show the total daily shadow of a tree in the same places, resulting from the sun's trajectory. An evergreen tree due west of a house will therefore not shade it at all in mid-winter, but will provide shade on a summer afternoon. Deciduous trees between a house and the low winter sun show their branch-pattern in winter and are perfectly lit in summer.

Boston
42°N

June 1st   January 1st

June 1st

January 1st

59.7   121.7
N   E   S
300.3   238.3
W

Miami
26°N

June 1st   January 1st

June 1st

January 1st

65.4   115.8
N   E   S
294.6   244.2
W

Italian cypress) provides a good frame for what is beyond, whereas a solid billowing shape like a sycamore or oak, or a broad dark pyramid like a fir, gives the impression of blocking off the view – even if it really hides no more of it.

The strongest effects are undoubtedly obtained by letting one form dominate a scene, using another only to emphasise how very cloudy, moundy, towery or whatever your principal theme is. To have one of everything is bound to produce too diffuse and uncertain an effect; a problem Repton called 'flutter' – he distinguished 'flutter' from 'intricacy'.

I also rather fancy you would arrive at a state of 'flutter' by planting two contrasting forms in equal numbers; say a homogeneous mixture of oak and larch. Both would be more appreciated if there were twice as much of one as of the other. Of course this is not a rule which only applies to trees: equal areas of grass and paving in a garden produce a similarly uneasy effect.

Pattern and texture are only slightly less important than form – though perhaps harder to pin down into categories. The most obvious example of pattern is the bare deciduous tree, where the balance, the boldness or delicacy, the thrust or swoop of its twigs and branches are dominant in the winter scene. But another is the positive modelling of some trees; beech with its graceful layers of foliage; oak with its firm hummocks; or palm with its arching fans.

Huge leaves (the tree of heaven's for example) create patterns; small ones (of elm or many of the Japanese maples) are more a matter of texture. The glitter of English

holly or the marvellous mattness of the fern-leaf beech, absorbing all light, are other examples of distinct tree textures.

Here light is the crucial factor. Modelling and texture (and also colour) are obliterated if the light is behind them; bare branch patterns are lost if the light is behind you, the viewer. This is a question that has exercised great minds. Leonardo da Vinci was firm: 'The trees which are between you and the sun are far more beautiful than those which have you between the sun and themselves.' Humphrey Repton held the same opinion, illustrating it with two views of the Thames at Purley. 'All natural objects' (he went so far as to say) 'look best with the sun behind them; all artificial objects with the sun on them.'

But then both were thinking big: of great landscapes where detail was lost in distance and where there was more colour from the shafts of the sun or the lilac haze of distance than from jolly variegated shrubs and

Colorado blue spruces in the foreground.

In garden terms the message is that views to the south (in the northern hemisphere) should always be treated as having the light behind in winter, and from both sides and behind in summer. And views to the north as having the light in front in winter, and from both sides and the front in summer. Bearing in mind of course that the sun in mid-winter is about a quarter as far above the horizon as in mid-summer, which makes an enormous difference to what it reaches.

So the place for deciduous trees is to the south of the house and for evergreens to the north (where they also, happily, give shelter). But for trees of any kind whose colour or texture (or flowers) you particularly enjoy – assuming that the house is your viewpoint – the south is the angle to avoid. This is only to touch on the question of light in the landscape, which can obviously be elaborated for gardening, as it can for painting, ad infinitum.

In a Riviera garden: an unusual example of tree forms to provide shade. In the foreground a tight group of London planes shades the terrace. Beyond a regular planting of mop-head acacias makes a pattern of shade on the lawn.

Planning for Planting

'It is difficult to lay down rules for planting. Time, neglect and accident will often produce unexpected beauties'–Repton again.

The trick is to know a 'beauty' when you see one, and to be able to make the most of it.

Planning and planting are subjects in the round. There is no one right approach to them. One can consider the available material; the objectives; the techniques. Yet there remains a body of lore gleaned from long experience that is worth fitting to the circumstances.

A Dutch landscape designer (a change from Repton, at least) produced an epigram that bears a lot of thinking about: 'The axe is my pencil.' If Repton had thought of it he'd have said it, because three-quarters of the grand new effects he created for his clients, and demonstrated to them in advance with before-and-after 'slides' (as he called them) in his famous Red Books, he contrived simply by selectively cutting down what was there already. This is cold comfort for the owner of a new garden in the middle of an old airfield. But it is surprising how often it does apply once you start to look at a place with open eyes, to sum up what Lancelot Brown referred to as its Capabilities.

There is besides a wicked satisfaction in cutting down trees and clearing bushes which anyone who only plants, and would defend any growing thing with his life, should experience and realize. The most memorable moments to me in taking over a new garden have been when a tree came down, to almost feel the new view rushing in to make its contribution.

Heaven forbid that anyone should think I am advocating indiscriminate clearing, which is generally the misconceived act of developers (who later find, to their chagrin, that they have bulldozed away a good part of the value of their new houses with the trees). The modern world is full of unlovely things crying out to be hidden by trees. Taking stock should be a lengthy business. One must contrive to 'see' the place as it will be with some of the existing trees removed. One must wait four seasons, to find out how leaf-fall changes the total effect. One must go through the site with great care, even if it is only 'scrub': there may be saplings in it which will make a marvellous new start if they are left in place. And finally one must do the job by degrees, and be ready to call a halt if an unexpected effect is achieved. 'Accident will often produce unexpected beauties.'

What one can hope for by clearing is to 'borrow' some of the surroundings for one's own enjoyment. In the 18th century nobody

One of Frank Lloyd Wright's most famous houses, Falling Water (at Bear Run, Pennsylvania) is a brilliant example of the use of existing trees as part of an architectural whole. Where most developers would have cleared the birches Lloyd Wright used their delicacy to interact with his massive slabs. In winter sunshine their lacy handwriting combines with light reflected from the water to make concrete fluid.

thought it particularly wilful if a landlord shifted the village a mile or two to clear a new prospect from his library windows. It is surprising how much one can achieve even while leaving the village exactly where it is.

There was a church spire two blocks away from my old London garden. In winter you could see it looking rather glum and grey through the branches of a sycamore. But I only had to take two branches off the tree to make a leafy frame so that in summer when the light fell on the spire it was as good as in the garden.

'A plain space near the eye gives it a kind of liberty it loves.' This time a quote from Shenstone, an 18th-century English poet whose garden (the famous Leasowes, near Birmingham) was rather more distinguished than his verses.

It sounds rather like another excuse for clearing, or at any rate for not planting. It can't apply, in any case, where the whole

The human eye takes in a vertical picture 80° deep. Only 27° is above the horizontal line of your eye – at say five feet from the ground. The diagram (right) shows how a tree need

therefore be only 17½ feet high to give the impression of complete enclosure at a distance of 25 feet. At 200 feet you can take in the whole of a tree 107 feet high.

garden is 'near the eye' and a plant must either be there or nowhere. It was a basic tenet of the English landscape school, though, that the house should be set in plain lawns and the eye encouraged to go out to the limits of the ground (and beyond). Balustraded terraces round the house came later as part of the general Victorian fussiness. It is lovely to look out from under trees, but not to gaze slap into the side of a big one at short range. William Robinson went (characteristically) too far when he said 'No forest tree should ever be planted near a house'. Close in to the wall is often an excellent place for a tree, if the foundations are sound and you are prepared to take a little trouble directing the young branches. I will always remember a house in Connecticut that had been built round a stand of pines, with an upstairs gallery right among the trees, so you could touch them. It wouldn't have been up Shenstone's street, though.

'Plant close together' – expensive advice from almost every landscape designer (and not just from the nursery trade). Trees like the company of other trees. To 'dot a few starveling saplings on an open lawn' is a recipe for slow-starting, discouraged specimens. Capability Brown always planted in thick clumps – which his clients usually forgot to thin out later as they were meant to. The technique in those days was not to pay a nursery for a few very expensive standard trees (which in any case take years to shake off the dish-mop look and develop much real character) but to plant lots of small ones, mixed in with shrubs. In the open country five or six hollies or hawthorns went in for every one big tree. The trees at that size needed no stakes, which was a real saving (and looked better).

The great argument for planting big trees today is that they are harder for vandals to kill. In public places this overrides everything else. But it is doubtful whether they get away faster in anything except the short

term – up to say five years. In ten to 15 years it is very likely that a tree planted at half the height will have raced ahead.

It is not necessarily a natural look you are after in planting a garden. But Nan Fairbrother (whose book *New Lives, New Landscapes* puts her among the most influential – and enjoyable – of modern writers on the subject) had a few words to say about the Fitted-Carpet Complex. She points out that the normal situation in nature is a tree layer above a shrub layer above a herb layer. Anything that separates these is a garden style. Public authorities are all too prone to plant the trees and then simply mow under them (at great expense) to produce the fitted carpet look, on the mistaken assumption that it is either easier, or tidier, or both. She instances roadsides where the householders have to watch the traffic across a wide strip of grass between tree trunks, whereas the natural regeneration of the area, with a nudge in the right direction and a spot of fertilizer, could have given them a belt of beauty, with a rich mixture of self-sown native trees and shrubs punctuated by the row of trees (if, indeed, a row as such was needed at all).

How much you can use perspective and other tricks to enlarge the apparent size of your garden – or for that matter reduce it – is a question to ponder. Trees here are the crucial factor. They play the essential role of visually linking land and sky. Without them there is a sense of bleakness: man's puny six feet is too open to comparison with the globe, not to mention the firmament. You have only to stand in the middle of the vast and treeless parterres at Versailles or Vaux-le-Vicomte to know the moon-walking feeling.

Happily, however, the human eye, which scans the surroundings for 90 degrees from left to right, peeps out through a comparative slit at the scene above the horizontal. Your eyebrows limit you to seeing 27 degrees of the scenery above eye-level at,

say, five feet from the ground.

A simple diagram at the top of the page demonstrates that in order to make you feel well and truly enclosed a tree at a distance of 100 feet needs to be only 60 feet high; at 50 feet only 30.

Various ways suggest themselves of using this information. Essentially, you have here the clue to the future effect of new tree planting, and of establishing a vertical scale as well as a ground plan to the picture.

A surveyor's pole, ten feet high with the feet marked off in alternate red and white stripes, was Repton's instrument for gauging the interaction of height and distance. He is guilty of the truism 'objects appear great or small by comparison only'. Your Japanese with his 'distancing pine' would of course agree. You plant the big trees at this end of the garden and the small ones at the far end, and (without a ten-foot pole to give the game away) your boundary slinks off into the middle distance.

There is a point about colour that is worth a thought here. Hot colours (yellows and reds) seem nearer to the eye; cool ones (blues and greys) farther from it. Given a reasonable distance for the illusion to get a start you can certainly increase the effect of depth by grouping foliage in this way. It would mean, for example, keeping red-leafed maples near to the house and planting bluish cypresses or a silver lime farther away from it.

It has always been a planter's axiom to use uneven numbers of one kind of tree. Three trees, or five, or seven, but never two, or four, or six – unless in an avenue or as a definite pair flanking a gate. The point that matters is that you should decide whether an effect is supposed to be regular or not – and in either case go the whole hog. Irregularity means trees of different sizes, spaced widely in one place, crowded together in another. Regularity should be exact, or it looks tatty. In the long run, as any ancient avenue will tell you, irregularity wins.

The art of planting to look natural was keenly studied by the 19th-century landscapers. These two illustrations from Humphrey Repton's Art of Landscape show (left) how even irregular planting can easily look artificial and (right) how,

by planting some trees very close together, by planting trees and bushes of different heights at the same time, even by planting some trees at an angle to each other, you can create the effect of natural open woodland.

Trees for Shade, Shelter and Seclusion

The Japanese, with their formalized style of garden design, would never decide (or should I say dare?) just to stick in a tree where they thought it would look nice. They would have to rationalize the situation—in practice by giving the tree a title. That is the Tree of the Sun at Tea-time, or the Gasworks-Hiding-Tree, they would say.

There is a lot to be said for their approach. In a small garden with no space to spare it is almost essential for each tree to have a *raison d'être*. Even in a big one the more controlled and purposeful the planting the greater will be the effect.

Besides, there is no end to the functions of trees once you start to analyse them.

There is shelter (from the weather). Near-ly always essential on at least one side of a garden; the side of the prevailing wind. And often essential on the side of the cold winds of early spring as well. Shelter-belts should consist of native trees if possible, to blend in with the landscape. If they are evergreens they give the garden the same feeling of having a protecting shell all the year around. Sylvia Crowe in her *Landscape Design* says such wise words that I would be doing you a disservice not to quote her. She says, in essence, 'Shelter-belts should always be homogeneous: two species are plenty. Get an idea and make a thing of it: a belt *can't* be too tall and thin, for example: if that's the character you're after, make it a single line of Lombardy poplar. Never be indeterminate; to go all out for something is the only way to a rich effect with simple (or any) materials.' That is what she says about shelter-belts, but it is wisdom for any aspect of the garden when you think about it.

There is shade–the avowed purpose of all the street trees in America. In southern Europe (in relatively unpolluted areas) pines and other conifers are widely used to great effect. Deciduous trees are much more popular in the United States, their leaves having a more cooling effect in very hot weather–and indeed casting more shade. A big shade tree very near a house can be almost like air-conditioning. (It can also, however, play havoc with its roots and branches if you are not careful.) In England

Few gardens *in the western world are planned with the functional precision of the Japanese style. Yet purposeful tree-planting defines the structure and scale of all well-designed gardens. The pictures above illustrate aspects of one old garden in eastern England, at Saling Hall, where big old specimens of the regional natives, oak and elms, have been the background to original and intelligent tree-planting for the last 35 years.*

Top *Looking southeast from the front of the house. The only evergreen is a round-headed Thuja orientalis and a yew hedge defining the front yard. But a simple screen of Lombardy poplars on the west, giving shelter from prevailing winds in* summer, *provides a strong structural base line and emphasises the perspective of the view, without hiding the low winter sun. The matching crowns of tall English elms on the left also emphasise the distance.*

Above left *In May the sun sets in the northwest, behind just-leafing hybrid black poplars. A white cherry (Prunus avium 'Plena') shows off its flowers against a dark Monterey cypress (providing shelter from northwest winds).*

Above *Trees give shelter, seclusion, shade in summer and a frame to the view both of the house and (top left) from it. A 25-year-old Japanese flowering cherry, 'Shirofugen', is massively horizontal in contrast to the upright Lombardy*

few trees are planted primarily for shade—but we seek the shade of trees in grass to lie under every summer none the less.

There is seclusion—also known as screening. This can involve anything from a whole airport to a bathroom window. In most cases trees are the only possible medium. The point to bear in mind here is that the screen planted near the eyesore has to be far bigger than the one planted near the eye. You can hide a whole house with one bush in the foreground; over against it you will need a whole row of trees.

There is structure: the role of hedges and walls where the scale is fairly modest, but in the landscape the job of trees: to define spaces. The old English landscape of wood, field and meadow, all compartmented by tall lines of elms, or lower barriers of hawthorn, is the perfect example. In a garden in winter the structure tends to fall back on the ever-greens; the thing to remember when planting them.

There is the sense of scale—a speciality of the Japanese gardener, who would persuade you that he has half the coastline of Japan in his back-yard. His Distancing Tree is a small pine on a small mound which with half-shut eyes you *might* take for a big pine on a mountain. Trees influence the whole sense of the size of a garden—and more. This aspect is discussed and illustrated on the previous pages.

There is the question of framing of views, which we touched on on the previous pages. It is worth noting how photographers instinctively scramble to the nearest tree to frame a picture of a new hotel or generating station. I suspect they often have to take a branch with them to hold in front of the camera.

And finally there is the tree as sculpture; triumphant, central, and intended to be admired for its own sake. In Japanese gardens this is often the tonsured pine leaning negligently over a stone at the water's edge. In western terms it is usually known as 'the lawn tree'. It is worth long pondering whether a magnolia or a cedar or a strawberry tree or a weeping ash deserves this place of honour.

poplars. Beyond it a bird cherry and Prunus *'Kanzan' have reached 30 feet. A low grey willow draws attention to the pond in the foreground. Beyond the roof of the house a 65-foot Scots pine has the effect of a vegetable pediment.*

Top right *A walled garden to the west of the house is sheltered from the north by a screen of hybrid black poplars 50 feet high (though only 13 years old). Their leaves are copper-pink in spring. The trees within the walls are planted formally: a*

regular row of clipped upright cypresses along each wall and a row of apple trees pruned into a contrasting flat mushroom shape on the lawn. Being kept low they give shade on the lawn but not on the flower beds. Old pear

trees in the centre are used as a framework for clematis, and a purple-leafed plum is trimmed into an upright shape and also smothered in summer with clematis. Two tall clipped Irish yews flank a gateway in the far end wall.

Above *A little pool in a hollow, approached by stone steps, has been thickly planted on the north and east sides with lush-foliaged trees to give a sense of privacy. From right to left they are smokebush,* Parrotia persica, *swamp cypress,*

Liquidambar *and a Caucasian maple whose red summer shoots contrast spectacularly with the blue foliage of Scots pine behind. On the extreme left a feathery grey-green Lawson cypress, 'Pottenii'.*

Planting Trees

Moving full-grown trees
is no new notion: though
modern machinery has
made it much less labori-
ous. But even under ideal
conditions and at the
right season (in autumn
or spring) there is a considerable risk of killing
the tree.

Trees are sold by a
nursery with their roots
either **bare of soil**, in
which case they must be
planted, either temporarily
('heeled in') or perman-
ently, straight away;
balled (i.e. lifted from

the ground with a ball of
earth round the roots and
wrapped in burlap or
sacking; these also need
rapid planting); or grown
in **pots** or **cans**: these can
be moved at any time but
preferably not in summer.

Broadleaf trees can be
bought at different ages
and sizes, trained in
different ways. Left,
bush-form (i.e. un-
trained) is best for multi-
stemmed trees, or any tree
you want to train yourself.

Feathered (i.e. with all
the lower branches intact)
is normally the best way
to buy specimen trees.
They are cheaper and
have all their natural
character. It is up to you
whether you leave the
lower branches or not.

Semi-standard and
standard are respectively
smaller and larger
versions of the same thing:
a tree with its lower
branches removed and the
upper branches trained
into a balanced head with
a more or less definite
leader.

Semi-mature trees are
standards grown on in
the nursery to 12 feet or
more. They tend to be
disproportionately
expensive and should
only be used where the
threat of damage to
smaller trees is too
great.

The first step in planting
any tree is to dig a hole
big enough to accom-
modate the roots fully
spread out. The soil
should be dug out and
mixed with a fertilizer (or
best of all leafmould) to a
depth of at least two feet—
depending on the size of

If you are prepared to take enough trouble
you can move a tree of almost any size without killing it. The catch is that the trouble
increases sharply above a fairly small size,
perhaps 15 feet, while the chance of success
diminishes. Sir Henry Steuart would not
agree with me, and neither would Arbor-
Haul Consolidated (if there is such an
enterprise). But for us ordinary folk it is
one of life's trying little facts.

Old Sir Henry was a 19th-century Scottish
landowner who shifted full-grown trees
round his park like milk-churns round a
dairy. He boasted that he had never lost a
tree, and never spent more than 12 shillings
(call it two dollars) on moving one. When
you consider that for this he employed ten
men for two weeks disinterring every scrap
of root and reinterring it just down the
road (so beautifully that his trees never
needed stakes or guy-ropes) you will see
why America filled up so quickly with
ingenious Scotsmen in the 19th century.

To have any hope of successfully moving
a big tree you need either a vast labour-
force or a huge machine. However huge the
machine, though, it will probably kill the
tree unless it has been laboriously prepared
beforehand. It means digging a trench first
round one side of the tree, then the other
(with a year in between) and filling the

trench with leaf-mould. The tree will react
by filling the leaf-mould with fibrous feeding
roots, making a compact enough root-
system to move without losing half of it.
Nurseries that grow trees with the intention of selling them extra-large annually
undercut the roots with the same object.
Unless this is done, and the tree moved at
the right season, the chances are it will die.

The easiest trees to shift, and ones that
amateurs can move around within their own
gardens, are typical garden conifers: cypresses and *Thujas* which have small zones
of dense root close to the foot. It is easy
for two men in a day to prepare a new hole
(the first move) and then unearth and transfer a tree up to say 20 feet, hardly losing
any root. With a good stake or guy-ropes
and constant watering for at least a year
there should be no problem.

But it is best to buy trees small. As a
counter-blast to the feeling of impatience
which small trees seem to engender in most
people I can do no better than to quote the
inevitable Humphrey Repton—at his most
dogmatic. 'There is no error more common
than to suppose that the planter may not
live to see his woods unless they consist of
(fast-growing) firs and larches . . . . man
outlives the beauty of his trees, where
plantations do not consist of oak.'

Semi-standard and larger trees must be securely tied to a stake for the first two years after planting (left). The inset picture shows a practical form of tree tie consisting of a plastic belt with a buckle, going through a band which keeps the tree and stake apart.
The tree (left) has a tall wire guard, normally necessary only in public places. Damage from rabbits (or lawn-mowers) can be prevented with a special plastic sleeve which covers the bottom two feet of the trunk. In hot-summer areas the bark of young trees can suffer from scorching after planting out. Paper wrapping material can be bought to shield it.

Above is a method of attaching a conifer to a stake: it can be difficult to get the stake near enough to tie the trunk in the usual way: the branches can be used instead.

It is easy to forget the exact name of a tree, and especially the date that you planted it. A permanent label is not easy to devise. This one is a small rectangle of sheet aluminium, the name and date punched on it with a steel letter-punch.

Lacking the facility Repton must have had of glancing the other way for 20 or 30 years, I have an alternative case to make: that in fact the planter, as soon as he has planted his small tree, begins to get great pleasure from it: greater even perhaps than the pleasure he will have when it is big.

I have kept a letter I had from Alan Mitchell, one of England's greatest dendrologists, when I first started planting. 'Very young trees', he wrote, 'have singular advantages that seem to escape many people . . . There is great aesthetic pleasure in seeing trees at their formative and most vigorous growth . . . when flourishing young foliage is at eye-level and leading shoots four feet long can be seen and measured.' Which is my experience exactly.

Planting a tree seems simple. You dig a hole and stick it in. This, literally, is the way forestry trees in their tens of thousands are planted: there is no time for fancy business. There are touches of finesse, however, that make a great deal of difference to garden trees (which are normally planted considerably bigger). Some of them are outlined on the left.

In places with a deadly winter all planting is best left to early-to-mid spring, when the ground is thoroughly thawed and not too sodden. In more temperate places, deciduous trees are best planted about the time their leaves fall. Their roots can grow surprisingly in mild winter weather, giving them a better chance to put on leaves than if they were planted in the spring. Cold spring winds are also less likely to dehydrate them if they have had a winter in the ground to make roots. Evergreens in the same places can be planted either in early autumn or spring: if in the spring not until the ground is well warmed up and the danger of frosty winds is over. Broadleaved evergreens would rather have some of their leaves cut off than bear the full strain of their transpiration. A jet-age alternative is 'transplanting spray'; a thin plastic coating that reduces transpiration.

Trees in pots or cans are in theory safe to plant at any time. Obviously the best planting season for them is the same as for any other trees. If you plant them in midsummer you must water them much and often. In many nurseries, however, the flourishing-looking tree has been in the can quite a lot too long: its roots are going round and round looking for a way out. For this tree proper planting is going to be quite as much a trauma as for a tree sold bare-rooted. Unless you unscramble the roots (which means shaking the soil off them) they will go on going round and never get a good start in their new home.

A shallow basin over the root area is a simple way of making sure irrigation water reaches the roots.

Where water is precious, roots can be irrigated by perforated pipes driven into the ground.

'Mould-planting': even swamp trees like to be raised a little above very wet ground when planted.

'Basin-planting': in very dry areas trees can be planted in little hollows to encourage water flow.

tree. Break up the bottom of the hole with a fork to ensure good drainage. Anything bigger than a feathered tree (see above left) needs **staking**. Drive a strong wooden stake into the hole at one side deep enough to keep the tree rigid.

Try the tree in the hole. Note that with bare-root trees the **soil-line** on the trunk must be the same as before. If necessary refill the hole until the tree is the right height. Then spread the roots out into their natural position (mainly horizontal).

Start **backfilling** by hand, sifting soil carefully between all the roots and rootlets. Pack them in tight. Mix the backfill soil with compost or leafmould to make it crumbly if necessary.

When the hole is full (all the soil should go back in) **firm the ground** round the trunk by stamping on it. Pull the tree upwards by the trunk: it should not move at all.

Maintenance

A gang was once chopping down a great fir in the Northwest. After a week of axing they thought they heard an echo to their axes. Their foreman mounted his horse and rode round the tree, to find another gang chopping at the other side. Many ingenious devices like the one below were invented to ease the labour of tree-cutting. But only in the last generation has the chain-saw revolutionized it.

I don't know if anyone has sat down cold-bloodedly to calculate how many of the trees planted for ornament survive to do their job. Forestry trees have a good record: 90 per cent success is the average. I suspect that with ornamental trees the failure rate is far higher, despite the fact that so much more trouble is taken, and despite the expensive nursery rearing. It is not only harder to get a four- or five-year-old tree off to a good start, but the risk of damage and the consequences of neglect are more serious. Trees need maintenance. There is a huge difference between a property where the trees are looked after and one where they are supposed to look after themselves.

The first need of trees in the year after planting is water. If the rainfall of the area is less than 30 inches a year, reasonably spaced out through the seasons with a good proportion in the spring, three or four heavy waterings in the first year, and for the next two or three years if possible, will make an enormous difference. Heavy watering means at least 25 gallons to a tree poured on slowly just where the roots are. Irrigation is rarely practised for established trees (i.e., trees that have been planted for more than four or five years) except in areas of notorious drought.

The roots of a newly-planted tree are so near the surface, and so limited in extent, that grass growing over them competes for whatever rations are going. The tree's response is to shade out the grass with its branches – but nursery training removes the low branches that would give the shade. The tree must be helped. Botanical gardens and new commercial orchards always keep a three- to five-foot circle of earth hoed free of grass and weeds round every young tree. In a normal garden this is laborious and not very pretty. The alternative is to mulch the tree with something that will keep down grass and weeds and at the same time help to keep the soil moist. In short grass the perfect material is to hand: the turf you have

There is an art in safely cutting down a tree and making it fall exactly where planned. The first stage is the 'undercut': a wedge of wood is removed with two cuts, one horizontal and the other

at an angle downwards to meet it. The undercut must point exactly where the tree is intended to fall. The second stage, the felling cut, is made from the opposite side starting at a point just above the

undercut and sloping slightly down to it. The tree will pivot on a 'hinge' of wood and the direction of its fall will be controlled. Big trees with hard wood can be further controlled if the felling cut is

stopped short and the tree pushed over by driving in a broad iron wedge with a sledge-hammer.

cut out to plant the tree, simply turned upside down and stamped down again round the stem. In long grass the answer is a thick pile of cut long grass (and weeds) to cover the ground for two or three feet all round the stem to a depth of four to six inches. Nothing can grow through the pile: it slowly rots down to add a layer of humus to the soil.

There is normally no need to interfere with the branches while the tree is small. It knows what is expected of it. The temptation is there, none the less, to see the twigs of today as the limbs of the day after tomorrow and make sure they form a

A branch should never be cut off in one piece: the bark will tear. The first step is to cut off the greater part a foot or two from the trunk or main limb. Start even this cut from underneath.

Saw upwards under the remaining branch-stub as close as possible to the tree until the saw starts to 'bind' in the cut.

Take off the stub by cutting downwards to meet the undercut, again as close to the tree as possible so that no stump is left.

Clean off any rough bits of wood or bark with saw, knife or chisel and paint the surface of the wound thickly with fungicide paint. The tree can now rapidly heal the wound with a covering of new bark.

harmonious, balanced pattern. Most of all to see that the trunk or a central leader has the dominance that will give the tree stature.

Some trees grown in the open without competition begin to be complacent, to stop growing upwards and round out their crowns while they are still quite small. It is perfectly sound practice in such a case to shorten the side branches and give the tree a vertical emphasis again. Rather than just cut back any branch and leave a stump in mid-air it is always worth finding a fork with a shorter angled branch you can leave, cutting off the longer arm of the branch flush at that point.

This sort of adjustment to older trees, particularly where it is concerned with repairing damage and fighting disease, is called tree surgery. It is scarcely a job for amateurs. There are real tree-cowboys who can stand (no hands) on a branch 80 feet from the ground while they use a chain-saw. I have got as far as learning to use the ropes and harness to get up there, but I shudder at the thought of actually doing anything (except hang on) at that height.

The tree-surgeon's bible is a book called *The Pruning of Trees, Shrubs and Conifers* by George E. Brown, Assistant Curator at Kew. I cannot attempt here to reproduce its lore and learning. There is, however, one basic lesson to be learned: how a tree heals itself. Bark will grow over a flat clean cut flush with the trunk – but a tree cannot heal a stump. A stump is the royal road for rot, bugs, disease and death.

Never take off a branch in one piece. There is nothing you can do to stop it falling by its own weight before the cut is finished, and taking with it a torn piece of the bark. Remember that the life of the tree lies just inside the bark.

Above *A tree surgeon uses a chain-saw high in an old Scots pine.*

The only reliable method is to cut the branch off a foot or two from the trunk (undercutting to prevent tearing) and then make a separate log of the short stump you have left. Saw from underneath until the blade jams in the cut. Then saw downwards as close to the trunk as you can get to meet the undercut. If there are ragged bits of wood where the two saw-cuts met, saw or chisel them off. Then paint the cut thickly (this is vital) with tree-paint, which is a tarry substance containing a fungicide. If you can't get tree-paint, ordinary household exterior paint is better than nothing. All wounds on trees, and certainly all wounds over one inch in diameter, should be dressed like this. Big wounds, over which it will take the bark several years to grow, should be painted again every year or two.

Unfortunately the gardener quickly learns that many trees which to him are a feast to the eye are quite a different sort of feast to all manner of creatures. A tree stripped of leaves by caterpillars or aphids is a pathetic sight and trunk-borers which work out of sight are no better: they can kill a tree.

Nature is redder in tooth and claw in this regard in North America than in Europe. The extremes of the continental climate, above all the wrecking power of ice-storms, also help to make tree upkeep much more of a problem in the U.S.A. and Canada. On pages 320-1 is a review of some of the commoner pests and diseases that threaten trees, with measures to combat them. The General Index mentions particular susceptibilities to forewarn you of the possible need to keep a spray-gun handy.

The Sitka spruce (right) had a diameter of two inches after 20 years on poor land. In 1960 70 lbs. of phosphate per acre was applied. The tree added half an inch diameter that year. By 1966 the diameter was six inches.

Some of the tools used in pruning and maintaining trees are shown on the left, (not to scale). From left to right and top to bottom they are: a bow-saw, which can be used by one man or two. This is the ideal implement for removing branches. The narrow flexible blade is easy to pull through the wood, but it needs fairly frequent 'setting' (that is, splaying the teeth) and sharpening. Lopping shears have a curved cutting blade pressing on a shallow hook that fits round a small branch. Long handles give great leverage. A good tool for branches up to one inch diameter. Secateurs are for pruning twigs and unwanted new growth. A folding pruning-saw is a useful pocket implement for minor bits of surgery. It can be used with more precision than lopping shears for similar work. A bill-hook should only be used for clearing dead wood or scrub, or 'brashing' (taking small sidebranches off felled trees). A carpenter's saw is preferred to a bow-saw by some tree-surgeons, but only for small branches. The axe is used more for splitting logs than felling trees today. The old forester's axe had a six-pound head on a three-foot ash-wood handle. The chain-saw with a petrol engine is the standard tree-felling tool today. A chain carrying alternate blades and 'rakers' to clear the saw-dust runs in a track round a steel plate. It is noisy, hot and heavy, but much quicker and easier than the axe.

The Effect of Fertilisers

During their first years, when their roots suffer competition from grasses, trees need food. It is wise to plant them with some fertiliser – and for four or five years to keep a circle at least three feet in radius clear of grass and well mulched.

Each of the three main ingredients of fertilisers, nitrogen, phosphorus and potassium, has a specific effect. Nitrogen promotes strong vegetative growth and enriches leaf colour. Phosphorus is necessary for good root-growth and potassium induces fruiting, and the proper ripening of wood and fruit. Excess nitrogen inhibits fruiting and, by inducing late growth, prevents proper ripening of wood.

At planting, mix a few ounces of super-phosphate with the soil in the hole; as growth starts, add a top dressing of fertiliser with a high nitrogen content. Sandy soils need more fertiliser after heavy rain.

Old trees on closely mown lawns suffer from malnutrition, becoming thin in the crown and prematurely senile. They are best fed by drilling holes over the area and filling them with general fertiliser.

Pruning and other Arts

Hedges are the everyday example of trees bidden by man. We accept the idea of enough beech trees, say, or yews, to make a substantial wood, all being restrained by cutting every year to take the form of a mere wall. Yet other forms of tree-discipline are frowned on as unnatural.

The Japanese think differently. To them a natural pine, whether compact or straggling, is less appealing than a bidden pine engineered into dancing a sort of pine-ballet. The garden is a stage, and the actors are called upon to do more than just stand around in their ordinary clothes passing the time of day.

Are we in the west perhaps too functionally minded? We cordon an apple tree to make it bear more fruit. We pollard a willow to get osiers for fencing and baskets. But if we have any fancy notions about shapes it is usually to carve quite unvegetable things in topiary – be it quasi-architecture, the Sermon on the Mount (in an ancient Warwickshire garden) or even a hunt in full cry, which is frozen in yew on the point of crossing the drive to a French château.

Not that functional forms are without beauty. The methods for maintaining the maximum number of fruiting spurs on an apple or a pear tree give the symmetry and order of the espalier, the fan and the cordon. Where there used to be a demand for regular supplies of long straight poles there are woods of coppiced hazel or chestnut: every six or seven years each tree was cut back to the ground, where it formed a 'stool' and sent up a porcupine of new shoots. They were not very lovely perhaps when they were in production; but old, abandoned coppice is some of the prettiest woodland. In gardens the idea is taken up with trees distinguished for their foliage; regular cutting down giving a bush, usually with bigger leaves than those of the natural tree, forced by roots out of proportion to the top. I have seen eucalyptus, golden poplar, catalpa, box elder all hacked mercilessly to

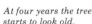

Bonsai can start with a one-year-old seedling.

Next year the main stem is cut off leaving a branch.

At three years the process is repeated.

At four years the tree starts to look old.

the ground, all bounding back in the same year with eight-foot shoots covered with mammoth leaves.

Pollarding is simply the coppice principle applied six feet above the ground, where grazing beasts can't reach the new shoots. It is the coppice of the meadow, as opposed to the woodland. The word pollard has the same root as poll – meaning head.

Willows are the most commonly pollarded trees, but oak, ash and hornbeam have often been cut for firewood in this way in the past. Sometimes in fact with old spreading trees it is hard to see whether they were once cut off six feet above the ground or not.

Generally you can say that if all the branches start from the same point on the trunk they were.

Pollarding is little used for ornament. The happiest effect I have seen achieved with it has been that of instant fen-land; a group of willows with brilliantly red-barked young shoots standing glowing in the winter sunlight above their reflections in a pond.

Bonsai is the end of the road. The deliberate use of all a tree's forces and (as it were) instincts to make a toy is gardening of a very sophisticated kind. It has special value for a city-dweller, whose chance to observe the forces of nature is limited and

Fruit trees are often pruned and shaped to prevent them growing vertically. They react by producing more fruit. Three shapes are used against walls and along wires. **Right** *the espalier.*

Left *The cordon, more often used on wires, is shown here before and after its annual pruning. Side branches are reduced by three-quarters in winter to induce flower and fruit formation.*

Right *A fan-trained tree, usually grown against a wall. The central leader is cut off after strong side branches have formed the basic fan. No branch is allowed to grow vertically.*

All conifers for bonsai must have their growing tips regularly shortened. **Top left** *Needle-leaf trees must be carefully pinched back (A) as cut needles (B) will turn brown. Scale-leaf trees (C) need a few tips nipping off more or less daily in spring.*

The process of turning a small pine into a bonsai pine-grove is shown in the drawings above. The tree, its shoots controlled by pinching back (1), is lashed into a horizontal position. Stiff wire is wound round its branches

to train as many as possible upwards (2); the rest are cut off. Wire is also used to bend the trunk. The tree is then transplanted to a wide flat container (3) and held down on to the soil with wires passed through the

drain-holes. The soil is kept level with the trunk (4) and the tree left in a sheltered light place out of the sun where it will form roots from the trunk.

– adapted from Bonsai-Saikei *by Toshio Kawamoto and Joseph Y. Kurihara Nippon-Saikei Co., Tokyo.*

Topiary is gardening with a sense of humour. This garden at Box Hill in the south of England, blends the whimsical and mock-monumental effects which can be achieved by

carving dense-leafed trees and bushes like yew and box. Because it can never be taken completely seriously topiary suits cottage gardens better than formal ones.

distorted to the point of psychological danger. One little tree in a pot can teach you more than a fortnight in a forest about the processes of plant life, if you work with it, as the Japanese do, to bring out its essential character.

Some of the techniques of bonsai are illustrated on the left. Big-tree modelling comes to much the same thing, with the difference that the roots have no restrictions: the size of the tree is only controlled by the amount you stop each year's growth. In practice of course this does restrict the roots, too.

One underlying principle affects all pruning: every time you cut off a growing tip you transfer the energy due to it to the next bud or growing tip back down the line. There is no guesswork in what will happen when you cut off a twig. The last remaining bud will take up the struggle and go whichever way it is pointing. If you want a branch to grow to the right you must choose a bud pointing that way and cut off what lies beyond it, as close to the bud as possible (leaving no 'snag' or stump to die and attract fungi or disease).

Any branch you cut below its lowest bud, simply leaving a stump, will do one of two things, neither of which you want. Either it will die or it will produce epicormic shoots (see page 10) of no beauty or value; just a bunch of straight whiskers.

With this in mind it is not difficult to pick on the branches you want to encourage to grow straight on and those you want to change direction; those you want to shorten or remove and those you want to make dense and bushy.

The trick is to see the tree's natural tendency and help it along. If it tends to form, for instance, flattened whorls of branches with all their leaves facing upwards, remove everything which doesn't conform to the horizontal pattern. The Japanese go further and clip the top of each tier of a pine-tree like a lawn to make it dense and even.

A common form of pollard in fen country; the willow (or osier) cut back every year or two for its pliant new rods for weaving into baskets or fences. The trunks of such pollards usually rot inside and become hollow sleeves, still supporting a flourishing crown. Varieties with coloured young bark treated in this way in spring are gay shock-heads the next winter.

In a bonsai nursery near Tokyo ready-made bonsai, such as the miniature grove of pines (right, middle-ground) fetch high prices. Enthusiasts, not content with buying off-the-peg, walk in wild mountain areas looking for stunted seedlings to take home, sometimes even starting to train them in situ. Of all trees, pines and junipers make the most natural-looking miniatures. Flowering trees are popular, but nothing can shrink the blooms. Well-tended bonsai trees can live over 100 years.

The urban pollard, symbol of a tidy-minded municipality. All over continental Europe one sees such trees, usually (as here, at Ghent in Belgium) London planes, cruelly cropped of each year's shoots till they develop great fists at their extremities. The volume of green produced by such trees and the length of its season are both minimal.

The Conifers

Conifers bear cones. That is their hallmark. Not all cones look like cones. Nobody would suspect a juniper berry, for instance, of being any such thing. But technically a plant whose female flower offers its eggs naked to the world for fertilization, and then develops into a 'fruit', usually of wood, to enclose them while they ripen, is a conifer. And all conifers are trees—or at least woody plants. There are no herbaceous conifers.

The conifers include the world's biggest plants—by far. There is a startling gap between the record heights of broadleaf trees and conifers. In the American championship table there are no broadleaves over 180 feet or so. Then a pause. Then an astonishing list of champions from 250 feet right up to 350 feet—all conifers.

Again, conifers hold all the age records. Millenarians are commonplace. The arguments concern how many thousands of years the oldest of the pines have been growing.

In the natural course of evolution the heyday of the conifers is over. They are one of the oldest plant families. They flourished long before the broadleaves. But they have been on the decline, numerically and territorially, for millions of years.

Yet man has found them a more efficient plant for his purposes, for timber and paper, than the up-to-date broadleaves. Partly it is their willingness to grow under the unlikeliest circumstances; on land too poor or wet or exposed—above all too far north—for farming. Partly it is their simple design with all the emphasis on a thick trunk—the branches being no more than something to hang the foliage on. But mainly it is their speed: the conifers are adapted to use the low sun of the higher latitudes to its utmost; they nearly all keep their leaves and thus have the means to make and store food the year round. Under northern conditions, therefore, they add wood to their bulk at a rate unsurpassed by any broadleaved tree.

There are about 650 species of conifers, in 50 genera in only eight families. They all grow in the temperate zones—most of them moreover in the colder parts; if they grow in the tropics at all it is only on mountains with a temperate climate.

The vast majority—33 out of the 50 genera—are confined to the northern hemisphere. Nearly all of them are evergreen trees with tough, dark-green needle-like leaves which make dense and deeply shady forests. In the gloom their lower branches rapidly die and drop off; their trunks develop into flawless pillars, often rising to an awesome height.

Yet from the same race, through odd freaks and sports, come small, precisely formal and even miniature trees of exquisite detail and often brilliant colouring—man's other reason for taking the conifers under his protection.

The Ginkgo or Maidenhair Tree

The ginkgo has not changed its design in 150,000,000 years. This fossil leaf found at Scarborough in Yorkshire is part of the evidence that the ginkgo grew world-wide. Eventually it retreated to the mountains of central China.

One feels a certain respect for a creature which has simply declined to evolve. I believe there are lowly crabs, and also insects, which have been much the same for 100 million years or so. But for a forest tree to survive its relations, its descendants, the conditions which gave it birth: to look unmoved on the drift of continents, the rise of mountain ranges, the coming and going of aeons of reptiles and ages of ice–to survive all this unaltered, for 200 million years, argues a degree of tenacity. Not to mention a sound design.

The ginkgo's unmistakable leaf is as startling as Man Friday's footprint among the tangle of tree-ferns in fossil strata of the Paleozoic era. The tree ranged world-wide in those days. Before the modern conifers evolved, long before the rise of the broadleaves, the ginkgo flourished in America, in Asia, in Australia; and on the Isle of Mull. It went into decline even before the Ice Ages, it seems. And yet it remained viable. There was still somehow a niche for this strangely sophisticated primitive.

By the time man came on the scene the ginkgo had retreated to the mountain forests of Chekiang in easternmost China, and Szechwan in the far west. It may still exist there in a natural state. Nobody seems sure. But its re-emergence is due to the priestly planting of it in temple gardens, first in China, then in Japan. An eighth-century Chinese writer mentions it. A 16th-century

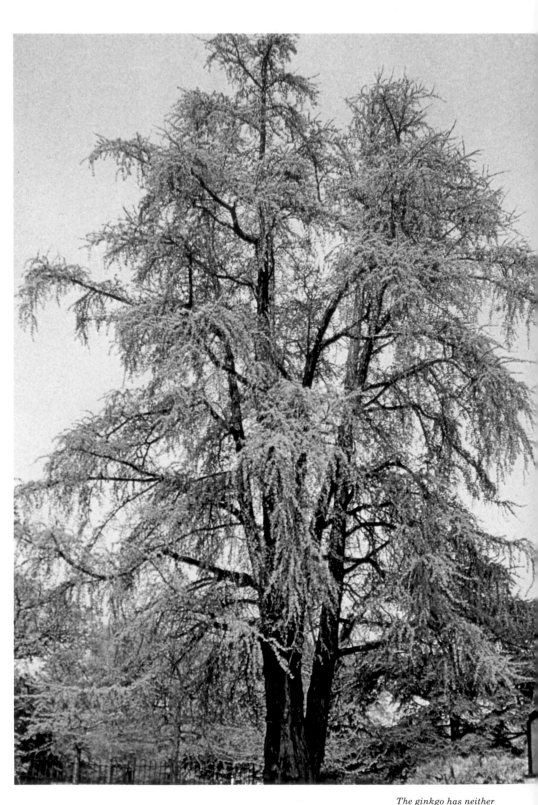

The ginkgo has neither needles nor cones, yet you might guess its ancestral relationship to the conifers from this picture. Trunk and limbs ascend stiffly; the top is like a spire; the small foliage softens the shape without disguising its basic outline.

The female flowers of the
ginkgo come with the
leaves from a short woody
spur like a peg. Trees are
either male or female; in

the lower picture the male
catkins are seen emerging
in clusters with the young
leaves from the same pegs
on a male tree.

The fruit of the ginkgo is
rarely seen; female trees
are avoided because the
fleshy covering of the
edible nut rots with a
powerful and unpleasant
smell.

one calls it the duck's-foot tree – referring to the shape of its leaves. Its modern name is the Japanese version of the Chinese yin-kuo, meaning 'silver-fruit'. (The fruit was another reason for planting it: the kernels, roasted, were eaten when liquor was flowing freely; the peanuts and cashews of the ancient Chinese.)

The West heard of the ginkgo when Kaempfer wrote of his visit to Japan in 1690. In 1730 the first plant arrived in Europe, in Utrecht, and in 1754 Kew Gardens bought the tree which still grows there from a nurseryman in east London. It was at this stage that it was christened maidenhair tree ('adiantifolia') from the maidenhair fern, the only plant with leaves of similar shape. Thirty years later it was introduced to the United States, to Philadelphia . . . and its new lease of life began.

One of the advantages of living on after your era is that your enemies have all, as they say, gone before. Doubtless there were epidemics of ginkgo disease, and hordes of ginkgo-eating insects – millions of years ago. But today, as oaks wilt and elms wither, the ginkgo can just look inscrutable. Even air-pollution in its deadliest form – on Fifth Avenue for example – leaves its odd duck's-foot leaves fresh and wholesome. It will even grow in shallow concrete tubs at the pavement's edge where buses breathe their unbreathable breath. It is the answer to the Parks Department's prayer.

Neither in Europe nor America, though, is it planted very often simply as the eccentric beauty it is. A young ginkgo's branches rise stiff and straight, rather like an Atlantic cedar's: in summer much softened by the pale green leaves drooping on long stalks; in winter sculptural – if you like it, or stark, if you don't. With age the branches dip at the end and fan out. It may just be fancy, but the ginkgo's distant relationship to the modern conifers seems to be reflected in its stance even in old age.

The tree's best moment is in the late autumn, when the leaves turn from their well-sustained green to clear butter-yellow, without a hint of orange or brown. They fall soon after, but the fleeting effect on a big ginkgo, fuller and more pendulous in figure, is marvellous.

Seventy or 80 feet is normally full size: one at Milan reached 125 feet. Hot summers will certainly have helped it. As to the spread, much depends on the clone: there is a very narrow upright one known as the 'sentry' ginkgo propagated in America for street planting, but the most graceful trees are the broad and droopy kind. One of the advantages of the 'sentry' is that it is a male tree: ginkgo fruit, if any, is malodorous when ripe.

Above *Ginkgo autumn colour is short-lived but lovely; a clear yellow which emphasises the fineness of the foliage. Here at Sheffield Park in* *Sussex, a garden famous for its autumn display, a ginkgo is flanked by its great grandchildren: cryptomeria (left) and oriental spruce (right).*

Above *The autumn colouring of ginkgo leaves emphasises their peculiar shape; like long-stemmed fans with more or less wavy edges and a notch in the middle. Leaves on young shoots are divided almost in two by the notch.*

The Pines of North America

Pines are to the conifers what oaks are to the broadleaves: the most widespread, most varied and most valuable trees of their order. The biggest family of conifers goes by their name, the *Pinaceae*. It includes the firs, spruces, cedars, larches – almost all the needle trees. But the actual genus *Pinus*, the pines proper, is limited to 100 or so species with certain clear and obvious characteristics, of which the easiest to see and remember is the relatively long evergreen needles in tight bundles, each bundle (of from two to five needles, according to species) wrapped at its base in a papery sheath.

The yearly growth of each shoot of a pine takes the form of a 'candle'. Firs and spruces and the rest add to their branches every year more or less horizontally; pine-candles tend to grow vertically, only settling down to their place as part of the branch later, as they grow heavier.

In contrast to its aspiring new shoots, however, a pine is much less forceful than its cousins in its defiance of gravity. A fir or a spruce is a spire as a young tree, and a spire it remains. Most pines, where they have room to expand, take a course in middle age which brings them nearer to the wide-spreading broadleaves. The result – an eccentric flourish of bold branches, often on a bare stem, usually with beautifully coloured and patterned bark – is one of the most triumphantly picturesque of all trees.

As old trees pines are the standard-bearers of the skyline. But the owner of a young pine has, if anything, even more to enjoy: a vigorous plant at eye level, fantastically rich in its detail, its thick and sappy shoots bristling with bright new needles, embossed with male and female parts of splendidly original and suggestive design.

The natural range of the pines is enormous. They grow from the Arctic Circle to the Equator. If anything they favour rugged conditions: drought and extreme exposure on mountains; on sandy seashores, where the subsoil is permanently frozen; or, like the famous Jeffrey pine, on a rocky dome high above Yosemite, where there seems to be no soil at all. If pines have a headquarters in our era it is in Mexico, whose tropical highlands they seem to relish. With their evolutionary tactics of interbreeding they keep botanists busier there than anywhere else on earth.

Of the hundred-odd known pine species 36 are natives of North America. They divide readily into northeastern, southeastern and western stables. Anyone planting one should certainly consider the trees of his own area first – not forgetting, of course, the imports from Europe, Asia and Mexico.

The great pine of the northeast is the

The needles of the Montezuma pine are pale greyish green, up to a foot long, grouped round bright red-brown buds. Unfortunately this beautiful tree is particularly susceptible to hard frost.

Above *Given the space, light and air the billowing broadleaf shape comes as naturally to most pines as the narrow spire. One of the most beautiful of all is the Mexican Montezuma pine, whose long (up to 10 in.) bluish-green needles droop gracefully from the branches. This specimen is in the garden of the Villa Melzi on the shore of Lake Como in northern Italy.*

Sugar pine (on the right of the picture) in the mountains of California. Long horizontal upper branches and the longest of all cones make it one of the easiest pines to recognize. Sweet resin

from the trunk, used by the Indians as food, gave the tree its name. The world's biggest pine tree is a sugar pine growing in Siskiyou National Forest, California.

Ponderosa pine shares the same California mountain country as sugar pine and grows to almost the same size. Beautiful fissured bark ranging in colour from ochre to pink is characteristic of

ponderosa. So are the needles in stiff round bunches at the ends of shoots. The tree between the trunks is another ponderosa, showing the typical crown shape.

Right Northern pitch pine is the almost indestructible pine of dry barrens in the northeastern United States. Chalk soil is the only thing it won't stand. It makes a medium-sized tree with long branches and an open crown. The picture shows its habit –unique among pines– of producing tufts of needles from the trunk. The needles are 3½ 4½ in. long and grouped in threes.

white or Weymouth pine (*Pinus strobus*). The old New England forest, which was relentlessly butchered over a period of 300 years, contained vast stands of it, with trees 200 feet high and eight or nine feet across. Its beautiful soft white wood supplied half Europe's needs, as well as building boats and panelling mansions throughout the eastern States. It was introduced to Britain in the 18th century by Viscount Weymouth, who planted it at Longleat. In Britain it has never been a great success: but in France and Germany there are good woods of it. Its thin, pale needles of a delicate blue-green make it a beautiful garden tree; it will keep long branches low-down, where you can see them. But it will make a giant eventually– far too big for the ordinary garden. Neither of the other two northeastern pines shown on page 73, the red pine (*P. resinosa*) and the pitch pine (*P. rigida*), are nearly as big or as beautiful. The red is a sombre tree, dark green with dark red bark, its foliage heavy like that of the Corsican pine; the pitch pine is generally considered a last-resort tree for really rough conditions, where it can cut a rugged, romantic figure. Its peculiarity of sprouting tufts of green leaves from its trunk makes it easy to pick out. In Canada the jack pine (*P. banksiana*) and in the eastern States the scrub pine (*P.*

virginiana) are small trees which play similar tough roles.

Southeastern pines are of enormous economic importance, and of great interest and vigour. They cover thousands of square miles of torpid, otherwise unprofitable country. Yet none of them is exactly a beauty.

The strange one is the longleaf pine (*P. palustris*). Long indeed are its needles–as much as 18 inches. But its real quirk is to crouch, a mere grassy mound of potential pine tree, for as much as three or four years before it starts to put on height. In its 'grass stage' it can survive forest fires and at the same time build up a strong root system to boost its later growth.

The southern forester uses four principal pine trees, and does a complicated equation to know which to plant where (the factors are speed, quality and resistance to rust disease). Longleaf is slow-growing but fairly resistant. Shortleaf (*P. echinata*) is even slower, but more resistant. Loblolly (*P. taeda*) is the biggest, best and fastest, at any rate on rich land, but highly susceptible to rust. Slash pine (*P. elliottii*) is the best and fastest on poor soil, but again liable to the disease. Slash has another advantage: a thicker bark, which makes it possible to burn the forest floor to suppress competition while the trees are young. ▶

The Jeffrey pine differs from the very similar ponderosa pine in its longer (5–10 in.) bluish-green needles, usually grouped in threes, and in its purple, grey or black bark.

Male flowers cover the entire shoot below the new tuft of needles on a bishop pine, native of the South California coast.

The Pines of North America

Opposite *Pines are adapted to a wide range of climatic conditions.* **Right** *A young shore pine in the snow at Bluff Lake, Oregon.* **Middle right** *Monterey pines luxuriate in the temperate climate of Monterey Bay in California.* **Far right** *Knobcone pines flourish near Bear Basin in California.*

▶ The western pines are in a rather different league. David Douglas, having canoed and portaged for weeks on end to find the sugar pine (*P. lambertiana*), called it 'the most princely of the genus: perhaps even the grandest specimen of vegetation'. Having met the grandfather of all sugar pines in a valley in the Siskiyou mountains of Oregon I can only say Amen. The monster stands 270 feet or so, not as a pole with a shaggy top, as western giant trees tend to be, but mightily branched most of the way up; a forester's nightmare.

Sugar pine branches are straight, and of immense length. Even a 200-foot tree tends to be a well-proportioned T, so each branch near the top must be 70 feet long, weighed down only slightly with its colossal two-foot cones at the tips. Nobody would call it a garden tree, or even a beautiful one. In European collections it has grown to about 100 feet and then perished, being, like all American five-needled pines, liable to the rust disease.

The only other western pine which reaches a comparable size is the ponderosa (*P. ponderosa*), which grows alongside the sugar pine on the same mountain slopes, and reaches its apogee (246 feet) in the same Siskiyou valley. The early settlers' name for the ponderosa was the bull pine, which well expresses the weight and vigour and solidity of this most impressive production. The bark forms into huge rectangular plates of warm pink, etched in grey. The needles are dense and stiff, up to almost a foot in length. In ideal conditions ponderosa has grown 120 feet in 50 years, perfectly straight and only slightly tapering. Of all the big western pines this is the one to choose for a (big) garden in Europe. It transplants well to almost any soil.

Jeffrey pine is similar to ponderosa with more of a liking for high places. Western white pine (*P. monticola*), in the mountains, is not unlike sugar pine–though a far better garden tree, the western equivalent of the New England white pine, with beautiful soft foliage. It has the same rust problem, though. Of the other California mountain pines perhaps the most rewarding to grow is the bigcone (*P. coulteri*)–not a tall tree but a broad one. The reward here–and hence the name–is the cones, as big as a baby's head and armed all over with eagle's claws.

Of the bristlecone pine (*P. aristata*), the oldest living creature on earth, I have written on pages 20–21. Anyone who wants to try this patriarch in his own garden will find it very slow. For the first few centuries the curious little dew-drops of resin on the leaves are probably the best part. The knobcone (*P. attenuata*) is another small and slow species. Its curving cones, as solid as hand-grenades, stick close to the trunk and never fall or open until a forest fire comes their way.

The shore pine (*P. contorta*) seems to be the most adaptable. It grows from the sea-coast right up to 11,000 feet (where the variety is called lodgepole). Not only is it adaptable and hardy, but it has beautiful dense foliage, usually from head to foot, and striking red buds which make it look as though it is flowering. Happily it is turning out to be a first-class forestry tree in Britain, suppressing even Scottish heather with its rapid early growth. After the Sitka spruce it is the most-planted species–and should be more so in gardens with acid soil.

The remainder of the western pines belong on the coast, in milder conditions, with the on-shore gale as their chief foe. The most important is the Monterey pine (*P. radiata*), perhaps the lushest and most lordly of the whole tribe. Nature had restricted this incredibly vigorous, but rather tender, plant to a few square miles round Monterey in southern California. Man has changed all that: it is now the chief forestry pine of the southern hemisphere. Results in New Zealand are sensational. In its fifth year one tree there put on 20 feet. Where it is happy the

■ Bigcone	■ Loblolly	■ White (or Weymouth)	▨ Red
▨ Bristlecone	▨ Lodgepole	▨ Sugar	■ Slash
▨ Pitch	■ Monterey	▨ Shortleaf	■ Jelecote
▨ Ponderosa	■ Longleaf	■ Western white	▨ Mexican white
■ Torrey	▨ Jeffrey	▨ Knobcone	▨ Montezuma

Monterey pine grows vast branches and keeps them densely clad in bright bottle-green needles. Even in southern England it grows four feet a year, not even making a resting bud in winter but charging right on, only pausing in cold weather.

The bishop pine (*P. muricata*) is along the same lines, but slightly duller in colour, often somewhat slower and hardier–an excellent front-line defence against sea winds.

In the same seaside context the Torrey pine (*P. torreyana*) has a limited southern range. It is a short, open, spreading tree with its bundles of five needles as heavy as darts: the leaves of plants below are punctured by them as they fall.

In New Mexico the piñon pine (*P. cembroides*) is grown for its seeds rather than for its looks. They are the pine-nuts which were an important food for the Indians. Mexico also produces three species which should be much better known. Perhaps the best-looking pine of all is the Montezuma (*P. montezumae*). It spreads pale grey needles in wide whorls round deep, resinous, orange buds almost like some titanic Michaelmas daisy. An old tree is a vast low dome of these stiff, brush-like shoots. Such specimens are rare–and there are less dramatic varieties under the same name from other parts of Mexico.

The jelecote or spreading-leaf pine (*P. patula*) could hardly be more different. The most feminine tree of all the pines, it has pale, drooping needles, as thin as threads, hanging from the tips of gently curving limbs. For all its delicate appearance it grows like the devil in a warm climate.

The third Mexican pine which occurs here and there in collections abroad is the Mexican white pine (*P. ayacahuite*). To the non-expert its smooth grey bark and fine needles make it a recognizable relation of the white pines of the eastern and western States–and come to that of the Himalayas.

The maps on the left show the natural range of North America's most important pines. The illustrations (below) show the needles, the cones and the manner of growth of sixteen of them. The trees shown are in their prime, shaped as they would be if growing in open ground. In forests they would be narrower with longer trunks clear of branches; with greater age they will grow wider in the crown and more branchy without putting on much more height.

Bigcone pine: P. coulteri; *small mountain tree; clawed cones weigh up to 5 lbs. Needles at 90° to shoot.*

Bishop pine: P. muricata; *small tree for poor or swampy soil. Needles stiff; cone has sharp prickles.*

Eastern white pine: P. strobus; biggest most beautiful conifer of northeast. Has grown to 220 ft.

Jelecote pine: P. patula; *small graceful Mexican tree. Footlong bright-green needles droop.*

Loblolly pine: P. taeda; *biggest (to 150 ft.) and fastest southern pine on good land. Weak wood.*

Lodgepole pine: P. contorta latifolia; *small vigorous mountain tree, hardy to 11,000 ft.*

Longleaf pine: P. palustris; *important and pretty southern forestry pine; 18-in. needles.*

Monterey pine: P. radiata; *beautiful, fast and dense tree; dark grassy-green needles.*

Pitch pine: P. rigida; *small and spreading; needs light; good by sea; stiff needles stick out.*

Ponderosa pine: P. ponderosa; *most important western timber pine with huge range. To 240 ft.*

Red pine: P. resinosa; *fast, dense, well-shaped; good on sandy soil.*

Shore pine: P. contorta; *vigorous coastal form of lodgepole. Big red buds.*

Slash pine: P. elliottii; *best and fastest southern pine for poor land.*

Sugar pine: P. lambertiana; *the world's biggest pine; to 270 ft.*

Western white pine: P. monticola; to 180 ft. in Idaho; soft blue-green.

Whitebark pine: P. albicaulis; *small mountain tree of northwest.*

The Pines of Asia

Looking at a photograph of Japan it is sometimes hard to know whether the scene is wild coastline or suburban garden. The lanterns and the carefully-placed stones soon give the game away, but the main visual element which links the two, and carries at least a momentary conviction, is the pine trees. Wind-contorted, shank-shrunk dotards of pine trees are the soul of the Japanese landscape. A gardener's business is to bend a sapling to his whim, to give it premature grey hairs by constant bullying, by weighing down branches, by pinching out shoots, by a salon-full of cosmetic tricks.

The principal victim of all this flattering attention – and the one on the willow-pattern china – is the Japanese white pine (*P. parviflora*). Its natural form already suggests the more highly-coloured coiffured version. It is short, wide-crowned, often with several stems; it holds its twigs and needles in flat plates, facing upwards. The needles are short, dark, grey-blue, with a slight twist and a paler inner surface which gives them a certain vivacity.

Japanese trees came west with a rush in the 1860s. The Japanese white, red and black pines all appeared here within ten years. The red pine (*P. densiflora*), however, is so similar to the Scots pine that there is little need for it, except to a collector. This is the skyline pine of the Japanese garden: the ragged, red-barked head on the quasi-distant hill. Its semi-dwarf variety, 'Umbraculifera', is the most interesting for the western gardener. It makes a broad dome, no more than seven feet high but with age perhaps twice as much across; a tent full of snaking branches. There is also a variety called

The shadow of a Japanese white pine snakes across rock and raked gravel in a formal Japanese garden. The white pine is the small and often contorted tree in the famous willow pattern.

The Japanese umbrella pine, so called because its needles look like the spokes of an umbrella, is quite different from the umbrella or stone pine of Italy. It forms a tall, bright green bush; very hardy on lime-free soil.

dragon's-eye with variegated foliage.

There would be no difficulty in growing either of these species in any temperate garden–or in a tub, or even on a plate, as bonsai. The red is very much faster than the white to start with; apparently it has reached 100 feet in California, but 50 feet is the most it has done in Britain. On the other hand the white, like most five-needled pines, transplants well when it is bigger.

The Japanese black pine (*P. thunbergii*) can be bracketed with the European black pines–particularly the Corsican. It has proved itself the best of all windbreak trees for the seashore in New England. Poor sandy soil does not worry it: it slowly forms a head of long unpredictable branches, bearing tufts of dark foliage–another opportunity (which the Japanese do not miss) for crimping and curling and theatrical effects.

The repeating pattern of black, red and white pines, whether it has a sound botanical basis or not, certainly helps one to classify, to recognize and remember certain types. There are two more Asiatic trees with typical 'white pine' characteristics–silky light green foliage, with the young bark smooth and grey. The Himalayan white pine is fairly well known under various names (*excelsa*, *griffithii*, the Bhutan and the Nepalese pine, as well as the up-to-date name, *wallichiana*). In *Trees for American Gardens* Donald Wyman names Seattle and Philadelphia as two places where it does particularly well, whereas Boston is too cold for it. The best trees in the British Isles (over 100 feet) are in Devon and Ireland, the mildest areas. It is one of the few five-needled pines to resist the rust disease. It grows quickly to start

with, then settles down at 50 feet or so as a broad, open tree of beautiful colour and gleaming texture.

The Chinese white pine (*P. armandii*) is much rarer. I have seen splendid young trees with long, grey-green needles growing at the French National Arboretum at les Barres, south of Paris. But by all accounts the eventual tree is less attractive than the Himalayan one.

The connoisseur's Chinese pine is the lacebark (*P. bungeana*), a tree which often

The dwarf Siberian pine is a bushy Asiatic version of the Alpine cembran pine. Its stiff and twisted needles are grey-blue; its male flowers brilliant red.

makes several stems–and the more the better, since the bark is the main attraction. Areas of white, buff, grey, rust-red, purple and green are revealed where the bark comes off. The bole is smooth and bulky, in fact not at all unlike a London plane in feeling. There are trees you can plant for immediate satisfaction, but the lacebark pine is not one of them: it is essentially a tree to bequeath (or inherit).

Apart from these two rare species, Chinese pines are oddly absent from the West. Korea makes an excellent contribution with a pine rather like the Swiss cembran, only, to my mind, much more decorative. The Korean pine (*P. koraiensis*) has the same way of keeping its upholstery from top to bottom, but it is a fine shade of deep grass-green, with what seems an abnormal amount of needles. The National Arboretum in Washington D.C. has a remarkable 20-foot specimen on which all the needles change direction by about 45 degrees a quarter of the way along. It is a well-proportioned tree, and this extra bushiness makes it quite vibrant with colour and life.

One more valuable tree from the Far East must find a place here–though it is only the most distant relation of the pines. The *Sciadopitys* is usually called the umbrella pine, because its long, succulent, bright green needles radiate from the branches like the spokes of a half-open umbrella. It grows slowly in a perfect full-dress cone-shape: a formal but very satisfying feature on a lawn or among low shrubs. There are 100-foot umbrella pines in Japan (and a 75-foot one in Kent) but 30 feet is a more probable maximum in most gardens.

Mature and immature cones of the Japanese red pine. The green female flowers are ripening to become real cones. The botanical name P. densiflora refers to the dense clusters of male flowers which result in such tight-packed cones.

A lacebark pine, one of the most ornamental of all pines, growing near Sochi in the USSR. In the wild the lacebark tends to have an almost white bark. In cultivation the bark is grey-green, flaking to show a patchwork of colours.

The Pines of Europe

Nobody would deny pride of place to the Scots pine (*P. sylvestris*) among the pines of Europe – even perhaps among the pines of the world. I find its beauty unrivalled. The richness of its colouring, its wild poise set it apart. No matter how grey the winter's day, the papery bark, flaking in butterfly wings of salmon and green, glows with the warmth of a fire in the sky. And if the bark is richly red, the leaves are no less richly blue. To handle a heavy, resinous spray and see the unripe cones, little jade carvings in the deep sea lights and shadows of the needles, is an intoxication.

In its natural range, from Siberia to the Highlands to the Mediterranean, the Scots pine is unique. It was the sole north European pine to survive the Ice Ages. In the Alps the cembran came through in some mountain refuge. Only along the shores of the Mediterranean and the Atlantic did half a dozen other species survive.

Of the great Caledonian forest where the Scots pine grew only a few remnants have come down to us, among them one of the most beautiful and romantic woodlands in the world: even its name, the Black Wood of Rannoch, has primeval vibrations. It lies at the head of a glen, on the high moorland round Loch Rannoch, in the centre of Scotland. Among the vast pines, not tall but broad and somehow darker than their descendants, widely spaced in the heather and bilberry, grow great fountainous gold birches, at the same time taller and more weeping than any you have seen. A little alder grows by the burn which slides on long granite slabs to the loch. A rowan stoops under a hundredweight of scarlet berries.

Until recent times, hard as it is to believe, these few pines of Rannoch Wood were the only pines in Britain. Early man had massacred the rest. An untravelled contemporary of Shakespeare's would never have seen the tree the English have come to know, with cheerful ignorance, as 'the fir'.

North Germany, the Baltic and Scandinavia grow the same pine. At higher latitudes and altitudes it narrows its crown, becoming almost a spire. But the Alps have their own pines: the slow, solid, columnar cembran or Arolla of Switzerland (*P. cembra*) and farther east the Austrian black pine (*P. nigra* var. *nigra*), closely related to the black pine of Corsica and the south of Italy (*P. nigra maritima*). Of all European pines the Austrian is probably the toughest: it will transplant well even at ten feet tall; it will grow in clay (which most pines would shun); it doesn't mind lime in the soil. It has special value in growing on ground which has been

Above *The Bosnian pine grows in naked rock in the mountains of northern Italy and Yugoslavia. It thrives in drought and chalky soil; dense, dark but full of character. Its cones are blue.*

Left *The female flowers of Scots pine are dark red, in bunches of two to five on the end of vigorous new shoots: they take two years to ripen seed, in the meantime turning dark green. New needles are bright green but turn steel blue in a season.*

Left *Male flowers of Scots pine cover weaker shoots in May, while their needles are still emerging. Varieties of Scots pine include a very blue one, 'Argentea', and a small form, 'Aurea', which turns brilliant light gold in late winter.*

Tall, spreading Scots pines on the shores of Buttermere, Westmorland. Forms vary through its wide range; snowy Scandinavia has some very narrow trees. This is not a slow pine; two or three feet a year is normal growth for 20 or 30 years.

Pinaster pines growing on the land which their forefathers helped to reclaim—the vast areas of barren sand-dunes around the Bay of Biscay, now known as the forest of the Landes. The pinaster grows well on a wide range of soils, but prefers a mild climate.

The stone (or umbrella) pine of Italy is one of the classic Mediterranean landscape trees. It has been widely planted for centuries. Here at Ravello near Naples it grows over the Church of the

Annunciation. Its shape is remarkably constant, in formal gardens and in the wild. A famous tree at Kew with four stems has an enormous table-like top. The large seeds of the stone pine are edible.

Below *The mountain pine (P. mugo) is very hardy and tolerant of poor, limy soil, forming a dense, sagging bush or a low tree of many grey, curving stems with dark green mopheads.*

Below right *The Corsican pine is southern Europe's biggest. In southern Italy it has grown to 180 feet; a long-branched tree with dense, black foliage. An excellent windbreak.*

churned up by contractors, where the topsoil has been buried or pilfered. You see it in such unpromising places as Kennedy airport and the filling-stations on Italian autostradas, where its big bushy crown makes a quick sight-screen and windbreak. It is a rough and rather dark and dull tree, but I have one to break the northeast wind behind the house, and I wouldn't be without its long strong branches for all the flowering cherries in Japan. The Crimean variety of the same tree, *P. n. caramanica*, is even more heavily branched and more handsome.

Both the common black pines of Europe are trees of use rather than beauty. The Corsican version, which is also the Calabrian, is a useful forestry tree for poor sandy ground, quicker than the Austrian, narrower and less branchy. At home in Calabria it has grown as tall as 180 feet, and in Corsica to 150. The Italian navy used it for masts—but the French thought that too much resin made it 'as hard and translucid as horn'. The size for a Scots pine mast (which was the best), in the terms of the 18th-century mast-brokers of Riga on the Baltic, was over 18 inches diameter and about 80 feet long. Smaller trees were sold as spars or termed 'Norway masts'—since Norway had no big trees to sell.

Unquestionably the most distinctive of

European—perhaps of all—pines is the stone (or umbrella) pine of Italy (*P. pinea*). It was a godsend to the Roman and Renaissance gardeners, who were in the habit of confusing vegetation and architecture: it provided them with the perfect foil for the black pillars of their cypresses—a dense black canopy on a nice tidy pole. The pine tree's tendency to flatten out on top is epitomized in the stone pine: its twigs seem to multiply in the crown to leave no chink for light—while all the lower branches disappear without a trace. It is a reasonably hardy tree and could be grown in more northern gardens than it is. Indeed it should be, for there are few big trees which interfere less with what goes on underneath.

In the kind of country where the stone pine grows there is often another less shapely pine with grey-green needles and a crooked leaning trunk; the Aleppo pine (*P. halapensis*). Typical Aleppo pine country (the hills between Marseilles and St. Tropez are an example) is perilously inflammable. Old trees are rare.

In some ways the most useful pine, though not a glamorous tree, has been the pinaster (*P. pinaster*). The pinaster's place is the seashore. It was the means by which the biggest man-made forest on earth was developed on shifting sand in southwest France during the last century. In 1789 M. Bremontier started to plant 12,500 acres of sand dunes, open to the Bay of Biscay, with pinaster and broom seed together. He laid brushwood over the top, and waited. The result was to fix what was thought unfixable. Three million acres were added to cultivation in the wake of his experiment. Today the pines of the Landes are still tapped for turpentine and used for coalmines and railways—but it is the third and fourth generations of them, and in the meanwhile their roots and needles have made the land so fertile that farms are taking it over.

One scrub pine of the Alps (*P. mugo*), not really a tree but a bush, is well known to rock-gardeners in various forms. But there are two other European hill pines which are little known, and which are even tougher and less choosy about soil than the cembran. The Bosnian pine (*P. leucodermis*) is one we should see more of, especially in small gardens. It grows slightly quicker than the cembran, is certainly more attractive in youth, and has bright blue young cones into the bargain. The other, also from Yugoslavia, is the Macedonian pine (*P. peuce*). It makes a broad, dark, well-furnished spire under almost any conditions. At the Conifer Conference in 1972 it was described as 'undoubtedly the most useful five-needled pine for landscape planting'.

Above *Pines can adapt to impossible conditions. Macedonian pine is here invading the upper slopes of Mount Olympus in Greece. The strata of the bare rock are plainly visible—yet the trees can find enough soil to grow.*

The cembran pine is the typical tree of the Alps; a column with dense leaves from base to tip. Its female flowers are red among the yellow-green foliage. Being slow-growing and shapely this pine could be used more in formal garden layouts.

The Silver Firs of North America

To most of us the silver or true firs are probably the least familiar of the common members of the pine family. The word fir is loosely bandied about. It has been applied to every pointed tree; almost every evergreen. But the true firs are a conservative genus. They rarely dominate the scene; each species keeps to a relatively narrow range: many, indeed, are well on the way to extinction. Superficially they look very like spruces and moreover all firs tend to dress rather alike.

Yet as a sensuous experience the fir tree is hard to beat. There is, first of all, its smell. Firs have been called balsams in North America for a long time. They seem to exude the scented gum from every pore. Their barks carry fat blisters of sweet resin; their shoots are full of it; their leaves, crushed, coat your hands with the delicious glue. Every species has its own peculiar scent: of lemon, or turpentine, or tangerine.

The form of the tree expresses vigour under stern control. Within the strictest spire shape of any tree, the liveliest branching pattern darts into space. The view up the side of a fir tree is of thousands of little aircraft zooming out from the centre: shoots and side-shoots create a design of crystalline energy and rigour against the sky.

A juicy rigidity is equally well expressed in the needles: plump, leathery and firm, apparently adhering to the stout shoots with little round sucker pads. Dried branches of most firs keep their needles firmly on: spruce sprays disintegrate. There is rigidity in the way the branches thrust out horizontally in regular whorls, rarely drooping as spruce branches do. The cones stand up on the branch-ends, and, when they break up and scatter their seeds, leave their centre spikes standing there; spruce cones hang down, and fall off, leaving nothing on the tree. There is a simple test to tell whether a tree is a fir or a spruce. Pull a living needle off a twig. If it leaves a neat round mark, a slight dent, it is a fir. If a little piece of bark comes too, leaving a torn scar, it is a spruce. When spruce needles fall naturally, though, the minute pegs which form their bases stay on the twig, making it rough to the touch. Fir branches are pegless, and consequently smooth.

The cones of firs are the most attractive cones of all, but since they mostly grow high up on tall trees they are hard to collect. Some species have green or brown ones; most are dark and dusty purple, and so solid-looking that their habit of collapsing in your hands is quite disconcerting.

Botanists have named about 40 species of the firs. In a tribe as homogeneous as this there arise disagreements over what is a

Fir needles are attached to the shoot by round sucker-like bases. This magnified (× 6) shot of the underside of a noble fir shoot shows the roundish needles, marked with white pores.

species and what a variety. Populations sometimes flow into each other with enough intermediate specimens to keep everyone guessing. All are limited to the cooler hills and mountain-ranges of the northern hemisphere. On the whole they are relatively self-indulgent trees, liking deep moist soil and not attempting the cold dry hills of the far north.

North America has nine of the firs; two in the east and seven in the west. The eastern species, the balsam fir of Canada and the Lake States (*Abies balsamea*), and Fraser's fir (*A. fraseri*), of the Great Smoky Mountains, are on an altogether smaller scale than the western ones, hence more often grown in gardens. The balsam certainly puts up with the worst climate of any of them, growing slowly to a maximum height of about 60 feet. It keeps a good shape, a dark spire complete with lower branches, even when crowding has killed the foliage. The scented needles are used to give the 'pine-woods' smell to soap and such – and in Quebec the resin from the trunk is collected as glue. 'Canada balsam' is the finest cement for glass in optical instruments. The wood, strange to say, is the one part which has no smell of resin.

It was, inevitably, David Douglas who discovered the biggest of all the firs, the grand fir (*A. grandis*). This tree of prodigious vigour thrives where the rainfall is highest – Vancouver Island has grand firs

Left The female flowers standing upright on the branches of the alpine fir are dull crimson. All the silver or true firs have upright cones, contrasted with the spruces, whose cones hang down.

Above Alpine fir grows high in the mountains of the Olympic Peninsula of Washington. It is sculpted by the snow; where the snow lies round the base thousands of short shoots make a broad skirt.

Left *New growth on the flat, comb-like shoots of the grand fir. On lower branches, as here, the long needles grow in even rows on either side. Higher up the tree they curl upwards.*
Below left *Grand fir, the biggest of its genus, reaches 300 feet on the coastal plain of the Pacific northwest.*

Below *Red fir growing in the Sierra Nevada of California. Most firs have stronger, more horizontal or upswept branches than spruces. The blackish trunk of the trees on the left is typical of red fir. The tree on the right is a Balfour pine.*

Cones of noble fir cluster round the top of the tree. Since fir cones fall to pieces on the tree, leaving only their centre spike standing, they are rarely seen complete. These are typical in being barrel-like with overlapping scales and extruding bracts.

nearly 300 feet high. But even more startling is its speed. Atlantic rain apparently suits it as well as Pacific, or better: trees in Scotland have grown 160 feet in 50 years. Even in drier areas it is a quick grower.

There is a childish simplicity about its design. The leaves are straight, parallel-sided, of shiny mid-green, neither dark nor light. They are set each side of the twig in flat rows, as straightforward as the teeth of a comb. Their undersides have two pale blue lines—but these you rarely see; the branches hang flat and low.

Where it stands above its fellows, exposed to the wind, the grand fir often loses its top. But an accident like this is only an excuse for another display of strength; three or four new tops will grow as tall as the first, creating a massive square head.

The red silver fir (*A. amabilis*) occupies ground only slightly higher; it too likes to have its roots in deep soil, to have a long growing season and an equable climate.

But its name is for beauty rather than size or speed. Its Latin name translates literally as lovely fir. Thick lustrous leaves set off its pale and smooth grey trunk blotched with white stains of resin. Though a foothill tree, it bears the pointed crown which is usually the mark of the snow-covered heights.

The red fir (*A. magnifica*) and the noble fir (*A. procera*) keep the middle altitudes of the Cascades and the Sierras from Canada to southern California. Noble fir has the north of the territory and red the south. In the middle is the Shasta fir of Mount Shasta, a variety of the red.

There is no striking difference between these trees. The noble fir has the biggest cones of any, and bears them most freely. Its needles are shorter, more crowded, with grooved upper-sides (which red firs never have). But their general appearance is the same: of immense vigour somehow restrained within a narrow space, as if there were a glass funnel inverted over the tree.

In western gardens both do equally well; in exceptional eastern gardens fairly well; in European gardens the noble fir, on the whole, rather better. In nature it is the bigger tree–to nearly 250 feet.

One of the mountain firs, oddly enough, is the most cultivated in gardens. The Colorado white fir (*A. concolor*) seems to be the most adaptable to conditions in the east and in Europe. Its natural range is enormous; it grows all the way from New Mexico to Oregon, where its variety Low's silver fir (*A. c. lowiana*) merges with grand fir. The tendency of its long needles towards blue-green has produced garden cultivars in shades of piercing silver-blue: 'Candicans' and 'Violacea' are two of the best known. The alpine fir (*A. lasiocarpa*) has a similar, rather more northerly, range, yet its garden performance has not been good. Its variety the cork fir (*A.l. arizonica*), from the southernmost part of its range, is healthier, and also prettier, with silvery-blue needles.

The Santa Lucia fir (*A. bracteata*) is the odd one out. It is a rare tree, not often cultivated and found naturally only in canyons in the Santa Lucia mountains, behind Monterey and Big Sur overlooking the Pacific. To me it is the most beautiful and memorable of all firs.

Where the others have plump needles with blunt ends, crowding and curling along the shoots, Santa Lucia's needles are long, slim, straight and hard, brilliant green with two white lines underneath ending in a sharp point. They fan out below the shoot; on top they surge forward to the tip where, in place of a fat, round, resinous bud, there is an elegant parcel of folded parchment.

The cone is equally eccentric: a fat little brown barrel decorated with what look like long green feelers.

Best of all, though, is the Santa Lucia's shape: a sharp, broad-based spire, terraced with branches which dip in the middle under the weight of drooping branchlets, and turn up at the end like a spaniel's tail.

■ Balsam
■ Fraser
■ Red
■ Shasta
■ Noble

■ Alpine
■ Grand
■ Santa Lucia
■ Cork

■ Red silver
■ Colorado white
■ Low's silver

The Silver Firs of Europe and Asia

Decorative, strong-growing species of fir abound in Asia, but not all of them have been properly tried out in the western world. Since most of them are too big for widespread garden use, and forestry prefers local kinds, they remain in a quite unwarranted obscurity. Even among Europe's three native firs only one, the common silver fir, has been planted widely. The Spanish and Greek firs are acknowledged handsome and hardy; yet we are only just beginning to put them to use.

The silver fir of Europe (*A. alba*) was for many millennia the second tallest European tree. In Britain it was the tallest until its reign was brought to an end (at 180 feet) by a Douglas fir in 1955. From its natural home in the mountains in a band stretching from the Pyrenees through Burgundy and the Vosges as far as Poland it was introduced as a forestry tree throughout Europe. It reached Britain in 1603 and grew so big that it was forgiven its susceptibility to spring frosts. Until the northwest American coni-

fers came on the scene more than 200 years later it had no competition for speed of growth and eventual height. Even then it was a relentless aphid which decided the question in favour of the newer exotics. None of the first trees survive, but there are some 17th-century specimens still left in Scotland. They tend, perhaps because of frost damage, to make big-branched trees rather than spires: huge, open-headed, grey-barked, dark-foliaged constructions of no special elegance or beauty. They are at their best when, as younger trees, their bark is as silvery as a beech's.

Two firs which are very much alike, perhaps survivors of the same race long decimated by the Ice Ages, have taken up their residence at the extreme corners of southern Europe, *A. cephalonica* in Greece and *A. pinsapo* in the mountains behind the Costa del Sol in southern Spain. This Mediterranean strain gives blue-grey trees with stiff, hard leaves emerging hedgehog-like from

all round the shoot; uncomfortable to handle. *A. numidica* is another, from Algeria—a rather denser and less prickly tree. Where the Spanish and Greek firs are particularly worth planting is in chalky, well-drained districts where other firs have reservations about growing. They are not fast, but they have character from the start.

Caucasian trees in general have a fine reputation. The Caucasus mountains lie on the same latitude as northern California (and Tasmania, another rich plant-kingdom, in the southern hemisphere). With the Black Sea on one side and the Caspian on the other, with Russia to the north and Persia to the south, they are one of the great meeting places of weather-systems; and also of genetic contributions. Mount Ararat lies just to the south. One might easily fancy the garden of Eden was in these hills—in which case the Caucasian fir (*A. nordmanniana*) would have been one of its more distinguished decorations.

A young plant of the Caucasian fir is the most delectable of evergreens. You look down on dense tiers of long, shiny, deep green needles. Underneath they have two icy stripes marking the pores. The tree is always one of the happiest, best-fed looking of the firs, right into its gianthood when its long branches, still dense and shining, cascade in rich tiers to the ground.

The supply of beautiful firs from farther east, from the Himalayas, China, Korea and Japan is almost overwhelming. Probably the best known of them at the moment is the Korean fir (*A. koreana*) which is obliging enough to cone prolifically at eye-level. The ripe cones remind me of those decadent displays of Fabergé imitating confectionery in ivory and rubies, or scrambled eggs in amber and gold; they are plump, and piercing purple, with brown contour-lines and spangles of translucent resin—and like presents in dreams they crumble when you pick them up.

Two Japanese firs, the Nikko (*A. homo-*

Above *Nikko firs on Hokkaido, the northern island of Japan. The Nikko makes a very large, hardy tree with a pale and faintly pink bark, turning an attractive purplish grey-brown with age.*

Above *Forrest's fir from southwest China is one of the handsomest. Its bright green leaves grow stiffly all round the shoot and its flowers and cones are blue. The buds are just bursting and the male flowers are prominent in this photograph.*

Left *A branch of the Caucasian fir, whose bright green foliage, remaining dense throughout the life of the tree, makes it one of the best firs for gardens. It has reached 144 feet in the south of England.*

Below *The Korean fir is the one most often grown for its cones. Even as a young tree it can bear heavy crops like this. They start deep purple and turn brown before they split up.*

The common silver fir was until the 19th century the most important forestry tree in western Europe, growing at altitudes of up to 6,000 feet. It is illustrated here in Zwinger's Theatrum Botanicum, 1744.

lepis) and the Veitch (*A. veitchii*) from Mt. Fuji are comparatively widely planted. The latter is one of the easiest to recognize, at least as a big tree, from its odd habit of forming an armpit in the trunk under each rather spindly branch. It is a gleaming tree, with the white bands under the leaves very conspicuous on the new shoots. The Nikko fir has the same effect; each leaf strains upwards, hiding its green side and showing its white.

There are fine differences of leaf-length or -shape between these species. But often the most noticeable feature is the colour of the new shoot within the covering of leaves. The Veitch fir has brown shoots, the Nikko fir white; a third Japanese species, Maries' fir (*A. mariesii*), has almost red shoots and its winter buds are coated with resin.

A short list of the best Chinese firs would certainly include George Forrest's variety of the fir named after the Abbé Delavay, who virtually initiated botanizing in west-central China. *A. delavayi* var. *forrestii*, as it is dauntingly called, sums up for me the juicy feeling of well-being which makes the firs such satisfying trees. My notes here get as far away from objectivity as they do at the end of a good wine-tasting: 'thick squirrel-brown shoots: needles crowding all round, brilliant white beneath; buds are red globes, shiny and succulent with resin; very bunchy and rich-looking'.

Another on the list would be *A. fargesii*, which was brought back by E. H. Wilson from the same area. Another would be the Manchurian version of the Nikko, *A. holophylla*, which Alan Mitchell at the 1972 Conifer Conference singled out as a good doer.

One couldn't close the list without at least one of the Himalayan firs. *A. spectabilis* (a tree very like the *A. delavayi* I have described) grows on the highest Himalayan slopes and *A. pindrow* on lower ground. *A. pindrow* (the west Himalayan fir) has distinct long thin needles dividing at the end into two tiny spikes.

Left *The East Himalayan fir, A. spectabilis, grows at about 10,000 feet in temperate rain-forest, with rhododendrons as the shrub layer. Old trees in this picture are covered with moss and ferns.*

The forest of Puck and Titania; Midsummer Night's Dream is set in 'the forest near Athens'. Here, 4,000 feet up on Mount Parnis, the Greek fir, a stiff grey-foliaged tree, is as lichen-covered as the rocks.

The Douglas Fir

A tree with the forester's idea of perfect form: a Douglas fir, nearly 200 feet high and five feet thick at the base, tapering gradually with no branches at all for the first 100 feet.

The bark of an old Douglas fir is deeply creviced and richly brown. This tree in the Mount Rainier National Park in Washington is in typical Douglas country. This tree would be about 400 years old.

The soft green foliage of Douglas fir with an unripe cone showing the unique trident-shaped bracts between the scales. For forestry purposes the exact provenance of the seed is vitally important. It decides the length of the tree's growing season.

With the greatest respect to the giant sequoias, the Douglas fir (*Pseudotsuga menziesii*) can be fairly called the world's biggest *beautiful* tree. There is no suggestion of the amazing survival from another era about the Douglas; it is in the prime of life, with a natural range all the way from Canada to Mexico—as well as close relations in China and Japan.

The Douglas is alone in its botanical compartment. It is not a silver fir. Its cones hang down, and remain in one piece. It is not a spruce either. Its leaves have tiny stalks and suckers like the fir's. It deserves better from botanists, however, than the Latin name they gave it. For *Pseudotsuga* means 'false hemlock'. The 'pseudo', with its implication of moral turpitude, I (on its behalf) most categorically refute. It was never a hemlock, and it never pretended to be.

Happily the rest of the Douglas's nomenclature celebrates the two deserving explorers who found it and introduced it to cultivation. Menzies, sailing with Vancouver's expedition in 1791, was the first. David Douglas, the tireless envoy of the London Horticultural Society, sent home the seeds in 1827. Some trees planted in 1828 still stand in Britain today.

The forest that Douglas found is also still unplundered in a few spots in the northwest. Mount Rainier National Park is one. Penetrating even 100 yards into a stand of old growth Douglas fir makes it hard to believe that this is the country Douglas crossed and recrossed, sometimes with Indian guides, often on his own. Every few yards a fallen log the size of a truck stops your progress. Great rotting snags tower above the brilliant emerald of the mounting young trees; Douglas and red silver fir, western red cedar, red alder. Rivers, of course, were the only way of covering long distances. But to portage through these woods . . . !

The seeds from which those first cultivated Douglases grew crossed the continent in this way. The cones were entrusted to the Hudson's Bay Company's 'express'—an annual expedition of a score of *voyageurs* who paddled and clambered 2,000 miles from Hudson Bay to the mouth of the Columbia River to collect pelts.

The Douglas is a relatively easy tree to recognize. The clearest indicators are the buds at the ends of the twigs, which are reddish-brown and pointed, very much like rather fat beech buds. If the tree has cones, they are unlike any others: egg-shaped, hanging, with three little paler points, an upside-down trident, extruding from beneath each dark-brown scale. The bark of a big Douglas is unmistakable: immensely craggy and rutted with dark corky cracks.

The hang of the whole tree is distinctive too: the foliage is dense and dark and soft, weighing down the side-shoots in swags below the branches; eventually weighing down the longest branches until they dip to the ground.

In the hills of the northwest occasional trees are so pendulous that they could, at a distance, be Brewer's spruce. Like all the western trees, though, they become stiffer, narrower and paler as they go south and higher into the mountains. The Rocky Mountain form of Douglas fir has the varietal name of 'Glauca'—though it is by no means bright blue—and is hardy where the big vigorous green tree is not (in northern New England for instance). 'Glauca' is also happier on chalk or lime. Ordinary Douglas will grow in a limy soil but, at least in my garden, turns yellow-green. When I first saw it I thought it was a golden cultivar.

Given reasonably good soil the Douglas is one of the best timber trees on earth. It makes wood like good quality pine at a prodigious rate. A tree planted 80 years ago is now, at 175 feet, one of the tallest trees in Britain. It stands by a woodland pool on the Duke of Atholl's estate in Dunkeld in Scotland. But Scotland has a long way to go. The tallest sequoia is 20 feet taller than this tree and its reflection added together.

The Spruces of North America

The spruces remind one more than any other conifer that they evolved in the age of reptiles. Those thin unwavering shoots groping at the sky are like tentacles. Few spruces, indeed, are very graceful. They seem to lack the plump poise of the firs, their nearest relatives. They are uncomfortable trees; their needles hard and spiny, their twigs rough, the bark thin and scaly. With age they become gaunt and gappy, their branches skeletons of corroded old twigs. The beauty of their new shoots is out of reach as they grow old. You have to be a forester to appreciate the sturdy pole which holds the tattered top against the sky.

There are about 40 species of spruce, as there are of silver fir. The spruces, on the other hand, are more varied than the firs in their habit, their colour and manner of growth. They contain in their number a handful of trees more strikingly ornamental than any other conifers–so ornamental, in fact, that it is hard to know whether to think of them as *haute couture* or Carnaby Street.

The spruces far outnumber the firs. From the mountains of the south, where the two share the same tastes and habits, the spruces fan out northwards into much colder, wetter country. The tree-map of the great land-masses of the north, Siberia, Canada and Alaska, shows the astonishing hardiness of the race.

Three spruces, the red (*Picea rubens*), the black (*P. mariana*) and the white (*P. glauca*), grow in the far north. Their range extends south to the Great Lakes–the red as far as the mountain tops of the Great Smokies. Their importance lies in their wood, which makes some of the best paper pulp. As

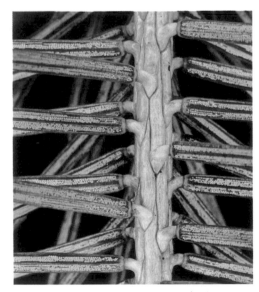

Above *The shoot of a Sitka spruce, magnified five times, shows the woody pegs at the base of the flattened needles and the plaited effect* *of the ribbed shoot itself. The leaves are dark green above; this shot from below shows the breathing pores, white with a waxy coating.*

Left *Ripe cones of Sitka spruce. Each scale has opened and released a seed. The cones of all spruces hang from the upper branches of a tree and fall in one piece shortly after they have dropped their seeds.*

Above *Sitka spruce from the coastline of British Columbia has become one of Europe's most important forestry trees. This young plantation is in Bavaria. Snow provides useful protection from drying winds.*

ornamental trees they are only planted where nothing else will grow. But the spruces have the peculiarity, much more than the firs, of producing odd branch 'sports' of dwarf form or unusual colour – and the northern spruces are no exception. *P. glauca albertiana* 'Conica', a bright green bushy form of the white spruce which was found in the Rockies in Alberta, is one of the best-known garden conifers – though bearing little resemblance to its parents. *P. mariana* 'Doumetii' is a similar production of the black spruce.

The biggest member of the spruce family (*P. sitchensis*) comes from the land of giants – the northwest. It takes its name from Sitka, the old Russian capital of Alaska on Baranof Island off the southeast Alaskan coast. Along the fog-bound straits and inlets there, where whales and log-rafts loom up intermittently out of the gloom, the spruces grow trunk to trunk to the water's edge. Melancholy ramrods of trees almost 300 feet high are found, their moss-grown bases splaying out as though to get a purchase in the saturated soil.

Farther south, on the Oregon coast, the Sitka is the first tree to front the sea-wind on crags and promontories above a beach buried deep in jetsam lumber. The grey water-worn snags below, the grey wind-torn branches above, epitomize the staying-power of the spruce. The same qualities have made it one of the most-planted forest trees in northern Europe in this century. One of Douglas's originals still stands in Ireland, 160 feet high. During its life-time some 2,000,000 acres of swampy exposed ground have been made productive by its kin.

It is barely 100 miles from the coast where Sitka grows to the heights of the Siskiyou mountains. But the spruce of the Siskiyous belongs to a different world. Brewer's spruce, or the weeping spruce (*P. brewerana*), is certainly the most beautiful tree of its race – possibly the most beautiful of all conifers. Its mountain home, above the valley where the world's biggest pine trees grow, is a garden of rare and graceful plants: the Lawson cypress is wild here, growing with pendulous western hemlock and Douglas fir, tufted incense cedar, tangerine-scented white fir, brilliant-leafed dogwood and bigleaf maple, and neat, dark-green bulwarks of Sadler oak. The weeping spruce, though, would stand out in any company. Its arching branches carrying long shawls of green-black lace hold arcs of sunlight or snow, receding tiers in different angles of profile; an exquisitely satisfying design.

But whereas Lawson cypress, equally limited in nature, has been prolifically fast

and easy in cultivation, Brewer's spruce needs wooing. It is slow to start, demands moisture (in the air as well as in the ground) and takes several years before its weeping habit really shows. Branch cuttings weep sooner, but need staking to develop a leading shoot. In the eastern States it rarely does well: in Europe, on the other hand, there are superb examples. One in the British National Arboretum at Westonbirt has grown to 40 feet in 35 years. It is a tree to try, and to keep trying.

There could not be a greater contrast than the blue spruce of Colorado (*P. pungens*). High altitude and bright light give the species its stiff habit of growth, the grey-blue cast in its leaves. But the cultivars a rejoicing nursery trade has found are surely bluer and stiffer than God ever intended. They include the most piercingly ice-blue of all plants. Various forms of the cultivar 'Glauca', notably 'Koster' and 'Moerheim', have a totally artificial air: they rise in stiffly perfect terraces of ice to a stiffly perfect pinnacle. They are perhaps the hardest of all plants to place successfully in a garden; and it is worth remembering that they are best in youth; gaps and dead twigs show up all too clearly on a pale ground.

The answer is to compromise, and plant the much less common, softer and more graceful Engelmann spruce (*P. engelmannii*). The 'Glauca' version of this is also very pale blue. But in place of the stiff icy terraces it has long furry tails for shoots; the needles run along the shoots towards the tip. The species is an important timber tree of the Rockies, with a more northerly range than the Colorado blue spruce.

__Above and left__ The handsomest of the spruces; Brewer's weeping spruce from the Siskiyou mountains in western Oregon. It is still rare in gardens, taking years to establish its weeping habit. Mature trees are highly prized.

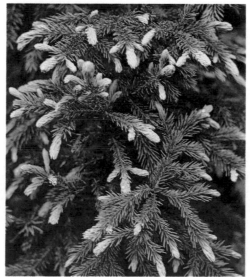

New growth on black spruce from the northeastern States. All spruces look best in the spring when the soft young shoots in paler colours light up the tree. The crushed foliage of the black spruce is strongly scented of balsam.

A stand of Engelmann spruce, a native of the western States, ranging from Alberta to New Mexico. In the wild Engelmann can reach 150 feet; in cultivation it tends to make a much smaller tree with a narrow, pointed crown.

The Spruces of Europe and Asia

Half of all the species of spruce are natives of China. We have two or three good ones from Japan and the Himalayas. As usual, Europe's contribution in numbers is minimal–only two species. On the other hand they are probably the two most important of all the spruces to the gardener.

The Norway spruce (*P. abies*) is Europe's tallest native tree: 200 feet is within its reach. It was the first of the pointed trees to re-enter Britain, whence the Ice Ages had expelled it. As long ago as 1500 it was planted and admired. As the source of much of Britain's light lumber (deal, as we call it) which was bought in the Baltic, it also

Left and above *Serbian spruce is shapely, quick-growing and adaptable; one of the best garden conifers. It grows with the same narrow spire-shape in the wild (above) in Yugoslavia.*

Above *The Himalayan weeping spruce growing in the foothills of the Himalayas in Kashmir. In cultivation it is often more distinctly weeping than these wild trees. It has reached 124 feet in Scotland.*

brought the word spruce into the English language: it derives from Pruce, the old English name for the Kingdom of Prussia. Today in most of northern Europe it is, at any time of year, 'the Christmas tree'.

From the forestry point of view it has one advantage over the faster-growing Sitka: it is frost-hardy from the start. There are cold areas where sapling Sitka suffers. For the gardener its importance lies in its profusion of off-beat cultivars. It comes in drooping, upright, golden, dwarf, bush, prostrate, tabular, globular, congested and exploded forms. A few of them are shown on pages 118–19. They could afford the subject of a whole collection in themselves.

More beautiful and useful in its normal form, however, is the Serbian spruce (*P. omorika*) from the mountains of eastern Yugoslavia. There are no difficulties with limy soil, or indeed soil of any kind, with this adaptable tree. Moreover, it can manage in city air. It grows tall (but not too tall), stays slim (but is satisfyingly solid at the bottom), forms a strong but graceful pattern with its short arching branches. It flatters buildings by introducing a harmony and rhythm which they often lack. Most important of all, it grows fast; two or three feet a year to about 50 feet. In fact it is hard to think of anything else you could stand on a ten-foot square base which would do the environment so much good.

The oriental spruce (*P. orientalis*) is not quite as exotic as it sounds: it comes from nearest Asia; from the Caucasus mountains–the home of a number of our best garden trees. One can't be dramatic about the oriental spruce: its strength is simply in its neatness. It has short needles which sit tidily on its twigs; a model of grooming. For all that, it makes a big tree, and a handsome one. It also has a cultivar, 'Aurea', which greets the spring with startling creamy-white (instead of green) new shoots. A bit gimmicky, but effective none the less.

None of the far-eastern spruces can be reckoned essential garden material, like the above. Encomiums have been lavished on one or two, particularly the Sargent spruce (*P. brachytyla*), from western China. The dragon spruce, which has been called China's version of the Norway spruce, is one of the best known, valuable for its densely needled, dark and stolid appearance. Its Latin name, *asperata*, celebrates the way it identifies itself to anyone who is rash enough to stroke its branches: a file is less asperate.

It is probably easiest to remember the Japanese tiger-tail spruce by linking it with the dragon. The dragon's bark is its bite, but beware of the tiger-tail's needles. Its

Latin name, *polita*, suggests the opposite of *asperata*. But its shoots bristle with arms like those of medieval Japanese knights.

Of the other Chinese spruces one very pretty one is well known for its flowers–indeed it is probably the only conifer which is planted primarily for that reason. The Likiang spruce (*P. likiangensis*), from Yunnan in southwest China, becomes spectacularly uxorious in the spring, loading its branches with crimson male and bright red female flowers, the females (the cones-to-be) standing up boldly at the tips of the branches until pregnancy weighs them into the correct spruce position, dangling down. It is

Above *The dull green of the Norway spruce is enlivened in May with the bright yellow-green of the new shoots. They decorate the tree for about two months before darkening.*

Top *Cones of the Norway spruce hang from the tips of the upper branches. They have leathery scales and are twice the size of the cones of the Sitka spruce, the other widely-planted forestry species.*

fair to add that this performance only starts when the tree is 25 or 30 years old.

Of all the Asiatic spruces possibly the best known is the Himalayan weeping spruce (*P. smithiana*). Were it not for the existence of Brewer's this would be a respectable entry as *the* weeping spruce. As it is, this much bigger (to 118 feet in the south of England), broader, less densely furnished tree, tending indeed to become decidedly skeletal with age, must take second place. It may be the answer in places like New England, where Brewer's is unhappy. But, as a young tree, it has trouble with late spring frosts.

Norway spruce is Europe's tallest native tree, reaching about 200 feet. Here it is growing in the Italian Tyrol, in the Alpine foothills.

The Hemlocks

One or other of the hemlocks (*Tsuga*) is a familiar sight from Alabama to Nova Scotia, and from San Francisco to Alaska; between them the four local species cover most of eastern America and most of the west coast. In Europe, on the contrary, it is a surprise to most people that there is such a tree at all. (If hemlock means anything to them it is the waterside weed which Socrates is supposed to have taken as poison.) The hemlock is one of the few important races of conifer which occur in America and Asia but have no representative in Europe; it has scarcely been planted outside its native habitat—very much to Europe's loss.

In appearance the hemlocks (all except one) come somewhere between a spruce and a yew. They are botanically close to the spruces; the yew likeness lies in their flat, blunt-ended, relatively broad needles. The hallmark of the hemlock, however, lies in its manner of growth. Of all the needle trees it is perhaps the most graceful in texture and

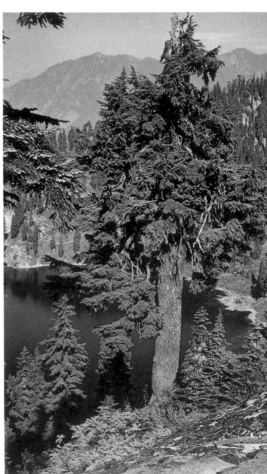

Above *The western hemlock, biggest and best of its race, grows with Douglas fir in the Pacific northwest. Open-grown it makes a broad pyramid with a characteristic drooping leading shoot.*

Left *Hemlock foliage is soft and fine, with the needles arranged in two ranks on the shoots. Shelter and moisture are essential for its lush growth.*

The mountain hemlock; an old tree, its top gone, at Snow Lake, 4,000 feet up in the Cascade Mountains of Washington.

Eastern hemlock is often a several-stemmed, spreading tree. Its weeping form is small and slow-growing; one of the best conifers of this shape. The ordinary variety makes dense and hardy hedges, much used in New England.

detail. Without drooping or dangling it suggests elegant repose.

You need to look no further than its leading shoot to see the hemlock's philosophy. It nods in a sleepy curve. Instead of neat ranks, or jostling crowds, its needles look faintly dishevelled. The side ones are longer than the top ones, and no two exactly agree on the direction to go. But they are a lovely soft green on top, marked white underneath, and dense enough to create an almost furry appearance.

The important differences between the hemlocks are questions of habit and habitat rather than twigs and leaves. They all answer the description above except the mountain hemlock of the Pacific northwest (*T. mertensiana*), whose needles surround each shoot, pointing onwards and outwards. Soft hemlock-green, in this case, is also overlaid with the bloomy grey cast typical of the mountain-tree – a subtle and telling colour in the garden.

The familiar pattern repeats itself: the eastern hemlock is the hardy one, usually shorter in stature. The western one (*T. heterophylla*) is the giant, the spoilt child of moist ferny litter, tall shelter and perpetual mist. Where it succeeds (and the moisture and shelter are both important) it can be breathtakingly graceful. Its long branches form loose layers, softer and more sloping than those of a cedar but almost as broad and architectural. It keeps a tall, narrow crown with a nodding shoot even as a tree 140 feet high. What clinches it for me is the foliage – a sort of subdued brilliant green . . . This is the one for the two-acre lawn.

The eastern hemlock (*T. canadensis*) very often grows up with several leading shoots, to make a spreading shape more like a typical broadleaf parkland tree. Its foliage has an odd feature in a line of little blunt needles lying upside down, with their white undersides showing along the top of the shoot. Eastern American gardeners have

found it so adaptable that they think of it more as raw material for shaping (particularly into a hedge) than as a tree with ideas of its own. Among its own ideas (it has almost as many as the Norway spruce) are gold, upright and dwarf versions, and an extremely effective weeping one – perhaps the best low evergreen weeper for the lawn. The maximum height of this form (*T. canadensis* 'Pendula') is nine or ten feet, but its spread might be 20 or 30.

The Carolina hemlock (*T. caroliniana*) is to all intents a local form of the eastern one. If there is any advantage in either of the two Japanese hemlocks (*T. diversifolia* and *T. sieboldii*) it is only a still-denser supply of needles. The sole discouragement from growing any of this graceful group is their distaste for limy soil, which is strong in the western, the Japanese and the Carolina, and less so in the mountain hemlock. The obliging eastern one hardly seems to be bothered by lime at all.

At Crater Lake in Oregon. mountain hemlocks at higher altitudes have the short branches and narrow profile of trees accustomed to long

months of snow. Their leaves have a grey-blue sheen like most high-altitude conifers, but their nodding tops proclaim them hemlock.

Male flowers of western hemlock shedding pollen. The short leaves are blunt, with little notches in the tips. Underneath they are marked with two broad white lines where waxy resin accumulates round the breathing pores.

Unripe cones forming from the female flowers of western hemlock. They ripen dark brown but remain only an inch long. Hemlock seeds germinate freely even in the shade of big trees.

The True Cedars

The cedar of Lebanon at Wilton House in Wiltshire is typical of the cedar's long association with noble country-house architecture. This tree, 85 feet high and 28 feet in girth, was probably planted in the 18th century. Many of them lose their high dome and become flat-topped.

The layman uses the name cedar for any tree with dark, spice-scented timber. Thus America has the incense, the western red, the eastern red, the Alaskan yellow and the Port Orford cedar; Japan the plume cedar and the Hiba cedar. The botanist uses much stricter rules and recognizes only four, none of them from America (or the Far East) and none of them remotely like the American 'cedars'. For once I would say (as a committed layman) that the botanist is right.

There is nothing like the true cedars in the whole coniferous kingdom. Not even the pines produce a tree of such majestic architecture. Partly no doubt because of their biblical background–they are the trees most mentioned in the Bible, and always as an image for fruitfulness and strength–Europeans regard them with something approaching awe. Countless cedars in English churchyards and on the lawns of country houses are celebrated in village lore as having come back with the Crusaders. Villagers' geography, in this case, is better than their history. Few of the giant trees which cut such a timeless figure are more than 150 years old. On the other hand crusading country is just where they do come from.

Three of the four species of cedar come from the shores of the Mediterranean; the fourth comes from the western Himalayas. The cedar of Lebanon (*Cedrus libani*) is the most celebrated and by far the oldest in cultivation. The remaining grove of ancient trees on the slopes of Mount Lebanon (at 6,200 feet–4,000 feet below the summit) has been a place of pilgrimage for centuries; from all accounts the cedars have remained exactly the same since travellers began writing about them. There are roughly 400 of them, the biggest 48 feet in girth and calculated (by guesswork) to be about 2,500 years old. The biggest natural woods of Lebanon cedar surviving are in the Taurus mountains in southeastern Turkey.

A grove of the great cedars from which King Solomon is said to have built his temple still stands on the slopes of Mount Lebanon, 4,000 feet below the 10,000 foot summit. In biblical times the cedar stood as a symbol for everything fertile and abundant. Its wood was highly prized for its strength, colour and scent.

The young female cones of the cedar of Lebanon are surrounded by clusters of protecting needles. The white, waxy lines of pores on the dark yellow-green needles are clearly seen in this picture.

The blue Atlantic cedar is the most popular cedar and one of the most popular of all conifers today; the picture shows a garden version of the tree from the Atlas mountains of Morocco. The first tree to be introduced to Britain, planted by Lord Somers in Herefordshire on the Welsh border in 1845, is still healthy.

The great Sir Joseph Hooker, incidentally, poured cold water on the idea that Solomon's temple was built of these trees. In his view builders' merchants of Solomon's day were no better botanists than they are nowadays: the wood they called cedar was probably a sort of juniper.

Despite such recollections of antiquity it is still remarkable that the first cedar of Lebanon to be planted in Britain, the forerunner of a great revolution in English gardens, is alive today. It is in the rectory garden at Childrey in the Thames valley, planted there by Dr. Pocock, the rector, in 1646, soon after his retirement as the Embassy chaplain in Constantinople. Today its trunk is 25 feet in girth, whereas the next oldest tree of known date, at Biel near Edinburgh, measured 23 feet in 1967.

John Evelyn did his best to popularize the cedar of Lebanon in the 1670s, but it was not until the earliest trees started to bear cones that they could be planted on a massive scale. In the mid-18th century they became a craze. The Duke of Richmond planted 1,000 at Goodwood in 1761. The trees on the lawn at Wilton House, illustrated on the left, belong to this era. They were the only exotic trees which Capability Brown used in his landscapes, and they continued to be planted in great numbers until the 1830s, when the new giants from Douglas's travels began to take their place.

The cedars, in fact, are not nearly so slow-growing as their stateliness might suggest; they can reach 50 feet in 30 years in good conditions, and grow stout and impressive in an equivalently short time. The tallest in Britain, at Petworth in Sussex, is 132 feet. Not until they are getting on in years, though, do they strike their splendid attitudes, forming black plateaux low over the lawn, at rooftop height, and again, high above pediment and belfry, spreading a black table in the sky.

The Atlantic cedar (*C. atlantica*) does not plant them. One sees their desperate pale-blue gestures over every little garden wall in some parts of France–particularly the southwest. It is hard to think of any tree less suitable for a small space: colossal spread is its very essence. And heaven knows how you would fell it in a back-yard.

The Deodar (*C. deodara*) is better as a small tree. With longer needles in a quieter colour, a lovely soft silver-green, it nods and droops in delicate attitudes. It tends to maintain its basic conical shape into maturity, rather than rearing all its upper branches together to a high plateau. In its native Himalayas it makes what must be some of the world's loveliest forests.

The fourth true cedar comes from Cyprus. Compared with the others it is unspectacular–and consequently a rarity in cultivation. It grows slowly to about half the size of a Lebanon cedar, and is notable only for its much shorter leaves–whence its Latin name, *brevifolia*.

The weeping form of the blue Atlantic cedar is the most spectacular of all weeping conifers–and also one of the rarest; a difficult tree to grow.

Above right *The Deodar is very beautiful as a young tree; the softest in shape and colour of the cedars. This adult tree is at Nymans, Sussex.*

have quite the same classical education as the cedar of Lebanon. Its arrival, from the Atlas mountains of Morocco, was not until 1839. A forest of it was planted in 1862 on Mont Ventoux in Provence–a magnificent sight today. It is a bold man, however, who claims to be able to tell the difference between the Lebanon and the Atlantic. The only certain way is with a magnifying glass: the Atlantic's needles have a minute translucent spine at the tip.

The ordinary green Atlantic cedar is not planted nearly so much as the variety 'Glauca', the blue one which is said to be the most popular of all ornamental conifers today. I have not actually seen one in a window box, but it is remarkable where people do

The growing stem of many germinating conifers lifts the seed above the ground. Here the seed-leaves of a cedar are pulling themselves free of the husk and are expanding to begin photosynthesis.

Right *Mature cones of the blue Atlantic cedar are plump and pink-brown, sitting up like over-fed skittles on the boughs of brush-like blue foliage.*

Above *A very different version of an adult Deodar cedar growing at Child Okeford in Dorset. This tree has grown tall and open–more like the Deodar in its native Himalayas.*

The Larches

The larches make their mark in autumn when they turn from the anonymity of forest green to warm gold. Here in the Pacific northwest the western larch, the tallest and narrowest of the larches, grows with the alpine silver fir.

Of all the conifers which are widely planted as forest trees the larches make the prettiest woods. It must be because they celebrate the seasons that we find them so friendly and amenable. The advantages of evergreenery are obvious enough—yet we love the larches for being different: for flushing feathery green in April; for glowing gold in November; even for spending the winter as a tangle of bare black rigging, when their colleagues are demonstrating the superiority of their leathery leaves.

Their leaf-dropping lets in the light so that a rich undergrowth of shrub and herb and creature can flourish, and contributes year by year to the fertility of the forest. Yet it by no means detracts from their vigour, as you might think it would do. The larch is one of the fastest-growing of all trees; certainly the fastest to make strong and heavy wood with almost oak-like qualities.

Close to, the larch's summer rig is remarkably like the cedar's. They are clearly the closest kin, with their leaves in little rosettes like those of no other tree. The larch bears no resemblance at all to the two other deciduous conifers, the swamp cypress and the dawn redwood; the confusion comes in telling larch from larch.

North America has three larches, two of them excellent trees. Both Russia and China have two species—of which one forms the world's northernmost forest, on the latitude of the northernmost point of Alaska. The Himalayas, Japan and Europe have one species each. Possibly more important than any of the species, however, is a hybrid, the fruit of a union romantically formed at a ducal seat in the highlands of Scotland.

The family of the Dukes of Atholl has had trees in the blood for generations. It was James, the 2nd Duke, who first saw the possibilities of the larch for reafforesting his naked Perthshire hillsides. The European larch (*Larix decidua*) had been brought to England from the Alps, its native home, in 1620; Evelyn had described it; but it had remained a rarity. In 1738 the Duke planted his first larches beside Dunkeld cathedral on the banks of the Tay, in sight of some of the best salmon water in the world. One of these famous 'mother' larches, as they are always called, can still be seen. It is a matronly figure, as broad as it is high (which is 105 feet) with massive curving limbs; more like an oak than a larch. The seeds from this tree and its companions were planted on a steep slope nearby called Kennel Bank. One of them now stands 131 feet high; its trunk, scarcely tapering at all, soars 90 feet without a single branch, then on to a distant, delicate head of pale, weeping branches.

Right *In spring bare larch branches sprout rosettes of pale green needles. This branch of the European larch is typical in its masses of hanging short shoots. Needles on new lengthening shoots are single and not in rosettes.*

Right *The female flower and cone of the larch are truly flower-like and often called a 'larch rose'. On the Japanese larch shown here cones are sometimes strung like beads with the shoot going through their centres (just visible above).*

The 4th Duke was so smitten with the larch that he planted 17,000,000 of them. His example was followed all over Britain, so that by the mid-19th century larch was the most important plantation tree. At that stage an aphid started to prey on it, with disastrous results.

In 1861 the nurseryman Veitch introduced the Japanese larch (*L. kaempferi*) to cultivation. The 7th Duke of Atholl, as larch-minded as his forebears, was quick to plant it, alongside Kennel Bank. By 1904 the first hybrids had come into the world.

As so often happens, the hybrids were better than either parent. The Dunkeld larch proved faster, more resistant to insects and disease, and just as beautiful. Today all three are planted in America and Europe, but the hybrid tends to be first choice.

The two American larches are similar in all respects except size. The tamarack, or eastern larch (*L. laricina*), ranges from Alaska to Illinois. It is a characteristic tree of swampy ground, and rarely grows taller than 75 feet – much less where the ground never dries out. It is ideal for gardens in really cold areas; its little rose-like cones are very decorative. The western larch (*L. occidentalis*) is a native of Montana and Idaho, where it can reach 175 feet – scarcely a garden tree.

The Himalayan larch (*L. griffithiana*) makes a graceful garden tree in milder regions. But the one which deserves to be far better known is a Chinese tree which carries the stigma 'pseudo' – the false larch. The structure of the false larch (*Pseudolarix amabilis*) is no different from that of the larch proper – except that it grows very wide and not so high (or fast). What is different is its texture. The perfect little open rosettes of needles are the softest, silkiest green; there's a porcelain quality about the depth and texture of its autumn apricot-gold. It would need a broad space in a garden – perhaps 30 feet across eventually. But it would be my first choice.

Above *The 18th century saw a craze for larch planting, particularly in Scotland. One of the early trees still stands at Dawyck by the Tweed in the Lowlands. Old larches reach out immense horizontal branches.*
Left *Immature cones on the false larch are the same brilliant fresh green as the needles. Gnarled and often lichen-covered wood increases the contrast with the delicate new growth.*

James, the 2nd Duke of Atholl, who was the first man to plant the larch on a wide scale for forestry.

Left *Male flowers and tender young rosettes of leaves form on tiny, woody, peg-like shoots. This is the false larch from China, a small tree but perhaps the most beautiful in colour and texture of all the larches.*

Above *Larch is a native of the Alps. It grows with silver fir at lower altitudes and with Norway spruce to 7,500 feet. Twigs of the European larch are buff-coloured (making the bare trees in this picture stand out against the dark spruce).*

The True Cypresses

Trees of the pine family have enough in common with the broadleaves for their parts to be easily recognizable. A twig is a twig, a bud is a bud, a leaf, though exiguously narrow, is a leaf. The trees of the cypress family are so different that they seem to have no way of growing, as we usually understand it, at all. You can't see the twigs for the leaves–or, in a sense, the leaves for the twigs. And buds there are none.

'Them ferns' is what an Essex countryman calls the 50-foot Lawson cypresses in my garden. Tree-ferns, if it didn't already mean something palm-like and entirely different, would be a good term for them. They seem as different from other trees as bracken is from a rose-bush. So much so that when in maturity they show their trunks, as stout and straight as any fir's, they look quite incongruous.

All the difference, in fact, lies in the foliage. The little leaves are so closely applied to the twigs they spring from that on most of the more recent shoots leaf green is all you can see: no wood shows through. Without twigs or buds or any of the usual points of reference the foliage is oddly homogeneous. Instead of forming the next year's shoot in miniature during the summer, and protecting it during the winter resting period in a covering of scales, the cypresses merely pause in their tracks during cold weather–and set off again in the spring. A cypress spray in time becomes a cypress branch simply by intermittent expansion.

There is no difficulty, then, in recognizing a member of the family. Certain parts of it, particularly the junipers, distinguish them-

selves by unambiguous signs–in their case, by having what seem to be berries instead of cones. With the two genera of cypress proper and false cypress, however, we catch a glimpse of the botanical backroom, where all is by no means so cut-and-dried. The *Thujas*, too, are a group of easily confusable trees, not only among themselves, but with the false cypresses.

And as though this weren't enough, along comes the woodsman and calls three-quarters of the cypress family, indiscriminately, 'cedar'.

On the whole this family is less important to the forester and more important to the gardener. The wood is excellent–durable, light and often sweet-scented. Hence the name 'cedar': a luxury rather than a staple. The Japanese pay thousands of dollars for a big Port Orford cedar (alias Lawson cypress) from Oregon, which they apparently use for lining coffins. There are no great forests of it.

Nurseries, on the other hand, are full of funny cultivars. There is hardly a gawky shape or a gaudy colour which doesn't find an admirer somewhere, particularly among the dwarf trees and little bushes with which the family abounds. On the other hand some of the finest species, fast, hardy and beautiful trees, get overlooked.

Cypresses proper, the nub of the whole family, are trees whose twigs, closely covered in tiny scale-like leaves, branch again not only sideways in one plane, as it were east and west, but north, south, and points between as well. This, together with their much bigger cones, distinguishes them from the false cypresses which (like the thujas) keep their sprays flat. If you hold a false cypress spray horizontal, you will find no twiglets heading upwards or downwards–only on the level.

The classic cypress (*Cupressus sempervirens*), *the* cypress of literature, is the dense dark column of the Italian garden, of the Greek olive grove–of all the sunwashed landscapes of the Mediterranean where its point of exclamation, alone or in combination with umbrella pines, contributes the essential architecture of the scene. There is no better columnar tree where it is hardy–and we are probably too ready to assume, because of its southern connotations, that it won't be hardy in our gardens. It grows well in the Edinburgh Botanic Garden; the Arnold Arboretum puts it in hardiness zone 7, which brings it as far north as mid-Tennessee and, on the coast, Atlantic City. If it is planted out very young in a reasonably sheltered place it is certainly worth a trial even farther north–although only southern nurseries are likely to stock it. It may have been because the cypress didn't take to the ▶

The tiny male flowers on a spray of the smooth Arizona cypress. These flowers will develop within several months into the cones shown on the right. Cypress twigs branch radially, making an open conic shape like tiny Christmas trees.

The Mediterranean cypress has a unique formality which sets off architecture to perfection. These fine specimens, keeping perfect shape even in old age, stand by the 15th-century convent of Pantanassa at Mistra, northern Greece.

Male flowers (yellow tips) and unripe cones on a smooth Arizona cypress. As they ripen the cones turn dark grey. They hang on the tree for several seasons, gleaming among the dense, dusky foliage like decorations.

Growing wild among the olive groves of Kato Figalia in Greece, the cypress masses into stately ranks which give the landscape the feeling of a garden. Classical landscape gardening leant heavily on the cypress for this effect. Farther north, where the cypress will not grow, Lombardy poplars are used for the same purpose.

The True Cypresses

▶Po valley in northern Italy that the Lombards took up their perpendicular poplar as a substitute. There is no real substitute, though, for the peculiar glossy blackness of this tree with its gleaming cones in constellations, towering 50, even 100 feet above the nymphs and gravel of an Italian garden.

The next best tree for texture, though not for form, is the Monterey cypress (*C. macrocarpa*) from California. In hardiness it may have a marginal advantage where winters are wet as well as cold–though zone 7 is given as its limit, as well. Tree-talk returns again and again to Monterey. The same wind-battered bit of Pacific coast which gave us the fastest-growing pine, and the best-looking silver fir (and more besides) has the only two natural groves of *C. macrocarpa*, at Point Lobos and Cypress Point.

The extraordinary junk-yard tangle of the trees which have grown up in the teeth of a gale is no indication of how a Monterey cypress will behave in a garden. What is fairly constant is that it will have several, perhaps many, stems. Whether these all go upwards, or spread to an oak-like head, may be a question of breeding, and is certainly a question of light, for which the tree is conspicuously greedy. Shaded branches die without more ado. The biggest and best of the species I have seen are in the Melbourne Botanic Garden in Australia: they are immensely broad domes. Often, on the other hand, one sees narrow, plume-like specimens, or ones with three or four of these plumes, all playing the leader. In San Francisco there are some which look at a distance like cedars of Lebanon.

The two-year-old you buy in a pot is curiously misleading if you expect the mature tree to look like that only bigger. It is a much paler green than the adult, which is very dark indeed. Transplanting of older trees is not a good idea–nor is it necessary, as cypresses grow at least three feet a year.

The Monterey cypress has spawned various golden forms. 'Lutea', 'Donard Gold' and 'Goldcrest' are all well known. Of these 'Goldcrest' is probably the best shape and 'Donard Gold' the best colour. It has also produced a weeping form (very rare) and two or three pigmy ones–even one which lies flat on its front.

Odd pockets of cypresses with just enough differences to count as species proliferate in California. Often there is only one stand, reached by a botanist-beaten path. *C. abramsiana* is one such. It lives on the southwest slope of Ben Lomond, about seven miles east of Bonnie Doon School in the Santa Cruz mountains. It is interesting as an indication of the good things still to come–if the one specimen in England, at

The foliage of the Arizona cypress shows the heavy wax coating, which protects it from drying out in the parched desert conditions. Some of the best blue garden conifers come from arid areas of the Rockies or the southwestern States.

The Monterey cypress is limited in nature to the gale-swept promontory of Point Lobos in southern California. The winds make stunted

but still thriving trees with characteristic antler-like branch formations. The same tree introduced into gardens is one of the most popular of all conifers.

Hillier's nursery in Hampshire, is a guide: it grew 50 feet and five feet round in the first 15 years. The Gowen cypress, which is similar, is already in circulation.

More to the point for gardeners north of zone 7 is *C. bakeri*, from 5,000 feet up in the very north of California, which the Arnold Arboretum at Boston has found totally hardy, and as fast as any tree there.

The dark green of all these is an excellent background colour for flowering trees and shrubs. By going inland into Arizona one finds, as in the other conifers, the lighter colours, the grey-greens and grey-blues, of drought-resisting species. The smooth Arizona cypress (*C. glabra*) is one of the best; an extraordinary tree to examine. The twigs look no more leafy than lengths of sash-cord, covered (like sash-cord) with a fine coating of wax. The cultivar 'Pyramidalis' is pale grey with a hint of blue. So cold a colour that you could almost use an enclosure of them, with perhaps an icy eucalyptus, for shooting snow-scenes in mid-summer.

The Mexican cypress, which owes its Latin name, *lusitanica*, to its early popularity in Portugal (Lusitania) is the south-of-the-border version. The name cedar of Goa – whoever thinks of these names? – makes it the only true cypress to be called a cedar.

Of the numerous true cypresses of Asia only one has really found favour in western gardens: the so-called Kashmir cypress (*C. cashmeriana*), a tree not only silvery-blue but softly weeping. This is really tender, though: at Kew (zone 8) it lives in the temperate house under glass. I can find no mention of it growing in America, but there are clearly places where it could.

There is also room to wonder why nobody grows the alerce (*Tetraclinis articulata*), the North African relative of the true cypress. The ancient Romans apparently rated its scented, bird's-eye-figured wood highly, and called it citrus (a change from cedar, but still further from the truth). A little grows in Spain .. Why not in Italy, if the Romans prized it so highly?

And few people grow the two cypresses of the southern hemisphere – though the Chilean *Fitzroya* is distinctly decorative, and the Australian *Callitris* very handy if you have a parched plain to furnish.

Fitzroya makes a big tree in its native Andes, and has reached 58 feet in Scotland. It is like a broad cypress whose hanging branchlets seem to be made of green plastic chain . . . except that it is really very pretty. Its possible role in modern gardens has yet to be explored.

The False Cypresses

From the four common species of this minor branch of the cypress family (minor in nature, that is) so many decorative cultivars have arisen that false cypress might be called the flowering cherry of the conifer world.

In gardens in many parts of the world (the south of England and the north of France are two) false cypresses are such a cliché that it is hard to see them with fresh eyes, or to use them effectively. Yet good specimens are graceful and satisfying plants.

The commonest in gardens, by far, is the Lawson cypress (*Chamaecyparis lawsoniana*). Lawson was a famous Edinburgh nurseryman, and fitting it is that such a nurseryman's staple should bear a nurseryman's name. If I occasionally address my trees as Port Orford cedars it is only to reinforce their dignity a little. For, though botanically way off mark, this is their forest name in the narrow tract of the northwest that is their home.

Port Orfords are common, but never dominant, in the forest which starts on the foggy coastline of Oregon and works back into the Siskiyou mountains, up to that extraordinary Eden populated by the Brewer's spruce. As far inland as the sea's influence is felt in mist and moisture-laden winds, the Port Orford is dotted, singly or in small groups. It stands out as a paler, more finely-detailed tree than the spruce, the Douglas and the western hemlock. On higher and drier spots its place is abruptly taken by the brighter, more tufted, incense cedar. Its love of moisture is a point gardeners should bear in mind. New England and most of California are too dry for it to flourish; it will grow there, as it will all over Europe, but it can be a drab thing where it is unhappy.

What more than anything has singled out the Lawson (to come back to its nursery persona) for intensive cultivation is its tendency to pop up in the seed-bed in eccentric–sometimes quite unrecognizable –forms. No conifer has so many faces. Den Ouden and Boom, authors of one of the standard reference books on conifers, list 200 cultivars of tree or big bush size and some 50 dwarfs.

The main variations are in colour, habit of growth and in leaf shape and arrangement. Some of the best are particularly soft and graceful by virtue of having permanently juvenile foliage–fronds which never reach the size, firmness and flatness of the adult tree. This state of affairs was misunderstood when it was first noticed. It is not peculiar to false cypresses, but occurs in *Thujas* and junipers and even *Cryptomerias* which are not members of the cypress family at all. All were thought to belong to a separate genus, which was labelled 'retinospora'; Victorian gardening books are full of retinosporas. As a genus it was a chimera: on the other hand it is a perfectly valid concept, and all these trees do share an attractive quality.

Two other fairly frequent aberrations of foliage are a sort of congestion, in which twice the usual ration of twigs and leaf-scales crowd into the same space; and the opposite, where they are freakishly spaced out along hanging sprays as thin as strings. The name 'filiformis' (string-shaped) is given

Top *The first of scores of garden versions of the Lawson cypress was 'Erecta Viridis', a tall (to 90 feet) column of emerald-green foliage. Wind and snow tend to break its erect branches unless they are tied up.*

'Fletcheri' is another of the popular-garden Lawson cypresses. It has a bluer tone and more feathery foliage than 'Erecta Viridis' and grows much more slowly; the biggest specimen is 40 feet tall.

The flat sprays of foliage of the Nootka false cypress hang vertically. They are thick, rough and heavy. Thousands of male flowers are visible at the shoot-tips all winter. The female flowers are dark grey; they take two years to ripen to brown peas with five claw-like points.

The cones of the Lawson cypress are full-grown but still green and unripe here. A few of last year's cones, brown and with their scales opened, still hang above them on the drooping spray.

The red male and black female flowers of the Lawson cypress become conspicuous all over the tree in early spring before any new growth starts.

to this type of foliage.

There are other differences in branching which it is harder to classify; ones which hold their sprays upright but side-on to the audience, or loose and nodding, or one with odd, twisted branch tips.

The first and still the greatest of the cultivars actually arose from seeds shipped from California to Britain in 1855, so it has been almost as long in cultivation as the species itself. It is sometimes called 'Erecta Viridis', sometimes just 'Erecta', but the first name describes it exactly: bright green upright–to 90 feet sometimes. Up to a certain age, and barring accidents, it is the best of all sentinel trees, as formal as a footman and as groomed. When most green cultivars turn grey in winter, it seems greener than ever. But accidents do happen to older trees: their fine fronds are pulled away from the column by wind or snow and never recover.

The best of the gold-leaved Lawsons are 'Lutea' and 'Lanei'; of the blue (for brightness) 'Spek', 'Pembury Blue' and the ultimately huge 'Triomf van Boskoop'; for combination of blueness and narrow upright form 'Columnaris'. For a broad upright habit like an Irish yew, 'Fletcheri' and 'Ellwoodii'. You can find Lawsons to fit any scheme or decorative plan. . . . One can't help thinking of them as garden wallpaper.

It is easy to confuse the ordinary Lawson cypress with other false cypresses or with thuja, which is often found in the same gardens. The best way to recognize it is to look at the underside of the foliage. A faint but distinct pattern of little white crosses marks the lines of pores.

The Nootka (false) cypress (*C. nootkatensis*) has never caught on to the same extent. Its real claim to fame in modern gardens is in being one of the parents of the Leyland cypress (see page 101). In nature the Nootkas are the northern neighbours of the Lawsons. Under the name Alaska cedar, ▶

False Cypresses and Leyland Cypress

▶or yellow cedar, they are common among Sitka spruce along the coast from Alaska to Vancouver, and farther south (on Mount Rainier for example) at an altitude much higher than the Port Orford cedar. The Nootka of their name is an inlet in the ocean side of Vancouver Island, where the botanist Archibald Menzies first caught sight of them.

The usual garden form of Nootka is different from the Lawson chiefly in the hang of its foliage. The sprays are heavy, and coarse to the touch. They droop as though the tree were desperate for water; and their rather dingy yellow-green suggests it may be too late. The form 'Pendula' is relatively rare in cultivation but superior in every way. Where Nootka just mopes, 'Pendula' is heartbroken. Each long branch bears a cascade of weeping fronds. If Forest Lawn were to revert to the 19th century notion of a graveyard which really looks like a graveyard this would be the tree they would plant by every skull-studded sepulchre.

Two species of false cypress grow on the east coast of the United States. The white cypress, *C. thyoides*, has by far the biggest range of any; being happy in wet ground from Maine to Mississippi. (Florida has its own species: *C. henryae*). It came into cultivation 150 years before the western and oriental species, but today they have more or less eclipsed it. Its best-known forms in modern gardens are the dwarfs, 'Andelyensis' and 'Ericoides'.

The Japanese Sawara cypress (*C. pisifera*) has identity problems like the Lawson. Indeed, if the species itself rather than one of its cultivars were grown few people would recognize it. In two areas of aberration it is conspicuously successful; the string-leafed and the juvenile (or retinospora). It goes so far in the latter that two different degrees of juvenility have separate terms: if it is merely childish it is 'plumosa'; if it is positively infantile it is 'squarrosa'–vernacularly, 'moss'. Seventy feet is not an impossible height for a 'squarrosa' with the finest and fluffiest foliage. One often sees hacked-about specimens ruining the rockeries where they were planted as pigmies years ago. Some of the best true dwarf forms are shown on pages 118–9. A compromise, and probably the best cultivar of all, is a 'squarrosa'-type called 'Boulevard' which grows slowly to 15 feet, and eventually a little more. Its leaves, if you can call them that, are like a silvery froth all over the plant.

The 'filiformis' ones, which come in green and gold but not blue, are even less vigorous than the retinosporas. None the less you finally get a huge gold (or green) bun–as much as 30 feet high and 20 feet through.

The other Japanese false cypress, Hinoki, or *C. obtusa*, is more consistent and in many ways a better tree, keeping dense and healthy-looking when many a Sawara has tired of life.

The hallmark of the Hinoki is the blunt-ended spray of deep shiny green, which gives the whole tree a compact, well-nourished look. Both the species and its golden version 'Crippsii' are first-class garden trees.

The most popular cultivar, and probably the best, is 'Nana Gracilis'; a big bush comparable with *C. pisifera* 'Boulevard' both in size and in its remarkable finish. It consists of a dense random heap of small vivid-green scallops; an unmistakable plant in the millions of gardens which give it pride of place.

Compactness goes berserk in some of the other cultivars; the foliage becomes a congested jumble which would look like a nasty spot of virus trouble if they weren't such sturdy, bright-coloured plants. 'Filicoides', 'Lycopodioides' and 'Tetragona Aurea' seem to make whole trees out of witches' brooms. The last is a good gold colour, but the others, to my mind, have no great virtues to balance their essential freakishness.

Top left *"Ellwoodii" is a bluish cultivar of the Lawson cypress which grows slowly to over 20 feet, keeping a dense, tight and narrow columnar shape as a young tree and broadening with age.*

Above *'Lanei' is one of the best of many golden cultivars of the Lawson cypress. Its soft golden branch-ends contrast prettily with the green of the older leaves. It will eventually reach 30 feet.*

Top right *'Lutea' is a bright, crisp-looking gold cultivar of the Lawson cypress; narrow, with a maximum height of 50 feet or so. All golden forms are brightest in early summer.*

Above *'Nana Gracilis' is the outstanding small cultivar of the Japanese Hinoki cypress: it makes a large bush (to about 10 feet). Its jumbled shell-like growths are brilliant dark green all year.*

'Filifera Aurea' is the best of the string-foliaged golden versions of the Japanese Sawara cypress. It makes a broad bright dome of unique texture.

Up to 1925 the two groups of trees we now call the cypresses and the false cypresses were considered one. So when in 1888 the pollen from a Monterey cypress lit on the female flowers of a Nootka false cypress in the grounds of a Welsh country house the affair was perfectly legal. Hindsight (in the shape of a taxonomic dictate of 1925) has since declared the two parents members of separate genera and their offspring, therefore, a mule.

The mule is the Leyland cypress (*Cupressocyparis leylandii*). It is still relatively little known in America, but in the last 15 years or so it has been recognized in Britain as one of the most useful trees in the whole list: a paragon combining hardiness, shapeliness, density of foliage and excellent colour. And it grows like the devil.

In normal British gardening conditions the Leyland is the fastest-growing conifer bar none. Cuttings, which root easily, are ready for planting out in one year. Thereafter growth only pauses in really cold weather. The first year out the plant will double in size; three years from a cutting it should be at least six feet tall. It will make a 30 foot specimen in ten years or so, and it has reached 100 feet in 55 years.

There are faster trees for milder climates.

Eucalyptus can go like a train. Even in the north spruces have made six feet in a season. But Leyland is not only tough: it has the good manners of a garden plant: it makes the ideal rapid hedge or tall screen, without gaps or bare patches; it gives a perfect even grey-green background for coloured trees or flowers. Even at 100 feet it keeps its smooth shape like a great green flame with a slightly leaning tip.

Some trial plants in California have taken on a different habit, becoming much broader, more bushy and less elegant. A trio of them in the Golden Gate Park in San Francisco are rather tubby things. Probably it is a tree for cool-temperate areas with decided seasonal changes (which, of course, San Francisco lacks).

The Leyland of the name was C. J. Leyland of Haggerston Hall, Northumberland. It was he who first spotted the hybrid at his brother-in-law's home, Leighton Hall, in Montgomeryshire on the Welsh border. In fact the cross happened both ways: in 1888 it was the Nootka which was the mother, but in 1911 (by the strangest coincidence on the same estate) the Nootka pollinated the Monterey cypress. Leyland's first find is now referred to as 'Haggerston Grey'. It is the common Leyland of commerce. The second cross bears the name of 'Leighton Green'; being harder to propagate it is not so often seen.

To every nurseryman's delight the Leyland has obliged with 'golden' (or at least yellow-green) sports. In 1970 'Castlewellan' appeared, followed five years later by the—slightly brighter—'Robinson'. Both seem to share all the admirable qualities of the green forms.

Above left *The soft mossy and silvery little Sawara cypress called 'Boulevard' originated in an American nursery in 1934. It has become one of the most-planted of all the miniature false cypresses.*

Above right *The Hinoki cypress cultivar 'Crippsii' is one of the most interesting-shaped golden plants. It grows slowly to 20 feet or more and keeps a bright colour even without much sun.*

Left *The white cypress* (Chamaecyparis thyoides) *has produced fewer ornamental cultivars than most, but 'Ericoides', bright green in summer and purplish in winter, is a superb small plant.*

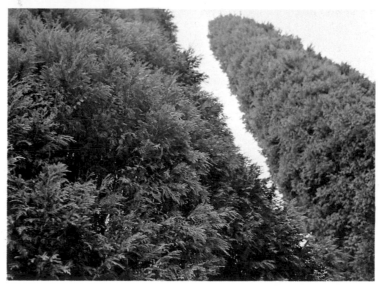

The Leyland cypress, a hybrid between the Monterey and Nootka cypresses, has all the qualities of the ideal background tree for gardens (or hedge): fast growth, good colour, dense and even foliage. It is hardy and reliable.

The Thujas or Arborvitae

It is comforting to know that the great Bentham and Hooker, authors of *Genera Plantarum*, one of the definitive systems of arranging plants, lumped *Thuja* and false cypress together. One doesn't feel quite such an idiot. The same flattened fronds, the same well-furnished conical form make the species infinitely more like each other than their own varieties. In the garden *Thuja plicata*, the western red cedar (or giant arborvitae, for it has nearly as many names as branches) and the Lawson cypress are almost interchangeable.

If the trees have cones it is easy to tell which are the thujas: the scales of their tiny, rosehip-shaped cones all hinge at one end. False cypress cones open round a central point: the scales point up and down as well as sideways, forming a sort of skeletal sphere. Perhaps the other most telling point of recognition which applies to all the thujas except one, is their powerfully pungent smell; something between balsam and turpentine. The leaves fairly exude it; you become aware of it just by standing nearby.

The two American species of thuja are by far the best-known. The familiar pattern repeats itself: a small, immensely hardy, not particularly attractive tree shows the flag in the east while out west its great brawny country cousin luxuriates in perfect conditions, developing to a size and beauty which makes it almost a match for the Douglas fir.

The eastern tree, *Thuja occidentalis* ('white cedar')–the roll call of 'cedars' is still not exhausted–was the first American tree to be grown in Europe. There is a record of one in Paris in 1553, almost 200 years before the trees of North America began to make their great impression on the world's gardens.

Its importance today, however, is based on its quirks and foibles in the seed-bed rather than its intrinsic value. It is second only to the Lawson cypress in the number of offbeat seedlings it produces. Professor C. S. Sargent of the Arnold Arboretum, Boston, once said that if anyone sowed a quantity of seed he 'would be sure to find forms among the seedlings as novel and interesting as any now in cultivation'. The competition, as represented in nurseries today, includes mainly dwarf and several juvenile-leaved varieties, but one of the classic golden conifers, 'Rheingold', is a bush form of *T. occidentalis*.

Thujas on the whole are strong on gold cultivars, shifting from bright gold to dull, bronzy old-gold at the onset of winter. The billowing flanks of a 12-foot 'Rheingold' (12 feet is about its maximum) can be one of the best things in a bleak winter landscape. The winter shift of colour is much less effective on a green tree. Hardy though it is, the white cedar tends to go drably brown as the pigmentation changes in very cold weather. A number of cultivars have been selected for constant colour, among them 'Wintergreen', 'Lutea', an excellent full-size golden form, and 'Spiralis', which is slim, compact and dark green with distinct formal possibilities.

In all except very northerly or badly-drained gardens the western red cedar is a much better tree; greener and more glossy, leafier and of course larger. Old lawn specimens are sometimes creatures of extraordinary character. Their lowest limbs rest on the ground and take root, to spring up and surround the tree with a grove of green buttresses, a tabernacle cavernous and perfumed within, floored and ceilinged in bracken-brown and raftered with branches.

In Washington and Oregon they grow to 200 feet with vastly buttressed bases as much as 35 feet through. One sees old red cedar butts grounded along the shores of Puget Sound, great wooden whales which decay, apparently, can never touch. The Indians hollowed out 50-foot canoes from them and carved them into totem poles. As 'cedar' in commerce today they provide outdoors all-weather wood for shingle roofs, greenhouses and football posts.

The gardener can hardly avoid using such

Western red cedar, the giant of the thuja family, growing in an experimental forest in Britain. In the Pacific northwest it grows to 200 feet and produces the fragrant 'cedar' of the building trade.

Above *A group of young western red cedars (Thuja plicata); ultimately, they will take on a majestic height and form.*
Left *Details of the branchlet system of western red cedar (Thuja plicata) with cones that have released their seeds.*

Above *Thuja occidentalis 'Aureospica' has yellow young shoots, gradually maturing to bronzy gold.*
Right *Cones of western red cedar. Soon they will turn pale brown and gape open, so that the seeds can be dispersed by the wind.*

Left *The Japanese arbor-vitae* (Thuja standishii) *is rare in cultivation outside Japan. In many ways it is a smaller version of* Thuja plicata. *Its blunted leaves are blue-white underneath. They have a rich lemony scent.*

Left *Eastern white cedar or arborvitae* (Thuja occidentalis) *is usually of columnar form, with rather drab foliage, especially in winter. In cultivation it is usually represented by dwarf and coloured foliage forms, such as the bright green 'Wintergreen' and 'Lutea', a narrow pyramid of golden foliage.*

Right *Under ideal conditions the zebra-striped western red cedar* (Thuja plicata 'Zebrina') *can be a most striking and ornamental specimen tree. The twigs are banded green and gold, or more heavily suffused with gold as in this specimen* (T.p. 'Zebrina Extra Gold') *at Bedgebury, Kent.*

an adaptable tree. It is happier than almost any conifer on chalk soil and in drought conditions–strange when you consider its moist, luxuriant origins. It will start life slowly but surely in quite heavy shade. Given better conditions it can grow three feet a year. It makes an excellent hedge.

'Zebrina', one of the forms of *T. plicata*, is the biggest of any golden conifer. It has reached 70 feet: a remarkable sight in its summer colouring. In winter it settles down to a mixture of gold and green which is still, in such bulk, extremely eye-catching.

Golden varieties are also the main attractions of the Chinese thuja, *T. orientalis*. The green tree is small, often a multi-stemmed, round-headed, substantial bush. One in my garden has been reduced to two of its original five stems, leaving a neat dome on bare poles which is extremely effective. Its sprays, fine and small-scale for a thuja, have a certain springy way of turning on their sides which gives it a tousled look. It is not glamorous, but its green is bright and one grows fond of such things.

This is the only thuja without a pungent smell, and the only one with little down-turning hooks on the scales of its cones: an easy tree to identify. 'Conspicua' and 'Elegantissima' are two of its best-known golden forms of small tree size. 'Aurea Nana' is a particularly good golden dwarf.

The Japanese thuja, *T. standishii*, is a rarer tree than the related *Thujopsis*, another native of Japan. Many conifers flirt with green plastic artificiality. Thujopsis goes the whole way. Its scale-leaves, firmly (and very prettily) marked with silvery-white below, are a conifer in kit-form from a cereal box: the precise, shiny, yellow-green of a stamped-out plastic conifer.

Though with a possible height of 60 feet or so it could not be classed as a dwarf conifer, it grows slowly in its early years so that you could happily plant it in a small garden. Young plants may grow only an inch or two a year for as long as ten years.

Above Thujopsis dolabrata, *showing the striking white pattern on the undersides of the plastic-like leaves. The green cone above is not yet mature; the previous season's brown one has opened and shed its seeds.*

Right *The Chinese thuja has claws on its round cones which make it easy to identify. As the cones ripen the waxy white bloom fades to brown and the scales gape open.*

Above *The Chinese thuja is a many-stemmed bright green tree, seldom more than 30 feet. Its golden cultivars are more popular than the species itself. This is 'Elegantissima', growing in the Trompenburg arboretum in Rotterdam, Holland.*

The Incense Cedars

Far left *The incense cedar from the forests of northwestern America has become the best of all narrow-column trees in cultivation. It stays narrow for many years, eventually broadening to a huge tower (left).*

Above *Its inch-long cones start off fleshy. When ripe they are woody and open like a book.*

If the incense cedar grew only in its native woods in the Pacific northwest it would rate little more attention than a cousin of the better-known *Thujas* with the peculiarity of holding its branchlets on edge instead of flopping horizontally. It is a common tree in the lower mountains of Oregon and California. The 'incense' of the name is a sweet resinous scent in the leaves and wood—no more so than in many other conifers. But there is more to it than this. It is one of only two conifers with almost identical relations south of the equator—so close that one might almost say its range runs from Oregon to New Zealand. And in cultivation it has given northern parts what is easily their grandest columnar tree, a formal upright more magnificent in size and much richer in colour and texture than the Mediterranean's cypress.

As far as the northern hemisphere is concerned the incense cedar, *Calocedrus decurrens* (catalogued as often as not under the name *Libocedrus decurrens*), is the sole representative of its genus. Colonel Fremont of the U.S. Corps of Topographical Engineers (an officer whose career embraced everything from botany to mutiny, and who eventually found himself the owner of one of California's richest gold lodes) discovered

the tree in 1848, flourishing in the drier and sunnier spots of the mountains of Oregon and California.

The tree he found is very distinct in colour and texture. Its firm, bright green tufts, vertically set, are a cheerful part of the character of the sunny slopes. It is never one of the tallest trees; rather it makes its presence felt by keeping more branches than most of the forest trees; often being clothed for most of its length in foliage, giving the woods a dense, well-furnished look. Only in old age does it tend to grow gaunt.

It doesn't, on the other hand, have the habit which makes the garden version so outstanding. In nature the incense cedar is a bushy, irregular tower of foliage, broadest about its middle reaches. Whereas the same tree grown in gardens in Europe and the eastern States soars up with completely parallel sides, the most regular and densest column to the greatest height of any tree. The best have reached 120 feet in 100 years or so, the only unevenness being a faint billowing of the rich greenery—the *embonpoint* of a courtier.

A variegated version also exists, but it is a poor thing, merely sprinkled with yellow branch-tips as though something were lacking from its diet.

The male 'flowers' of the incense cedar are like tiny cones whose scales open to release the pollen. In the wild the tree has none of the statuesque quality it has mysteriously assumed in gardens.

The Junipers

Reading accounts of desirable conifers I sometimes begin to despair that they all want the same (to me unattainable) conditions: acid soil and lots of moisture. What hope of these arid and alkaline acres ever having anything worthwhile to show? And then I remember the yews–and the junipers.

The juniper in particular desires and does almost the exact opposite of the general run of conifers; even of the rest of the cypress family. Where they grow relatively fast she grows at a snail's pace. Where they love shelter she loves the south slope of the hill–unmitigated sunlight. Where they need damp luxurious leaf-mould she likes to get her wiry roots into mineral soil. Where they have both male and female flowers on one tree she (again like the yew) has either one or the other. They have woody cones; she has fleshy berries.

Her slow growth rules her out for the forester, except for such small-scale and specialized uses as providing the scented wood for pencils. The same quality makes the juniper a basic stand-by in planning gardens–particularly small gardens. But the great majority of garden forms of juniper fall far short of tree stature: there is probably more grown as ground-cover than in any other role.

The common juniper (*Juniperus communis*) is the only tree species which occurs naturally in Europe, Asia and America. It is usually dismissed as scrub; its only claim to fame is that its berries provide the flavour for gin. To give it a fair hearing, however, I must quote Gertrude Jekyll, whose sensitive eye made her one of the greatest gardeners of this century. She feels differently. 'Its tenderly mysterious beauty of colouring . . . as delicately subtle in its own way as that of cloud or mist, or haze in warm, wet woodland. It has very little of positive green; a suspicion of warm colour in the shadowy hollows and a blue-grey bloom of the tenderest quality

imaginable on the outer masses of foliage.' She goes on in the same vein, admiring the way the plant recovers from snow damage, the silver lichen on its stems, 'the infinitely various position of the spiny little leaves'. One is driven by such words at least to take a second look.

In fact no nursery will supply the common juniper today except in one or other of its cultivar forms. Three of these are pale grey-green columnar plants of considerable merit: the tallest 'Suecica', as much as 40 feet ultimately; the commonest the Irish juniper, 'Hibernica', perhaps 15 or 20 feet; and the baby, which has no business here but is such a gem I can't leave it out, 'Compressa'; about 18 inches of drum-tight fuzz; one of the best of all miniature trees for a sink garden or rockery.

All common juniper incidentally comes into the category of retinospora–having nothing but juvenile foliage. Some other junipers tend to be very variable, having some branches adult (with scale-leaves, quite cypress-like) and others, or just individual sprays, with fine sharp-pointed leaves: the juvenile form.

The two junipers which between them give more garden varieties than all the rest are *J. virginiana*, better known as eastern red cedar, and the Chinese juniper, *J. chinensis*. Both have this characteristic of variable foliage. The eastern red cedar is widespread in the wild throughout the eastern United States. Occasionally it makes a 100-foot tree of a battered conical outline; but only in the south of its range, south of (say) Pennsylvania. There are said to be 40 cultivars of eastern red cedar in all; nurseries looking for shapeliness concentrate on the narrower, smaller, northern ones. 'Glauca' is a good blue-grey upright one; 'Canaertii' is a selection made in a Belgian nursery: dark green and firmly conical, with the added attraction of regular masses of blue-bloomed berries.

There is not a great deal of difference between the eastern and the Rocky Mountain junipers, or between the Rocky Mountain (*J. scopulorum*) and several other local western forms. According to Sunset Magazine, which caters exclusively and exhaustively for western gardeners, the juniper is the 'most widely-used woody plant in gardens in the west'. I can make no attempt to sort out the Utah from the one-seed or the Californian; the varieties of the world-wide ones are enough to be getting on with. The Rocky Mountain contributes half a dozen good garden varieties, mainly columnar. 'Columnaris' in fact comes from North Dakota. In the wild, to give you some idea of its unhasty progress, it has

The pale green berry-like male 'flowers' of the common juniper are borne in the angles of the whorls of spiky leaves. Here they are mature and have released their pollen.

Left *The common juniper has little pointed 'juvenile' needles and berry-like cones. In form it varies from prostrate mats to spire-like trees: usually it is bush-size.*

105

The Junipers

▶been measured at 14 feet in 40 years, 18 feet in 80 years, and 30 feet in no less than 300 years. The western juniper, *J. occidentalis*, is something different, by the way; a rough, big-limbed, unshapely tree from dry sites in eastern Oregon and western Idaho.

Most original of the American junipers is the one known as the 'alligator', *J. deppeana pachyphlaea*. All other junipers have thin bark which peels off, if at all, in brown vertical ribbons. The alligator's cracks up into square patches like the carapace, if that's the word, of the terror of the Everglades. Its leaves are light blue, fine and spiny as befits a tree from the near-desert of Texas and New Mexico.

The Chinese juniper (*J. chinensis*), like the common juniper, is the raw material of dozens of cultivars. It is not often seen in the form nature intended. There is no striking difference between it and the eastern red cedar (*J. virginiana*) unless it be the considerably larger berries of the Chinese plant (when it has berries at all). Both carry foliage of two types, fine-prickly, and cypress-like with scale-leaves. Some of the selected forms break this rule, however; the size of the berries, if any, is probably the most consistent trait to watch for. One cultivar, 'Femina', has been selected on the strength of its profusion of pretty berries.

Of the other selections the golden one, 'Aurea', is probably the most popular, as one of the most reliably bright gold conifers for a small garden. It may reach 40 feet, but it will take 60 or 70 years. 'Keteleeri' is a tidy, solid, dark-toned tree, a broad cone in shape–again very slow. 'Kaizuka' (also known as the Hollywood juniper) is a harum-scarum sort of bush, launching long limbs of bright green in unexpected directions: a good one for a mid-lawn position where it can freely yawn and stretch as wide as 15 feet. In straightforward columns most shades from bright green through grey to blue are available under one name or another. Nursery names often depart from

the strictly botanical; the great thing is to see the tree and like it.

One occasionally sees a very different oriental juniper, a tree with great character which could be used much more: the temple juniper, *J. rigida*. Not column- or cone-shaped, the temple juniper puts out pine-like branches to make a small but venerable-looking open head. Spiky dark foliage droops densely from the branches with an effect like Spanish moss on an old swamp cypress. Thirty feet would be a big one.

In 1930 another drooping juniper was discovered in the Burmese foothills of the Himalayas. This one, *J. coxii* (after Euan Cox, its finder), has almost the effect of a weeping willow at a distance. The long camouflage-green sprays, so dense and soft to the touch that you can squeeze them like sponges, hang from arching branches. It is more of a forest tree than most junipers; shade, especially near a woodland pool, suits it well.

To stick strictly to the trees of the family I should ignore the much better-known Himalayan juniper, *J. squamata*, whose form 'Meyeri', a prickly, icy-blue bush with drooping shoots, is familiar in so many gardens. I should also fail to mention the ubiquitous *J. chinenis* 'Pfitzeriana', child of a union between the Chinese juniper and the shrub *J. sabina*, the Savin of southern Europe. 'Pfitzeriana' (and also *J.c.* 'Hetzii') are vigorous V-shaped bushes capable of covering a remarkable amount of ground. Being capable of growing in pure chalk, dry as a bone and in deep shade, they are the workhorses of the family, inevitably seen in problem corners.

In southern gardens one sometimes sees the Greek juniper, *J. chinensis* 'Pyramidalis'; a tight grey column. From the best accounts the Syrian juniper, *J. drupacea*, is much hardier and more tolerant, as well as being (I quote Alan Mitchell, in his *Conifers in the British Isles*) 'a fresh light green colour unique among junipers'.

Top *A remarkably shapely specimen of the pencil juniper (J. virginiana 'Pseudocupressus') in the Schlossgarten at Baden Baden in Germany. Its many cultivars include bushy and weeping forms.*

Above *The 'Swedish' juniper is an upright form of the common juniper which grows wild in Scandinavia and north Germany (here on Lüne-berg Heath near Hamburg).*

Above *The spreading prickly juniper (Juniperus oxycedrus) with 'juvenile' leaves is common all round the Mediterranean. It varies in size from a low shrub to a 30-foot tree.*

Right *The drooping juniper of the Himalayas (Juniperus recurva) is here (in its native land) trimmed and shorn by the weather to a more compact and stiffer shape than it assumes in gardens.*

The Phoenician juniper growing on the Acropolis in Athens. It can live for 1,000 years, and has spread from the East throughout the Mediterranean and to the Canary Islands.

The Phoenician juniper of the Mediterranean has typical mature foliage (compare the prickly juniper opposite). Its berry-cones lose their bloom as they ripen and turn reddish-brown.

The Yews

I am not sure that one could rightly describe the yew as beautiful. My feelings, at least, are not so much of admiration as of respect. The yew is old and wise. It is the colour of ancient widows' shawls; as unkempt and wispy as their hair. Yet senile as it seems, its berries are bright red and there are lusty new shoots from the old trunk. From some secret place in its dark boughs it shakes bright yellow dust to catch the springtime sun.

Folk must always have felt like this about the yew. They have so lavished legend upon it that there is not a 200-year-old churchyard yew which isn't in Domesday Book. My favourite fable is built round the old tree (what is left of it) at Fortingall in the Scottish Highlands. It appears that Pontius Pilate's father was an Imperial official in that area and the stripling Pontius (or so they say) romped beneath those very branches. He scratched P.P. in the bark of the tree and he even added a date: 15 B.C.

The unusually tall yews in the churchyard at Kergrist in Brittany are estimated to be 1000 years old. The usual shape of yews is more squat and spreading, with branches to the ground.

Left *The tiny female 'flowers' of the yew consist of a pair of naked ovules surrounded by overlapping scales. The needles are flat, dark green, pointed, with a faint 'backbone'.*

Sober report has it that this particular yew is 1,500 years old and thus one of the oldest living inhabitants of Europe. There are no annual rings to count, though. For yews, unlike redwoods, have no thick rind to protect them. Their heart-wood, immensely durable as it is, eventually decays and they become hollow. The Fortingall tree has no centre left at all: it is a palisade of living fragments. Two hundred years ago it measured 52 feet round, but it would be hard to know which bits to measure today.

The association of yews and churchyards is so widespread that everyone has his own explanation of it. I find it easy to believe that people have always respected this ageless evergreen. In England, moreover, it was the only conifer (save the bushy juniper) throughout the middle ages. Along with holly and ivy (both equally associated with Christianity) it was the only green thing in the brown winter world. A practical consideration is that the yew's leaves are poisonous and the churchyard is one of the few places fenced against stock.

For garden purposes it is not the species of yew that matters, but the form. Some authorities, indeed, say there is only one species, and that it alters slightly in leaf size and colour from place to place. *Taxus baccata*, the European species, is in any case the yew of yews. If there is any argument for growing either *T. canadensis* (the northeast American native one), *T. brevifolia* (the Pacific coast version), or *T. cuspidata* (the Japanese yew) it is only a question of local conditions. North of New York, for example, the Japanese yew is recommended; *T. baccata* suffers in winter. But the biggest and best-looking yews are all European—and it is the European yew that has spawned the most celebrated garden forms.

It is one of the oddest coincidences in gardening that the two most distinguished cultivars of the yew arose within a couple of years of each other at the end of the 18th century. In 1777 a Mr. Dovaston at West-felton in Shropshire in the English west midlands spotted a weeping yew among the seedlings offered by a pedlar. And in 1778 or '79 a farmer called Willis saw two female versions of what is now the famous Irish yew (*T. baccata* 'Fastigiata') growing in the wild near Florencecourt in County Fermanagh. They were moved to the Earl of Enniskillen's garden nearby and from them, by cuttings, are descended the millions of upright yews all over the world.

One sees far fewer Westfelton yews—largely, no doubt, because they take up so much space. What the ordinary yew tree lacks in poise and harmony this graceful one provides. It makes a broad symmetrical

Two stages in the development of a yew 'berry' or single-seeded fleshy cone. The lower ones show the acorn-like cup which later swells up with sticky red pulp. Both the leaves of the yew and the seeds are poisonous.

Left *Male yew 'flowers' or pollen-producing cones are usually borne in abundance on the undersides of the twigs. In February and March they scatter yellow clouds of pollen on the wind.*

Below *Rugged, windswept yews on a hillside in Borrowdale, Cumberland. Common yew grows equally well in the shade of a forest or completely exposed on a bare hill.*

Right *A magnified (× 5) close-up of a male yew 'flower', showing the lobed, umbrella-shaped scales. Yews and junipers are the only common conifers which have separate male and female trees.*

Irish yews, thick columns in nature, clipped into a goblet shape in a churchyard in Tiverton, Devon. All yews thrive with regular clipping and make the best of all hedges.

tree like a huge pavilion, rising to a conical centre. The branches all round have weeping swags of near-black branchlets and often a good crop of red berries in autumn.

Yews are unusual among conifers in being either male or female. The male tree has much bigger flower buds on the new shoots. It is important to distinguish a tree's sex if you either want the berries or don't want the prodigious clouds of pollen that gild the countryside around a virile yew.

Both the weeping and upright yews, at the Great Gardener's command, have done the sporting thing and produced golden cultivars. The golden upright (*T. baccata* 'Fastigiata Aurea') is much the brighter and more effective. Both the golden and green Westfeltons sometimes fail to develop central leaders and flourish as spreading bushes with much less to recommend them.

Yew is incomparably the best hedging plant. It is so dense and even-textured that one can easily think of it as architecture. Many of the greatest gardens have their structure defined in clipped yew: it makes a perfect background for colours in shrubs or borders. It answers the shears perfectly, yet somehow always contributes its own weight to the effect: there is no such thing as a straight line in yew, yet you can hardly perceive just where it sags and softens the design. If the hedge is grown from seedlings there is a constant play of different colours where one plant merges into the next: no two are ever exactly the same green. When the new growth starts in spring a warm coppery bloom spreads in broad jigsaw pieces over the hedge.

If yew hedges are planted much less today than hedges of *Thuja* or Lawson cypress it is partly a question of price but more, I suspect, a question of impatience: yew has the name for growing at a snail's pace. We should learn from the Hon. Vicary Gibbs, who in 1897 planted some seedlings which he fed liberally with nitrate of soda. Eight years later, in 1905, he had trees 12 feet high and 16 inches in girth. Better to wait four years for a six-foot yew hedge which needs clipping only once a year than two for a thuja which bristles with new growth after every rain.

If Gibbs had waited another three years before planting he could have tried the hybrid between the European and Japanese yews, raised in 1900 in Massachusetts. *Taxus × media*, as it is called, was reported at the Royal Horticultural Society's Conifer Conference in 1972 as being 'slightly coarser in texture than English yew, much quicker growing; easily rooted from cuttings'. The last part is important: it could bring down the price of yew hedges.

The Plum Yews and Podocarps

I have yielded here to the temptation to lump together the two families of the yew's relations. They have so much in common that a taxonomist in mild mood might have done the same. They come from California and the Far East. Their leaves are much longer, more spaced-out and lighter green than the yew's. Their fruits are nuts enclosed in flesh like a small plum, not open at one end as the yew's fruit is. They both grow into small, irregular, rather open trees whose main charm is in the strong pattern of their leafing.

The Chinese plum yew, *Cephalotaxus fortuni*, is probably the most-planted of the group. Its long, soft, light green leaves are ranked along the sides of its shoots so that each branch presents a flat upper surface like a young grand fir branch, but bolder in detail. The Japanese plum yew (*C. harringtonia drupacea*) is similar, a bush rather than a tree perhaps, with the leaves tilting up to give a V-shape to the shoot. An excellent form of this imitates the Irish yew almost to the life, with the same way of leafing radially all round the upwards-pointing branches; the only obvious difference being that the leaves are bigger. The fruits of both (it is hard to think of them as cones) are light green ripening to purple, juicy and inviting-looking. Squeezed hard they exude delicious-smelling milky resin. They are plants that grow well in the shade and tolerate chalky soil, and would certainly make a worthwhile contribution to many gardens.

The California nutmeg (*Torreya californica*, named after the same botanist as the rare Torrey pine) makes a bigger tree–the biggest in Britain is 75 feet, to the cephalotaxus's 35 feet. In texture it is much spikier, its needles hard and coming to positive points. The fruit is similar, perhaps a shade bigger. A Japanese species of torreya (*T. nucifera*) has smaller, relatively broader leaves. Neither is a tree that would justify itself in a small garden where other conifers would malinger.

Above *The Huon pine of Tasmania* (Dacrydium franklinii) *is a most distinguished weeping conifer, very like the true cypresses in leaf and twig. All dacrydiums suffer in hard frost.*

Below *The big-leaved podocarp* (Podocarpus macrophyllus) *is one of the exotic Asiatic conifers we have hardly started to appreciate as a garden tree. Its leaves are as big as six inches by half an inch.*

Top *This small specimen of the California nutmeg* (Torreya californica) *is typical of its form in gardens. In its native mountain woods it reaches as much as 90 feet and a nine-foot girth.*

Above *The Chinese plum yew* (Cephalotaxus fortuni) *is the best-looking tree of its genus. Its single-seeded fleshy 'cones' look like plums– but are totally inedible.*

Above *The California nutmeg takes its name from the shape and appearance of its fruits– here in their unripe green state. The ripe fruit is streaked with bands of purple. The fleshy part is thin and resinous.*

The podocarps are largely a submerged clan as far as European and American gardeners are concerned. They are (with the *Araucarias*) the principal conifers of the southern hemisphere. In South Africa, for example, yellow-wood (*Podocarpus latifolius*) is the chief source of timber. Podocarps, in fact, are almost the only native South African conifers. In Australia 'brown pine' and 'black pine' are both podocarps. In New Zealand *P. dacrydioides*, the biggest of the family, up to 200 feet, is called 'white pine'. But only one exceptional species of podocarp, a native of Japan, belongs in the northern hemisphere and the few excellent hardy species from New Zealand and Chile have hardly been used at all.

The fruit of the podocarp (technically a cone) is a purple or red berry in which a nut is embedded. Podocarp leaves vary from yew-length to willow-length; all narrow but the longest ones too tapering at the ends to be described as needles. Perhaps their best quality is their rich yellow-green glossiness, a subtropical quality that draws you to the tree, particularly in winter. *P. salignus*, the willow-leaf podocarp from Chile, and *P. macrophyllus*, the Japanese member of the family, both have this effect. Where they are hardy (zones 7 and 8 respectively) they will eventually grow into fair-sized trees. The biggest willow-leaf one in Britain at present is 64 feet; in the southern States 60 feet is not exceptional for *P. macrophyllus*.

One of the short-leaved podocarps, the Chilean *P. andinus*, is remarkably like the yew for such a distant relation. To make matters worse it has been christened the plum-fruited yew, to the chagrin (one imagines) of the plum yew.

Another yew-like podocarp from Chile was made memorable by being called after the husband of Queen Victoria; *Saxegothaea conspicua* (Prince Albert's family name was Saxe-Coburg-Gotha). 'Prince Albert's yew' is certainly worth planting. It looks like a rather slender weeping willow with black foliage–or at least it does in Edinburgh, where it is perfectly hardy.

The podocarps have their cypress-types as well as their yew-types and willow-types. The *Dacrydium* branch of the family has scale-leaves that suggest cypress (or perhaps juniper). The New Zealand Rimu (*D. cupressinum*) is another small, soft-foliaged, weeping tree, happy in the moderate warmth of San Francisco. The Tasmanian Huon pine (*D. franklinii*) has shown itself a shade hardier. If you can imagine a cypress weeping willow you are somewhere near it. Such a tree, if only one could find it (few nurseries yet have them), would be a superb acquisition for a garden in zone 8.

Above *A mature Huon pine weeps gracefully. Young trees make some of the most elegant of pot-plants for conservatories in zones that (like most of Britain) are too cold to grow them out of doors.*

Below *The distinctive branched clusters of male 'flowers' of plum fruited yew (Podocarpus andinus). Here they are shedding pollen. Male and female flowers usually occur on separate trees.*

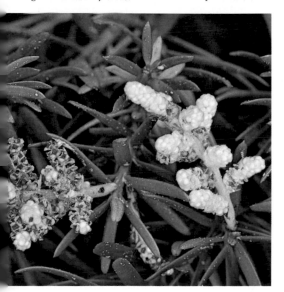

The plum-fruited yew, Podocarpus andinus *(from Chile), is surprisingly like a yew in every way except in its fruit, which look like small plums. They change from blue- to yellow-green and eventually turn black.*

Above *The New Zealand Kahikatea or 'white pine',* Podocarpus dacrydioides, *grows in swampy ground in both North and South Islands. Captain Cook measured a specimen with a clean bole to 90 feet. In Britain it is tender,* making a slender, pretty tree only in the mildest garden.

Swamp Cypresses and Dawn Redwoods

A pretty mixed bunch of trees are grouped under the family heading *Taxodiaceae*. No single feature proclaims them: it is rather a combination of the symptoms they have with those they lack. Conifer naming is much more confident with the nuts and bolts of varieties and cultivars than with the bafflingly broad horizons of families that have been in existence 100 million years or more. One might say that the big divisions into families and orders are provisional. But a pigeon-hole is a pigeon-hole, whether it has the right label or not. The species would be much harder to remember if they were not organized at all.

One thing the swamp cypress (*Taxodium*) and its class-mates have in common is great age. Another is colossal size. To this group belong the redwood and the giant sequoia, the Japanese 'cedar' and Chinese 'fir' (the biggest timber-trees of their respective countries) and the biggest conifer of the eastern United States, the swamp or, as it is known in America, bald cypress.

It may seem odd to recommend a conifer for being deciduous, but the swamp cypress, like the larch, makes a virtue of its seeming disability by being the freshest-looking of all the needle trees while it is green, and turning colour superbly in autumn. It complements the larch beautifully, in fact; they should be planted together. For when the larch turns from dark green to autumnal gold, the swamp cypress shifts from pale green by deepening stages to a ripe ginger brown. The two colours together in my garden, interspersed with the steel blue of Scots pine, are one of autumn's most compelling compositions.

Why is the swamp cypress not planted more? Partly, no doubt, on account of its size. Yet of all tall trees in a small garden it can make the most effect while casting the least shade. Partly, I suspect, because everyone assumes it needs a swamp. Curiously, it seems indifferent. For a tree whose home-ground (if that's the word) is the brackish water of swamps in the sub-tropics, it does remarkably well in dry ground in the sub-arctic winters of New England. It needs a good warm summer–it fails on the mild west coast of Scotland–but it freezes without flinching, as the 80-foot tree at the Arnold Arboretum in Boston shows.

The only attraction you will probably lose by planting it in ordinary garden soil is the eventual growth of its unique 'knees' from the roots. Science is puzzled by these spongy knobs, which arise over the points where its deep sinker-roots descend into the mud. Sometimes they form a whole village of odd mounds like ant-hills, coming out of the water or out of the waterside ground.

It seemed reasonable to think that they supplied air to the roots, which would otherwise be in danger of drowning. Yet they seem to have no means of doing this. Like earlobes or little toes they are just there.

The swamp cypress includes two other

Left *Female flowers of the swamp cypress are like tiny open green cones at the tip of the old shoot before the new leaves have emerged. The eventual cone (far left, unripe) is a little ball only one inch across.*

The trunks of swamp cypress in Cypress Gardens, Charleston, S. Carolina, show the fluted, flaring base of a tree adapted to wet, unstable ground. The 'knees' (right of big trunk) may be a way of supplying the roots with oxygen.

The daunting Latin species name given to the dawn redwood—glyptostroboides—is derived from the Greek words gluptos meaning engraved and strobus meaning pine cone. It alludes to the slit on the edge of each cone-scale. The tree is photographed here in its autumn colour at Wisley.

Left *Swamp cypress has no objection to a hard winter. By a Swiss lake it forms the same knotty and knobbly roots as by a Florida swamp. The first examples planted in Europe in the 17th century are still healthy trees.*

The dawn redwood was only discovered in 1941 in China. Already it has produced cones in cultivation in several places. These were photographed in the Donaupark, Vienna. They closely resemble the cones of the swamp cypress.

trees in its rather special genus. The pond cypress (*T. ascendens*) is a local form, restricted to the southeastern part of its huge range, which runs from Delaware to the swamps of eastern Texas. Although it is not so hardy, the pond cypress is in some ways an even better tree for the garden: smaller and upright, with its leaves set spirally all round the branches instead of in two ranks.

The other taxodium is evergreen at home in Mexico, only losing its leaves where it is planted near the limit of its hardiness. One specimen, the Montezuma cypress (*T. mucronatum*), can safely be called the world's fattest tree: it is 115 feet in girth. Postcards from Tule, Oaxaca, show nothing but El Gigante: there is no room for anything else.

Asia's nearest approach to a taxodium was a tree of great rarity, reported as living a swamp cypress-like life near Canton in the south of China. Whether there is any *Glyptostrobus* left in the wilds nobody seems sure. There is one in the University of Washington arboretum at Seattle and three tiny ones grow in the south of England, distinguishing themselves by turning a lovely warm pink-brown in autumn.

Then in 1941 a Japanese scholar found the fossil remains of a similar tree in Tokyo. He called his find *Metasequoia glyptostroboides* –an indication, perhaps, of his state of scholarly indecision, rather than of his barbaric ear.

What seems almost incredible is that in the same year, 1941, thousands of miles away, half-way up the Yangtze river in eastern Szechwan near Chungking, a botanist stumbled on three trees of this same unknown genus. It was 1944 before specimens were collected and 1946 before a thorough search of the region was made by the National University. By September that year the Arnold Arboretum, for which Wilson had done most of his collecting in that very area, had joined the search. There were plenty of these trees; they were known to the people as water-larch and fed to the cattle. In 1948 seeds germinated in Boston and Britain and within a year the tree was being planted all over the world.

Like the ginkgo, this survival from among the fossils seems to have left its enemies behind. It grows much faster than the swamp cypress, at least to start with; there are

dawn redwoods (the name that was coined for it) 60 feet high in collections already. So far it has grown as a regular, pointed tree with very light, indeed rather twiggy branches. It remains to be seen whether it will broaden out with age, as swamp cypresses do, to the splendid, branchy, irregular head it possesses in its native habitat. It already shows signs of developing a flaring, fluted bole and of having a special fondness for water: both typical swamp cypress traits.

The ready way to distinguish between the two is by the arrangement of the leaves. Though both have green branchlets in two ranks along the main shoots (which fall in autumn with the leaves) those on the metasequoia are opposite each other, while the swamp cypress's are placed alternately. The same is true of the tiny soft-green needles themselves. Perhaps easier to see is the metasequoia's unique habit of having the next year's buds underneath the branchlets.

Dawn redwood (above and below) holds its light green colour until late in the season. Then it colours well; sometimes creamy-gold, often pinkish; always ending with shades of amber. The

dawn redwood's only drawback as a garden tree is its tendency to put out leaves before the last frost. Yet it repairs damage quickly with more long feathery sprays of its fragile little needles.

Above *Ancient specimens of the swamp cypress completely lose the tidy pyramidal look they had in youth. Old trees in the Everglades of Florida have huge limbs which semaphore with hanging curtains of Spanish moss.*

Right *In the 25 years it has been cultivated the dawn redwood has maintained a neat and narrow profile of perfect symmetry. Time will tell whether it will go on to imitate the gestures of the swamp cypress above.*

Trunks of bigger specimens of dawn redwood are often a maze of deep flutings which writhe down the trunk for two or three feet and then stop. Many of them are rich ginger-red with the bark coming away in strips.

Giant Sequoias and Coast Redwoods

Subject to an unconcluded debate about whether early Australians were just bragging when they reported eucalyptus trees 470 feet high, the redwood is the tallest tree we know and its cousin, the 'big tree' or giant sequoia, is the biggest.

Just how big they are in relation to more everyday trees comes across well in the comparison made by the American dendrologist Rutherford Platt. The lowest branch of the biggest of the 'big trees', in his report, is 150 feet from the ground; but this branch is six feet in diameter and 150 feet long – a branch alone bigger than the biggest elm tree in the world, held horizontally more than an elm tree's height above the ground.

It took even 19th-century Californians in all their vigour and rapacity quite a time to think of a way of cutting down such formidable creatures. There is a note of hysterical triumph in the account of five men working for three weeks boring holes round the trunk of a tree 100 feet in circumference to fell it. It never occurred to them to leave it where it stood.

In times past, before the Ice Ages, redwoods grew in many parts of the globe. Fossil remains of them have turned up in Cornwall, in the southwest corner of England, among other places. But like so many trees they have retreated to the one place on earth that offers them ideal conditions, and as so often that place is California.

There is a recipe for instant confusion in the fact that there are two trees in this story, not one. To make matters worse the tree known to botanists as *Sequoia sempervirens* is called the redwood (or coast redwood) while the tree known to laymen as giant sequoia or 'big tree' is botanically separate in the genus *Sequoiadendron*. It is the only species: *Sequoiadendron giganteum*.

Superficially the two are similar enough. Their foliage in fact is quite different; but what distinguishes them far more is their tastes and habits. The coast redwood reaches its preposterous heights in dense stands in the coastal fog belt of northern California; the 'big tree' builds its bulk in open groves with white fir and ponderosa pine and incense cedar in the relatively dry and extreme climate of the western Sierra, where most of the precipitation comes as snow.

A redwood forest is like no other. The best stands are on rich alluvial flats sheltered by the coast range but still within 30 miles of the sea. Bull Creek Flat in the Rockefeller Forest near Highway 101 is one of the best remaining, with about 10,000 acres of superb trees. The biggest surprise on seeing them for the first time is not so much the height of the trees, for it is almost impossible to stand

One of the biggest of the 'big trees': 'General Grant' is 267 feet high, 80 in girth, and weighs over 2,000 tons. 'Big trees' grow in groves with other species – in contrast to the coast redwood which forms dense stands on its own.

The 'big tree' of the Californian Sierras has succeeded splendidly in cultivation in Europe. Here at the Younger Botanic Gardens at Benmore in western Scotland 70-year-old trees make a perfect avenue between 130–150 feet high.

Right *The foliage of the 'big tree' is scale-like (compare with the redwood's, opposite). The cones here are full-size but still green: they turn dark brown on ripening and release scores of tiny angular seeds.*

back and survey one; it is the way they stand shoulder to shoulder, sometimes leaving scarcely room for a man to squeeze through between two trunks each 20 feet thick.

The whole grove seems to grow from one giant skein of roots. Nothing else except a few ferns can grow in that half light. It is a solemn and simple environment: the soft brown floor of litter; the surrounding trees more like walls than pillars, the dusky brown of their bark lit occasionally with a needle of light from far above. The style of the architecture is distinctly Gothic: the bark splits in deep grooves which end in a narrow Early English arch every ten or 15 feet.

The 'big trees' in the Sierra are more impressive to visit as a spectacle. There is all the fairground stuff of being able to drive through holes in them. You can stand back and see the whole monstrous vegetable: its untapering shaft going up like a road to the tangle of heavy branches that make its head – perhaps 100 feet of lively sprouting above 200 feet of simple, unadorned log. The tallest, a towering 320 feet, is only 47 feet short of the tallest redwood. A tree 100 feet in circumference at the base is 3,500 years old and some of the largest are at least 4,000 years old; there is no question of 'second-growth' trees ever supplanting these, except for logging purposes.

In nature since the trees never grow together there is no opportunity to compare them. In cultivation their foliage – if you can reach it – is the simple way of telling them apart. The 'big tree' is essentially scaly: somewhere between a cypress and a monkey puzzle in size of scale but inclined to the monkey puzzle's reptilian look. The redwood has two kinds of foliage: a little on new shoots like the 'big tree' but most of it more like a yew with regular rows of flat, taper-ended needles. The needles grow steadily shorter towards the end of the shoot, so that each individual shoot is roughly boat-shaped. The texture of both trees is stiff and coarse.

In cultivation the 'big tree' has proved much the hardier and more adaptable. Its arrival in Europe in 1853 caused a sensation. The craze for the cedar of Lebanon was almost over: the 'big tree' took its place. It was christened 'Wellingtonia' in honour of the Iron Duke. There was not a landowner in Britain who failed to plant one. And British conditions suited it perfectly: the trees survived and flourished so that today there is one on every estate; the tallest (in 1970) is in Devonshire and stands 165 feet high.

In the United States there was some attempt to counter-christen the tree 'Washingtonia' – a name already pre-empted by a palm. It is hardy as far north as Rhode Island on the east coast. But it has never been regarded quite as rapturously as it was in Europe, perhaps for lack of the private parkland in which its opulent symmetry is so telling.

Open-ground cultivation gives the drooping lowest limbs of the 'big tree' the opportunity to layer themselves round the base. Some of the most magnificent specimens have formed vast pyramids in this fashion. The siblings moulded into the general mass are all the more beautiful because the younger growth is noticeably more grey, or silvery-green, than the dark spire above.

It is the nature of the coast redwood to dwell in groves. Single trees tend to resent the exposure to frost and wind. The best specimens outside California, where it is widely used, are in southwest Britain where it has reached 135 feet. But in central France, for example, where the wellingtonia grows well, it is not happy.

I feel obliged to mention what to me is the ugliest tree in the world – the weeping wellingtonia. This freak from a French nursery has branches that grow straight downwards, as near the trunk as they can get. As it gains height it begins to topple from the tip, sometimes curving almost into a loop. To grow one seems to me rather like exhibiting Siamese twins.

Left *Coast redwood sprouts vigorously from the base of the stump. Cut-down trees put up dense clumps of shoots. The foliage consists mainly of needle-leaves; a few shoots are scaly like those of the 'big tree'.*

Above *Spongy red bark gave the coast redwood its name. It is remarkably fire-resistant; a factor which has helped redwoods survive for up to 2,000 years.*

The coast redwood thrives in the coastal zone of northern California. The remaining acres of old-growth redwood are guarded by the Save-the-Redwood-League, one of the earliest conservation groups in the United States.

The Pacific 'Cedars' and 'Pines'

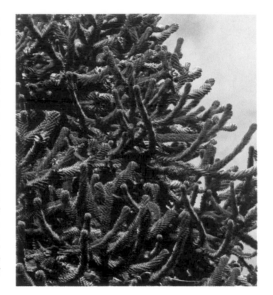

'A tree of the pine tribe, and perhaps the most miserable-looking ever introduced; something like an *Araucaria*, it is usually full of dead twigs.' Thus William Robinson in *The English Flower Garden*, writing of the glorious, vigorous, shapely (but not terribly hardy) *Cunninghamia*.

Robinson did not approve of the vogue that had set up monkey puzzle trees (or Chile pines, *A. araucana*) as thick as television aerials in the suburbs of late-Victorian England. The highly-flavoured taste of the time would combine these reptilian relics with bogus-rustic arbours and geometrical beds of scarlet salvias. But at least the monkey puzzle flourished. The cunninghamia sinned twice by turning brown.

James Cunningham was the first western plant-hunter ever to reach China. On that voyage in 1700 he discovered and described two magnificent trees, unlike anything then known. The one that bears his name is China's principal timber-producing tree,

coming second only to bamboo; his other find was the *Cryptomeria*, which plays the same role in Japan.

Genealogically these two trees link the sequoias with the weird araucarias of the southern hemisphere. The cryptomeria is very like the giant sequoia in foliage; the cunninghamia, as Robinson says, is like the monkey puzzle. Yet botanically the two belong to the same family.

They are both uncommon if not actually rare trees in gardens today. Only a juvenile-foliaged or retinospora form of the cryptomeria is well-known – as *Cryptomeria japonica* 'Elegans'. It justifies its popularity in every way: its soft plumey foliage changes with the seasons from a pale opal in summer to a bold brick-purple in the coldest months. It is no dwarf: 60 or 70 feet is within its reach. If it does grow so high, though, it has a tendency to topple over or even to bend double under its own weight, and layer its long curving branches in the ground.

Left *Immature male cones of the monkey puzzle. It is unusual to see such a perfect whorl of five cones together, ones and twos being the norm. When mature, each cone will be the size of a small coconut.*

Above *A vista in one of the great monkey puzzle forests of Chile on the slopes of Volcan Llaima. Here the trees extend up to the snow line and thrive in soil that seems to be no more than ash and clinker.*

Top *The reptilian-scaly branchlets of the monkey puzzle (or Chile pine). Each leaf is hard and tough as leather, tipped with a sharp point. At the top of the tree partly mature rounded cones can be seen.*

Typical arching branchlets of Cunninghamia lanceolata, *the Chinese fir. The handsome glossy dark green foliage is only seen at its best in sheltered humid areas; frosts and icy winds will sear or kill it.*

There is a strong argument for bringing back the cryptomeria proper, a tree like a more elegant and lightweight wellingtonia with softer foliage and a less rocket-like silhouette. And also, in milder areas, for re-installing the cunninghamia.

My ideas about these bold reptile-trees (there is no other way of describing their bright green scaliness) were abruptly altered when I saw them being tried out in what are known as 'forest-plots' on the west coast of Scotland.

Where one monkey puzzle (or cunninghamia) looks quite embarrassingly stiff and self-conscious—at least as a young tree—a whole clump of them takes on quite a different air. Seven or eight araucarias, six feet apart and 20 feet high, would make the most magnificent garden sculpture: fairly ferocious-looking, I'll admit.

The other araucarias, the Norfolk Island pine (*A. excelsa*), the candelabra tree (*A. angustifolia*) and the bunya bunya pine (*A. bidwillii*) are too tender, alas, for northern Europe or most of the United States. Alas because they are really much better-looking trees than the monkey puzzle. The Norfolk Island pine is the beauty of the family. It grows for many years with the hypnotic symmetry of a paper cut-out, each perfect whorl of branches holding aloft four perfectly-matched green combs of leaves.

The Pacific Ocean is completely encircled by this family: the redwoods in the northeast, the Chile pines in the southeast, cryptomerias in Japan and the araucarias in Queensland and Norfolk Island. The most southwesterly of all is a genus peculiar to Tasmania, an island with many excellent and original plants. The King William pine (*Athrotaxis selaginoides*) and the smaller *A. cupressoides* and *A. laxifolia* are nearest to the cryptomerias in appearance; hardy and good-looking, but still very much collectors' pieces. In a tub (as they are often grown) they look quite artificial.

Part of the vast cryptomeria forests of Japan, where it is the most important timber tree and is cultivated with great skill. Cryptomeria needs a high rainfall to grow fast and well. Like the monkey puzzle it had a vogue in Victorian gardens.

Above *Two ages of cryptomeria cones. At the top are partly matured green specimens; below can be seen cones of the previous season; the angular seeds have been dispersed by the wind.*

Below *The scuffling of human feet and the erosive force of rain have combined in laying bare this pattern of cryptomeria roots near a Japanese temple at Kyoto.*

The Dwarf Conifers

When the nurseryman says sport he doesn't mean violent exercise: nor does he mean jest. He means the tendency of plants and parts of plants to have a mind of their own; to deviate from the norm. The nurseryman's business is to follow up the most promising deviants to see how they develop. It happens in the seed-bed: out of 200 cypress trees one or two may be blue or yellow instead of green, or thin and narrow instead of pyramidal or bushy. It also happens occasionally on one branch of an otherwise blameless tree. There is suddenly a confusion of twisting, twining little shoots. The nurseryman pounces. If he can propagate from this oddity, either by getting a cutting of it to take root, or by grafting it on to other roots, he has a new design of tree of his own. In the past he has celebrated the fact in appalling pseudo-Latin: today he must use a vernacular name.

Sports of conifers which grow very little, or at least slowly, are particularly valuable. They are permanent, often pretty and they take up practically no space. In town gardens which have no room for real trees they offer, pollution permitting, the chance to enjoy the lovely variety of the conifer world in miniature.

There is no clear dividing line between conifers and dwarf conifers. Natural smallness may or may not be permanent; but it can always be made so. By a simple borrowing from the technique of bonsai–just lifting and replanting every few years–it is possible to keep any small conifer (or even any big one) from getting the bit in its teeth and growing away.

On this page are some of the outstanding miniatures. The broadleaf world has no equivalent–only relatively few stunted arctic forms. A certain amount of tact is needed in using dwarf conifers effectively; their scale works best if they are kept to themselves, in a bed or on a rock garden of their own, perhaps with low heather to cover the ground between them.

The most effective way of using dwarf conifers is in a self-contained landscape. This is the famous Pigmy Pinetum at Devizes, Wiltshire, made by H. J. Welch, author of Dwarf Conifers; the standard work on the subject. The plants in the picture are:

1 Juniperus chinensis 'San Jose'; a blue dwarf ground-cover form.

2 A golden version of Chamaecyparis lawsoniana 'Ellwoodii': 'Ellwood's Gold'. It is slower than the green form; a dense little column of gold.

3 'Boulevard' is an American improvement on what was called the 'moss retinospora' (Chamaecyparis pisifera 'Squarrosa'). It is a beautiful colour, and can reach 15 feet or more.

4 Even the coast redwood has a dwarf form: Sequoia sempervirens 'Prostrata'. Full-size shoots that appear need cutting off.

5 A dwarf form of one of the best false cypresses: Chamaecyparis lawsoniana 'Wisselii Nana' has clustered radially arranged shoots of dark bluish-green. Strong-growing shoots need pruning to keep it small.

6 Chamaecyparis pisifera 'Plumosa Aurea' is a rich-gold mossy bush which can live among dwarfs for several years.

7 A dwarf form of the well-known cultivar Chamaecyparis lawsoniana 'Ellwoodii', one of the best of the soft blue columns.

8 A white-variegated round bush form of the Chinese juniper (J. chinensis 'Variegata'): eventually much more than dwarf size, becoming pyramidal with densely packed branches.

A tidy little gold ball: Thuja plicata 'Rogersii'; a far cry from its giant parent the western red cedar. It will take 30 years to grow to about three feet each way.

Right *The Waukegan juniper (Juniperus horizontalis 'Douglasii') is one of the best of the blue-grey ground-cover junipers humping up into low billows. In winter it takes on a purple tone.*

Right *A wild form of the Balsam fir from New Hampshire: Abies balsamea 'Hudsonia'. It makes a flat spreading shrub with short, broad leaves of a good green. Slow enough to be treated as a dwarf.*

Chamaecyparis law-
soniana 'Nidiformis'–the
name means 'nest-shaped'
–slowly makes a broad
arching mound of
graceful grey-green
sprays. Only in the short
term is it a true dwarf.

12 *The Hinoki cypress
(Chamaecyparis obtusa
'Nana') is shapely,
brilliant green, and one of
the slowest-growing
dwarfs.*

13 *One of the smallest
and brightest Lawson cy-
presses; C. lawsoniana
'Minima Aurea' is a
golden cone in spring,
growing only a foot in
ten years.*

14 *'Fletcheri' is a Lawson
cypress cultivar, too tall
for dwarf status. But it is
neat, soft and bluish–and
one can always trim it.*

15 *Cryptomeria japonica
'Pygmaea' or 'Nana'–a
low flat-topped bush
version of the Japanese
cedar with tiny leaves.*

16 *The only non-conifer
in the picture: Hebe
lycopodioides from New
Zealand: a conifer-mimic
until its white flowers
appear in summer.*

17 *The best small golden
thuja (T. occidentalis
'Rheingold'). Grows
slowly to become a bronze-
gold bush with superb
winter colour.*

18 *Another ground-
hugging juniper (J. pro-
cumbens 'Nana') makes a
blue-green mat.*

19 *An excellent small
juniper: J. communis
'Hornibrookii' moulds its
miniature green silver-
backed foliage to the
shape of the ground.*

20 *The prostrate Christmas tree (Picea abies
'Procumbens') starts flat
on the ground, then heaps
up close-pressed tiers of
foliage to make a wide-
spreading, flat-topped
bush. It is one of the most
vigorous prostrate forms
of P. abies.*

Above *A new, as yet
unnamed form of
Cryptomeria japonica.
Such sports are con-
tinually arising in
nurseries. Worthwhile
ones are given names and
propagated.*

Above *The bizarre
cockscomb growths of
Cryptomeria japonica
'Cristata' make it perhaps
the most obviously
freakish of conifer
cultivars. It grows slowly
but can reach 30 feet.*

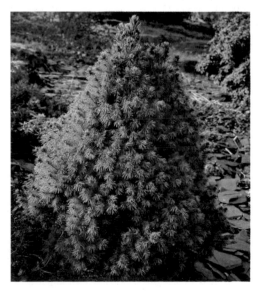

9 *The golden Chinese
thuja that appears on
page 102 (T. orientalis
'Elegantissima') is slow
enough to live among
dwarfs for several years.
In winter the leaves turn
bright reddish-brown.*

10 *A miniature version of
the Asiatic 'Schrenk's
spruce'–Picea schrenk-
iana 'Globosa'; a broad
low cone of short but
typical spruce branches.
This form is now rare in
cultivation.*

11 *Another Hinoki
cypress, C. obtusa
'Mariesii', makes a tiny
but untidy cone shape.
The variegated foliage is
creamy-white in summer,
yellowish-green during
the winter.*

Left *A young form of
eastern hemlock, Tsuga
canadensis 'Pendula';
eventually it will become
a dome-shaped bush with
pendulous branchlets. It
was first introduced into
cultivation in the 1870s.*

Above *The dwarf
Alberta spruce (Picea
glauca albertiana
'Conica') grows very
slowly to six feet: a neat,
bright green, well-
furnished cone. It was
found wild in the Rockies
in 1904.*

The Palms

The palms, the potent symbol of the tropics, occupy a by-way of evolution. In the remotest past they parted company with the family which contains the water-lilies and the magnolias. In strict botanical terms, being properly called flowering plants, which the conifers are not, they come closer to the broadleaves. But unlike any broadleaf tree they come into the class of plants with one seed-leaf, the monocotyledons. The implications of this abstruse detail are far-reaching. From it springs the totally different design and construction of the palm trees.

Palms don't and can't have any real branches. They have no annual rings of growth: they grow taller without growing thicker. All their leaves are produced from the top of the stem, and their flowers and fruits from among their leaves. The workings of a palm tree are shown in the illustration on the right.

There are certain crucial disadvantages in their design. The biggest is that they depend utterly on the cabbage-like bud at the top of the stem . . . . which happens to be a very tasty morsel, much sought by the evolving beasts of every age up to and including man. Its defence has therefore been an important part of their evolutionary story. Witness the fact that mainland palms tend to be more or less furnished with spikes to make them uncomfortable to climb, whereas on remote and mammal-less islands in the Indian Ocean they have no spikes at all.

A hundred and twenty million years ago most of the globe suffered the same tropical climate. Then came the cooling that ended with the Ice Ages. The palms retreated before the cold in just the same way as the rest of the trees, but very few were left in the temperate zone and not many in the sub-tropics; they needed the tropical extreme. Most of the 3500 species of palm need heat and moisture as a way of life.

To palms, therefore, even the subtropical climate of southern California or Florida is chilly. A world-wide group of a very few species venture into the world of frost. Only one, a Chinese species, is at home in a truly northern climate. Overleaf some of the best-known on the borderlines of hardiness are illustrated.

The study of palms is relatively new. The first and still the most considerable work on them was done by the Dutch in the East Indies in about 1800. The classic palm drawings of that period have not been surpassed. For the plain fact is that you have to be a blend of botanist and steeplejack to get very far. Not surprisingly, most botanists stick to trees with branches. ▶

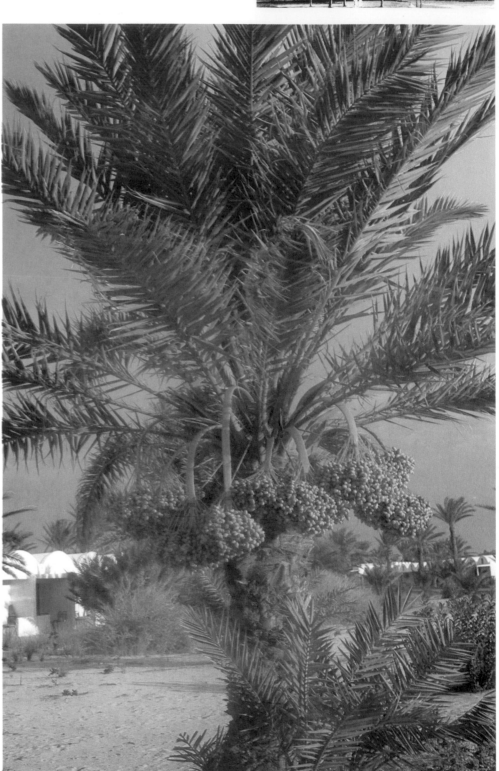

A date palm heavily laden with its bunches of fruit. The date palm is a native of North Africa, but today planted in places with a similar climate all over the world. Suckers can be seen arising from the base of the trunk.

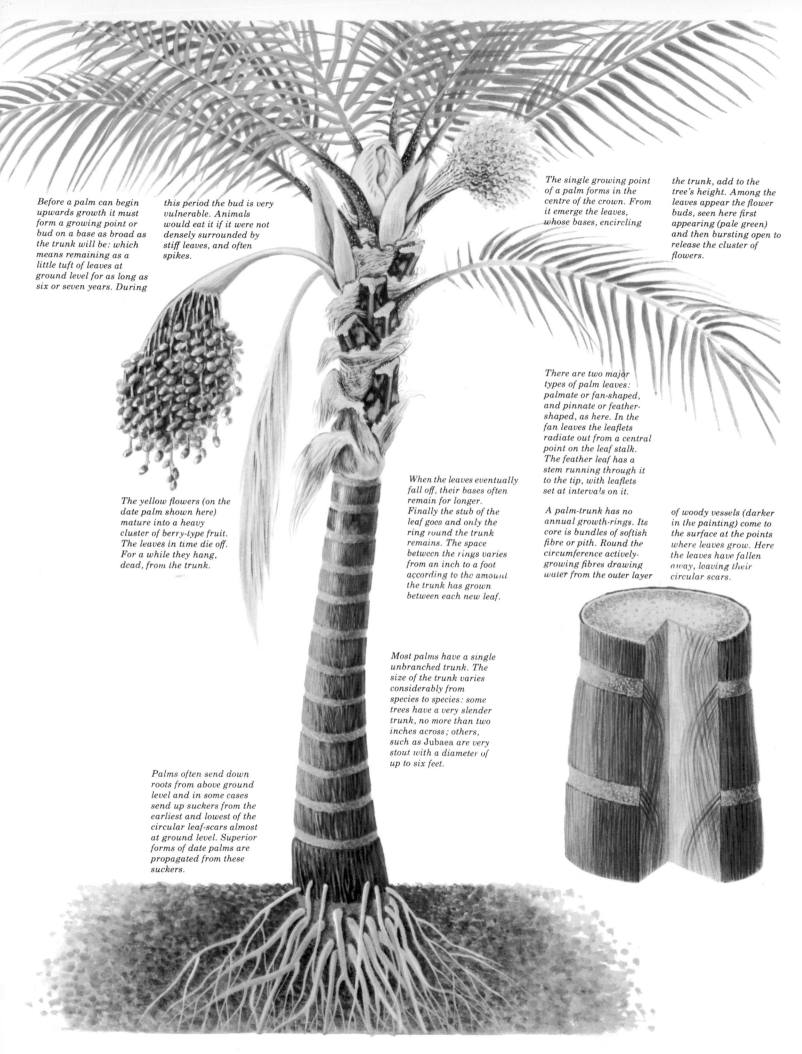

Before a palm can begin upwards growth it must form a growing point or bud on a base as broad as the trunk will be: which means remaining as a little tuft of leaves at ground level for as long as six or seven years. During this period the bud is very vulnerable. Animals would eat it if it were not densely surrounded by stiff leaves, and often spikes.

The single growing point of a palm forms in the centre of the crown. From it emerge the leaves, whose bases, encircling the trunk, add to the tree's height. Among the leaves appear the flower buds, seen here first appearing (pale green) and then bursting open to release the cluster of flowers.

There are two major types of palm leaves: palmate or fan-shaped, and pinnate or feather-shaped, as here. In the fan leaves the leaflets radiate out from a central point on the leaf stalk. The feather leaf has a stem running through it to the tip, with leaflets set at intervals on it.

The yellow flowers (on the date palm shown here) mature into a heavy cluster of berry-type fruit. The leaves in time die off. For a while they hang, dead, from the trunk.

When the leaves eventually fall off, their bases often remain for longer. Finally the stub of the leaf goes and only the ring round the trunk remains. The space between the rings varies from an inch to a foot according to the amount the trunk has grown between each new leaf.

A palm-trunk has no annual growth-rings. Its core is bundles of softish fibre or pith. Round the circumference actively-growing fibres drawing water from the outer layer of woody vessels (darker in the painting) come to the surface at the points where leaves grow. Here the leaves have fallen away, leaving their circular scars.

Most palms have a single unbranched trunk. The size of the trunk varies considerably from species to species: some trees have a very slender trunk, no more than two inches across; others, such as Jubaea are very stout with a diameter of up to six feet.

Palms often send down roots from above ground level and in some cases send up suckers from the earliest and lowest of the circular leaf-scars almost at ground level. Superior forms of date palms are propagated from these suckers.

The Palm Family/*Palmae*

The Palms

Top left *The crown of the coconut palm with its feather-leaves up to 20 feet long. Up the trunk of this tree growing in the West Indies climbs* Scindapsus aureus.

Above *The Canary Island date palm is a squatter, broader tree with a much thicker trunk than the date palm of Egypt. The flowers can be seen appearing from among the leaves.*

Middle *The date palm is an important food plant in North Africa, its original home, and in many parts of the world with a similar climate. Here in Tunisia the ripe dates are being stripped by hand from their heavy clusters.*

Above *The royal palm makes one of the best street trees for the tropics with its pale trunk, bulging interestingly at the base and again in the middle.*

▶ Only one palm has come to terms completely with snow and ice: *Trachycarpus fortunei*, the Chusan or windmill palm of the Far East.

It is no beauty. Each year it grows two or three fan-leaves, three or four feet across, and sheds their yellowed forebears. The old leaf-bases remain, covering the trunk with brown furry fibre. As a young tree, a cluster of green fans on a short stalk, it has definite merit, but in age, a 15- or 30-foot column of tatty fur with a tuft of leaves on top, it is a sad creature. Still, a palm is a palm, and the raffish Riviera air it can lend an innocent rose garden is not to be underestimated.

The Riviera, indeed the whole Mediterranean, has its own native palm, a similar fan-leaved affair. *Chamaerops* is not quite so hardy and rarely grows so high. It often forms a bush with a cluster of short trunks, each carrying a bunch of completely rigid fans. At most it will grow, single-stemmed, to 20 feet, and look like a better-groomed Chusan palm.

Most of the palms on the border-line of the temperate zone belong to the group with fan-leaves: in the tropics the feather-leaf is much more common.

There are two other fan-leaf palms, not as hardy as the first two but certainly acquainted with freezing temperatures—the

FAN PALMS

The hardiest palms have fan leaves (right). They will survive in temperate zones but only one, the Chusan palm, is fully frost-proof.
1 *The Chusan palm (Trachycarpus fortunei) can survive temperatures of 10° F. or even lower. It grows slowly with an untidy fibrous trunk.*
2 *The Mediterranean fan-*

palm, seen growing far right in the south of France, is more often a many-stemmed bush or even a hedge.

CABBAGE PALMS

A group of palms with fan-leaves formed round a distinct mid-rib (right) include several moderately hardy species for Mediterranean-climate regions (zone 8).
3 *The cabbage palm (Sabal palmetto) grows to 90 feet with immense fans on stiff spines curving out and down. Its dried leaves furnish the crosses for Palm Sunday services.*
4 *Livistona is a genus from Australia and China. The slow-growing Chinese form has gracefully drooping tips to the lobes of its fans.*

5 *Washingtonia, a sturdy-looking tree surviving temperatures down to 22° F. The Mexican W. robusta is one of the fastest-growing palms, but not as hardy.*
Far right *A young Livistona australis.*

MODIFIED-FAN PALMS

A third form of palm-leaf continues the progression from fan to feather (right); leaflets are curled almost into tubes where they attach to the leaf-spine. Trees with this form of leaf are more tender than fan palms.
6 *The date palm of commerce is planted worldwide in regions with a climate similar to Egypt's. A temperature of 20° F. will defoliate a date palm, but the trunk may survive even lower temperatures.*
7 *The Canary Island date palm is the most impressive of its genus. The less hardy Senegal date palm (Phoenix reclinata) forms graceful clumps of thin stems.*
Far right *The date palm in the Algerian Sahara.*

FEATHER PALMS

The feather-leaved palms (right) are mostly tropical trees with little or no resistance to frost. Their leaves may be as long as 20 feet. The hardiest tree is the Chilean wine palm.
8 *The king palm grows to 70 feet with a smooth green trunk and a broad shapely head.*
9 *The queen palm grows*

rapidly and keeps ramrod-straight to 40 feet with an open crown of long pendulous leaves.
10 *The coconut palm with its curving trunk grows only in frost-free regions, such as, far right, Tahiti.*
11 *The royal palm is at the borderline of its hardiness in southern Florida. Its pale trunks line avenues in many tropical cities.*

1

2

3

4

5

6

7

8

9

10

11

Palm-like as it looks, the tree fern (here a species of Dicksonia *in Tasmania) is no relation; but a normal fern with its rhizome or root vertical instead of horizontal in the ground. The illustration is from* A Narrative of a Visit to the Australian Colonies, *published in 1843.*

Caribbean cabbage palm (*Sabal palmetto*) and the Australian (and Asian) *Livistona*. In both, the leaf-stalk extends through the fan, giving it a distinct mid-rib. That of the cabbage palm–the common palm of South Carolina and Georgia and many beaches of Florida–curves the whole six-foot leaf outwards and downwards. *Livistona australis* is in some ways the most graceful of the fan-leaved palms: the points of the fan's score of fingers are as long as whips and dangle from the crown.

California's only native palm, the petticoat or California fan (*Washingtonia filifera*) is also fan-leaved and moderately frost-proof. The petticoat's peculiarity is to keep its dead leaves indefinitely. They hang round the trunk, eventually making the whole tree look like an Alpine haystack.

The move from fan to feather advances a stage with the date palms. In the date genus (*Dactylis*) leaflets of leaves that are obviously feathers meet the stalk in a pleat with its curling edges facing upwards, a characteristic which apparently relates it to the fan-leaf. Date palms have magnificent crowns–as many as 200 leaves each 20 feet long. They are hardy enough for southern California and central Florida; the Canary Island date (*Phoenix canariensis*), which has an immensely thick stem, being hardier than *Phoenix dactylifera*, the Egyptian date palm. Left to their own devices certain cultivars of the date palm often produce so many suckers from the base that their trunks are lost in fountains of greenery.

There are two more magnificent feather palms hardy enough for southern California and central Florida: the king palm of Australia (*Archonthophoenix alexandrae*) and the queen palm (*Arecastrum romanzoffianum*) of Brazil. The king has a worthy crown of short, substantial leaves, rising from a glossy green crown-shaft at the top of a 70-foot trunk. The queen is less than half the height, with a distinctive top.

The royal palm and the coconut palm make no pretence of hardiness. The royal palm (*Roystonea regia*) comes from Cuba, the coconut (*Cocos nucifera*) from almost everywhere in the tropics. Both make enormously stately trees: the royal palm perfectly straight, pale-trunked with a gentle swelling at the base and again half-way up; the coconut tall but never straight, characteristically inclined towards the surf over a dazzling white beach.

The hardiest of the feather-palms seems to be the Chilean wine palm, *Jubaea chilensis* (or *J. spectabilis*). It does very well in California and of all palms has perhaps the most impressive trunk. It can be as much as six feet in diameter.

Above *The Joshua tree,* Yucca brevifolia. *Yuccas, like palms, have only one seed-leaf; they are native to Mexico and the southern United States. The Joshua tree is the most tree-like of the genus. It grows to over 30 feet.*

The Broadleaves

The broadleaf trees belong to the earth's dominant group of plants: the flower-bearers, in the strict sense of the word. Unlike the conifers the families of the broadleaves include plants that are not trees at all. They stem back to tropical climates (where by far the greater number of species still live). In the course of adapting to temperate conditions—above all to freezing winters—they have had varying degrees of success. Only a minority of species has come through as trees. All our herbaceous plants had tree-ancestors in the ancient tropical forests and many of them have tree-cousins still to be found in the forests of today.

Broadleaves originated as an evolutionary improvement on the conifers. What they managed better, above all, was the circulation of sap. The structure of their wood adapted to allow a much freer and stronger flow: this in turn allowed them leaves which could evaporate more water, photosynthesize quicker and thus get more value out of the summer sun.

Having made leaves that were more efficient for the conditions in which they grew, they were in trouble when (in the course of geological time) colder weather came. Some modified their leaves, giving them a tougher structure and a thicker skin: made them, in fact, more like the leaves of their conifer ancestors. These are our broadleaf evergreens.

Some simply became herbaceous, going underground in winter. These no longer exist as trees.

Most adopted a third plan: they went

deciduous. By dropping their leaves they could make the best of the sunny season with big, delicate and efficient leaves, capable of the maximum photosynthesis; but suffer no damage in winter (when they would not be missing much sun anyway).

As far as flowers were concerned the big step forward by the broadleaves was pollination by insects rather than by the wind. It seems to have started with beetles eating the flowers of members of the magnolia family. The great advantage of insect pollination is that it does not need a great crowd of trees of the same species to have a fair chance of success. There is less drain on a tree's protein supply because less pollen is needed. (The nectar that attracts bees is made not from protein but from more easily obtainable sugars.)

The other development, crucial to the science of taxonomy, but without much advantage for the broadleaves, was the introduction of an ovary to contain the seeds. The term Angiosperm, which covers all the flowering plants, refers to this and distinguishes them from the naked-seeded conifers (Gymnosperms).

'In a large group an imperfect organization is better than no organization at all.' So writes Arthur Cronquist, the Senior Curator of the New York Botanic Garden in his *The Evolution and Classification of Flowering Plants*. I am glad I can quote him, because the organization of the broadleaves is a mine-field for the amateur–or, come to that, for the professional. My debt to Dr. Cronquist goes much further, though: the order in which the families appear in the following pages is entirely his. It is based on the relative primitiveness or sophistication of the families, as demonstrated (chiefly) by their flowers. Thus the magnolias, which are accepted as belonging to the most primitive order of all the flowering plants, come first. The rest follow in increasing order of sophistication and modernity.

The common oak, Quercus robur, *in the forest of Fontainebleau, France.*

The Tulip Tree and the Magnolias

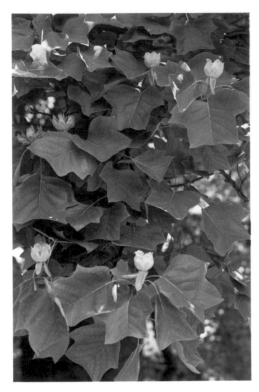

Every magnolia is the apple of someone's eye. To be conspicuous but to manage an air of frailty is a good recipe.

There are 80 species of magnolia and two of tulip trees (*Liriodendron*) in the magnolia family. Nearly all have flowers larger than any other tree and leaves bigger than most. They range from the tallest of American broadleaves to cafe-umbrella size. None comes from Europe; some big ones are natives of the southeastern United States; almost all the pretty little garden ones come from China and Japan. Frailty is deceptive: these last tend to be the hardiest.

The tulip tree is the grandfather of the family. It sounds rather less glamorous under the name foresters know it by: yellow poplar. As the tulip tree it sounds like a Walt Disney production. Imagine: 190 feet high; all covered with tulips. The only trouble is that the two selling points cancel each other out. It's true about the tulips, but you often need binoculars to see them.

You can hardly grow a more adaptable, less demanding tree, or one that grows faster. In the wild it grows in the Great Smokies and along the Ohio River, but its range reaches from the Great Lakes to the Gulf of Mexico. It should be planted small: like all magnolias it has vulnerable fleshy roots and one of them is a deep taproot. Ideally it likes deep loose soil and a wet spring. A seedling with all its prayers answered has grown 50 feet in 11 years. But tulip trees soldier on in polluted air, mutilated by amateur tree surgeons, in disease (they catch few) and drought (provided there is a moist sub-soil).

They offer an individuality that makes one think of the ginkgo. There is no other leaf quite this shape. It sets off like a maple leaf, with pointed lobes at the sides, but where the third and biggest lobe should come to a point it is cut off short. Again ginkgo-like, it keeps up an even, fresh, medium green from spring to autumn, then changes to a clear light yellow. I can never understand the prejudice that autumn colour is not colour unless it is red. A hundred feet of fresh farm butter is a stirring sight.

As for the tulips, which open in May or June, it's a pity they are not often within reach: they are sumptuous flowers, beloved by bees, with pale green petals opening to show a soft orange lining and a noble array of parts.

The tree has a remarkably similar Chinese counterpart; less different indeed than one or two odd cultivars which have cropped up. There is also an upright one, a variegated one and one without the side lobes so that the leaves are virtually rectangular.

Magnolias proper can reach almost the same colossal heights, but many stay obligingly near eye-level. It is probably in terms of size that they can be most usefully catalogued; that, and the crucial question of when they flower.

There are really three major types of magnolias. One is the evergreen, of which *Magnolia grandiflora*, the bull bay of the Deep South, is the prime example. The second is the deciduous magnolia that flowers in summer, so that its leaves set off (or hide, as the case may be) the flowers, which are tulip-shaped, opening to saucers. The third is the kind that flowers before the leaves. Most of them are small trees, some are shrubs, and all are from the Far East. There is a superannuated subgenus name for these: *Gwillimias*. It has no more modern validity than *retinospora*, but I like the Welsh feeling about it–and why not make a distinction of plants that are, to you and me, distinct?

Gwillimias in turn can be divided first into tulip-flowered and star-flowered kinds and then into the few big trees (all tulip-flowered) and the rest, which are small-to-medium.

The bull bay (what a dreadfully hearty name for such a voluptuous plant) must be counted the all-round champion of the

Top *The highly original leaves of the tulip tree seem to have the middle lobe cut off. The beautiful orange flowers often occur too high up to be clearly seen.*

The tulip tree is one of the tallest natives of eastern North America: specimens nearly 200 feet high have been known. Its foliage turns pale yellow in autumn.

Magnolia grandiflora, the bull bay of the south-eastern States, is the best evergreen member of the family, even tolerating city air (as here, in London). In northern parts it is often grown against walls.

Left *A magnificent close-up of the fruit of Magnolia grandiflora, splitting to disclose one of its bean-like seeds. They germinate the following spring, but the plant takes ten years or more to flower.*

The leaf, flower and fruit of the yellow cucumber tree of Georgia and the south, Magnolia cordata, are shown here in the painting by the 18th-century botanist André Michaux.

magnolias. In the forests of the south it grows to well over 100 feet and regularly delivers a heavy, creamy, scented flower on every shoot, making sackfuls of seed. Its leaves are beautiful: best when they unfold with a layer of velvet rust underneath, but always glistening and trim. Furthermore, they dry well and keep for ever: year after year we have, as Christmas decorations at home, some little artificial orange trees made of them.

Towards the north of its range (Philadelphia is about the limit on the east coast; it is hardy in most of Europe and all of Britain) the custom is to grow it up a high south- or west-facing wall, which it totally buries in its magnificent evergreenery. It prefers no lime (but is tolerant of it) and lots of nourishment. Once it gets going it flowers steadily (though not all over except in the south) from June or July to October. Some clones start flowering at a much earlier age (four or five years) and have bigger flowers than others. An 18th-century English selection called 'Exmouth' (or 'Exoniensis') is one of the best on both counts. Another good one, with whopping flowers, is called 'Goliath'.

The first magnolia to reach cultivation was the swamp bay (*M. virginiana*). It lacks the magnificence of the bull bay, either in leaf—it is only a committed evergreen in the south—or in flower. Its compensations are a delicious fragrance in flowers which persist (at Kew) even into December and almost luminous blue-white undersides to the leaves—but many other magnolias share this.

The bigleaf magnolia (*M. macrophylla*) from the southeastern States has its detractors, but I find it superb. This one is definitely not an evergreen, but then its leaves are really startlingly big—getting on for banana size. Its flowers, moreover, are in proportion. They come in summer, beaming through the two-foot, luminous-green ▶

In climates like that of its native south (here in northern Italy) the bull bay (Magnolia grandiflora) makes a magnificent evergreen tree, growing as high as 90 feet and flowering profusely.

Top *The scented creamy flower of Magnolia grandiflora. Some forms of bull bay, notably 'Goliath', have flowers up to ten inches across, produced in great numbers from mid-summer on.*

Above *The evergreen sweet or swamp bay was the first of the family to be grown in Europe, as early as the 17th century. It lacks the vigour, hardiness and gloss of the bull bay.*

Top *The Chinese evergreen rival to the bull bay, Magnolia delavayi, has much bigger leaves with milky-green undersides. It is just as hardy, but has never achieved the same popularity. It flowers in late summer.*

Above *The bigleaf magnolia, with the biggest leaves of all, up to two feet long, is another native of the southern States, but deciduous. Its huge flowers (up to 12 inches across) are sweetly scented.*

The Magnolias

▶ leaves. In autumn, if the tree is well sheltered from the wind (this is essential) and the leaves hang on in good condition, they can turn anything from malted milk to espresso. Not classic fall colour exactly, but even more arresting.

I have strayed from the evergreens. The other one is *M. delavayi* from western China. This is the compromise between the bull bay and the bigleaf: it is evergreen, and its leaves are quite big enough to satisfy most people. Its flowers come and go very quickly: the leaves would be the reason to plant it, but again, only if you have a wind-proof corner. It is as hardy as *M. grandiflora*.

The bigleaf is, in fact, a member of class two; deciduous, summer-flowering magnolias. The champion for flowers in this department is the Japanese 'whiteleaf' magnolia (*M. obovata*). Its flowers are long-petalled, white and sweet-scented and the leaves really do set them off: they are long enough to be slightly floppy: their undersides are milky white; and if you are lucky enough to be standing under the tree on a sunny day you will see how they have the translucency of tropical sea-water; a pale green glow suffuses everything beneath.

The cucumber tree of the eastern States (*M. acuminata*) is probably the tallest magnolia in the flower-with-the-leaves department, but it would be misleading to class it as an ornamental flowering tree; the flowers can scarcely be seen in the towering mass of big shiny leaves. In every way the yellow cucumber tree (*M. cordata*), which has been considered a variety, is more of a garden proposition. It is half the size or less, but has masses of yellow flowers, among leaves half the size. The same cucumbery pods appear on both.

Wilson's (*M. wilsonii*), the Chinese (*M. sinensis*) and the Oyama (*M. sieboldii*) are a group of three oriental species without significant differences as far as the gardener is concerned: all flower from May or June onwards, sometimes intermittently for two

or three months. All have flowers which hang their heads so that you have to be underneath to see the red stamens in the white shades and all tend to be big bushes rather than real trees. There is a famous hybrid of *M. sinensis* named *highdownensis* which proved, at Sir Frederick Stern's famous chalk garden at Highdown near Worthing on the south coast of England, to be perfectly happy to grow on that uncompromising rock.

The gwillimias, now. These are the really spectacular ones, covering their bare branches with waxy flowers before a leaf appears, and often while there is still a good chance (in Britain at least) of a frost to wreck the show. *M. campbellii* is the giant tulip tree of the Himalayas. I think I can imagine one 150 feet high and holding aloft no leaves but thousands of big, pink, waxy flowers, but it does set the mind to boggling. It is pretty good at 60 feet, the highest it grows in England. There are several forms with flowers from white to pink/purple, but many demand patience: *M. campbellii* has no flowers at all for 25 years or so. There is one particularly hardy variety, *M. c. mollicomata*, which gets under way rather quicker at about 15 years.

A quick start is obviously a major consideration with a tree which is grown for its flowers. The excellent *M. kobus* has been largely superseded because it takes 15 years or more to start flowering. The ones which start soonest are *M. stellata*, the low bush with white star flowers you see almost everywhere, its more vigorous and splendid hybrid *M. × loebneri*, and the most popular and free-flowering of the tulip-flowered kind, *M. × soulangiana*.

The trick with the very-early flowering kinds like *M. stellata* is to grow them in a comparatively cold spot where their buds will not be wooed open by the spring sunshine too soon. *M. × stellata* and *M. × loebneri* are hardy enough to flourish in a north exposure. *M. × loebneri* grows twice as fast, however, and has bigger flowers, either pink or white to taste.

There are at least a dozen clones of the hybrid *M. × soulangiana*, varying from white through the grades of flush and blush which are typical of the race to a fairly livid purple. They are not trees at all, but spreading shrubs which consume a fair amount of space. Having flowered, they fill the space with not very fascinating foliage. To my mind it is a big garden which can spare the space for them. The Japanese willowleaf magnolia (*M. salicifolia*) is the narrowest-growing gwillimia, and an ardent flower-bearer; perhaps the best for a small garden.

Of the species other than *M. campbellii* which are relatively leisurely about flowering, the Chinese Yulan (*M. denudata*) is the classic. Its flowers have broad, pure white petals of the substance and thickness of an ivory paper knife. The leaves are milky-white beneath.

There is a hybrid between this and the Himalayan giant *M. campbellii* (under the name *M. × veitchii*) which has grown to 85 feet in Cornwall and apparently covers itself with hundreds of pink flowers. Neither of these last two would be at all happy in an alkaline soil.

The catalogue could go on and on, but these are by and large the best, and certainly the best-known, of the big family. There is one more, which doesn't exactly fall into the gwillimia class because, although it starts flowering early, it goes right on into mid-summer. This is the bush-size lily magnolia (*M. liliiflora*), whose variety 'Nigra' is almost new-wine purple on the outside of the petals. I would say crocus rather than lily for the shape of the flowers, though.

The positioning of magnolias is worth some thought. Wind and rain can soon destroy their fragile flowers. Shelter is the vital factor; light woodland shade provides the ideal conditions.

Above *The star-shaped flowers of the Japanese* Magnolia stellata, *the shrub on the left of the big centre picture. It grows slowly, rarely to more than ten feet, often wider than its height.*

Below *The darkest form of the lily-flowered magnolia is known as 'Nigra'. It is a smaller plant than the normal species but flowers even more freely, going on all summer in a good year.*

Above centre *Two of the most popular garden magnolias; the big pink* Magnolia × soulangiana *and the smaller white M. stellata: both are reliable and profuse flower-bearers before the leaves in spring.*

Of the many forms of the hybrid Magnolia × soulangiana *'Rustica Rubra' is one of the darkest pink. The 'lily-flowered' magnolia in the picture to the right is the parent that gives the colour.*

The shrub-sized lily-flowered magnolia of China (Magnolia liliiflora) starts flowering before the leaves and goes on far into the summer. It is one of the parents of M. × soulangiana.

The Bays and Laurels

Below left *Sweet bay or laurel was the emblem of victory to the ancient Romans, and poets were crowned with laurel wreaths. For more than 2,000 years it has been used for decoration, medicine and cooking.*

It is as well, first, to denounce the common laurel as the usurper of an honoured name. *The* honoured name, you might say, since the true laurel, to us the bay tree, sweet bay or bay laurel, is the Latin *Laurus nobilis*, whence poets laureate, winning your laurels, passing your baccalaureate and all the rest. Wreaths for distinguished brows were made, in fact, of the leaves we put in courts-bouillon and milk pud. The noble tree of the ancients is the one they clip like a poodle outside the Hôtel de Paris in Monte Carlo and casinos and hairdressers the world over. Whereas the common laurel (page 203) is an evergreen cherry.

Laurels are fairly close to the magnolias. They have in common striking, rather big leaves, usually simple ovals (and where not, as in the tulip tree and *Sassafras*, quite odd and original shapes). They share an aromatic principle: their chemistry is not identical, yet your nose tells you there is something in common between magnolia, bay, camphor and sassafras smells. What they lack, of course, is the fancy flowers. They are essentially foliage trees.

The bay tree comes into the same class as the yew and the box as material for vegetable sculpture. It is a slow grower; naturally a dense cone to no more than 40 feet. But it can easily be trimmed to a pyramid, or more laboriously pruned up to make a ball on a stick. It survives in a tub, or anywhere where the drainage is good. Very hard frost can hurt it, but it is by no means tender.

There is an unusual narrow- and rather wavy-leaved variety of bay (*L. nobilis angustifolia*) which is apparently hardier. Like the golden bay (*L.n.* 'Aurea'), it is not common in cultivation.

Bay is a Mediterranean tree. It has two far-flung relations that are similar in general effect, but curiously different in their (very powerful) smells. The smell of camphor is familiar enough. Camphor comes from the camphor laurel (*Cinnamomum cam-*

phora) of southeast Asia. But there is no short way of describing the smell of *Umbellularia californica*, the California laurel—or, as Oregonians have it, Oregon myrtle. It is the sort of smell that somehow spells danger to me. I would no more put it in my soup than I would petrol—though Californians (and no doubt Oregonians too) play chicken with it in the kitchen, scorning the pungent bay as a spice for weaklings. The crushed leaf has a reputation for giving headaches. I'm prepared to take it on trust.

A smell is not a tree, however. The umbellularia is a very fine evergreen. The biggest one, near Santa Barbara, California,

Above Looking up into the crown of an ancient bay tree in Italy. Although it is hardy, the bay never grows to this sort of age and size except in a warm climate. But it stands clipping into formal shapes.

Left Bay is not grown for its flowers; they are small and cream-coloured. But they can appear in dense masses, to be followed by little black cherry-like berries. The French 'baie' —whence the name— means berry.

Sassafras is an eastern American relation of the bay. Its deciduous leaves vary from ovals to three-lobed (like maples') or two-lobed (like a mitten), rich green above with a blue-white patina below. Sassafras will grow to about 60 feet.

thick black branches. This is for southern parts only.

The deciduous sassafras, the only other hardy member of a family which (like so many) has its real headquarters in the tropics, is by far the most beautiful (and the best-smelling) of the collection. The bark and the roots used to be used to make a fragrant and refreshing pink tea, known colloquially as 'saloop'. Sassafras is rare in Europe, but in its native eastern States it is common enough–and it has a vast natural range, all the way from Florida to Maine and west to Texas.

Sassafras leaves can't even agree among themselves: some are plain, some lobed rather like maple leaves, some lobed on one side and looking like mittens. They stay a really edible, succulent green as late as September; then they turn orange and scarlet.

This excellent tree doesn't take up too much room: its branches are noticeably short for its height. Only its very positive likes and dislikes tell against it. It needs well-drained sandy loam; alkaline soil kills it. It doesn't like being moved except in infancy, and it clearly prefers summers that are summers and winters that are winters; Europe's wishy-washy arrangement gets it confused. The difference shows in the size. The biggest known in Europe is six feet round–although it was introduced nearly 350 years ago. The biggest in America, in Kentucky, is 17 feet round and 100 feet high.

The pawpaw (*Asimina triloba*) is a not-so-distant cousin of the laurels. It had a great name among the early settlers in America as a food in the wilds. John Bartram sent it over to England in 1736. Yet today it is far from common. To collectors of the curious its pleasures are its big, drooping, oval, deciduous leaves; its small, browny-violet flowers and its short brown pods which are edible–but not, I'm told, a gastronomic experience.

is 80 feet high and 100 feet wide. It is a tree that will grow in deep shade before its turn comes to cast it. The big ones have rather wandering trunks of wood, so hard that folk who up and move house (in the land where moving house means moving house) just put umbellularia rollers underneath and shove. It is not so hardy as bay but even in England grows to a bigger tree. Certainly it has a much more interesting shape.

In California the camphor laurel is beginning to be fancied as a street tree. It is slow (like all the family) and rather greedy for a small garden, but it supports a wide canopy of lovely shiny big leaves on

Witch Hazels, Sweetgums and Parrotias

The witch hazel family stands at the head of a broad class of plants that show symptoms of having developed very early in the evolutionary scheme of things. The class includes a good chunk of the biggest hardwoods of the temperate world: the oaks, elms, beeches, chestnuts, planes, walnuts and hickories. Their relationship is proved only by unobvious technical points: the structure of their wood and pollen in particular. But there are other indications: most of them have catkins for flowers and rely on wind-pollination – possibly because in their day (so to speak) few pollinating insects had evolved. With wind-pollination goes a tendency to flower early in the spring before the forest's leaf-cover gets in the way. There are obvious catkin-trees like the willows and poplars outside this group; but not many.

The witch hazel's own family of close relations gives us some of the best autumn colour outside of the maples in the sweetgum (*Liquidambar*) and the Persian ironwood (*Parrotia*). The witch hazel itself is one of the best winter-flowering shrubs – though scarcely a tree. And two other closely allied families give us a useful range of Australian evergreens, the *Pittosporums*, and one of the most delicate and beautiful of all big trees for the garden, the Japanese katsura or *Cercidiphyllum*. Nobody seems to have come up with a vernacular name for this. It might sell well as the Valentine tree; its leaves are perfect little hearts which turn all kinds of sweetheart colours at the end of the year.

None of these trees survived the Ice Ages in Europe. The witch hazel, which gives the sweet-scented soothing lotion for bruises, was the first one known to botany; the eastern American *Hamamelis virginiana*. Hazel because of its soft oval leaves like the nut tree's; witch, presumably, from witch.

The most tree-like of the witch hazels is the Japanese *H. japonica* 'Arborea'. The best for winterflowering in gardens is the Chinese species, *H. mollis*. They all have beauti-

Top *The sweeping layers of its branch-pattern combine with its little heart-shaped leaves to make* Cercidiphyllum japonicum *(in Japanese 'katsura') one of the most graceful of all medium-sized trees. It needs deep soil and moisture.*

Disanthus cercidifolius *has leaves exactly like the cercidiphyllum's (top) but with brighter autumn colour. A rare member of the witch hazel family, it makes at best a small tree. It needs lime-free woodland soil, moisture and shade.*

ful pale yellow leaves in autumn and all tend to grow with a broad horizontal emphasis, covering a fair bit of ground.

The relationship of the sweetgum to the witch hazel is far from obvious. It looks much more like a maple, with leaves lobed in just the same way. It is another tree that ended up everywhere but in Europe. The eastern American version (*Liquidambar styraciflua*) is by far the best known; but the Turkish *L. orientalis* and the Chinese *L. formosana* are very pretty; especially the Chinese, which produces lavender-coloured young leaves in spring.

Sweetgum is not all sentiment in the United States. Any tree that grows to 125 feet and 20 feet round is forestry material. I have seen it grown as the moist bottomland hardwood in Georgia, with its masters expecting quite some performance from it.

It is a fairly slow grower in Europe (10 feet in 12 years), and furthermore is a tree that must be planted small; it has fleshy roots that sucker furiously if they are disturbed. The biggest in England (at Syon House near London) is none the less 93 feet high and a beautiful sight, turning from the same sort of rich shiny green as the sassafras to an autumn motley of scarlet and crimson. There are two simple ways of recognizing the sweetgum. All maples have their leaves and shoots in pairs opposite one another on the twig; the sweetgum's are arranged alternately. And the bark, even of the twigs, has deep ridges of corky material like that of a number of elms.

Its liking for damp ground (though not bogs or floodland) suggests the bank of a pond as the ideal place to plant it. The reflection can be sensational.

Shiny succulence of leaf doesn't always count as a botanical characteristic, but if you see the sweetgum and the parrotia side by side (a good idea, by the way) you can sense a relationship. The parrotia is known to gardeners as a low tree that grows more sideways than up–as does the witch hazel, in fact. I have the word of Roy Lancaster, the curator of Hillier's nursery/arboretum near Winchester, that in Persia he has seen it straight as an arrow and 60 feet high, but the biggest I have seen in captivity is the Arnold Arboretum's tree; a broad fan with a good dozen stems to maybe 35 feet.

Parrotia, drooping as it does, tends to show you here and there a cascade of rich deep green leaves from above. Other branches will take off like flapping wings of a big bird, making the tree a free-form performance you need to stand back from. Its little blood-red flowers, rather like the elm's, make a lovely early spring incident. In England its autumn colour is patchy, some leaves going orange or red while others stay green, or parti-coloured. The snag is that the ones on the end of the long branches drop off before the inner ones have turned, so you seldom have the whole tree furnished and coloured at the same time.

What with the colours and the flapping I was prepared to believe that it was the parrot which lent the tree its name. Now I read that it was named in honour of a Herr Parrot, the second man to the top of Mount Ararat (Noah being the first) in 1829.

Among all this lush foliage the cercidiphyllum strikes a blow for quiet good taste. An old tree makes distinct terraces with its swooping, almost-horizontal branches. On them each small, long-stalked leaf stands out precisely; a neat heart in pale green. One of its lovely habits is to produce single leaves from the old wood of its inner recesses, so that when they turn almost pure white as they often do in autumn you catch a glimpse of white hearts against dark bark. Overall it can turn anything from deep pink to ivory; the paler colours stressing all the more the marked separateness of each leaf. Eighty feet is the tallest it has yet grown in England, but it shows promise in America of reaching 100 feet. Virtually pest-free, this is one of the first-choice garden trees.

Above *The sweet gum or* Liquidambar *has leaves like a maple's. Its ridged and corky bark and alternate pattern of branch and leaf are the easiest ways to distinguish it.*

Below *The deep green glossy leaves of parrotia in summer. Before the leaves the parrotia opens petalless crimson flowers like the elm's. They are followed by hard oval capsules.*

Above *Persian parrotia (or ironwood) colours brilliant red and yellow in autumn. It tends to a broad horizontal shape. Mature trees have flaking bark making patterns like that of the London plane.*

Right *Seed capsules of* Pittosporum tobira *on the point of ripeness. They develop from yellow flowers with an orange-blossom scent. Several species are popular in California, where they grow well by the sea.*

Left *The pittosporums are evergreen Australian relations of the witch hazel family, making small trees in a sub-tropical climate. Here the seed capsules of* Pittosporum tobira *are splitting open to show the red seeds.*

Above *A young sweetgum starting to change colour in autumn. The leaves hold a good bright green until late in the season, then take on tones of scarlet and orange. It is the biggest tree of the family, growing to over 100 feet.*

The Plane Family/*Platanaceae*

The Planes

An avenue of young London planes in Belgium. They have been regularly pruned to produce a mop-head effect. Planes take well to such treatment, but it totally destroys their winter beauty of branch-tracery.

The London plane growing by the Thames in a painting by John Varley (1811). Since the 18th century this hybrid between the oriental and American planes has been London's principal tree.

It was calculated in 1920 that more than 60 per cent of the trees in London were London planes, most of them planted in the previous 25 years. If that isn't daredevil monoculture I don't know what is. The figure is not very different today, for the fact remains that the plane is, in the words of the Chairman of the tree planting committee, the 'most biddable tree' there is.

The London plane is generally believed to be a cross between the two sorts of plane that occur in the wild. There is an eastern plane (*Platanus orientalis*), native to Turkey and Greece; and the western plane (*P. occidentalis*) which Americans call either buttonwood or sycamore. The first record of the London plane was in England in 1663 – which of course has not prevented the botanists calling it *P.× hispanica*, the Spanish cross. It certainly shows the sort of vigour associated with hybrids. Given a good bit of clay it grows two or three feet a year from the start.

Familiar as the plane is, it is hard to fault it for style. Its great attraction is a trunk as tall as an English elm's, not getting lost in a maze of branches but weaving purposefully to the top, dappled with big patches where the dark outer bark has flaked away and left the inner layer; green ripening to buff. Its winter silhouette is one of the most graceful of all; a tracery in which the weeping twigs form countless little Gothic arches, diversified with dangling black balls, three or four to a string.

The power of this form to save city architecture from itself has been realized for 200 years. It has never been more needed than today. There remain authorities, notably round the Mediterranean but also in the suburbs of most cities, who hack the branches off planes as a symbol of municipal power over nature. This is what is meant by the plane being biddable: it just shoots again undaunted. But streets where it is allowed to fulfil itself, as it is in countless Provençal villages, are among the most stately, be the houses mere hovels.

The three most important planes (there are of course others, of which the Californian, *P. racemosa*, is the most notable) are easily distinguished by their leaves. They all have what are, basically, maple leaves, but the eastern plane's are deep-lobed, the buttonwood's very shallow-lobed and the London plane's something between them. What is odd is that they could hardly

be farther from the maple in the evolutionary sense.

Of the three, the London plane is the most widespread today. It will grow in an astonishing variety of climate and latitude, ranging from North Africa to New Zealand. The French Ministry of Forests has suggested planting it in place of the ubiquitous poplar for its quick-growing timber. But to a tragic extent the range of forestry trees is controlled by what the market is accustomed to.

Where the buttonwood is grown for timber in the southeastern States you can see that the poplar analogy is no exaggeration. A trunk 45 feet high and nine inches thick in ten years is not bad going. Unfortunately this beautiful tree, in many ways even better-looking than the London plane and certainly more handsome than the rather dumpy eastern one, demands the continental climate of the eastern States. Spring frost makes it hard to grow in Britain.

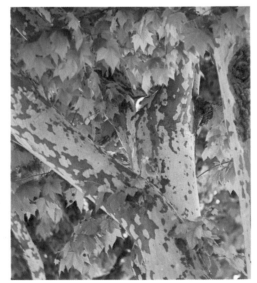

Above The leaf, fruiting ball (left) and flower clusters of the American plane, known as buttonwood or sycamore. Compare this leaf with that of the oriental plane in the picture to the right. The lobes are very much shallower.

Right Late spring foliage of the London plane with young, partly-developed fruiting clusters. The London plane has two to four fruit balls on a stem; the oriental plane four to six and the American buttonwood one or two.

Above The deeply-lobed maple-like leaves of the oriental plane, one parent of the London plane, take on warm russet tints in autumn. It is a shorter, less graceful tree which remains rare in cultivation in the West.

The smooth flaked and marbled bark of the London plane is derived from its American parent, the buttonwood. It gives even enormous trees (the tallest, at Bryanston, Dorset, is 145 feet) the appearance of youth and vitality.

A much-loved London vista and the world centre of nannydom: the 200-year-old planes in Kensington Gardens with the sun setting over the rooftops of Kensington Palace and the spire of St. Mary Abbot's church in the background.

The flaking bark of the American buttonwood. The irregular plates of outer bark are continually falling away, especially in summer, to reveal the creamy inner layer, which changes to a mosaic of green and fawn.

135

The Elms

A dismal cloud hangs over the elms. Nobody could write without emotion of this most majestic family of trees being under the threat of extinction. In many townships as far apart as New England and East Anglia elms *were* the landscape. Whether the local species is the American elm, immensely high-arched and spreading; the English elm, tall-trunked and balancing a broad fan far above the fields; the wych elm, wide-crowned and weeping, or any of a dozen others it set the scale for life in its countryside. In our flat country it did service for the non-existent hills.

Dutch elm disease is a fungus carried by a beetle. It grows in the new ring of wood, just inside the bark, on which the tree relies almost totally for its flow of sap. When it blocks the sap vessels, the branch dies—and very soon the tree. Two-hundred-year-old trees can be killed in one season. Because the disease battens on wood that is being created that year little can be done to protect the tree. The only hope is to kill the beetles with a DDT-type spray and to inject the sap-stream with fungicide. But this is an expensive operation which might have to be repeated year after year. To whole populations of millions (70 per cent of the hedgerow trees in the English Midlands and eastern counties were elms) it is impossible.

We can only hope that as the disease passes some of the abundant hedgerow sprouts will prove immune and provide our descendants with these irreplaceable trees.

There are about 45 species of elm: nobody is quite sure how many. Donald Wyman in *Trees for American Gardens* says there are 200 or so named clones. There are certainly five species that count, and perhaps another six hybrids and cultivars. Which you consider *the* elm depends entirely on where you were brought up.

I was brought up in the heart of elm-land, in the southeast of England, where three species and several elusive crosses and crosses of crosses clumped or filed all over the landscape. Our chief glory was the English elm (*Ulmus procera*) which, because it sets no fertile seed but reproduces entirely by new saplings springing up from the roots of old trees, maintains its blood free from taint. In a sense all English elms are parts of one gigantic tree, and look like it; the pattern of branching in a line of them is hypnotically repetitive. They all have short horizontal or slightly drooping branches on the lower part of the trunk, then very often a distinct waist half way up, then an almost-symmetrical, half-open fan of long branches forming the top third of the tree. William Gilpin, who wrote late in the 18th century about the

aesthetics of trees, pronounced magisterially: 'No tree is better adapted to receive grand masses of light.' The grand masses are not exactly of light, but of the dark green, small-leafed foliage whose cloud-formations seem to hold it. Constable, a native of this landscape, was constantly trying to paint it: and yet his oaks are better than his elms.

The leaves stay green on the English elm longer than on the others; even into November. Their autumn colour is a fine light gold, which coincides with autumnal mist to create effects I can't begin to describe. It is a savage irony that that lovely colour comes early now, and means death.

Elm is the traditional wood for coffins. There is a trenchant old jingle which makes the link between this and the tree's famous tendency to drop a big branch, without warning, on a still summer's day.

Elem hateth man
And waiteth.

It is customary in books about trees to repeat this warning and advise against planting elms anywhere where people might walk under them. Well and good; but where does that leave us? There is a much higher death toll from getting run over by lawn-mowers than from standing under elm trees. How often do you hear of anyone being slain in this honourable fashion? ▶

The smooth-leaved elm, Ulmus carpinifolia, *growing on fen-land near Cambridge.*

The Elms of Europe and America

The English elm is essentially the hedgerow, often the parkland tree; not so frequent now in towns. It has been as successful in North America as in Europe. 'Chinese' Wilson in his *Aristocrats of the Trees* remarked that not only did it flourish in New England, but it showed no sign of doing its branch-dropping act.

I have the honour of living in Saling, the village with the biggest smooth-leaved elm (*U. carpinifolia*)—as far as anyone knows—in the world. It isn't what it was (in 1841 it was 114 feet high) but it is 22½ feet round and that, for an elm, is big. In the last 130-odd years it has grown five feet in girth. It must

have been planted between 1600 and 1650, which happens to be just when my house was built. It is all too easy to get damp-eyed about the historic associations of trees, but it is a quality they possess that one can't pass over in silence.

At a casual glance a smooth-leaved elm and a wych elm (*U. glabra*) can look very much the same. They usually fork fairly low and broaden out (like the American elm) into an immense explosion, from the extremities of which the twigs come tumbling in intricate cascades. They are at their most beautiful in winter, when their tracery is on display; not even the grand masses of light

Elm flowers (here on a wych elm) have no petals, but appear as a red bunch of stamens on the bare twigs in very early spring. They can be borne densely enough to colour the whole tree red.

Left *The fruit of the elm often covers the branches so densely (especially on the wych elm, seen here) that the tree appears to be in premature leaf. It turns brown and falls as the young leaves appear.*

Below *The weeping wych elm forms a broad crown of branches which climb slowly in shallow arcs, sometimes to a considerable height. Its flat top has earned it the alternative name of the tabletop elm—an ideal tree for a large garden or park.*

can compare with what is surely nature's very best pen-and-ink work.

If you can reach a leaf you have your answer to the identity of the tree: the smooth-leaved elm's leaf is smooth (on top) and shiny; the wych elm's is bigger and raspingly rough. The English elm's has the same sandpapery feeling. The trade-mark of all elm leaves is a lop-sided base.

The flowers of the elm are often dismissed as being invisible from the ground, and so not worth bothering with. It has no showy catkins, but early in the spring it carries so many tiny red flowers, which are really just bunches of stamens appearing from a bud, that the whole leafless tree, caught by the sunlight, glows misty crimson. Still before the leaves appear come the winged fruit; little discs more or less the shape of a fried egg, which colour the tree green. They ripen brown and fall as the leaves expand. The fertile ones germinate as quickly as they ripen: the whole performance from flower to new elm is a matter of eight weeks or so.

On a tree like the American elm, which often hangs its branchlets so low that you can examine the twigs, you can see from late summer on which buds are going to produce leaves and which flowers. On the whole the leaf buds congregate near the branch tips, where they will get most light. The flower buds, a little higher up the hanging spray, are twice the size. If you open one with your fingernail you will see that it is all ready to go; packed with pinky-crimson fluff.

One of the many crosses between the smooth-leaved and wych elms, or rather a whole group of such crosses, constitutes most of the elm population of continental Europe, under such names as the Belgian and Dutch elms (*U.* × *hollandica* 'Belgica' and ditto 'Major'). Wandering down to Italy they become the support for many a promiscuous vine; a role they have filled since Virgil's day. Several selected clones have shown themselves more able to resist Dutch elm disease than others. Two offspring of

U. × *hollandica,* 'Christine Buisman' and 'Bea Schwarz', were at one time much fancied as saviouresses – but neither has proved fully immune.

A similar cross, a tree which fountains up to a spectacular height and spread, has long been known and admired in England as the Huntingdon elm (*U.* × *vegeta*). One Huntingdon elm clone called 'Commelin' is also reckoned fairly disease-resistant. Of the local French types that have been selected (as opposed to the unstudied multitudes of the fields) the most widely-adopted is the Jersey elm (*U.* × *sarniensis*) whose narrow head of long ascending limbs makes it possible for (wide) streets and gardens where others would be in a straitjacket.

The really weeping forms of elm you sometimes see on broad lawns (weeping, that is, not just in branchlet and twig, but in the whole branch from the top) are varieties of the wych elm: the lower and rounder 'Camperdownii'; the taller and more angular 'Pendula'.

There has not been such planting of the lesser-known American elms, either in the United States or in Europe. The slippery elm (*U. rubra*) with its big velvety leaves (slipperiness, being in the inner bark, is not an obvious character) and the narrow, short-branched rock elm of the Great Lakes have been overshadowed by the far-ranging American elm (*U. americana*) itself.

There are no native elms west of the Rockies. The lack has been supplied partly from the eastern States and Europe, but also from Asia. The Chinese elm (*U. parvifolia*) – though not remotely elmy to the untutored eye – is a highly desirable garden tree: all rather miniature; its leaves decidedly so; dark green, shiny, almost evergreen, colouring red before its late leaf-fall. In cold places the similar (but less attractive) Siberian elm (*U. pumila*) does service for it. An Asian hybrid under the name 'Sapporo Autumn Gold' holds out hopes of becoming a big disease-free elm.

Left *The narrow pyramidal crown of the Jersey (or Wheatley) elm makes it one of the best elms for streets and avenues. The perfect avenue seen here in early spring is at Cranborne Manor, Dorset. The Cornish (or Goodyer) elm is another species of similar shape.*

Far right above *Disease has drastically reduced the population of American elms, whose wide-spreading crowns used to be landmarks all over the eastern States. A survivor, photographed here, formerly stood in New England.*

Above *The rugged bark, stained green with algae, and (right) the characteristic shape of the English elm, growing by the Serpentine lake in Hyde Park, London. English elms all conform closely to this narrow-waisted shape.*

Zelkovas and Hackberries

The elms are a homogeneous lot; more so even than the oaks. None is evergreen; none has wildly eccentric leaves. Their relations also toe the line. The excellent *Zelkova* (if ever a tree deserved a good common name) is thoroughly elmy, though only a cousin. And the nettle-tree or hackberry (*Celtis*) has much of the same family look about it.

Very few trees have had such a good press as the zelkova. With no flowers or fruit to speak of and with leaves like those of the elm (only singly toothed; elm leaves have paired teeth) it manages it on composure alone. It is a graceful, well-proportioned, short-trunked, many-stemmed, broad-domed, soberly coloured ordinary tree.

Both the zelkovas (the medium-rare ones; there are more, but they are really rare) answer this description. I turned up William Robinson's *The English Flower Garden* to find myself echoed with another forest of commas: 'The longer points, sharper teeth, more numerous nerves and leathery texture, together with the fact that they hang longer, may enable anyone to tell the leaf of the Japan Zelkova (*Z. serrata*) from that of the better-known Caucasian tree (*Z. carpinifolia*).'

I would add to the list of distinctions the thin bark of the 'Japan Zelkova', which in flaking off reveals enticing little patches of quite startling orange. With the wide spread of the long branches from a mere five feet above the ground there is plenty of bark to contemplate.

It is the fruit that distinguishes the hackberries from the elms. Though it is scarcely a reason to grow them, it consists of red, yellow or blackish berries compared with the elm's dry, flattened, winged fruit. Otherwise in proportions and general aspect they are small (rarely much higher than 50 feet) spreading, bush-topped and rather bright green elms, with much to be said for them as street or small garden trees.

One point in their favour is that they root deep. You can grow shrubs under them – if the shrubs can take dense shade, which is what they deliver. Their deep roots, once they have found their depth, are virtually drought-proof.

The best part about the common hackberry (*C. occidentalis*) of eastern North America (which will grow more or less anywhere) is its highly original bark. Corkiness is in the family (several elms have corky twigs) but the hackberry handles it differently. By middle age the tree has deep flanges of cork, widely spaced, running more or less north-south but wandering about on its surface. As a tree for public places the common hackberry is apparently discredited for its habit of forming witches' brooms from which

A superb specimen of the Caucasian zelkova growing in Devon. The short buttressed trunk and extraordinary system of crowded upright branches are unique to this tree. It was discovered in 1760, yet remains almost unknown.

The relationship of zelkova to the elms can be sensed in this picture of the leaves of the oriental Zelkova serrata, *despite their characteristic serration. This is a broader-spreading tree than the Caucasian species opposite.*

the congested twigs fall off and make a mess. This shouldn't put anyone off planting a good and unusual tree in his garden. In its place the authorities plant either the Mississippi hackberry (*C. laevigata*), with mainly untoothed leaves, the Chinese hackberry (*C. sinensis*) with shiny, bright green leaves, or the southern European hackberry (*C. australis*). '*Australis*' in this usage simply means southern. The most unexpected fact about this tree is that its small, dark purple berry is the Lotos of Tennyson's mild-eyed, melancholy Lotos-eaters, no less. I'm afraid the spectacular pollination the poet describes–'Round and round the spicy downs the yellow Lotos-dust is blown'–would be quite beyond it. Did I say the berries were no reason to grow them? I'm not so sure.

The *Eucommia* is a lone Chinese species that offers proof to the sceptical of the closeness of the elms and the fig family (see next page). The figs include among their tropical members the rubber plant. The eucommia looks like a small elm, but has rubber in its veins. If you tear one of its leaves in half the barely-visible strands hold the two halves together. It is the only hardy tree that does contain rubber; not enough to make it a commercial proposition, but in an attractive and easily-grown tree perhaps enough of a reason to plant it.

American Nettle Tree.

The same species as the tree opposite: the Caucasian zelkova in summer (and comparative youth). At this age it is very like the American elm in shape. Cities hit by elm disease are planting it in the elm's place.

The leaves of the Caucasian zelkova are less toothed than those of the oriental species above. They turn yellow or bronze in autumn. The fruits are hard little nuts, unlike the elm's flat wafers and the hackberry's berries.

The American hackberry is much more like a small elm in general appearance than its leaves and certainly its berries would suggest. It is fast-growing and well-shaped; mature trees have a corky, thickly-ridged bark.

141

The Figs and Mulberries

Below *A mulberry tree planted by the poet Milton in the garden of Christ's College, Cambridge, was a place of pilgrimage in the 19th century. Centenarian mulberries often need props and wear a look of immense antiquity.*

What can you grow that gives a garden such a sense of established well-being as a fig tree or a mulberry? I've no doubt it is just witless harking back to a three-quarters-mythical past: the fig-tree mentioned so often in the Bible and popping out from under every fallen marble frieze in the ruins of the classical world, and the mulberry appearing from China in the Dark Ages—maybe long before—and with it the Secret of Silk.

Historical stuff apart, it would never have occurred to me that they belonged together, particularly as the one fig species hardy enough to grow in the temperate zone happens to be the only one with distinctly un-mulberryish, deeply-lobed leaves.

All the mulberry family have in common the white sap that contains latex. In the fruit department things are more complicated: mulberries, paper mulberries (*Broussonetia*) and osage oranges (*Maclura*) having essentially raspberry-like fruit, all globules and pips where the old flower-cluster was; the fig having a design of its own in which the flowers bloom (if that's the word) on the inside walls of a little fleshy funnel, which then swells around the pips to become the fig.

The hardy species (*Ficus carica*) can scarcely in fairness be described as a tree at the northern extremes of its range. It is more of a sprawling shrub, whose thin grey branches need support from a wall to reach any height. With a bit of care, however, it can be persuaded to ripen fruit in the south of England and in the United States as far north as New York. The trick to get it to fruit well is to give its roots the minimum space to ramble; feed them well in a tub. Certain cultivars can set fruit without pollination. Of all the late-summer garden pleasures there is nothing to beat a forage through the heavy, dusty-smelling leaves of the tree to find ripe figs. Their own leaves make a plate for them beside a bowl of cream cheese among the wine glasses. I cut them, not because biting them open isn't a pleasure, but to see the purple-violet-indigo of their livery opening to the silver of the knife.

Mulberries are gastronomically neglected. They are somehow not quite right as fruit, combining the extremes of squashiness and pippiness—yet the flavour, searchingly sour and hauntingly sweet, is very special.

The mulberry is an easy, though rather slow, tree to grow. You can plant cuttings even five feet long in autumn with every hope of starting something. The great question is where. It is ultimately a wide, sprawling, low-profile tree with fruit which,

Above left *A young mulberry on the west lawn at Polesden Lacey house, near London. Mulberry trees were much planted in England in the 17th century in the hope of starting a silk industry.*

Lower left *Light and shade in a mulberry tree in summer. The raspberry-like fruit ripen from light to dark red; few people today appreciate their sweet-acid flavour.*

Above right *The silk-moth has been cultivated in the orient for so long that it can no longer fly. Here an adult female moth sits with her eggs beside her silken cocoon.*

Lower right *An almost fully-fed silkworm (the caterpillar of the silk-moth) feeds on a black mulberry leaf. Silk is spun from the very fine thread with which the worm makes its cocoon.*

unless you eat it, falls abundantly to stain everything under it a fine shade of crimson. That is the black mulberry; the eating one. If you want to keep silkworms you will want the white mulberry, which grows a bit quicker. But the black makes a better garden set-piece: few small trees grow so gnarled and ancestral-looking.

The paper mulberry helps to link mulberry and fig; in terms of leaves, not fruit. Some of its leaves are more or less heart-shaped like the mulberry's; most are lobed and figgy. The fruit, not edible but pretty, is like a round red mulberry.

Some of the earliest Chinese paper was made from the bark of the paper mulberry by soaking it, smoothing it and finishing it with rice paste. In Japan it is still an important source of super-quality paper. As a tree it has some of the qualities of the common elder; it grows rank and tousled with soft and pithy wood almost anywhere.

One thoroughly off-beat American tree, the osage orange, limited in nature to parts of Kansas, Virginia, Georgia and Texas, can be dimly perceived to be a relation through the formation of its remarkable fruit. It does indeed look like an orange, but its bumpier surface suggests the same composite structure. Each fruit is in fact composed of many smaller ones tightly welded together.

Above *The parts of the flower and fruit of the black mulberry (letters a to g) and the common fig (letters h to v). A cluster of female flowers (f) of the mulberry develops into a cluster (c) of fruitlets (d)* *which is a mulberry. The fig-flowers (h) are clustered inside a swelling at the end of the stalk (in cross-section in s and complete in k). The male flowers are at the top; the female further in.*

Below *The common fig is a native of the Near East, at home in a Mediterranean climate but hardy surprisingly far north. In Britain it needs shelter and a good summer to ripen its soft sweet fruit.*

Right *The fig turns a bloomy purple and wrinkles when it is ripe. Fresh figs go beautifully with raw Italian ham or with cream cheese at the beginning or end of a meal.*

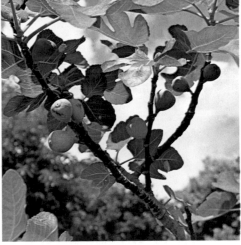

Left *The osage orange has little globular heads of flowers like the mulberry. They fuse together as they develop to form orange-sized yellow (inedible) fruit.*

The Walnuts

What makes a man proud and happy about having a walnut on his lawn? There can scarcely be a tree that puts on less of a show. It is one of the last bare trees of spring and the first of winter. Its leaves fall a sullen brown. Its catkins are by no means ornamental, coming with the leaves; nor is its fruit. It is stocky, heavy of detail and thick of limb and twig.

Can trees communicate extra-sensorily? A walnut can. It speaks of fatness and fertility even while it stands looking like a puritan about to close the theatres. What it offers is of the highest quality: the best timber and the best of all nuts.

Of the eight or nine species of walnut which inhabit Asia and America two are widely planted – the American (or black) and the English (or Persian). Hickories – those quintessentially American trees – are distantly allied. There is an Asiatic branch, too, the wingnuts, with very similar character and perhaps more beauty than either.

What all the family have in common are catkins; compound (often slightly fragrant) leaves with anything from five to 25 leaflets along a stalk up to two feet long; bold buds above pronounced scars from the old leaves; and nuts. Their twigs are distinctly knobbly and substantial, full of slight changes of

Walnut wood has some of the most beautiful colour and 'figure', or patterns of graining, of any tree. This portable writing cabinet was made in England in the early 18th century.

planted in a more desultory way, in hedge-rows and gardens. Grenoble in southeastern France has the great name for walnuts as fruit; the Dordogne in the southwest for walnuts as wood. In the Dordogne a walnut tree can be an important family asset. Demand ran away with supply many wars back. Walnuts are indispensable trees for gunstocks: for weight, elasticity and smoothness of touch there is apparently no comparable wood. Today the famous gunsmiths of London make special journeys to the Dordogne to find the best; the rest, one imagines, goes to make 17th-century furniture for the antique shops of Paris.

Circassian ('Persian') walnut from the Caucasus has always had the name for the most beautiful figure of all. It is like a troubled, swirling pool of browns, from parchment to near-black, on the brink of a weir that draws the ripples towards it.

The common English walnut (*J. regia*) grows slowly. It never makes such a big tree as the American (*J. nigra*), either in height or spread. The only attraction it has which the American lacks is a gleaming pale-grey bark: the black walnut's is blackish-brown. America's biggest black walnut is 111 feet high and 125 feet across from branch-tip to branch-tip, with a trunk 21 feet round. It grows almost as well as this in Europe, compared with our native's best performance of 80 feet or so.

The English walnut in fact is first choice for nuts. The American is the choice for ornament or timber, unless your family is prepared to wait twice as long for the ultimate quality; a chancy philosophy.

The American walnut has one nasty habit you should watch: it is capable of poisoning neighbouring trees and shrubs, particularly fruit trees (including its own offspring) with a substance called juglone in its roots. Apple trees near walnuts are often known to die mysteriously. It is a sinister development in the battle for survival; happily a secret the walnut can't impart to other trees.

direction that give them character compared with, say, the ash, which has similar leaves.

With so much in common it is often a job to tell them apart. The way to know a walnut from a hickory (in the absence of a nut) is to slice a twig longways: if the pith is solid it is hickory; if divided with air-pockets, a walnut or a wingnut. If it's a wingnut you're in an arboretum.

The walnut has a history of cultivation as long as the fig's. Its Latin name was concocted for it by the Romans when it came to them (via Greece) from Persia. *Juglans* was derived from *Jovis glans*–Jupiter's acorn.

Our name for it means simply 'foreign nut', from the same old German word Welsh as again meaning simply 'foreign'.

As a fruit tree the walnut has had a good deal of attention paid to it: there are a score or more of named clones, chosen for bigger fruit or more of it or thinner shells. The most famous, perhaps, is *J. regia* 'Franquette', a vigorous wide-spreading French tree with long, oval nuts, not specially big but full of meat, and the meat full of flavour.

The biggest orchards of the English walnut are in central California (125,000 acres) In Europe orchards are rare and it is

One of the best of the lesser-known walnuts is the Texan Juglans rupestris, *a small tree with dense masses of very narrow leaflets that give it a feathery look. It is hardier than its southern origin suggests.*

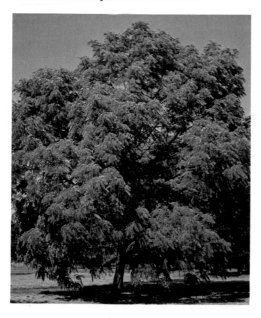

Hickories and Wingnuts

If the walnuts inherited the dignity in their family, it was the hickories and the wingnuts which inherited the looks.

The hickories are hardly known in Europe; not even for their superlative wood whose smoke goes up like incense from the barbecue-pits of America. Yet the vast forests of the eastern States, with their vitality and variety undreamed of in the Old World, have hardly a more characteristic ingredient.

It is not hard to characterize the hickories as a race. They are like taller and more graceful walnuts; more finely textured; in brighter colours. Their catkins, instead of being a single tassel, fork to become three-pronged. Their wood is the finest of all for the traditional offices of ash—for tool handles and firewood.

The most distinguished of them is the pecan (*Carya illinoensis*). It is also, alas, the least hardy: a native of the Mississippi basin, in Europe not happy north of central France, but ripening fruit in Bordeaux. If the walnut (nut, not tree) has a superior it is this.

Given the soil it likes (deep and moist) the pecan is the fastest of its race and makes the biggest tree—taking spread into account as well as height. A pecan in Tennessee, 106 feet high, is 136 feet in total width. The leaves are composed of many leaflets, the

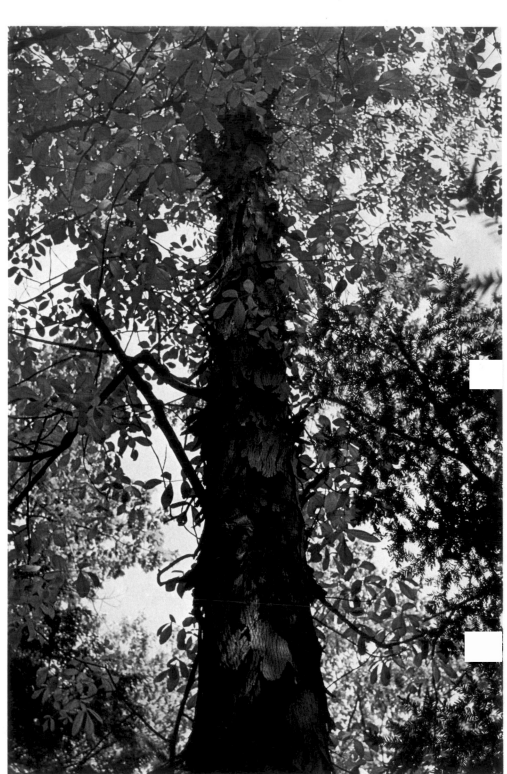

The hickories are the beauties of the walnut family, with long sweet-scented and rich-textured compound leaves. The shagbark hickory has the fewest and biggest leaflets. All hickories colour well in shades of warm yellow in autumn.

The trunk of a tall shagbark hickory is covered with stiff curling and crackling bark—possibly a defence against nut-hunting animals. The shagbark covers a vast territory, and grows as well in Europe as in North America.

Below *The leaves and fruit of four important hickories. Left, the bitternut, a magnificent tree (see photograph below) but with inedible fruit.*

The shagbark: on the right behind the leaf is a typical three-branched hickory catkin. The shagbark's nut is white and always quartered.

The mockernut: planted chiefly for its drooping sweet-scented leaves; a smaller tree than the bitternut. The name refers to the fact that the nuts are often empty.

The pecan has the longest leaves and the sweetest fruit of all the hickories. But it is less adaptable than the other species, demanding hot summers to grow well.

longest of all the hickories', and every leaflet is gracefully curved. Bulk and grace combine to make a most impressive tree.

The pecan has only one problem. All the hickories have it and so to some extent do the walnuts: they hate being moved. Nurseries don't like them, and often don't stock them, for this reason. At best they sulk; usually they die. The only thing to do is to plant them out tiny—or bury some nuts.

The easiest hickory to identify is the shagbark (*C. ovata*). If ever there was a case where the botanist who christened the tree in Latin should have seen it first it is this. But he was Philip Miller, 3,500 miles away at the Chelsea Physic Garden, and all he had was a few leaves and a few (oval) nuts. Had he seen the amazing trunk of the tree he would have ransacked mythology for some old witch in moth-eaten rags to express its appalling look of wear and tear.

It is when the shagbark comes to fruiting age, at 30 or 40 years, that its trim trunk starts to tatter. It may well be an evolutionary adaptation which has proved successful in keeping squirrels away from the nuts. Certainly the sharp-edged strips of bark, still rigid although apparently ready to fall, must present them with a problem.

The shagbark has fewest leaflets per leaf; only five; the end one bigger than the rest.

It is an upright, tower-headed tree, its spread only half its height or less. The tallest, 132 feet high and 64 feet across, is in Texas.

The bitternut (*C. cordiformis*) has a pale yellow bud, curving and without covering scales, which is unlike any of the others. This is the most widespread of the family and the commonest, reaching as far north as Minnesota and Maine, where it turns from its gay green to a lovely straw yellow in autumn. It is also unfortunately the one with totally inedible fruit.

The mockernut (*C. tomentosa*)—its fruit, almost empty, is the mockery—has the alternative name of bigbud, which tells its story precisely. The velvety grey end bud is twice as thick as the twig behind it. This is the commonest southern hickory; not a big tree compared with the others, but excellent for timber and liked, also, for having sweet-smelling leaves.

One more, the pignut, is important and relatively distinctive for the smoothness of bud and twig, and glossiness of the undersides of its leaves, which give it its Latin name of *C. glabra* (literally, smooth hickory). It has the same range as the shagbark.

The Caucasian wingnut (*Pterocarya fraxinifolia*) comes into that class of trees, like the worthy *Zelkova*, which are strong, trouble-free, easy to grow, decorative and in

every way to be recommended, but which are hardly ever planted, simply because they are strangers. Ideally it likes a climate more continental than the British; the eastern U.S.A. up to say New York would be ideal for it. It also likes moist ground. Given these it quickly forms a huge dome on a short trunk with the liveliness of millions of leaflets on long stalks. By July its winged nuts are developing from the catkins in long yellowy-green streamers all over the tree. The hybrid *Pterocarya × rehderana* from the Arnold Arboretum is even more prolific in catkins: a tree to stop and gaze at, and at a time of year when flowering trees are few.

The bitternut is one of the tallest and most vigorous of the hickories: easy to identify in winter by its bright yellow buds. Hickories must be planted out small: they never grow well after transplanting at larger sizes.

The wingnuts are another group of trees that deserve to be better known. They grow fast to oak-like shapes with long elaborate leaves and catkins, followed by chains of nuts. These are the nuts of the Chinese wingnut (Pterocarya stenoptera).

The dangling nut-chains of the ash-leaved wingnut from the Caucasus, a bigger tree than the Chinese, but with a liking for damp soil and a hot summer.

Top *The wingnuts are at their most ornamental in summer when their pale nut-chains hang all over their spreading crowns. A cross between the Chinese and Caucasian, Pterocarya × rehderana is the most vigorous and splendid of all of them.*

Above *An expanding shoot-tip of the Caucasian wingnut, covered in a layer of brown wool. The embryo leaves are still tightly folded like fans and the flower spikes before expanding are like little brown catkins.*

The Beeches

A painting of a famous old beech tree at Windsor by the English artist Paul Sandby, 1832. Beeches are not as long-lived as oaks: they rarely survive to become as bulky and gnarled as this tree.

The beech family in its broad sense, embracing beeches, oaks and sweet chestnuts, is the royal family of the broadleaves by any reckoning. It has the oak for king and the beech for queen.

Oaks spread over more of the temperate world than any other broadleaf tree. There are some 450 species, evergreen and deciduous. There are shrubs among them, but most of them are big trees.

There are fewer beeches and less beech forest. None the less, the beech grows in the three northern continents and appears again in a modified but recognizable form in the southern hemisphere. It is the only broadleaf tree to be established in force on both sides of the equator.

The chestnut, closely kin to the oak, is the third major member of the family. What marks all three of them as close relations is their fruit. Acorns, chestnuts and the 'mast' of beeches are all formed in the same way: by the woody base of the female flower growing to form a husk round the seed.

If there is a royal seat it is surely Normandy. It is there that the beech grows to perfection, in woods of amazing purity and grandeur. At Lyons-la-Forêt, near Rouen, illustrated on these pages, beeches that seeded themselves during the French Revolution now soar clear and smooth-boled to 100 feet, into a green canopy 30 feet deep shutting out the sky. One cannot avoid the feeling that the inspiration for the great Norman cathedrals came from the ancestors of this solemn forest.

The beech is a much-shorn tree, excellently adapted for making hedges. Appropriately enough, the monarch of all hedges is of beech. It stands at Meikleour, about ten miles north of Perth in the Highlands of Scotland, a green wall 580 yards long and no less than 95 feet high. It is kept trimmed up to 60 feet—but beyond that ingenuity (and courage, I shouldn't wonder) is exhausted. ▶

The fruit of the beech family clearly links its members. Their nuts are all more or less enclosed in a woody sheath which grows up from the base of the female flower. The 'mast' of the beech (top left) has two nuts completely enclosed until they are ripe and the husk splits open as here. The acorn of the oak has one, sitting in an open cup. The chestnut has one, two or three nuts wrapped entirely in a prickly shell.

The autumn colour of beeches varies from yellow to russet to deep foxy red. They are a small and homogeneous race of trees, easily recognizable even in their ornamental and exotic forms.

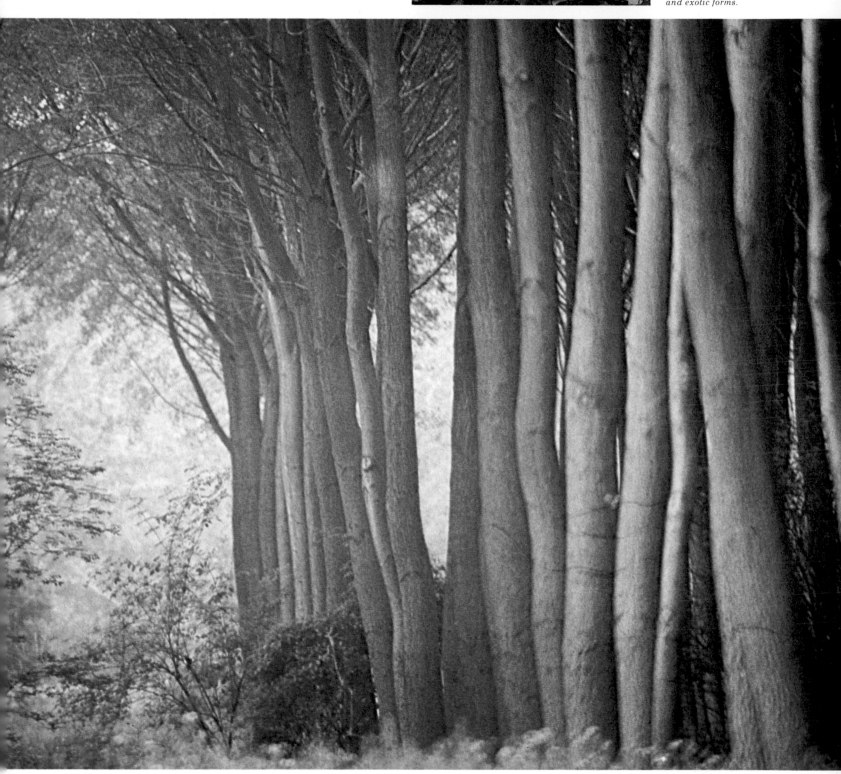

Century-old beeches in one of the great beech-woods of Normandy, at Lyons-la-Forêt near Rouen. The beech makes dark woods, casting deep shade with its layers of leaves. All the lower branches die off to leave tall trunks of silver-grey.

149

The Beeches

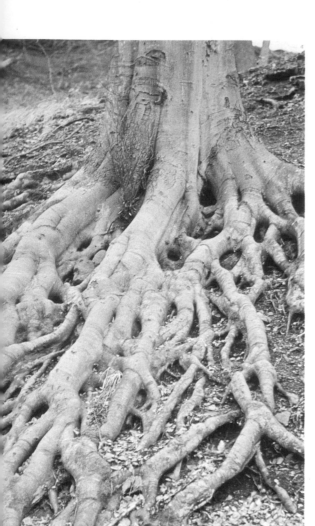

Above *The erosive action of rain has laid bare this labyrinthine pattern of beech roots. Surface-rooting is one of the factors that make beech a very competitive tree, able to starve out other species.*

Below *The darkest of the copper or purple beeches is named 'Riversii' after the 18th-century English nursery firm of Thomas Rivers. Many shades of purple exist but all grow darker in late summer.*

▶ Odd that the beech has not seen fit to diversify in the same way as the oak. The eight or nine species are almost interchangeable, save for a bigger, smaller, longer or rounder leaf. The beech is clearly the logical end of its own evolutionary road, just as it is the final winner in a struggle for dominance in the forest.

An old beechwood has the longest echo of any woodland: a sound so eerie and disturbing that I remember it vividly from when I was a boy of four living on the chalk hills of Buckinghamshire. (The 'Buck' of Buckingham in fact means beech.) The beech thrives on lean chalk where other trees flag. In due course it takes it over completely; scarcely a bramble, barely a toadstool grow in the moss below the massed beech boles of the Chiltern hills. Their layered canopy lets only threads of sunlight through. Hence the long-answering echo; the echo of an empty room.

The beech's domineering methods, of filling the surface of the ground with fine roots, and covering it with heavy shade, certainly don't show in its face. Of all the big trees it is one of the daintiest; one of the most graceful in angles and movements, one of the lightest and most feminine in colour, one of the smoothest in texture.

Rather than accumulate calloused old corky stuff to form a protective layer of bark, the beech's cambium stays almost on the surface; its trunk remains smooth and silvery and fresh-looking. By the same token it needs the shade it is so good at making with its layer upon layer of leaves, all horizontally aligned. A beech grown in the open keeps branches right down to the ground to protect its trunk from sunlight. To see the sun playing on its pale curves and hollows – paler in the American beech, like the bloom on old aluminium – is one of the winter pleasures. You could argue that the beech is best in early winter. Its leaves turn sometimes to the colour of golden burnt butter, sometimes to the clear coppery red of a fox's brush, before they fall. But one in ten of those on young trees hangs on to the lower branches up to eight or nine feet from the ground. Between the red drifts on the ground and the red spume in the air (and dare I mention the azure firmament behind?), the silver shaft is dazzling. Summer with its geraniums has no monopoly of nature's colours.

The American beech (*F. grandifolia*) is reluctant to grow in Europe. The European (or common) beech (*F. sylvatica*) has no such qualms about America: which is just as well, since it is the one with all the interesting cultivars. Beech's commonest manifestation in gardens is in hedges, for which it is perfectly suited. But next after hedges comes, undoubtedly, the purple or the copper beech

– understandably popular as by far the biggest red thing there is to grow.

Red beeches have turned up many times in the wilds – usually, for some reason, in the middle of Europe: in Switzerland, Bavaria or eastern France. At their earliest appearances they were inevitably rumoured to be the mark of nature's disapproval of some unnatural crime – the blood refusing to lie down. Redness is a fairly stable characteristic of these trees; often their seedlings are red too. A number of shades of red are registered in different varietal names. 'Cuprea' has been used for the lightest, supposedly copper-coloured; 'Rivers Purple' for the darkest, a full-blooded purple. But nurseries don't often offer a choice – and since beeches all go through the whole range of colours, from new leaves of rosy-red silk to a browny-purple final stage in autumn, it is hard to know which colour is the one to put a name to.

The fern-leafed beech (*F. sylvatica heterophylla*) is a more subtle and, truthfully, far more beautiful tree. Its leaves are deeply cut into narrow points that somehow give the whole tree a much finer and less shiny texture: a matt effect which soaks up the light. It is difficult to see why this tree is quite as effective as it is; and yet if any tree in old

Left *Mature leaves of the common European beech and three fully-grown, but not yet ripe, fruits. Beech fruit, known as 'mast', splits into four and releases two triangular nuts.*

A beechwood in autumn. The floor is bare of all save beech-leaves, thanks to the shade cast by the horizontal layers of foliage. Being shallow-rooted, beech is apt to be blown over in a gale.

Above *The Botanical Garden at Leiden in Holland has one of the biggest and most splendid weeping beeches in the world.*

Left *The upright, or Dawyck, beech was discovered in a Scottish garden in the last century. It makes a superb tower of pale shining green.*

A hybrid between the cut-leafed beech (whose leaves are almost as fine as these) and the copper beech: a remarkable tree called Fagus sylvatica 'Ansorgei', which is not too vigorous to grow on a moderate-sized lawn.

parkland has people streaming up for a closer look it is always this one.

I am probably alone in thinking the weeping beech a monstrosity. But it comes near the bottom of my list of weeping trees; the ash and the elm both weep far more convincingly. The beech's are surely crocodile tears, or indeed – as Hillier's *Manual* perceptively suggests – elephant's. I quote: 'the enormous branches hang close to and perpendicular with the main stem like an elephant's trunk'. Nothing like as bad as a weeping sequoia, which looks like a boa-constrictor trying to take off. But still far from graceful.

Possibly the most useful of all the variants is still a fairly new tree; clearly with a lot of planting ahead of it. It was Mr. Naesmith of Dawyck who found it. Dawyck is an estate in the Tweed valley in lowland Scotland which has been in the hands of tree lovers since Elizabethan times. Mr. Naesmith was the incumbent in 1860 when up sprang a beech with the stance of a Lombardy poplar, the perfect compromise for people who want a beech tree but haven't got room. The Dawyck beech (*F. sylvatica* 'Dawyck') is formal when young, but big ones are huge leafy ovals. As a street tree, where shade was not the main need, it would be hard to beat.

Above *The demented growth of the 'Tortuosa' beech. These rare trees occur in a line through Denmark, Champagne, and Le Cosquer in Brittany (above). A radioactive meteor centuries ago may have caused the malformation.*

151

The Southern Beeches

The world has been pretty thoroughly ransacked for trees. It is unlikely that even in China any significant genus remains undiscovered. There is, however, one highly significant and decorative one which is still virtually unexploited and unknown: the southern beeches. Here is a race of trees of remarkable singularity, style and speed. But where do you see them? Few nurseries have ever heard of them.

The southern beeches are *Nothofagus*; the beeches, *Fagus*, of the southern hemisphere. The botanical differences between the two are relatively minor. They are very different trees, though, to look at. Some of them are deciduous, some are evergreen, but the hallmark of most is a tiny leaf—at biggest, perhaps half the size of a beech leaf: at smallest, smaller than a box tree's.

What is the advantage of a tiny leaf? To the gardener it is a question of texture. Evenness and flatness may not sound very exciting, but they are the qualities that draw the crowds to the fern-leaved beech (see the previous page).

Close to, it is a question of the pleasure taken in anything miniature and precise. In the Antarctic beech (*N. antarctica*), for example, the leaves are disposed in two neat rows along the slender twigs, each leaf a crinkled, nervy, shell-like *objet*.

There are southern beeches in both Australasia and South America; a fact which confirms that the southern land-masses have separated relatively recently. The hardiest and best-tried are the Chilean species. Novelty can't be the reason for their remaining in an esoteric niche; two of them were introduced to botany in the 1820s.

Of the deciduous Chilean species the Antarctic beech is perhaps the most characteristic and the least rare. It has a tendency in Britain to make a wide bush rather than a tree; one I have seems to be modelling itself after a corkscrew.

The evergreen southern beech Nothofagus cunninghamii *from Tasmania is typical of the genus in its tiny leaves. The red of the new shoots recalls the autumn colour of its deciduous relations.*

'Black beech', Nothofagus solandri, *growing in the foothills of the Southern Alps of New Zealand. It forms enormous pure forests ascending to the snowline.*

The Antarctic beech from Chile, Nothofagus antarctica, *sometimes fails to make a straight trunk at all, but spreads into a huge shrub-like form of twisting branches.*

The deciduous leaves of the Chilean Antarctic beech are almost as small as those of the black beech. Clusters of yellow flowers hang from the branches in spring.

As a piece of autumn colour the Antarctic beech is also quite remarkable; it changes colour leaf by leaf, and into several different shades. The effect is a mosaic of green, red, orange and brown, all over the tree. Its rather obvious and fish-bony branching pattern adds point to the performance.

Two other Chilean deciduous beeches *N. procera* and *N. obliqua*, have bigger leaves. *Procera's* leaves are paler with more marked veins, not unlike a hornbeam's. Its buds stand out from the twigs at an angle like the beech's. *Obliqua*, darker green with shinier and more toothed leaves, looks more like a chestnut. Both are enormously fast-growing and colour well in autumn.

The only evergreen species I have had a chance to get to know is the Chilean *N. dombeyi*. The fishbone branching pattern in this is almost as pronounced as in some young elms. In leaf it is like the Antarctic beech, only darker, the leaves set alternately and rather close together on red twigs, flecked, as the branches of some cherries are, with white horizontal streaks. On the grey trunk these white streaks persist, scaled up.

Another Chilean evergreen, *N. betuloides*, the New Zealand black beech, *N. solandri*, and its form *cliffortioides* are very similar. The Chilean ones are reckoned hardier in Britain, but in a climate like California's they would all grow, one would think, like beans. Their only dislikes are wind and lime in the soil.

Most of the southern beeches are easy to propagate by cuttings. Surely a few more nurserymen must be tempted?

Above and below *The prominently veined leaves of another of the Chilean deciduous southern beeches,* Nothofagus procera, *are some of the biggest of the genus—up to four inches long. They are remarkably like those of the hornbeam. In autumn (above) they take on various warm shades of pink and brown. The fruit of procera (below, unripe) is very like that of the familiar beeches.*

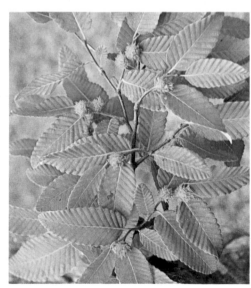

A typical upright fan-shaped spray of the ever-green black beech of New Zealand. It makes a slender tall tree whose tiny leaves give it great elegance. The form Nothofagus cliffortioides *is a close relation with even smaller leaves.*

The Oaks

'"Robur, the Oak". I have sometimes considered it very seriously, what would move Pliny to make a whole chapter of one only line.' So John Evelyn begins the first chapter of his *Sylva*.

Pliny, and Evelyn, were right. The oak carries such a cargo of symbolism that embroidery is counter-productive.

Robur, the Oak.

'I wonder if you ever thought of the single mark of supremacy which distinguishes this tree? The others shirk the work of resisting gravity; the oak defies it. It chooses the horizontal direction for its limbs, so that their whole weight may tell; and then stretches them fifty or sixty feet . . . to slant upward another degree would mark infirmity of purpose; to bend downwards, weakness of organization.'

This is Oliver Wendell Holmes, *The Autocrat of the Breakfast Table*, chapter Ten. I beg you to find the book and read on to where he goes to look for New England's biggest elm.

In Britain it seems as though a sort of race memory still exists of the time when the whole country was oakwood. Even in Henry VIII's time, 450 years ago, one-third of the whole island was still covered by oak trees. Still, today, if good land is left fallow, oak will very likely find its way there and cover it before ten years are out.

There are 450 species of oak in the world. There is one that started the legend. Oak grows in every form: as tree, as bush, as scrub; deciduous or evergreen: in Europe, Asia and America. But the oak of imagery is the English oak: broad and slow, angular and ponderous-branched; *Quercus robur*.

I should hasten to say that there are two species of oak in England and northern Europe, *Q. robur* and *Q. petraea*; that they are quite distinct (though they often hybridize) and that I have no evidence (or not much) for offering one as the original of the oak-image and not the other.

Typically, the English, common, or pedunculate oak (*Q. robur* has all these names) is the broad tree, not specially tall, that the *Autocrat* was talking about. Typically the durmast or sessile oak (*Q. petraea*) is a taller, more upward-reaching tree.

True, it depends above all on where they are growing. In an open field both will be broad and spreading; in close forest both need to aspire towards the overhead light. You have to remember, therefore, that the pedunculate oak has its acorns on peduncles or stalks; the durmast has them sitting on the twig. The leaves are the other way round: the short-stalked leaves of the pedunculate form stiff rosettes at the ends of the twigs, making the canopy broken, with patches of sky showing through. The stalked leaves of the durmast oak give an even coverage; a shaftless, uniform shade.

The great oak forests of central France where Europe's tallest oaks grow, above all the Forêt de Tronçais, planted by Colbert for the French navy in the 18th century, are durmast woods. In the west of England durmast is in the majority. In an eastern, or midland, or southern English park on the other hand, the huge, broken-headed hulks, reputed (often rightly) to have been there 500 years or more, and all their gnarled and leafy offspring are common oak. As far as the navy was concerned, there were never enough of these trees. Their awkward, angular way of growing gave the shipwright the hugely powerful brackets and angle-pieces that held a 74-gun ship together as she blundered through the troughs on her way into the line.

Queen Elizabeth's Treasurer, Lord Burghley, was the first man to plant oaks. He sowed acorns and holly berries together, shrewdly giving his saplings evergreen cover that would never smother them. It was held that bigger acorns make better trees, so they were sieved and only the biggest were planted.

Intensive cultivation produced its crop of ornamental cultivars. An excellent upright version of the common oak, Lombardy-poplar style (*Q. robur* 'Fastigiata'), is perhaps the best. The rest are rare, but there exist a cut-leafed version (*Q.* × *rosacea* 'Filicifolia'); a purple version (*Q. robur* 'Atropurpurea'); a golden version (*Q. r.* 'Concordia'); and a rather anaemic variegated version (*Q. r.* 'Variegata').

By the mid-18th century most of the oaks of Europe and the Mediterranean region were well known and enthusiastically cultivated. A number of hybrids of permanent value arose in the nurseries, where oaks quite foreign to each other were planted side by side.

1 *English oaks in the snow* 2 *The leaves and acorns of an English oak in the late summer* 3 *A young pedunculate oak in a French hedgerow* 4 *The male flowers of the English oak (magnified)* 5 *The embryo acorns of the cork oak formed in the angles of its (evergreen) leaves.*

Turner's oak, the Fulham oak and the Kew oak are all examples that have been famous in their time. The most famous and the most used today was a chance seedling in the Exeter nursery of Lucombe & Pince in 1762. The parents were the vigorous Turkey oak (*Q. cerris*) and the evergreen cork oak (*Q. suber*). The Lucombe oak (*Q.* × *hispanica* 'Lucombeana') has the most useful attributes of both its parents short of providing cork. It is a most distinguished and huge-growing almost-evergreen, with beautiful glowing-green leaves with a golden cast.

Oaks continue to plant themselves, but not many are planted today. Mainly, one supposes, because they are notoriously slow. It is worth examining, therefore, just how fast or slow they are.

On a piece of land which was completely cleared 15 years ago I have oaks 25 feet high, from acorns presumably sown by jays the year the land was cleared. True, if they were poplars they could be 60 feet by now, but is 25 feet in 15 years (or say conservatively 15 feet in 10 years) so slow? It's certainly a satisfying rate of progress to watch.

One should not underestimate young oaks as ornament. The Lammas shoots which make all oaks glow with new life in mid-summer show up most on a young tree. Last year one particular tree was so covered with new pink and golden leaves that no flowering cherry could have been more spectacular; and it took them six weeks to fade through pale green to dark. The same tree, in a sheltered place, has kept its brown leaves on all winter like a young beech. In that tree's future there is really something to look forward to.

The Oaks of Europe and Asia

The tendency to keep their leaves late in the season, dead or alive, is clearly an oak family trait. The oaks as a whole give the impression that evergreenery is never very far away. Many of the oaks of the south, whether in Europe or America, are outright evergreens. Others (especially the big-leafed species) hang on to their leaves for as long as they can. In northern Europe this is often until January. In the south it is until the new crop of leaves takes over in spring.

The holm oak is by far the most familiar of the Mediterranean species and far and away the biggest and best broadleaved evergreen we can grow as far north as Britain. (In the U.S.A., as far north as Washington D.C.) It seems to break all the rules, exposing a mass of leaf to the cruel winter winds. Yet it takes a severe winter to defoliate it, even partially – and even then the tree is often unharmed.

The name 'holm' (and also the Latin name, *Q. ilex*) means holly. It may have been the shock of seeing another green broadleaf in winter which caused the comparison, because, though its young leaves are spiny, the adult leaves have nothing like the shine nor the spines of the holly. Holm oak leaves vary from plain ovals to distinctly toothed shapes, from thumb-nail size to three inches or so, and from quite pale green in shade to a dark gloss in the sun. The tree's best moment, like the yew's, is when the young growth of the spring shows against the near-black background of the old. A white moss of hairs covers the fresh leaves; as they open they glow amber and tawny. The broad dome of a big tree, dressed with drooping branches to the ground, and creaming over with these quiet colours, is spring's most solemn celebration.

Being such good shade-bearers makes close-grown holm oaks quite remarkable. They grow tall and slim like any forest tree, but without losing their lower leaves and branches. I have seen full-dressed trees 60 feet high and not ten across in a forest clearing; perhaps the most elegant of all evergreens. There is no better tree for the architectural backbone of a garden or park.

The other evergreen oak of the Mediterranean is the cork oak, *Q. suber*. It is not quite so hardy as the holm oak, neither is it such a big and good-looking tree. Its interest lies in its bark, which is usually displayed (as the elephant-skin bark of the holm oak is not) by its open and haphazard way of growing. Old cork oaks usually lean at perilous angles which go with the exaggerated cragginess of the trunk to make a convincing picture of age. Cork as a commercial proposition is still pretty well confined to Portugal and Spain. South of the Tagus in Portugal the country is orchard-like for mile

Left *The sessile or durmast oak, native of most of Europe and western Britain, is often a taller and less spreading tree than the common English oak. France's finest oak-forests are of this species.*

Below left *The Turkey oak is the fastest-growing and most adaptable European species. Its acorn is distinctive for its densely mossy cup. The rough leaves vary in shape from oval to oblong.*

Above *The cork oak of Spain and Portugal is still the world's principal source of cork. The thick, rugged bark is stripped off every ten or 15 years.*

Below *The male catkins of durmast oak are yellow and easily visible. The female flowers sit, like the acorns, stalkless in the angles of the leaves. The durmast's leaves are generally bigger than those of the closely allied (and similar) English oak.*

after mile among the spreading, stunted cork-trees. Recently, though, there have been plantations in California and the southern States.

In many ways the ideal plant for a public place is one that is slightly larger than life. Not a ferocious-looking exotic that makes the native greenery look dowdy, but a close relation with a touch of extra ginger. Just enough to wake people up with the surprise of, let us say, an oak with such big leaves.

This alone would be reason enough to bring back the neglected big-leaf oaks of southern Europe, even if they were not in

their own right singularly splendid, vigorous and adaptable trees.

There are three outstanding oaks which once were famous: the Hungarian (*Q. frainetto*), the Algerian (*Q. canariensis*) and the Caucasian (*Q. macranthera*). They all have leaves about six inches long – not as long as some of the American oaks', but long enough to give a distinctively tulgy look.

The Caucasian and Algerian oaks are easily confusable; the Hungarian has much deeper lobes – even two inches deep – in its splendid leaves. All are eventually trees of the biggest size.

Another distinctive pair of oaks from the

The oaks of the orient are still rare in western gardens. Quercus glauca *is a beautiful small evergreen species from China with blue-white undersides to the leathery little leaves.*

Several southern European oaks have bold and shiny leaves twice the size of the common English oak. The Caucasian Quercus macranthera *is one of these noble and eye-catching trees, perfectly hardy in northern Europe.*

The English oak has produced several ornamental cultivars, among them the slow-growing but attractive 'Atropurpurea'; the leaves and shoots are suffused with a rich purple, turning greyish-purple on mature trees.

Left A lion's head, carved in oak, from the French royal palace of Fontainebleau. This carving is a work of the school of André Gobert, the court woodcarver to Louis XIV.

Right At Dyrham Park in Gloucestershire a row of holm oaks under a bank have inclined steadily outwards from the shade of the trees above. Given the option, holm oak will choose the light, but it grows well in shade and (amongst other difficult conditions) near the sea.

Leaves of the holm (or holly-leaved) oak are glossy but without the glitter of holly. They fall in early summer and resist rotting, which can make them a problem in gardens. The acorns take 18 months to ripen.

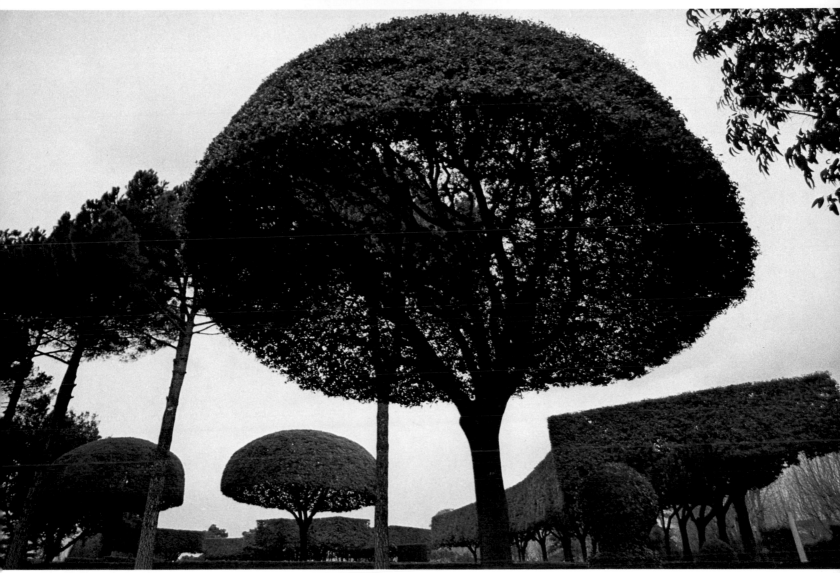

Near East have narrow leaves, not lobed (i.e. with the wavy coastline of most oak leaves) but with a regular row of little points, or teeth; ten or 15 a side. The general effect is very much like a chestnut leaf. One of them, in fact, is called the chestnut-leafed oak (*Q. castaneifolia*); the other the Lebanon oak (*Q. libani*). Like chestnuts' their leaves are dark green and shiny; like oaks', they hang on until the new year.

The only one of this southern group which could be called at all common is the Turkey oak, *Q. cerris*. It has the reputation of being the fastest-growing and could perhaps make in time the tallest tree. At one time the navy had great hopes of it, but its wood proved a disappointment. Its leaves are all points and angles, not oversize but eye-catching. Most important, perhaps, it grows well on unpromising dry and chalky soil.

The oaks of the Far East in cultivation are not (yet, at any rate) such big trees. The outstanding ones are the sawtooth oak (*Q. acutissima*) from Japan, a very similar tree to the chestnut-leafed oak, and the daimyo oak (*Q. dentata*) which has the biggest leaves of any, sometimes over a foot long. *Q. acuta* and *Q. glauca*, both small evergreen trees, and *Q. variabilis*, the Chinese cork oak, occasionally turn up in collections.

Above The evergreen holm oak of the Mediterranean makes massive hedges and thrives under clipping almost as well as yew. It will grow on all types of well-drained soil. This garden is at the American University in Rome.

In the middle ages oak was important as a source of pig-food. Forests were assessed by the number of swine which could live on their acorns. The swineherd was still a familiar figure in 16th-century Germany when this engraving was made.

157

The Oaks of North America

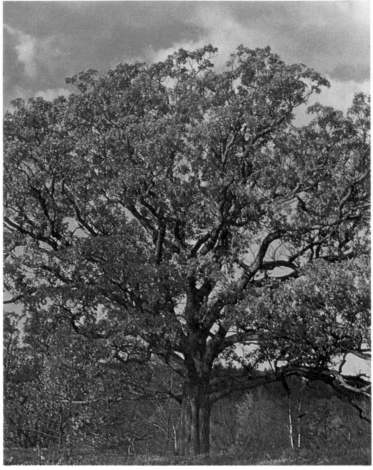

The American Oaks

The oaks of North America present a daunting picture at first. Yet there are certain key features which help one to classify and recognize the individual species. The chart on the right shows the leaves and acorns of 25 of the most important ones. The trees are divided according to their black/white affinities, the shape of their leaf (lobed or unlobed), whether they are deciduous or evergreen, and their native habitat – whether they belong east or west of the Rockies.

Left *The black oak of the eastern States* (Quercus velutina), *one of the tallest of all oaks; a tower of dark glossy green, turning red in autumn, up to 140 feet in good moist soil.*

Above *The white oak, most characteristically oak-like of all the American species with its mighty dome. The leaves turn from autumn purples and reds to golden brown.*

Left *The red oak* (Quercus rubra) *is more amenable to transplanting than either the white or the black and grows faster than any other American oak. It has golden new shoots and red autumn colour.*

Above *The California white or valley oak is the biggest oak of the west, the tree that makes parts of the Central valley look like a park. The best specimen today is 120 feet high, 103 feet in spread and 28 feet in girth.*

White

East

Deeply lobed

Burr (or mossycup)
Q. macrocarpa
Very big long-trunked drought-resisting oak of the mid-west.

Overcup *Q. lyrata:*
Wet ground oak of south. Acorn almost enclosed.

Post *Q. stellata:*
Slow drought-resisting upland oak commonest in eastern Texas.

White *Q. alba:*
The classical oak of America, native from Maine to Texas. Wide-spreading.

Shallowly lobed

Chestnut
Q. prinus:
Limited north-eastern range; medium-sized; biggest acorn of all.

Chinkapin (or yellow chestnut)
Q. muehlenbergii:
Fast limestone-loving, uncommon; acorns sweet.

Swamp chestnut (or basket)
Q. michauxii;
Big southern oak, rich yellow autumn colour.

Swampwhite
Q. bicolor.
Wide-branched shaggy oak with flaking bark from northern midwest.

West

California white (or valley) *Q. lobata:*
Biggest western hardwood: broad, spreading.

Oregon white *Q. garryana:*
Similar to Eastern white; only oak of north-west.

Black

East

Deeply lobed

Black *Q. velutina:*
Very tall, fast, relatively short-lived with wide range throughout east.

Nuttall *Q. nuttallii:*
Grows with sweetgum on Mississippi; fast, tall, smooth-trunked.

Pin *Q. palustris:*
Most popular and graceful oak for eastern/mid-western suburbs; likes wet ground.

(Northern) Red
Q. rubra:
Common, adaptable, vigorous, spreading. Good autumn colour.

Scarlet *Q. coccinea:*
Eastern upland oak, fast growth to medium size. Best autumn colour of all.

Shumard *Q. shumardii:*
Uncommon but splendid tall southern oak, north to Ohio.

Southern red (or Spanish)
Q. falcata:
Common southern upland oak with a long trunk and high dome.

Unlobed

Laurel *Q. laurifolia:*
Tall, dense, deep-southern almost evergreen. Unusually fast early growth.

Shingle *Q. imbricaria:*
Once used for roofing, now uncommon. Eight-inch shiny leaves are downy beneath.

Water *Q. nigra:*
Similar to laurel oak with wider range; fast-growing and tall; leaves persistent, unlobed on mature trees.

Evergreen

Live *Q. virginiana:*
Huge-domed, moss-covered oak of the south. Vast horizontal limbs.

Willow *Q. phellos:*
Big oak of east and south with fine texture of a willow. Superb ornamental.

West

California black
Q. kelloggii:
Similar to eastern black; leaves bristle-tipped. Medium to big.

Canyon live
Q. chrysolepis:
Small yellow-downy evergreen, common from Yosemite to Oregon coast.

Coast live *Q. agrifolia:*
Superb broad shade tree from San Francisco southward, often dotted in golden grassland.

At times the great American forest seems like an oakwood with intruders—so many splendid species are there. Eighty grow in North America and 60 of them are full-fledged trees.

There can be few people who have mastered the whole catalogue, though when you start breaking it down into the more obvious distinctions—region, deciduous or evergreen, whether the leaves are lobed or not and the colour of the bark—the process of identification works pretty quickly. The truth is, however, that in most parts of America there is an obvious oak to plant—the one that grows there already.

The most noticeable distinction is between the live oaks (as the evergreen species are called) and the deciduous ones. The live oaks in fact are few: one in the east and half a dozen in the west.

The real botanical distinction is between white and black oaks (which include the red oaks and all the live oaks). There is no single great give-away here, but enough clear differences to make it quite easy.

In the northeast *the* white oak, *Quercus alba*, has its domain. In what way is it typical of its group? Its name, it seems, comes from the colour of its trunk, which is grey and scaly, contrasting with the blackish and furrowed trunks of the black oaks. The deep lobes of its leaves are rounded at the ends, without points or bristles. Its acorns are reasonably sweet to eat, their cups are shiny inside. And they stay on the tree for only one season; they fall in autumn and germinate straight away—often to be killed by frost before they have got established.

The red oak (*Q. rubra*) is the protagonist of the blacks. Its bark is blackish-brown and corrugated. The leaves have less indented bays, but their lobes are sharp-pointed and their points have little bristles. Acorns last two years on the tree; when they fall they wait until spring before germinating. Their meat is bitter and their cups are downy inside instead of shiny.

By and large the rules of identification apply. Often one of the typical features is missing. There are no bristled lobes, for example, on the (black) willow oaks. In the last resort the botanist's criterion has been the wood structure, which divides the two groups perfectly in accordance with the other evidence. White oak timber is, on the whole, much the better. It is an odd side-light that the white oaks are miserable in Europe and hardly grow at all, while the black have done excellently.

The big variations in leaf shape that occur within each group help the identification process considerably. The chart above shows the principal trees—far more black than white, and far more in the east than in the west. The map overleaf shows the total range of the two groups and the site of the biggest known tree of each species—an indication of where it feels most at home. ▶

The Oaks of North America

▶ Differences in acorns and leaves seem to suggest that there is considerable variation between the species of oaks–but how much, in fact, do they differ in life style?

In outright hardiness they vary surprisingly little; some of the southern oaks will grow even in New York, though they lose the leaves they might have kept, at home, through most of the winter. They all have their favourite haunts: moist river bottoms, gravelly gullies or rocky open hills. In overall size they can certainly vary: from the cliff-like 125 feet of occasional black oaks to the mere 50 feet of, say, the blue oaks of California, not to mention some of the scrub oaks that never make a tree. On the other hand, most oaks with space to spread settle for a medium height: 70 feet or so.

There are three characteristics in particular that single out certain oaks as trees of real beauty: their habit of branching, their texture and their autumn colour.

The classic oak branch pattern–bold, wide and angular on a stocky trunk–is best expressed by the white oak. The Oregon white and the burr oaks are similar. The others in their group approach it, though they are rarely so perfect in form. Overcup oak, for instance, often has a crooked trunk.

Among the second group of white oaks, those with chestnut-style leaves, the trees are often taller in relation to their spread, with shorter or upward-trending branches. They are less typical of the oaks both in figure and in leaf.

The red and the black oaks tend to be narrower than the white; the total effect more tower than dome. The shumard and the Spanish (or southern red) oaks are typically taller and narrower trees; the scarlet oak more branchy and open. The fastest-growing oaks all belong to this group.

Of these the tree most often planted in America for its profile is the pin oak, which has, instead of stout wandering branches, an abundance of thin and straight ones. The upper branches climb to make a rather narrow crown; the lower ones droop, often as low as the ground, hiding the trunk. For an oak it is a lightweight tree; the more so because of the fine texture of its deeply-divided leaves.

The live oak of the south is the most characteristic of all in its shape: it grows twice as wide as it is high. The champion is 138 feet across by a mere 71 feet high.

All oak leaves are lively: the oak is never dull in texture. The burr oak, which has the biggest leaves (sometimes a foot long) has an extraordinarily emphatic pattern. Yet perhaps the finest-textured make the most beautiful trees: fine either in having deep-

cut leaves like the pin oak, or in having them slim and small like the willow oak. Small leaves on a big tree do not have the busy effect you might expect: they make a perfect patina for the terrific sculpture of crown and bough.

What matters more to the parks department than the exact shape of tree or leaf is the way the tree transplants. Tap-rooting oaks are notoriously reluctant to move: the white, scarlet and black oaks are all examples. Among the easiest to transplant, and hence the most popular, are the red, water, pin and willow oaks. The last three, alas, need acid soil.

Above *The canyon live oak, a common evergreen species in California, is the oldest American oak. It is a medium-sized spreading tree with smooth pale bark and gold-fuzzy acorn cups.*

Below *The Oregon white oak takes over from the valley oak in north California. It has similar twisted branches but makes a smaller deep-rooting tree. The leaves are deeply lobed.*

Deciduous Black Oaks
1. Black
   *125' h. 85' s.
   Warrensville Heights,
   Ohio.*
2. Blackjack
   *47' 4" h. 76' s.
   nr. Wakita, Oklahoma.*
3. California black
   *124' h. 115' s.
   Siskiyou National
   Forest,
   Oregon.*
4. California blue
   *55' h. 87' s.
   Nevada County,
   California.*
5. Laurel
   *102' h. 116' s.
   Waycross, Georgia.*
6. Nuttall
   *130' h. 80' s.
   Rolling Fork,
   Mississippi.*
7. Pin
   *93' h. 85' s.
   nr. Carrollton,
   Missouri.*
   *134' h. 99' s.
   nr. Smithland,
   Kentucky.*
8. Red
   *118' h. 128' s.
   Berrien County,
   Michigan.*
   *88' h. 88' s.
   Ashtabula County,
   Ohio.*
9. Scarlet
   *65' h. 80' s.
   Massapequa, New
   York.*
10. Shingle
    *80' h. 80' s.
    Wayne County, Ohio.*
11. Shumard
    *130' h. 111' s.
    Brooksville,
    Mississippi.*
12. Southern red
    *128' h. 149' s.
    Harwood, Maryland.*

The blue oak of inland California has a bluish cast to its leaves, often the mark of a tree which can withstand drought conditions. In the foothills of the Sierras it grows with little moisture, wide-spreading, rarely over 50 feet.

White Oaks

18. Basket
75′ h. 100′ s.
Northport, New York.

19. Burr
128′ h. 104′ s.
Algonac, Michigan.

20. California white
120′ h. 103′ s.
nr. Gridley,
California.

21. Chestnut
130′ h. 86′ s.
nr. Urania,
Louisiana.

22. Chinkapin
72′ h. 62′ s.
Ross County, Ohio.

23. Oregon white
98′ h. 72′ s.
Douglas County,
Oregon.

24. Overcup
120′ h. 83′ s.
Rolling Fork,
Mississippi.

25. Post
86′ h. 42′ s.
nr. Hartwell,
Georgia.

26. Swamp white
104′ h. 119′ s.
nr. Tompkinsville,
Monroe County.

27. White
102′ h. 158′ s.
State Park,
Wye Mills,
Maryland.

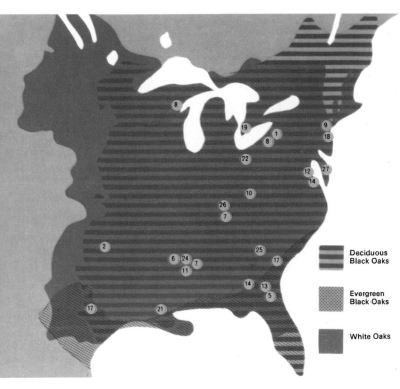

Deciduous
Black Oaks

Evergreen
Black Oaks

White Oaks

13. Water
106′ h. 105′ s.
nr. Waycross, Georgia.

14. Willow
125′ h. 106′ s.
Queenstown, Maryland.
112′ h. 125′ s.
nr. Hillman, Georgia.

Evergreen Black Oaks

15. Canyon live
72′ h. 80′ s.
Cleveland National
Forest, California.

16. Coast live
108′ h. 129′ s.
Chiles Valley, Cal.

17. Live
44′ h. 89′ s.
Goose Island State
Park, Texas.
71′ h. 138′ s.
Beaufort County,
South Carolina.

Top *The live oak of the Deep South; one of the widest-domed of all trees, nearly always decked with shawls of grey Spanish moss which give it an indescribable grace. It will grow on most soils.*

Above *The willow oak (named for its narrow, unlobed, willow-like leaves) has the finest texture of all and makes one of the most magnificent, yet graceful and lightly-built, trees.*

Most brilliant of all oaks in autumn, the scarlet oak has a natural range of nearly a third of the United States and grows excellently in Europe. Its long, relatively slender branches and open crown cast a light shade.

The pin oak is easy to recognize by the hang of its thin branches; the lower ones always sweeping to the ground and the upper ones forming a tidy dome. Deep-cut leaves give it a fine texture in keeping with its almost feminine shape.

The water oak of the southeast will grow considerably north of its natural range and in relatively dry ground. Like many southern oaks it keeps its leaves for half the winter or more, according to the climate.

The Chestnuts

It is hardly a step from some of the chestnut-leaved American oaks to the chestnut itself. Botany has made stepping stones rather than a linking path between the two, preferring to give the golden chinkapin and the tanbark oak, two American species which come firmly between oak and chestnut, and *Castanopsis*, a Japanese one, the status of separate genera. But from the acorn, part in its cup and part out, to the chestnut, all inside, each stage of wrapping is represented.

When you get to the chestnut tree there is no mistaking it. Vivid leafiness proclaims it. Big tongue-shaped leaves, every vein making a valley and every valley ending in a holly-like point. Very commonly the leaves are all the evidence you have of what it is. In Europe because of a still-flourishing industry in chestnut poles, for which the wood is coppiced; cut to the ground every seven or eight years. But in North America because disease has in the last 60 years killed every big chestnut. If anyone is complacent about the elms, let him look at the fate of the chestnuts. At the beginning of this century they were one of the chief components of the eastern forest, bigger than almost any oak, spreading from Alabama to Maine. In 1906 a bark fungus very like the elm disease was introduced accidentally from the Far East. By 1940 the chestnut was expunged from the list of American forest trees. Only because of its immense power of sprouting from the base (which makes it ideal for coppice) does it survive at all, as leafy fountains from where huge old trees formerly stood.

Uncoppiced and unblighted, standing on a lawn, the chestnut is a dense, substantial-looking tree, forming a billowing pyramid of light-catching leaves. In July it is variegated by its long yellow-green catkins. In them lies its only disadvantage: a sickly smell that haunts high summer.

The Spanish or sweet chestnut (*Castanea sativa*) of Europe gets its name from an

Above *Sweet (or Spanish) chestnut in mid-summer, covered with its creamy spikes of flowers. In its native Mediterranean it is the longest-lived of all deciduous trees.*

Below *The catkin-like flower spikes and glossy toothed leaves of the sweet chestnut. The flowers give off a sickly smell but the leaves make it one of the handsomest trees for parkland.*

Below *The fruit of the sweet chestnut: the only beech-family fruit commonly eaten by the human race today. The sweet brown nuts are enclosed in a prickly green case until they are* ripe: one, two or three nuts to each shell. Varieties with extra heavy crops of good nuts have been selected: 'Marron de Lyon' is the most famous. There are forms with yellow or white leaf margins.

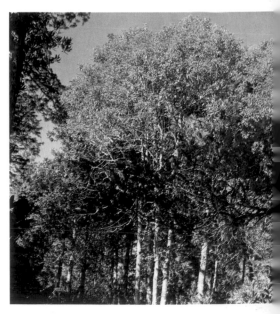

Left *The deep and regular fissures in the bark of the chestnut have the habit of swirling round the trunk in a spiral; often the quickest way to identify a chestnut tree in winter.*

Right *The giant chinkapin is an evergreen relation of the chestnut from northern California and Oregon. It has valuable wood, good fruit and beautiful foliage. It could be planted much more outside its natural range.*

A record-size specimen of the giant chinkapin growing near Saverdun in the foothills of the Pyrenees. The whole tree takes on a fluffy bronze look in mid-summer with its thousands of flowers. Where it will not make a full-size tree (i.e. too far north) the chinkapin is worth growing as a shrub.

ancient city in what is now Turkey: the city of Kastanaia, whence the Latin name; *châtaignier*, the French; and chestnut. The horse chestnut, of another family entirely, has merely borrowed it because its nuts are similar, at least in size and shape.

Where the chestnut demonstrably feels most at home is half-way up a full-sized Mediterranean volcano. The most colossal hulk of a tree ever recorded still flourished in the last century on the eastern slopes of Mt. Etna. It was 204 feet round, counting all the fragments, and supported a small industry of nut-gatherers, who in their simple Sicilian way eventually killed the goose by cutting off its branches to stoke the fire to cook the nuts. At 2,500 or 3,000 years of age (having been an old tree when Plato lived in nearby Syracuse) it finally succumbed to souvenir-hunters.

The Spanish and American chestnuts are as close cousins as any two trees on opposite sides of the Atlantic. Which means, alas, that the Spanish chestnut is susceptible to the blight and can't be planted in America.

To take its place American nurseries have introduced the Japanese and Chinese chestnuts (*C. crenata* and *C. mollissima*). Of the two, the Chinese has the sweeter nuts and makes the bigger and better tree–but still only half the size of the native species.

There are beautiful variegated versions of the Spanish chestnut, with leaf-margins ivory-white or yellow. But these of course are blight-prone in America too.

Happily the stepping-stones are immune. Both are evergreens from the northwest States, Oregon and North California. The more chestnut-like of them in fruit is the golden chinkapin (*Chrysolepis chrysophylla*, formerly *Castonopsis chrysophylla*).

For one of the most original and charming of relatively hardy broadleafed evergreens, this tree remains curiously uncommon outside its natural range. Its leaves vary from willow-slim to broad as bay, dark green above and beneath permanently upholstered

in brown-gold down. Its nuts are very like chestnuts, and can be eaten.

Once golden chinkapins–the name is the Indian for chestnut–grew on a truly western scale, 150 feet high among the redwoods and Douglas firs in the coastal hills. But their wood was too good to last in a region where hardwood is the exception.

The tanbark oak (*Lithocarpus densiflorus*) has less to attract the gardener. It is like a chestnut in leaf and identical to an oak in fruit. Its very tannic bark makes it important for the leather industry, but in gardens it has proved wilful and demanding, without offering very much in return.

Left The evergreen foliage of the giant chinkapin (sometimes known as the golden chestnut) is elegantly tapered, dark green above and densely covered below with gleaming gold-amber felt.

Above The American sweet chestnut, which, until 60 years ago, rivalled the tulip tree as the tallest deciduous tree of the eastern forests. In the '20s and '30s, it was wiped out by a bark fungus very like the Dutch elm disease.

Above Chinkapin is an American Indian word for chestnut. The tree bears its edible fruit in gold-spiky clusters: another aspect of its year-round value as an ornamental garden plant.

Below At the beginning of the century a quarter of the hardwoods of the Great Smokies were chestnuts. Today almost the only relic of them is the shingle roofing of the old settlers' cabins.

The Birches

The evolutionary group that started with the witch hazels and included the elms, the beeches and the oaks ends with the birch family: the birches, the alders, the hornbeams and the hazels.

Both the birches and the alders, the closest cousins, are lightweight trees of the forest's edge, adapted to poor land and extremes of either drought or damp. The birches are the hardiest of all the broadleaves; the only trees native to Iceland and Greenland.

There are some 60 species of birch. It circles the globe in the higher northern latitudes without varying very much in stature (save in tundra where it dwindles to scrub) or in stance; remaining always a light-branched, thin-twigged and graceful tree. Birch species are notoriously difficult to identify. In collections they lose no time in hybridizing–which only makes matters worse. They vary (but not very much) in leaf shape, colour and texture; more in leaf size–up to the six-inch heart-shaped leaves of the monarch birch of Japan, *Betula maximowicziana*. Where they vary most is in the birch's most original feature: the colour of its bark.

The common silver birch of Europe has chalk-white bark; the American canoe (or paper) birch whiter still; the yellow birch yellow; the gray birch white streaked with black; the cherry birch cherry-like brown; the river birch dark shaggy brown; Forrest's birch a purply brown; the Himalayan birch buff or cream; the Chinese paper birch a range from pink to oxblood satin.

In all these (except the river birch) the coloured layer is a stage in the bark's development from a reddish brown to an eventual craggy black. During this stage the outermost layer peels off in the thinnest of ribbons. It has incredible endurance. Pieces of birch bark hundreds of years old have been found intact in peat bogs. In Siberia (at Dworotrkoi, to be exact) it has even been found in its original state attached to wood that has fossilized. To dwellers in the north it is indispensable. Indians make canoes of it; Lapps cloaks and leggings; Norwegians roofs, covering a layer of bark with a foot of earth. When all is sodden in the forest birch bark will burn. To Russian leather (which is tanned with it) it gives its peculiar musty scent. ▶

Left *A dense natural stand of the canoe or paper birch of North America, one of the tallest and most vigorous of the birches, whose waterproof bark formed the hulls of Indian canoes. The biggest tree (in Maine) is nearly 100 feet.*

The outermost layer of bark of a birch is in a constant state of replacement. Few other trees have peeling bark. Above is the bark of the paper or canoe birch; it provides writing material, weatherproof covering or instant kindling for a fire.

Right *The Russian rock birch* (Betula ermanii) *is another of the northern Asiatic species that have proved a success in northern gardens. A tall tree with pinky-white peeling bark on the trunk and orange-brown branches.*

Left *Northern Asia is the home of dozens of species and varieties of birch.* Betula costata *(it has no English name) is one of the most decorative. It has pinky-cream bark, narrow oval leaves and glorious autumn colour.*

Below *The North American river or black birch has crackly dark brown bark very different from the usual silky sheath. It is the best species for wet ground. Its diamond-shaped leaves turn clear yellow in autumn.*

The silver birch of Europe is not quite the glowing warm white of the paper birch, nor does it grow so big. But its crown has an unrivalled fountaining elegance. It often seeds itself abundantly and forms dense stands on burned-over woodland.

The bark of the yellow birch (Betula lutea): *yellow more in its magnificent autumn leaves than in its peeling bark, which is amber or golden brown. This is the tallest of the American birches, reaching over 100 feet in the Allegheny mountains.*

Right *The gray (or poplar-leaved) birch is often a short-lived, many-stemmed tree colonizing derelict land. Its grey-white trunk is marked with black lines where young branches have been.*

The Birches

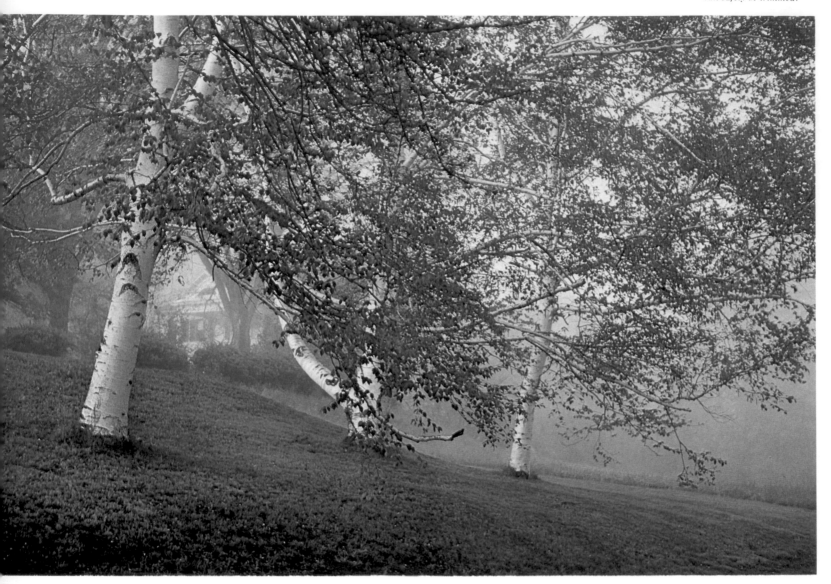

▶ Bark apart, the birch's beauty lies in its poise; the way it puts dense swarms of lacy twigs in the air with the flimsiest engineering. Perhaps its best time is in spring, when its natural droop is emphasized by the weight of catkins. Beside an oak, or a pine, its natural companions, it looks unmistakably feminine. Coleridge called it 'The Lady of the Woods'. There is no avoiding the inevitable image.

But then there is autumn. Birch leaves turn the purest, most sovereign gold of any tree's. It begs to be planted against a background of dark conifers, where the slender pallor of the trunk, fountaining up to fall in shining leaf tresses can really be seen. Plant birch to the north of your house: not only is it a tree that wants the light shining on, rather than through it, but the moss which tends to grow on the trunk and hide its colour concentrates on the north side of the tree.

Birches are trees to plant in clumps rather than singly, for the maximum effect from their bark. Or you can cut a sapling back right to the base: it will sprout up again as a cluster of stems – but they will take a few years to turn white. The American gray birch (which is perfectly white with interesting dark marks at intervals on the trunk) forms clumps naturally.

There is no need to look for exotic species. The common birch of damp ground in Europe, *B. pubescens*, is not so beautiful as the more drooping silver birch (*B. pendula*) of sandy heaths – above all in Scotland. The common birch has downy twigs; the silver birch rough and warty ones – you can tell them apart even as young trees while their bark is still brown. There are extra-graceful versions of the silver birch: the Swedish birch 'Dalecarlica' with deeply lobed leaves, the cultivar 'Tristis', narrowly soaring and weeping, and Young's weeping birch with a low domed head are all striking

Left *The natural weeping form of the silver birch is exaggerated in several cultivars; the most extreme is Betula pendula 'Youngii', whose branchlets all hang perpendicularly. Here it is turning to autumn gold in an English October.*

Below *A mature silver birch can be the most perfectly poised and graceful of all trees. With age the bark loses its silky whiteness but the airy crown grows more pendulous. This is typical of the form of birch found in Scotland, photographed at Dawyck, near Peebles in the Lowlands.*

Above *The long heart-shaped leaves of the Russian rock birch. The monarch birch of Japan (Betula maximowicziana) has the biggest leaves of the genus: up to seven inches long by five across.*

Below *The leaves of the silver birch with its catkins, conspicuous on the tree all year. One particularly pretty cultivar of this tree, 'Dalecarlica', has its leaves deeply divided and almost ferny.*

and excellent trees. Young's is peculiar for having branches as bare as curtain-rods with all the foliage hanging below them. But can one honestly say they are more beautiful than the species itself? Or than the straightforward canoe birch? Or the Japanese silver birch, *B. platyphylla japonica?*

The coloured-bark species compare with the snake-bark and paper-bark maples as trees with a special value in winter: trees to plant near the house, or at any rate near a path where you will see them at close quarters. Their satin glow seems to reach its warmest on a cruel snowy day.

The paper birch, shown here growing by a lake in New Canaan, Connecticut, is the most widespread of all the American birches, ranging in its natural habitat from Labrador to Nebraska. In the north the bark is used for roofing.

Above *The southern white Chinese birch (Betula albosinensis septentrionalis) is a supreme collector's tree; its bark of pale coppery silk with a greyish bloom makes it perhaps the most beautiful of all birches.*

Middle *The birch of the western Himalayas, Betula jacquemontii, in its native Kashmir. Himalayan birch is variable; its bark sometimes white, sometimes cream or brown. Our knowledge of the birches of Asia is far from complete.*

The Alders

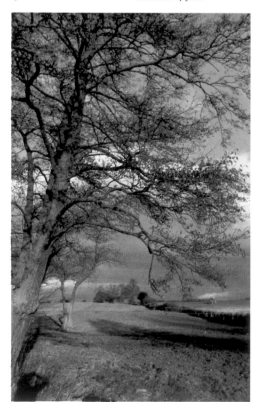

Below *Early in the year the alder puts on its most telling performance with its catkins and fruit on its bare branches. When low wintry light strikes the tree it seems to glow with ripeness.*

Above *Alder is the stream-side tree. Its common forms (here the common European alder, growing by a Yorkshire 'beck') tend to be neglected, although pretty at all times of year.*

Alders must be the easiest trees to overlook, or simply to accept as part of the scenery. I lived for 30 years before I became aware of them. Perhaps that's why they give me so much quiet pleasure now.

Alders have their moment in late winter. They are the dark-brown silhouettes at the water's edge, often in single file along a streambank, which gradually become more and more cluttered with dangling bits and pieces as the winter wears on. By spring their silhouette is noticeably denser; the transparency of a winter tree is gone. In its place is an abstract of clustered catkins and cones. Cones on a broadleaf? The alder is the only one that has them.

Having spotted the alders in winter I watched them into full leaf and discovered that their silhouette is still their hallmark. By coincidence they tend to be neat and narrow, as short and lightly-branched as conifers and with their branches almost as regularly arranged. Their leaf-shapes vary in detail from species to species, but all are round or fat-oval in general outline and all tend to be held horizontally. From below, therefore, an alder floats black discs across the sky.

Alders are humble trees. Their place is boggy bottoms in the wild. Since clogs went out of fashion (if fashion is the word) nobody has wanted their timber, even though half of Venice is built on alder piles. Only in the Pacific northwest, where hardwoods are the exception, is it used for furniture. In gardens the alders tend to be equally ignored.

There is little call, it's true, to plant the common alder of Europe or the American speckled (or grey) alder from the east or red alder from the west – unless to vary the endless willows and poplars that tend to be stuck in wherever ground is boggy.

But the genus has a dressy member in the Italian alder; and a tree, moreover, that seems completely impartial about site and soil. As to soil, indeed, it actually improves

The bunches of male catkins of the red alder of the Pacific northwest are often up to six inches long. Red alder grows densely in swampy land near the sea in Oregon and provides good timber for furniture.

Left *Alders by the sea in Normandy, with Mont-St-Michel visible over the tide-flats. A narrow silhouette with dark leaves is typical of the alder. Its wood is still used for clogs in Normandy.*

Above *The Italian alder is tall and hardy, with strikingly shiny leaves. Alder is the only broadleaf to bear cones—though their resemblance to those of conifers is mere coincidence.*

what it finds, having (like the pea family) the trick of introducing nitrogen with its roots.

I first saw the Italian alder (*A. cordata*) growing by the terrace of a mansion that had been burnt down and its ruins demolished. The garden was rank and dispiriting: the ponds choked, the once-trim columns of yew toppling and coming apart. What were those gleaming dark green trees still formal and polished as butlers in the chaos? They made a great impression on me, which has been reinforced wherever I have seen them in a garden (which is not often, I admit).

To be specific: a tall (to 90 feet) and narrow tree, though with branches more horizontal than upright. Substantial (up to four inches) heart-shaped leaves like a birch's, but darker green and glossy. Remarkable little cones: black eggs standing up on the branch-tips in trios.

Natural variation of the common alder of Europe (*A. glutinosa*; so named for the stickiness of its buds and twigs) and the grey alder (*A. incana*, or in America the very similar *A. rugosa*)—grey of leaf—has produced a few garden forms of these unpretentious trees. The most successful are the cut-leafed versions (*A. glutinosa*–or *incana*– 'Laciniata' and *A. glutinosa* 'Imperialis') and the golden ones (*A.g.* or *i.* 'Aurea').

Garden forms of the alder include several golden varieties. This is the golden form of the common alder of Europe (Alnus glutinosa 'Aurea'). There are also alders with ferny, deeply-cut leaves: a leaf-form which gives a lovely texture to the tree.

169

The Hornbeams and Hazels

The alder is not the only sleeper in its family. It's a long time since there was exactly a craze for hornbeam.

Hornbeam's fate is to be passed over as beech, with the feeling that the beech is a bit short of beechiness—the silver trunk and silky leaf we prize it for.

Certainly there is only one superlative that applies to hornbeam. It is the hardest. Iron-wood is another name for it. Before iron became cheap and plentiful the load-taking parts of machines—cogs, axles, spokes—were made of hornbeam. So was the sweet and simple furniture of the dairy: the yoke, the scrubbed white milkpails and the churn. But its engineering role past, what part has it to play today?

The distinctive quality of hornbeam is its texture. An old parkland hornbeam is simply a good broad-headed tree of something less than terrific height, colouring well (the American hornbeam, *Carpinus caroliniana*, splendidly) in autumn. At close quarters, though, the subtle corrugation of its surface gives it special interest. Where the bole of the beech is smooth and round the hornbeam looks as though muscles were straining within, making irregular flutes and ridges. And where the beech's leaves are slips of well-ironed silk, the hornbeam's are corrugated with ribs between the veins.

Where this texture can best be seen and appreciated is in a hedge. Not even the beech takes to the shears so well as the hornbeam. It makes a sturdy windbreak on almost any soil, like the beech keeping many of its dead leaves through the winter. One couldn't call their shade of brown a festive colour, but it has warmth.

Biddable as it is, the hornbeam will do more interesting things than a simple four-square wall. Its most effective use is at Hidcote, the Gloucestershire garden where hedges attain almost the status of art. Hornbeam here makes a hedge-on-stilts, pleached, as the old word is, into a perfect box-shape carried on wide-spaced immaculate stems four feet off the ground. The European *C. betulus* is best for hedge-work.

In hedging hornbeam you lose, of course, its natural shape. You also lose its fruit. The ordinary hornbeams of Europe and North America have little clusters of hanging winged nuts which catch the eye in autumn. But the Japanese ones (*C. cordata* and *japonica*) seem to be covered in bunches of drying hops when the leaves fall.

Hornbeams have a close relation which carries the hop theme far enough to be called the hop-hornbeam. The hop-hornbeams (*Ostrya* species) flourish in America, Europe and Asia, all looking remarkably alike and like hornbeams, save for their

Top *The fruit of the common hornbeam consists of short chains of three-winged nuts. It can hang high in the tree after the leaves fall, a help in distinguishing hornbeam from the similar but unrelated beech.*

Above *Hornbeam is one of the best broadleaf trees for hedging. This famous 'pleached' alley of common hornbeam is at Hidcote Manor in Gloucestershire. It keeps its perfect box shape with only one annual clipping.*

One of the world's great
woods of hornbeam:
Epping Forest to the
northeast of London. For
centuries the hornbeams
of Epping were a source
of timber and fuel. All the
older trees are pollards:
gnarled stumps below a
cluster of ascending
stems. It is easy to mistake
the bare-floored forest for
beechwood.

Right *The Japanese hornbeam* Carpinus cordata
*has more substantial
tassels of green fruit, and
bigger, broader leaves
than the European or
American hornbeams. It
makes a small spreading
tree, worth growing for its
hop-like display of fruit
in autumn.*

shaggy bark, which recalls the shagbark
hickory. Their long catkins add spring to
their season of display; like the hornbeams
they colour richly yellow in autumn.

The most familiar catkins of all are those
of the homely hazels and filberts, species of
Corylus, which with one exception are
bushes rather than trees. In their lowly
ranks there are some very attractive individuals. There is no more velvety leaf, for
example, than the Californian hazel's (*C.
californica*). And the purple hazel (*C.
maxima purpurea*) is one of the best purple-
leafed shrubs. But the one tree the hazels
can boast is a splendid one. It was brought
to Europe from Turkey at about the same
time as the horse chestnut. Vienna on the
fringe of the old Turkish empire has always
specialized in it. The Turkish hazel (*C.
colurna*) is just a greatly magnified (to 75
feet) version of the familiar one; a shapely,
many-branched tree, bearing trios of nuts
enveloped in whiskery husks.

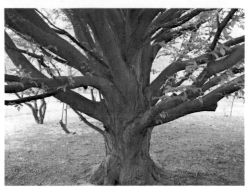

Left *Catkins of the
common hazel come in
late winter, undeterred by
frost. In February they
turn soft yellow. There are
pendulous and also
corkscrew-like forms of the
common hazel.*

Above *'Fastigiata', a
form of the common
hornbeam, makes an
attractive medium-sized
tree. Although it starts off
narrow, with age it
becomes vase-shaped with
a short trunk, as here.*

*The common European
hazel is typical of the
genus with its roundish,
hairy leaf and nut (here
immature, still green) in a
frill of leaf-like material.
The shape of the frill is
the principal way of
distinguishing the
different species.*

Right *Hop-hornbeam is a
smaller tree than the
hornbeam, pretty both in
spring with long catkins
and in autumn when its
yellow leaves show off its
brown fruit. The fruit has
each little nut in a tiny
bladder.*

The Trees of the Tea Family

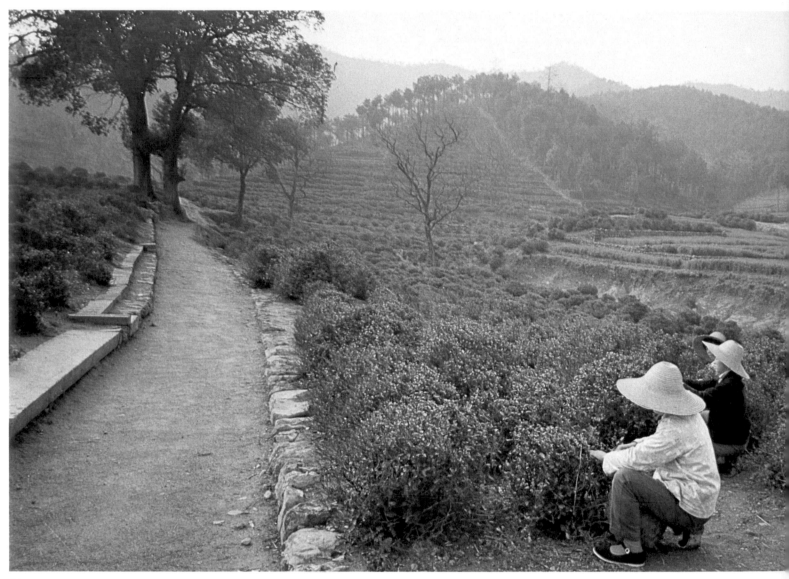

The tea family is a link in the ancestral chain between the great group headed by the primitive magnolias and a yet more diverse group that includes the heath family, the limes and – strange to say – the willows. Between the magnolias and their kin, and tea and its kin, come the peonies, a genus without trees, at least in our era. The grounds for such deductions are technical in the highest degree, starting with, of all things, the firing order of the stamens. Thus evolutionary links are obscured by infinity of variation and length of time.

The least spectacular member of the tea family is the tea-tree itself (*Camellia sinen-*

sis). Its little nodding white flowers hardly prepare you for the glory of its sisters the camellias of the garden, nor the curiously-named trio of *Franklinia*, *Gordonia* and *Stewartia* which represents the family in North America. In Europe, ice-ravaged as ever, there are none.

Nurseries have developed a huge range of camellias from the original species. The process began centuries ago in China. *C. japonica*, the common species, is totally submerged in a sea of hybrids and cultivars. Two other species, however, are still important, both in their own right and for the magnificent hybrids they have generated. *Cam-*

ellia reticulata from Yunnan in China is one; *C. sasanqua*, from Japan, the other.

All camellias are capable of making small trees (or very big bushes) in time, given the summer heat of Virginia and southwards (in Europe, of Bordeaux or the Italian Lakes), and given the right peaty soil and the right degree of woodland shelter. *C. reticulata* (which flowers in early spring) and *C. sasanqua* (which flowers from late autumn onwards) are or can be the most tree-like of them. Their flowers come in such a range from white to scarlet and from single to double and convoluted that they can match almost any human emotion. But even in

Above *The modest white flowers of the tea-bush seem to have little in common with their cousins the camellias. The tea-plant is kept small by the repeated drastic pruning of the* *harvest. High-quality tea was introduced from China (above, in Hang-chow province) to India in the last century by the British botanist Robert Fortune.*

Left *These splendid trees of* Camellia japonica *in the garden of the Duchess of Campo Bello in Portugal were planted in 1560, some 150 years before the 'official' introduction of one of Asia's greatest flowering plants to Europe. This species of camellia has produced hundreds of large-flowered varieties.*

Right *The deciduous stewartia is perhaps the most valuable tree of the tea-family for temperate gardens where it can grow to 50 feet or more. Here the leaves of the Japanese* Stewartia pseudocamellia *show their characteristic vein-pattern as they begin to turn rich shades of red and purple in autumn.*

Above *The Korean stewartia is a slightly smaller tree than the Japanese, but with bigger flowers. It too has rich autumn colour, and an attractive flaking bark.*

Right *The single camellia-like flower of the Japanese* Stewartia pseudocamellia.

Left *A typical Japanese hybrid of the common camellia, 'Haku-rakuten'. It makes a small but vigorous upright tree.*

regions where growth is slow and flowers are often spoilt by frost it is worth thinking of camellias for their foliage.

The stewartias are by comparison committed trees. (The 'Stewart' in question was John Stuart, the Earl of Bute who was unofficially the first Director of Kew Gardens.) Stewartias are native to both North America and the Far East, but the ones grown to such effect in gardens are Japanese (*S. pseudocamellia*) and Korean (*S. koreana*). Both are small-to-medium trees, often low-forking and branchy, with white flowers like single camellias coming in summer, often for eight weeks on end; and leaves that

turn episcopal shades of crimson and purple before they fall. Their intricately-flaking bark is my reminder of the connection with tea: its colours are the shades of gentle brown in strong tea just clouded with milk.

Franklinia and gordonia are both prizes of the great John Bartram, who collected them for his (and America's first) botanic garden in Philadelphia in the 1760s. He found them down in Georgia, where the gordonia is still to be found as the loblolly bay, but whence the franklinia has totally disappeared.

All the franklinias grown now must be descendants of Bartram's plants. The tree is

not unlike a stewartia, but smaller; less hardy but less fussy about soil – the only members of the family in fact which are happy to grow on lime. They flower rather later, with creamy flowers, and they too colour richly in autumn.

The Franklin, I should add, was Benjamin. Gordon was a London nurseryman, James Gordon of Mile End, supplier of many plants to the infant Kew. His loblolly bay is perhaps the least distinguished of a very fine bunch. It is grown in the southern States for its evergreen foliage like the bull bay magnolia's, but its flowers are out of their class in such company.

Left *The camellia has been coaxed by breeders into every size, shape and colour since the Chinese emperors began to collect it over 1,000 years ago. The process still goes on. 'Yours truly' is a modern hybrid, in this case a slow-growing bushy form.*

Limes, Lindens or Basswoods

Left The famous lindens of Berlin: a walk in the Tiergarten as October frosts turn the leaves.
Above *The common European lime or linden has the soft, translucent, heart-shaped leaves typical of the genus, midway in size between its two parents; the small-leafed and big-leafed limes.*
Right *The scented flowers are borne on stalks coming from a long leaf-like bract.*

How many of the great country-houses of Europe do you approach along drives of rearing twiggy monsters: England's limes; France's tilleuls; Germany's lindens; the basswoods of America? It must have been in the 17th century that they first came into fashion as the show-trees of the great. One can see why they were thought the very thing for avenues. They take the form of a tower; a huge rectilinear tree, not spreading wide but with the upper branches going up and the lower ones down. Of all the biggest class of trees they are the most softly leafy, with fine-textured, heart-shaped leaves as big as the palm of a (lady's) hand. And in mid-summer they sweeten the air most mellifluously with the scent of their flowers.

Yet despite its benefits the lime is one of the few trees whose vices outweigh its virtues.

The common lime (*Tilia × europaea*) is a hybrid; a cross between Europe's big-leafed and small-leafed limes (*T. platyphyllos* and *T. cordata*). It has all the vigour associated with hybrids; it has reached 150 feet in England, making it the tallest broadleaf in the country. Its problem is its suckers, which spring up all round the base and grow furiously in ungainly competition with the crown. The same exuberance produces great whiskery nobs on the trunk: pruning only makes matters worse. Miles Hadfield, the English tree historian, blames the wide circulation of the common lime on the Dutch nursery trade, which found it one of the easiest, most profitable trees to grow.

But both its parents are widespread natives of Europe, and both are much better trees. The big-leaf lime is often the bigger in stature as well as leaf; otherwise the differences between them are unimportant. Today these are the ones that are commonly planted; particularly the red-twigged form of the bigleaf (*T. p.* 'Rubra')–which makes an excellent hedge, distinctly warm-looking in winter–and a narrow cultivar of the

Left Limewood is the softest wood for sculpture. The work of the English sculptor Grinling Gibbons, never surpassed for exquisite intricacy, was all done in limewood. This piece (from 1691) is at Trinity College, Oxford.

Hoheria glabrata, one of the New Zealand ribbon-woods which are related to the limes. As sweet-scented small trees or large shrubs, often stooping under bushels of soft white flowers, they deserve to be better known in the northern hemisphere.

Below *Young specimens of the silver lime, Tilia tomentosa, in the valley of the Loire in western France.*

Right *One of the rare but very pretty and silvery Chinese species of linden or lime, Tilia henryana, has finely-toothed leaves. T. oliveri is similar. These flower-buds of T. henryana were photographed in July on a 30-foot tree at the French National arboretum at les Barres.*

Below *The underside of a spray of the silver linden or lime, Tilia tomentosa. This tree and its weeping counterpart, T. petiolaris, are the best-known of a number with silver-backed leaves which glint in the breeze. The flowers (here fully mature) can have unfortunate effects on bees.*

small-leaf, the 'Swedish Upright'.

The search for a fault-free lime continues, however. All the foregoing have another problem. They are the regular diet of aphids which cover their leaves all summer with honey-dew. Honey-dew is not the pleasure it sounds; it blackens the leaves and drops stickily on to everything below.

Sad to say the American basswood (*T. americana*) is just as much a victim. It should be a spectacular tree; it has by far the biggest leaves of the family–up to a foot long. But by the end of the summer they can be a sorry sight; blackened and sucked dry, curling and turning brown.

The most aphid-proof of the limes has turned out to be another hybrid, known as the Crimean lime (*T. × euchlora*) So far this has good reports; if not for its overall shape, at least for its glossy leaves. The only catch here is the mystery of its flowers, which draw the bees in swarms only to knock them out with a narcotic dose that often proves fatal. Feebly buzzing bees cover the ground below the tree.

The same problem is the only possible reason for not planting the two most beautiful trees of the genus, the silver lime and the weeping silver lime (*T. tomentosa* and *T. petiolaris*). Both these trees have the backs of their leaves richly silvered with fine hairs so that when the wind ruffles them they glisten and wink. The weeping version has leaf-stalks twice as long, which makes its leaves stir more readily and gives more glimpses of silver. As weeping trees go it is not, however, the full cascade that say the willow can be.

Does this leave us any lime totally free of faults? There is one lime, or so I'm told, which clears up all the points. Wilson brought it from China in 1900 and called it *T. oliveri*. Alan Mitchell says: 'It has an open upright crown of grey smooth branches bearing very flat, large leaves . . . Each leaf is pale green above, silver beneath and elegantly toothed.'

Above *The big-leafed lime of Europe (Tilia platyphyllos) is a much better park tree than its offspring, the common lime, which tends to send up ungainly suckers. The tower-shape of this specimen is typical of the bigger Tilia species.*

Middle above *The leaves of the big-leafed lime are sometimes six inches long, but those of the American basswood, Tilia americana, can be twice the size or more. Here the flowers of the broadleaved species have ripened into round fruits.*

Above *Limes can grow to a tremendous age. This big-leafed lime at Upstedt, near Hanover, Germany, was planted about A.D. 850 and is mentioned in a document of 1100. Its diameter five feet from the ground is 25 feet.*

The Willows

The willow family has evolved along a distinct path of its own as a client of the four winds. Although the construction of its flowers puts it in the line of descent from the tea family, it stands on its own in being specially adapted to give the wind its seeds to sow. There are only two members of the family; the willows and the poplars. Both have male and female catkins on different trees and offer nectar to the bees for fertilizing them. Poplars get their other name of cottonwoods from the seed's flying apparatus: all willows and poplars use the same bit of fluff to carry the seed away.

The seed has to be very light, which means it can carry no endosperm, the food supply most seeds include in one form or other. Seed without endosperm has a very short life; germinating conditions must be right straight away. Which may be why willows and poplars tend to grow in moist ground.

Vigour is another family quality, but in this the poplar is more consistent than the willow. For one of the odd things about this original tree is that, fast as it can grow, most of its 250-odd species are shrubs.

America, Europe and Asia share most of the tree species of willow – all except the most famous of all, the weeping willow, which grows wild only in the west of China.

Stories abound of the introduction of *Salix babylonica*, the original weeping willow. Before it was established that it came from China it was thought to have been the tree by the waters of Babylon where the Jews in captivity sat down and wept. Its entry into western gardens came early in the 18th century, from the Middle East, or, according to another story, as a withy used to tie a parcel sent from Spain to Lady Suffolk in London. W. J. Bean recounts how the poet Pope, 'noticing one of the twigs was alive, begged it, and planted it at Twickenham, where it grew into the celebrated weeping willow of his villa garden'.

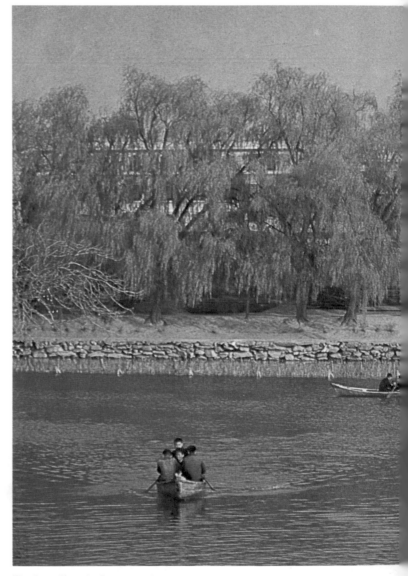

White willow is one of the fastest-growing of all big trees: a silver cloud with a leaning spine, usually growing straight but rarely perpendicular. Countless fine twigs and white-silky leaves give its reflection in dark water a subtle beauty.

Weeping willows in the grounds of the summer palace, Peking. The weeping willow picked up the name of babylonica on its travels from China to Europe. Most weeping willows in gardens today are hybrids between this and the white willow.

Although the Chilean Maytenus *is no relation of the willow (or any other tree in this book) this is the only place for it. It looks remarkably like a small evergreen weeping willow: a rare but highly desirable tree for any garden.*

The English landscape movement had mixed feelings about this noticeable tree. William Gilpin held that it was 'not adapted to sublime subjects. We wish it not to screen the broken buttresses . . . of an abbey . . . These offices it resigns to the oak, whose dignity can support them. The weeping willow seeks an humbler scene; some romantic bridge. which it half conceals. . . .'

Most books agree that what really popularized the tree was Napoleon's fondness for one on Saint Helena. So fond was he that he asked to be buried under it, whereupon the poor thing was torn twig from limb by tourists. Most Victorian weeping willows claimed to be cuttings from that tree.

The blood of *Salix babylonica* runs in every weeping willow's veins, but the species itself is rare today. Finding that it was none too hardy, nurserymen (or possibly in the first place nature) produced various crosses of it with hardy native willows. The commonest of these in Europe is *S. × chrysocoma,* which is *S. babylonica* crossed with the golden form of the common white willow (*S. alba* 'Vitellina'). In America other crosses are popular; notably the Thurlow and the Wisconsin weeping willows (*S. × elegantissima* and *S. × blanda*) which are crosses between *S. babylonica* and the crack willow (*S. fragilis*).

The Thurlow has reddish shoots, the Wisconsin a bluish sheen in both shoots and leaves. They weep less than *S. × chrysocoma. S. × sepulcralis* (which is a cross between *S. babylonica* and *S. alba*) is the most vigorously and grandly ascending of weeping willows. The magnificent trees round the lake at Kew are this hybrid.

Today it is accepted that a weeping willow is almost indispensable to any biggish body of ornamental water. Water is not necessary for the tree, but the reflected light apparently encourages it to extend its twigs in that direction. ▶

Right *Male catkins of the grey sallow (*Salix cinerea*). This, the similar goat willow (*S. caprea*), and *S. discolor* of North America are all known as pussy willows. The male catkins appear before the leaves.*

Top *Hoar-frost accentuates the writhing pattern of the twigs and branches of the twisted willow of Peking,* Salix matsudana *'Tortuosa'. It makes a fast-growing small tree; its leaves are are among the first to come and the last to go.*

Above *Willows are either male or female plants. In the foreground a female grey sallow has bright silver-green catkins. Behind and slightly to the right is a male tree with yellow catkins (see also close-up in the picture below left).*

The Willows

▶ Gilpin went on to call the weeping willow 'the only one of its tribe which is beautiful'. Evidently he was never invited to Woburn Abbey. There the 7th Duke of Bedford made a complete Salicetum: a collection of every known species. For a time the Salicetum was like the Pinetum, the collection of conifers, a desirable–if not essential–part of the grounds of a great house. The importance of osier beds as a way of using undrainable land provided an economic excuse. But the point was that willows are pretty.

Catkins in the early spring are the first obvious attraction. The prettiest catkin-bearers tend to be the shrubby kinds of willows, or sallows–which also fortunately have their catkins within reach. It is the male plants that have the bigger and brighter catkins. There are red-catkinned ones like *S. gracilistyla*, but it is hard to beat the common European pussy willow (*S. caprea*), with its fat pearly-furred catkins

ripening to saffron yellow.

Coloured bark is the other willow speciality. Many of the shrubs, and several of the trees, have brilliantly-painted new shoots. They come in scarlet, yellow, green, orange, white, purple and brown. The colour is brightest on new stems in their first winter. The trick, therefore, is to cut them back hard in the spring, to give them all summer to grow. If you cut them to ground level it is coppicing; to shoulder-level pollarding. Uncut, if the thing becomes a tree, it is scarcely less bright waving in the sky. I can see an ordinary golden white willow (*S. alba* 'Vitellina') from my desk. Winter morning sun makes it easily the brightest spot in the landscape. The best red is another variety of the white willow (*S. alba* 'Chermesina'); the best purple (overlaid with a soft white bloom), *S. daphnoides*.

The typical willow leaf is racing-boat-shaped: long, narrow and pointed at both ends. Many are bloomy-silvery, the common

The power of the willow to brighten a dull wintry landscape: these red-stemmed white willows were twigs on a tree two years ago. Any willow twig stuck deep in the ground in autumn will start growing as a new tree the next spring.

White willows by the Stour, in eastern England typical white willow and bat-willow country. The smallest trees here are three years old, the biggest 12. Conditions are ideal: plenty of water and full sunlight.

Left *The peach-leafed
willow (Salix
amygdaloides) is found by
wild water-courses from
Quebec to Oregon
(photographed here in
Wyoming). The similar
almond-leafed willow*
*(S. triandra) plays the
same role from Europe to
the orient. It has long
been cultivated for basket-
making. Although it is a
workaday tree its glossy
leaves with pale under-
sides make it very pretty.*

white willow (*S. alba*) perhaps most of all.
There are surprising variations, though, in
this too. The bay willow (*S. pentandra*) has
glossy dark-green ovals which look – and
even smell – like a bay tree's; *S. magnifica*
from China has leaves as big as a magnolia's.

One inspired variation is the twisted leaf.
A variety of the original weeping willow
(*S. babylonica* 'Annularis') has leaves like
little ringlets. In the corkscrew willow
(*S. matsudana* 'Tortuosa') the vibrations
go right through the whole tree: every inch
of twig as well as leaf wiggles. It sounds
bizarre: in fact it is elegant. I know of only
one willow which has gone too far: *S. ×
erythroflexuosa* tries to do everything at
once: to twist, to weep and to look cheerful in orange-yellow bark. The result is a
neurotic-looking bush.

The white willow, the crack willow (*S.
fragilis*, so-called because its twigs snap off
if you pull them) and their super-vigorous
hybrid the bat willow (*S. × caerulea*) are
the common tree-willows grown not for
their beauty – beautiful as they are – but for
their wood. The willow combines first-class
timber with rocket-like growth. Whether
for cricket bats, the bottoms of quarry
carts that have to endure the shock and
scrape of stone, or in the terms of the
naval timber manual which called it 'the
best wood without exception for the formation of small, fast-sailing war vessels',
willow is strong.

As for speed, a normal rotation period
for bat willow, from planting to felling, is
15 years. By then, on a good site, the tree is
70 feet high and five feet round.

Willow-growing is made absurdly easy by
the readiness of the twigs to take root. The
sets used for willows are ten feet long;
simply a young branch driven into the
ground for half its length. 'Sets' are planted
in February; by May they are in leaf and
growing as new trees. You can even stand a
young willow on its head. The branches
can become roots and vice versa.

This wonderful instant tree must have
its drawbacks. It has several, from its
liability to the fatal disease of canker to
its attractiveness to aphids; also, curiously
for such strong wood, its liability to split in
a bad storm. But to me they are outweighed
by the advantages: its ability to grow so big
and beautiful so quickly.

Above *One of the most
exquisite of all big shrubs,
without even a flower to
its name: the Chinese
Salix moupinensis, with
broad oval leaves from
sealing-wax red buds.*

Above *The woolly willow
(Salix lanata) is one of
the prettiest of the shrub-
size willows. Its name is
derived from its woolly
catkins and its young
branchlets which are
covered with grey wool.*

Below *Willows are as
ready to root in water as
in earth: looking down
the trunk of a waterside
white willow. A big
willow tree drinks and
transpires up to 400
gallons a day.*

179

Poplars, Cottonwoods and Aspens

The willow family includes, in the weeping willow and the Lombardy poplar, the two most famous and distinctive of all ornamental trees: a text-book pair of forms planted together for contrast in almost every park in the world.

The weeping willow is a true species: its seed comes up weeping. The Lombardy poplar is a cultivar, in the sense that its seed may or may not grow bolt upright. It is propagated by cuttings, which luckily are as easy to persuade to take root as the 'sets' of willows.

But neither tree is typical of its race. They are exceptional not only in shape but in being considered ornamental at all. Poplars on the whole are thought of, like willows, as wood factories. Like willows they grow alarmingly fast. A cottonwood (*Populus deltoides*) planted on Mississippi bottom-land grew 98 feet in 11 years.

Like willows, poplars hybridize among their kind with abandon. As racing trees they have also been subject to a great deal of stud activity. Hence, as J. L. Reed irresistibly puts it in *The Forests of France*, 'their social history is like one of those exhausting novels which describe the adventures and alliances of several generations of an international family established in different capitals'.

The four branches of the family are the black, white, trembling and balsam poplars. The black are the biggest branch, containing all the poplars which aren't white under the leaves, don't smell of balsam in bud (or if the twigs are bruised), and don't tremble (as the aspens do).

The white poplars are natives of Europe, long since established in North America. The basic white poplar (*P. alba*) is an eye-catching tree, even where (which is often on poor land) it grows no higher than 20 or 30 feet. Its leaves toss at the merest breeze to show their silver-white undersides. The standard poplar leaf-shape is more or less like a heart; the white poplar's are lobed like a maple's. In America, furthermore, they often turn red in autumn. In Europe, like other poplars', they turn yellow.

There is an upright version of the white poplar ('Pyramidalis' or 'Bolleana') which is like a rather beamy Lombardy with the distinct advantage of the winking white leaves, and a charming smaller form of the tree known as Richard's poplar, with leaves buttercup yellow on top and white below; unassuming and easy to grow but potentially a knock-out against a background of heavy shade.

The balsam poplars are some of the earliest trees of all to come into leaf. Their big pointed buds on curiously ribbed twigs are sticky with balsam in late winter. In the south of England the strong sweet smell is one of the clearest heralds of spring.

Of the American balsams the confusingly-named black cottonwood (*P. trichocarpa*) (which is neither black nor strictly speaking a cottonwood) is, if the record figure of 225 feet is right, the tallest American broadleaf.

Balsam poplar leaves are markedly shiny and rich green; the long necklaces of yellowish catkins usually arrive just ahead of them. It sounds attractive, yet I would never recommend anyone to plant either the monster black cottonwood or the more modest-sized balsam (or tacamahac) poplar (*P. balsamifera*), or the hybrid balm of Gilead (*P.* × *candicans*). They have no real grace of growth; their winter silhouette is always really that of a huge branch stuck in the ground. The Chinese poplar (*P. simonii*) may be an exception to this–I have seen a row in Seattle which had much softer and less rigid skeletons with hanging twigs.

For the balsam smell alone one can well plant any of them and treat it as coppice: cut half the shoots right to the ground every year. The result is extra-big leaves on wands which are ideal to scent the house. Indeed there is a variety of the balm of Gilead poplar called *P.* × *candicans* 'Aurora' which has creamy, pink-tinged leaves, balsam and all. ▶

Poplars and willows, members of the same family, completely dominate the landscape in many low-lying parts of Europe, as here in the Seine valley. At all seasons they are light and airy trees in pale colours.

*Renoir, Monet, Pissarro . . .
poplars in autumn seem to
sum up the vision of the
French impressionists.
This is 'Robusta', a
hybrid black poplar which
is now planted in millions
in northern Europe.*

Poplars, Cottonwoods and Aspens

Top *Several upright forms of the black poplar, of which the Lombardy is the best-known, have occurred in nature. This Lombardy-like tree was photographed by the 1972 Everest expedition in the Himalayas.*

Above *The female catkin of the Japanese* Populus maximowiczii *starting to ripen into fruit. Each green capsule will split in mid-summer and release a cotton-wrapped seed: hence the American name cottonwood.*

The cypress-like pattern of the branching of Lombardy poplars is seen here in a stormy light against a hillside in the Lot valley in southwest France. Male trees tend to be very narrow like those on the right, female ones to grow a little more beamy.

Top *Poplars, like willows, are either male or female. The female catkins of the aspen are typical: short woolly tassels before the leaves. The weeping aspen, a male variety, has pretty purplish-grey catkins in February.*

▶ The cottonwood of the western creekbeds is the most familiar black poplar in the wilds. A film director is bound to aim his cameras at it or through it when it is the only tree in the landscape. Its range runs from the Atlantic to the Rockies; in the east it is less conspicuous until it snows cotton in July.

The union of the cottonwood with the black poplar of Europe (*P. nigra*) has brought about most of the rapid commercial poplars that – in France especially – have made their own style of valley landscape. The ordinary black poplar is not distinguished; its varieties 'Italica', the Lombardy poplar, and 'Plantierensis' (which often steps in to take the Lombardy poplar's place) are the important ones. Their value as landscape trees is always before one's eyes: either the single huge tower, sometimes 100 feet high or more, dominating some Alpine valley; or the elegant file through fenland, leading to a lonely farm; or the grand approach to an urban institution. There is no tree which creates an architectural incident so quickly and surely.

The black poplars have made a race of varied merits, all fast and some beautiful in a light-leaved, summer-meadow way. 'Robusta', for example, leafs late but coppery – an autumnal colour in May. Its narrow, light-branched crown (which it shares with 'Eugenei') can look like a feather on the skyline. 'Regenerata' and 'Marilandica' are denser and broader; 'Serotina' can make a huge cloud-like head. In the Melbourne Botanic Garden there is a golden poplar (*P. serotina* 'Aurea') a good 120 feet high and built like a sunlit thunder-cloud.

Since all poplars have leaf-stalks and many of them long ones, the wind always sets them aflutter. The difference with the aspens, the trembling poplars, is that they feel breezes when the whole world is becalmed. You can lie under an aspen on a stiflingly still day and listen to its incessant whisper. The trick is in the leaf-stalk, a narrow ribbon set at right-angles to the hanging leaf-blade.

The American quaking aspen (*P. tremuloides*) is the tree with the widest distribution on the whole North American continent. It grows from Labrador to Mexico and to the Bering Strait, leaving out only the southeast and part of the midwest. Its life is short and vigorous: it demands light and offers bigger and more permanent trees a light shade for their early years; then they overtake it and it dies. In the east of its range it grows with its sister, the bigtooth aspen (*P. grandidentata*), which has bigger, toothed leaves.

Its favourite place to seed and start a new colony is where fire has been. According to J. C. Loudon, the European aspen (*P. tremula*) took over the ruins of Moscow in 1813, the year after Napoleon had reduced most of the city to ashes.

It is similar to the American aspen, lacking only its pale smooth bark. Both are (or were when Europe had such things) the beaver's favourite tree. Despite its astringency he loves the inner bark. Both species have small weeping forms, particularly pretty with their grey catkins in early spring and again in autumn, when aspens turn a shining yellow.

Aspen crossed with white poplar has produced grey poplar (*P. × canescens*), a common and on the whole stately tree beside French roads. It has a bad habit (which it gets from both its parents) of throwing up suckers. It is a good catkin tree before the leaves come, and the leaves can be almost as silvery as the white poplar's in a breeze. Poplar wood is not generally sought for special qualities, except perhaps its readiness to split into narrow shavings, good for matches and lightweight fruit baskets. Basically it is grown today for pulp. Grey poplar, however, has smooth, non-splintering, non-warping and lightweight wood which has many uses, from silk-rollers to barn doors.

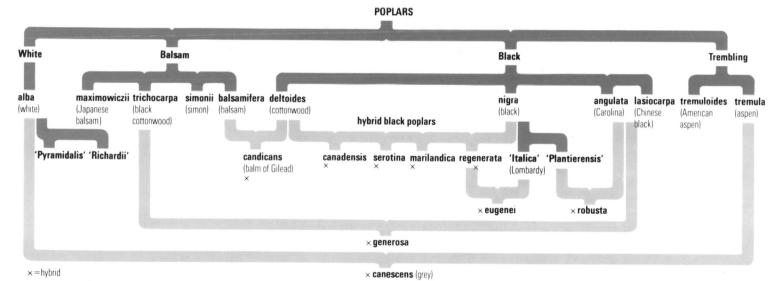

POPLARS

White	Balsam					Black			Trembling
alba (white)	maximowiczii (Japanese balsam)	trichocarpa (black cottonwood)	simonii (simon)	balsamifera (balsam)	deltoides (cottonwood)	nigra (black)	angulata (Carolina)	lasiocarpa (Chinese black)	tremuloides (American aspen) / tremula (aspen)
'Pyramidalis' 'Richardii'				candicans (balm of Gilead) ×	canadensis × / serotina × / marilandica × / regenerata ×	'Italica' 'Plantierensis' (Lombardy)			

hybrid black poplars

× eugenei   × robusta

× generosa

×=hybrid

× canescens (grey)

The interbreeding of the four different groups of the poplars has given us some of our most useful and fastest trees. The diagram above shows the family story so far as it is known: many of the crosses are intentional, but others happened in nature.

Poplar catkins have a beauty of their own. A male aspen catkin (here magnified twice) shows its purple stamens and their outer covering of white hairs.

The Chinese species Populus lasiocarpa has the largest and lushest leaves of any poplar: shiny green hearts up to a foot long. It was introduced from China in 1900 by E. H. Wilson.

Heather and Strawberry Trees

The heath (or heather) family is the backbone of the gardening style which has distinguished the great gardens of this century. It is the family of the rhododendron and the azalea: the mounds, drifts and terraces of evergreen foliage that unobtrusively back up every garden picture, to burst into life in spring with improbable quantities, sizes and shapes of flowers in every colour, save true blue. So universal are rhododendrons in the great woodland gardens, especially in Britain and the United States, that gardeners who don't have those flourishing mounds of evergreenery to give their gardens substance and backbone often feel at a psychological disadvantage. There are ways round that, but the fact remains: the classic woodland scene is a fantasy largely borrowed from the rainy lower slopes of the Himalayas (and to some extent the mountains of western North America) where conifers and heaths flourish together in ecological harmony on a soil composed of centuries of fallen leaves. A soil without the smallest trace of lime.

The heaths are part of a race derived from the tea family, which through the ages has developed cooperation with soil organisms called mycorrhizae. For some heaths this has gone so far that they are totally dependent: without their fungus friends they can't make their own food at all. The mycorrhizae attached to most of the familiar heaths need acid soil: therefore rhododendrons do too.

The most tree-like of the family are also those that are least particular in this regard. They are the tiny-flowered arbutuses from California, the Mediterranean and Killarney. Southwest Ireland is one of the warmest points in the British Isles and thus a logical outpost for a Mediterranean plant, but in fact the strawberry tree (*Arbutus unedo*) is hardy in much colder places; almost anywhere in Britain and to zone 7 at least in North America.

The flowering of the strawberry tree is a charming piece of understatement: the clustering of hundreds of tiny near-white pitchers among handsome bay-like leaves. It happens in the autumn when flowering trees are few. But the best thing about it is that the fruits from last year's flowers ripen red at the same time. They are more like cherries with roughened, pimply skins than strawberries. The overall effect is of a

The great sweep of the heath (or heather) family is summed up by the flowers above, those of the only true heather (Erica) to grow to tree size – and the flowers opposite, those of a modern rhododendron hybrid. Despite the huge difference in size the family resemblance is clear. The strawberry tree (below) has flowers very like the heather, although it makes a substantial tree.

Above *A red-flowered form of the strawberry tree,* Arbutus unedo *'Rubra'. The normal form has white flowers (as on the left), perhaps just blushing pink. The strawberry tree is evergreen with handsome bay-like foliage.*

Right Clethra arborea *of Madeira is known as the lily-of-the-valley tree. Again, the heather relationship is clear from the flowers; the rhododendron kinship is suggested by the leaves.* Clethra *needs an oceanic climate.*

quietly prolific plant in glowing good health; a happy thing to have around.

The California version, the madrone (*A. menziesii*) flowers more conspicuously, at the branch-tips, in spring. It is altogether much more of a tree; to 80 or 90 feet. The strawberry tree's maximum is 30 or 40 feet.

The madrone's real beauty lies in its combination of rich green foliage and beautiful smooth red bark on a graceful curving and forking trunk and limbs. A big tree in evening light can show up on a hill-side two or three miles away. In flower, in fruit (which is red, yellow or orange) or in mid-winter, when its evergreen foliage is all the more telling, it is one of the finest trees hardy enough for northern Europe. There is a 55-foot specimen in the glorious collection at Hergest Croft on the Welsh border.

The strawberry tree, and also its Greek cousin *A. andrachne* and the splendid hybrid between the two, *A. × andrachnoides*, are content to grow with a modest amount of lime in the soil; the madrone would much rather not.

Arbutus flowers betray the relationship of the genus to the heathers; the same little pendant pitchers cluster among the conifer-like foliage of the biggest of the heathers, *Erica arborea* (a big bush, seldom a real tree), and the broad leaves of the madrone.

They appear again in long streamers on the sorrel tree, *Oxydendrum arboreum*, of the eastern United States. Sorrel tree is a deciduous member of the family, the only one of its kind and a plant of very decided character. It wears a sort of oriental grace, its shoots falling away rather like the multiple eaves of a pagoda to form a tall pyramid – as high as 70 feet in the wilds. It flowers very usefully in late summer, is hardy to Cape Cod, and colours fiery red in autumn. Given good rhododendron country, every garden needs one.

And again the tree *Clethra* (*C. arborea*) from Madeira has the same flower design. Most members of the clethra family grow only to large shrub size but *arborea* can make a very attractive multi-stemmed tree, up to 25 feet. In late summer the tree is a cascade of fragrant, white, bell-like flowers on delicate spiky stalks. Sadly it is a very tender tree and will thrive only in the mildest of climates. Ideally it likes a rich, acid soil.

Left *The Pacific madrone is the western American version of the strawberry tree: a magnificent evergreen with a red trunk and red fruit, both contrasting splendidly with the dense green foliage.*

Above *Fruit of a strawberry tree, turning from yellow to red. Flowers can be seen (left of centre).*
Right Arbutus × andrachnoides *combines the hardiness, vigour and warm red bark of its parents the strawberry tree and* A. andrachne.

The Rhododendrons

Left *A pink form of the tree rhododendron, Rhododendron arboreum 'Roseum', has its trumpet-like flowers marked with red spots inside. There are also white varieties, one of which, 'Sir Charles Lemon', has red-brown felt under the leaves.*

The first known tree rhododendron, Rhododendron arboreum, has been a vital part of the genetic heritage of hundreds of hybrids. Here it is growing near Senchal lake in Darjeeling in the eastern Himalayas.

Below *Among the Himalayan species Sir Joseph Hooker introduced was Rhododendron falconeri, whose big stiff leaves have a thick buff felt beneath. The flowers are creamy-yellow bells splashed with purple.*

Left *The flower bud of a rhododendron holds up to 20 flowers packed tightly within its leaf-like scales. Nine out of ten rhododendrons flower in spring, sometimes going on into mid-summer.*

Below *The creamy-white flowers of the tree-sized Rhododendron fictolacteum open in April or early May. The leaves – up to 12 inches long – are covered with a thick brown felt on the underside. This species was discovered by Delavay in western China about 1884.*

Right *A rhododendron flower with some of its petals and stamens removed to show its structure. The female parts are the long curved pistil (right) and the small green ovary at its base. The male parts, the stamens, are the thin filaments to the left of the pistil. Their tips produce pollen.*

For a non-fanatic to write of rhododendrons at all is foolhardy, but to try to distinguish those that should be called trees, at least without long experience in the Himalayas, is almost suicidal. There never was a rhododendron with the sort of long straight trunk that would tempt a forester, that is certain. Yet who would call a plant 90 feet high, however curving and many-stemmed, a shrub?

Until 1820 the European and American rhododendrons were the only ones known. Of these the rosebay rhododendron, *R. maximum*, from the eastern States, was the biggest – though scarcely a tree.

In 1820 the first seeds of *R. arboreum* arrived in England from the Himalayas, packed by the prudent Nathaniel Wallich in brown sugar. With them arrived the glorious red blood that transformed the relatively tame and dowdy colours of the rhododendrons then known. For though *R. arboreum* was tender at first, and needed a conservatory in Britain, it soon hybridized and started hardy strains. Waterers, the famous nurserymen of Surrey, were the pioneers in adapting this tender giant to cultivation. Most modern rhododendron varieties, even small ones, have the blood of *R. arboreum* in their veins.

Sir Joseph Hooker's expedition to the Himalayas from 1847 to 1850 set the seal on the rhododendron as the supreme flowering evergreen. He introduced 43 species, including the tree-size *R. falconeri*.

Magnificent as they are in flower, a yet greater virtue of the bigger species is their leaves: great glossy tongues of darkest green, often backed with thick brown felt.

Left *These rhododendron hybrids at Squerryes Court, Westerham, Kent, are over 80 years old. Careful training of a single trunk can, as here, create a small tree even of bush-size species.*

The 'bearded' rhododendron (Rhododendron barbatum) might have been better named the unshaven: its twigs and leaf-stalks are covered with bristles up to half an inch long.

Western China has given us one of the hardiest of the tree-rhododendrons with huge evergreen leaves: Rhododendron calophytum.

The Himalayas have more great rhododendron species than California has kinds of pine. Rhododendron thomsonii was another of Hooker's discoveries: a very distinct tree with rounded leaves and deep red waxy bells of flowers.

Persimmons, Silverbells and Snowbells

The mainly tropical race that takes its name from the ebony tree of India and Ceylon is another remote descendant of the tea family on lines roughly parallel to the heaths. The ebony (*Diospyros ebenum*) has jet-black heartwood of great value. Its temperate-zone relations are better known for their fruit, the persimmon.

The persimmon is one of many trees which the chances of history have left in China and eastern North America and nowhere else. The Chinese tree (*Diospyros kaki*) gives the edible persimmon; a succulent yellow fruit the size and shape of an apple. The American tree (*D. virginiana*), which is much more impressive, has fruit that is edible only late in the season, after a frost (when it is soft and sweet, but still without flavour). As ornamental trees, however, both have merit. The smaller Chinese tree has long leaves of a glossy green that can turn orange, yellow or purple in autumn. The American is tall and narrow to 60 or 70 feet and its bark is one

Left *The common persimmon of the eastern States makes a straight and stately tree with a distinctive dark bark in a four-square pattern and fine yellow autumn colour. Its fruit is edible.*

Above *The Chinese persimmon is a smaller (up to 40 feet) but more ornamental tree. Though its flowers are green and well-camouflaged, its leaves are broad, glossy and attractive.*

The fruit of the Chinese or kaki persimmon ripens orange as the leaves turn to a noble shade of purple. These are the sweet persimmons or date-plums of the fruit-basket, grown in Japan, the southern States and in the south of France.

of the most arresting of any tree's: clear and regular fissures mark it both ways, dividing it into rectangular blocks of sooty grey. In Washington's National Arboretum it grows well in swampy ground by a stream, among dark-barked river birches. There were no leaves left when I saw it, but I picked the squashy yellow fruit which hung on the dipping boughs.

Persimmons claim no beauty of flower. But three neighbours of theirs on the evolutionary tree (neighbours rather than close relations) are among the trees with the prettiest flowers: the American snowdrop or silverbell tree; the Japanese snowbell; and the American-named Chinese fragrant epaulette tree.

There are two silverbells (called snowdrop trees in Britain): the shrubby Carolina version (*Halesia caroliniana*) and the much more noticeable mountain one (*H. monticola*) from the Great Smokies, which grows to 90 feet and wears big bunches of its bell-flowers on its bare shoots like cherry-blossom in the spring. The flowers are succeeded by fruits – also bell-like but with four little wings – which can hang a whole year.

The Japanese snowbell tree (*Styrax japonica*) seems more decorative in intention, for when it flowers in June it contrives to put the flowers just where you can best see them, in long rows along the long, low branches. It is a tree with a strong horizontal inclination, often twice as wide as it is high.

The leaves perch in pairs like butterflies along the tops of the branches while the dainty little white flowers hang beneath. *Styrax obassia* has fragrant flowers on erect spikes as an added advantage, but its bigger leaves are less neatly disposed.

As for the fragrant epaulette tree, *Pterostyrax hispida*, the lavish way it covers itself with creamy cascades of sweetly-smelling flowers could make it a mid-summer successor to the laburnum. It is the least particular of its group in the matter of soil – the others all shun lime.

Roses, Shadblows, Mespilus and Cotoneaster

Above *The Himalayan musk rose* (Rosa brunonii) *is among those with the vigour to climb to the top of a tall fruit tree and give it a second flowering season. The white flowers are richly scented.*

Below *The Allegheny serviceberry. Amelanchier laevis, produces myriads of delicate white flowers with pink young leaves in May. A hardy small tree, it grows best on soil with no lime.*

The fruit of the rose family varies more than its flowers. These three cross-sections show the flowers and fruit of the rose (above), the apple (below) and the plum (foot of page).

In each case the ovaries of the flowers are contained in a receptacle which is an extension of the flower-stalk. It is this receptacle that swells to become the flesh of the fruit.

In the rose-hip (top) the receptacle swells very little. It swells much more round the five seeds in one ovary of the apple (above) and the single seed in the ovary of the plum (below).

The thin bony membrane round the apple-seeds is the ovary wall: the ovary wall of the plum hardens to become the shell of the plum-stone.

The scope of the rose family is staggering. In the widest botanical sense the broad group of plants or Sub-class that bears the rose's name, the *Rosidae*, contains a third of all the species of flowering plants with two cotyledons. In the narrower Order, the *Rosales*, one-third of this one-third, one-ninth of the vast number belong: about 20,000 species. Of these some 2,000 species belong to the rose family proper; the *Rosaceae*.

Most of our fruit trees and ornamental blossom trees belong to this one family. The cherries, crab-apples, hawthorns, black-thorns, pears, apples, mountain-ashes, whitebeams, quinces, fire-thorns, shad-blows, laurels, cotoneasters, medlars, almonds, peaches, apricots and plums are all members. The next 18 pages are full of them, and this is only a selection of the best.

Hardiness is a feature of the family: there are few tropical members. There is no nonsense about acid soil either; to this family alkalinity is a positive virtue. In flower structure the family is distinctive; both sexes are present in the same flower and most flowers have five petals (though the number is often increased in the 'double' flowers that are bred for show).

How near together or far apart in ancestry the various members of the family may be has not been fully determined. There have been some surprising instances of cross-breeding between two very dissimilar trees: *Amelanchier* (the shadblow or snowy mespilus) and *Sorbus* (the mountain ash) for example. On the other hand *Malus* (the crab-apple) will not even graft on tò *Sorbus* or *Pyrus* (the pear), let alone hybridize with them. There can never be a cross between an apple and a pear.

There are no tree-roses, or rose-trees. The only way a rose can reach tree height is by climbing, using strong hooked thorns on long shoots as crampons. Some roses can go 40 feet or even higher. Species such as *Rosa filipes* 'Kiftsgate' or the Himalayan musk rose (*R. brunonii*) will scramble out into the sunlight at the top of an old fruit tree and send down astonishing cascades of a hundred sweet-scented flowers in a spray. If there is an old tree in your garden you consider dull you could do much worse than give it such an adornment as a Christmas present.

But even a 40-foot rose is only a shrub with long shoots, as liable to lie on the ground as to ascend into the air.

The tree known in America as shadbush or shadblow or serviceberry, in England as juneberry or snowy mespilus, is one of the most delicately beautiful of the rose's relations, and perhaps the one that gives a

The shadblow, tallest of the Amelanchiers, *reaches 50 or 60 feet in the eastern States. Its silvery leaves which accompany the white flowers in May turn scarlet and orange in autumn.*

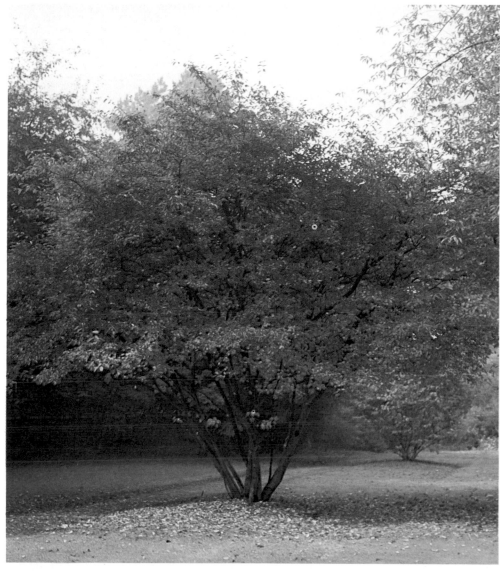

Left 'Snowy mespilus' is a bushy form of Amelanchier which grows wild in southern Europe, as here in Provence.

Below All Amelanchiers can be treated as garden shrubs; they readily sucker and form a thicket of stems. Their typical autumn colour is a sustained glow, effective even in grey weather.

small garden best value. *Amelanchier* (here is a case where an international name is obviously a relief) is a tree–or sometimes a bush–to watch carefully, even when it is not putting on its main performances.

The genus on the whole is lightly built and all its parts are cast in a fine mould: thin, pale grey limbs and pointed buds, emerging leaves of pale pink and coppery bronze, silver-haired (only a few cherries have the same combination) and accompanying the masses of star-shaped white flowers which froth it over lightly (though in warm weather, admittedly, for only a few days). By June there are bunches of berries like blackcurrants in shining green foliage. And in autumn, for a relatively long spell, the leaves turn the softest red, orange and brown; a glow rather than a flame.

North America has three or four amelanchiers, but there is often some confusion about which is which. When you say shadblow you mean the bush which blows–or blooms–when the shad are running in the rivers in April . . . or so the story goes. *Amelanchier canadensis* is the name most often used for the tallest, a tree often as much as 50 feet high. But if you follow the latest edition of W. J. Bean, which is much the wisest course, you must call this *A. arborea*. The Allegheny serviceberry is generally smaller, but has the prettiest unfolding leaves and sweet-tasting berries–as the birds know. And there is a hybrid between these two with pink-tinted flowers. Again this is often called *A. canadensis*, although its real name is *A. × grandiflora*. The true *A. canadensis* grows as an upright shrub in wet ground: a wildling.

Strictly speaking (to complete the picture) snowy mespilus is none of these but the European *A. ovalis*, a medium-sized to large shrub, which is snowy in its downy new leaves as well as its flowers.

Here among the rose tribe the shrub-barrier is crossed and recrossed so many times that a distinction must be arbitrary. Most of the species of *Cotoneaster* are shrubs without qualification. Indeed, some have a marked fondness for lying flat on the ground. But up rears the excellent *Cotoneaster × watereri*; a more than half-hearted attempt at an evergreen tree. In my garden it loses most of its dark green leaves by Christmas but keeps its incredible crop of red berries: almost a solid dome of scarlet 15 feet high and the same across. True it has 20 stems, but each one carries a tree's baton in its knapsack. For some reason the pheasants are in no hurry to gobble this crop; in mid-March there is still a good third of it beaming in the sun. Perhaps this restaurant knows more about serving than seasoning.

Shadblow fruit ripening from yellow through red to an eventual purple-black. When fully ripe it is edible though too small to be worth more than an inquisitive nibble.

None of the rose family bears fruit more abundantly, reliably and brilliantly than the almost-evergreen near-tree Cotoneaster cornubia and its improved forms. The scarlet bunches hang on long into the new year.

The Hawthorns

'Whenever I smell a May tree I think of going to bed by daylight.' This is William Morris, remembering his childhood on the edge of Epping Forest. Marcel Proust, thinking of Normandy, said the same thing (in a hundred times more words). Hawthorn blossom *is* the smell of early summer in the country.

To the layman there is scarcely a simpler or more consistent genus of tree than the hawthorn. It is a dense, compact, always a wild-looking tree, never a big one. It flowers in a sheet of haunting-scented blossom in May. Its blossom can be pink, is occasionally red, but (says the sentimentalist) ought to be white. It is fiercely armed with thorns, and covered with dark red berries as the year wears on.

In northern Europe it is the hedgerow tree; or rather it is the hedgerow. Its name means hedge-thorn, and long before barbed wire it made it very clear where my property ended and yours began. It was 'laid'

Above and below *The common hawthorn, otherwise known as 'May' or 'Quick', is northern Europe's commonest hedging material; below, in meadows in Burgundy. It is hard to beat for beauty of flower, for scent or for profusion of flower and fruit. Above, its little white flowers are peppered with darker stamens; they come after the deeply-lobed, polished leaves in late spring.*

by being cut half-through with a bill-hook and bent horizontally, to make a barrier that neither man nor beast could pass. Or often where no such fence was needed it grew to make an orchard-shape tree. The meadows (unpurged with selective weedkillers) shone with buttercups just at the season when the hawthorns gave them their dazzling frame.

But if it seems almost elemental to the layman, to the botanist it is a genus to dream of. A thousand species have at one time or another been identified in North America alone. How deceitful that apple-like blossom; those simple, shiny, dark green, tooth-edged leaves . . . that we should have been happy to think of them all as hawthorns, and never suspect. . .

The major differences that need concern a planter lie in the colour of the flower, the colour of the fruit, and the length of time the fruit hangs on the tree. Many species have red or orange leaves in autumn, too.

The best for flower colours, or at least

Left *The common hawthorn has a single seed in each berry or 'haw'. The other famous European species,* Crataegus oxyacantha, *has two or three seeds. It also has more different varieties with more ornamental flowers.*

the most varied, is the English hawthorn, *Crataegus oxyacantha*–not the common May or quick of the hedges, *C. monogyna*, but a tree differing in having two or three seeds to the berry instead of one. There are single- and double-flowered versions of the English thorn in white, pink and red. The best-known cultivar is the famous 'Paul's Scarlet'. Double-flowered cultivars on the other hand bear little fruit; nor does the English hawthorn colour well in autumn.

The common or hedgerow hawthorn has grown to almost 50 feet–and the oldest known is ten feet in girth. It usually has white flowers, but has them in such profu-sion that they hide the whole tree. The date of its flowering has a strange fascination for people. It was a point of pride that it should flower by May Day, the first of the month, in time for the traditional celebrations of spring (and of course socialism). The poor tree has had a hard time keeping to schedule since 1751, when the calendar was altered by 12 days.

It is a variety of this thorn (*C.m.* 'Biflora') that has earned itself a legend by habitually bearing a precocious crop of flowers at Christmas. The legend goes that Joseph of Arimathea, who visited England to preach Christianity after the Crucifixion, was getting nowhere with a sceptical Somerset audience on Christmas morning when God made his staff (which he had stuck in the ground) burst into leaf and flower.

Some of the American thorns have much bigger fruit than the English (the downy hawthorn, *C. mollis*, is an example) but more have as their advantage orange or red leaves in autumn. The Washington thorn (*C. phaenopyrum*) turns scarlet; the wide-spreading cockspur thorn (*C. crus-galli*) orange or red; the glossy-leaved thorn (*C. nitida*) the same. The hybrid *C. × lavallei* has both shiny leaves which last until the end of the year and red fruit which hangs on till spring. The combination is almost like holly in November.

There are also two Chinese hawthorns of character, *C. pinnatifida major* with big leaves, big bright fruit and good autumn colour, and *C. laciniata*, whose leaves are deeply lobed and grey with down and whose fruit is orange.

Above *The brightest and most 'double'-flowered hawthorn is the cultivar 'Paul's Scarlet', which makes a low spreading small tree. No fruit is produced by these sterile flowers.*

Below *The only variegated hawthorn is a variety of the common 'May'. One advantage of the hawthorns is that they are among the first deciduous trees to be green in spring.*

Above *The leaves and blossom of the late-flowering hybrid Crataegus × grignonensis. The flowers are followed by big red fruits; the leaves stay green until well into the winter.*

Below *Long-fingered grey leaves and orange berries make the far-eastern Crataegus orientalis one of the most original and decorative of the hawthorns. It is very tough and hardy.*

Above *The dark and glossy hawthorn Crataegus × lavallei is a cross between the American cockspur thorn and a Mexican species. Its fruit hangs on throughout the winter.*

Below *The American cockspur thorn has the longest (up to three inches) thorns of its prickly genus. Its glossy unlobed leaves colour well in autumn. Its flowers are profuse and its fruit long-lasting.*

Right *The 'Bronvaux medlar' (Crataegomespilus dardarii) is a strange cross between hawthorn and medlar (see pages 194–5), originally formed by grafting one tree on the other. It is more like a miniature medlar than a hawthorn.*

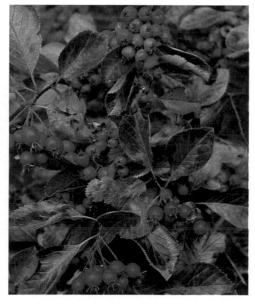

Quinces, Medlars and Crab-Apples

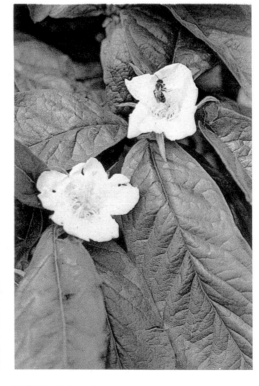

Fish is about the only thing we eat on a large scale today which is not specially bred for our consumption–perhaps the reason why we think of it as a luxury. The relationship of our wheat to the original grass, our heifers to the original wild cattle is pretty remote. As for the unselected, unimproved food which is all around us, we leave it for the birds.

In the rose family you can see every stage of selection and improvement–for every purpose. Selection has produced cabbage roses from sweet hedgerow briars, our big juicy apples from sour crabs. In the case of orchard apples it has concentrated on the fruit; in the case of crab-apples it has sought to perfect the flowers.

There remain other trees within the rose family, however, where the fruit has never come up to the standard of interest or flavour (or glamour) that is needed to make it a commercial proposition. It is eccentric to eat medlars or to grow quinces today; they are neither flesh nor fowl; that is, neither standard rations nor spectacular bearers of blossom. They come into the same category as mulberries–and make as alluring a tree to have on the lawn.

The medlar, both in flower and leaf, quickly becomes a centre of interest. It grows short and often crooked with a broad spread of generous leaves, hairy underneath (and in autumn a lovely russet colour). In May–already leafy–it carries quantities of soft round-petalled pinkish-white flowers. Watching these become medlars you can see exactly how, as in roses, the seed receptacle behind the flower's facade of petals swells into ripeness–without even closing at the end in the medlar's case, but leaving ajar the end where the petals were. The medlar is like a big brown rose-hip, perhaps two inches across. In the terms of a healthy Shakespearean exchange of insults, however, 'You'll be rotten ere you'll be half ripe'. The medlar is not ready for eating until it has been 'bletted' by the frost: gone 'sleepy', as they say of pears, with incipient rottenness. And then, truth to tell, it is no gastronomic experience.

The quince on the other hand is a tree to grow for the fruit. You can buy all the apples and pears you need, but the quince is the truffle of the orchard; the mysterious savour that makes an apple pie come alive as no apple–except possibly an old-fashioned russet–can. In Portugal quince jelly in granular pinky-amber slabs is a common confection; the quince ripens better there. Britain is a shade too cool for it. The haunting lemony fragrance hangs about the tree, however, and fills the kitchen.

There is not very much to choose between

Top *The fruit and (above) the flowers of the quince: one of the most beautiful of fruit trees, like an exotic pear with leaves silvery beneath and big yellow fragrant fruit. In time quinces make wide-spreading trees of great character.*

Top *The fruit and (above) the flowers of the medlar: like the quince, a fruit tree which calls to mind the well-stocked larders of old country-houses. The medlar has long softly hairy leaves and fruit like big rose-hips.*

quince and medlar as trees: their habits are similar. The quince has leaves richly white-felted below; flowers a little showier perhaps; fruit–a shining pale yellow pear–much prettier. The slightly more tender Portuguese quince is the best for flowers and has softly downy fruit; but any quince is a source of pleasure.

In the Middle Ages the crab-apple was important in the kitchen as the source (or a source) of verjus, a powerfully acid liquid that seems to have played the role of vinegar in salad recipes and recipes for preserving. In those days before bottles, when so much wine went bad in the barrel, it is a wonder they needed any other vinegar. But in Elizabethan cookery books there is still a great call for it. In addition, of course, crab-apples make refreshing jelly.

It was not until the end of the 18th century when the Siberian crab was introduced into cultivation that exciting hybrids began to appear with far more telling flowers than the modest white blossom of the old hedgerow tree.

Native American and later Chinese species joined in the criss-cross of breeding so profitably that the pedigree of a modern hybrid would have more 'begats' than the Book of Genesis.

Today crab-apples come second only to flowering cherries for excellence and popularity among flowering trees. Indeed before planting a flowering cherry it is very well worth examining the claims of the crabs. They have certain marked advantages that usually get overlooked.

In tough conditions of either soil or climate the crabs on the whole are more adaptable and hardy than the cherries. And under any conditions they are normally longer-lived. Like the cherries they rarely have good autumn colour but in compensation they often have very pretty fruit. What's more in many cultivars the fruit stays on the tree long after the leaves have gone–even into the following February or March. A crab with this peculiarity soon becomes a centre of curiosity and astonishment. I know of one (a 'Golden Hornet') that has nearly caused nasty accidents. It stands, dripping with yellow apples, near a sharp bend in the road. On a brilliant winter day you can't help looking at it as you go by. . . .

Crabs often bear as many flowers as cherries, but few have the weight of petals; the flowers have never quite developed into the same sort of extravaganzas. Some think that with fewer petticoats they have more charm.   ▶

Early spring in the département of Calvados. Cider-apple trees share the fields of Normandy with cattle. The cider from the sour apples is distilled to make Calvados apple-brandy; the cattle give superlative cream and cheese.

The Crab-Apples

Left and below left *The Japanese flowering crab has the simplest little single white flowers. It gains its extraordinarily beautiful effect from the backs of the petals, which are cherry-red before they open. Its flowering is delayed until the leaves have expanded, so white, red and bright green are intermingled on the arching tree. This was one of the first flowering trees to be introduced from Japan in 1862.*

Above *'Charlottae' is a superior form of one of America's native crab apples, Malus coronaria. Its big but delicate and subtly-scented flowers come in late spring or early summer.*

Right *A complicated parentage of Chinese and Japanese crabs has produced hybrids with a red tint in both flowers and leaves. One of the most popular cultivars, with deep red flowers, is Malus 'Lemoinei'.*

Above *The hybrid Malus × purpurea is one of the most conspicuous crabs with its profusion of reddish-pink flowers and its dark purple-green leaves. The fruits are like large cherries and hang on dark red stalks.*

Above and left *The Siberian crab is the hardiest of its race; a small tree which regularly smothers its branches in fragrant white flowers. Its fruit is as small as a berry, usually yellow as here but sometimes red.*

The crab apples are more
often distinguished for
autumn colour than the
cherries. The Japanese
Malus tschonoskii is
worth planting for its
autumn scarlet alone. Its
upright carriage makes it
very suitable for street
planting.

▶Several of the species of crab-apples that have contributed most to the breed in the stud book are still very much in circulation in their own right.

Perhaps the best of them is the Japanese crab (*Malus floribunda*), which is one of the first to flower; a thrilling sight in April when its flowers open from bright red (the backs of the petals) to white (the front). The new leaves are still shining grass green and very small; the flowers waiting to open look like scarlet berries among the white stars of those that already have. All this happens at eye level: it is only a short tree and the branches tend to arch and hang. Most important, it does its stuff every year; a number of otherwise excellent crabs take alternate years off.

There is another Japanese species, Sargent's crab (*M. sargentii*) which is as beautiful in flower (white flowers with gold centres) and in its bright red fruit, but which is only a big bush eight or nine feet high and wide.

The selected, bigger-flowered forms of two native American species, themselves closely related, compete in the flowering-cherry league with big soft double pink flowers. Bechtel's crab (*M. ioensis* 'Plena') is a form of the prairie crab–no relation of the prairie oyster–which sacrifices fruit for extra petals. The less temperamental tree of the two, *M. coronaria* 'Charlottae', has the great advantage of noticeably larger and toothed leaves, which colour well in autumn.

Of the many superb Chinese species– China has the richest natural supply–the cutleaf crab (*M. toringoides*) is the most un-usual on account of its leaves, which are not only deeply cut with lobes but colour well in autumn to set off the big red and yellow apples. *M. halliana* 'Parkmanii' has double pink flowers on red stalks; *M. spectabilis* 'Riversii' (or Rivers' crab) is fairly early with its profuse red-bud-pink flower combination; the Hupeh or tea crab which E. H. Wilson found (*M. hupehensis*) is a strange thing with branches which, when they flower late in the season, are like long tentacles of pink and white.

Different parts of Siberia have given us different improvements on the Siberian crab, *M. baccata*. *M.b.* 'Mandshurica' is the Manchurian candidate, a big early-flowering tree with fragrant white flowers. In the tree horrifically named *M. niedzwetzkyana* southwest Siberia or Kazakhstan has made an important contribution of red blood: *M. niedzwetzkyana* has a red pigment that shows in its new shoots, its clusters of purply-red flowers and its plum-coloured fruit. Some of the reddest of the hybrids have this 'blood' in their veins.

'Lemoinei' is a typical example with rich red flowers. The more recent 'Profusion' is another and 'Red Tip' a third. 'Echtermeyer' is a tree with the same colour scheme but a weeping habit. I confess to a quiet loathing of a dark red tone in almost anything except wine–but don't listen to me.

There is obvious confusion lying in wait in the two excellent hybrids called 'Red Jade' and 'Red Sentinel', both of which sound like fellow-travellers but in fact have white flowers. 'Red Jade' is a small weeping tree, 'Red Sentinel' a bigger one. The great value of both lies in the bunches of red crabs bigger than cherries that hang on and on through the winter.

Of the trees with yellow fruit the 'Golden Hornet' I have mentioned is certainly one of the best and 'Dorothea' (a product of the Arnold Arboretum) is said to be very good. Dorothea's flowers are pink and double.

Even this trugful by no means exhausts the catalogue. 'John Downie' is possibly the best known cultivar of the old English wild crab, *M. sylvestris*. For a crab it makes a big tree which is generous with substantial red and yellow fruit: several crabs make good jelly material but John Downie's fruit is actually good to eat off the tree.

The Siberian crab has a Manchurian variety (Malus baccata 'Mandshurica') which is the first of all the crabs to blossom, though later than some of the early flowering cherries.

Left *The 'cherry' crab (Malus × robusta), a hybrid of the Siberian crab, is another form with particularly striking fruit.*

Above *'Golden Hornet' is a crab apple worth growing for its fruit alone. It is a neat domed tree with unremarkable white flowers but a regular crop of brilliant yellow fruit which stays long after the leaves have fallen.*

The Flowering Cherries of Japan

The flowering cherry is not so much a tree as an event: a milestone in the year which even the most ungardening citizen recognizes. It is (as the Japanese have long known) a suitable object for a cult. Would thousands flock out from the city to see the crabs, the laburnums – even the magnolias – in flower? They do to see the cherries.

The cherry alone manages to look both virginal and voluptuous. It is easy (and fashionable) to turn up your nose at it; to consider it tainted by the suburbs which have become its second home. Yet nature offers no experience of profusion and delight so strong. To stand among the low branches in the fragility of millions of pale petals is in the range of natural experiences that are totally distinct and all-embracing; like standing under a waterfall, or flying through racing scraps of cloud.

It is also, to westerners, a modern experience. Japanese cherry-worship is a thousand years old, but the garden cherries perfected in Japan were not seen in the West (or had not grown to full size) until this century. Most of the work that has led to their popularization was done by one man who is still alive: Captain Collingwood Ingram.

The Japanese have firm notions about which cherries should be planted where. The elaborately double-flowered forms they keep for important sites, where they plant them singly. For the massed effects of hundreds of trees they use single-flowered species and they stick to one kind. The most famous cherry-viewing district near Kyoto is planted entirely with the hill cherry (*Prunus serrulata* var. *spontanea*). It flowers late enough (the second half of April) for the weather to be perfect when its broad crowns turn white against black pines and the pattern of dark and light is reflected in the Kamo River.

The biggest (to 90 feet) and longest-lived (to 1,000 years at least) of these half-wild single cherries is the spring cherry (*P. subhirtella*). But its little pale pink flowers are not up to the standard of cultivated varieties. The important forms of the spring cherry are the weeping *P.s.* 'Pendula' (which was the first Japanese cherry to reach the western world in the middle of the last century); the double-flowered *P.s.* 'Fukubana'; and the winter-flowering *P.s.* 'Autumnalis'. One can forgive the flowers their weak colour and puny size when they are the only ones in the garden. In a mild winter in the south of England the performance is continuous from late October on; most of the flowers clustering tightly round little wispy shoots from the trunk – ideal for cutting and taking indoors. In a harder climate 'Autumnalis' often flowers in Novem-

ber and again in the early spring.

The most popular cherry in Tokyo today is a relatively modern hybrid, the Yoshino (*P.* × *yedoensis*), which flowers early and fills the suburbs with the scent of almonds. Its advantage for a shifting population is that it grows and flowers quicker than the others. The flowers come in tens of thousands, white stained with pink, on branches that droop at the ends as though under their weight. Nurseries often offer selected droopy forms.

Noblest of the common species is the tall great mountain cherry. Picture it on the middle slopes of Mt. Fujiyama. It is known to the West by the name of Professor Sargent of the Arnold Arboretum. Sargent's cherry (*P. sargentii*) candies over with bright pink flowers before the leaves, but the leaves catch up and mingle their ruby-brown with the pink. On a tree 40 or 50 feet high the effect is pretty powerful.

Cherries as a whole are not great autumn-colour trees. Sargent's cherry is an exception, particularly conspicuous for turning orange and red in September while most trees are still green. Its long oval leaves turn their points down and hang rather sadly as summer ends, but when they catch fire the display is all the better for seeing their whole length.

The Japanese use the term *sato zakura*, which means village cherries, for their cultivated productions. There are 40 or 50 of them in cultivation in Europe and America. When they first arrived they were given Latin names relating them all to the species *P. serrulata*, but the tendency today is to use their Japanese names alone without trying to trace the intricacies of their parentage.

The most popular of them all, by far, is the variety called 'Kanzan' (or often, but wrongly, 'Kwanzan'). Its vigour, its freedom with its many-petalled flowers, and above all their piercing pink colour combine to make a fatal appeal. Pink is tricky. There are agreeable clear pinks, salmon pinks, tawny pinks and rosy pinks, but as soon as pink is stained with blue it starts to shriek. Kanzan is calmed by a white background, but its stridency in combination with red brick walls has alone been enough to give the cherries a bad name.

As a little tree in the nursery Kanzan looks well-adapted for a narrow space. Its branches climb steeply in a narrow V-shape. At ten or 15 years, however, the narrowness is a thing of the past: 25 feet or more is a normal spread.

Several other cherries have the same vase-shape, at least in youth. 'Ukon' is a very pretty one with white flowers just

touched with enough lime-green to give a sulphury effect. 'Hokusai' is another, eventually spreading wide, with hundredweights of pale pink flowers slowly being overtaken by pinky-brown emerging leaves.

The only flowering cherry that really fits permanently into a narrow space is 'Amanogawa', which is built like a stripling Lombardy poplar; a shape which (soldier-like as it is) makes a laughable combination with petticoat-pink flowers. 'Amanogawa' is a mistake in the open lawn. At the back of a bed or among shrubs where its shape is not overstressed it could be a very useful tree, though.

Tokyo's favourite flowering cherry is the 'Yoshino' (Prunus × yedoensis). *Its faintly pink flowers come early and scent the April air with almonds. Though it grows eagerly to start with it never makes a big tree.*

Flowering cherries have been an important theme in Japanese art and literature since the 12th century. This 17th-century painted screen shows cherry and plum blossom.

Flowers of the 'hill' cherry, simple and white with bronzy-green young leaves, are the archetype of Japanese cherry-worship. This is the tree planted in groves near Kyoto, the object of pilgrimages in early May.

The weeping form of the 'spring' cherry is so graceful a little tree that even without its early white (or very pale pink) flowers it would be planted, like the weeping birch, for its elegance.

What the flowering cherries really want to do, or look as though they want to do, is to reach long branches low across the lawn. The trees that do this offer you a whole universe of coloured petals to swim in at head height–even to wade in at waist height.

'Shirofugen' is a May-flowering, long-lasting one, pink in bud and maturing white, which does this. 'Shirotae' is an earlier, scented, pure-white one, which makes wonderful use of the bright green of its new leaves to show off its hanging clusters of flowers. The leaves remain a feature of 'Shirotae': their edges are fringed with deep teeth and they have long points. 'Shimidsu' is a third, with pink buds opening late to wide white flowers on stalks six inches long.

The best of all spreading cherries, and all white cherries, however, is 'Tai Haku'–a tree with a fascinating history. In 1923 the owner of a garden in Sussex showed Captain Collingwood Ingram a tree without a name. It had the biggest flowers he had ever seen on a cherry; simple five-petalled flowers, shining white with gold stamens, displayed among huge copper-red young leaves. He promptly took grafts and put it into circulation, knowing nothing of its name or where it originally came from.

On his next visit to Japan Ingram was shown an 18th-century book of flower-paintings. In one of the paintings he recognized his new white cherry. But, he was told, it had been lost to cultivation since the painting was made. There was no 'Tai Haku' in Japan; the Japanese certainly didn't believe it could exist in England.

How it came to that Sussex garden remains a mystery. All the 'great white' cherries in cultivation today, however, are its offspring. Ingram himself recommends planting it by still water where its roots can drink deep and its beauty be reflected.

Top left *Sargent's cherry opens its tens of thousands of single clear pink flowers early in the season, making one of the great landmarks of spring. In autumn, again very early, its leaves turn the fieriest colour of any of the cherries.*

Bottom left *'Amano-gawa' is the only upright cherry: a little column of ascending branches like a baby Lombardy poplar. Its pale pink slightly scented flowers come late in the season. In autumn it turns pinkish amber.*

Top right *The piercing pink and frilly flowers of 'Kanzan' have made it the most popular of the Japanese cherries in the western world. It is a vigorous, wide-stretching tree, growing quickly to over 20 feet.*

Bottom right *The great white cherry has the biggest blooms of any, in the purest white. At the same time the young leaves have a coppery glow. A big 'Tai Haku' near water is the finest sight the Japanese cherries can offer.*

The Flowering Cherries

The *Prunus* branch of the rose family has such a strangely various bunch of components that it used to be divided into a number of different genera. The cherries then were *Cerasus*; the almonds and peaches *Amygdalus*; the plums, *Prunus*; the apricots, *Armeniaca*; the bird cherries *Padus* and the laurels, or cherry laurels, *Laurocerasus*. The botanical argument, though, is that they all have a single female organ in a five-petalled flower, and consequently a single-stoned fruit.

Japan has no monopoly of the flowering cherries. In fact Captain Collingwood Ingram, enumerating the species, counts 13 for Japan (not counting, of course, the countless varieties), 23 for China, six for North America and five for Europe. Europe's best have long been known and used both for ornament and for their fruit. For both purposes the leading species is the gean, mazzard or simply wild cherry which flourished over the whole European continent, in Britain and as far east as the Caucasus. Its small cherries are sweet or relatively sweet in the wild; in cultivated varieties of course they are delicious. Seduced by the Japanese varieties, however, we have forgotten how beautiful the gean can be. Its double-flowered variety (*Prunus avium* 'Plena') not only rivals the *sato zakura* in its billowing white flowers but is hardier. The biggest gean, moreover, is of forest tree size, almost 15 feet in girth, and specimens 80 or 90 feet high are not unknown. This is the tree whose wood makes so much splendid French furniture and whose fruit makes the potent Kirsch of Switzerland, the Black Forest and the Vosges.

Above *The wild cherry of Europe, the mazzard or gean, is a tall woodland tree greatly prized for its timber and very beautiful in early spring. Its double-flowered form is among the best white cherries for the garden.*

Left *Leaves of the wild cherry in early autumn. Few cherries are noted for autumn colour, but many turn gentle amber shades and hang their leaves like this. The wild cherry often goes on from this stage to deep red.*

The sweet-fleshed eating cherries are cultivars of the European wild cherry. Morello cherries (here growing in Switzerland) are derived from the sour cherry (Prunus cerasus). The Swiss use their fruit for jam.

Left and below *Bird cherries make their little white flowers conspicuous among their early-appearing leaves by carrying them in spikes like the butterfly-bush buddleia. The American choke and rum cherries do the same. The showiest of them is Waterer's bird cherry (Prunus padus 'Watereri'), shown here.*

Of still older use as a garden ornament is the sour cherry *P. cerasus*, the parent of the dark Morellos from which the Swiss make their marvellous jam. The white double-flowered version of this (*P.c.* 'Rhexii') has been known to gardeners since Elizabethan times at least.

The bird cherry (*P. padus*), which grows all the way from Britain to Japan, is different in having its flowers in spikes; much smaller individually, but almost as effective in being crowded together. Of this too there are selected versions: *P.p.* 'Watereri' with extra-long flower-spikes, 'Colorata' with pink ones and *commutata*, an oriental form which produces leaves exceptionally early.

North America's native cherries have produced no spectacular ornamental trees; the best of them, *P. serotina*–the black or rum cherry–is the equivalent of the bird cherry. It is very common in the woods of the east, but neither its short spikes of white flowers nor its little red cherries attract much attention. The choke cherry (*P. virginiana*) is another 'bird' type with flowers in spikes. The wild red cherry, *P. pensylvanica*, has clustered flowers and fruit like the gean.

E. H. Wilson brought back a number of cherries from China. The most important in cultivation have been *P. conradinae* which he found in Hupeh, whose variety 'Semi-Plena' is singularly weather-proof; *P. serrula* from western China, whose flowers are not up to much but whose bark is in the birch class, glistening squirrel-brown; and *P. campanulata*, which he picked up in Formosa as a contribution to the gardens of the south. It is one of the reddest-flowered of cherries, but for a warm climate only.

It was not Wilson but an earlier traveller who brought *P. maackii* back from Manchuria to the Arnold Arboretum. It remains rare, but makes a stout tree with bark of a glorious polished golden-brown. There is one like a barrel of honey at Wakehurst Place, Kew's country garden in Sussex.

Nurseries meanwhile have been busy with hybrids and selections; far too many to catalogue. One of the very best was produced by Hillier's and called *P. × hillieri* 'Spire'. Their description of it as 'possibly the best small street tree raised this century . . . flowers soft pink; leaves with rich autumnal tints' is fair comment.

Given a good start in life the cherry is such an easy tree to grow in most soils (it prefers a little lime and good drainage) that its performance is more or less assured. There is one thing it doesn't like, and that is to be hacked about; it tends to go on producing gum from a bad cut until it dies. Its motto is 'Don't Prunus'.

Left and below *Cherry bark is easy to recognize by its scattered horizontal scars, or lenticels. A few cherries have satiny, birch-like bark, emphasising the stripes. Most beautiful and striking is* the Chinese Prunus serrula *(left). The Manchurian cherry (below) with flaking honey-coloured bark is less common but a much hardier tree. Neither has spectacular flowers.*

Left *The wild red or pin cherry is common in woods in parts of the eastern States. It has white flowers before the bright green, finely-toothed leaves–and shiny little red cherries in great abundance.*

Left *The fruit of the bird cherry is small, black and bitter: far from being the favourite of the birds, which often leave it on the tree all the winter.*

Peaches, Plums and Cherry Laurels

The frivolity of the flowering cherry has been contagious. Peach, almond, apricot and plum have all caught it and produced more or less fruitless varieties with a short season of stunning display.

It comes most easily to the almond, *Prunus dulcis.* Even in countries where the almond is grown seriously for the kernels of its fruit, orchards are a tourist attraction. In Sicily, for instance, they are frothing pink in a countryside not given to such femininities – and as early as February. The fruit is not up to much in northern parts, but the trees are hardy and flower just as well. *P.d.* 'Roseoplena' is the almond's nearest approach to a cherry: pink, many-petalled, and one of the first trees in blossom. Well-protected with evergreens it can be the best thing in a drear March garden.

An almond is a peach with a lean fruit: or a peach is an almond with a fat one. In any case there is little difference besides the sweet flesh. They are close enough kin to breed together. The most ornamental upshot so far was conceived in Australia at the turn of the century and given the name *P. × amygdalo-persica* 'Pollardii'. Pollard was the nurseryman; *amygdalus* was in those days the specific name of the almonds (*dulcis* is today) and *persica* of the peaches. The fruits of this hybrid are like hard green peaches; the main attraction is its big pink flowers – bigger and pinker than either of its parents'. Again, a first-class tree for early blossom.

The peaches flower just after the almonds. A well-planned group of trees could use a flowering peach to link the blossom-time of the almond to that of the first cherries so that from early March (or sooner in the south) through to June there would always be a tree in flower. Of the peaches selected and sold for their flowers the most telling are perhaps the double-flowered red or rose-pink cultivars. The best-known is *P. persica* 'Klara Meyer'. Peaches, however, are not the rugged self-supporting individuals that cherries and even almonds are. They have a range of problems, from a curling and crumpling ailment of their handsome long leaves to relatively early decline and death. Growing peaches (or even better their smooth-skinned sisters nectarines) against a wall for fruit is another matter.

The fruit-tree apricot from China (*P.*

In the very earliest spring almond blossom comes to lighten the Troodos mountains in Cyprus. Even in a northern climate the almond is one of the first trees to flower: often as early as mid-March.

armeniaca) is nothing much to look at, though it is hardy and early in bloom. For its fruit, of course, it is eminently worth growing anywhere warm enough to ripen it. The Japanese apricot (*P. mume*) is the one for flowers. It is a shade less hardy than the almond. Double white, double pink and pendulous forms of both are to be had. Their 'floral ardour', as Collingwood Ingram warmly puts it, depends on the sunshine of the summer before.

Most of the domestic plum-trees are thought to be forms of an ancient hybrid between the sloe or blackthorn (*P. spinosa*) and the myrobalan or cherry plum *P. cerasifera*, which originally came from eastern Europe and western Asia. Neither is a very impressive tree in its own right; the blackthorn more often a suckering bush. The blackthorn's flowering, tiny though the white flowers are, is such a feature of hedgerows at the end of March that the spell of cold weather which often occurs in northern

Europe at that time is known as the blackthorn winter.

I was surprised to discover that there is a fancy purple-leaved variety even of the humble blackthorn. The purple version of the cherry plum is all too well known: the grossly over-planted purple-leaved cliché of suburban streets. The culprit for this tree was M. Pissard, the French gardener of the Shah of Persia 100 years ago – whence its name of *P. cerasifera* 'Pissardii'. There are other, slightly different cultivars, but all of them are trees of dreary hue.

It is quite hard to make the mental jump from the deciduous trees of *Prunus* to the big shiny-leaved evergreen shrubs which have borrowed from the bay tree the name of laurels. What could have less in common with a flowering cherry? Yet *Prunus* species they are.

The cherry laurel is the common one that flourishes in the dankest shade. It has a dozen variants; different leaf-shapes,

The almond and the peach are closely related. The ripe fruit of the almond (left) is like a green peach without the thick layer of juicy flesh. Though the almond is remarkably hardy it takes a Mediterranean climate to ripen fruit regularly.

The Japanese apricot, Prunus mume, introduced to the West in 1844, is a pretty little tree with almond-scented pink flowers. It has produced several splendid varieties, including the form shown here: 'Alphandii'.

The wild apricot of China has naturalised itself in parts of Europe. Here it blooms in March above Lake Lugano in Switzerland.

Right *The beautifully-bloomed but intensely sour sloe is the fruit of the blackthorn (Prunus spinosa). Blackthorn in the hedges is a sheet of tiny white flowers just before the more voluptuous pear-blossom appears.*

Below *A cross between the peach and the almond, Prunus × amygdalo-persica, was first made in cultivation in 1623. One of its most ornamental forms is 'Pollardii' which has big, deep pink flowers.*

Bottom *The Chinese Photinia serrulata looks more like a cherry-laurel than its nearer relation the hawthorn. Its great value to gardeners is its almost year-round succession of new shoots bearing bright red young leaves.*

The purple-leaved plum has a short-lived display of almost daisy-like pink flowers, appearing with the coppery-red young leaves. During the summer the leaves grow darker and darker, becoming almost black by autumn.

The evergreen cherry laurel successfully disguises its close relationship to the cherries until its fruit ripens red. Victorian shrubberies have given this magnificently-leaved little tree (or big shrub) a bad name it scarcely deserves.

colours and habits, the most striking of all a tall one with bold curling leaves, *P. laurocerasus* 'Camelliifolia'. The Portugal laurel (*P. lusitanica*) is a very smart round-topped tree up to 30 or 40 feet, glossy and a good bright green all the year round. Game birds enjoy the little cherries. Forms with broader leaves (*azorica*); narrower leaves ('Angustifolia'); and variegated leaves ('Variegata') can be found. The capabilities of these trees as the evergreen foundations of gardens on poor and chalky soil have scarcely been explored.

Better still is the Chinese *Photinia serrulata* – as yet an almost unknown member of the rose family but a hardy, uncomplaining and thoroughly original tree/shrub. This photinia is constantly producing new shoots of brilliant orange-red leaves, which slowly fade to gleaming green. The effect is of a tree never-endingly in flower. I have not seen a photinia as big as the biggest reported – 50 feet – but it must be quite a sight.

Pear Trees, Whitebeams and Mountain Ashes

Pears, whitebeams, mountain ashes–they seem strange bedfellows. Two, in fact, the superficially unlike whitebeams and mountain ashes, belong in the same genus–that of *Sorbus*. The pear is *Pyrus*, on its own.

What are the real differences between apples and pears? Flavour is obviously the most important. The pear tends to have a fleshy stalk, not joining the fruit in a dip but on a bump. Its flesh is granular in texture; gritty when unripe and once ripe, soon rotten.

Pears are wild in Europe and Asia; not in the New World. The common pear from which all the orchard varieties are derived occurs frequently in the south of Europe, and is not uncommon in the north. It is one of the longest-lived of fruit trees and eventually reaches a remarkable size: there are records of pear trees 16 feet in girth, and 60 feet is not an exceptional height.

Old common pears are densely twiggy; black and emphatic in winter–which makes their regular early spring covering of delicate white blossom all the more effective. Few (if any) are planted on purpose; where they happen to come up they are none the less very much enjoyed. Their wood is the 'fruit-wood' of French provincial furniture; the light brown that glows in old armoires and dressers.

There are two Chinese wild pears that have a following in the United States these days as ornamental trees. One is the work of the Plant Introduction Station at Glenn Dale, Maryland. From their stock of *Pyrus calleryana* they chose a seedling (known as *P.c.* 'Bradford') which has all the makings of a good medium-sized shade tree; a dense pyramid with plenty of flower and red autumn colour. The other is the Ussurian pear (*P. ussuriensis*) which has a more northerly range. Neither gives edible fruit.

The only pears one would normally consider planting for their beauty in the garden are those with white or silvery young leaves–*P. nivalis* from the Mediterranean and above all the willow-leaved pear (*P. salicifolia*) from the Caucasus. For the particular combination of summer-long silveriness and a weeping habit this has no competitors. If anyone is looking for an instant feature, a theme to form the basis for a new garden, or a corner of an old one, they could hardly do better than this. It has a tendency to overbranch and make a tousled head; this is its only fault (and it can be cured by pruning). I have made a silver plantation using it beside a weeping silver lime in a thicket of silver sea-buckthorn. Some common juniper (also in part silver) is dotted about. Have I overdone it? Very likely.

Above and below *The most decorative of pear trees is the weeping willow-leaf pear: a small tree with narrow silvery leaves, simple creamy-white flowers and a dense, rather congested but generally pendulous way of growing. Its pale silvery green shows up brightly all summer. The fruit is small, brown and shaped like a top. The form 'Pendula' is more common in cultivation.*

Above and below *Of all garden trees not bred or selected for beauty of blossom, the pear gives the best display. Old pear trees are like clouds of white and gentle green in early spring. Above is a typical old domestic pear, a cultivar, probably nameless, of Pyrus communis, by a farmhouse in Normandy. Below is pear blossom, white touched with pink, bunched and stiff on the spray.*

Above *Summer leaves and newly-formed fruit of the common pear.*

Right *The autumn colour of pear leaves. They emerge slightly white-furry in spring, but become glossier as the season advances. Pear trees will live to a great age, becoming the stateliest members of their family.*

It is almost a relief, after the frenzied flowering of so many of the rose family, to come to a group of trees which arrange their nuptials more discreetly. Neither whitebeam nor mountain ash, the two broad classes of *Sorbus*, is worth planting for the sake of its flowers. They are white or cream, and although there are plenty of them in broad heads they come with the leaves which not only tend to hide them but are in themselves more eye-catching. The leaves are the strong point of both sections of sorbus, different though they are. And after the leaves, in many cases, the heavy bunches of little coloured berries.

The whitebeams have single, simple leaves; usually just toothed but sometimes lobed, very often white-felt-backed. The white side of the leaf gives the tree its name. The mountain ashes have compound leaves; anything from three to 30-odd leaflets on a stalk. In the days of more naïve botany this was enough to prove them ashes. None of the trees in either class grows to enormous size. Seventy-five feet would be a record.

The mountain ashes outnumber the whitebeams but remain pretty consistent wherever they grow. There are four distinct whitebeam strains; a splendid one of several species with huge leaves in the Himalayas; the locally variable whitebeam (again several species, but very similar ones) of northern Europe; a couple of trees with leaves deeply enough lobed to remind one of the maple, also in Europe; and a superb Japanese tree with hornbeam-like leaves which is the best of all for flowers and fruit. America has no native whitebeams.

It is the way in which the leaves appear that first draws your attention to the whitebeam in the spring. They emerge from the bud rather as the petals do in the tulip, forming a chalice-shape with their points up and displaying their undersides. At this stage the underside (in most cases indeed the whole leaf) is covered with a silvery silk that reflects the light like metal. In the wild the tree is characteristic of chalk and limestone hills; it winks from copses of pale beech or the bronzy black of yew.

By July the brilliance of the leaves has gone. In many years insects get to work on them and leave mere fretwork. But if all is well they have a second stint in October in shades of russet and amber, setting off heavy bunches of red berries.

This is the wild one of Europe, *Sorbus aria*. Cultivation has polished up its performance without greatly changing it in the cultivars *S.a.* 'Lutescens' and 'Majestica' (which has bigger leaves and berries). It has also produced a pale yellow form (*S.a.* 'Chrysophylla') and a weeping one (*S.a.* 'Pendula') which are both very pretty trees.

The Himalayan whitebeams are recognizably the same tree, but with much bigger leaves, rich glossy green on top, chalk-white beneath, and as much as ten inches long. *S. cuspidata* has broad-oval or long, tapered leaves; *S.* 'Mitchellii' almost round ones; both are supremely lush and well-nourished looking trees, whose livery of dark green and white lasts well all summer. Their berries are crab-apple size, but not brightly coloured. The place to plant either would be in a wood where their big leaves are given some protection from the wind. They stand out magnificently among the busy patterns of oak or beech.

There are three whitebeams with lobed leaves. The Swedish whitebeam (*S. intermedia*) is just that – intermediate; the second is a native of most of Europe including England with the curious name of the wild service tree; and the third is *S. hybrida*. Learned discussion has produced two alternative theories for the meaning of 'service'. One gives it the same Latin root as *cerveza*, the Spanish word for beer, on the grounds that a drink was once brewed from its berries. The other, more earthily, reckons it is no more than a corruption of sorbus. In any case people with wild service trees tend to be rather pleased with themselves; not because the tree is spectacular (though its leaves like a handsome maple – without a felty side – and its speckled brown berries make an intriguing combination) but because it is wild and native. There are butterflies which get people in the same way. ▶

Left and below The Swedish whitebeam (Sorbus intermedia; *left, in autumn*) and S. hybrida (*below*) appear to be links between the oval-leafed whitebeams and the closely related but very different mountain ashes with their divided ash-like leaves. The Swedish tree has slightly lobed leaves; the 'hybrid' deeper lobes, becoming actual divisions towards the base of the leaf.

Its silvery-hairy leaves make the whitebeam (Sorbus aria) conspicuous. The flowers (like those in the picture on the left) are pretty, but less noteworthy than its young leaves. It is a common wild tree on chalk or limestone soil in Europe.

Pear Trees, Whitebeams and Mountain Ashes

► The wild service tree has hybridized with the ordinary whitebeam to produce the service tree of Fontainebleau (*Sorbus latifolia*) which has both lobes and felt lining. The other hybrids of the family link the whitebeams with the mountain ashes. The upshot in these cases, *S. hybrida* from Scandinavia (now considered a true species) and *S.* × *thuringiaca*, originally from Thuringia in what is now East Germany, is just what you would expect; compromise leaves with a whitebeam-type oval at the end and a clutch of mountain ash-type leaflets. From the whitebeam they keep white bottom-sides.

An upright version of the Thuringian white-mountain-ash-beam (*S.* × *t.* 'Fastigiata') earns praise on all sides as a street tree which doesn't take up too much room.

The Arnold Arboretum is also full of praise for the Japanese/Korean sorbus, which is hard to place in either section of the family. This is the one with leaves very like a hornbeam, having the same corrugation where the veins go. Botany has described its leaves as alder-like (its name is *S. alnifolia*) which seems a bit far-fetched. In any case it is the gayest of the race in flower and the most conspicuous in fruit, keeping its red berries long after the leaves have turned red and fallen.

It follows from its leaf-design that the mountain ash is a less substantial, more feathery-looking tree than the whitebeam. It grows to about the same size and has the same flowers and fruit, but otherwise it is remarkably different.

One basic model of mountain ash with only stylistic variations in colour of leaf, size of leaf and colour of berry runs right round the world. Its most famous representative is the rowan; a tree, like the Scots pine, identified inextricably with Scotland (though it is native to most of Europe). I have seen landscapes there in which full dress tartans would have simply disappeared

Whitebeam fruit ripens in glowing colours while the leaves turn shades of buff and yellow. The fruit is rose-hip size and very popular with the birds. Whitebeams never grow much taller than 50 feet.

Above *The Japanese whitebeam* Sorbus alnifolia *is one of the best for autumn colours. It is highly prized by the Arnold Arboretum for its clusters of tiny bright-red fruit that hang on the tree long after the leaves have gone.*

Above *The whitebeams of the Himalayas (here* Sorbus mitchellii) *have huge and handsome leaves, dark shiny green above and furry-white beneath. Their fruit is like a tiny pear.*

Below *The leaves and ripe fruit of the wild service tree, an unusual whitebeam with maple-like leaves, growing to 60 or 70 feet. It is a native of Europe, Asia Minor and North Africa.*

Below *The mountain ash or rowan of Europe is a small tree of the wilds but a willing recruit for gardens, with remarkable quantities of gaudy fruit. Here it is growing with larch in the French alps.*

Above *(both pictures) Among the Chinese mountain ashes E. H. Wilson found this rich-toned widespreading tree: Sorbus sargentiana. Its winter buds are*

crimson and sticky, its young shoots (left) also crimson, its summer colour dark green, its fruit bright and generous and its autumn leaves dark red nudging crimson.

Below *The American mountain ash and the European are very similar. If anything the American has larger leaves and less fruit. It has been known in cultivation since 1782.*

into the background as a perfect disguise. The heather gives a purple ground on which the larches and the birches display their yellow gold. The rowan is gold of a richer tone, set with preposterous carbuncles of scarlet fruit.

It is hard to improve on the common rowan. Various nursery productions offer alternatives; of yellow fruit, for example, in *S. aucuparia* 'Xanthocarpa'; of finely divided, ferny leaves in *S.a.* 'Aspleniifolia'; of a narrow upright head in *S.a.* 'Sheerwater Seedling'; even of edible fruit in *S.a.* 'Edulis'.

North America's native *S. americana* is a similar tree, usually smaller and with smaller fruit. *S. scopulina* is a western version with bigger leaves and fruit – on, if anything, a smaller tree.

The most valuable of the dozen or so Asiatic mountain ashes are those with different coloured fruit and leaves. *S. hupehensis* and *S. cashmiriana*, for example, with grey-green leaves and white or faintly pink fruit; either of them a lovely misty sight in the gloaming. Or *S. sargentiana* which is dark green, with very long leaves with red stalks, red autumn colour and scarlet fruit which hangs on into the winter.

S. discolor (otherwise known as *S.* 'Embley') is very much recommended as a street tree because its branches slant sharply upwards out of the way. It has both big red fruit and red leaves at the same time. Several of them in fact have the same trick of branching: *S. pohuashanensis* from the north of China and very hardy; *S. harrowiana* from the south and rather tender; *S. insignis* from Assam with pink fruit which lasts right through the winter.

Among the best for autumn colour, regularly turning orange, red, purple and everything between, is a gracefully spreading little tree from China called *S. vilmorinii*. A Scottish gardener has told me that birds which lose no time in stripping the other species of their fruit leave this one (whose fruit is white blushed pink) entirely alone.

Left *One of the very best mountain ashes, both for its neat shape with erect branches and for the powerful autumn colour of its leaves and fruit together: Sorbus discolor, alias S. 'Embley'.*

Above *There are mountain ashes with fruit of almost every colour. The Chinese Sorbus prattii is a delicately-formed little tree with ivory-white fruit in small hanging clusters.*

Above *The yellow-fruited mountain ash is one of the forms of the common European rowan. Another form 'Edulis' has fruit which ripens sweet and is quite pleasant to eat.*

China's huge stock of mountain ashes includes the exquisite Sorbus vilmorinii, with grey-green leaves as fine as ferns, thinly arranged on an elegant arching little tree. Its fruit (right) varies between deep pink and blushing white.

Locusts and False Acacias

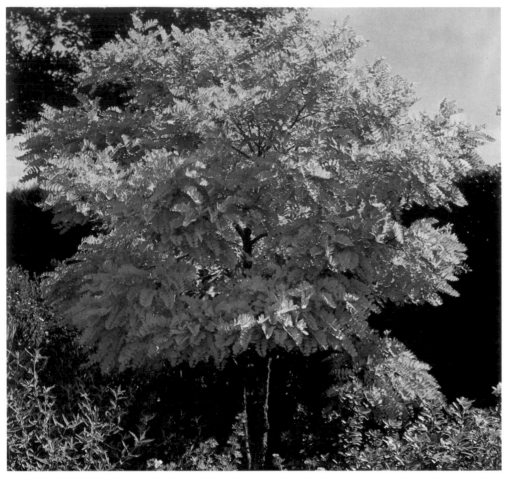

Peas and pea-trees of various kinds grow everywhere on earth. The tropics are their natural base; in the temperate zones they appear more often as herbaceous plants than trees. Peas, beans, lupins are all examples. Even the big trees of the family, however, share the pea-likeness to a remarkable extent. The *Robinia* (which goes by the name of the black locust, false acacia or acacia according to where you happen to be) is the first one that springs to mind. Big tree though it is, it has essentially pea-like flowers, pods for fruit, and much the same sort of finely-divided foliage as all its kin.

Most of the family are cultivated for their flowers. Of the bigger trees grown for their stature, timber and shade four are natives of eastern North America. Europe has been poorly endowed in this department.

The term locust, which has stuck with several members of the family, started as the Latin word for lobster. From lobsters it got transferred to the swarming grasshopper-like insect of the Middle East which, with wild honey, was said to be the diet of John the Baptist in the wilderness. Learned discussion produced the verdict that what he was eating was really the fruit of the carob tree, which thereupon took the name of locust. Thence, via the Bible-reading colonists, the name was attached to the American trees with the same sort of pod: *Robinia* became black locust and *Gleditsia* honey-locust.

The black locust was one of the first American trees to be sent back to Europe. By about 1600 Jean Robin, Henry IV's herbalist, was growing it in Paris. It derives its generic name of *Robinia* from him and its specific name of *pseudoacacia* from its obvious similarity to the subtropical acacias of Africa. There are no European acacias. The acacia can hardly have been a well-known plant in the 17th century. Yet for some reason its name stuck and to this day in England acacia means robinia. (Real

Above *One of the most graceful and decorative of all small garden trees: Robinia pseudoacacia 'Frisia', a cultivar of the false acacia produced 40 years ago in Holland. Its rich yellow colour from* *spring to autumn shows off feathery and graceful leaves which are typical of the pea family.*

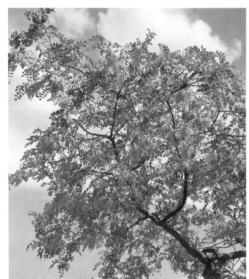

Above *A cross between the false acacia (or black locust) and the lesser-known clammy locust of the southeastern States has produced two delicate little pink-flowering garden trees: (here) Robinia × ambigua 'Bella-rosea' and 'Decaisneana'.*

Left *The false acacia or black locust looks, for a native of the eastern States, remarkably like a Chinaman. Its branch-pattern is usually decidedly picturesque, both in zig-zag main limbs and in mazy fine twigs.*

Above *The flowers of the false acacia are scented, but scarcely conspicuous enough to enhance the foliage.*

Left *The biggest tree among the peas is the magnificent honey locust of eastern North America, which grows to the proportions of the spreading American elm, yet still with fresh and delicate leaflets. Here its pea-like pods are ripening.*

acacia from Australia we call mimosa.)

Whatever the natural range of the black locust may have been, somewhere in the Alleghenies, today it grows wild in large parts of North America and most of Europe. Greedy though it is, with shallow and competitive roots, it is usually welcome. It grows very fast and makes wood which rivals oak for strength and permanence. In the wine-districts of France a copse of 'robinier' is a valuable asset; vine-stakes from it will not need replacing for 50 years.

Moved by its performance and its manifest usefulness, the English journalist William Cobbett came home from America in 1823 to sing its praises. In his enthusiasm Cobbett had started a nursery on Long Island and raised thousands of seedlings for the English market. He sold them, and they grew; but unfortunately crooked-trunked and useless.

Crooked or straight, though, from the ornamental point of view the black locust is an exciting tree. Its signature in the winter sky is unmistakable: branches like forked lightning zig-zagging out from a pale grey trunk with deep-shadowed furrows. It seems to have no over-wintering buds on the twigs; where each bud should be the ridge is crowned with two short sharp thorns.

Like the walnut, it is a black shape for more than half the year. The leaves are late to come and early to fall. They come out tender and yellow-green, deepening to a bluer shade when the white flowers appear. Then for a fortnight there is a faint sweetness in the air and the gaunt framework is transformed into as delicate a salad as anything in the garden.

But the black locust takes up a lot of space for what it does, and casts practically no shade. Nursery work has made a better version of it for street-planting; the cultivar *R.p.* 'Inermis' which has no thorns – and alas few flowers – but which forms a dense round head of the most mouth-watering green. In town squares in southern Europe it is an ideal shade-tree, leafing only when the sun grows hot and always keeping a neat shape.

For the garden proper there is a smaller golden version, *R.p.* 'Frisia', which is one of the most desirable of all golden trees. Its annual programme is from pale gold through golden green to golden copper.

The other locust, the honey locust (*Gleditsia triacanthos*), has also been called acacia in its time. There is no mistaking this tree in nature; it grows thorns in vicious clusters, even on the lower part of the trunk. It will grow to twice the size of the black locust: to 130 as against 70-odd feet. The biggest honey-locust, in Michigan, is 115

feet high and 124 in spread.

The search for an elm-substitute has lit on this tree as being tall, shapely, singularly beautiful in its fine, almost ferny, foliage and not subject to too many pests. Sad to say, though, it has had to be emasculated; disarmed of its thorns and made barren of its long shining brown pods, to satisfy the parks departments. The thornless locust comes by many names from different nurseries: 'Moraine' is perhaps the best known cultivar.

Better still for gardens is the smaller Japanese species of the same tree (*G. japonica*) which has leaflets so small (about half an inch long) and in so many millions as to look exactly like a big billowing fern.

Honey locust and its near relation the Kentucky coffee tree (*Gymnocladus dioicus*) are unusual in the pea family for having regularly petalled, not pea-like, flowers. Since in both cases they are green they are of no ornamental importance. If the coffee tree is planted it is for its leaves, the biggest and boldest in the family; up to three feet long, easily 18 inches wide. Bare of leaf the coffee tree remains a landmark. For a while the long leaf-stalks hang on. When they fall the tree seems bereft of all its twigs; what is left is so sparse and each shoot so thick.

The American yellow-wood (*Cladrastis lutea*) is the last of the locust-relations from the same astonishingly species-rich forest of the east. It would pass for a specially showy black locust selected for longer streamers of bigger white flowers. The way to identify it is to look for its buds. They lurk all summer inside the hollow stalks of the leaves.

Its oriental counterparts, the *Maackias* from Manchuria (*Maackia amurensis*) and China (*M. sinensis*) are rare but highly-prized little trees: the Manchurian for its upright blue-white flower heads in summer, the Chinese for ravishing young shoots in spring, emerging dark and bluish with a covering of silver-silk down. ▶

Above *'Sunburst' is a recent cultivar of the honey locust with bright yellow young leaves. Its shoots lack the sharp thorns of the ordinary honey-locust, making it a better street tree.*

Below *Older specimens of the honey locust develop dangerous branching thorns on the main trunk. Most barbarously armed of all is the Caspian locust from northern Persia, seen here.*

Left *The American yellow-wood is like a smaller false acacia with longer streamers of white flowers in June, falling like wisteria from its rounded crown. Here the tiny pods which succeed the flowers are half-ripe. In time they turn brown.*

The Chinese yellow-wood flowers in mid-summer, a month after the American (see top of page) and with upright flower-clusters tinged with pink and cream. Yellow-woods are a useful size: up to 40 or 50 feet at most.

Laburnum, Redbuds and the Silk Tree

▶Europe's biggest pea-tree is the original locust, the carob (*Ceratonia siliqua*) of the Mediterranean. Apart from the occasional experimental bite into the fleshy brown pod (which is mildly chocolaty; not bad at all) nobody pays the carob much attention. Because it is evergreen its eight-inch pods often escape notice. It merges into the background: short, gnarled, ageless-looking.

But experimental bites into pods are not something to encourage. The little laburnum tree is poisonous in every part. Were it not so beautiful, so regular in profuse flower and so ready to grow anywhere it might well have been banned as a public danger. As things are it is almost as universal in small gardens in Europe (where it is native) as the flowering cherry, with the same drawback: that its big moment is only two weeks of the late spring.

There is common laburnum (*Laburnum anagyroides*), Scotch laburnum (*L. alpinum*; hardier, with shinier leaves and longer spikes – a better tree) and a hybrid between the two (sold either as *L. × watereri* or *L. × vossii*) which seems to flower even more lavishly than either. Any of them used in calculated masses for knock-out effect or scattered among light woodland like natural accidents can be the most telling of all hardy yellow-flowering trees – unless you count broom, another pea-cousin.

Most brooms are shrubs. But it has needed only a slight help from a wall to windward to egg on a Mount Etna broom (*Genista aetnensis*) to 20 feet in my garden. On the way up Mount Etna you pass through a belt of this broom growing in black lava soil: a more startling monochrome landscape it is hard to imagine.

The best of the hardy Asiatic pea-trees, the pagoda tree (*Sophora japonica*), is more in the vein of the American locusts. Among the curiosities of Kew Gardens there is a specimen that reclines its trunk as though

Below *The poisonous pods of the common laburnum, which hang on the tree for months on end. The thickened upper edge of the pod helps to distinguish the common laburnum from the Scotch.*

Above *The laburnum tunnel in the gardens at Bodnant, North Wales, is perhaps the world's most spectacular use of this almost universal tree. It is made of the hybrid* Laburnum × vossii.

Left *Scotch laburnum is a slightly showier tree than the common laburnum. Here its young flower racemes are developing with the yellow flowers still folded.*

Right *The pea family likeness can be traced in the evergreen leaves of the Mediterranean carob tree. In the top right corner of the picture young pods are ripening. When they are brown they are edible and sweet.*

Left *The silk tree from Persia is a remarkably hardy member of a largely tropical family. It makes a low wide-spreading tree covered with pink flowers in mid-summer.*

Above *The hardiest of the true acacias is silver wattle, here growing wild in southern Australia. It needs a Mediterranean climate to reach tree-size, surviving hard frosts only with artificial aid.*

'Moroccan broom' is one of the biggest of the shrubby Cytisus *branch of the pea family. Its laburnum-like leaves have a silver-silky sheen and its orange-yellow flowers in summer a pineapple scent.*

The young translucent seed-pods of the Judas tree clearly relate it to the peas. They grow to about five inches and ripen purple. The Judas tree and the related redbud flower from old wood, producing flower-buds even from the main trunk near the ground.

on an invisible chaise-longue. It was planted in 1762–one of the first two or three Chinese trees to reach Europe direct through the offices of M. d'Incarville. In the same year the garden's ten-storey pagoda was finished. Did the sapling gaze up at the 163-foot tower and realize it would never make it?

The pagoda tree remained relatively unknown in the New World, perhaps because the black locust (which was there already) is so similar. Yet a month after the black locust has dropped its leaves the pagoda tree will still be fresh and green. Its chief justification, fine foliage apart, is that it flowers notably late, in August. Its flowers are creamy-white. The variety *S.j.* 'Pendula', a graceful small tree with long weeping branches, would succeed much better than a weeping willow in very dry soil.

The New Zealand kowhai (*S. tetraptera*) is an evergreen relation that needs the mild winters of the south to get beyond the shrub-stage. Its flowers are bigger and bright yellow, coming in May among ferny young grey-green leaves.

Yellow is one characteristic pea flower colour. The other is purply-pink. The red-bud (*Cercis*) genus, represented in Europe by the Judas tree, is probably the most familiar instance of the second kind–aside from sweet peas. The North American redbud (*C. canadensis*) flowers with the dogwood in the woods of the east from Pennsylvania southward, the only native tree with this flowering-cherry colour.

Europe's best display must be the grove of 50-foot Judas trees in the Retiro gardens in Madrid. I remember seeing them being watered one sunny morning by a jet with a great plume like a fire-hose. The big trees, arched with rosy blossom, were entirely covered with drops of water; the sun caught a crystal in each of the million tiny flowers. The tree's peculiarity is to flower not only on young twigs but even from the most calloused old bark of the main trunk.

China has a similar redbud, and also another whose flowers hang in short streamers (*C. racemosa*). They are all worth having for their glossy green heart-shaped leaves, quite apart from their flowers.

The legend that this was the tree from which Judas Iscariot hanged himself marches on. The French name for the tree, however, explains all. They call it *l'arbre de Judée*–the tree from Judaea.

All these trees adhere to the pea's own asymmetrical flower design. It is the mimosa group that rocks the boat. Their ring-leaders are the acacias–the true acacias of the tropics. In the sub-tropics they have concentrated in the southern hemisphere. After the eucalyptus they are Australia's

commonest trees. Mimosa-type flowers are radially designed and symmetrical.

The silk tree (*Albizia julibrissin*) is the one hardy tree of this group that belongs in the northern hemisphere. It was first found in Persia (julibrissin is its Persian name) but its range runs all the way to China. Like the true acacias it has doubly-divided leaves of the finest texture. Unlike most of them it is deciduous and its fluffy heads of flowers are a rather washy pink. In southern gardens it is often called mimosa. A better form (*A.j.* 'Rosea') has been introduced from Korea for the north; both hardier (zone 5) and stronger in flower-

colour, though not happy in Britain. The top of the low, wide-reaching tree is never without a few pink plumes from July to September.

Of the 500 species of Australian acacia, or wattle, only half a dozen are usually attempted in gardens outside the sub-tropics. Only one has ever made a substantial tree in England: the one the Piccadilly flower-sellers call mimosa; the silver wattle (*Acacia dealbata*).

For Californians and Floridians and gardeners on the Mediterranean the wattles to try (apart from the silver) are the cootamundra, the black and the Sydney.

Above *The first pagoda tree* (Sophora japonica) *in Britain was planted at Kew in 1762. It is still alive and well, but for some strange reason has adopted a reclining position. Mature trees are covered with white flowers in late summer.*

Right *The eastern redbud blooms in early spring with the dogwood in the eastern States, especially from Pennsylvania to Virginia. A white-flowered form is also available from nurseries.*

Above left *The flowers of the New Zealand kowhai or* Sophora tetraptera. *Their tubular form is unlike that of other pea flowers. Kowhai is evergreen in mild areas, and flowers in late spring.*

Top right and above *A young shoot of the Judas tree grows with a zig-zag gait. The rounded heart-shape of the leaf can clearly be seen. The purply-pink flowers are tiny, but densely massed.*

The Eucalypts or Gum Trees

Left, below and right
*The flower-bud of a
eucalyptus (here, the
blue gum) is like a little
urn (left) with a lid. The
flower has no petals, but
as the stamens expand
they push the lid off
(below, the lid coming off
and – on the right – the
expanding stamens ex-
posed). Right, the
flower opens.*

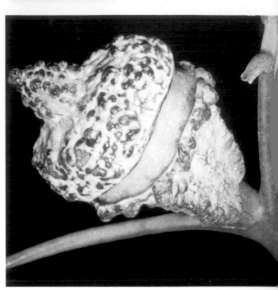

Australia is more closely associated with *Eucalyptus* than any other country with any other tree. Three-quarters of all the forest trees of Australia are eucalypts–from the snowy passes of Tasmania to where palms and tree ferns take over in the tropical jungle of northern Queensland. Their ecological range is thus enormous.

The eucalypts are members of the myrtle family, which was probably in ancient times a branch of the rose family. Most of the myrtles (including the eucalyptus) have simple, untoothed, unlobed, straightforward leaves appearing opposite each other in pairs. Very often the leaves have tiny translucent dots which are visible against the light. The eucalyptus is unique in having a flower bud with a lid which comes off when the sexual mechanism inside is ready to receive insects (for whom it supplies abundant nectar). It also has unusually well-marked stages in the two-year growth of its evergreen leaves. Juvenile or new

leaves are one shape–often round; mature leaves are totally different, usually long and narrow like larger-than-life willow leaves. More often than not they are grey with wax, at least while they are young. They all have a fragrant oil inside. And finally the bark of many eucalypts is as deciduous as most trees' leaves, resulting in patterns of flaking or tattered strips which are half the tree's character.

Typical eucalyptus country, in South Australia for instance, is strangely like the ghost of a great English park. If you half-shut your eyes those soft contours with grazing sheep, those huge hummocky broadleaf trees, here in a clump, there standing alone in massive maturity, suggest a Petworth or a Longleat drained of all colour, condemned to everlasting summer, to bone-grey and bone-brown.

In the arid parts towards the desert, where grass gives way to bare earth and stone, the scrubby types of eucalyptus known as

The gum trees have a vast range of habitats, from the tropics to such cool mountain sites as Crater Lake, Tasmania (above), where Eucalyptus cocci-fera *submits to wintry storms. In garden conditions this tree has brilliantly blue-waxy leaves.*

The ghost gum is so-called for its smooth almost luminous white bark. In very hot climates (here in Dampier, western Australia) gum trees get by with very little foliage to minimize transpiration losses. Their roots also plunge deep for water.

Right *Red resinous gum pours from a wound: hence 'gum tree'. Eucalypts also have a very marked oily fragrance in most of their parts. The oil has many uses, from disinfectant to boot polish, and it also makes a soothing embrocation.*

mallee take over as dense brush. And in the towns and villages the red-flowering ones (principally *E. ficifolia*) line the streets like flowering cherries.

There are 600 or so species. Some are very local; others, like the river red gum (*E. camaldulensis*), are native to every State, growing wherever their niche – in this case the riverbank – can be found. There are huge variations in hardiness within a species. In the very common snow gum, for example, it is essential to know whether the seed comes from Tasmania or New South Wales, and from what altitude, before it is possible to say if it will survive in northern Europe or the eastern States.

On the whole eucalypts must be regarded as subtropical trees. In England the commonest, by far, is the Tasmanian cider gum, *E. gunnii*. High altitude strains of the snow gum, *E. niphophila*, from 7,000 feet on Mt. Kosciusko in New South Wales in particular, have also come through seasons of

icy winds unharmed. The University of Washington arboretum at Seattle finds this the hardiest, and also grows the startlingly silver-grey Tasmanian snow gum, *E. coccifera*. They are pleasant enough trees, yet somehow they always look spindly and top-heavy; their grey-green foliage always looks as though it has been slept in; they look uneasy among the busy burgeoning and quick corruption of northern summers. Perhaps the most effective use of eucalyptus in a northern climate is to coppice it. This way the foliage is perpetually juvenile: the effect is of a cool little shrub.

In the south it is another matter. California saw the first invasion of the United States by eucalyptus in the 1880s. The blue gum was widely planted with the fanciful notion that it would absorb the 'noxious gases' which were then supposed to be the cause of malaria. The blue gum did so well it gave the whole gum-tribe a bad name. It seeded itself everywhere and filled good ▶

Eucalyptus growing against the mysterious red wall of Ayers Rock, a vast monolith in the flat central desert of Australia. Rainfall in this area is limited to 30 days a year and rarely exceeds ten inches.

Right *Gum tree bark comes in almost every colour, but always has the character of skin, often peeling or flaking away in thin layers to make beautiful patterns, as here on the blue gum. Sometimes the peeling layers hang on the trunk.*

Above *Snow gums in the snow in Tasmania. Eucalyptus niphophila, the snow gum, is one of the hardiest species; a small slow-growing tree worth having in a garden for its beautiful bark (picture on left).*

Eucalypts, Silk Oak, Fire-Bush and Oleasters

Right *Woodward's gum (Eucalyptus woodwardii) is a tender species with its wax-red flower-buds opening to golden flowers.*

Below *The western Australian Eucalyptus miniata has bright orange flowers.*

Below right *The red-flowered Eucalyptus leucoxyla 'Rosea' is widely grown in Mediterranean climates for its almost cherry-blossom effect.*

Left *The tallest known broad-leaf (327 feet) is a* Eucalyptus regnans, *the species seen here (in the foreground) growing in the Styx valley of Tasmania. The smaller trees are Eucalyptus obliqua. Neither species has been extensively tried in the northern hemisphere.*

Left Myrtus apiculata *makes a beautiful ever-green in regions without hard frost; it is photo-graphed here in Cornwall.*

Right *The cider gum (Eucalyptus gunnii) is rather less spectacular than the trees above, but very hardy and fast growing. It is the one relatively common eucalyptus in British gardens.*

Below *The only real tree of the true myrtles, the Chilean Myrtus apiculata, shows its kinship with the eucalypts in its peeling trunk.*

ground with its greedy shallow roots. None the less it looked splendid, and still does, its blue-rinsed tresses and chaotically shaggy forking trunk mingling magnificently with the native oaks and pines.

If Californians curse the blue gum it is only fair to say that Ethiopians bless it. Its introduction at the end of the last century probably saved their capital city. The native timber had all been cut and the seedlings grazed: Addis Ababa was without fuel. No native tree would grow at anything like the speed of this exotic.

Speed trials with eucalyptus species are going on now in the southern States. The Chinese, with their well-known fertilizing techniques, claim figures so astonishing that every forester is intrigued. But everyone is wary of eucalyptus statistics–from the original claim of a 470-foot tree onwards. What is certain is that the tallest species in Australia, *E. regnans*, is easily the tallest non-conifer in the world. There may be trees 350 feet high in western Australia.

Of the gum-trees I know (which is admittedly a minute fraction of the field) the one that stands out for beauty–alas a tender one, but worth growing even in a greenhouse–is the lemon-scented gum, *E. citriodora*. It possesses a trunk as slim and white as a goalpost, but a goalpost with hips.

Right *The little light-limbed and often almost weeping Eucalyptus caesia, hardy down to about 25°F., has some of the prettiest flowers of the genus, in loose clusters in early spring, often recurring later.*

The oleaster or Russian olive (Elaeagnus angustifolia) is one of the best small silver-leaved trees, suggesting an olive tree both in colour and in its many-stemmed spreading shape.

Europe's sea buckthorn has even narrower leaves than the oleaster (left) and often makes a thicket rather than a tree. Female plants bear orange berries (in autumn) only when a male plant is nearby.

Is it a coincidence that most of Australia's trees come in a rush at this stage of evolutionary history? Between the *Eucalyptus*, the *Acacias* which came just before them, and the *Grevilleas* and *Hakeas* which turn up now in their order of *Proteales*, we have accounted for a high proportion of all Australian trees.

The silk oak *(Grevillea robusta)* is more familiar in the northern hemisphere as a pot-plant or summer bedding plant than as the big tree (to 120 feet) it makes in Australia and California.

The name 'oak' as applied to trees so very unlike oaks as the *Grevilleas*, or the 'she-oak' *Casuarina* (an apparently leafless Australian with bamboo-like twigs), derives from the properties of their timber, which has oak-like broad medullary rays. In California the silk oak grows fast, looks lush and thrives in desperately dry areas. The pincushion tree *(Hakea laurina)* is the other member of the family Californians grow, for its pink and gold pincushion flowers.

Gardens as far north as southern and western Britain can grow the Chilean fire-bush (*Embothrium lanceolatum*). If there is a more spectacular tree than this in flower I have never seen it. In May and for several weeks the fire-bush covers its whole 20 or 30 feet with scarlet tubes, which curl back at the mouth like bells. The effect of flame is almost realistic.

There is nothing so showy in the allied *Elaeagnus* or *Oleaster* family. The family likeness lies in a subtle silvery-scaliness. In the main they are a collection of the most useful and cheerful of evergreen shrubs, with silver-backed leaves. The one small tree among them (*Elaeagnus angustifolia*, sometimes known as the Russian olive) has the silver-scales both sides of its narrow, willowy leaves. The general effect is like a small olive-tree; even to the olive-like fruit, the many trunks, and the domed top. This and its cousin the sea-buckthorn (*Hippophae rhamnoides*), which needs a bit of pruning to make a tree-shape, are two of the best small silver-leaved trees; they deserve a place in the sun with a dark background. When the sea-buckthorn is covered with its orange berries all along its twigs among the leaves (you need both male and female plants to get fruit) the effect is of fire-light on silver hair – a truly autumnal theme.

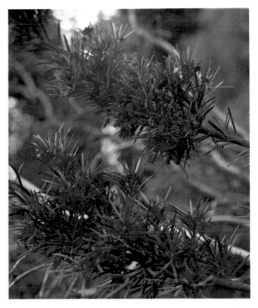

Left *The flowers of the evergreen Chilean fire-bush (Embothrium coccineum) are here about to open. In mild climates this elegant tree becomes a pillar of fire in late spring.*

Above *The ferny leaves of the silk oak (Grevillea robusta) are silver underneath and golden green above. In cold climates in the north it is used as a summer bedding plant for its foliage alone.*

Australia has a number of trees that mimic conifers with their drought-resisting needle-like leaves. 'Sweet' hakea (Hakea suaveolens) is a useful small tree in hot dry places. H. laurina is more showy with red and gold flowers.

Right *Rosemary-leaved grevillea is hardier than the silk oak, but reaches only six feet in cultivation. It looks like rosemary with red flowers all summer.*

The Dogwoods

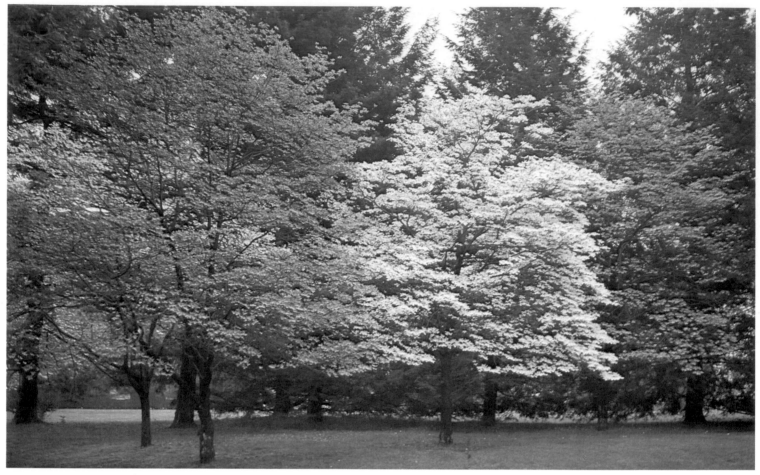

The name dogwood covers more different kinds of shrub and tree than one name rightly should. It covers creeper ankle-high; shrubs waist-high; little trees window-high and big trees of the high forest. There are almost as many designs of flowers as there are sizes. The leaf, always an oval with veins curving to meet the centre axis at both ends, is the only clearly visible link between them all.

Although the dogwood trees have two very different flower designs they are all so whole-hearted about it that the effect comes to much the same thing: a spread of warm white, of branches obliterated under table-cloths of massed flowers which have no equal – not even among the cherries. The common flowering dogwood of eastern north America, the Pacific dogwood and the Japanese dogwood are the proponents of one system of flowering. The giant dogwood of China leads the other school.

What seem to be petals on the flowers of the first are really no such thing: they are the modified leaves known as bracts, which usually play a humble supporting role protecting the unopened flower. Inside that ring of four (sometimes six) white pseudo-petals the real petals are tiny: miniature parts of a cluster of miniature flowers. The second school simply has bigger clusters of bigger flowers, and no fancy bracts.

It is the way the dogwood grows almost as much as its floral ardour that makes it such a spectacle in spring. Its tendency is to throw out long branches sideways. Every flower tells because it is held face upwards on these branches.

From the point of view of habit and flower there is little to choose between the flowering dogwood (*Cornus florida*) of North America and the (normally rather smaller) Japanese dogwood (*C. kousa*) – except their flowering times, which are staggered . . . making it worthwhile planting both.

Unfortunately the American dogwood demands a continental climate; Britain is too temperate for it, and so is the northern Pacific coast. We therefore miss the pink varieties which only occur in this species. The Japanese model does triumphantly in England, however, and in France both succeed as well as they do in New York or Pennsylvania. The Chinese variety of the Japanese (*C. kousa chinensis*) is said to be even better, more vigorous and ardent in flower, than the species.

Having seen dogwood in flower in Connecticut I was prepared to settle for that. It would have been absurd to ask for more. More is what they get on the west coast, though. The most memorable of many stirring forest sights is the Pacific dogwood in mid-October high in the hills of Oregon, not only lighting the depths of the Douglas fir and hemlock with flurries of golden and scarlet leaves, brighter even than the big-leaf maple on the same hill, but lighting its own brilliant branches with a second crop

The autumn leaf colour of the American dogwood in its native land is as great a display as its spring blooming. Unfortunately in Britain we can rely on it for neither.

The true flowers of the dogwood are the un-remarkable little cluster, here about to open, in the centre of each set of four big petal-like bracts. These are the 'flowers' of Cornus florida 'Rubra'.

Below *The giant dog-wood of the orient has a superb horizontal habit of growth, coming in time to look almost like a cedar in the snow when its branches are covered in dense masses of creamy flowers in May.*

Above *Strange straw-berry-like fruits follow the yellow flowers of Cornus capitata. In very mild winters this dogwood is evergreen, although some leaves will turn purplish and fall.*

Below *The white blooms of 'Goldspot', a form of the pacific dogwood, are some of the biggest of any dogwood's. 'Goldspot' flowers even as a two-foot plant and has a very long flowering season.*

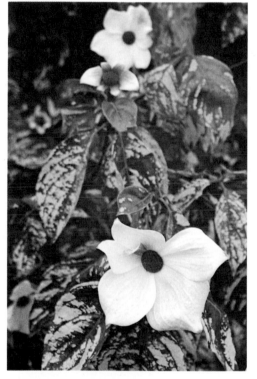

of its huge white clematis-like flowers.

Alas this, the biggest of the dogwoods, able to grow to 100 feet in its own woods, is less happy abroad. In the east it suffers from the cold. In Europe it is good, but short-lived and never a big tree.

The biggest tree of the dogwoods we can grow in either Europe or the eastern States is the giant dogwood of China, *C. contro-versa*. This is the one without big white bracts, but with broader clusters of little flowers which at a distance have almost the same effect.

The horizontal branching pattern is most marked in this tree. There are specimens, perhaps slightly aided and abetted by the gardener, which have made perfect wedding-cake tiers year after year on which the flowers lie like a covering of snow. Its freer form is perhaps even more dramatic. The branches go like the swirl of a dancer's skirt or the tipping horizons of distant alps. By 50 feet with most trees a degree of round-headed anonymity is creeping in. Not with the giant dogwood: it builds another majes-tic plateau for its 50th birthday.

Gardens where such an empire-builder would soon take over have the alternative of an exceedingly pretty variegated-leaved version of the same tree, *C. controversa* 'Variegata'. Like most trees with a short share of chlorophyll it grows slowly, but with the same deliberate pattern of whorled branches. The leaf margins are white, so whether the tree flowers much or not makes little difference: you have your wedding-cake all the summer.

The dogwood family is by no means exhausted with these. There is the cornelian cherry (*C. mas*) of Europe, which flowers yellow before the leaves in February, and like all dogwoods gives a good account of itself with autumn colour. For southern gardens there is an evergreen, *C. capitata* from western China, which has pale yellow bract-flowers.

Left *The oriental equivalent of America's flowering dogwood has pointed bract-petals and fades from white to white-and-pink. Flowering is conveniently a month later, making it worth planting both species.*

The 'Cornelian cherry' is so-called for its edible red fruit. It is Europe's big-gest native dogwood; a large shrub or small congested tree that flowers on its bare twigs in mid-winter or earliest spring.

Dove Trees and Black Gums

The dove tree grows to about 60 feet and as much across: a light-limbed and airy tree. The 'doves' (or 'handkerchiefs') grow along the whole length of its long branches in late spring, mingling with its bright green to make a most refreshing sight.

The dove tree looks rather like a linden (or lime) with over-size dogwood flowers. The two 'petals' of each flower have a leaf-like construction and one is four times as long as the other.

So many of the trees of North America have turned up again as survivors of the Ice Ages in China that there is considerable excitement when a family is found that holds out in only one of these refuges.

Leaving aside the ginkgo, no individual tree has caused quite so much wonderment as the *Davidia*, which, in 60 years, has become known as the dove tree, the ghost tree and the handkerchief tree.

Father David, the French missionary who first reported the panda, was also the first to report—in 1869—a beautiful new tree in the mountains of western China. He told of huge white flowers, hanging like handkerchiefs (or fluttering like doves, according to the weather) from the branches.

Not until 1897 did another missionary, Father Farges, collect seed from the tree and send it home to France, to the great tree-collector Maurice de Vilmorin. Of the 37 seeds he sent only one germinated, but M. de Vilmorin planted it out in his arboretum at les Barres, and it did splendidly. It flowered in 1906 and the West saw its first dove (or handkerchief).

But Veitch's nursery, the most enterprising in Britain at the time, knew nothing of this Gallic transaction. They had just engaged the young Ernest Wilson and the first job they gave him was to collect the davidia. He set off in 1899. His only information about the tree came from Dr. Augustine Henry, the famous amateur botanist who

The fruit of the Davidia *is a green ball, purple-bloomed at first, containing a single hard, ridged, inedible nut. E. H. Wilson brought enough of these back from central China to recoup the costs of his expedition to find the tree.*

had lived in China for nearly 20 years. First Wilson had to reach Henry, who was in Yunnan in the southwest. Then, with Henry's instructions, he had to travel the 900 miles to Ichang in central China where the tree was. Henry drew Wilson a map—to show a solitary tree in an area the size of England.

Wilson was boat-wrecked in rapids. He was travelling through country that was notoriously unsafe; it was the time of the Boxer Revolt; and his Chinese guide was an opium addict.

He found the tree, though. Its stump was standing by a house that had just been built from its wood. 'I did not sleep that night,' he wrote in his diary.

Eventually, by combing the neighbourhood, he found a grove of davidias and collected their seed. When he sent it off to London he was sure it was the first ever to leave China.

He was bitterly disappointed when he came home to find that de Vilmorin already had the tree in his collection. But on closer examination it turned out that there were two different varieties. Farges's was named *Davidia involucrata* var. *vilmoriniana*, Wilson's *Davidia involucrata*.

The two varieties are almost identical, the only difference lying in the colour of the buds and the under-surface of the leaves. But oddly there is a big enough ecological difference for Farges's to be fully hardy in Boston, at the Arnold Arboretum, while Wilson's is not. The arboretum's original (about 1910) specimen of *D. involucrata* is still alive, but every winter cuts down the year's shoots to the ground. It is an interesting case of the borderline between a tree and a herbaceous plant, although few trees would stand such attrition for more than a few years.

The botanists' first impression of the davidia was that it belonged to the dogwoods. For just as in the dogwoods, the apparent petals of the huge white flowers turned out to be bracts. Where the dogwood has four equal ones, however, the davidia has two—and one is four times as long as the other. The leaves, moreover, are heart-shaped; more like those of the linden tree. It was not a dogwood, but it was a close relation. So it was given its own family of *Davidiaceae*.

Nothing but a botanist's word would have convinced me that the nearest relation of the davidia, nearer even than the dogwoods, was the tupelo or black-gum, *Nyssa sylvatica*. Tupelo is an eastern American tree; common, though scattered, on moist ground throughout the whole of the eastern States. It has relations in China . . . other tupelos. But it has neither bracts nor heart-shaped leaves; the evidence for its connection with davidia lies in the intricacies of the little flowers and fruit. When tupelo is planted as an ornamental tree it is for its generally glossy and wholesome appearance—a strong and shiny green—and for its whole sunset of autumn colours. It goes with *Liquidambar* as one of the trees for a damp site on the sunny side of a pond. All summer long it deepens the water with its dark reflection; then suddenly in autumn it lights the surface with the reds and yellows of a flaming evening sky.

The Hollies

*English holly has produced dozens of different varieties, making a fascinating collection of subtly different leaf-shapes and colours. **Right** and overleaf are some of the outstanding cultivars and species— most of them growing slowly into big bushes or small trees.*

It must have struck you by now that the evolutionary order of things is a pretty funny one. To leap from poplars to strawberry trees; from laburnums to eucalypts to dogwoods to hollies seems like no kind of order at all. This, however, as far as we know, was how, over tens of millions of years, new trees developed. We can only be thankful that the randomness of evolutionary mutation and selection did produce such a mixed bunch; and wonder humbly how each one of them in its own way manages to be so intricately and originally beautiful.

There is no objective reckoning by which one tree is more beautiful than another. But one can have favourites. One of mine is the holly. And I find I am in good company: this is what John Evelyn had to say (about his holly hedge): 'Is there under heaven a more glorious and refreshing object of the kind than an impregnable hedge about four hundred feet in length, nine feet high, and five in diameter, which I can show in my now ruined gardens at Say's Court (thanks to the Czar of Muscovy) at any time of year, glittering with its armed and varnished leaves?'

Poor Evelyn. His fractured syntax makes it plain that he was distracted by having the Czar in the house. Peter (later the Great) was his tenant. He had come to England to learn about shipbuilding, and needed a house near the naval dockyard at Deptford. Who but a Czar, having discovered that his landlord was a passionate gardener, would have set about wrecking the garden?

The story goes that the Czar amused himself by having his staff wheel him through the holly hedge in a wheelbarrow. But apart from the difficulty (not to mention discomfort) of being any part of an assault on five feet by nine feet by 400 feet of holly, Evelyn's own words seem to contradict it. He goes on '. . . It mocks the rudest assaults of the weather, beasts, or hedge-breakers.' Whichever of the three he considered the Czar, it sounds as though the hedge survived.

Evelyn was, of course, talking about English holly, *Ilex aquifolium*. There are 400 species of holly, even deciduous ones (the American 'Possumhaw' for example). But it is a tree that has been in cultivation for ornament so long that the cultivars and hybrids outnumber the species. Most of the best of these are either variants on the English holly, or forms of a cross between the English holly and the native holly of the Azores.

Strangely, for a native, English holly is not 100 per cent hardy in England. Only a once-in-a-century winter will actually kill a holly tree, but really sharp weather can strip it of leaves. In consequence, its range

in the eastern States is limited to zone 6– from Connecticut southwards. Northwards the American holly (*I. opaca*) is hardy, and can be good for berries. But it lacks one of the English holly's principal virtues; what Evelyn calls its 'varnished leaves'. At its best it makes a distinctively matt, greyish or yellowish-green small tree (the biggest, 53 feet high, is in Texas) on which a good crop of red berries (or in the cultivar 'Xanthocarpa' yellow berries) shows up well.

The typical English holly, left to nature but given some woodland shelter, is slightly bigger (the tallest is 74 feet, the thickest 11 feet round) and almost as pointed as a Christ-

mas tree. But such trees tend to be thin and transparent. The best-looking ones are in hedgerows where the wind has a pruning effect: shorter shoots keep the foliage dense and stress the contrast of glitter and darkness that is half the pleasure. For this reason holly is best in summer, when the new shoots emerge so soft and shiny that they look (and even feel) wet. The new leaves glow with pink, brown and purple tones as well as green.

Most holly trees are either male or female, which means they need a mate if they are to bear berries. Many of the variegated cultivars, unfortunately, are male, and will never ▶

'The holly bears a blossom As white as the lily flower.'– The famous old carol gives the holly the crown of 'all trees in the greenwood'.

Top *Common English holly (Ilex aquifolium) with berries, borne only on female plants. They often last all winter.*

Upper middle *A narrow-leaved variety: I. aqui-folium 'Angustifolia'.*

Lower middle *Hedgehog holly, I.a. 'Ferox', has fierce spines on all surfaces of its leaves.*

Bottom *I.a. 'Elegantis-sima' has wavy leaves with a white edge and faintly marbled centres.*

Top *Holly flowers in early summer, inconspicuously but with a sweet scent.*

Upper middle *I.a. 'Hastata' is a strange variety, with leaves long-spined at the base but with rounded tips.*

Lower middle *The silver hedgehog holly (I.a. 'Ferox Argentea') is both bright and bristly.*

Bottom *'Silver Queen' is a male (berryless) holly with yellow leaf-margins surrounding green and grey-mottled centres.*

Top *One cultivar (I.a. 'Bacciflava') has yellow berries, often in strikingly large quantities.*

Upper middle *I.a. 'Crispa' has thick leaves curling in bizarre contortions.*

Lower middle *Perry's silver weeping holly is a beautiful little dome of a tree. Masses of berries line its drooping branches.*

Bottom *I.a. 'Argenteo-marginata' is one of the several cultivars with silver-edged leaves.*

Holly and Box

▶ have berries. One would hope and expect that their names would give some indication of their sexes–especially as the most famous of them are called either Kings or Queens. But the Joker must have stepped in. 'Golden King' is a female; 'Golden Queen' a male. There is no 'Silver King' but 'Silver Queen' is also a male. These are all variegated with a band of either silver or gold round the margin of the leaf and green in the middle.

The two 'Milkboys', 'Golden' and 'Silver' (both male, reassuringly), have the alternative form of variegation; green round the edge and a beautiful mixture of apparent brush-strokes of dark green, light green and gold (or silver) in the centre. It is these plants with centre-variegated leaves that have a built-in tendency to revert to plain green. If you see any plain green shoots on them you simply cut them off. Sometimes, on the other hand, shoots with no green at all, leaves exactly the colour of that Swiss white chocolate appear.

On the left is a selection of the leaves of some of the best and most distinct hollies. Leaf-shape varies as much as colour. There is hedgehog holly (*I.a.* 'Ferox'–the fierce), both green and green-and-white, which has spines on all the surfaces of its strange hunch-backed leaves. There is 'Crispa', a rare cultivar on which everything–leaf, twig, branch and trunk–curls and contorts: a slow-growing, but ultimately unmatchable, specimen for a courtyard or a lawn. There is weeping silver-variegated holly (*I.a.* 'Argenteomarginata Pendula')–bright as a button and not in the least doleful. There is yellow-berried English holly ('Bacciflava'); there are purple-stemmed, unarmed, narrow-leaved and broad-leaved English hollies. And there are combinations of most of these characteristics. It is hard to think of any tree more worthwhile collecting, or more rarely collected.

Moreover, the crossing of English holly and *I. perado* from the Azores has produced another whole range known as the Highclere hybrids (*I.* × *altaclerensis*). On the whole these tend to be more vigorous than English holly, and less prickly. One of the most magnificent varieties is the camellia-leaved holly (*I.* × *altaclerensis* 'Camelliifolia') which has very few prickles, and those only on the lower branches. 'Golden King' is in fact supposed to come from this stable. 'J. C. van Tol' is famous for his (her) profuse berry-bearing. 'Silver Sentinel' is one of the tallest growing variegated hollies, and female. 'Purple Shaft' has tremendous deep purple shoots. 'Lawsoniana' has gold centres like the 'Milkboy'. . . . There are 20 or so: another whole collection.

Top *Hollies with gold or white margins (here, 'Golden Queen') often produce shoots with no green in the leaves at all.*
Upper middle *'Camelliifolia' is one of the best Highclere hybrids: very vigorous with numerous berries.*

Lower middle *'Lawsoniana' is another of the Highclere hybrids with golden variegation in beautiful brush-strokes and few prickles.*
Bottom *American holly, Ilex opaca, is similar to English. It has good berries but matt leaves.*

Top *'Golden Milkboy' is one of the best centre-variegated hollies, a variety of the English holly. It has no berries.*
Upper middle *'Golden King' is perhaps the most popular Highclere hybrid: a female with broad yellow leaf-margins.*

Lower middle *Ilex pernyi from China is one of the most elegant species with tiny leaves, often making a tall thin bush.*
Bottom *The surprising Ilex pedunculosa is a Japanese holly whose berries are carried on very long individual stalks.*

Below *Formal box. Box is the traditional material for low hedges round flower-beds in formal gardens, as here at Hampton Court Palace near London.*

Bottom *Natural box. Left to themselves, box trees are often many-stemmed and straggling. Their hard, even-grained wood is perfect for wood-engraving blocks.*

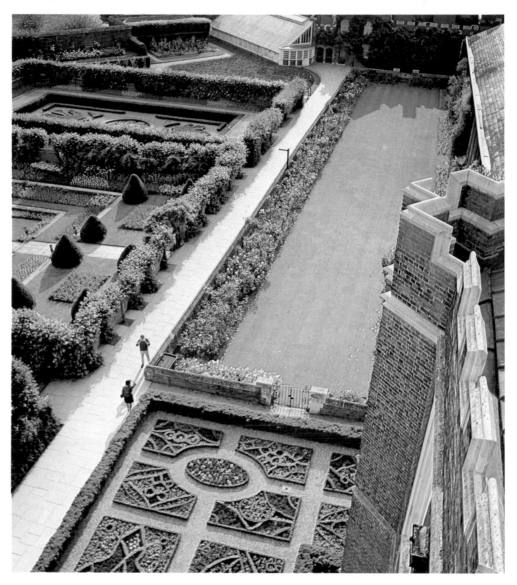

Among the species, which come from almost everywhere in the northern hemisphere, my own favourite is Father Perny's holly (*I. pernyi*) which was found by yet another of the French missionaries in western China. It has the smallest leaves of any; each one a crisp green diamond. It makes a sparkling little tree.

At the other extreme the Japanese broadleaf holly (*I. latifolia*) you would take for a cherry laurel, with its long, wide, serrated but unprickly leaves. The Dahoon holly (*I. cassine*) of the southeastern States is also unarmed, but tender. There is a prettier and much hardier one from Japan which carries its berries on stalks as long as the leaves (*I. pedunculosa*).

There is only one word of warning needed about hollies: they do not like being moved after two or three years. It is very risky indeed to move them without a big ball of soil containing as much as possible of the roots. And even then it is better to move them in very late summer or mid-spring, when the roots can make some headway before the full demand of transpiration starts to dry out the plant. If a holly does seem to be under this sort of stress, take off some, or even all, of the leaves. It can recover from being denuded, but not from drying out. Do not assume, by the way, that a holly is its own protection against grazing animals; rabbits will eat an unprotected little plant down to the ground.

Defenceless box on the other hand they leave alone. Its smell, which is so attractive to us, the smell of old walled gardens in summer, they apparently shun. Box is more of a social than a botanical connection of holly, but it has some of the same virtues and is too modest a tree to have any vices. It seems equally happy cropped down to a six-inch hedglet grilling by a pathway in the sun or reaching up in permanent gloom as the undergrowth of thick woods. Wherever it is its neat, almost round, yellow-green leaves give it a satisfying texture.

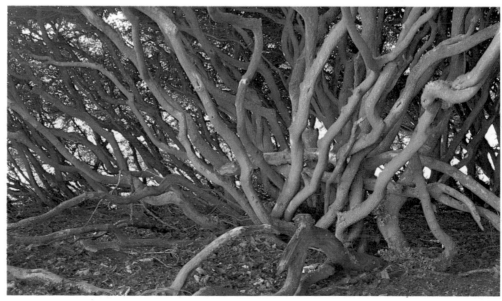

Horse Chestnuts and Buckeyes

Far left, below left and below *The fruit, the flowers and the tree in flower. Horse chestnut, the biggest of our ornamental flowering trees, is a native of northern Greece. It is decoration pure and simple, with no economic value.*

There are no identification problems with the horse chestnut. It peddles a whole catalogue of its own patented paraphernalia. Item: one sticky bud–take indoors for an instant spring. Item: one huge fingered leaf, with no competitors for boldness of design. Item: one tall candle of flowers, as original as orchids. Item: one prickly green container, holding the most succulently shiny of inedible fruit–the conker.

Despite its manifest entertainment value, the horse chestnut gets a bad press. It is proclaimed 'dirty': which means it drops things. Its foliage is described as 'coarse': which means its leaves are big. And those responsible for public trees get themselves into terrible knots over the favourite sport of every nine-year-old: chucking sticks up at the conkers.

The horse chestnut was brought into western cultivation from Turkey in Elizabethan times. It soon proved to be not only the biggest of all flowering (or rather ornamentally flowering) trees, but to be completely hardy, to grow fast and to grow in any soil. Also to grow old. The oldest dated trees in Britain were planted in 1664 and one of them (in Surrey) is still 125 feet high.

Yet it remains essentially an ornamental tree, the sign of human habitation, of a park or a village. There are no woods of it:

its timber is hardly worth having. We plant it because we love its paraphernalia, but also its billowing, drooping outlines, its bright shade of green in early summer and its early autumn colouring of a warm yellow. It is one of the first trees to hang out its limp green flags in the spring.

America has its own set of close relations of the horse chestnut: the buckeyes. There is the red buckeye (*Aesculus pavia*) of the south; the sweet buckeye with yellow flowers (*A. flava*) from the Appalachians; the Ohio buckeye (*A. glabra*) with creamy flowers and the California buckeye (*A. californica*) with pink or white flowers. The

first three of these are medium-sized trees. The last, and also *A. parviflora* from the south, are elegant lounging shrubs.

The inevitable cross between the imported horse chestnut and the native buckeye (in this case the red one) has given us the red-flowered horse chestnut, *A. × carnea*. It is fashionable to regard this as the ideal horse chestnut for parks; its red (or rather dark pink) flowers and its small stature being regarded as advantages. But truth to tell it is a bit of a runt, and distinctly dowdy, beside the majesty of a full-scale horse chestnut flashing white flowers from ground level up to its cloud-like crown. If you must have

The sticky bud of the horse chestnut swells and begins to open in early spring: among the first trees to come into leaf.

The bud-scales fold back as the growing tip emerges. Six compound leaves and a spike of flowers are all packed into this little parcel.

The inner bud-scales hinge back as the white-furry shoot pushes the swelling leaves clear. An analysis of a horse chestnut shoot appears on pages 10-11.

The fledgling contents of the bud sort themselves out. The year's whole growth is made in this one flush: the thick shoot has all summer to ripen into wood.

The bold design of horse chestnut leaves is magnificent in autumn yellow. The tree colours more reliably in Europe than in America, however, and the leaves fall early.

Right *One distant horse chestnut relation, Koelreuteria paniculata (the 'golden-rain tree') comes from China. Its flowers are similar, but hang down. Its bladder-fruit is very different. A wide small tree with beautiful feathery leaves and good autumn colour.*

Above *Japanese horse chestnut flanked by cedar and golden yew at Westonbirt, Gloucestershire. It has splendid three-foot-wide leaves and yellowish-white flowers with red spots.*

Below *The sweet (or yellow) buckeye is a tall tree in the central eastern States with yellowish flowers. Hybrids between this and the red buckeye have red-and-yellow or reddish flowers.*

Above *A hybrid between the white and red-flowering horse chestnuts, Aesculus × plantierensis has pale pink flowers but no fruit – often considered an advantage.*

Below *The red horse chestnut is unusual among hybrids in having fertile fruit which produces trees identical to the parents. It has one variety, 'Briotii', selected for deeper pink flowers.*

a smarter version the Swiss cultivar 'Baumanii' with double flowers (and no conkers) is a better choice.

Some of the common horse chestnut's oriental relations offer it serious competition. The Japanese horse chestnut (*A. turbinata*) has leaves as much as three feet wide. And the Indian horse chestnut (*A. indica*) brings into the family an indefinable grace and polish. The leaves are a little shinier, with perhaps a little more emphasis on the centre leaflet of the seven. It is different enough to catch your eye as an extra-handsome specimen, rather than a different and exotic species.

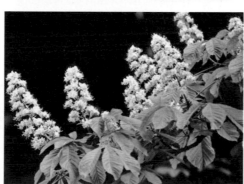

Left *Young leaves of the red buckeye of the southern States have a reddish tinge. Although it is one parent of the red-flowering horse chestnut it is an uncommon tree in cultivation.*

Above *The flowers of the Indian horse chestnut, perhaps the most graceful and distinguished member of its family. It flowers in mid-summer; another reason to plant this admirable tree.*

Above *The southern buckeye, Aesculus parviflora, has the most delicate flowers of the family in late summer. Strictly speaking this buckeye is a shrub: it spreads wide with no central trunk.*

The Maples of North America

The oaks, the hollies, the mountain ashes and the southern beeches get through to the semi-finals. But in the finals there is no competition. The maples are the trees with the most beautiful and varied foliage of all the broadleaves.

The maples' own rules are fairly lax. Among the 115 species there are shrub-sized maples and very big trees. Though there is a tendency to a hand-shaped leaf, interpretation runs through everything from a simple oval to a filigree of 15 fingers. Bark is almost as varied. Nearly all are deciduous. Though autumn colour is very much part of the game, there are maples whose leaves turn crisp and dismal brown, rattling to the ground with the first good frost. Very few maples make a show of flowering. Where their family loyalty is strongest is their fruit: they all have 'keys', consisting of two little nuts with one wing each, linked together by their bases; and in their almost universal rule of branching: two twigs at a time, opposite each other on the shoot.

Maples group curiously well by geography. America provides big and handsome ones, given to brilliant autumn colouring. Eastern Asia contributes small and intricate ones, carefully shaped and often beautifully coloured all summer. Europe has the strong silent ones; the bull of the family, the sycamore, for instance; or the workhorse, the field maple.

Europe has never seen anything like New England's maples in October. There is no describing, nor photographing satisfactorily, the trumpet-pitch of red their leaves achieve. And strangely you never seem to see two trees with the same tone side by side: the whole gamut of the highest-frequency colours is in use.

Sugar maple (*Acer saccharum*) and red maple (*A. rubrum*) grow together through most of the eastern States (though sugar maple not in the south). Both colour supremely well in the northern part of their range, where they get the right combination ▶

Keys are as much the hallmark of maples as acorns are of oaks. Every species has a different shape. Here, from top to bottom, are the keys of the sycamore, field maple, silver maple, bigleaf maple, sugar maple and Japanese maple.

Sugar trapped in the dying leaves of maples turns them an infinity of fiery colours. New England, where cold autumn nights alternate with sunny days, has the most pyrotechnical palette of anywhere on earth.

The Maples of North America

▶of sunny days and freezing nights. Over part of their northern range, they are joined by the black maple (*A. nigrum*) which is very like the sugar maple. None, unfortunately, gives quite such a performance in Europe.

It is easy to confuse the sugar and red maples. They are in the same size range; medium to big, but never giants. They are dense trees, close-branched and rather upright; oval shapes in silhouette. Extremely upright forms of both (*A. rubrum* 'Columnare'; *A. saccharum* 'Temple's Upright') have been propagated. The clues are the red buds, flowers and leaf-stalks of the red maple. Its leaves have more acute angles; the sugar maple's leaf-lobes are separated by curves. The red maple grows faster, flowers earlier and often turns red earlier in autumn. Given moisture it will stand city conditions; sugar maple is essentially a countryman.

Silver maple (*A. saccharinum*) is the third one with a similar range. In summer it is a more obviously decorative tree. Its leaves are a cheerful light green backed with a soft silver lustre; their lobes are longer, parted with deep indentations almost like the red oak's. Unfortunately there is a history of accidents with the silver maple. Evidently it was over-commended for its beauty and speed (it is very fast) at the turn of the century in areas where conditions are too tough for it. It got a name for splitting in storms. Yet of all the big American maples this is the happiest in Europe. It makes a beautiful light-shaded wide-crowned tree remarkably quickly and turns a happy pale yellow towards the end of October. There are also cultivars with yellow-green leaves and deeply cut, almost shredded leaves (*A. saccharinum* 'Lutescens' and 'Laciniatum').

One has come to expect the west coast to produce something bigger. In maples it is the leaves. The tall-tree maple of the west coast is the bigleaf or Oregon maple (*A. macrophyllum*), which has whoppers. In the Pacific forest, where broadleaved trees (even narrow-leaved ones) are far outnumbered by conifers, the foot-wide foliage of the bigleaf stands out everywhere. In autumn when it is yellow or orange a single leaf shuffling to the floor among the dark fronds of Douglas fir is an incident worth watching. Bigleaf maple, like many western trees, thrives in Europe but not in the eastern States.

The native maple of the middle-west, so common there that it is often regarded as a weed, is the box elder (*A. negundo*). 'Elder' is easy to understand; it grows to about the same size in the same disorganized bushy way. 'Box' is more difficult. Box elder departs from the expected maple leaf-shape, simply by treating three (or sometimes five) lobes as three (or five) separate short-

Above *The sugar maple has rounded angles between the leaf-lobes, and its trunk is furrowed with distinct vertical lines, almost like boarding. It is one of America's best trees for autumn colour.*

Below *The red maple grows alongside the sugar maple and colours almost as brilliantly in autumn. Red maple leaves have sharp angles between the leaf-lobes.*

stalked leaves. It is the only American maple with this character; in the East there are several more.

There is scarcely an easier or more undemanding tree to be had. It can, and often does, grow in the dustiest and driest places. On the other hand it is dull in form, dull in colour and makes no special effort in autumn. It is one of the rare species in which the variegated form is superior to the normal one in almost every way. *A. negundo* 'Elegans' has yellow edges to its leaves and 'Variegatum' has white. Both are extremely conspicuous trees.

The west coast has its shrubby maple too;

Red maple makes a medium-sized tree, fast-growing and a tidy shape for street-planting. Autumn colour can be yellow (above left) or any shade of red: it rarely colours well on chalky soil. This picture was taken in Vermont.

Below *The flowers and half-grown leaves of the bigleaf maple of Oregon. Full-grown leaves of this tree can be a foot or more across, and the tree 100 feet high with luminous yellow-gold autumn colour.*

Below *Flowers of the red maple have just formed into tiny keys. It flowers early: the leaves are still in bud. Buds, stems and flowers of red maple are red. Young branches have bark (as here) as silvery as beech.*

Below *The box elder has its male and female flowers on separate trees. Here the male flowers appear with the opening leaves, which are in three pieces – each lobe on a separate stalk. Box elder is a common wild tree from New York to the Rockies.*

Below *The vine maple is seen here in the Cascade mountains of Washington in its usual company: giant firs. It is an insubstantial tree, sometimes literally a vine, but its leaves are eye-catching.*

Right *'Moosewood' (Acer pensylvanicum) is the striped-bark maple of America: a slender, light-shading tree with leaves tending to oval. The young stems are jade green and white.*

the vine maple (*A. circinatum*), so-called because in the tangle of the forest it often fails to make a real trunk, but wanders vine-like on the ground and up other trees. It is possible to make a tree of it, but more interesting to let it sprawl. It is one of the most worthwhile small maples for a garden; excellent in autumn and very pretty in spring with its purple and white flowers.

America has one striped-bark maple; a ravishing tree which the settlers christened, with inimitable earthiness, moosewood (*A. pensylvanicum*). A few Asiatic maples have the same characteristic: the constantly smooth, fresh green bark of a tree with its living cambium almost on the surface, vertically striped with bold chalk-marks.

Moosewood is a tall thin tree, as though in a hurry to get out of the moose's reach. Its rather sparse and spindly branches are a beautiful clear green like the trunk, or in one cultivar (*A.p.* 'Erythrocladum') a pretty pale pink, which turns red in winter.

Moosewood leaves are like ovals with wings; a totally different and memorable design. It can be too sparse a tree to plant in the middle of a lawn; one would tend to see right through it. Its place in nature is in light woodland, where its pale snake-bark blends with the fleeting shadows.

The Maples of the East

Right *Late-summer leaves and keys of the aconite-leaved Japanese maple (Acer japonicum 'Aconitifolium'), another low tree of richly distinctive texture which colours crimson in autumn.*

The maples, with the flowering cherries and the pines, are the cornerstone of Japanese gardening. They are the second annual event: April brings white and soft pink to the gardens and the woods; October the flame colours of ripening maple leaves. Composing tone poems with maples, however, is a less exact art than it is with cherries. For you never know exactly what colour a maple will turn. And cherries are constant year after year; maples louder or fainter according to the season.

None of the maples of the East is a big tree. Fifty feet is about as high as any of them go. But they have an incomparably rich range of variations on their elegant theme. Central China is the great reservoir of species. Many of the Japanese trees were imported from China in the distant past.

As far as the West is concerned *the* Japanese maple is the little shrub-size but tree-shaped plant with a domed head and fine-cut, often dark red, foliage. This particular tree, the most popular of all garden maples, is *A. palmatum*. 'Atropurpureum' is the dark red variety. Nurseries have concentrated on two variables; leaf colour and leaf shape. There are bright green, pale gold and bronzy green, as well as various mottlings and marginations, besides the red form. There is a second group, all known as *A. palmatum* 'Dissectum', with their leaves cut right down to the stalk in a series of almost needle-like lobes. These are the weakest-growing kinds, never reaching tree height. They also come in red, bronze, purple and green. And there is a third group of relatively vigorous small trees with bigger leaf-lobes; normally seven of them, each with a serrated edge. Three of the best of these are *A. palmatum* 'Senkaki', which has red twigs and colours a thrilling clear yellow in autumn; *A. palmatum* 'Linearilobum', whose green or red leaves are shredded as deeply as the 'Dissectum' maple's; and 'Heptalobum Osakazuki', which simply turns furnace-red for a fortnight in October. The original 'Osakazuki' tree, imported from Japan in 1886, is at the British national arboretum at Westonbirt; 30 feet high with half a dozen stems. Although it is well-shaded by a huge red oak it lights its dark corner like a lantern. A glade at Westonbirt is given to seedlings of *A. palmatum* (which, being seedlings, have no more exact name). The range of shapes, sizes and colours is extraordinary.

The maples which botany knows as Japanese (i.e. the *A. japonicum* group) are not very different. The species tends to have more leaf-lobes (from seven to 11) and to grow a bit bigger, but the detail of a downy leaf-stalk is the only crucial distinguishing mark. The three named cultivars of *A. japonicum* are all outstandingly beautiful small trees. 'Vitifolium' (vine-leaved) for its broad, fan-shaped leaves; 'Aconitifolium' for its deep-cut leaves and 'Aureum' for its pale warm-yellow leaves. The first two colour magnificently in autumn; 'Aureum' tends to be scorched by the sun and turn brown. With a little guidance all these trees will make wonderfully harmonious shapes, putting on a terrace of leaves here, a terrace there like the hand-movements of a Japanese dance.

Japan has one totally different maple, with simple oval leaves. Only the keys and the opposite branching give away the hornbeam maple (*A. carpinifolium*). It has the same corrugations between the leaf-veins as the hornbeam.

Some excellent species share the characteristic of the box elder: having the lobes of their leaves completely separate and on stalks. One of the rarest and most beautiful of all small trees, the paper-bark maple, *A. griseum*, has little three-leaf leaves, greyish underneath as the name suggests. The bark of this tree is much more like a birch than a maple; it peels away in tatters of rich red-brown. Even the bark of quite thin twigs starts crackling and coming away. As it does

For a combination of elegant shape with brilliant colour there is no small tree to compare with the Japanese maple (Acer palmatum). A score of its cultivars have different leaf shapes and colour. Here A. palmatum 'Osakazuki' blazes in autumn.

Right *The Japanese maples with very finely-divided leaves (here, Acer palmatum 'Dissectum Atropurpureum') never grow higher than low mounds which perfectly display the beauty of their almost ferny texture.*

Below *The paperbark maple adds to the delicacy and autumn brilliance of its foliage the beauty of birch-like peeling bark in the warmest tones of red-brown. It is among the bigger oriental maples, growing as high as 45 feet, though slowly.*

Below *One of Japan's snake-bark maples, Acer rufinerve, has three-lobed leaves very similar to those of the American moosewood. Its variegated form 'Albolimbatum' is a superb tree.*

Above *The vine-leaved Japanese maple (Acer japonicum 'Vitifolium') has bolder and broader leaves than the others: magnificent as they turn by degrees to their final autumnal scarlet.*

Left *The nikko maple has leaves divided into three separate pieces like the American box-elder. In autumn colour it is far superior, turning shades of brilliant red or purple.*

Above *Japan's hornbeam maple departs entirely from the typical maple leaf design. The leaves are similar in shape and size to the hornbeam's and turn the same autumn colour.*

raced shape. It colours rich yellow in autumn. *Hersii* and another species, *A. grosseri*, have botanists in a tangle about whether they are two or one. Hers was a Belgian railway engineer, who improved his leisure, while hunting up timber for his tracks, by some very distinguished botanizing. For the gardener's purposes, rather than the botanist's, it is fair to consider his, David's and *A. grosseri* as one group; immensely decorative and valuable trees.

None of these trees is by any means common. The purple horned maple (*A. diabolicum purpurascens*), the biggest of the red-leaved maples of Japan, is more often planted—both for its leaves and its profuse pink flowers. The trident maple (*A. buergeranum*), with leaves that suggest the name, is popular in California. And the Amur maple (*A. ginnala*), from the north of China, whose leaves are similarly three-pronged but with teeth and a long central lobe, is grown a good deal in the north.

There remains one maple (*A. giraldii*) that tries to combine all the attractions; a paperbark trunk with snake-bark shoots; big sycamore-like leaves with long pink leaf-stalks; beautiful autumn colour with a rich crop of keys. It only fails in its shape: it tends to long-branched stiffness. Needless to say it is the rarest of them all.

so it catches the light, so that the interior of the tree is always full of reddish lights and shadows. The leaves turn scarlet, and so do its thousands of tiny keys lining the branches. Unfortunately very little of this harvest is fertile: hence the tree's rarity.

The nikko maple (*A. nikoense*) is not common anywhere, even in Japan. Among the three-leaf species it is easily distinguished by having densely furry stems. The whole of a young tree bristles like a moss-rose. It grows into an upright fountain shape and colours brilliantly.

Another group of a good half-dozen has snake-bark more or less like the American moosewood. *A. davidii* and *hersii*, both from central China, are probably the best-known. *A. davidii* is a conspicuously coloured tree all year, with green-and-white bark, shiny green leaves which are heart-shaped and toothed rather than lobed, and bright red leaf-stalks. One of Westonbirt's examples is a wide-spreading tree of a beautiful ter-

Hers's Chinese maple (Acer hersii), left, and the very similar A. davidii have some of the best striped bark. The leaves of David's turn yellow in autumn. Hers's turn bright red.

Above *One form of the Japanese horned maple (the keys are 'horned') has purple foliage and purply-pink flowers, more conspicuous than those of most maples.*

Top *Acer davidii 'George Forrest' makes an open, spreading small tree with tiers of rich yellow foliage in autumn. It was introduced by Forrest from Yunnan in 1921 and is now the commonest form of David's maple in cultivation.*

The Maples of Europe

Europe hasn't many maples. What she has on the other hand are exceptionally useful. Two of her maples are now basic planting material far beyond her frontiers. The sycamore and the Norway maple are among the fastest, hardiest and least demanding of all big trees. And both of them are prolific in coloured versions for ornament. One would not claim exquisite grace of design for any of them, but they are easy, colourful and on the whole tough and vigorous.

The sycamore-maple (*A. pseudoplatanus*) is the giant of the maple family. Also the beanstalk: it reaches full height in 60 years. It makes a great girthy tree, longer in branch than in trunk, with pale rough bark breaking into plates like rhinoceros armour. Its green winter buds break to produce so many dangling yellow-green flowers that a tree of mine that flowers with a neighbouring laburnum almost rivals it in beauty. The big leaves of the sycamore darken during the summer to yew-green, often overlaid with black by 'tar-spot' fungus. They have no autumn glory; but in compensation they soon fall after a frost.

You can tell a sycamore in spring without raising your eyes from the ground. It sows its seed with such abandon that the ground below is a lawn of its little strap-shaped seed-leaves uncurling. The town-dweller as a result often sees sycamore in the most unlikely and undesirable places. He comes to regard it as a tree weed.

Scotland (where it is known as the 'plane') is where the sycamore grows in its greatest beauty. On the windswept moors of the border country wind-shaped sycamores are drawn like hoods around the cowering farms. In the 'policies' (as they call the parks) of mansion and castle the 'plane' is the dark green cumulo-nimbus that defines where pleasure-grounds end and country begins. Above all the sycamore is the front-line defence against the salt-laden sea-wind. It may crouch, but at least it grows, and provides that minimum shelter in which other plants can start to grow.

Dark as the sycamore is, a purple pigment comes naturally to it and suits it very well. The purple sycamore *A.p.* 'Purpureum' or 'Spaethii' is a subtle tree; green at first glance, but with crimson flashes where the wind lifts a leaf. On top the leaves are green; underneath they are dark purply-red.

The golden sycamore *A.p.* 'Worleei' also works well, particularly in the spring. It is not such a big tree as the green or purple. But the doll of the family, without a doubt, is the almost-miniature *A.p.* 'Brilliantissimum', a little mop-head with leaves of a lovely faint pink at first, turning pale greeny-gold, then a bronzy colour with

Above and right *The European sycamore is one of the biggest of the maple family; fast-growing, immensely hardy and prolific with its seedlings. It makes a broad tree in the open, casting a heavy shade with its big dark green leaves.*

Left *The Montpellier maple (Acer monspessulanum) is the common hedge maple of southern Europe. Its neat three-lobed leaves distinguish it from the five-lobed hedge maple of further north.*

Below *is the excellent gold-leaved form of A. campestre, called 'Postelense'.*

The medium-sized maples include the Caucasian Acer cappadocicum 'Rubrum' (right), whose new shoots are blood red and the Italian A. opalus (below) whose flowers (seen here) cover the tree with autumnal gold in spring. Both colour yellow in autumn.

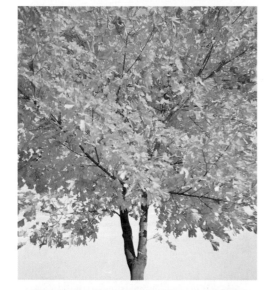

Above left and left *The Norway maple is one of the fastest-growing and most adaptable trees, beautiful in flower (left) and in autumn colour (above left). It has produced a dozen coloured varieties, including some very dark purple ones.*

veins etched in green. Maples as a race are shy of the hottest sun. 'Brilliantissimum' should be kept in a light shade.

The Norway maple (*A. platanoides*) is looked on as a more refined tree and often used for street planting. It has many of the sycamore's qualities of speed and indifference to conditions, but less of a liking for the sea. Its leaves are of thinner fabric and a paler colour, and they turn splendid gold, rather briefly, in autumn. A Norway maple should be encouraged to branch as low as possible; its yellow-green flowers are early and relatively conspicuous. They repay a closer look.

Hardly any broadleaf tree, at least big tree, has given us such an imaginative catalogue of forms. There are mop-head, upright, cut-leaf, variegated and red forms, and one with strange angular leaves known as the eagle's-claw maple. The red pigment is not altogether satisfactory in this tree. Either there is too much or not enough. Some forms ('Goldsworth Purple' and 'Faassen's Black' are examples) start wine-red but turn a depressing dull purple-brown by summer. Some on the other hand – and these are much preferable – run out of red and end the season an original kind of bronzed green. 'Schwedleri' and 'Reitenbachii' are of this school. None of the fancy ones is as

good as the straightforward species.

America appreciates Europe's little hedge (or field) maple (*A. campestre*) more than Europe does. On the continent it is used to form hedges, but in Britain its growth is mainly wild. When I see it growing on the chalk downs in Kent I almost wish it came from Japan so that someone would make a fuss of it. Its yellow-gold is not exactly rapturous in autumn, but it makes a neat little tree with its very small leaves, and answers the shears as well as a beech. No doubt with a good choreographer it could adopt poses as graceful as any. Its golden form, *A.c.* 'Postelense', is exceptionally pale and fine.

Towards the Mediterranean its place is taken by the Montpellier maple (*A. monspessulanum*) which has three lobes to its leaves, a little like clover, instead of five.

The Italian maple *A. opalus* and the Turkish *A. cappadocicum* are both uncommon outside their own countries, but both well worth considering, the Italian maple for its yellow flowers, as early as March, and the Cappadocian for its dome of pale yellow in autumn. The variety of *A. cappadocicum* called 'Rubrum' has startling blood-red new shoots in summer. They are all trees of moderate stature; the convenient size for street-planting that urban authorities are always on the lookout for.

Cashews and Sumachs

The pistachio tree has poplar-like male catkins on separate trees from the female flowers. The true pistachio, source of the nuts, demands a Mediterranean climate. The Chinese pistachio is fully hardy with fine foliage and brilliant autumn colour, but inedible nuts.

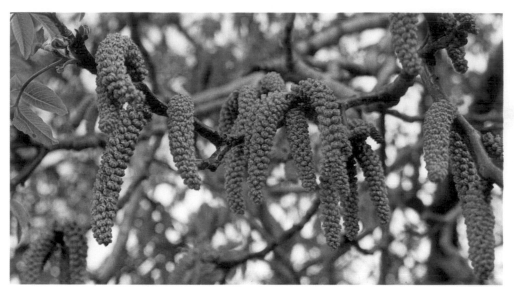

The nuts and leaves of the pistachio tree, by the French artist Redouté. He painted details of over 400 trees for Le Nouveau Duhamel *in 1801–19.*

The sinister principle of poison links the members of the cashew family. They all have to some degree the faculty of giving you a nasty rash. Poison ivy is the extreme example. But even the unroasted husks of cashew nuts can be irritant. Even mangoes (another tropical relation) can give people who eat them raw an extremely sore mouth.

The cashew is a Caribbean tree, a native of Haiti. The hardier nut-bearer of its race is the pistachio (*Pistacia vera*) of the eastern Mediterranean. Anyone who has sat in a cafe in Athens knows that the pistachio is a very profitable item of commerce in that part of Greece; old men and little boys are waiting in the wings to sell you a tiny bag for a huge price. There is another pistachio tree in the same area that produced the chewing gum (mastic; hence masticate for chew) which was issued to the inmates of harems to give them white teeth and sweet breath. Californians and Italians could have a shot at growing either of these useful trees. There is a *very* hardy pistachio (*P. chinensis*), but it has no comestibles to offer. It is grown for its upright shape, moderate size and first-rate autumn scarlet. It will perform in the same way at Palm Springs and Kew Gardens.

The graceful pepper tree from South America (*Schinus molle*) is also limited in Europe to parts with a Mediterranean climate and in America to zone 9. The pepper part of it is its little red berries. But what makes it so popular is the combination of thick gnarled trunk and branches with

The pepper tree of Peru is a feathery evergreen for a warm climate. Its autumn cascades of fruit like red peas make it popular in southern Europe.

The smoke tree envelopes itself in a haze of minute buff-coloured flowers, seen here becoming fruits. Their stems show up clearly against the foliage of the purple-leaved form. All smoke trees colour red in autumn.

The most elegant garden form of the stag's-horn sumach (Rhus typhina 'Laciniata') has fretted leaflets on its big compound leaves, here in their autumn colour. The sumachs grow in most soils.

droopy, almost weeping branchlets. It reaches its ultimate height and equal spread of 35 or 40 feet in only 20 years. People are apt to install pepper trees in brand-new gardens, only to find that they have commandeered the whole place.

The two members of the cashew family important in northern gardens are *Rhus* and *Cotinus*. Rhus is best represented in the species known as staghorn sumach, from its antler-like growth with supple bends and very few twigs—and also for its antler-like texture; when stag's horns are 'in velvet' in the spring they have the same mossy covering. The species (*Rhus typhina*) is a native of the eastern States; a hardy and tenacious plant despite its exotic, subtropical appearance. Plant it in a border where its roots get pronged when you are forking around and it suckers freely. But it is a little tree well worth having for its scarlet lollipop fruit and its fiery autumn leaves.

Chinese rhus (*R. verniciflua*) is the source of lacquer for furniture. E. H. Wilson gives the recipes for the various colours in his account of his journeys. The natural colour of the dried sap (which can also give you a rash) is black. Oil from *Aleurites fordii* (tung, or Chinese wood-oil tree) is added to make it brown; mercuric sulphide to make it red. Apparently only in a hot climate does the sap give the right results.

Cotinus is the smoke tree. The European *C. coggyria*, common in gardens with its purple leaves and fawn fuzz of flowers, can hardly claim tree status. America's *C. obovatus* is more upright, and by all accounts one of the best-colouring plants even in the fire-box of an eastern autumn.

The Citrus Trees

Rue is a little herb with a strong smell. Few of the 1,600 plants that sail under its flag as *Rutaceae* are trees, but the few include the highly decorative and useful genus *Citrus*; also the eastern American hop-tree or wafer-ash and the Amur (which means, roughly speaking, Manchurian) cork tree.

Their flower structure puts them in the same evolutionary category as the maples. What singles them out as associates of rue is having in their leaves translucent glands filled with aromatic oils. Fastidious Frenchmen of the 18th century 'stopped their noses' with rue.

The orange tree, prettiest of the citrus family and the most able to stand relatively low temperatures, came into cultivation in Arab lands from the Far East at least 1,000 years ago. In 17th-century Europe the orangery, a room with big windows and a stove for over-wintering orange trees, became a craze. The huge white tubs containing the trees were manoeuvred into it in the early autumn and out into the garden again in the spring. The trees barely existed through the winter and would have died without their summer out of doors.

It was an essential part of the upkeep of the ornamental oranges in those days to hose them down regularly – even daily – to keep pests and disease at bay. Oranges are singularly prone to both.

A winter temperature in the upper forties is enough for an orange to thrive and set fruit. Spring is the season of blossom, so sweet-smelling that in orchard areas it can become too much of a good thing. The fruit takes a long time to come to maturity. The following winter is the normal harvest

Top *The charm of orange trees lies in their glossy evergreen foliage against which white flowers and bright orange fruit stand out like decorations – often both at the same time, since fruit takes a year or more to ripen.*

Above *Lemon trees are less hardy than oranges, but no less ornamental. Here at Marlia in Italy the lemon garden has trees in pots. They are put out in the spring and taken indoors for the winter.*

Right *The 'orangery' is a 17th-century invention: a building with tall windows for sheltering oranges through the winter. Here, at Fontainebleau, the orange trees are in their summer order in front of the orangery.*

Right *The soft blackish bark of the Amur cork tree from northern China at the Trompenburg arboretum, Rotterdam. The trunk often forks low and massive furrowed branches take over, making a most impressive wide-spreading shade tree.*

Left *The very hardy cork tree has big bright green leaves like the tree of heaven's and small black plum-like fruit. Only the aromatic essence in glands in the leaves suggests its relationship with the rue family.*

period in subtropical conditions, but in cooler parts oranges are not ripe till the following summer–hence the charming combination of fruit and flowers on the same tree together.

The citrus list is formidable. Apart from the sweet oranges there are Seville oranges (bitter; the best for marmalade) tangerines with their reach-me-down skin, lemons (the least hardy trees), limes (which gave their name to all the 'limeys' who sailed on British ships and drank lime-juice to ward off scurvy), grapefruit and its forebear the shaddock, citron with its thick skin, used for flavouring cakes. The list of hybrids is as long. There is the ugli (a cross between grapefruit and tangerine), the citrange, the limequat, the tangor, the orangequat and even the citrangequat. The -quats involve the blood of China's shrubby, sour-fruited kumquat (*Fortunella margarita*), which is a hardier plant.

The Japanese bitter orange (*Poncirus trifoliata*) is hardy even in Britain and up to Boston. It can scarcely be called a tree, but it has plenty of flowers and little oranges that make adequate marmalade.

The same chemistry gives the little hop-tree (*Ptelea trifoliata*) one of North America's best-smelling flowering seasons, and in a smaller degree pervades the Amur cork tree (*Phellodendron amurense*) and the Korean *Euodia daniellii*. Euodia is occasionally planted as a hardy small tree with mid-summer scented flowers. The Amur cork tree is planted more for its corky bark, which looks impressively bulky on its thick, wide-reaching branches. Both these Asiatic trees have long compound ash-like leaves.

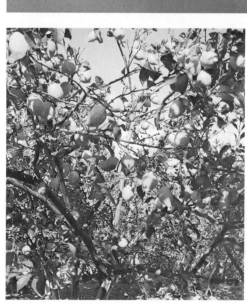

Above *Lemon trees need less summer heat than oranges to ripen their fruit–but they also need warmer winters. They should be able to survive where temperatures never fall below about 44° F.*

Above *In the tropics oranges ripen while they are still green–and so unsaleable. Hence subtropical areas like southern Spain and Florida are the main commercial producers.*

Below *The oriental Euodias (here E. hupehensis) are unexpected citrus-relations with big compound leaves, viburnum-like flowers, and clusters of red or black berries.*

The Ashes of North America and Europe

Right *The weeping ash is a spectacular lawn tree, particularly in winter when its stiffly hanging rod-like branchlets are visible. Weeping branches can be grafted on to a normal ash at any height: even 100 feet up.*

Not even the oak carries quite such significance out of the murk of legendary time as the ash. In which cold land of myth-making was it such a conspicuous tree? Somewhere on the Baltic shores where the Vikings' ancestors spent the dark evenings scaring themselves with sagas and dreaming up dragons, primeval ash-woods must have held them in awe. To them the ash was Yggdrasil, 'the greatest and best of all trees. Its branches spread over the whole world, and even reach above heaven.' At the top (so they said) sat an eagle; at the bottom a dragon. In between a squirrel scrambled up and down like Henry Kissinger relaying endless threats and counter-threats.

Was it size alone that promoted the ash to this position? Certainly it is one of the tallest of Europe's broadleaves. It has reached 150 feet in modern times. Linnaeus' name for it, *Fraxinus excelsior*, stresses its height.

It is not exceptional in leaf: best perhaps when its grey-green leaflets stream in the wind. It is more conspicuous in winter: notably austere, grey-barked and sparse-branched. Dryden wrote 'nature seems to ordain the rocky cliff for the wild ash's reign'.

Botanically the ashes belong to the olive family, which also includes (among common garden plants) privet, lilac and jasmine. The family traits are by no means obvious (unless you count opposite branching, which is common to most of them, but to thousands of other plants too). The fruits of ash and olive could hardly be less alike.

Most of the world's 60 or so ash species conform to the general style of *F. excelsior*. They have compound leaves; the leaflets arranged in opposite pairs (except for the

The manna ash is always a tree to watch, from the tulip-like unfolding of its grey-green buds into leaves and copious flowers to the gentle autumn colouring of its dense and shady foliage.

The common ash seeds itself widely and comes up fast, making a tall, wide-spreading, grey-barked tower of the finest quality timber. This typical tree is in the south of England, at Hambledon near Portsmouth.

Below *The flowers of the common ash colour the bare branches well before the leaves (which come late to this tree).*

Below right *'Keys' of the ash are rather like half a maple key. They hang in dense bunches, often right through the winter, and germinate almost as prolifically as those of the sycamore.*

Right *The ash carries leaves and buds in opposite pairs, making a branch pattern that often makes a young tree in winter easy to recognize. The common European ash has matt black winter buds unlike any other tree's.*

odd one at the end) on a green stalk seldom more than a foot long. They have simple, single-winged keys for fruit. They are vigorous, dense-rooted and demanding of the soil: easy to transplant but bad to grow near shrubs: liable to commandeer all the rations.

All North America's common ashes follow this general pattern. The white ash (*F. americana*) is the tallest, best for timber and most commonly planted. The basic hardiness of the race comes out in the fact that it grows as well in Europe as in America; not true of American oaks, beeches or elms. White ash is white and downy beneath the leaves; in autumn purple in the north; yellow farther south.

Red ash and green ash (*F. pensylvanica* and *F.p. lanceolata*) are varieties of one species; the green one (green beneath the leaflets) the commoner of the two, with the biggest natural range of any of them. These, and several other American ashes, have a great advantage as street trees: they are

fast-growing at first, but slow down and form round crowns at about 60 feet.

The same size range includes black ash (*F. nigra*; a far-northern swamp tree), blue ash (*F. quadrangulata*) from the southeast and velvet ash from the southwest. Blue ash has twigs with a square cross-section, and bark which makes blue dye. Velvet ash (*F. arizonica*) has a downy layer on both twigs and leaves, together with a dense fashion of leafing that makes it a good shade tree.

Only the Oregon ash of the northwest (*F. latifolia*; a Douglas discovery, named by him for its broad leaflets) grows to the same sort of height as the white ash.

There are European ashes that give relief from this generally business-like approach. There are narrow-leaved kinds (two different species: *F. angustifolia* and *F. oxycarpa*); an odd one with only one leaf at a time (*F. excelsior* 'Diversifolia') instead of nine or 11; one with dandelion-yellow bark (*F.e.* 'Jaspidea') which is remarkably con-

spicuous in winter; and above all the weeping one: to me the best of all weeping broadleaf trees. Weeping ash (*F. excelsior* 'Pendula') manages to be both stiff and graceful together. It is made by grafting weeping branches on a stem already grown to the required height; this has been done, successfully, to a tree 90 feet high. It is a particularly fine sight in winter when its hanging ramrods of branches are like wooden rain.

But the biggest departure from what we expect of ashes comes in the group that flaunts its flowers. Of these the manna ash of southern Europe (*F. ornus*) is by far the best known. The flowers are showy, creamy-white, in May. But they are only half the story. The whole tree is so voluptuous in glossy leafage that others look quite abashed beside it. It stands out in staid parkland like the velvet-framed bosoms of Nell Gwynn and her contemporaries on ancestral dining-room walls.

A storm-cloud picks out the pale bark of the green ash – America's most widespread species. America's tallest ash is a hybrid between this and the white ash – a 'pumpkin' ash 130 feet high in Missouri.

The yellow ash (Fraxinus excelsior 'Jaspidea') is a fine form of the common ash which colours gold in autumn (the common ash stays green till leaf-fall) and has distinctly yellow bark – very striking in the winter sun.

Olives and Fringe-Trees

If your fairy godmother would let you grow just one tree from outside your climate-zone what would it be? For me the answer is not the coconut palm nor even the lovely weeping blue cypress of Kashmir. I would choose the olive.

Olive-trees have Homeric style. I cannot see flowering cherries in the Elysian fields. I can see grey olive-orchards, black cypresses and pines. Grace and gravity the olive has, living as long as yew, growing as gnarled, yet still leafing with a silver spray.

The olive tree is given to branching low, and its branches to wandering. Down into them through leaves like the white willow's pours Mediterranean light. The range of the olive in Europe has always been taken as the limits of the Mediterranean world. Wherever olives are planted they bring their mood. No Doric columns, no transplanted temple ever brought the classical world into America as powerfully as an olive grove.

Olives love the sun and dread humidity. They like the soil deep but dry. Florida is not such good olive country as California, and of California the south and the central valley is best. They are slow trees to grow. But they have one great advantage: by diligent digging and packing of its roots, you can move even an ancient olive.

The best imitation olive tree I have seen in a northern garden was its cousin *Phillyrea latifolia*, a favourite Victorian evergreen. Phillyrea can be remarkably olivey in shape: only very dark green.

To turn from olive to its cousin privet sounds at first like a descent from the sublime to the ridiculous. And is privet a tree? Common privet isn't: just one of the necessary evils of gardening. But its Chinese counterpart with glossy leaves (*Ligustrum lucidum*) is one of the best hardy (to zone 7) evergreen trees.

Vogue would no doubt call this the wet-look privet. Its leaves are long, camellia-size, dark green and glossy. In summer it carries upstanding batons of white flowers

Olive wood is hard but smooth-grained and ideal for carving into implements. Monks in the monasteries of Mount Athos have made a small industry of olive-wood spoons and bowls.

Far left and left *Unripe green olives and the swollen, wrinkled, oily black ripe fruit. Olives for oil are left on the trees to ripen: eating olives are picked both half-ripe and ripe.*

Above *The ancient marriage of oil and wine; olive trees and vines grow together on the terraced hillsides of the island of Samos in the Aegean, punctuated with black spires of cypress.*

The glossy privet of China is in a class apart from common hedge-privet. It makes a beautiful and hardy small evergreen tree with pointed shiny leaves and masses of white flowers in autumn.

Left *Olive-trees can live for 1,500 years or more. They share with yews the distinction of being Europe's oldest trees. In age they become grotesquely gnarled, in wonderful contrast with their light silvery foliage.*

Below *The olive-harvest in the Mediterranean takes place in the winter. The ripe olives are beaten from the trees with long poles and gathered from the ground. In this close-planted grove in Dalmatia the trees are growing unusually straight and tall.*

with the rather sickly privet smell. Thirty feet (fairly fast) is about as high as it grows, but 30 feet of such intense dark green gloss can be quite a showpiece–especially with such a heavy load of flowers.

One of the stranger tales E. H. Wilson told of backwoods China is the story of the wax-insect. It seems almost as though the insect sensed that the privet and the ash are of one family. In one valley in the west (at Chien-ch'ang to be exact) the wax-insects breed on the leaves of the Chinese ash, *Fraxinus chinensis*. In May they are collected in boxes and carried by coolies, travelling only at night (it being too hot for the insects during the day) for 200 miles to their feeding ground –the leaves of the privet-trees of Kiating. Such extraordinary pains are rewarded by three months of unrelenting wax-laying, when the insects weigh down the privet with hundredweights of the finest wax–used for candles, for coating paper and polishing jade. Whether the Cultural Revolution left the wax-coolies in business we may one day find out. But how did the business start?

With a bit of imagination one can see the fringe-tree (*Chionanthus*) as the missing link in the olive-ash family; close enough to the ash to be grafted on its roots, flowering rather like the flowering ashes and with fruit not unlike the olive.

But a fringe-tree in flower, more fringe than tree, needs no botanical footnotes. Like the ashes it comes late into leaf, but almost at once, in June, puts on a covering of white flowers: five spidery-thin petals joined at the base (whence 'fringe'). It is one of the most stunning small trees (or big shrubs) that a northern garden–on any soil–can grow.

Olives for oil are first crushed with a stone roller (left) then pressed like grapes in a huge vice (right). The ancient process is shown here in a 16th-century Flemish engraving.

There are two species of fringe-tree: Chinese and North American. The American (above left) has drooping flowers in enormous quantities (but not as a young bush). Its leaves appear very late in

the spring. The Chinese fringe-tree (above right) carries its dainty and fragrant flowers in erect clusters – by the million. Both species do best in a continental climate.

241

The Tree of Heaven and the Cedrelas

It is possible for a tree to be too easy and prolific–to devalue itself by appearing whether it is invited or not. The tree of heaven, *Ailanthus altissima*, makes this mistake. But before dismissing it as an urban weed we should look closer. Its leaves, often dismissed as 'coarse', are among the most impressively tropical-looking of any hardy tree's: plumes, sometimes a yard long, of as many as 30 substantial pointed-oval leaflets. Yet with these splendid leaves it contrives to remain open and light-shaded; often forked and wide-spreading; rarely more than 60 feet high.

Trees of heaven are (usually) either male or female. There are disadvantages to both; the male flowers smell nasty, but then the female has offspring. The female, however, is definitely the tree to buy if you have a choice: its fruit, bunches of propeller-like keys ripening bright red, is as good as a flowering season.

There is said to be no limit to the range of soils and other substances (ash, gravel, garbage) in which the tree of heaven will seed itself and thrive. On the other hand moving bigger trees is not so certain. I have been disappointed by standard trees set in good soil with loving care.

The way many people take advantage of such noble leaves without having to accommodate a whole tree is to cut the whole thing back every year as coppice. The effect in a border is of some ferocious fern, in which you will observe a curious habit: the leaf-stalks, usually in such compound leaves as deciduous as their leaflets, seem undecided as to whether they are leaf-stalks or permanent twigs. Often they let their leaflets fall some time before they let go themselves.

All the tree of heaven's close connections are tropical: the West Indies is the home of several *Quassias* that are relations. The West Indies is also the headquarters of the mahogany family, of which one branch, the Spanish cedar (*Cedrela odorata*) and its Chinese counterpart (*Cedrela sinensis*) is remarkably like the tree of heaven.

The Spanish cedar gets its inappropriate name from its scented wood; the wood of cigar-boxes. The Chinese cedrela or toon has little-known gastronomic potentialities. Its young shoots and leaves, which are delicate shades of pink and cream, are said to be delectably oniony: to the Chinese a vegetable. I can't help wondering how long the ones in the streets of Paris would remain so leafy if this were generally known.

The Chinese toon has other advantages over the tree of heaven: its yellow autumn colour and its bigger (and unscented) flowers. On the other hand it is a smaller tree and not quite so hardy.

Only in the south of Britain, and then only as a shrub, can we grow *Melia azedarach*, its near-eastern subtropical relation. Melia is fast-growing and shady; pretty in leaf but prettier after leaf-fall, when the yellow berries stay glistening in its crown.

Above and left *The bead tree or chinaberry; an ideal fast shade-maker in a hot climate, needing little moisture. The small, pale-lilac flowers, left, are fragrant. Above, the tree in early winter, a tangle of yellow berries. The berries remain on the tree long after the leaves have fallen. The hard, bony seeds inside them were strung together to form rosaries, hence the name 'bead tree'.*

Right *Three-foot ash-like leaves are perhaps the strongest point of the tree of heaven. They can lend an exotic subtropical air to any group of trees. Cut right down to the ground regularly and* *heavily manured an* Ailanthus *base will throw up monster leaves which can be an exciting ingredient in a shrub or herb border. The variety 'Pendulifolia' has even larger, drooping leaves.*

Left *The Chinese* Idesia polycarpa *(the only tree of its genus) has been described as 'like a small-leaved catalpa', with a splendid autumn display of red berries in heavy clusters.*

Top and above *The ash-like fruit of the tree of heaven (on female trees only) is normally faintly coloured like the example at the top. The variety* 'Erythrocarpa' *(above) has darker green leaves and bright red fruit which makes a good show from late summer into autumn.*

Above *The tree of heaven gets its name from its height. Tall trees like this, however, are the exception. America's biggest, on Long Island, is 60 feet high and 80 wide.*

Above *The cedrela (or 'Chinese cedar', or 'toon') has lagged behind the tree of heaven in popularity, although it makes an admirable street tree in Paris (as here) and has the bonus of onion-flavoured leaves.*

Right Ehretia *is another small Chinese genus of trees which remain rare, though they are easy and rewarding to grow. E. dicksonii develops rapidly into a short broad tree with ten-inch leaves and June flowers.*

Empress Trees and Indian Beans

Left *The catalpa (or Indian bean) of the southern States is a remarkably hardy garden tree, suffering only from strong winds which bruise its big soft leaves.*

Below *Catalpa leaves are heart-shaped, softly furry, and as much as ten inches long by eight wide—in young trees even larger. The purple tint of new leaves makes the new shoots conspicuous.*

Big pale crushable leaves give a tree the look of being in tropical kit. In Florida or Cap Ferrat you wouldn't give the *Catalpa* a second glance: which makes it all the more effective in Philadelphia or Frinton.

The catalpa and the *Paulownia* (or empress tree) are two trees northern gardens can grow as a reminder of the jacaranda and other tropical excesses. They are so similar in most ways that one is surprised to find them in different botanical families—respectively the *Bignoniaceae* and the *Scrophulariaceae*. What they have in common are flowers like foxgloves, weak and pithy young wood, and their oversize leaves. The

most obvious difference is that catalpa's flower-clusters hang while the paulownia's stand erect. And that catalpa flowers are white spotted with purple, while paulownia's are purple all over.

Catalpa's other name of Indian bean tree only reinforces the tropical impression. But Indiana bean tree would be nearer the mark. It is a mid-western native; another of the trees that turn up only in North America and China; nothing to do with India—only with Indian beans; its pencil-like pods.

There are two American catalpas: the southern *Catalpa bignonioides*, more common in gardens, and the northern *C.*

speciosa, a far bigger tree, making (surprisingly, considering its pithy shoots) timber that will lie on the wet ground for a century and not rot.

The southern catalpa is also the commonest in Europe. It tends to spread, even to sprawl, from a short trunk, or from none. Its heart-shaped leaves start hairy in the spring, growing shiny above as they reach their full nine or ten inches, at flowering time in mid-summer. Young trees produce only leaves, but old ones sometimes perform prodigiously with clusters of their extremely elaborate flowers.

The place for a catalpa is on a lawn that

Left *The empress tree or royal* Paulownia *is well-named: a conspicuous but impractical tree with huge leaves, weak and pithy wood, and flowers which appear in bud in autumn and often succumb to frost. Its fruit follows the flowers on tall spikes.*

Jacaranda is a flamboyant Brazilian cousin of Catalpa *and* Paulownia: *a gaudy tree in flower even by tropical standards. Its ferny-fine leaves are almost evergreen and its habit horizontal, making it a first-class shade tree for tropical and subtropical cities.*

Left *Some of the younger branches and shoots of* Kalopanax pictus *are armed with stout, sharp prickles.*
Below *The glossy green leaves of* Kalopanax pictus *are similar in shape to those of the sweetgum or a maple. The tree carries white flowers in flat heads in autumn.*

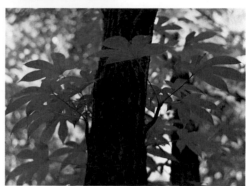

Left *The scented foxglove-shaped flowers of* Paulownia tomentosa *are a pale shade of heliotrope which easily merges with a bright sky. They need to be offset by a dark background.*

Below *The golden Indian bean tree,* Catalpa bignonioides *'Aurea', is one of the most striking of all yellow-leafed trees. The leaves are big and velvety in texture.*

has both space, sun and shelter from wind. Such rare spots are not lightly allotted, though. A tree must be more than merely conspicuous to compete. There are hybrid catalpas (American crossed with Chinese species) that offer further distractions: double-size leaves in the case of *C.× erubescens* 'J. C. Teas'; purplish ones in the case of *C.×e.* 'Purpurea'. Best of all is the golden cultivar of the southern catalpa, *C.b.* 'Aurea'; the nearest thing to a permanently sunlit hill.

The empress tree (*Paulownia tomentosa*) can be disappointing for flowers in northern gardens. It has the rather illogical habit of forming substantial flower-buds in autumn, which winter-cold often kills. Some gardeners for this reason forget about them altogether and coppice the plant, taking advantage of its natural vigour to force huge furry leaves out of it. It seems that the more recently introduced *P. fargesii* from China may do better with flowers–and also make a bigger tree.

No botanical considerations, only the arresting strangeness of the tree, brings the rare *Kalopanax pictus* in here. With the related thorny shrubby *Aralias* (Hercules' club and the Japanese angelica tree) it is botanically nearer the dogwood, with the same little massed florets and seeds arranged in a ball. *Kalopanax pictus* (sometimes called the castor aralia) is most like a succulent sycamore or a sweetgum in leaf: a striking pile of glossy greenery. But it is its winter frame that is really distinctive: its few, thick and forky twigs make memorable sky-writing. There could be no better tree to sharpen up bland avenues of plate-glass offices.

Aralia is more often shrub than tree. The most worthwhile of the genus are the variegated forms of the Japanese angelica tree (*A. elata* 'Variegata'). The leaves are huge and many-leafleted. In mottled green and creamy-white they look both ferociously tropical and innocently pretty.

The Elders

Evolutionarily new-fangled as they are, elders are still ancient in human history. The Latin *Sambucus* takes us back, via Greece, to very ancient things . . . among them the sackbut that accompanied the Psalms. Elder still makes whistles, as every schoolboy knows, and wine, as every grandmother did.

The elders and viburnums are close kin, as their flat flower-clusters show. The viburnums are unusual in sometimes having two kinds of flowers in one cluster: some working (i.e. sexual) and some purely to attract insects. The related hydrangeas do the same. Most insect-fertilized flowers, as W.J.Bean puts it, 'do their own advertising'. Yet here in this relatively recent design a division of labour is introduced.

In playing to the gallery like this they have played into the nurseryman's hands. The snowball tree (*Viburnum opulus* 'Sterile') is a form of the 'guelder rose' in which the sterile parts have been kept and the sexual rejected: the flower is all the showier.

The elder of elders is the truly tree-like blueberry elder (*Sambucus coerulea*) of the Pacific northwest. It grows in the wild to 50 feet and staggers under its late-summer load of bloomy fruit.

Common elder (*S. nigra*) will be a bush (and very likely a weed, too) if you let it. But such a vigorous and uncomplaining - and immensely hardy - plant can easily be harnessed into service. It will grow in dense shade, on a minimum of soil - and deliver barrow-loads of berries. Its worst point is its smell - not of the flowers (though this is a matter of opinion) but of its pithy new wood. Flies apparently agree: carters used to make chaplets of elder to keep the flies from their sweating horses' heads.

Several viburnums reach tree stature - though not strictly speaking the wayfaring tree, the only one with a tree name. Wayfaring tree (*V. lantana*) is a European hedge-row bush with white-wool-backed leaves which have much the same effect as the whitebeam. It was William Turner the Elizabethan herbalist who likened it to a wayfarer come from a dusty road.

The eastern American blackhaw (*V. prunifolium*) and the sheepberry or nanny-berry (*V. lentago*) are the principal viburnums of North America which make small trees. Both are worth growing for their autumn colour, apart from their edible fruit and masses of white (or off-white) flowers.

John Evelyn must have the last word: the pleasure he took in matching trees and words comes so clearly over 300 intervening years. He is speaking of inflammation. 'An extract of elder is efficacious to eradicate this epidemical inconvenience.'

Left *A typically vigorous common elder (here in North Wales). The elder is considered too coarse and vigorous (and free-seeding) for gardens. American blueberry elder is the most ornamental tree-sized species.*
Below Left *The wayfaring tree is conspicuous in spring with its dusty-white shoots and in autumn for its jewel-like fruit which turns from red to black.*

Above *The common elder is weighed down with sweet-scented flowers in early summer. The broad flat heads make heavy clusters of sweet black berries.*
Below *The berries of the 'guelder rose'* (Viburnum opulus) *turn and remain ruby-red, hanging on far into the winter. It is a tree or tall spreading bush for wet or boggy ground. The lobed, maple-like leaves colour richly in autumn.*

A-Z Index of Tree Species

This index of tree species and varieties is organized alphabetically by internationally accepted botanical Latin names. To look up a tree whose name you only know in English, first turn to the general index — pages 332-336 — which will give the English name followed by the Latin name. (Not all trees, by any means, have vernacular names; those without a vernacular name only appear in this index, not in the general index.) General notes on the genus are at the head of the entry, followed by specific notes on species and varieties in alphabetical order.

As well as listing trees referred to in the main text of the book, this index includes about 100 more species with particular interest for beauty, scarcity or both. The conservation of unusual and rare trees by growing them in gardens is becoming an increasingly important facet of their cultivation — although what is unusual in one place may well be common in another.

The hardiness zones (e.g. 'Zone 9') referred to are those mapped on pages 30-31.

The sign × before a name denotes a natural hybrid; the sign + a graft hybrid.

The words 'big', 'medium', 'small' in relation to leaf size are based on the following measurements: 'big' — 7 in (17.5cm) upwards; 'medium' — 2-6 in (5-15cm); 'small' — to 2 in (5cm).

The height given is that of a mature tree in its native land.

The speed of growth given is that of a known tree in good but not exceptional conditions. Statistics are not available for all species.

An * indicates that the tree is illustrated.

For space reasons, certain geographical abbreviations have been used, including C. — central, E. — eastern, etc.

Trees that have been chosen by the Royal Horticultural Society for the Award of Garden Merit, the internationally recognized commendation of an outstanding garden plant, have the legend 'A.G.M.' with the date of the award at the end of their specific entry. (The last list of awards was published in 1969 and has long been overdue for updating.)

Trees Scarce in Gardens and Collections

The following species and varieties are all relatively scarce in cultivation — a fact that adds considerably to the desirability of planting them where conditions are suitable. They may not be easy to find, but the effort is worthwhile.

ABIES
A. balsamea
A. bracteata
A. cilicica
A. concolor 'Candicans'
A. concolor 'Violacea'
A. fargesii
A. firma
A. holophylla
A. kawakamii
A. magnifica shastensis
A. mariesii
A. nebrodensis
A. numidica
A. religiosa
A. squamata
A. sutchuenensis
A. vejari

ACER
A. amplum
A. argutum
A. buergeranum
A. caudatum
A. diabolicum
A. diabolicum purpurascens
A. distylum
A. forrestii
A. giraldii
A. henryi
A. hyrcanum
A. lobelii
A. micranthum
A. miyabei
A. nigrum
A. pensylvanicum 'Erythrocladum'
A. platanoides 'Globosum'
A. platanoides 'Lorbergii'
A. sempervirens
A. syriacum
A. tartaricum
A. triflorum
A. truncatum
A. villosum

AESCULUS
A. glabra
A. pavia

ALNUS
A. incana 'Aurea'
A. japonica
A. maximowiczii

ARAUCARIA
A. angustifolia
A. bidwillii

BETULA
B. forrestii
B. grossa

BROUSSONETIA papyrifera

CARPINUS
C. cordata
C. japonica
C. laxiflora
C. orientalis

CASTANEA
C. crenata
C. mollissima

CASTANOPSIS cuspidata

CATALPA
C. × erubescens 'J. C. Teas'
C. fargesii

CEDRUS
C. brevifolia

CELTIS
C. australis
C. laevigata
C. sinensis
C. tournefourtii

CERCIS
C. canadensis
C. chinensis

CHAMAECYPARIS
C. henryae
C. thyoides

CHRYSOLEPIS chrysophylla

CINNAMOMUM camphora

CLADRASTIS
C. lutea

CORYLUS
C. californica

CRATAEGOMESPILUS
dardarii

CRATAEGUS
C. monogyna 'Biflora'
C. tanacetifolia

× **CUPRESSOCYPARIS**
× C. notabilis
× C. ovensii

CUPRESSUS
C. abramsiana
C. bakeri
C. forbesii
C. goveniana
C. guadalupensis
C. sargentii

DIOSPYROS
D. lotus

DIPTERONIA sinensis

EHRETIA dicksonii

EMMENOPTERIS henryi

EUCOMMIA elmoides

EUODIA (EVODIA)
E. daniellii
E. hupehensis

FAGUS
F. grandifolia
F. orientalis
F. sylvatica 'Ansorgei'
F. sylvatica 'Tortuosa'

FRANKLINIA alatamaha

FRAXINUS
F. americana
F. chinensis
F. mariesii
F. pensylvanica
F. quadrangulata
F. tomentosa
F. velutina
F. xanthoxyloides

GLEDITSIA
G. caspica
G. japonica

GLYPTOSTROBUS lineatus

GORDONIA
G. lasianthus

IDESIA polycarpa

ILEX
I. cassine
I. latifolia
I. opaca
I. pedunculosa
I. verticilluta

JUBAEA spectabilis

JUGLANS
J. cathayensis
J. mandshurica

JUNIPERUS
J. ashei
J. deppeana
J. distans
J. excelsa
J. formosana
J. monosperma
J. virginiana 'Pendula'

KETELEERIA davidiana

LAGERSTROEMIA indica

LARIX
L. gmelini
L. laricina
L. occidentalis

LINDERA obtusiloba

LIQUIDAMBAR
L. formosana

LITHOCARPUS densiflorus

MAACKIA
M. amurensis
M. sinensis

MACLURA pomifera

MAGNOLIA
M. fraseri
M. sargentiana

MALUS
M. coronaria 'Charlottae'
M. niedzwetzkyana
M. toringoides

MANGLIETIA insignis

MAYTENUS boaria

MELIOSMA veitchiorum

MICHELIA doltsopa

NOTHOFAGUS
N. moorei
N. pumila

NYSSA sinensis

OSTRYA
O. japonica
O. virginiana

PICEA
P. asperata
P. brachytyla
P. engelmannii 'Glauca'
P. koyamai
P. polita
P. rubens

PICRASMA quassioides

PINUS
P. albicaulis
P. aristata
P. attenuata
P. bungeana
P. cembroides
P. cooperi
P. densiflora
P. echinata
P. gerardiana
P. lambertiana
P. massoniana
P. monticola
P. palustris
P. pumila
P. pungens
P. resinosa
P. rigida
P. roxburghii
P. sabiniana
P. sylvestris 'Fastigiata'

P. tabulaeformis
P. torreyana
P. virginiana

PISTACIA
P. chinensis
P. vera

PLATANUS
P. racemosa

POPULUS
P. deltoides
P. maximowiczii
P. simonii
P. tacamahaca
P. wilsonii

PRUNUS
P. campanulata
P. conradinae
P. conradinae 'Semiplena'
P. cornuta
P. 'Kursar'
P. mahaleb
P. pensylvanica
P. serrulata spontanea
P. virginiana

PSEUDOTSUGA
P. japonica
P. macrocarpa

PYRUS
P. calleryana
P. nivalis
P. ussuriensis

QUERCUS
Q. acutissima
Q. agrifolia
Q. alba
Q. aliena
Q. bicolor
Q. chrysolepis
Q. dentata
Q. douglasii
Q. garryana
Q. glandulifera
Q. glauca
Q. incana
Q. infectoria
Q. kelloggii
Q. laurifolia
Q. × ludoviciana
Q. lyrata
Q. macedonica
Q. michauxii
Q. muehlenbergii
Q. nigra
Q. nuttallii
Q. pontica
Q. prinus
Q. robur 'Concordia'
Q. shumardii
Q. stellata
Q. variabilis
Q. virginiana
Q. warburgii
Q. wislizenii

ROBINIA
R. viscosa

SEQUOIADENDRON
giganteum 'Pendulum'

SORBUS
S. americana
S. harrowiana
S. scopulina

TAXODIUM
T. mucronatum

TAXUS
T. canadensis
T. cuspidata
T. × media

TETRACENTRON sinense

TETRACLINIS articulata

THUJA
T. standishii

TILIA
T. chinensis
T. dasystyla
T. henryana
T. insularis
T. kiusiana
T. mandshurica

TORREYA
T. nucifera

TSUGA
T. caroliniana
T. diversifolia

ULMUS
U. rubra
U. serotina
U. thomasii

ZELKOVA
Z. cretica
Z. serrata

Abies alba
Silver fir

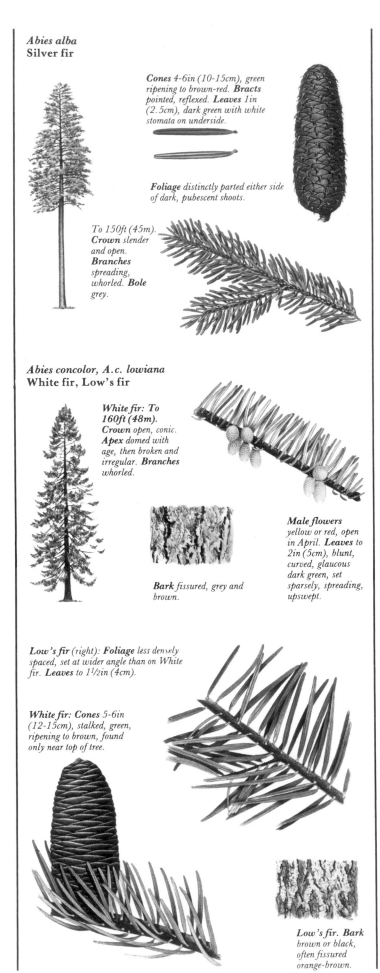

Cones 4-6in (10-15cm), green ripening to brown-red. **Bracts** pointed, reflexed. **Leaves** 1in (2.5cm), dark green with white stomata on underside.

Foliage distinctly parted either side of dark, pubescent shoots.

To 150ft (45m). **Crown** slender and open. **Branches** spreading, whorled. **Bole** grey.

Abies concolor, A.c. lowiana
White fir, Low's fir

White fir: To 160ft (48m). Crown open, conic. **Apex** domed with age, then broken and irregular. **Branches** whorled.

Bark fissured, grey and brown.

Male flowers yellow or red, open in April. **Leaves** to 2in (5cm), blunt, curved, glaucous dark green, set sparsely, spreading, upswept.

Low's fir (right): **Foliage** less densely spaced, set at wider angle than on White fir. **Leaves** to 1¹/2in (4cm).

White fir: Cones 5-6in (12-15cm), stalked, green, ripening to brown, found only near top of tree.

Low's fir. Bark brown or black, often fissured orange-brown.

A

ABIES 78–81, 326, 327
Evergreen trees, big, mostly conical. Leaves either spreading around shoot, or directed forward, often notched at tip, smell of turpentine when bruised. Sexes separate on same tree: male 'flowers' in clusters on underside of branches, often brightly coloured; female 'flowers' catkin-like. Cones have spreading scales, cylindrical, upright on branches, breaking up and leaving a central spike on the tree. Some years many, others few or none. Seeds winged. Bark usually resinous. Dislikes shallow chalk. Susceptible to certain insect pests, e.g. woolly aphid and rust fungi in Europe and America.

A. alba* **80, 81,** 318 Common silver fir, European silver fir. Europe. Zone 4. To 150ft (45m), sometimes with huge branches. Leaves in 2 ranks, upper shorter than lower, dark shiny green. Cones clustered near top of tree, pale green becoming brown-red. Young foliage susceptible to late frosts. 35ft (10.5m) in 20 years.

A. amabilis 79, 83, 319 Pacific silver fir, Red fir. W. United States. Zone 5. To 250ft (76m). Leaves flattened, crowded on upper surface of twig, brilliant white bands beneath. Cones dark purple-brown. Most soil types, except dry or chalky. Requires deep soil or high rainfall. 30ft (9m) in 20 years.

A. balsamea 42, 78, 319 Balsam fir, Balm of Gilead. E. Canada, United States. Zone 3. To 75ft (23m), dense, narrow. Leaves flat, dark green above, whitish near tip, silvery-white beneath, very sweet-scented. Cones purple. Not suitable for chalk. 15ft (4.5m) in 20 years.

A. borisii-regis 318 Sturdy, big tree from Balkan Peninsula.

A. bracteata 79, 319 Bristlecone fir, Santa Lucia fir, Fringed spruce. Mts of S. California. Zone 7. To 150ft (45m), broad-conical shape with hanging branchlets. Buds pale, slender, conical. Leaves large, spread horizontally into 2 opposite sets, curved and flattened with sharp tips, icy-white underneath. Grows on deep soil over chalk. 30 ft (9m) in 20 years.

A. cephalonica 80, 81, 318 Greek fir. Mts of Greece. Zone 5. To 100ft (30m), broadly conical, becoming more open. Leaves spread round shoots, mostly above; dark shiny green above, 2 narrow white bands beneath, prickly. Male 'flowers' in dense clusters beneath shoots. Cones often at top of crown, green-brown. Early foliage often frost-damaged. Disease-free. Likes chalk. 28ft (8.5m) in 20 years.

A. cilicica 318 'Cilician fir', from Mt. Lebanon, similar to *A. nordmanniana.*

A. concolor* **79,** 319, 327 Colorado white fir, White fir. S.W. United States. Zone 4. To 160ft (48m), narrow. Leaves 2in (5cm) long (longer than most other species), blue-grey, dull green with age. Cones oblong, olive-green becoming purple. 30ft (9m) in 20 years.

    A.c. 'Candicans' 72, 327 Handsome form. Leaves silver-grey to white.

    A.c. lowiana* **79,** 319 Low's silver fir, Pacific white fir. S.W. United States. Zone 6. To 250ft (76m). Leaves horizontal and curving upwards, dark blue-grey or green. Cones green, brown with age, big, smooth barrels. 45ft (13.5m) in 20 years.

    A.c. 'Violacea' 79 Leaves waxy blue-green.

A. delavayi 318 W. and C. China. Zone 7. Medium-size. Densely set leaves, bright shiny green above, gleaming white below. Cones dark bluish-violet. Buds very resinous.

    A.d. forrestii 80, 81 Forrest's fir. W. China. Zone 7. To 60ft (18m). Cones deep blue. 40ft (12m) in 20 years.

A. fargesii 81 W. and C. China. Zone 5. To 100ft (30m), with massive branches. Leaves long, spreading horizontally in 2 or more ranks, upper rank ½ length of lower. Cones purple to red-brown. 35ft (10.5m) in 20 years.

A. firma 319 'Japanese fir': big tree, leaves bright green, thick and broad; bark pinkish.

A. fraseri 78, 319 Fraser's fir. S.E. United States. Zone 4. 50 to 70ft (15 to 21.5m), open. Leaves short, dark shiny blue-green, 2 broad white bands beneath. Cones purple. Prone to disease.

A. grandis 26–7, **78–9,** 319 Grand fir, Giant fir. W. United States. Zone 6. To 250ft (76m), columnar, becoming rounded, sometimes multiple-topped. Leaves double-ranked horizontally, upper shorter than lower, bright green above, 2 bands of silver-white beneath. Cones green-purple in summer. Moderately lime-tolerant. Vigorous on many soils. 55ft (17m) in 20 years.

A. holophylla 81, 319 Manchurian fir. Manchuria, Korea. Zone 5. 100 to 150ft (30 to 45m), narrow conical or spreading. Leaves medium length, bright green, 2 grey-green bands beneath, sharp pointed. Cones green ripening to light brown.

A. homolepis 80, 81, 326 Nikko fir. Japan. Zone 4. 80 to 90 ft (24.5 to 27.5m). Leaves, lower at right angles to shoot, upper directed outwards and upwards, dark green shiny above, two conspicuous white bands on lower leaves. Cones purple, brown when mature. Tough, adaptable, tolerates some pollution. 25ft (7.5m) in 20 years.

A. kawakamii **318** Small silver fir with white bark from Formosa.

A. koreana **80, 81,** 318 Korean fir. Korea. Zone 5. To 40ft (12m), conical, or low, bushy. Leaves nearly covering upper side of shoot, curve upwards or near vertical; black-green above, 2 broad white bands below. Male 'flowers' on side-shoots, ovoid, dark red-brown; female 'flowers' dark-red to purple or pink to bright yellow. Cones freely from early age, dark purple. 10ft (3m) in 20 years.

A. lasiocarpa **26–7, 78, 79** Alpine fir. W. United States. Zone 2. Sometimes to 130ft (40m), beautifully narrow spire (Washington). Leaves irregularly double-ranked, medium length, shorter on higher branches, waxy, blue-green. Cones dark purple. Seeds with a shining purple wing. Does not grow well in lime as *Adelges* make gouty swellings on shoots.

A.l. arizonica **79** Arizona cork fir, Corkbark fir. Arizona. Zone 2. 100 or 130ft (30 or 40m), neat, conical, blue tree. Leaves 1in (2.5cm) long, striped blue-grey each side; flat, upward-curving, those in midline covering the stem. Cones dark purple. Seeds with a purple wing. Tolerant of many soils. 15ft (4.5m) in 20 years.

A. magnifica **79,** 319 California red fir, Red fir. W. United States. Zone 5. To 200ft (60m), narrow. Leaves blue to blue-green, later, 4-angled, lower horizontal, upper leaves curve upward. Cones purple-brown. Dislikes chalk. 30ft (9m) in 20 years.

A.m. shastensis **79** Shasta red fir. Zone 5. To 125ft (38m). Leaves 4-faceted, curved.

A. mariesii **81** Maries' fir. Japan. Zone 5. To 80ft (24.5m). Leaves 1in (2.5cm) long, shiny, dark green, 2 white bands beneath. Cones violet-blue at first, becoming dark brown, oval.

A. nebrodensis **318** Small silver fir from Sicily.

A. nordmanniana **80, 81,** 318, 326 Caucasian fir. W. Caucasus. Zone 4. To 200ft (60m), conical, becoming columnar, pointed or flat-topped. Bright green leaves forward-pointing, 2 sets on lower sides of shoots, upper set shorter. Cones pale green becoming brown, resinous. Generally disease-free. 35ft (10.5m) in 20 years.

A. numidica **80,** 318 Algerian fir. Eastern Algeria. Zone 6. 70 or 100ft (21.5 or 30m), conical. Leaves short, flattened, stiff, broad and thick, dark shining green, broadly banded grey all round shoot, curving upwards. Cones brown. Best *Abies* near towns.

A. pindrow **81,** 318 West Himalayan fir. Afghanistan to Nepal. Zone 6. To 200ft (60m), narrow, pyramidal with short branches becoming open with age. Leaves mainly below shoot. 2 to 3in (5 to 7.5cm) long, dark shiny green. Cones deep purple, becoming brown. Requires high rainfall and cool summers.

A. pinsapo **80,** 318 Spanish fir. Mts of S. Spain. Zone 6. To 100ft (30m), narrow cone, becoming more irregular. Leaves all round shoot, very short, blunt, broad, straight or slightly curved, noticeable bands on both sides. Male 'flowers' abundant, round, beneath shoot, bright red, opening late spring. Cones tapered, purple-brown. Tolerates lime, chalk, and any dry soils. 25ft (7.5m) in 20 years.

A. procera **78, 79,** 319 Noble fir. W. United States. Zone 5. To 250ft (76m), dome-headed. Leaves slightly 4-angled in section, flatter than *A. magnifica*; pointed, crowded on upper side of twig, blue-green. Cones olive-green to purple. Dislikes chalk. 30 to 45ft (9 to 13.5m) in 20 years.

A. religiosa **319** 'Sacred fir' from Mexico. Hardy in Britain.

A. sibirica **319** Siberian silver fir.

A. spectabilis **81,** 318 East Himalayan fir. Himalaya, Sikkim, Bhutan. Zone 7. To 150ft (45m), broad, columnar, eventually flat-topped. Leaves on a large scale, dense, in 2 ranks, lying slightly forward. Cones pale grey-blue, becoming dull, dark purple by winter. Susceptible to late frosts. 35ft (10.5m) in 20 years.

A. squamata **318** 'Flaky fir', small silver fir with peeling brown bark from W. China.

A. sutchuenensis **318** 'Szechwan fir': small silver fir, rare in cultivation.

A. veitchii **81** Veitch's silver fir. C. Japan. Zone 3. 60 or 70ft (18 or 21.5m). Leaves as *A. nordmanniana* but softer to touch. Male 'flowers' orange-red, minute, becoming round, red-brown; female 'flowers' red cylinder. Cone purple-blue to brown. Trunk deeply fluted. Dislikes chalk; thrives in semi-urban conditions. 40ft (12m) in 20 years.

A. vejari **319** Silver fir from Mexico similar to *A. religiosa*.

ACACIA **208, 209, 211,** 326

Mostly evergreen trees and shrubs. Leaves usually doubly pinnate, often replaced by flattened structures developed from leaf-stalks. Flowers bisexual, yellow, winter or spring. Full sun, acid or neutral, dry soils. Tender.

A. baileyana **211,** 327 Cootamundra wattle, Bailey's mimosa. Australia. Zone 10. To 20ft (6m) or more, often weeping. Leaves divided into numerous

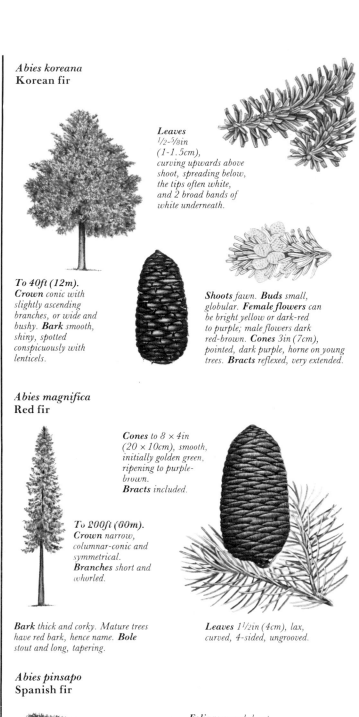

Abies koreana
Korean fir

Leaves 1/2-5/8in (1-1.5cm), curving upwards above shoot, spreading below, the tips often white, and 2 broad bands of white underneath.

To 40ft (12m). **Crown** conic with slightly ascending branches, or wide and bushy. **Bark** smooth, shiny, spotted conspicuously with lenticels.

Shoots fawn. **Buds** small, globular. **Female flowers** can be bright yellow or dark-red to purple; male flowers dark red-brown. **Cones** 3in (7cm), pointed, dark purple, borne on young trees. **Bracts** reflexed, very extended.

Abies magnifica
Red fir

Cones to 8 × 4in (20 × 10cm), smooth, initially golden green, ripening to purple-brown. **Bracts** included.

To 200ft (60m). **Crown** narrow, columnar-conic and symmetrical. **Branches** short and whorled.

Bark thick and corky. Mature trees have red bark, hence name. **Bole** stout and long, tapering.

Leaves 1 1/2in (4cm), lax, curved, 4-sided, ungrooved.

Abies pinsapo
Spanish fir

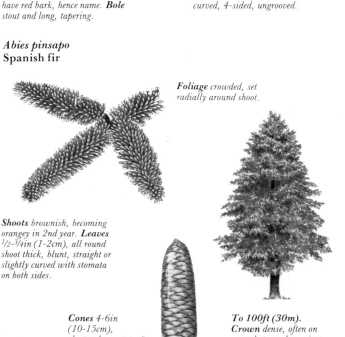

Foliage crowded, set radially around shoot.

Shoots brownish, becoming orangey in 2nd year. **Leaves** 1/2-3/4in (1-2cm), all round shoot thick, blunt, straight or slightly curved with stomata on both sides.

Cones 4-6in (10-15cm), clustered near top of tree, ripening to purple-brown.

To 100ft (30m). **Crown** dense, often on several stems, becoming rugged. **Bark** dark, in small plates.

Acacia dealbata
Silver wattle

Leaflets *1/4 × 1/20in (5 × 1mm), finely haired.*

Leaves *5in (12cm), bipinnate.* **Pinnae** *in 10-20 pairs, each with 30-50 pairs of linear leaflets.*

Flowers *1/6-1/4 (3-5mm) across, yellow in panicles of up to 30 globular heads, fragrant, first appearing in January.*

Acer campestre
Hedge or Field maple

Buds *1/4in (5mm), apex hairy.* **Winter shoots** *often glossy.*

Leaves *4in (10cm) across, 5-lobed with basal pair small or absent, sinuses acute. Paler and downy underneath, turns golden yellow in the autumn.* **Vein axils** *hairy.* **Margins** *ciliate.*

Leaf stalk *slender 2-4in (5-10cm), with milky sap.*

Seed keys *in about 4 pairs, hairy.* **Wings** *each 1 1/4in (3cm) at 180°, brown when ripe.*

Bark *grey, cracked and fissured.*

Acer ginnala
Amur maple

Flowers *in erect showy panicles of about 50, opening late in May. Yellowish white, very fragrant.*

Leaves *3 1/2in (8cm), bright dark green above, scarlet in autumn.*

To 20ft (6m). Crown *round domed.* **Branches** *slender.* **Bole** *small, winding.* **Bark** *smooth, dark.*

Seed keys *hang in small clusters. Red and conspicuous.* **Wings** *large, 1in (2.5cm), translucent, set almost parallel.*

Teeth *irregular.*

Petioles *1 1/2in (4cm).*

long, narrow leaflets, obliquely pointed, evergreen, waxy, silvery. Flowers, clusters of small, roundish heads. Fruits in pods 2 to 3in (5 to 7.5cm) long.
A. dealbata* 209, **210, 211,** 316, 319, 327 Silver wattle, Mimosa. Australia. Zone 8–9. To 50ft (15m), spreading. Leaves fern-like, downy, silver-green. Flowers, clusters of small, round heads, fragrant. Seed pods flat, 2 to 3in (5 to 7.5cm) long, blue-white. Sun-loving; can be killed by severe or prolonged frost. 50ft (15m) in 20 years.
A. decurrens See *Acacia dealbata*
A. longifolia 211, 327 Sidney golden wattle. Australia. Zone 8/9. To 20ft (6m), spreading. Leaves long, lance-shaped, simple, evergreen, leathery, dark green. Flowers small, round heads, bright yellow, in spikes 2 to 3in (5 to 7.5cm) long. Seed pods 3 to 4in (7.5 to 10cm) long. Fairly lime-tolerant.

ACER 226–33, 327
Maples. Deciduous, rarely evergreen trees. Opposite, normally lobed leaves often with brilliant autumn colours. Clustered uni- or bi-sexual flowers. Fruits are paired nuts or keys. Usually pest-free. Tolerant of most soil-types.
A. amplum 318 Small maple from central China with shiny green stems.
A. argutum 319 Small Japanese maple, five-lobed leaves with conspicuous veins.
A. buergeranum 231, 318, 326 Buerger's maple, Trident maple. E. China, Japan. Zone 6. 20ft (6m) high, rounded. Leaves 3-lobed, simple, bright green above, paler, waxy beneath, toothed, stalked. Flowers in a flattish cluster.
A. campbellii 318 Medium-sized Himalayan maple; leaves lobed.
A. campestre* 233, 327 Hedge or field maple. Europe (incl. British Isles), W. Asia. Zone 5–6. To 25ft (7.5m), rounded, dense. 5-lobed leaves, 4in (10cm) across, downy beneath, yellowish in autumn. Small green flowers in small clusters, early May. Keys 1in (2.5cm) long, downy. Grows on chalk. A good hedge or screen plant.
A.c. postelense 233 Hedge maple. Europe (incl. British Isles), W. Asia. Zone 5–6. To 25ft (7.5m), rounded. Leaves golden yellow in spring, turning clear yellow, sometimes flushed red, in autumn.
A. capillipes 319, 327 Small Japanese snakebark maple.
A. cappadocicum 233, 318 Caucasian maple. Caucasus and W. Asia to Himalaya. Zone 5 or 6. To 65ft (20m), spreading. Leaves 5- to 7-lobed, 3 to 6in (7.5 to 15cm) across, glosssy green, yellow in autumn. Small yellow flowers. Keys in clusters. Shade tolerant. 30ft (9m) in 20 years.
A.c. 'Rubrum' 233 New shoots blood red.
A. carpinifolium 230, 231, 319 Hornbeam maple. Japan. Zone 5. To 35ft (10.5m), vase-shaped with a number of stems from the base. Leaves opposite, otherwise hornbeam-like, unlobed, 3 to 4in (7.5 to 10cm) long, golden brown in autumn. Green flowers in spiky clusters. Keys have curved wings. 15ft (4.5m) in 20 years.
A. caudatum 318 *(A. papilio)* Maple with five-lobed, toothed leaves; E. Himalayas.
A. circinatum 228–9, 319, 326 Vine maple. W. United States. Zone 5. Small tree, to 40ft (12m), wide-spreading with several branches from the base. Leaves almost circular, 7 to 9 lobes, orange to red in autumn. Flowers white to purple in drooping clusters, late April. Red keys. Shade-tolerant. 15ft (4.5m) in 20 years.
A. cissifolium 319 Small Japanese maple with three-piece bronzy leaves.
A. crataegifolium 319 Hawthorn maple. Japan. Zone 5. Small, spreading, to 35ft (10.5m). Leaves variable, shallow lobes. Yellowish-white flowers on small erect spikes, April. Striped bark. 15ft (4.5m) in 20 years.
A. davidii 231, 318, 327 David's maple. China. Zone 6. To 50ft (15m), rounded head. Oval, pointed leaves up to 8in (20.5cm) long, dark, shining green, yellow and purple in autumn. Keys green flushed with red, hanging along branches in autumn. Bark green striped with white. 30ft (9m) in 20 years.
A. diabolicum 231, 319 Horned maple. Japan. Zone 5. To 40ft (12m). Big, 5-lobed leaves. Yellow flowers, April, in hanging clusters. Bristly red fruits.
A.d. purpurascens 231 Horned or Red devil maple. Japan. Zone 5. To 30ft (9m), round-topped. Young leaves red, purplish in autumn. Drooping clusters of salmon-pink flowers in spring. Young keys purple, bristly. 15ft (4.5m) in 20 years.
A. distylum 319 Larger Japanese maple, simple leaves unfolding pink.
A. divergens 318 Similar to *A. campestre* leaves three- or five-lobed.
A. forrestii Lovely little Chinese snake-bark maple with long graceful branches, red young shoots and leaf-stalks. The centre one of three lobes is much the biggest. Likes acid soil. 12ft (3.5m) in 20 years.
A. ginnala* 231 Amur maple. China. Zone 2. To 20ft (6m), upright, rounded, dense branching, vigorous, 3-lobed leaves, toothed margins, bright dark green above, scarlet in autumn. Keys red and conspicuous. Flowers yellowish white, very fragrant, May. 15ft (4.5m) in 20 years.

A. giraldii **231** Yunnan. Zone 6. Medium to large with rather gawky habit. Broad-lobed leaves not unlike sycamore, bluish-white and veined beneath. Drooping clusters of big fruits. Bright autumn colours. 25ft (7.5m) in 20 years.

A. griseum **230–1,** 327 Paperbark maple. C. China. Zone 5. To 30ft (9m). Leaves compound, 3 leaflets on a downy stalk, scarlet in autumn. Downy winged fruit. Most striking 3-leafed maple. 15ft (4.5m) in 20 years. A.G.M. 1936.

A. grosseri **231,** 327 Grosser's maple. C. China. Zone 6. Small, to 20ft (6m). Leaves sometimes lobed, toothed, Good autumn colour. Keys in long hanging clusters.

A. heldreichii **318** Medium-sized maple with deeply 3-lobed leaves.

A. henryi Elegant spreading Chinese maple with three-part leaves and grey-striped bark. Yellow flowers just before the leaves, and stalkless red fruits. 15ft (4.5m) in 20 years.

A. hersii **231,** 318, 327 Hers's maple. C. China. Zone 5. To 30ft (9m). Leaves usually 3-lobed, dark dull green above, paler beneath. Fruits in hanging clusters. Young bark striped with white. Very similar to *A. grosseri,* but commoner and slightly hardier. 30ft (9m) in 20 years. A.G.M. 1969.

A. hyrcanum **318** Small version of *A. opalus* from eastern Mediterranean.

A. japonicum* **230–1,** 319, 326, 327 Full-moon maple. Japan. Zone 5. Small bushy tree, 30ft (9m), rounded. Leaves 2 to 5in (5 to 13cm) long, roundish, 7 to 11 lobes, bright red in autumn. Purplish-red flowers, April. Keys in clusters. Best in woodland shelter. 10ft (3m) in 20 years.

   A.j. **'Aconitifolium'** **230,** 326 Japan. Small tree or large bush. Leaves deeply cut and divided, soft green, turning rich crimson in autumn. Flowers red in drooping clusters. Grows well in moist, well-drained positions sheltered from cold winds. A.G.M. 1957.

   A.j. **'Aureum'** **230,** 326 Japan. Soft yellow leaves, liable to scorch in full sun. Slow-growing. A.G.M. 1969.

   A.j. **'Vitifolium'** **230, 231,** 326 Wide, fan-shaped leaves, 10–12 lobes. Beautiful autumn colour.

A. lobelii **318** An erect form of the Caucasian maple.

A. macrophyllum* **228, 229,** 319, 326 Oregon or Big-leaf maple. W. United States. Zone 6. To 100ft (30m), round-headed. Leaves, 6 to 12in (15 to 30cm) across, dark shining green, orange and scarlet in autumn. Flowers small, yellow, in hanging clusters, fragrant, May. Keys in hanging clusters. 35ft (10.5m) in 20 years.

A. mandshuricum **319** Small Japanese maple like shiny-leaved *A. nikoense.*

A. micranthum Delicate bushy Japanese maple. Small five-lobed leaves can colour bright red.

A. miyabei **319** Small Japanese version of the Norway maple.

A. mono **319** Larger Japanese maple, lobed leaves turning yellow in autumn.

A. monspessulanum **233,** 318, 327 Montpelier maple. S. Europe, W. Asia. Zone 5. To 30ft (9m), rounded. Leaves 3-lobed, simple, virtually smooth, dark green above, paler beneath. Flowers in drooping, loose clusters, greenish. Fruit red, profuse, winged.

A. negundo* 42, 64, **228, 229, 230,** 319, 327 Box elder. North America. Zone 2. To 65ft (20m), spreading and rather open. Leaves compound, 3 to 5 leaflets, bright green above, paler beneath. Sexes on separate trees. Male flowers in dense clusters, female flowers in slender drooping clusters. Keys in drooping clusters. 20ft (6m) in 20 years.

   A.n. **'Elegans'** (or **'Elegantissimum'**) **228,** 326 Leaves with bright yellow margins. Young shoots with white bloom.

   A.n. **'Variegatum'** **228** Leaves white and green.

A. nigrum **228** Black maple. Eastern N. America. Zone 3. To 120ft (36m). Leaves 3-, occasionally 5-lobed, simple, furry beneath, dull green above, paler beneath. Flowers in weeping clusters, pale green. Fruit smooth.

A. nikoense **231,** 318, 326 Nikko maple. Japan, C. China. Zone 5. To 50ft (15m), round-topped or vase-shaped. Leaves compound, on a stout hairy stalk. Brilliant red or purple in autumn. Yellow flowers in threes on a hairy drooping stalk. Keys with hairy nutlets. 20ft (6m) in 20 years.

A. opalus **233,** 316, 318, 326, 327 Italian maple. S. Europe. Zone 5. To 50ft (15m), rounded head. Leaves 2½ to 4½in (6.5 to 11.5cm), wide, 5 shallow lobes, toothed, dark green and hairless above, paler and downy beneath. Clusters of small yellow flowers, March. 20ft (6m) in 20 years.

A. palmatum **230,** 319, 326, 327 Japanese maple. Japan, C. China, Korea. Zone 5. To 25ft (7.5m), low, rounded head. Bright green leaves, 5 to 7 toothed lobes, bronze or purplish in autumn. Small purple flowers on erect stalks. Fairly chalk-tolerant; prefers shelter from cold winds. Moist well-drained loam preferred. 15ft (4.5m) in 20 years. A.G.M. 1969.

   A.p. **'Atropurpureum'** **230,** 326 Bloodleaf Japanese maple. Leaves with 5 to 7 lobes, crimson-purple in summer. 20ft (6m) in 20 years. A.G.M. 1928.

Acer japonicum
Full-moon maple

Leaves *5in (13cm), bases cordate.*
Lobes *7-11, coarsely toothed, cut shallowly.*
Veins *hairy below.*

Autumn leaves *especially fine while turning.*

Fruit wings *each 1-1¼in (2.5-3cm).*

Acer macrophyllum
Oregon or Big-leaf maple

Leaf sinus *deep, acute, rounded.*

Shoots *stout, green.*

Buds *stout, conic with red-brown scales.*

Teeth *blunt.*
Margins *ciliate.*

Leaf *paler below.*

Leaf blade *very large, 6-12in (15-30cm) across, 5-lobed, thin-textured.*

Flower panicles *narrow, small, yellow, in hanging clusters.*

Leaf stalk *long, 6-14in (15-35cm), red or green, clasps stem closely, almost hiding bud.*

Seed keys *big, each wing 2in (5cm) at 90° or less.*

Acer negundo
Box elder

Leaflets *3-5 irregularly toothed.*

Leaves *bright light green with no autumn colour.*

Shoots *green, later bloomed violet.*

Leaf stalk *3½in (8cm), pink or yellow.*

Seed keys *in drooping clusters; ripen early, remain after leaf fall.*
Wings *¾in (2cm), set acutely, incurved.*

Male flowers *set in dense pendulous clusters of 12-16.*

Acer platanoides
Norway maple

Flowers open early April, before leaves, in erect yellow-green corymbs of 20-30. *Petals* ¹⁄₃in (8mm) wide. **Buds** ¹⁄₂in (1cm) tall, red-purple. **Shoots** stout, hairless, dark brown.

To 100ft (30m). **Crown** broad-domed, densely leaved. **Bole** Short. **Bark** grey-brown, finely ridged.

Seed key nutlets flat. **Wings** each 1¹⁄₄-2in (3-5cm), almost horizontal.

Leaf 4-7in (10-17.5cm) wide, cordate. 2-6 coarse teeth per lobe, edges of central lobes parallel. Bright green.

Blade underside paler.

A.p. 'Schwedleri' opens pink-red. Green by summer, then purple in autumn.

Leaf stalk long, 6in (15cm), with milky sap distinguishing it from similar maples.

Acer rubrum
Red maple, Swamp maple

To 120ft (36m). **Crown** tall, domed, fast-growing.

Veins red. **Blade colours** intensify during September.

Bark smooth, silver-grey, finally darker, scaling.

Shoots red-brown or maroon, slender. **Buds** very small, ¹⁄₆in (4mm) ciliate on scales red-brown, pointed. **Flowers**, small, red, in dense clusters, opening in March, before leaves.

Leaves 4¹⁄₂in (11cm), usually dark green, glossy above, silver below with waxy bloom.

A.p. 'Dissectum' 230, 326 To 10ft (3m), dome-shaped, fernlike. Green leaves with 7, 9 or 11 lobes. Slow-growing. A.G.M. 1956.

A.p. 'Dissectum Atropurpureum' 230 As above. Leaves deeply cut, purple. A.G.M. 1969.

A.p. 'Linearilobum' 230, 326 Leaves divided into narrow lobes, slightly toothed, reddish when young, green in summer.

A.p. 'Osakazuki' 230, 326 Possibly the most brilliantly-colouring Japanese maple. A.G.M. 1969.

A.p. 'Senkaki' 230, 327 Coral bark maple. Shrub or small tree. Young branches coral-red, effective in winter. Leaves yellow in autumn. A.G.M. 1969.

A. pensylvanicum 228, 229, 319, 326 Striped or Snake-bark maple, Moosewood. Eastern N. America. Zone 3. To 40ft (12m), open and irregular. Young stems green, becoming striped with pale green and white. Leaves 3-lobed, up to 7in (17.5cm) long, bright yellow in autumn. Flowers yellow, in hanging clusters, May. Unhappy on chalk. 20ft (6m) in 20 years.

A.p. 'Erythrocladum' 229 Young winter shoots pink-red, distinctive.

A. platanoides* 232, 233, 316, 318, 326, 327 Norway maple. Europe, Caucasus. Zone 3. To 100ft (30m), rounded head. Bright green leaves, 5-lobed, 4 to 7in (10 to 17.5cm) wide, yellow in autumn. Small yellow flowers in clusters, late April. 35ft (10.5m) in 20 years. A.G.M. 1969.

A.p. 'Columnare' 326 Erect columnar form becoming conical with age. Leaves smaller with shallower lobes than the type.

A.p. 'Dissectum' 326 Lobed leaves with crinkled edges and straight points.

A.p. 'Erectum' 326 Narrow pyramidal form with short ascending branches. Leaves bigger and darker than the type. Slow-growing.

A.p. 'Faasen's Black' 233 Leaves as *A. platanoides* 'Goldsworth Purple'.

A.p. 'Globosum' 326 Dwarf rounded form, dense. 10ft (3m) in 20 years.

A.p. 'Goldsworth Purple' 233, 326 Red-leaved form, becoming purple/black.

A.p. 'Laciniatum' 326 Eagle's claw maple. Big, upright tree. Leaves wedge-shaped at base; lobes with claw-like points.

A.p. 'Lorbergii' 326 Medium-size tree. Palmate leaves, pale green.

A.p. 'Reitenbachii' 233 Medium size. Leaves red at first, green later, red again in autumn.

A.p. 'Schwedleri' 233, 326 Large leaves and young shoots red-purple, bronzy green later.

A. pseudoplatanus 232-3, 318, 326, 327 Sycamore or Sycamore maple. Europe and W. Asia. Zone 5. To 100ft (30m), wide-spreading. Leaves usually 5-lobed, dark green above, paler below. Yellowish-green flowers in large drooping clusters. Keys in clusters. Succeeds in exposed positions, any soil. 35ft (10.5m) in 20 years.

A.p. 'Brilliantissimum' 232-3, 326 Small dense tree, young leaves pink, later yellow-green, finally green. 12ft (3.5m) in 20 years.

A.p. 'Purpureum' ('Spaethii') 232, 326 Purple sycamore. Leaves dark purply-red beneath.

A.p. 'Worleei' 232, 326 Golden sycamore. Medium-sized tree. Leaves yellow-green when young, leaf-stalks reddish. 20ft (6m) in 20 years.

A. rubrum* 42, 226, 228, 229, 319, 327 Red maple, Swamp maple. Eastern N. America. Zone 3. To 120ft (36m), round head, dense foliage. Leaves medium length, with 3 to 5 toothed lobes, dark shiny green above, waxy bloom underneath. Small red flowers on slender stalks, early spring. Bright red keys in hanging clusters. 35ft (10.5m) in 20 years.

A.r. 'Columnare' 228, 326 Columnar red maple. Big, upright, wide.

A. rufinerve 231, 319 Japan. Zone 5. To 35ft (10.5m). Young stems bluish-grey; older stems and trunk green and white striped. Leaves 3-lobed, similar to *A. pensylvanicum*; bright red and yellow in autumn.

A.r. albolimbatum 231, 319 Leaves mottled or edged with white.

A. saccharinum 43, 228, 319, 325, 326 Silver maple. Eastern N. America. Zone 3. To 120ft (36m), spreading head. Leaves medium length, 5 deep toothed lobes, bright green above, silvery white underneath. Clear yellow in autumn. Small greenish yellow flowers. Keys in hanging clusters. 50ft (15m) in 20 years.

A.s. 'Laciniatum' 228 Branchlets weeping, leaves deeply lobed.

A.s. 'Lutescens' 228 Pale yellow leafed form.

A. saccharum 43, 226, 228, 229, 319, 326 Sugar maple. C. and E. North America. Zone 3. To 120ft (36m), fluted trunk, rounded head. Leaves medium length, 3 to 5 toothed lobes, bright green, yellow orange or scarlet in autumn. Small greenish-yellow flowers in hanging clusters. Grey furrowed bark. 35ft (10.5m) in 20 years.

A.s. 'Temple's Upright' 228 Columnar, possibly rounded or oval.

A. sempervirens 318 'Cretan maple', similar to *A. monspessulanum*; keeps shiny leaves very late.

A. syriacum **318** Variable bushy tree from Syria and Cyprus.
A. tataricum **318, 327** 'Tatarian maple'. Large shrub or small spreading tree. Leaves dull, pale green, doubly toothed.
A. triflorum **318** Rare small maple like *A. nikoense,* brilliant in autumn.
A. truncatum **318** Small lobed-leaved maple, leaves truncated at base.
A. velutinum, A.v. vanvolxemii **318** Caucasian maples with enormous leaves.
A. villosum **318** Himalayan maple with very big leaves.

AESCULUS 224–5, 327

Deciduous trees or shrubs, compound leaves usually with 5 to 7 leaflets. Flowers in large conical heads, late spring to summer. 1 or 2 large seeds in a smooth or prickly husk. Hardy. All soils, if not too dry. Prefer open, sunny position. Leaf spot in Europe and America.
A. californica **224** Californian buckeye. California. Zone 7. To 35ft (10.5m), spreading tree or shrub. Leaves medium length. Flowers white to rose-coloured, 1in long (2.5cm) long, fragrant, April to Aug. Egg-shaped fruit, Aug. and Sept.
A. × *carnea* **224, 326** Red horse chestnut. Zone 3. Hybrid between *A. hippocastanum* and *A. pavia,* to 70ft (21.5m), pyramidal when young, becoming round-headed with age. Leaves smaller and darker than common horse chestnut. No autumn colour. Flowers rose-pink in upright clusters 10in (26cm) high, mid-May. 25ft (7.5m) in 20 years.
    A. × *c.* **'Briotii' 225, 316** Almost identical to the type, but the flowers are a deeper colour and in larger clusters.
    A. × *c.* **'Plantierensis' 225, 327** Damask horse chestnut. Zone 3. Backcross between *A. carnea* and *A. hippocastanum,* ¾ common horse chestnut and ¼ red buckeye. Flower cluster is like former, but flowers soft pink.
*A. flava** **224, 319** Sweet buckeye. S.E. United States. Zone 3. To 90ft (27.5m), round-headed. Leaves opposite, medium length, finely toothed, downy beneath, usually good autumn tints. Flower long, yellow, May to June. Fruit smooth. 20ft (6m) in 20 years.
A. glabra **224, 319, 326, 327** Ohio buckeye. S.E. and C. United States. Zone 3. To 30ft (9m), round-headed. Leaves oval to wedge-shaped, smooth with age. Flowers green-yellow. Fruit ovallish, prickly. 20ft (6m) in 20 years.
*A. hippocastanum** **224, 316, 318, 323, 326, 327** Common horse chestnut. Greece, Albania. Zone 3. To 120ft (36m), with a rounded spreading head. Leaves medium to long, scattered hairs below, hairless above. Flowers white, May. Fruit spiny. 40ft (12m) in 20 years.
    A.h. **'Baumannii' 224, 225, 327** Baumann's horse chestnut. Zone 3. To 85ft (27m), rounded at maturity. Flowers double, white, mid-May, lasting longer than the type. No fruit.
A. indica **224, 318, 327** Indian horse chestnut. N.W. Himalaya. Zone 7. To 100ft (30m), often with a short, thick trunk. Leaves large, toothed, hairless, dark shiny green above. Flowers 1in (2.5cm) long, white flushed with pink, July. Fruit tough. 30ft (9m) in 20 years. A.G.M. 1969.
A. neglecta **'Erythroblastos'** Slow-growing small American buckeye comparable with *Acer pseudoplatanus* 'Brilliantissimum' for the pale creamy pink of its spring foliage. Yellow-green later. Subject to spring frost-damage in parts of Britain.
A. parviflora **224, 326** Shrubby pavia, Dwarf buckeye. S.E. United States. Zone 4. To 15ft (4.5m), a spreading, suckering shrub with several slender stems. Leaves medium to long, shallow-toothed, beneath. Flowers white with red anthers, July, Aug. Fruit hairless, nearly egg-shaped. Tolerant of shade. 10ft (3m) in 20 years. A.G.M. 1969.
A. pavia **224, 319, 327** Red buckeye. S. United States. Zone 5. To 20ft (6m), shrub or small tree. Leaves medium length. Flowers crimson, June. Fruit nearly egg-shaped, August.
A. turbinata **224, 326** Japanese horse chestnut. Japan. Zone 5. To 100ft (30m), with a thick trunk. Leaflets up to 16in (41cm) long, toothed, on a long stalk. Attractive autumn tints. Flowers yellowish-white, June. Fruit pear-shaped, rough. 35ft (10.5m) in 20 years.

AGATHIS australis 319

Kauri pine. New Zealand. Zone 9. Leaves large, evergreen, leathery, stalked, in opposite pairs, 1in (2.5cm) apart, tapering to a blunt point, dull grey-green. Male and female 'flowers' on same tree, but separate. Cones round to oval. Seeds winged. Tender in Britain. 12ft (3.5m) in 20 years.

AILANTHUS altissima* 242–3, 317–8, 326, 327

Tree of heaven. N. China. Zone 4. To 90ft (27.5m) usually less. Leaves compound, deciduous, leaflets ovallish, with unpleasant smell, toothed near base. Flowers in small clusters, greenish-yellow, sexes on separate tree, male flowers with unpleasant smell. Fruits dry, winged, reddish-brown, profuse,

Aesculus flava
Sweet buckeye, Yellow buckeye

Leaflets 6in (15cm), on ⁵/₈in (1.5cm) stalk.

Leaves have 5-7 leaflets with impressed veins.

To 90ft (27.5m), with fine autumn yellows and orange-reds. **Bole** straight. **Bark** grey or red-brown, smooth becoming scaly.

Flowers 1¹/₂in (4cm), dense, usually yellow, sometimes pink, on 4-6in (10-15cm) panicles. **Petals** (4) forward-pointing. **Fruit** 2¹/₂in (6cm), 2-seeded.

Aesculus hippocastanum
Common Horse Chestnut

Flowers white, numerous, up to 150 on 6-12in (15-30cm) panicles. **Petals** (5) have basal blotches.

To 120ft (36m). **Crown** tall, spreading, dense. **Mature branches** pendent, then upswept at ends.

Leaflets (5-7) 4-10in (10-25cm), sessile, unevenly serrate.

Fruit 2in (5cm).

Buds 1in (2.5cm). **Shoots** stout. **Leaf scars** horseshoe shaped.

Ailanthus altissima
Tree of heaven

Shoots stout with grey scars.

Bark smooth, grey-brown, with shallow cracks.

Leaves 24in (60cm), pinnate. *Leaflets* (13-31) ovate with 1-3 basal teeth, red-stalked, open red.

Fruit a samara or key. **Panicles** to 12in (30cm) deep.

Buds ovoid; no terminal bud. **Seed wings** thin, 1¹/₂in (4cm).

Alnus glutinosa
Common alder, European alder

To 80ft (24.5m).
Crown broad, conic,
often on 2 or 3 stems,
purplish.

Flowers open
on male and
female
catkins,
before leaves,
in late March.
Male catkins
2in (5cm) when
fully open.

Male
flowers
yellow.

Female
flowers
¹/₃in (8mm),
erect, red.

Catkins appear in
winter, purple-
brown.

Bark fissured,
grey, in small
plates.

Petioles 1¹/₂in (3.5cm), speckled.
Buds ¹/₃in (8mm), flat, on ¹/₁₆
(3mm) stalks, narrowed at base,
with 2-3 scales.

Fruit ⁵/₈in
(1.5cm), ovoid, set
in clusters of 1-4.

Seeds small
winged nutlets.

Shoots
purple by
autumn.

Leaves
glabrous,
paler below.
Vein axils
tufted.
Leaf margins
slightly waved.
Teeth irregular,
shallow.
Veins impressed.

Fruit woody by
the time it ripens
and releases seeds
in October,
very persistent as
empty 'cone'.

Leaves 4in (10cm), persist
until the very end of autumn.

Amelanchier lamarckii
Downy serviceberry

Flowers massed,
star-like, with 5
pure white obovate
petals, ³/₄in (2cm),
in conical upright
racemes.

40ft (12m). Crown low
rounded dome, often on
several stems, glowing
orange-red in autumn.

Leaves 3in (7cm), margins
finely toothed, dull green,
rounded or cuneate at base, new
leaves copper.

Fruit ¹/₃in
(8mm), purple-
black changing
to red, summer
to autumn.

on female trees only. Tolerant of dryness, shade, acid soil; sun-loving. 45ft (13.5m) in 20 years.
    A.a. 'Erythrocarpa' 243 Dark green leaves, bright red fruit.

ALBIZIA *julibrissin* **210, 211,** 316, 326, 327
Silk tree, Pink siris. Persia to China. Zone 7. To 40ft (12m), broad, spreading, flat-topped. Leaves doubly pinnate, 9 to 18in (23 to 46cm) long. Flowers light pink, brush-like, in rounded heads, June–August. Pods 5in (13cm) long, narrow between seeds, flat, Sept.–Nov. 15ft (4.5m) in 20 years.
    A.j. 'Rosea' 211, 328 Smaller form, pinker flowers, hardy to Zone 5.

ALNUS 168–9, 326, 327
Very hardy deciduous trees or shrubs. Toothed leaves. Long male catkins, short female catkins on the same tree form woody cones, ripe in autumn. Seeds are small flat nuts. Flowers produced before the leaves. Mostly moisture-loving, some lime-tolerant. Susceptible to die-back, leaf spot, tent-caterpillar.
A. cordata 168–9, 318, 327 Italian alder. Corsica and S. Italy. Zone 5. To 80ft (24.5m). Leaves roundish with abrupt point, medium length, bright green, glossy, finely toothed. Male catkins 2 to 3in (5 to 7.5cm) long, groups of 3 to 6. Fruit erect, egg-shaped, about 1in (2.5cm) long, in threes. Suited to all types of soil. 50ft (15m) in 20 years.
A. glutinosa* 168, 169 Common alder, European alder. Europe (incl. British Isles), W. Asia, N. Africa. Zone 3. To 80ft (24.5m), with sticky young growth. Broad, pear-shaped leaves, medium length; dark green and sticky above, pale green below. Male catkins in groups, 2 to 4in (5 to 10cm) long. Egg-shaped fruits in clusters. Suited to boggy ground. 40ft (12m) in 20 years.
    A.g. 'Aurea' 169, 326 Leaves golden yellow, particularly in spring and early summer.
    A.g. 'Imperialis' 169, 326 Leaves deeply and finely lobed, the lobes slender and pointed, not toothed. 25ft (7.5m) in 20 years.
    A.g. 'Laciniata' 169 Sturdy, rather stiff form; leaves not so finely divided as 'Imperialis'.
A. incana 168, 169, 318 Grey alder, American speckled alder. Europe, Caucasus, E. North America. Zone 2. Large shrub to medium-sized tree, to 65ft (20m). Leaves dull green above, grey beneath, downy, oval. Male catkins 2 to 4in (5 to 10cm) long in groups. Oval fruits clustered. Good for cold or wet situations. 50ft (15m) in 20 years.
    A.i. 'Aurea' 169 Young shoots and foliage yellow; catkins red-tinted.
    A.i. 'Laciniata' 169 Leaves dissected, grey on lower surface. Very hardy.
A. japonica Aristocratic Japanese alder with brown-tinted, finely veined and pointed leaves. Eventually a tall and shapely tree, with catkins in early spring.
A. maximowiczii A vigorous, often many-stemmed Japanese alder with broad, tooth-fringed leaves. Very hardy.
A. rubra 168, 319 Red alder. Western N. America. Zone 4. Medium-sized tree, to 65ft (20m), narrow pyramidal head, pendulous branches. Oval leaves medium length, upper surface dark green, lower surface pale or greyish. Male catkins 4 to 6in (10 to 15cm) long in groups. Fruits barrel-shaped in clusters. 40ft (12m) in 20 years.
A. rugosa 169 Smooth alder. E. United States. Zone 2. Small tree or large shrub. Long catkins in spring before leaves. Similar to *A. incana* but leaves almost egg-shaped and green beneath.
A. subcordata 318 'Caucasian alder'–big tree with broad leaves 6in (15cm) long, downy beneath, less cordate than *A. cordata*. Very vigorous. 30ft (9m) in 12 years.
A. viridis 318 Green alder; erect shrub from the Alps.

AMELANCHIER 190–1, 326, 327
Small trees or shrubs. Leaves deciduous. Flowers in small clusters, white, 5-petalled, spring, before leaves fully developed. Fruit berry-like, small. Some species lime-tolerant. Subject to rusts and fire-blight.
A. arborea See **A. canadensis**
A. canadensis 191, 327 Service-berry, June-berry, Shadblows. N. America. Zone 4. To 65ft (20m) upright, often narrow. Leaves oval to heart-shaped, simple, saw-toothed, stalked. Flowers in upright or drooping clusters, snow-white. Fruit round, fleshy, berry-like, green turning red and maroon-purple, early summer. Prefers lime-free soils. Susceptible to lacewing fly, various scales and fire-blight. Sun or semi-shade.
A. × grandiflora See **A. lamarckii**.
A. laevis 191, 327 Allegheny service-berry. N. America. Zone 4. To 40ft (12m), spreading. Leaves ovallish, simple, smooth; young leaves purple-bronze, turning rich orange-red. Flowers small, in pyramids, fragrant. Fruit

berry-like, purple-black changing to red, summer to autumn. Prefers lime-free soils. Sun or semi-shade. Susceptible to pests as *A. canadensis*.

A. lamarckii* **191,** 316, 327 Downy serviceberry. Accounts for 80% of Amelanchiers cultivated. Europe. Zone 4. 20 or 30ft (6 or 9m). Spreading. Leaves oval to oblong, simple, silky at first, red-copper. Flowers in large, lax bunches. Fruit small, purplish-black, containing several seeds. Prefers lime-free soils. Susceptible to pests as *A. canadensis*.

A. ovalis **191,** 327 Snowy mespilus S. and C. Europe. Zone 4. Medium-large, upright shrub. Flowers in large, upright heads. Fruits black.

ARALIA 245

American and Asiatic deciduous shrubs or trees. Bisexual flowers in clusters. Small berry-like fruits. Mostly hardy. All aralias do well under city conditions.

A. elata **317,** 326 Japanese angelica tree. Japan. Zone 3. To 50ft (15m). Most often a shrub renewing by suckers. Leaves compound, 3 to 4ft (1 to 1.2m) long, 2ft (60cm) wide, many oval, pointed leaflets, dark bright green. Flowers small, white. Black fruits. Sun or semi-shade. Fast growing.

   A.e. **'Aureovariegata'** Leaflets blotched and margined with yellow, fading to cream.

   A.e. **'Variegata'** 245 Leaves green and white.

A. spinosa **326** Hercules' club, Devil's walking stick. S.E. United States. Zone 4. To 50ft (15m). Very spiny stems. Compound leaves. Finer foliage in richer soil, but wood tends to be pithy on rich soil, and liable to frost damage. Greenish-white flowers. Black fruits. Grows fast, in sun or semi-shade.

ARAUCARIA 111, 116, 117, 327

Evergreen trees, big, pyramidal or rounded. Leaves oval, spirally arranged, leathery, overlapped dark green. Male and female flowering heads on separate trees usually; male heads cylindrical, possibly clustered. Cones round to oval. Seeds winged.

A. angustifolia **117** Parana pine, Candelabra tree. S. Brazil. Zone 9. To 110ft (33m), few branches, flat crown with long hanging branchlets. Leaves scale-like with curved spiny tips.

A. araucana* **116, 117,** 319 Chile pine, Monkey puzzle. Chile, Argentina. Zone 7. To 80ft (24.5m). Leaves triangular, long, yellow-green, hard, pointed. Male 'flowers' drooping at end of shoots, 6in (15cm) long, cylindrical, pollen in summer, female round, on upper side of branches, after 3 years dark green with long, yellowish spines. Disease-free. Tolerant of all but driest or most boggy soils. 20ft (6m) in 20 years.

A. bidwillii **117** Bunya-bunya. Queensland. Zone 10. To 150ft (45m), young trees broadly conical. Leaves overlapped, stiff. Male 'flowers' to 7in (17.5cm) long. Cones upright, round, 12in (30cm) long. Fairly resistant to insect pests.

A. excelsa See *A. heterophylla*.

A. heterophylla **117** Norfolk Island pine. Zone 10. To 150 or 200ft (45 or 60m), main branches very regular, spreading. Leaves of 2 types, either soft, bright green, incurving, ½in (1cm) long on young branchlets, or shorter, overlapping, with hard, incurving tip on older shoots. Cones 3 to 4in (7.5 to 10cm) long 3½ to 4½in (9 to 11.5cm) wide.

ARBUTUS 184-5, 326, 327

Small to large evergreen trees. Leaves simple, dark, shiny green, leathery. Flowers white or pink, pitcher-shaped. Fruits orange-red, globular, fleshy, edible but tasteless. Subject to crown die-back, leaf canker in America.

A. andrachne **185,** 318 Strawberry tree. E. Mediterranean region. Zone 7. To 35ft (10.5m) with cinnamon-brown stems. Leaves simple, ovallish. Flowers dull white, in broad clusters, March and April. Fruit ½in (1cm).

A. × *andrachnoides* **185** Hybrid between *A. andrachne* and *A. unedo*. 20 or 30ft (6 or 9m), with cinnamon-red branches. Leaves dark green, toothed. Flowers white, pitcher-shaped, ¼in (6mm) long in clusters, late autumn or spring. Fruit smaller and smoother than *A. unedo*. Tolerant of lime.

A. menziesii **185,** 316 Madrona. Western N. America. Zone 7. To 100ft (30m). Leaves oval, medium length, usually with entire margins, dark green above, bluish-white beneath. Flowers, May, in terminal panicles 3 to 9in (7.5 to 23cm) long, whitish, small. Fruit pea-sized berries. Transplants badly. Soil should be lime-free but can be poor and dry. Sun or semi-shade. 35ft (10.5m) in 20 years.

A. unedo* **184-5,** 316, 327 Killarney strawberry tree. Mediterranean region, S.W. Ireland. Zone 8 (7 with shelter). To 40ft (12m). Leaves medium length, narrow, oval. Flowers late autumn, in drooping clusters, small. Fruit strawberry-like, late autumn. Sun or semi-shade. Tolerant of dry and limey soils. 15ft (4.5m) in 20 years. A.G.M. 1969.

   A.u. **'Rubra'** Pink-flowered form, often fruiting well.

Araucaria araucana
Chile pine, Monkey puzzle

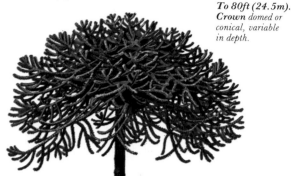

To 80ft (24.5m).
Crown domed or conical, variable in depth.

Bole very straight with occasional suckers. Bark dark grey, fissured, with old branch scars.

Branches in whorls, horizontal near apex of crown, drooping elsewhere, upturned at tips. Foliage remains green for 10-15 years, persisting after drying and turning brown.

Male cones 2½-4in (6-10cm), green at first then brown, dry, papery, hanging in clusters of 1-6 near branch tips, persisting 1 year.

Leaves 1½ × ½in (4 × 1cm), set spirally, interlocking around shoot, hard, leathery, sharply tipped, with parallel veins.

Female cone (right) large, 6in (15cm), ripening to brown in 2nd autumn when 1½in (4cm) seeds released as they break up.

Arbutus unedo
Killarney, Strawberry tree

Leaves 4in (10cm), variable, serrate, shiny, very dark above, paler below. Handsome, bay-like, evergreen.

Petioles ½in (1cm), hairy. Shoots long-haired.

Flowers ⅓in (8mm), white, frequently with a pink blush.

Fruit ¾in (2cm), warty, green-yellow, ripening to strawberryish orange-pink as new flowers open, so tree bears red fruit at same time as new flowers.

Panicles of 15-20 flowers open in October-December.

Betula lutea
Yellow birch

Leaves *have 12-15 pairs of veins, hairy below.* **Petioles** *³/4in (2cm), grooved.*

Bark *golden-brown, peeling, aromatic, inflammable even when wet.*

Fruit *1¹/2in (4cm), erect, sub-sessile, with spreading scales.*

Leaves *4¹/2in (11cm), elliptic, dull green.* **Margins** *irregularly doubly serrate.*

Apex *acute.*

Shoots *dull grey-brown, pubescent at first.*

Betula nigra
River birch, Black birch

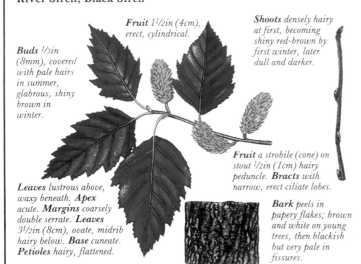

Fruit *1¹/2in (4cm), erect, cylindrical.*

Buds *¹/3in (8mm), covered with pale hairs in summer, glabrous, shiny brown in winter.*

Shoots *densely hairy at first, becoming shiny red-brown by first winter, later dull and darker.*

Leaves *lustrous above, waxy beneath.* **Apex** *acute.* **Margins** *coarsely double serrate.* **Leaves** *3¹/2in (8cm), ovate, midrib hairy below.* **Base** *cuneate.* **Petioles** *hairy, flattened.*

Fruit *a strobile (cone) on stout ¹/2in (1cm) hairy peduncle.* **Bracts** *with narrow, erect ciliate lobes.*

Bark *peels in papery flakes; brown and white on young trees, then blackish but very pale in fissures.*

Betula papyrifera
Paper birch, Canoe birch

Buds *¹/3in (8mm).* **Shoots** *warty.*

Petioles *1¹/4in (3cm), stout, pubescent.*

To 130ft (40m). Crown *stiff.* **Branches** *ascend.*

Leaves *4in (10cm) but variable, doubly serrate, upper surface full green.* **Leaf underside** *paler with black glandular dots, hairy on midrib.*

Catkins *with young leaves; male 4in (10cm) when ripe, female erect, smaller 1¹/2in (4cm).*

Bark *white, shreds off in papery flakes.*

Buds *green and brown.*

ARCHONTHOPHOENIX *alexandrae* **123**
King palm. Australia. Zone 9. To 70ft (21.5m), trunk 6ft (1.8m) thick, surface ringed with leaf scars. Short-stalked pinnate leaves 3 to 5ft (1 to 1.5m) long, green above, greyish-white beneath. White or cream-coloured unisexual flowers on same tree. Roundish fruit ½ in (1cm) long, red.

ARECASTRUM *romanzoffianum* **123**
Queen palm. Brazil. Zone 10. To 30ft (9m), trunk 1 to 2ft (30 to 60cm) thick, smooth ringed surface. Pinnate leaves 8 to 15ft (2.5 to 4.5m) long on a 3ft (1m) stalk. Leaflets green. Small cream-coloured unisexual flowers on a 3ft (1m) stalk. Fruit 1in (2.5cm) long, oval, yellow, fleshy.

Armeniaca **200**

ASIMINA *triloba* **131**
Pawpaw, S.E. United States. Zone 5. To 40ft (12m), deciduous. Leaves alternate, long, oval tapering to the stalk; yellow in autumn. Purple flowers in May. Small bottle-shaped edible fruit. Likes rich soil.

ATHROTAXIS **117**
Tasmanian cedars. Tasmania. Evergreen trees. Leaves small, overlapping, scale-like. Male and female 'flowers' on same tree, male flowering heads catkin-like. Cones small, woody, seeds winged. Some lime-tolerance.
A. cupressoides **117** Tasmania. To 20 or 40ft (6 or 12m) erect. Leaves minute, pressed closely to stem, blunt, dark-green. Wedge-shaped cones.
A. laxifolia **117** To 70ft (21.5m); oval to broadly conical. Leaves short, green, free only at incurved tips. Cones clustered or singly on the ends of short shoots, pale or bright yellow. 15ft (4.5m) in 20 years.
A. selaginoides **117** King William pine. To 100ft (30m), gaunt. Leaves lance-shaped, short, larger than in other species, leathery, keeled on the outer surface. Cones ½ in to ¾ in (1 to 2cm) long, larger than in other species. Less hardy than *A. laxifolia*.

AUSTROCEDRUS *chilensis* **104**
Chilean cedar. Chile, Argentina. To 95ft (29m), upright, spreading, evergreen. Leaves green or grey-green, short, flattened sprays of overlapping scales in fours, distinctive white marking, narrow band above, broad band below. Male flowering heads round to oblong. Cones with 4 scales, solitary, small. Slightly tender. 15ft (4.5m) in 20 years.

B

BETULA **164–7**, 326, 327
Deciduous trees or shrubs, mostly with silky, peeling, ornamental bark. Oval, pointed, toothed leaves turning yellow in autumn. Long male catkins form in autumn, expand in spring. Roundish female catkins on same tree. Fruit is a small winged nut. Mostly suited to poor sandy or boggy soil. Hardy. Fast-growing when young. Subject to galls, bronze birch borer, birch leaf miner, rust, fungal wood-rot, witches' broom.
B. albo-sinensis septentrionalis **167**, 318 China. Zone 5. To 100ft (30m). Leaves hairy on veins beneath. Beautiful bark, orange-brown with pink and grey 'bloom'. 35ft (10.5m) in 20 years.
B. allegheniensis **319** (See *Betula lutea*)
B. costata **165**, 319 N.E. Asia. Zone 5. To 100ft (30m). Small flower clusters and fruiting catkins. Conspicuous creamy-white bark.
B. ermanii **165, 167** Russian rock birch. N.E. Asia. Zone 5. To 35ft (10.5m). Branches medium length, smooth, with downy veins. Fruiting catkins barrel-shaped 1 to 1¼ in (2.5 to 3cm) long. A.G.M. 1969.
B. × *fetisowii* A Polish hybrid birch with narrow head, chalk-white bark.
B. forrestii **164** Forrest's birch. Zone 5. To 40 to 50ft (12 to 15m), tree or bush. Leaves oval to oblong, simple, silky above, short stalked. Catkins 1in (2.5cm) long. Bark brown-purple.
B. grossa **319** Japanese birch with dark grey bark.
B. jacquemontii **164, 167** W. Himalaya. Zone 7. Medium-sized. Leaves often doubly toothed, both surfaces almost smooth. Male catkins 2 to 2½ in (5 to 6.5cm). Fruiting catkins cylindrical, 1½ in (4cm). Bark white and peeling. 35ft (10.5m) in 20 years. A.G.M. 1969.
B. lenta **164**, 319 Cherry birch, Sweet birch. Eastern N. America. Zone 3. To 80ft (24.5m) in America, but smaller in Britain. Leaves medium length, dark green above, paler below. Male catkins 2 to 3in (5 to 7.5cm). 30ft (9m) in 20 years.
*B. lutea** **164, 165** Yellow birch. Eastern N. America. Zone 3. To 100ft (30m). Leaves dull green, medium length, initially downy. Fruiting catkins

upright, 1 to 1½ in (2.5 to 4cm). Bark golden-brown. 30ft (9m) in 20 years.

B. mandshurica See *B. platyphylla*

B. maximowicziana **164, 167,** 319 Japan. Zone 5. To 100ft (30m) in America, medium-sized in Britain, wide head. Leaves heart-shaped, largest of any birch. Male catkins 4 to 5in (10 to 13cm). Fruiting catkins 2 to 2½ in (5 to 6.5cm) in groups of 2 to 4. Seed wings large. 35ft (10.5m) in 20 years.

B. medwediewii **318** Handsome birch with alder-like leaves, yellow in fall.

B. nigra* **164, 165,** 319, 327 River birch. C. and E. United States. Zone 4. To 90ft (27.5m), pyramidal form. Leaves diamond-shaped, medium length, glossy above, waxy beneath. Male catkins 2 to 3in (5 to 7.5cm). Fruiting catkins on same tree erect, 1 to 1½ in (2.5 to 4cm), with downy scales. Bark whitish becoming shaggy and peeling blackish. One of best trees for damp ground; thrives in ordinary soil. 30ft (9m) in 20 years.

B. papyrifera* **164, 165, 166, 167,** 319, 327 Paper birch, Canoe birch. N. America. Zone 2. To 130ft (40m), with rather open head. Leaves medium length, irregularly toothed, upper surface dull green with scattered hairs, lower surface pale. Male catkins up to 4in (10cm). Fruiting catkins, on same tree, drooping, about 1½ in (4cm). White bark, peeling in thin papery layers. Most soils. 40ft (12m) in 20 years.

B. pendula* **164, 165, 166, 167,** 322, 327 Common silver birch, European birch. Europe, Asia Minor. Zone 2. To 75ft (23m), branches pendulous at ends. Leaves diamond-shaped and doubly-toothed. Cylindrical fruiting catkins. Bark white. Tolerant of dryness. 40ft (12m) in 20 years. Susceptible to bronze birch borer in United States. A.G.M. 1969.

   B.p. **'Dalecarlica'** 167, 326 Swedish birch. Sweden. Slender with drooping branchlets and leaves. Leaves deeply lobed, coarsely toothed, with long slender points. 40ft (12m) in 20 years. A.G.M. 1969.

   B.p. **'Fastigiata'** 326 Columnar head, straight upright branches. Leaves very dark green. A.G.M. 1969.

   B.p. **'Purpurea'** Purple leaf birch. A graceful little tree, dusky leaves.

   B.p. **'Tristis'** 166 Graceful tree with pendulous branches forming a narrow head. A.G.M. 1969.

   B.p. **'Youngii'** 167, 326 Young's weeping birch. Small weeping tree, dome-shaped. A.G.M. 1969.

B. platyphylla 326, 327 Manchurian birch. Manchuria, Korea. Zone 5. To 60ft (18m). Bark white. Leaves ovallish, medium length.

   B.p. japonica 167 Japanese white birch. Japan. Zone 4. Very beautiful. Leaves broad, medium length. White bark. 50ft (15m) in 20 years.

B. populifolia **164, 165** Gray birch. E. United States. Zone 3–4. To 30ft (9m) with thin pyramidal head. Leaves medium length, shiny on both sides. Male catkins 2 to 3½ in (5 to 9cm); smaller fruiting catkins with downy scales. Bark grey-white. Good on poor, damp or dry soil. 40ft (12m) in 20 years.

B. pubescens **166,** 327 Common white birch, Downy birch. Europe, N. Asia. Zone 2. To 65ft (20m). Leaves medium length, coarsely toothed, sometimes downy beneath. Bark white, peeling, eventually dark and rugged at base. Thrives on many soils, especially damp. 30ft (9m) in 20 years.

B. utilis **164, 167,** 318 Himalayan birch. Himalaya. Zone 7. To 60ft (18m). Leaves dark green above, paler, downy beneath, roughly toothed, stalked. Bark peeling, papery, creamy white or brown.

B. verrucosa See *Betula pendula*

BROUSSONETIA *papyrifera* 142, 143, 326

Paper mulberry. E. Asia. Zone 6. To 45ft (13.5m), wide-spreading, broad rounded head. Leaves variable, oval or lobed, dull green and rough above, woolly beneath. Deciduous. Flowers, sexes on separate plants, male flowers in woolly catkins 1½ to 3in (4 to 7.5cm); female flowers in small round clusters, May. Round orange-red fruits ¾ in (2cm) across. Any soil.

BUXUS *sempervirens** **223,** 327

Common box. S. Europe, N. Africa. W. Asia. Zone 5. To 35ft (10.5m), evergreen shrub or small tree. Leaves oval, tapering, notched at tip, short, profuse, leathery. Flowers pale green, insignificant, males clustered round female. Fruit, small oval or rounded capsule. Most soils. Sun or shade. Subject to leaf spot, twig dieback. 15ft (4.5m) in 20 years.

C

CALLITRIS *robusta* 97

Common cypress pine. Queensland, Tasmania. Zone 9. To 15 or 20ft (4.5 or 6m), evergreen, branches spreading or upright. Small leaves in whorls of 3, narrow or scale-like. Male and female 'flowers' separate but on same plant, males cylindrical, female conical. Cones single or clustered, 1in (2.5cm) long. 10ft (3m) in 20 years.

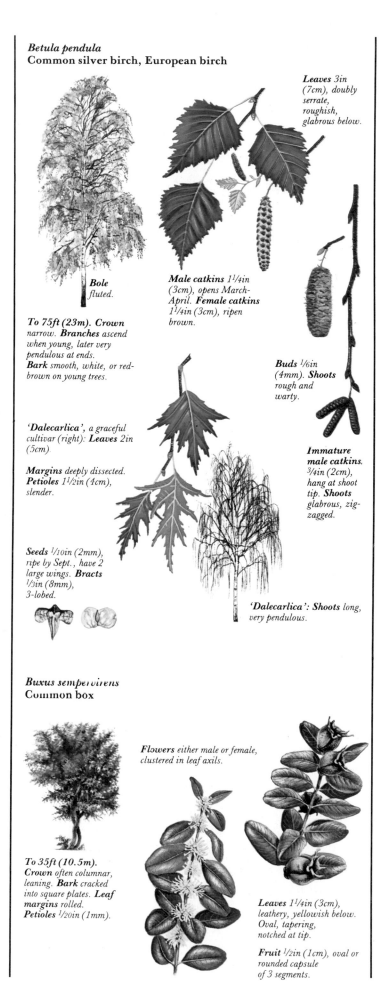

Betula pendula
Common silver birch, European birch

Leaves 3in (7cm), doubly serrate, roughish, glabrous below.

Bole *fluted.*

Male catkins 1¼in (3cm), opens March-April. **Female catkins** *1¼in (3cm), ripen brown.*

To 75ft (23m). Crown *narrow.* **Branches** *ascend when young, later very pendulous at ends.* **Bark** *smooth, white, or red-brown on young trees.*

Buds ⅙in (4mm). **Shoots** *rough and warty.*

'Dalecarlica', a graceful cultivar (right): **Leaves** *2in (5cm)*

Margins *deeply dissected.* **Petioles** *1½in (1cm), slender.*

Immature male catkins. ¾in (2cm), hang at shoot tip. **Shoots** *glabrous, zig-zagged.*

Seeds ⅒in (2mm), ripe by Sept., have 2 large wings. **Bracts** *⅓in (8mm), 3-lobed.*

'Dalecarlica': Shoots long, very pendulous.

Buxus sempervirens
Common box

Flowers either male or female, clustered in leaf axils.

To 35ft (10.5m). **Crown** *often columnar, leaning.* **Bark** *cracked into square plates.* **Leaf** *margins rolled.* **Petioles** *⅟20in (1mm).*

Leaves 1¼in (3cm), leathery, yellowish below. Oval, tapering, notched at tip.

Fruit ½in (1cm), oval or rounded capsule of 3 segments.

Calocedrus decurrens
Incense cedar

Foliage *dense, in irregular flat sprays, deep green outside, yellower beneath.* **Leaves** *to ¹/₂in (1cm), in unequal pairs with facial ones shorter.*

Cones *long, narrow, ³/4-1¹/4in (2-3cm), with only middle 2 scales carrying seeds, red-brown when fully ripe.* **Cone scales** *hooked.*

To 100-150ft (30-45m). Crown *columnar and slim in cultivation, far broader when wild.* **Branches** *short.* **Bark** *thick, furrowed, scaling.*

Carpinus caroliniana
American hornbeam

Leaves *4in (10cm), oval or ovate, long pointed, bright green above, light yellow-green below.* **Base** *rounded or cuneate, usually oblique.* **Veins** *slender, deeply impressed.* **Petioles** *¹/₂in (1cm), hairy, bright red when young.* **Leaf** *glabrous above, hairy in vein axils below.*

Margins *double serrate.* **Teeth** *sharp, spreading, glandular.*

Shoots *slender, initially with long silky white hairs, becoming red-brown, shiny, later dull grey, tinged red.*

Fruit *in 8-11 pairs, a nutlet subtended by trident bract, hanging in 3in (7.5cm) clusters on slender pubescent red-brown stems.* **Bracts** *sleafy, green ripening to brown.* **Involucre** *1¹/₂ × 1in (4 × 2.5cm), coarsely toothed, often only on one margin.*

Nutlets *¹/₃in (8mm).*

To 40ft (12m). Crown *usually bushy, dense and flat-topped.*

Catkins *1¹/₂in (4cm), appear with leaves in spring.* **Male catkins** *overwinter in bud, open in spring.* **Buds** *¹/₆in (4mm), ovoid, acute.* **Scales** *brown with white margins.*

Branches *zig-zag, slender, wiry, pendulous at tips.* **Bole** *short, characteristically fluted.*

Bark *smooth, with broad horizontal patches.*

CALOCEDRUS 104

Evergreen. Leaves flattened, scale-like, overlapping. Male and female 'flowers' on different branches of same tree usually, both solitary; males oblong to oval, females oval to oblong, woody. Cones woody. Seeds winged.
C. decurrens* 85, 90, **104**, 326, 327 Incense cedar. S.W. United States. Zone 5. Conical in wild, columnar in cultivation, 100 to 150ft (30 to 45m). Shoot covered in scales, becomes red-brown, vertical sprays of foliage, deep green outside, yellower beneath. Male flowers pale yellow. Cones pale yellow-brown, becoming red-brown. Bark dark red-brown, fragrant. Dislikes shallow soils, or very dry, exposed places. 35ft (10.5m) in 20 years.

CAMELLIA 172-3, 326, 327

Evergreen trees or shrubs. Leaves alternate, toothed, simple. Flowers bisexual, usually solitary, white to red, showy. Seeds big, oily, in woody capsule; rare in cultivated forms. Neutral, slightly acid soils. Shade-loving. Subject to leaf blotch.
C. japonica 173, 316, 318, 327 Common camellia. China, Japan. Zone 7. To 20ft (6m). Leaves ovallish, long-pointed, smooth, often black-dotted beneath, leathery, dark green, short-stalked. Flowers single, red, waxy, possibly slightly fragrant, late winter. 15ft (4.5m) in 20 years. A.G.M. 1930.
   C.j. **'Haku-rakuten'** 173 Erect form, vigorous growth. Flowers big, white, semi-double with curved petals.
   C.j. **'Yours Truly'** 173 Bushy. Leaves wavy. Flowers semi-double, pink streaked with deeper pink, bordered with white.
C. reticulata 172-3 Yunnan, China. Zone 8. To 35ft (10.5m), evergreen tree or compact shrub. Rigid leathery leaves, dark dull green. Flowers rose-pink. March. Prefers slightly acid soil.
C. sasanqua 172-3 Japan. Zone 7. Shrub or small tree. To 20ft (6m). Leaves narrowly oval, dark green, leathery. Flowers white, fragrant, early winter. Needs shelter. 12ft (3.5m) in 20 years.
C. sinensis 172 Tea-tree. Assam to China. Zone 7. To 45ft (13.5m), compact shrub or tree. Leaves variable, broad to lance-shaped. Flowers white, nodding, spring. Slow-growing.

CARPINUS 170-1, 327

Hardy deciduous trees or shrubs. Leaves toothed in two ranks. Hanging male catkins, spring. Narrow female catkins. Fruit in small ribbed nut, ripe in autumn. Bark smooth or scaly grey. Easily grown. Clay- and chalk-tolerant.
C. betulus 64, 170, 171, 327 Common hornbeam, European hornbeam. Europe, Asia Minor. Zone 5. To 75ft (23m), pyramidal, becoming rounder. Leaves oval, tapering; dark green, downy beneath, turning yellow and smooth by autumn. Unisexual flowers. Male catkins 1¹/₂in (4cm); fruiting catkins 1¹/₂ to 3in (4 to 7.5cm), with large, 3-lobed bracts. 35ft (10.5m) in 20 years.
   C.b. **'Columnaris'** 327 Small, compact form, conical becoming columnar. Slower than 'Fastigiata'.
   C.b. **'Fastigiata'** 171 Medium-sized tree, erect, columnar, broadening with age, 30ft (9m) in 20 years. A.G.M. 1969.
   C.b. **'Incisa'** 326 Leaves small, narrow, deeply toothed. May revert.
   C.b. **'Intertexta'** 326 Ascending, open. Branchlets drooping. Foliage blue-green, in flat sprays. A.G.M. 1969.
C. caroliniana* 170 American hornbeam, Blue beech, or Ironwood. E. United States. Zone 2. To 40ft (12m), branches spreading, arching at tips. Leaves oval, bright green, downy when young, sparsely hairy later; scarlet and orange in autumn. Male catkins 1 to 1¹/₂in (2.5 to 4cm) long. Fruiting clusters 3in (7.5cm) long. 15ft (4.5m) in 20 years.
C. cordata 170, 171 Japan, N.E. Asia, N. and W. China. Zone 5. To 40 or 50ft (12 or 15m). Leaves heart-shaped, pointed, simple, deeply-veined, hairy below, slightly so above. Male catkins with long hairs, female catkins 3in (7.5cm) long. Fruits small, green, clustered.
C. japonica 170, 171, 317, 327 Japanese hornbeam. Japan. Zone 4. To 50ft (15m), wide-spreading. Leaves alternate, oval, tapering; medium length, upper surface dark green, lower surface downy on veins, corrugated. Male catkins 1 to 2in (2.5 to 5cm) long with conspicuous scales. Fruit clusters to 2¹/₂in (6.5cm) long, persist on tree. 15ft (4.5m) in 20 years.
C. laxiflora 319 Japanese hornbeam with ornamental fruit.
C. orientalis 318 Small bushy tree or shrub from S.E. Europe and Asia Minor. Small, sharply toothed leaves.
C. turczaninowii 318 A very graceful thin, spindly hornbeam.

CARYA 132, **144, 145, 146, 147**, 326, 327

Big deciduous trees related to walnuts. Pinnate leaves. Sexes on same tree. Male flowers in branched, slender catkins; female flowers in small clusters. Fruit, nut surrounded by a husk. Deep loamy soil. Subject to canker, leaf

blotch and scab in America; pest-free in Europe. Resent transplanting.
C. cordiformis* **147,** 319 Bitternut. E. United States. Zone 4. To 90ft
(27.5m), broad, rounded. Winter bud scales yellow. Leaves long, 5 to 10
oval, toothed leaflets, yellow in autumn. Male flowers downy. Fruit in twos
or threes. 25ft (7.5m) in 20 years.
C. glabra **147,** 319, 326 Pignut. E. United States. Zone 4. To 120ft (36m),
narrow to round. Leaves long, 5 to 7 oval, toothed leaflets, yellow in autumn.
Nuts vary in size and shape.
C. illinoensis **146–7,** 326 Pecan. E. United States. Zone 5. To 150ft (45m),
rounded head, huge branches. 11 to 17 toothed, pointed leaflets, yellow in
autumn. Fruits clustered, oblong.
C. laciniosa 319 A shaggy-barked hickory from E. United States.
C. ovata **146, 147,** 319, 326, 327 Shagbark hickory. E. United States. Zone
4. To 120ft (36m), narrow and upright, irregular. Leaves long, 5 to 9 leaflets,
hairy beneath, rich yellow to golden brown in autumn. Male catkins hairy, in
threes. Fruits roundish. 20ft (6m) in 20 years.
C. tomentosa **147,** 319, 326 Mockernut, Bigbud hickory, S.E. Canada, E.
United States. Zone 4. To 90ft (27.5m), upright with a round head. Leaves
long, 5 to 9 toothed, pointed leaflets, dark green above, yellowish, downy
below. Male catkins downy, 3 to 5in (7.5 to 13cm) long. Fruit roundish. 20ft
(6m) in 20 years.

CASTANEA 162–3, 327
Leaves toothed, deciduous. Flowers, sexes on separate catkins; males long,
hanging, females shorter; both pale yellow, July. Fruit, nuts surrounded by
prickly husks. Tolerant of shade. Not suited to shallow, chalky or sandy soils.
Subject to chestnut blight in America, canker, die-back, leaf-spot.
C. crenata 163 Japanese chestnut. Japan. Zone 5. To 30ft (9m). Leaves
narrow oval, often hairy beneath. Nuts 1in (2.5cm), 2 or 3 in each husk.
C. dentata 163 American sweet chestnut. E. United States. Zone 4. To 100ft
(30m), upright, broad. Leaves hairless, dull green; narrowly oblong,
tapering. Flowers in catkins, unisexual. Fruit 1 to 3 nuts. 15ft (4.5m) in 20
years.
C. mollissima 163 Chinese chestnut. China, Korea. Zone 4. To 65ft (20m),
dense, rounded head. Leaves oval, tapering, sometimes hairy, with short,
hairy stalk. Usually 2 or 3 nuts in husk. 10ft (3m) in 20 years. Resists
chestnut blight.
C. sativa* 64, 132, 148, **162–3,** 317, 323, 325, 326 Spanish chestnut, Sweet
chestnut. S. Europe, N. Africa, Asia Minor. Zone 5. To 100ft (30m),
spreading. Leaves oblong, tapering hairy beneath at first. Flowers yellowish-
green, unpleasant-smelling. Ornamental, especially in flowers. Nuts edible.
35ft(10.5m) in 20 years.
    C.s. **'Aureomarginata'** 326 Leaves bordered yellow.
    C.s. **'Marron de Lyon'** 162 Bears fruit at a very early age.

CASTANOPSIS cuspidata 162, 163, 318
Small evergreen tree between oak and chestnut.

CASUARINA nana 215
Dwarf sheoke, She-oak. Australia. Zone 8. Small, bushy evergreen tree or
shrub, narrow, with rushlike stems and leaves.

CATALPA 64, 244–5, 327
Deciduous. Big, opposite leaves, long-stalked, sometimes lobed. Flowers
clustered, bisexual. Long, narrow seed capsule. All well-drained soils. Sun-
loving. Subject to leaf-spot in America.
C. bignonioides **244,** 317, 319, 326 Indian bean tree, Southern catalpa. E.
United States. Zone 4. To 65ft (20m), wide-spreading. Leaves broadly oval,
tapering, light green above, pale downy beneath, disagreeable odour when
crushed. Flowers upright, white and purple. 20ft (6m) in 20 years. A.G.M.
1960.
    C.b. **'Aurea'** **245,** 326 Golden Indian bean tree. Zone 4. Leaves rich
yellow and velvety.
C. × erubescens 319 To 30ft (9m). Leaves ovallish, 3-lobed and whole on
same tree, purple when unfolding. Flowers similar to *C. bignonioides* but
smaller and more numerous, late July.
    C. × e. **'J. C. Teas'** 245 Double-sized flowers.
    C. × e. **'Purpurea'** 245 Shoots and leaves black-purple, becoming
greener.
C. fargesii 318 Smaller-leaved catalpa with excellent summer flowers.
    C.f. **duclouxii** A form with wonderfully soft and smooth hairless leaves
with longer points.
C. ovata 318 To 40ft (12m). Leaves usually 3-lobed. Small white flowers
with yellow and red markings.

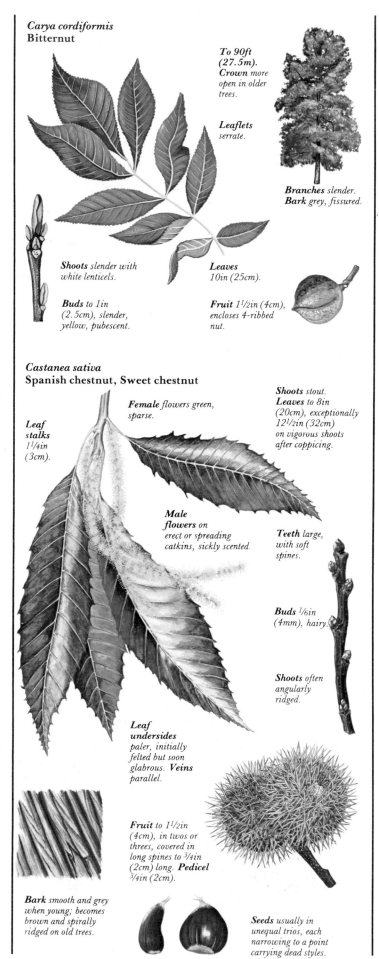

Carya cordiformis
Bitternut

**To 90ft
(27.5m).
Crown** *more
open in older
trees.*

Leaflets
serrate.

Branches *slender.*
Bark *grey, fissured.*

Shoots *slender with
white lenticels.*

Leaves
10in (25cm).

Buds *to 1in
(2.5cm), slender,
yellow, pubescent.*

Fruit *1½in (4cm),
encloses 4-ribbed
nut.*

Castanea sativa
Spanish chestnut, Sweet chestnut

**Leaf
stalks**
*1¼in
(3cm).*

Female *flowers green,
sparse.*

Shoots *stout.*
Leaves *to 8in
(20cm), exceptionally
12½in (32cm)
on vigorous shoots
after coppicing.*

**Male
flowers** *on
erect or spreading
catkins, sickly scented.*

Teeth *large,
with soft
spines.*

Buds *⅙in
(4mm), hairy.*

Shoots *often
angularly
ridged.*

**Leaf
undersides**
*paler, initially
felted but soon
glabrous.* **Veins**
parallel.

Fruit *to 1½in
(4cm), in twos or
threes, covered in
long spines to ¾in
(2cm) long.* **Pedicel**
¾in (2cm).

Bark *smooth and grey
when young; becomes
brown and spirally
ridged on old trees.*

Seeds *usually in
unequal trios, each
narrowing to a point
carrying dead styles.*

Cedrus libani
Cedar of Lebanon

To 100ft (30m).
Crown broad, often flat-topped and many-stemmed. Large, horizontal layers of dense foliage.

Branches massive, arching then level.
Bole huge, expands to support fast-growing branches on young tree.

Bark grey-brown, fissured; smooth, dark grey on young trees.

Cones from 3¹/₂-5¹/₂in (8-14cm). Apex sometimes depressed. Resinous.

Foliage dense, darkest green of the cedars, can be grey or glaucous. Buds ¹/₁₀-¹/₆in (2-4mm), brown, ovoid.

Shoots brown, pubescent.

Leaves narrow. Taper to sharp translucent tips. On young, long shoots: ³/₄in (2cm), set singly and spirally; on older ¹/₁₀-¹/₆in (2-4mm) spur-shoots: 1¹/₄in (3cm), in whorls of 10-20.

Celtis occidentalis
Hackberry, Sugarberry

Fruit ¹/₃in (8mm), an ovoid to obovoid drupe, in leaf axils. Pedicel ³/₄in (2cm).

Leaves 4in (9cm), ovate, with three veins at base. Base obliquely rounded. Veins pubescent. Petioles ³/₄in (2cm), silky. Leaf apex often at angle to midrib.

Fruit persists on shoots after leaf-fall.

Apex acuminate.

Bark silvery-grey, flaky, with warts and longitudinal winged ridges.

Shoots slender with long white hairs. Buds ¹/₃in (8mm), adpressed. Margins singly serrate towards apex, short-toothed at base.

C. speciosa 244, 317 Western catalpa. C. United States. Zone 4. To 100ft (30m). Leaves heart-shaped, tapering, lower side downy. Flowers slightly larger than *C. bignonioides,* less spotted with purple. 20ft (6m) in 20 years.

CEDRELA 242, 243
Deciduous or evergreen trees. Leaves alternate, usually pinnate. Flowers small, whitish or greenish, bisexual, in big clusters. Fruit, a capsule holding many winged seeds.
C. sinensis 242, 243, 318, 326, 327 Chinese toon. N. and W. China. Zone 5. To 70ft (21.5m), rounded and dense. Leaves pinnate, to 2ft (60cm) long, 5 to 12 pairs of leaflets, open red, yellow in autumn, deciduous, taste of onion. Flower clusters 1ft (30cm) long, fragrant, June. Any soil.

CEDRUS 69, 70, 83, 85, **90–1,** 94, 97–100, 102–6, 112, 114, 327
Cedars. Hardy evergreen, initially conical, spreading later. Leaves needle-like, in rosettes on old shoots, single on new. Male and female 'flowers' on same or separate trees, males yellow, profuse. Cones barrel-shaped, break up on tree after 2 years. Seeds winged. Few fungal diseases, susceptible to drought.
C. atlantica 91, 318, 326 Atlas cedar. Atlas Mts. Zone 6. To 120ft (36m), pyramidal when young. Leaves shorter but similar to *C. libani,* slightly more waxy and numerous. Male 'flowers' erect sugarloaf-shape, pale green in summer, purplish Sept.; females green, tinged pink in centre of rosette. 40ft (12m) in 20 years.
　　C.a. 'Aurea' 327 Leaves shorter than the type, golden yellow.
　　C.a. 'Fastigiata' 326 Narrow, pyramidal, ascending branches. Leaves light green above, bluish-green below, on short branchlets.
　　C.a. glauca 91, 163 Blue cedar. To 120ft (36m), more pointed, less liable to have multiple stems. Leaves light blue or waxy. Bark pale grey. 40ft (12m) in 20 years.
　　C.a. 'Pendula' 326 Small, pendulous branches. Leaves green or greyish green.
C. brevifolia 91, 318 Cyprus cedar. Mts of Cyprus. Zone 7. Narrowly conical. Leaves rich green to blue- or yellow-green. Cones smooth pale green. 20ft (6m) in 20 years.
C. deodara 91, 318, 326 Deodar. W. Himalaya. Zone 7. To 200ft (60m), pendulous. Leaves short, dark green, waxy or silvery, sharply pointed. Sexes usually on separate trees. 45ft (13.5m) in 20 years.
C. libani* 41, 43, **90–1,** 318, 325, 326 Cedar of Lebanon. Asia Minor and Syria. Zone 5. To 70 or 100ft (21.5 or 30m), often erect or ascending, flat-topped with age. Leaves short, green or waxy. 30ft (9m) in 20 years.

CELTIS 140-1, 327
Medium or large, related to elms. Leaves deciduous, simple. Flowers small, greenish. Separate sexes on same tree, male flowers clustered, female flowers in groups of 1 to 3. Fruit fleshy, single-stoned, sweet, ripe in autumn. Subject to leaf-spot where native, witches' broom in America. Any soil.
C. australis 141, 318, 327 S. Europe, N. Africa, Asia Minor. Zone 6. To 80ft (24.5m), round-headed. Leaves toothed, lance-shaped, soft down beneath, harsher above, short-stalked. Sun-loving. 10ft (3m) in 20 years.
C. laevigata 141 Sugar hackberry, Mississippi hackberry. S.E. United States. Zone 5. To 100ft (30m), spreading, sometimes weeping. Leaves oval to lance-shaped, smooth, dark green above, paler with some hairs beneath, few teeth. Male flowers separate from solitary females. Fruits small, oval, orange to black. Sun-loving. Fairly resistant to witches' broom. 12ft (3.5m) in 20 years.
C. occidentalis* 140, 141, 319 Hackberry, Sugarberry. N. United States. Zone 2. Usually to 40ft (12m), occasionally much more. Leaves oval to oblong, possibly downy, short-toothed near base. Flowers early spring. Fruit ripens purple, small, profuse. Bark warty, corky, rough. 12ft (3.5m) in 20 years.
C. sinensis 141 Chinese hackberry. E. China, Korea, Japan. Zone 6. To 65ft (20m), spreading. Leaves shiny, dark green, broad oval. Flowers as *C. laevigata.* Fruit small, red or yellow, edible. Sun-loving. Resistant to witches' broom disease. 20ft (6m) in 20 years.
C. tournefourtii 318 Small oriental tree, polished leaves and red and yellow fruits.

CEPHALOTAXUS 110–11, 327
Hardy evergreen shrubs or small trees. Leaves narrow, pointed, dark green above, obvious midrib. Sexes usually on separate trees; male 'flowers' round, females scarce, cup-shaped. Fruit in cup, single seed. Shade-tolerant.
C. fortunei 110 Chinese plum yew. C. and S.W. China. Zone 6. To 30ft (9m), slender or bushy. Medium length leaves. Male 'flowers' on short stalks

below shoot, females on separate trees. Small fruit, oval, green-white vertically striped green. Lime-tolerant. 12ft (3.5m) in 20 years.
C. harringtonia drupacea 110, 319 Cow's tail pine, Japanese plum yew. Japan, Central China. Zone 5. To 20 or 40ft (6 or 12m), wide-spreading, bushy crown, rounded. Leaves short, in double ranks, forming narrow V-shaped channel on upper surface of branchlets. Male 'flowers' small, short scaly stalks. Seeds pear-shaped, oily, brown or olive-green. Thrives on chalk soils. 8ft (2.5m) in 20 years.

CERATONIA siliqua **208, 210,** 326
Carob. St John's bread. Mediterranean. Zone 10. To 50ft (15m), rounded shrub or small tree. Leaves evergreen, pinnate, wavy-edged, glossy, dark green. Flowers, sexes separate, small, red, clustered, spring. Fruits, pods 1ft (30cm) long, edible, early autumn. Tolerates dry soils.

CERCIDIPHYLLUM japonicum **132, 133,** 326, 327
Katsura tree. Japan, China. Zone 4. To 50ft (15m). Pendulous branches, often with several stems. Leaves simple, deciduous similar to 'Judas tree' (*Cercis*), but opposite and smaller, superb varying autumn colours. Flowers, sexes on separate trees, females small with green sepals. Fruit, small pods, on short stalk. Chalk-tolerant, but not reliably coloured on these soils; tolerates dry conditions. Sun or semi-shade. 40ft (12m) in 20 years.

CERCIS 211
Small group of trees and shrubs. Leaves simple, deciduous, heart-shaped, medium length, untoothed, bisexual. Flowers usually in dense clusters on stems, before or with leaves. Fruits narrow, flat pods holding several flattened seeds. Prefers well-drained, loamy soils. Sun-loving. Hardy. Subject to coral spot fungus, leaf-spot and canker in America.
C. canadensis 211, 327 Redbud. S.E. Canada, E. United States. N.E. Mexico. Zone 4. To 40ft (12m) broad, rounded head. Leaves bright green. Flowers pale rose, spring. Acid and alkaline soils. Less free-flowering than *C. siliquastrum* in Britain. 15ft (4.5m) in 20 years.
C. chinensis 211 Chinese redbud. China. Zone 6. To 50ft (15m) often shrubby in cultivation. Leaves roundish, glossy green, yellow in autumn. Flowers rosy-purple, May. Rather tender in Britain. 15ft (4.5m) in 20 years.
C. racemosa 211 China. Zone 7. To 30ft (9m), flat-topped. Leaves dark green above, downy beneath, yellow in autumn. Flowers rose-coloured, May. 20ft (6m) in 20 years.
C. siliquastrum* 211, 316, 318, 326, 327 Judas tree. E. Mediterranean. Zone 6. To 30ft (9m), round-topped, bushy. Leaves roundish, waxy green. Flowers rose-purple, April–May. Pods red, Oct. through winter. 25ft (7.5m) in 20 years. A.G.M. 1927.

CHAMAECYPARIS **99–101,** 327
False cypresses. Evergreen, conical, becoming wide-spread. Leaves scale-like, small, awl-shaped in early stages. Male and female 'flowers' separate on same tree; males oval to oblong, tiny, red or brown; cones round. Seeds winged. Dislike dry, chalky soil. Subject to root-rot and rusts in America.
C. formosensis 318 Formosan cypress. Huge in Formosa, small but hardy in Britain.
C. henryae 100 S.E. United States. Zone 3. To 70 or 80ft (21.5 or 24.5m) pyramidal. Horizontal or upright spreading branchlets. Juvenile foliage green, adult yellow-green. Cones green.
C. lawsoniana* 85, 94, **98–9,** 102, 327 Lawson cypress, Port Orford cedar. S.W. Oregon, N.W. California. Zone 5. To 175 or 200ft (52 or 60m). Leaves in fours, 2 unequal pairs, leaf sprays flattened. Male 'flowers' pink or red. Cones ⅓in (7mm) wide, red-brown in autumn. Tolerates sunshine or shade. 35 to 45ft (10.5 to 12m) in 20 years.
  C.l. 'Allumii' A spire-like blue-grey variety. To 60ft (18m).
  C.l. 'Columnaris' 99, 326 Upright, narrow. To 30ft (9m). Leaves a good blue-grey. 25ft (7.5m) in 20 years. A.G.M. 1961.
  C.l. 'Ellwoodii' 99, 100, 118, 327 To 25ft (7.5m), upright. Leaves juvenile, feathery, turning grey-green. 15ft (4.5m) in 20 years. A.G.M. 1969.
  C.l. 'Erecta Viridis' 98, 99, 326 To 90ft (27.5m). Branches short, upright, deep green and erect; branching from base of tree. Cones narrow. 30ft (9m) in 20 years.
  C.l. 'Fletcheri' 98, 99, 119 Columnar, often many tops. Foliage blue-grey and green, feathery, juvenile. 20ft (6m) in 20 years. A.G.M. 1969.
  C.l. 'Kilmacurragh' Narrow-columnar, like a rich green Italian cypress. To 40ft (12m). A.G.M. 1969.
  C.l. 'Lanei' 99, 100, 326 Medium-small, columnar, dense. Leaves bright gold in ferny sprays. Male 'flowers' red. 30ft (9m) in 20 years.

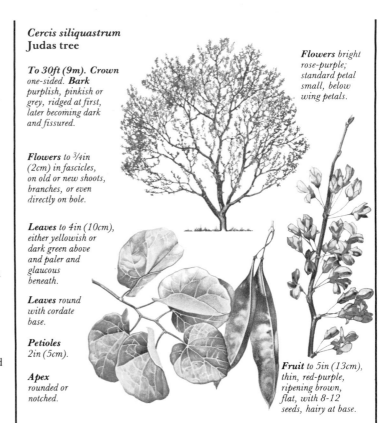

Cercis siliquastrum
Judas tree

To 30ft (9m). Crown one-sided. **Bark** purplish, pinkish or grey, ridged at first, later becoming dark and fissured.

Flowers to ¾in (2cm) in fascicles, on old or new shoots, branches, or even directly on bole.

Leaves to 4in (10cm), either yellowish or dark green above and paler and glaucous beneath.

Leaves round with cordate base.

Petioles 2in (5cm).

Apex rounded or notched.

Flowers bright rose-purple; standard petal small, below wing petals.

Fruit to 5in (13cm), thin, red-purple, ripening brown, flat, with 8-12 seeds, hairy at base.

Chamaecyparis lawsoniana
Lawson cypress, Port Orford Cedar

To 175-200ft (52-60m) in wild. **Crown** regular in young trees, less so in mature ones. **Stem** often forked. **Foliage** dense, pendulous, becoming spaced in old trees. **Leader** and new shoots always droop. **Terminals** wispy, unbranched near tips.

Cones ⅓in (8mm), globose, ripening from green or blue-green to red-brown. **Scales** (8) have short central spikes.

Bark smooth, ridged then scaly, dark red-brown, purplish on older trees.

Male flowers terminate weakest branchlets.

Foliage flat, fern-like. **Leaves** grouped in pairs: lateral ones keel-shaped, facing pairs smaller, adpressed. Each leaf has central translucent gland. Between leaf scales, stomata form thin, white lines. Especially clear on foliage underside; give best identification.

Chamaecyparis nootkatensis
Nootka cypress, Alaska cedar

Leading shoot *leans.*

Crown *is extremely regular.*

Foliage *very pendulous, in thick, flat, alternate sprays.* **Leaves** *¹/₁₀-¹/₆in (2-4mm), hard, rough, dull-green, in equal-sized pairs.*

Cones *¹/₂in (1cm), globular, with large scale spikes, green with blue bloom, ripening brown over 2 years.*

To 120ft (36m). **Bark** *stringy, peels.*

Chamaecyparis obtusa
Hinoki cypress

Foliage *in fan-like, feathery sprays.* **Leaves** *small, ¹/₁₀in (2mm) in blunt pairs, incurved, with white scale joints on undersides. The leaves and large, round cones distinguish the Hinoki cypress from other 'false' cypressus.*

To 75ft (23m). **Crown** *columnar, conic.*

Branches *level, then ascending.* **Bole** *straight.* **Bark** *fissured.*

Cones *¹/₂in (1cm), round, green, orange-brown when ripening.*

Chamaecyparis thyoides
White cypress, Atlantic white cedar

To 70 or 90ft (21.5 or 27.5m). **Crown** *columnar or broad conic.*

Foliage *very slender, ¹/₂₀in (1mm), short, fern-like, angular green or bluish-grey sprays.* **Cones** *set on small branchlets.*

Branches *short.* **Bark** *stringy. The wood of the White cypress is extremely strong and durable.*

Shoots *become brown in 2nd year.*

Leaves *very small, down to ¹/₂₀in (1mm), acutely pointed, incurved and close-pressed but freer on vigorous growth. Often have central resin glands and carry prominent white marks near bases, particularly on undersides.*

Cones *¹/₃in (8mm), glaucous blue-purple, ripening to red-brown.*

C.l. **'Lutea' 99, 100,** 326 To 40ft (12m), columnar, level branches with drooping shoots. Winter colour good. 25ft (7.5m) in 20 years. A.G.M. 1955.
C.l. **'Minima Aurea' 119** Dense dwarf, conical with sprays of golden-yellow foliage. A.G.M. 1969.
C.l. **'Pembury Blue' 99,** 326 To 30ft (9m), conical, very attractive, loosely-branched bushy tree. Silver-blue leaves. 12ft (3.5m) in 20 years. A.G.M. 1969.
C.l. **'Pottenii'** An upright form with very soft apple-green foliage, partly juvenile. To 30ft (9m).
C.l. **'Spek' 99** Blue-grey, broadly columnar. 20ft (6m) in 20 years.
C.l. **'Stewartii'** Commonly planted conical golden variety, turning yellow-green in winter. To 50ft (15m).
C.l. **'Triomf van Boskoop' 99,** 326 To 75ft (23m), coarse, open sprays of grey-blue, broadly columnar. Good bole. 35ft (10.5m) in 20 years.
C.l. **'Tamariscifolia'** The best bushy 'Lawson', with fine ferny-green foliage. To 15ft (4.5m). A.G.M. 1969.
C.l. **'Winston Churchill'** Probably the best year-round golden form. Conical. To 35ft (10.5m).
C.l. **'Wissellii' 118,** 326 60 or 85ft (18 or 27m), columnar, branches upward-twisting. Leaves deep blue-green, foliage bunched. Male 'flowers' prominent crimson. Very vigorous after slow start. 35ft (10.5m) in 20 years. A.G.M. 1969.
C. nootkatensis* **99–100, 101,** 319, 326 Nootka cypress. Yellow cypress. W. United States. Zone 4. To 120ft (36m), weeping foliage. Leaves hard, rough, dull green, sprays fern-like. Male 'flowers' small, yellow, spring. Cones green-brown, late spring or early summer. Withstands any soil, considerable exposure. 25 to 50ft (7.5 to 15m) in 20 years.
C.n. **'Pendula' 100,** 326 To 60ft (18m), raised branches, weeping shoots. Leaves dull green. Cones navy blue 1st year. 30ft (9m) in 20 years.
C. obtusa* **100** Hinoki cypress. Japan. Zone 3. To 50 or 75ft (15 or 23m), broadly conical. Fine branching system bears leaves in unequal pairs, 1 opposite pair larger than other, shiny bright green, leaf margin white below. Male 'flowers' tiny, terminal. Cones green, orange-brown when ripening. Prefers moist soils and air. 25ft (7.5m) in 20 years.
C.o. **'Crippsii' 100, 101,** 326 Broadly conical. Leaves in fronds, drooping slightly at tip, bright golden yellow. 15ft (4.5m) in 20 years.
C.o. **'Filicoides' 100** Fern-spray cypress. Small, bushy, branches straggly. Foliage in hanging, fern-like clusters. Leaves oval, often glandular. 15ft (4.5m) in 20 years.
C.o. **'Lycopodioides' 100** Small, sparsely branched, open-crowned. Leaves closely pressed to shoot, dark green, blunt-tipped, moss-like. 12ft (3.5m) in 20 years.
C.o. **'Mariesii' 119** Small, conical, open. Foliage in loose sprays, variegated yellowish to white in summer, yellow-green in winter.
C.o. **'Nana' 119** Flattened dwarf to 2ft (60cm). Foliage in shell-like sprays. Leaves very small, dark green.
C.o. **'Nana Gracilis' 100,** 319 To 15ft (4.5m). Shell-shaped sprays of dark green foliage. 6ft (1.8m) in 20 years. A.G.M. 1969.
C.o. **'Tetragona Aurea' 100** To 35ft (10.5m). Young trees gaunt, level branches upswept at tips with congested foliage in dense bunches of golden threads, wide-spreading. Leaves bright gold. 15ft (4.5m) in 20 years.
C. pisifera **100** Sawara cypress. Japan. Zone 3. To 50 or 75ft (15 or 23m), conical. Leaves in upturned spreading sprays, narrow-pointed, deep shiny green, becoming darker, white markings underneath. Male 'flowers' minute, pollen shed in spring. Cones abundant, small, green turning brown. Prefers lime-free soils. Fairly slow.
C.p. **'Boulevard' 100, 101,** 118 United States. To 12ft (3.5m). Leaves mossy, densely bunched silver-blue; colouration best in summer and in slight shade. 6ft (1.8m) in 10 years.
C.p. **'Filifera Aurea' 101** To 30 or 40ft (9 or 10.5m), pyramidal or conical, spreading branches, hanging sprays of golden-yellow foliage.
C.p. **'Plumosa Aurea' 118** To 30ft (9m), conical, ascending branches, golden-yellow foliage.
C.p. **'Squarrosa' 118** Japan. To 20 or 30ft (6 or 9m), broadly pyramidal, level-branched. Outer crown dense. Foliage blue-grey on irregular branchlets. Bark red-brown. 25ft (7.5m) in 20 years.
C. thyoides* **100,** 319 White cypress. E. United States. Zone 3. To 70 or 90ft (21.5 or 27.5m), conical. Tiny leaves laterally-paired, sharp pointed, with resin gland on reverse of leaves, waxy green, white edged. Male 'flowers' tiny, dark-brown. Cones small, waxy, blue-purple becoming red-brown. No serious pests or diseases. 25ft (7.5m) in 20 years.
C.t. **'Andelyensis' 100,** 327 To 20ft (6m), narrow, columnar sometimes with multiple spires. Branches crowded with short, blue-green aromatic leaves, turning bronze in winter. Bears a mass of pink male 'flowers'

and tiny cones. Prefers lime-free soils. Slow.
    C.t. **'Ericoides' 100, 101** Low, compact, pyramidal, usually reddish-brown in winter.

CHAMAEROPS *humilis* 122
European fan palm. Mediterranean. Zone 8. To 20ft (6m), trunk often covered with old leaf bases. Palmate leaves 2 to 3ft (60cm to 1m) across.on long, slender stalk. Sexes on separate trees, small yellow flowers. Brown or yellow rounded fruit ½ to 1½ in (1 to 4cm).

CHIONANTHUS 241
Deciduous trees or shrubs. Leaves simple, opposite. Flowers, sexes on separate trees, pure white, in loose, branched clusters. Fruit egg-shaped or oblong, fleshy, dark-blue with single seed. Moist loam and sun.
C. retusus **241** Chinese fringe tree. China. Zone 5. To 20ft (6m), spreading. Leaves oval, entire. Flowers in broad heads, petals strap-shaped, June–July. Fruit ½ in (1cm) long, blue-mauve, Sept.–Oct. 8ft (2.5m) in 20 years.
C. virginicus* **316** Fringe tree. E. United States. Zone 4. To 30ft (9m), shrub or tree, spreading. Leaves narrow, oblong, bright green above, paler, slightly downy beneath, yellow in autumn. Flowers May–June. Fruit ½ to ¾ in (1 to 2cm) long, Sept. 8ft (2.5m) in 20 years.

CHRYSOLEPIS *chrysophylla** 162, 163, 326
Golden chinkapin. W. United States. Zone 7. To 100ft (30m), pyramidal. Leaves leathery, pointed, dark green above, yellow beneath, evergreen. Flowers creamy-white, unisexual on same tree, fluffy spikes, June and July. Fruit, green prickly husk 1 to 3 nuts. Prefers well-drained acid or neutral soils. Tolerates drought.

CINNAMOMUM *camphora* 130, 131
Camphor tree. Tropical Asia, China, Japan. Zone 9. To 100ft (30m), upright. Leaves slender, oval, simple, evergreen, shiny, fragrant, stalked. Flowers greenish-white, in clusters, spring. Sun-loving, needs shelter.

CITRUS 236–7, 326, 327
Evergreen or semi-evergreen trees or shrubs. Leaves simple and aromatic. Flowers usually fragrant. Fruits are oranges, lemons, etc. Sun-loving. Medium growth. Some will grow in Zone 9 if low temperatures are not prolonged.
C. aurantifolia* **237** Lime. India, S.E. Asia. Zone 10. Small, spreading. Leaves ovate, evergreen, shiny green, edges slightly crinkly. Flowers in small clusters, white. Fruit round-oblong, pale green, acid-tasting, ripens irregularly. Pests as *C. sinensis.*
C. aurantifolia × *Fortunella* **237** Limequat. Zone 10. Branches become weighed down by fruits. Leaves lance-shaped, evergreen, thick, dark green above, paler beneath. Fruits oval, light yellow, shiny peel, acid-tasting. Almost hardy, but needs a long, warm summer.
C. **'Aurantium' 237** Seville orange. S. Europe. Zone 9. To 20 or 30ft (6 or 9m), spreading. Leaves oval, pointed, evergreen, winged stalk. Flowers small, white, in flat heads. Fruit round, orange-red, aromatic, bitter, acid. Hardier than *C. sinensis.*
C. limon **236–7** Lemon. India. Zone 10. To 20ft (6m), spreading. Leaves ovate, evergreen, smooth, dark-green, crinkly-edged. Flowers white, slightly flushed, single or paired. Fruit ripens irregularly. Pests as *C. sinensis.*
C. paradisi **237** Grapefruit. S.E. China. Zone 10. To 30 or 50ft (9 or 15m), pyramidal. Leaves ovate, evergreen, light green becoming darker, smooth, edges crinkly, stalked. Flowers in flat heads. Fruit large, pale yellow to orange, flavour pleasant, acid, bitter. Pests as *C. sinensis.*
C. reticulata **237** Mandarin orange, Tangerine. China. Zone 10. Small, spreading. Leaves narrow to oval, pointed, evergreen, dark green, stalked. Fruit flattened at both ends, smaller than *C. sinensis,* yellow to orange-red, sweet-tasting. Hardier than *C. sinensis.* Pests as *C. sinensis.*
    C.r. **'Satsuma' 237** Orangequat. Zone 9. Small bushy tree, sometimes spiny. Leaves ovate, dark shining green. Flowers small. Fruits broad, ovoid, thick, spongy peel, acid pulp. Hardiest of satsuma orange group.
C. sinensis* **236–7** Sweet orange. Cochin, China. Zone 10. To 25 or 40ft (7.5 or 12m), pyramidal. Leaves ovate, evergreen, smooth, shiny, dark green above, lighter beneath. Flowers white, solitary or in small clusters. Fruit roundish, orange or orange-red, smooth, large. Pests include scales, aphids, mites and also fungi and bacterial diseases.
C. **'Ugli' 237** Ugli tree. Zone 10. Upright and straggly tree. Leaves ovate, dark green. Flowers white. Fruit usually light lemon-yellow flushed with apple-green, roundish with thick, nobbly peel, sweetish, flavour between tangerine and grapefruit.

Chionanthus virginicus
Fringe-tree

Flowers in drooping panicles to 6in (15cm), very fragrant. *Petals* (4-6) narrow, ½in (1cm), with purple spots on inner base.

Leaves elliptic or obovate.

Leaves bright green, lustrous above. *Veins* impressed, hairy below *Petioles* ¾in (2cm), stout, hairy.

Margins entire.

Leaves 8in (20cm).

Fruit ¾in (2cm), in panicles to 6in (15cm), 3 per branch, oval, often bloomed. *Flesh* thin, with 1 seed (rarely 2).

Shoots stout with raised lenticels. *Buds* ⅙in (4mm), acute. *Bark* in adpressed plates.

Chrysolepis chrysophylla
Golden chinkapin

Shoots initially golden, flaking, later reddish brown.

Leaves 6in (15cm), oblong-lanceolate, thick, leathery, dark glossy green above, yellow below, evergreen. *Margins* entire, curled under. *Apex* sometimes acute.

Cupules split irregularly.

Seeds ⅝in (1.5cm), 1-3 per fruit, triangular. *Fruit* 1½in (4cm), ripens in second year. *Cupules* covered with branched, slender spines.

Citrus aurantifolia
Lime

Leaves 4in (9cm), ovate, shiny green, evergreen, edges slightly crinkly. *Fruit* round-oblong, pale green, acid-tasting. *Petioles* winged.

Citrus sinensis
Sweet orange

To 40ft (12m). *Crown* dense.
Branches horizontal. *Bole* short.

Shoots occasionally bear spines. *Leaves* 6in (15cm), oblanceolate to ovate. *Petioles* narrowly winged. *Flowers* 1¼in (3cm), white, fragrant, single or in small lax clusters. *Leaves* ovate, shiny, dark green above, lighter beneath.

Fruit 4in (10cm), globose, orange or orange-red, more rarely green or yellow, appear Oct-June. *Skin* shiny, smooth. *Flesh* red-orange.

Cladrastis lutea
Yellow-wood

Leaves *12in (30cm)*.

Leaflets *(5-11)*
4in (10cm),
obovate, widely
spaced.

Veins
impressed.

Bark *smooth, silvery*
grey or brown.

Shoots
slender, shiny.
Cladrastis,
meaning brittle,
refers to the
shoots.

Leaflets *usually alternate but*
variable. **Buds** *naked, in fours,*
hidden by base of petiole.

Cornus controversa
Giant dogwood

To 65ft (20m).
Branches *form tiers.*
Must be open to sun to
flower fully.

Shoots *dark*
red, glabrous.

Bark *grey, smooth, becoming*
cross-ridged.

Petioles
1½in (4cm).

Leaves *5in (12cm), shiny, alternate;*
those of **'Variegata'** *narrower,*
creamy yellow and green, twisted.
Flowers *each ⅝in (1.5cm), in*
upright cymes, June-July.

Cornus kousa
Japanese dogwood

Leaf
margins
entire.

Flowers *appear in dense*
mass in May-June. **Bracts**
2in (5cm), pointed, set
around flowers. **Flowers**
held upright above shoots.
Flower bracts *star-like.*
C. kousa *can be*
distinguished from C.
controversa *(above) by its*
opposite leaves.

Leaves *3½in*
(8cm), variable,
entire, soon glabrous except for
axil tufts, glaucous below.
Petioles *¼in (6mm).* **Shoots**
glabrous.

Fruit *sweet,*
strawberry-like, of
many fleshy drupes,
ripening late
summer.

CLADRASTIS 209, 326
Small group of deciduous trees. Leaves pinnate, leaflets big. Flowers bisexual, white, rarely pinkish, in flat-topped clusters, buds enclosed in swollen base of leaf-stalk. Fruit, narrow, oblong pods, flattened. Wood brittle. Sun-loving.
C. lutea* 209, 316, 327 Yellow-wood. S.E. United States. Zone 3. To 65ft (20m), rounded, spreading. Leaves long, wide oval leaflets, hairless, turning yellow before falling, stalked. Flowers slightly fragrant, June. Seed pods, autumn. Loamy soil; not long-lived on chalk.
C. sinensis 317 Chinese yellow-wood. China. Zone 5. To 80ft (24.5m), spreading. Leaves pinnate, shape variable, light green above, waxy below, rustlike on midrib, stalks downy. Flowers fragrant, summer. Pod long, smooth, Sept. Loamy soil.

CLETHRA 184–5, 327
Small ericaceous trees or shrubs; deciduous and hardy or evergreen and tender. Leaves alternate, simple. Flowers fragrant, white, usually in clusters Fruit a capsule holding many seeds. Lime-free soil.
C. arborea 184–5, 317, 327 Lily-of-the-valley clethra. Madeira. Zone 8/9. To 30ft (9m), large shrub or small tree. Leaves lance-shaped, evergreen, finely toothed, dark green above, pale with scattered hairs below. Flowers ½ in (1cm) wide. Requires mild area, sun or semi-shade sheltered position. 30ft (9m) in 20 years.

COCOS nucifera 123
Coconut palm. Tropics. Zone 10. To 80ft (24.5m), always leaning; trunk thickened at base, surface ringed. Pinnate leaves 10 to 20ft (3 to 6m) long, yellowish green. Unisexual flowers on same tree, on 4 to 6ft (1.2 to 1.8m) long stalk. Fruit, a big nut surrounded by tough fibrous husk.

CORDYLINE australis 319
Cabbage tree. New Zealand. Zone 4. To 40ft (12m), erect trunk forking into erect branches each with dense head 6 to 9ft (1.8 to 2.7m) wide. Leaves narrow, pointed, 6 to 9ft (1.8 to 2.7m) long, evergreen. Flowers small, creamy-white, in hanging clusters, fragrant. Fruit, small white or bluish-white berry.

CORNUS 216–17, 327
Deciduous, seldom evergreen trees or shrubs. Simple leaves, usually opposite. Small, bisexual flowers mostly white, in clusters. Oval, fleshy fruits containing a stone. Normally easy to cultivate. Subject to mildew in Britain, leaf-spot and crown canker in America.
C. alternifolia A fine-foliaged American dogwood, the only one with alternate leaves. Branches in 'wedding-cake' layers. No flowers to speak of, but good autumn colour. To 25ft (7.5m).
    C.a. 'Argentea' A white-variegated form, extremely graceful and eye-catching. To 15ft (4.5m).
C. capitata 217, 326 Bentham's cornel, Evergreen dogwood. Himalaya. Zone 8. Evergreen small tree, bushy. Young shoots downy. Leaves leathery, oval, lance-shaped, dull grey green, hairy. Minute flowers surrounded by bracts, sulphur-yellow. Fruit strawberry-shaped. 20ft (6m) in 20 years.
C. controversa* 216, 217, 326 Giant dogwood. Japan, China. Zone 5. To 65ft (20m), horizontal branches in tiers. Leaves alternate, oval, pointed, dark glossy green above, waxy beneath. Flowers white, in flattish heads, profuse. Fruit blue-black, roundish. Chalk-tolerant. 25ft (7.5m) in 20 years.
    C.c. 'Variegata' 217 Zone 5. Small tree, form similar to type. Leaves with silver-white to pale yellow border. 12ft (3.5m) in 20 years.
C. 'Eddie's White Wonder' A showy American hybrid (*C. florida x nuttallii*) with giant white flowers in spring.
C. florida 42, **216**, 316, 326, 327 Flowering dogwood. E. United States. Zone 4. To 40ft (12m), wide-spreading tree. Leaves oval, dark green with scattered down above, pale beneath. Flowers insignificant, spring, but four white bracts, 2in (5cm) long, expand in May after enclosing bud in winter. Red berries in winter. Sun or semi-shade. Dislikes poor, shallow chalk soils. 10ft (3m) in 20 years.
    C.f. 'Cherokee Chief' 216 Flower bracts deep rose red.
    C.f. 'Pendula' 326 Stiffly pendulous branches.
    C.f. 'Rubra' 216 Variable, flower bracts rosy pink. Less hardy than the type. A.G.M. 1937.
C. kousa* 216, 316–17, 326, 327 Japanese dogwood. Japan, Korea, Zone 5. To 25ft (7.5m), shrub or small tree. Leaves oval, pointed, crimson-bronze in autumn. Flowers small, inconspicuous, attractive large white bracts. Fruits strawberry-like. Dislikes poor, shallow, chalky soils. Moderately sunny location. 12ft (3.5m) in 20 years. A.G.M. 1969.

C.k. chinensis **216** Chinese dogwood. China. Taller, more open than *C. kousa*. Leaves slightly bigger, flower bracts slightly longer. A.G.M. 1969.
C. mas* **217,** 316 Cornelian cherry. C. and S. Europe. Zone 4. To 25ft (7.5m), shrub or small tree, dense branching. Leaves oval, pointed, dark dull green, reddish-purple in autumn. Flowers small, yellow, late winter, in short-stalked, flat-headed clusters on leafless twigs. Fruit bright red, edible. Resists insect or disease pests in America. Sun-loving; tolerates dryness and exposure. 20ft (6m) in 20 years. A.G.M. 1924.
　　C.m. **'Variegata'** Exceptionally pale, beautiful, white-variegated form.
C. nuttallii **216,** 316, 326 Pacific dogwood. W. United States. Zone 7. To 80ft (24.5m). Leaves oval, downy, good autumn colour. Flowers small, purple and green, surrounded by 4 to 8 large white bracts, flushed with pink; attractive. Dislikes shallow chalk soils, extreme cold. Sun or semi-shade. 25ft (7.5m) in 20 years.

CORYLUS 171, 327

Deciduous shrubs, rarely trees. Leaves oval, toothed. Flowers, male and female on same tree, male catkins hanging in winter, female flowers in small clusters, opening in spring. Fruit, ovoid nut held in toothed cup, mostly edible, ripen in autumn. Lime-tolerant, suited to chalk soil. Occasional bacterial blight in America, fungal fruit rot, bark fungi in Europe. Nut weevil attacks young nuts.
C. avellana* **64, 171,** 326 Hazel, Cobnut. Europe, W. Asia. N. Africa. Zone 3. To 11ft (3.3m), shrub or small tree. Leaves roundish, terminal half open lobed. Nuts in shallow lobed husk. Mainly attractive for male catkins, although leaves turn yellow in autumn. Sun or shade. 15ft (4.5m) in 20 years.
　　C.a. **'Contorta' 171,** 326 Corkscrew hazel, Harry Lauder's walking stick. To 10ft (3m), twigs twisted and curled. Attractive in late winter when in catkin. Slow-growing.
C. californica **171** Californian hazel. California. Zone 5. To 10ft (3m), shrub. Leaves downy beneath. Fruit bristly with a short beak.
C. colurna **171,** 326 Turkish hazel, Turkish filbert. S.E. Europe. W. Asia. Zone 4. To 80ft (24.5m), symmetrical, pyramidal form. Leaves pointed at apex; upper side dark green, lower downy along midrib. Nuts held in husk fringed with lobes, fine down, in groups of 3 or more. Thrives in hot summers and cold winters, as in central Europe. Sun-loving. 35ft (10.5m) in 20 years.
C. maxima **'Purpurea' 171,** 326 Purple-leaf filbert. Leaves and catkins coppery purple.

COTINUS 235, 326, 327

Deciduous shrubs or trees. Simple alternate leaves with slender stalks. Sexes sometimes on separate trees. Small, egg-shaped, fleshy fruit. 12ft (3.5m) in 20 years.
C. americanus (C. obovatus) **234–5** American smoke tree. S.E. United States. Zone 5. To 40ft (12m), shrub or small tree. Leaves wedge-shaped ovals, medium length, often reddish purple; brilliant autumn colouring. Flowers in greenish feathery masses; sexes separate. Fruit sparse. Richer soil gives poorer colour. Tolerant of dry soils. Sun-loving.
C. coggygria **235** Smoke tree. Venetian sumach. Central Europe. Zone 5. Shrub or small tree, to 15ft (4.5m). Smooth rounded green leaves, good autumn colours. Flowers fawn-coloured plumes, turning smoky grey. Preferable to *C. americanus*. A.G.M. 1969.
　　C.c. **'Royal Purple' 326** Leaves deep wine-purple. A.G.M. 1969.
C. obovatus See *Cotinus americanus*

COTONEASTER 191, 327

Evergreen and deciduous trees and shrubs. Leaves simple, without teeth and lobes, unlike the closely allied *Crataegus*. Flowers all similar, ⅓ to ½ in (7mm to 1cm) wide, white or rose-tinted, usually in profuse clusters, attractive to bees. Fruits round to oval; best types brilliant red, thornless. All soils. Sun-loving; some species tolerant of shade. Hardy. Susceptible to fireblight and some rusts.
C. **'Cornubia' 191,** 317 Zone 7. To 20 or 30ft (6 or 9m), spreading. Leaves narrow, oval, pointed, semi-evergreen, smooth above, slightly hairy below. Fruit profuse, large. Fast-growing. A.G.M. 1969.
C. **'Exburiensis'** A yellow-fruited arching little tree resembling *C. watereri*. *C.* 'Rothschildianus' is very similar. A.G.M. 1969.
C. frigidus* **318** Himalaya. Zone 7. To 20 or 40ft (6 or 12m), spreading. Leaves elliptic, deciduous, smooth, woolly below at first; dull green. Flowers, late spring or early summer. Fruit clustered, pea-sized, crimson, autumn to winter. 25ft (7.5m) in 20 years. A.G.M. 1925.
C. **'Hybridus Pendulus'** Cascading branches grafted on an upright stem. Good red fruit. Ideal for a very small garden.
C. **'Rothschildianus'** See *C.* **'Exburiensis'**

Cornus mas
Cornelian cherry

To 25ft (7.5m).

Crown spreading on several main stems. **Bark** scaly, becoming positively reptilian in old trees.

Bud scales valvate.

Fruit ⅝in (1.5cm). **Pedicels** ½in (1cm).

Flowers in clusters 1in (2.5cm) wide; appear before leaves.

Leaves 4in (10cm), with adpressed hairs on both sides. **Veins** forward-curved. **Petioles** ¾in (2cm).

Flowers ⅙in (4mm), with 4 bracts at cluster base.

Corylus avellana
European hazel, Cobnut

Male catkins 2in (5cm), open half-yellow in Feb.

Female catkins ¼in (6mm).

To 11ft (3.3m). **Crown** shrubby.

Nuts in papery, toothed bracts.

Nuts ¾in (2cm), delicious, ripen brown in clusters of 1-4.

Shoots covered in long stiff hairs with swollen tips. **Leaves** 4in (10cm), hairy above and below, doubly serrate.

Cotoneaster frigidus
Tree cotoneaster

Bark scaly.

To 40ft (12m). **Crown** wide, rounded, sometimes on several stems, often leaning. **Branches** arch, then level.

Flowers set in dense 2½in (6cm) heads, open June.

Leaves 5in (13cm), soft, entire, semi-evergreen; some forms more crinkled. **Fruit** ¼in (6mm), abundant.

Fruit ¼in (6mm), abundant. A pome with 2 nutlets, ripening September, persistent.

Crataegus crus-galli
Cockspur thorn

Leaves 3¹/₂in (8cm), dark green, smooth, with rich orange tints in autumn. *Fruit* ⁵/₈in (1.5cm), 2-seeded, sometimes persists in winter.

Leaves serrate, glabrous.

Shoots and spines purple-brown. Spines to 3in (7.5cm), vicious.

Crataegus monogyna
Common hawthorn, Single-seed hawthorn

Leaves 4in (10cm), deeply lobed, with few teeth. *Thorns to 1in (2.5cm).*

Veins pinnate.

To 35ft (10.5m). Crown dense. Bole short, fluted.

Flowers in corymbs of up to 16, appear with leaves in May.

Shoots purplish, stout. Buds ¹/₁₀in (2mm), glabrous, set in pairs at bases of spines, start to open in late winter.

Fruit ¹/₂in (1cm), 1-seeded, has persistent calyx, profusely set, ripening September.

Cryptomeria japonica
Japanese cedar

'Elegans' leaves (right) long, ³/₄in (2cm), soft, spirally set, becoming red-bronze in autumn and winter.

Cones ³/₄in (2cm), globular, ripening in 1 season. *Scales* (20-40) each with 4-6 hooked spines.

Crown narrow conic, unevenly dense. Branches spaced, horizontal or billowing, tips upswept.

Bark soft, fibrous, fissured, peeling on old trees.

Leaves of C. japonica *(above) long,* ⁵/₈in (1.5cm), set spirally, turning slightly bronze in winter.

C. salicifolius Tall arching Chinese evergreen, often with masses of fruit. Forms include ground-covering kinds.

C. × *watereri* **191,** 327 Zone 7. To 15ft (4.5m), spreading, hybrid. Leaves tapered at both ends, semi-evergreen, smooth when fully developed. Fruits small, in clusters. Fast-growing.

CRATAEGOMESPILUS dardarii 193

Bronvaux medlar. Zone 5. To 15 or 20ft (4.5 or 6m), spreading, grafted hybrid, consists of core of hawthorn enveloped with medlar. Leaves yellow to orange in autumn, ovallish, simple, deciduous, downy on both sides, possibly finely toothed, short stalk. Flowers white in domed heads, very fluffy. Fruits clustered, like small medlars. Occasionally thorny.

CRATAEGUS 192–3, 327

Hawthorns. Deciduous trees or shrubs. Usually thorny. Leaves simple, toothed or lobed. Flowers usually white and clustered, late spring/early summer. Fruit apple-like, small, variously coloured. Susceptible to fireblight, juniper rust, hawthorn blight, lacebugs, mites, leaf miners, various borers and others. Very hardy. All soils.

C. arnoldiana Vigorous American species (a variant of *C. mollis*) with dense thorny branches and good big fruit. To 20ft (6m).

C. crus-galli* **193,** 317, 319, 326 Cockspur thorn. E. and C. United States. Zone 4. To 40ft (12m), wide-spreading. Leaves wedge-shaped, shiny, smooth, dark green, stalked. Flowers small. Fruits, crimson, winter. Thorns 1½ to 3in (4 to 7.5cm) long, branched.

C. × *grignonensis* **193** Zone 5. Small hybrid. Leaves with 2 to 4 toothed lobes, green until winter. Flowers white, late summer. Fruits bright red.

C. laciniata (C. orientalis) **193** S.E. Europe, W. Asia. Zone 5. To 20ft (6m), rounded spreading head. Leaves with 5 to 9 toothed lobes, hairy above, woolly below. Flowers June. Fruit roundish, hairy, orange-red, October.

C. × *lavallei* **193,** 326 Zone 4. To 20 or 25ft (6 or 7.5m), spreading to upright, hybrid. Leaves long, shiny, dark green, often remain until mid-winter. Flowers small, numerous. Fruit orange to brick-red, autumn and winter. Thorns stout, few. To 20ft (6m) in 20 years. A.G.M. 1925.

C. mollis **193** Downy hawthorn. C. United States. Zone 4. To 35ft (10.5m), wide-spreading with stout thorns. Leaves oval with shallow lobes, downy. Flowers profuse, April and May. Fruit pear-shaped, red, Aug.–Sept.

C. monogyna* **192–3** Common hawthorn, May. Europe, N. Africa, W. Asia. Zone 4. To 35ft (10.5m), spreading. Leaves 3- to 7-lobed, dark green, stalked. Flowers in tight clusters, fragrant. Fruits small, red, usually single-seeded, autumn. Many short, rigid thorns.

   C.m. **'Biflora' 193** Glastonbury thorn. Leaves produced earlier than *C. monogyna*. Occasionally flowers in mid-winter (if mild) as well as spring; fewer flowers than species.

   C.m. **'Stricta' 326** Small upright form.

C. nitida **193** Glossy hawthorn. E. United States. Zone 4. To 20 or 35ft (6 or 10.5m), rounded. Leaves oblong, shiny, roughly lobed, double-toothed. Fruit round, dark red, persists through winter.

C. orientalis See *C. laciniata*

C. orientalis sanguinea **318** Red-fruiting form of *C. orientalis*.

C. oxyacantha **192–3,** 326, 327 Hawthorn, May. N.W. and C. Europe. Zone 4. To 25ft (7.5m) spreading. Leaves 3- to 5-lobed, smooth except at first, glossy, dark green, toothed, stalked. Flowers small, in flat heads. Fruit scarlet, autumn, several-seeded.

   C.o. **'Paul's Scarlet' 193** Double-flowered form. Fruit sparse.

   C.o. **'Plena' 316** White double flowers. A.G.M. 1969.

C. phaenopyrum **193,** 317, 326 Washington hawthorn. S.E. United States. Zone 4. To 35ft (10.5m), upright, narrow. Leaves triangular, possibly lobed, smooth, glossy, bright green, sharply toothed, stalked. Flowers numerous in flat heads, small. Fruit shiny, scarlet, winter persisting until spring. Slender-thorned. Good autumn colour.

C. pinnatifida major **193** Large Chinese hawthorn. China. Zone 5. To 18ft (5.5m), spreading. Leaves wedge-shaped to round, downy along the midrib above and below, deep lobe at base, often double-toothed, glossy dark green above, paler below. Flowers small, in flat heads. Fruit shiny, crimson, with tiny dots, winter. Thorns absent or short.

C. tanacetifolia **318** 'Tansy-leaved thorn'. A rare small thorn, from Asia Minor, scarcely armed, with deep-cut grey leaves like *C. laciniata* but yellow, small apple-like fruits.

CRYPTOMERIA 69, 98, 116–17

Evergreen tree, sun-loving, fairly hardy.

C. japonica* **116–17,** 326 Japanese cedar. Japan, C. China. Zone 5. To 150ft (45m), narrowly conical, older trees broader and domed. Leaves spirally arranged, short, blunt points. Sexes separate on same tree; male 'flowers' in terminal clusters, roundish, pale green in summer, pale yellow in winter; female 'flowers' green rosettes. Cones globose, rough, green ripening to dull dark brown. Likes moisture. 40 to 55ft (12 to 17m) in 20 years.

C.j. **'Elegans' 116,** 326 Broad, rounded tree to 70ft (21.5m). Leaves juvenile, spreading outwards and downwards, grey-blue, soft to touch, short, red-bronze in autumn and winter. Cones rare, smaller and smoother than *C. japonica*. 20ft (6m) in 20 years.

C.j. **'Lobbii' 316** Zone 5. Narrowly conical. Short branches upturned at ends. Foliage dense. Hardiest form. 35ft (10.5m) in 20 years.

C.j. **'Nana' 119** Dwarf, to 3ft (1m), erect twisted branches with crowded branchlets. Shoot tips curved. Slow-growing.

C.j. **'Pygmaea' 119** Compact round bush to 6ft (1.8m). Leaves short, needle-like, apple-green. Slow-growing.

C.j. sinensis **318** Commonest *Cryptomeria* in cultivation in the West.

CUNNINGHAMIA lanceolata **112, 117,** 318
Chinese fir. C. and S. China. Zone 7. To 150ft (45m), spreading, weeping branch tips, evergreen. Leaves in spirals, lance-shaped, bright green above, with 2 white bands beneath; bronze in autumn. Male 'flowers' in clusters of about 12, female 'flowers' with leafy scales; both open in spring. Cones single or clustered, oval.

× *CUPRESSOCYPARIS leylandii** 99, **101,** 326, 327
Leyland cypress. Zone 4. To 90ft (27.5m), broadly columnar, tapering. Evergreen. Very adaptable. 50ft (15m) in 20 years.

C.l. **'Castlewellan'** Zone 7. A greeny-gold form of almost equal vigour to the green, introduced in 1970. Green in winter.

C.l. **'Haggerston Grey' 101** Columnar but rather open form with irregular sprays of grey-green foliage.

C.l. **'Leighton Green' 101** Narrow columnar. Foliage green in flattened fern-like sprays.

C.l. **'Robinson's Gold'** Zone 7. A more recent (1975) golden form which stays more gold in winter than 'Castlewellan'.

× *Cupressocyparis notabilis* (*Chamaecyparis nootkatensis* × *Cupressus glabra*) Zone 7. Another vigorous bigeneric hybrid, introduced about 1960. more open in habit than the 'Leyland', palish green with flatter sprays.

× *Cupressocyparis ovensii* (*Chamaecyparis nootkatensis* x *Cupressus lusitanica*) Zone 8. A similar vigorous new hybrid, but darker green and more drooping like *C. nootkatensis*.

CUPRESSUS 94–101, 327
Cypresses. Evergreen, mostly columnar or pyramidal. Leaves minute, scale-like, pressed on branch. 'Flowers' separate on same tree; cylindrical heads on male 'flowers'. Cones round to oval. Tolerant of various soils but often tender.

C. abramsiana **96–7,** 319 Santa Cruz cypress. California. Zone 7. Conical to columnar. Leaves blunt-pointed, pale green; resin gland inconspicuous or absent. Cones green ripening brown. 50 to 60ft (15 to 18m) in 20 years.

C. arizonica See *Cupressus glabra*

C. bakeri **97,** 319 Modoc cypress. California. Zone 5. To 35 or 50ft (10.5 or 15m), open, conical. Leaves grey-green, short, pointed, with obvious resin gland. Cones grey-brown, warty. 15ft (4.5m) in 20 years.

C. cashmeriana **97,** 326 Kashmir cypress. Zone 8. Conical, spreading, ultimately pendulous. Leaves in opposite pairs, blue-white, sharply acute, hard. Grows fast under glass. 25ft (7.5m) in 20 years.

C. forbesii 319 Rare small cypress from California with flaking bark.

C. funebris 318 'Mourning cypress'. C. China. Zone 9. To 60ft (18m). Flat hanging branchlets. Leaves bluish-green. Cones small, dark brown.

C. glabra* **94–5, 96, 97,** 319 Smooth Arizona cypress. Central Arizona. Zone 6. 25 or 50ft (7.5 or 15m), conical. Leaves toothed, usually waxy, glandular, resin whitish. 30ft (9m) in 20 years.

C.g. **'Pyramidalis' 97,** 326 Conical or pyramidal. Shoots upturned at tips. Leaves blue-green, heavily white spotted. 25ft (7.5m) in 20 years. A.G.M. 1969.

C. goveniana 97 Gowen cypress. California cypress. California. 30 or 70ft (9 or 21.5m), dense, bright green, columnar in Britain; open, wide, conical in California. Leaves pale green or yellow-green, fragrant. Male 'flowers' small, yellow; females small, becoming grey. Cones shiny brown, bunched well back on main shoot. 35ft (10.5m) in 20 years.

C. guadalupensis 319 'Tecate cypress'. Vigorous, erect, fairly hardy cypress from Mexico. Red bark.

C. lusitanica **97,** 319 Mexican cypress. Cedar of Goa. Mexico, Guatemala. Zone 9. To 100ft (30m). Branches spreading, slightly pendulous. Leaves

---

Cupressocyparis leylandii
Leyland cypress

Cones (when present) 1¹/₄in (3cm), globular, brown.

Foliage dark green or grey, in irregular flattish planes (with neither the truly flat sprays of Chamaecyparis nor the more radial arrangement of Cupressus); less dense near leader. Leaves slightly incurved with ridged glands.

To 90ft (27.5m). Crown dense, columnar with conic or rounded conic apex. Branches ascend steeply. Leader leans slightly, not drooping as in Lawson cypress. Bark initially smooth, then ridged becoming stringy.

'Castlewellan' is extremely vigorous and its foliage, arranged in plumes, turns yellow-green in winter.

Cupressus glabra
Smooth Arizona cypress

Foliage open, branching at almost 90°.

Bark smooth, flaked, can be cherry-red.

Cones ³/₄in-1in (2-3cm), often clustered and persistent, bloomed at first. Scales have low, curved spikes.

To 50ft (15m). Crown conical or ovoid, fairly dense, with blunt apex. Branches ascend. Branchlets horizontal. Bole short. Distinguished by its bark (left).

**Cupressus macrocarpa
Monterey cypress**

Young crown columnar conic with erect leader.

*'Lutea'
(right):
To 80 ft
(24.5m),
perhaps
slightly hardier than the type.
Foliage thicker, grows more
slowly, greener when planted
in shade.*

Leaves small,
*¹/10in (2mm),
scale-like.*

Bark ridged.

Branches ascend at base,
level near apex.

To 110ft (33m). Habit: usually this shape
when mature but can broaden and
become flat-topped.

Foliage slender but set
densely, lemon-scented
when crushed.
Thicker, shorter on
older trees; salt-
resistant. **Shoots**
forward-pointing,
almost cylindrical,
covered by leaves.

Cones to
*1¹/2in (4cm)
when
mature,
with 8 or 10
peltate
scales.*

**Davidia involucrata
Dove tree**

*Flowers ³/4in
(2cm) wide.*

To 65ft (20m). Crown
domed. **Bole** short.
Branches radiate outwards.
Bark purplish, flaking
brown, with vertical fissures.

Bracts large, to 8in (20.5cm),
in uneven pairs, paper-thin.
Buds ⁵/8in (1.5cm), conic, shiny.

Leaves 6in (15cm), vivid green,
shiny above, softly hairy below.
Veins impressed. *Petioles* 6in
(15cm).

Shoots
glabrous.

Lenticels
pale.

Fruit 1¹/4in (3cm),
hard, fleshy, ribbed,
ripening purple, with
prominent lenticels.
Pedicels 4in (10cm).

pointed, grey-green. Cones small, waxy, brown when mature. Unsuited to cold climates. 40ft (12m) in 20 years.
C. lusitanica × macrocarpa Zone 8. A hybrid distributed by Hilliers, so far nameless but vigorous and intriguing with long dark horizontal branches almost recalling a cedar. 30ft (9m) in 20 years.
C. macrocarpa* 96, 97, 101, 319, 326, 327 Monterey cypress. California. Zone 7. 70 or 110ft (21.5 or 33m), columnar or conical, broadening with age. Leaves bright green, dulling later, triangular, close to stem. Cones purple-brown. May succumb to frost but withstands exposure, especially to sea winds. 45 to 60ft (13.5 to 18m) in 20 years.
    C.m. 'Donard Gold' 96 Medium height, conical or broadly columnar. Leaves golden yellow. 40ft (12m) in 20 years.
    C.m. 'Goldcrest' 96, 97 Medium height, narrowly columnar. Juvenile leaves rich yellow.
    C.m. 'Lutea' 96 50 or 80ft (15 or 24.5m) wide, columnar. Leaves yellow, becoming green. Cones yellow. Good against sea winds. 40ft (12m) in 20 years.
C. sargentii 319 'Sargent cypress'. Small attractive cypress from California.
C. sempervirens 94, 95, 96, 318, 326 Italian cypress, Mediterranean cypress. Mediterranean. Zone 7. To 75ft (23m), columnar. Leaves dark green, thick and dense on old trees. Male 'flowers' terminal, greenish. Cones shining green, becoming dark brown, each scale with central spike. 35ft (10.5m) in 20 years.
C. torulosa 318 Bhutan or Himalayan cypress. Tall and cedar-like. Not very hardy.

CYDONIA 194–5
Mostly deciduous trees and shrubs. Leaves simple. Flowers in clusters or solitary. Fruit with many-seeded cells distinguishing group from related *Pyrus*; fragrant, edible when cooked. All soils. Sun-loving. Hardy. Subject to leaf blight, fruit spot, mildew, fire-blight.
C. oblonga 194, 195, 327 Common quince. N. Persia, Turkestan. Zone 4. To 25ft (7.5m), spreading. Leaves ovallish, deciduous, underside covered with pale grey matted hairs, upper surface dark green, often turning deep yellow before falling. Flowers 2in (5cm) across, solitary, 5-petalled, white or pale pink, late spring. Fruit pear-shaped, golden yellow, acid-tasting when raw.

CYTISUS battandieri 211, 317, 327
Morocco. Zone 3. To 15ft (4.5m) or more, upright, rarely tree-like. Leaves compound, stalked, semi-evergreen or deciduous, with fine silver hairs. Flowers in ovoid heads, golden yellow, pineapple-like fragrance, summer. Pods upright, to 2in (5cm) long, hairy. Prefers neutral or acid soils; tolerates chalk if not too dry. Sun-loving. Subject to rust, fungal die-back.

D

DACRYDIUM 111
Evergreen trees related to yews. Juvenile leaves awl-shaped; adult leaves fine, scale-like on hanging branchlets. Sexes usually on separate trees; seed produced in fleshy cup. Few are hardy.
D. cupressinum 111 Rimu, Red pine New Zealand. Zone 9. To 60 or 100ft (18 or 30m), pyramidal and weeping at first, round-headed when mature. Leaves lance-shaped, small at first; mature leaves needle-like or incurved, blunt, with central ridge on reverse. Male 'flowers' small, green. 12ft (3.5m) in 20 years.
D. franklinii 111, 319, 326 Huon pine. Tasmania. Zone 9. To 100ft (30m), pyramidal, evergreen with drooping branches. Leaves small, dense, overlapping, bright green. Fruits nutlike. 12ft (3.5m) in 20 years.
Dactylis See **Phoenix canariensis, P. dactylifera**

DAVIDIA 218–19, 327
Hardy medium-sized trees related to dogwoods. Leaves simple, alternate, toothed, deciduous. Flowers small, inconspicuous, above 2 big, unequal-sized bracts. Male and bisexual flowers on same tree in dense round heads. Fruit, single, pear-shaped, contains hard nut. Any fertile soil.
D. involucrata* 218, 316, 326, 327 Dove tree, Ghost tree, Pocket-handkerchief tree. C. and W. China. Zone 6. To 65ft (20m). Leaves medium length, vivid green, broadly oval with fine point, upper surface with hairs, lower surface pale felted. Outstanding features include large creamy-white bracts, sometimes 8in (20.5cm) long, round flowers in early summer. Fruit green, purplish bloom. Prefers sun or semi-shade. 25ft (7.5m) in 20 years. A.G.M. 1969.

D.i. vilmoriniana 219, 318, 326, 327 (Same vernacular names as above). China. Zone 5. Leaves hairless. Fruits more oval than *D. involucrata*, horticulturally similar. A.G.M. 1969.

DIOSPYROS 188–9
Evergreen and deciduous trees and shrubs. Leaves simple. Flowers small, inconspicuous, unisexual on separate trees. Fruit is large, juicy berry. Mainly tender, some species hardy.
D. kaki 188, 317, 318, 326, 327 Chinese or kaki persimmon. China. Zone 7. To 45ft (13.5m). Leaves medium to long, oval, deciduous, tapering at both ends, glossy green above, downy below. Fruit up to 3in (7.5cm) across, orange to bright yellow, edible. Tolerates dryness. Sun-loving. 15ft (4.5m) in 20 years.
D. lotus 318 Date plum. Female trees bear purple or yellow tomato-like fruit.
D. virginiana* 188–9, 327 Common persimmon. N. America. Zone 4. To 100ft (30m), with pendulous branches. Leaves medium length, oval with pointed tip, glossy green above, pale beneath. Male flowers solitary, twos or threes; female flowers solitary, yellowish white. Fruit yellow to orange, edible after frost. 15ft (4.5m) in 20 years.

DIPTERONIA sinensis 318
Chinese shrub related to maples; red elm-like seed clusters in autumn.

DISANTHUS cercidifolius 132, 326, 327
Japan. Zone 7. To 15ft (4.5m), slender branches. Leaves roundish, dull bluish-green above, paler beneath, deciduous. Flowers small, dark purple, in pairs. October. Fruit, an oval capsule holding several shiny black seeds. Moist well-drained, lime-free soil, semi-shade.

DRIMYS winteri 319
'Winter bark': small evergreen with big leaves, fragrant white flowers in spring. S. America. Zone 7. Not for chalk soils.

E

EHRETIA dicksonii 242
China, Formosa, Liukiu Isles. Zone 7. To 35ft (10.5m), large shrub or small tree, deciduous. Young shoots slightly downy. Leaves oblong, downy hairs. Flowers clustered, small, white, beautifully fragrant, June. Fruit greenish-yellow. Young shoots slightly susceptible to frost. 20ft (6m) in 20 years.

ELAEAGNUS angustifolia* 215, 326, 327
Russian olive, Oleaster. S. Europe, W. Asia. Zone 2. To 25ft (7.5m), deciduous shrub or small tree, often spiny branches. Leaves medium length, alternate, silver-grey, scaly, simple, lance-shaped. Flowers clustered, bisexual, small, silvery outside, yellow inside, fragrant, petalless, bell-shaped. Fruit silvery-yellow, oval scaly berries, fleshy, sweet, edible. Dislikes shallow chalk soils. Sun-loving, tolerates dryness. Normally disease- and pest-free. 10ft (3m) in 20 years.

EMBOTHRIUM coccineum* 215, 316, 326, 327
Chilean firebush. Chile. Zone 8. To 40ft (12m), shrub or small tree, upright. Leaves medium length, dark glossy green, leathery, lance-shaped or oval, evergreen. Bark, smooth. Flowers orange-scarlet, in short clusters, May–June; short-lived. Needs lime-free soil. Shade- and shelter-loving. 35ft (10.5m) in 20 years.
    E.c. lanceolatum 215, 328 Norquinco Valley, Chile. Leaves long, narrow, strap-shaped. Flowers red, profuse, clusters. Dislikes alkaline soils. Hardy. 25ft (7.5m) in 20 years.

EMMENOPTERIS henryi
China. Zone 8. A very rare small tree of great quality. Large soft ovate leaves open bronze. Its white flowers with showy bracts have appeared in Italy, but not in Britain. 15ft (4.5m) in 20 years.

ERICA arborea 184, 185, 326, 327
Tree heath. Mediterranean. Zone 7. To 15 or 20ft (4.5 or 6m), rounded shrub or tree. Leaves minute, evergreen. Flowers small, round, whitish, fragrant, in big pyramidal clusters, spring. Fruit, small roundish capsules holding minute seeds. Dislikes lime, thrives on sandy soil.
E. canaliculata S. Africa. Zone 9. White to pale pink winter-flowering tree heath of great delicacy and beauty. To 25ft (7.5m).

Diospyros virginiana
Common persimmon

Flowers ³/₄in (2cm), open in July.

Bark black or dark grey, cracked into squares.

Leaves to 6in (15cm), waved, paler below.

Calyx 4-lobed, persistent.

Leaves dark, glossy above.

Fruit 1¹/₂in (4cm), yellow to orange.

Shoots slender, downy or glabrous. *Buds* small.

Elaeagnus angustifolia
Russian olive, Oleaster

Flowers ¹/₂in (1cm), bell-shaped, short-stalked, solitary or in threes at leaf bases. *Leaves* 4in (9cm), oblong or lanceolate.

To 25ft (7.5m). *Crown* rounded, spreading.

Bole often leans.

Bark fissured, peeling.

Shoots with silvery scales, sometimes spined.

Leaves dull, scaly above, silvery scaled, dotted below. Alternate, simple, fragrant.

Fruit ³/₄in (2cm), silvery-yellow, oval scaly berries, fleshy, sweet and edible.

Embothrium coccineum
Chilean firebrush

To 40ft (12m). *Crown* slender, often on several boles. *Bark* smooth.

Leaves 6in (15cm), entire, leathery, glossy above, glaucous green below, shape variable.

Flowers 2in (5cm), tubular, comprising 4 linear segments curving back to reveal long anthers. Orange-scarlet. *Racemes* 4in (10cm). *Fruit* to 2in (5cm), woody, on long, red peduncle.

Eucalyptus globulus
Blue gum

Juvenile leaves opposite, sessile, glaucous blue.

Leaves to 9-12in (25-30cm), lanceolate or sickle-shaped, blue-green, glossy, alternate, on a short petiole. They smell of camphor. Apex acuminate, often curved.

Flower buds glaucous, ridged, wrinkled, 1in (2.5cm).

Flowers 1¹/₂in (4cm), solitary or rarely in twos or threes, a cluster of creamy-white stamens.

Fruit 1¹/₄in (3cm), semi-spherical, ridged, sessile, blue-white.

Eucalyptus gunnii
Cider gum

Fruit in threes, ¹/₃in (8mm).

Adult leaves (left), 4in (10cm), stalked, alternate.

To 100ft (30m). Crown conic, with a wispy halo when growing fast. Bark peels in orangey strips to expose smooth, pale surface below.

Juvenile leaves sessile, opposite.

Eucalyptus niphophila
Snow gum

Flowers in clusters of 9-11, with mass of creamy-white stamens and common stalk. Buds set the previous summer.

Leaves sickle-shaped with hooked apexes.

Trunk distinctive green, grey and cream, often multiple. Bloomed snow-white, occasionally red-brown.

Leaves 5¹/₂in (14cm), thick, hard. Petioles ³/₄in (2cm), wrinkled.

ERIOBOTRYA japonica
Loquat. China and Japan. Zone 8. The largest-leaved evergreen hardy in most of Britain. Noble pointed leathery leaves with fawn felt beneath. Fragrant whitish flowers in mild winters. Edible yellow fruit. Best in shelter. 15ft (4.5m) in 10 years.

EUCALYPTUS 64, 101, 114, **212–14**, 326, 327
Evergreen trees, rarely shrubs. Adult leaves alternate and hanging, juvenile leaves opposite, often waxy greyish white. Flowers white, yellow or red, usually in small clusters; numerous stamens are main feature. Fruit funnel-shaped capsule holding many small seeds. Deep, moist loam. Fast-growing.
E. caesia 214 W. Australia. Zone 9. To 27ft (8m). Bark brownish, peeling to reveal green inner bark. All well-drained soils.
E. camaldulensis 213 River red gum. E. Australia. Zone 9. To 120ft (36m), often spreading, short, thick trunk. Juvenile leaves ovate; adult leaves to 1ft (30cm) long, stalked, narrow, tapered, dull, often pale. Stalked white flowers.
E. citriodora 214 Lemon-scented gum. Queensland. Zone 8. To 80 or 130ft (24.5 or 40m), narrow. Juvenile leaves medium length, oblong, stalked, bristly; adult leaves narrow, tapered. Flowers clustered in leaf axils. Fruit on long stalks. Bark smooth, white to pinkish.
E. coccifera 212, 213, 319 Tasmanian snow gum. Tasmania. Zone 5. To 110ft (33m). Juvenile leaves short, unstalked; adult leaves medium length with bluish-grey bloom. Flowers clustered in leaf axils, 5 to 7 on short stalk. Bark smooth, greyish. 55ft (17m) in 20 years.
E. ficifolia 213, 317 Red-flowering gum. S.W. Australia. Zone 10. To 30ft (9m). Juvenile leaves medium length, stalked, ovate, bristly; adult leaves longer, narrow or oval, darker above. Flowers red, 3 to 7 on long stalk.
E. globulus* 212, 213, 319, 326 Blue gum. Tasmania. Zone 9. To 180ft (55m). Juvenile leaves medium length, oval, unstalked; adult leaves longer, narrow, deep lustrous blue-green, stalked. Flowers white, single or in threes. Bark blue-grey, smooth. 70 to 90ft (21.5 to 27.5m) in 20 years.
E. gunnii* 213, 214, 319, 322 Cider gum. Tasmania. Zone 7. To 100ft (30m). Juvenile leaves short, oval, green or bloomed, unstalked; adult leaves medium length, narrow or oval, green or bloomed, stalked. Flowers in threes on stalk in leaf axil. Bark smooth, green and white. 75ft (23m) in 20 years.
E. leucoxylon '**Rosea**' 214 Zone 9. To 50 or 60ft (15 or 18m).
E. miniata 214 N. and W. Australia. Zone 9. To 90ft (27.5m). Bark grey to yellow on trunk, white on branches. Leaves dark green above, paler below. Thrives on sandy soils.
E. niphophila* 213, 327 Snow gum. Victoria. Zone 4. Crooked tree to 20ft (6m). Leaves large, leathery, grey-green. Trunk is green, grey and cream. 50ft (15m) in 20 years. The hardiest of the genus.
E. obliqua 214, 319 S.E. Australia, E. Tasmania. Zone 9. To 230ft (70m). Bark fibrous, deeply furrowed. Prefers deep moist loam.
E. papuana Ghost rum. W. Australia, Papua. Zone 9. To 30 or 40ft (9 or 12m). Bark smooth, white or grey-white. Adult leaves shiny yellow-green.
E. perriniana 213 Spinning gum. Tasmania. Zone 9. To 30ft (9m). Bark smooth, white. 18ft (5.5m) in 3 years.
E. regnans 214 Victoria, E. Tasmania. Zone 9. To 200 or 280ft (60 or 85m). Bark white, smooth.
E. woodwardii 214 Woodward's gum. W. Australia. Zone 9. To 35ft (10.5m), straggling. Bark white, smooth. Thrives on sandy soils in dry areas.

EUCOMMIA ulmoides 141, 318, 326
Hardy rubber tree. China. Zone 5. To 65ft (20m). Leaves simple, deciduous, oval, slightly hairy, becoming smooth above, leathery, glossy containing rubbery sap. Flowers, sexes on separate trees, insignificant. Fruit compressed, winged. 30ft (9m) in 20 years.

EUCRYPHIA cordifolia 225
Chile. Zone 7. Big evergreen shrub or broad, columnar tree, to 40ft (12m). Leaves heart-shaped. White flowers, conspicuous stamens. Fairly lime-tolerant.
E. glutinosa Chile. Zone 7. Of the same stature as the last, but deciduous with pinnate leaves and fine autumn colour. Covered with large white flowers in summer. Lime-free soil. A.G.M. 1935.
E. × **nymansensis (cordifolia** × **glutinosa)** '**Nymansay**' The most popular garden Eucryphia. Evergreen, vigorous and floriferous (in late summer). A tower — to 40ft (12m) — of glistening white in flower.

EUODIA (EVODIA) 141
Deciduous or evergreen trees or shrubs. Leaves opposite, pinnate. Flowers small, unisexual, in broad, flattish clusters. Fruit in capsule holding small shiny black seeds. Any soil.

E. daniellii **237,** 317, 327 Korean euodia. China, Korea. Zone 5. 20 or 30ft (6 or 9m), spreading. Leaves deciduous, leaflets ovallish, smooth above, downy on midrib below; edges finely toothed, short-stalked. Flowers white, pungent, late summer. Fruits red-black, autumn to winter. Sun-loving.
E. hupehensis **237** China. Zone 5. To 60ft (18m), wide-spreading. Leaves deciduous, leaflets long, slender-pointed, smooth, excepting few white hairs underneath. Flowers white, summer. Fruit red, clustered. Sun-loving.

F

FAGUS **150–3,** 326, 327 Big, hardy, deciduous. Leaves entire or shallowly toothed. Male flowers in round clusters, females in twos or threes on same tree. Fruits are paired triangular nuts in spiny husk. Moist soils. Surface-rooting and competitive.
F. englerana **318** Bluish-foliaged beech from central China.
F. grandifolia **150** American beech. E. United States. Zone 3. To 100ft (30m), pyramidal, spreads by means of root suckers. Leaves medium length, oval, tapering, toothed, hairy at first; green above, paler below.
F. orientalis **318** 'Oriental beech', with bigger leaves than *F. sylvatica*.
F. sylvatica* **148,** 149, 150, 151, 324, 326, 327 Common beech, European beech. Europe. Zone 4. To 120ft (36m), densely pyramidal or rounded. Leaves medium length, oval, pointed, glossy, veins and stalk silky-hairy; red-brown in autumn. Suitable for extreme acidity or alkalinity. 35ft (10.5m) in 20 years.
   F.s. **'Ansorgei' 151** Leaves very narrow lance-shaped, dark purple.
   F.s. **'Asplenifolia' 150–1,** 326 Fern-leaved beech. Leaf-shape varies, being narrow and cut or lobed, with feathery texture. 30ft (9m) in 20 years. A.G.M. 1969.
   F.s. **'Dawyck' 151,** 326, 327 Medium to large, narrow-columnar form, broadening with age. 35ft (10.5m) in 20 years. A.G.M. 1969.
   F.s. **'Pendula' 151,** 326 Weeping beech. Large weeping form, large branches horizontal or drooping, smaller branches vertical. 25ft (7.5m) in 20 years.
   F.s. purpurea **150** Purple beech. Leaves pale red, becoming dark purple. 35ft (10.5m) in 20 years.
   F.s. **'Purpurea Pendula' 326** Weeping purple beech. Small, dome-shaped, weeping. Leaves dark purple.
   F.s. **'Riversii' 150,** 326 Rivers purple beech. Big tree with purple leaves through summer.
   F.s. **'Rohanii'** A purple-leaved version of the cut-leaved 'Asplenifolia'.
   F.s. **'Rotundifolia'** A bizarre beech, short-branched with round cockleshell leaves. Rather pretty.
   F.s. **'Tortuosa' 151,** 326 Small, spreading. Branches very twisted, hanging at tips.
   F.s. **'Zlatia' 326** Leaves soft yellow at first; green in late summer.

FICUS **142–3**
Evergreen or rarely deciduous trees or shrubs. Leaves alternate, sometimes toothed or lobed. Flowers usually unisexual on same plant, borne inside hollow cup. Fruit pear-shaped, fleshy.
F. carica **142,** 143, 318, 326 Common fig. Zone 6. To 30ft (9m), low, rounded, spreading head. Leaves big, rounded lobes, rough with short, stiff hairs, deciduous. Fruit greenish brown and violet.

FITZROYA cupressoides **97,** 319
Chile, Argentina. Zone 7. To 45ft (13.5m), leaning over at top. Leaves free, in threes, hard, blunt ends curling out from the shoot; deep blue-green with 2 bright bands on each face. 'Flowers', separate sexes, can be on same tree. Small cones, wide and persistent. Seeds winged. Needs good rainfall. 15ft (4.5m) in 20 years.

FORTUNELLA margarita **237**
Nagami, Kumquat, S.E. China. Zone 9. 10 to 15ft (3 to 4.5m), spreading. Leaves lance-shaped, dark green, paler beneath, partly crinkle-edged, evergreen. Flowers solitary or in small clusters, white, spring. Fruit oval-oblong, pale orange, sweet, slightly acid.

FRANKLINIA alatamaha **172,** 173, 326, 327
Georgia, United States. Zone 5. To 35ft (10.5m), upright. Leaves medium length, narrow, oblong, deciduous, simple, shiny above, dark green, then red in autumn, minutely toothed. Flowers to 3in (7.5cm), white, cupped, waxy, single, fragrant, late summer. Fruit woody, round, capsule. Tender in Britain; requires hot summers. Acid or alkaline soil. 10ft (3m) in 20 years.

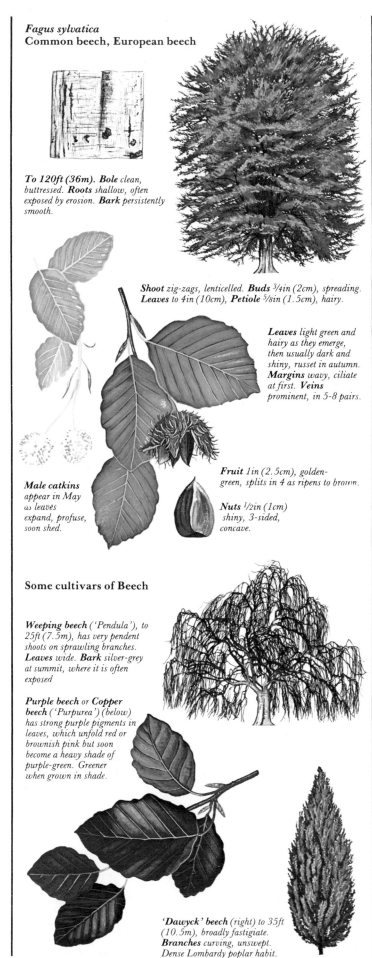

Fagus sylvatica
Common beech, European beech

To 120ft (36m). Bole *clean, buttressed.* **Roots** *shallow, often exposed by erosion.* **Bark** *persistently smooth.*

Shoot *zig-zags, lenticelled.* **Buds** $^{3}/_{4}$*in (2cm), spreading.* **Leaves** *to 4in (10cm),* **Petiole** $^{5}/_{8}$*in (1.5cm), hairy.*

Leaves *light green and hairy as they emerge, then usually dark and shiny, russet in autumn.* **Margins** *wavy, ciliate at first.* **Veins** *prominent, in 5-8 pairs.*

Male catkins *appear in May as leaves expand, profuse, soon shed.*

Fruit *1in (2.5cm), golden-green, splits in 4 as ripens to brown.*

Nuts $^{1}/_{2}$*in (1cm) shiny, 3-sided, concave.*

Some cultivars of Beech

Weeping beech *('Pendula'), to 25ft (7.5m), has very pendent shoots on sprawling branches.* **Leaves** *wide.* **Bark** *silver-grey at summit, where it is often exposed*

Purple beech *or* **Copper beech** *('Purpurea') (below) has strong purple pigments in leaves, which unfold red or brownish pink but soon become a heavy shade of purple-green. Greener when grown in shade.*

'Dawyck' beech (right) to 35ft (10.5m), broadly fastigiate. **Branches** *curving, unswept. Dense Lombardy poplar habit.*

Fraxinus americana
White ash, American ash

To 135ft (41m). Crown open, conical. Branches stout, spreading, pendent in lower crown, often very angular. Bole often forked, sometimes repeatedly. Bark grey, smooth at first but becoming evenly fissured into diamond-shaped ridges; older trees deeply fissured.

Leaflets (5-9) 5in (12cm), grey-green below. Petiolule ¹/₂in (1cm), except on terminal leaflet, to 1¹/₂in (4cm). Veins prominent; those on underside may be pubescent.

Wings pointed or notched at tip.

Fruit a samara, to 2¹/₂in × ¹/₃in (6cm × 8mm), in pendent clusters to 8in (20cm). Ripens from bright green to dull brown.

Leaves 12in (30cm).

Margins either entire or serrate, with forward teeth.

Fraxinus excelsior
Common European ash

Male flowers have stamens set more densely than females.

Female flowers spreading.

Buds ¹/₃in (8mm).

Flowers without petals or sepals, open in April, before leaves.

Terminal leaflet on ³/₄in (2cm) petiole.

Shoots green-grey with white lenticels.

Branches ascend.

Bole long.

To 130ft (40m). Crown light, open. Bark smooth when young, ridged, thick and grey in older trees.

Leaves 12in (30cm), pale and white-haired below. Rachis glabrous, grooved.

Leaflets (9-13) 5in (12cm), toothed, fall while still green.

Fruit 1¹/₂in (4cm), in pendulous bunches, ripening brown in October, persisting after leaves fall. Wing tips obtuse or notched.

FRAXINUS 238–9, 327
Deciduous trees, few shrubs. Leaves mostly pinnate. Flowers mainly insignificant, bisexual or unisexual on same tree. Fruits narrowly ovoid, winged, often propellor-like. Hardy.
*F. americana** **239**, 318 White ash, American ash. E. United States. Zone 3. To 135ft (41m), upright. Leaves pinnate, leaflets stalked, oval or near, dark green above, whitish-green and downy beneath; end of leaflet may be toothed. Flowers petalless. Prefers loamy soil, much moisture. Subject to oyster scale, canker in America. 25ft (7.5m) in 20 years.
F. angustifolia **239**, 318 Narrow-leaved ash. S. Europe. Zone 6. To 80ft (24.5m). Leaflets slender, lance-shaped, smooth, shiny, dark green above, toothed, stalked. Flowers few, petalless. 30ft (9m) in 20 years.
F.a. 'Lentiscifolia' Exceptionally small-leaved and graceful form but a fine, vigorous tree.
F. chinensis **241** Chinese ash. China. Zone 5. To 45ft (13.5m). Leaves with 5 to 9 leaflets, dark dull green above, paler beneath, often purple in autumn. Flowers in big loose clusters, fragrant, May. Fruit narrow, 1 ½ in (4cm) long.
*F. excelsior** 64, **238, 239**, 325, 327 Common ash. Europe (incl. British Isles), Caucasus. Zone 3. To 130ft (40m), spreading. Leaves pinnate, oblong, lance-shaped, smooth above, furry brown by lower midrib, dark green, toothed; leaflets stalkless. Flowers greenish-yellow, clustered, spring. Likes chalk soil. Susceptible to oyster scale. 30ft (9m) in 20 years.
F.e. 'Diversifolia' **239** One-leaved ash. Leaves simple or 3-part.
F.e. 'Jaspidea' **239**, 326 Branches yellowish, young shoots golden.
F.e. 'Pendula' **238, 239**, 326 Weeping ash. Height according to graft; spreading. Vigorous. Branches and branchlets stiffly hanging.
F. latifolia **239**, 319 Oregon ash. W. United States. Zone 6. To 80ft (24.5m), narrow, upright to broad. Leaves pinnate, leaflets oval or oblong, pointed, downy, dark green above, paler below; main stalk grooved. Flowers petalless. Fruit to 2in (5cm) long. Susceptible to oyster scale. 20ft (6m) in 20 years.
F. mariesii **239**, 318 Flowering ash, Maries' ash. C. China. Zone 7. To 30ft (9m), spreading. Leaves pinnate, leaflets oval, tip tapering, smooth, dull green, toothed or almost toothed, leafstalk purplish. Flowers in terminal clusters, creamy-white, late spring or early summer. Fruits winged, to 1 ¼ in (3cm) long, deep purple, autumn. Sun-loving. Susceptible to oyster scale. 15ft (4.5m) in 20 years.
F. nigra **239** Black ash. E. United States. Zone 2. To 75ft (23m). 7 to 11 slender pointed leaflets, dark green above, paler beneath. Sexes on separate trees. Fruits 1 ½ in (4cm) long.
F. ornus **238–9**, 316, 318, 327 Manna ash. S. Europe, Asia Minor. Zone 5. To 50ft (15m), spreading. Leaves pinnate, broad, oblong leaflets, rusty hairs along midrib beneath, dull green, toothed. Flowers clustered, off-white, spring. Fruit notched at tip. Sun-loving. Susceptible to oyster scale. 15ft (4.5m) in 20 years.
F. oxycarpa **239**, 318 S. Europe to Persia and Turkestan. Zone 5. To 30ft (9m), upright to spreading, but compact. Leaflets narrow, lance-shaped, shiny dark green, downy beneath, sharply toothed. Flowers without petals. Sun-loving. Susceptible to oyster scale. 30 to 50ft (9 to 15m) in 20 years.
F.o. 'Raywood' Bred in Australia, smoky-purple autumn colour.
F. pensylvanica **239**, 319 Red ash. E. United States. Zone 3. To 60ft (18m). Leaves big, 7 or 9 narrow oval leaflets, dull green, downy beneath. Sexes on separate trees. Fruit to 2in (5cm) long. Fast-growing.
F.p. lanceolata **239**, 327 Green ash. E. United States. Zone 2. To 60ft (18m), spreading. Leaflets oblong or narrowly oval, downy beneath, pale green, obscurely toothed. 18ft (5.5m) in 20 years.
F.p. 'Variegata' White mottling on grey-green makes this a conspicuous tree.
F. quadrangulata **239** Blue ash. C. and E. United States. Zone 3. To 80ft (24.5m), with square branchlets. Leaves big, 7 or 11 narrow oval leaflets, yellow-green. Bisexual flowers in clusters. Fruit, 1 to 2 in (2.5 to 5cm) long.
F. tomentosa **319** Ash with big downy leaves. E. United States.
F. velutina 318, **327** Velvet ash. S.W. United States, N. Mexico. Zone 5. To 45ft (13.5m), round-headed, fairly open. Suitable for dry alkaline soils.
F. xanthoxyloides **318** 'Afghan ash'. Small, rounded close-set leaflets on winged stalk.

G

GENISTA aetnensis 210, **327**
Mount Etna broom. Sardinia, Sicily. Zone 3. To 20ft (6m). Tiny, slender leaves, green, rush-like, sparse, simple, deciduous. Flowers profuse, pea-shaped, golden yellow, summer. Prefers well-drained, light loam; tolerates chalk. Sun-loving. Subject to rust, fungal die-back. A.G.M. 1923.

GINKGO *biloba** 68–9, 318, 324, 326, 327
Maidenhair tree. E. China. Zone 4. To 80ft (24.5m), varies from narrow, upright to broadly spreading. Leaves larger and more deeply cleft at first, green both sides, deciduous. Male 'flowers' rare, thick, yellow; female 'flowers' single or paired, pale yellow becoming orange. Fruits yellow, plum-shaped; offensive smell if crushed. Seeds edible. Tolerates lime. 25ft (7.5m) in 20 years. A.G.M. 1969.
   G.b. **'Fastigiata' 69,** 326 Columnar, upright-branched form.

GLEDITSIA 208–9
Deciduous trees. Leaves pinnate. Flowers small, insignificant, greenish, regularly-petalled, not pea-like as other *Leguminosae*. Most species have large thorns, some thornless. Sun-loving.
G. *caspica* 209 Caspian locust. N. Persia. Zone 6. To 35ft (10.5m), very spiny. Leaves, pinnate with 12 to 20 oval, toothed leaflets, or doubly pinnate. Pod thin, curved, 8in (20.5cm) long.
G. *japonica* 209 Japanese locust. Japan. Zone 5. To 70ft (21.5m), pyramidal, spiny bole. Leaflets roughly lance-shaped, midrib and stalk slightly hairy. Flowers, male and female on separate spikes, yellow-green, bell-shaped, June. Fruit, pods to 10in (26cm) long, curved, eventually twisted. 15ft (4.5m) in 20 years.
G. *triacanthos** 208, 209, 319, 327 Honey locust. C. and E. United States. Zone 4. To 140ft (42m), broad, open, spiny trunk and branches. Leaves pinnate, medium to long, glossy dark green. Flowers unisexual on same tree, clustered; males green, females more sparse, June. Pod brown, to 18in (45cm) long, curved, Oct.–Dec. Tolerates chalk soils and drought. 25ft (7.5m) in 20 years.
   G.t. **'Columnaris' 326** Columnar form.
   G.t. **'Moraine' 209** C. and E. United States. Wide-spreading form. Flowers as *G. japonica*. Fruitless; thornless. Many soils.
   G.t. **'Sunburst' 208,** 326 Medium-sized, thornless stems. Young leaves bright yellow.

GLYPTOSTROBUS *lineatus* 113
Chinese deciduous cypress. S. China. Zone 8. Small bush or tree. Leaves either short in 3 ranks, or scale-like, overlapping: both types pale sea-green, rich brown in autumn. Cones pear-shaped, long-stalked. Seeds winged.

GORDONIA 172, 173, 327
Tender evergreen trees or shrubs similar to *Camellia*. Dark glossy green leaves. Conspicuous flowers during the autumn and winter. Dislikes lime.
G. *lasianthus* 173 Loblolly bay. S.E. United States. Zone 8. To 60ft (18m), narrow. Leaves oblong, pointed, evergreen, simple, shiny, smooth, leathery, dark green, shallow-toothed. Flowers 3 to 6in (7.5 to 15cm) across, white, single, fragrant, mid-summer. Fruits oblong, hard.

GREVILLEA *robusta* 215, 326, 327
Silk-oak grevillea. Australia. Zone 10. To 150ft (45m) in Australia. Leaves feathery, simple, evergreen, white hairs on underside. Flowers bunched, honeysuckle-like, orange to golden yellow. Fruit a boat-shaped capsule. Needs well-drained, lime-free soil. Sun-loving. Tender in Britain.

GYMNOCLADUS *dioica* 209, 319
Kentucky coffee tree. E. and C. United States. Zone 4. To 90ft (27.5m), large branches, open. Leaves bi-pinnate (i.e. leafstalk has secondary stalks bearing leaflets), medium to long, green above, grey-green and hairy beneath, yellow in autumn. Small flowers unisexual, clustered, greenish-white, on same or different trees, June. Pods oblong, flat, Oct. through winter. Tolerates chalk. 18ft (5.5m) in 20 years.

H

HAKEA *laurina* 215
Sea-urchin, Pin-cushion tree. New Zealand. Zone 8. To 30ft (9m), shrub or small tree. Leaves oblong to lance-shaped, narrow, simple, evergreen. Flowers red-pink, tubular. Fruit a thick, woody capsule. Not lime- or chalk-tolerant. Sun-loving.

HALESIA 189, 327
Shrubs or small trees. Leaves simple, deciduous. Flowers hanging, snowdrop-like, clustered. Fruits, pear-shaped winged pods, pale-brown. Tolerates lime if enriched with peat or leaf soil. Sun-loving.
H. *carolina* 189, 319, 327 Snowdrop tree, Silverbell tree. S.E. United

Ginkgo biloba
Maidenhair tree

Buds *set spirally around shoots.*

To 80ft (24.5m). Crown *columnar, broadening with age.* **Branches** *very stiff, relatively thin, dipping when old.* **Bark** *ridged, fissured.*

Leaves *ribbed, variable, from 2¹/₂-5in (6-12cm), set in whorls of 2-5 on short, slow growing, older shoots; larger, set singly on new shoots.* **Veins** *straight, parallel, non-dividing.*

Blades *open pale yellow-green, golden in autumn.*

Gleditsia triacanthos
Honey locust

Bark *shallow-ridged with bunches of spines.*

Shoots *slender, often with single or 3-pronged spines.*

Bipinnate leaves *8in (20cm), with 8-24 pinnae of up to 32 ³/₄in (2cm) leaflets.*

Lower buds *small, hidden at first in petioles.*

Pinnate leaves *4-6cm (10-15cm), with 14-36 leaflets each ³/₄-1¹/₂in (2-4cm), remotely serrate.*

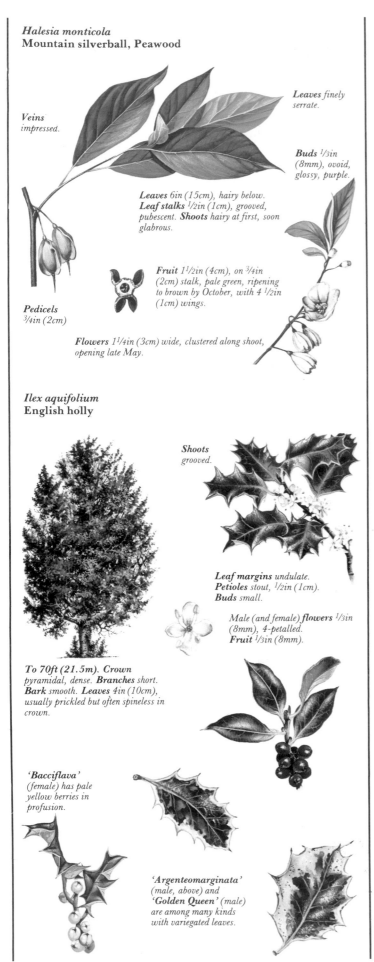

Halesia monticola
Mountain silverball, Peawood

Veins impressed.

Leaves finely serrate.

Buds ⅓in (8mm), ovoid, glossy, purple.

Leaves 6in (15cm), hairy below.
Leaf stalks ½in (1cm), grooved, pubescent. Shoots hairy at first, soon glabrous.

Fruit 1½in (4cm), on ¾in (2cm) stalk, pale green, ripening to brown by October, with 4 ½in (1cm) wings.

Pedicels ¾in (2cm)

Flowers 1¼in (3cm) wide, clustered along shoot, opening late May.

Ilex aquifolium
English holly

Shoots grooved.

Leaf margins undulate.
Petioles stout, ½in (1cm).
Buds small.

Male (and female) flowers ⅓in (8mm), 4-petalled.
Fruit ⅓in (8mm).

To 70ft (21.5m). Crown pyramidal, dense. Branches short. Bark smooth. Leaves 4in (10cm), usually prickled but often spineless in crown.

'Bacciflava' (female) has pale yellow berries in profusion.

'Argenteomarginata' (male, above) and 'Golden Queen' (male) are among many kinds with variegated leaves.

States. Zone 4. To 35ft (10.5m). Leaves ovallish, thick down beneath. Flowers small, white. Bark scaly. 12ft (3.5m) in 20 years. A.G.M. 1946.
H. monticola* 189, 316, 319, 327 Mountain silverbell, Peawood. Mts of S.E. United States. Zone 5. To 90ft (27.5m), pyramidal. Leaves medium length, ovallish, yellow in autumn. Flowers white, spring. Resistant to pests and disease. Sun or semi-shade. 25ft (7.5m) in 20 years.

HAMAMELIS 132–3, 327
Deciduous shrubs or small trees. Leaves alternate, with wavy or toothed edge. Flowers bisexual, clustered, thin yellow petals, late autumn to spring. Fruit, capsule holding 2 shiny black seeds.
H. japonica 'Arborea' 132–3, 327 Wide-spreading form sometimes making a small tree. Flowers rich yellow. 10ft (3m) in 20 years.
H. mollis 132–3, 326, 327 Chinese witch-hazel. China. Zone 5. To 25ft (7.5m), bushy. Leaves roundish, simple, hairy. Flowers fragrant. 8ft (2.5m) in 20 years. A.G.M. 1922.
H. virginiana 132–3, 326, 327 Virginian witch-hazel. E. United States. Zone 4. To 30ft (9m), often bushy. Leaves oval to triangular, simple, hairy on veins beneath, toothed, hairy stalk. 6ft (1.8m) in 20 years.

HEBE lycopodioides 119
New Zealand. Zone 7. To 2 or 3ft (60cm or 1m) with upright 4-sided yellow-green stems. Leaves minute, triangular, scale-like, evergreen. Flowers small, white, in small clusters. Fruit, small capsule. Thrives in industrial and seaside areas, on all soils.

HIPPOPHAE rhamnoides 215, 317, 326, 327
Sea buckthorn. Europe, temperate Asia. Zone 3. To 30ft (9m), deciduous shrub or small tree. Leaves short to medium length, narrow, lance-shaped, simple, greyish-green above, silvery-green below. Flowers, sexes on separate trees, small, clustered. Fruit, berry-like, small, orange-yellow, in winter; very acid. Tolerates dry soils, exposure; excellent in coastal areas, sandy soils. Sun-loving. 15ft (4.5m) in 20 years.

HOHERIA 174, 175
Evergreen or deciduous small trees or shrubs from New Zealand. Leaves alternate, toothed. Flowers white, bisexual, solitary or clustered, summer. Seed-case thin, sometimes winged.
H. glabrata 174 Ribbonwood. Zone 7. To 35ft (10.5m). Leaves alternate, toothed, medium length, lance-shaped. Fragrant white flowers in summer.
H. lyallii Zone 7. A small tree with leaves becoming grey-green by mid-summer, when it arches with white cherry-like blossom. A.G.M. 1926.
H. sexstylosa Zone 8. Erect-growing evergreen with narrow leaves. Summer-flowering. 25ft (7.5m) in 25 years.

I

IDESIA polycarpa 242, 317, 318, 326
Japan, China. Zone 6. To 45ft (13.5m), horizontal branching. Oval leaves, medium to long, red-stalked, deep green above, deciduous. Sexes usually on separate trees; small, greenish-yellow, fragrant flowers in hanging clusters to 10in (26cm) long. Red pea-like berries, autumn. Good in neutral or slightly acid, moisture-retentive soil. 30ft (9m) in 20 years.

ILEX 220–3, 326, 327
Deciduous and evergreen trees and shrubs. Leaves simple, stalked. Flowers small, off-white, males and females on separate trees. Fruit small. Most soils. *I. aquifolium* forms hardier than *I. altaclerensis* forms. Sun or semi-shade; injured by cold in N. Europe and America. Pest-free, except holly leaf miner.
I. × altaclerensis* 222, 326, 327 Highclere hybrid holly. Zone 7. A group of excellent vigorous hybrids. Small tree or large bush to 50ft (15m). Leaves evergreen, large, less prickly than *I. aquifolium*. Tolerates seaside and industrial areas. 25ft (7.5m) in 20 years.
　　I. × a. 'Camelliifolia' 222, 317 Vigorous, conical. Leaves evergreen, nearly spineless, purplish at first, dark green later. Large fruits. Bark purple. 20ft (6m) in 20 years. A.G.M. 1931.
　　I. × a. 'Golden King' 222, 326 Variegated female form. Leaves green, edges bright yellow, virtually spineless. 20ft (6m) in 20 years. A.G.M. 1969.
　　I. × a. 'J. C. van Tol' 222, 317, 327 Dark-green leaved form, nearly spineless. Masses of berries. 20ft (6m) in 20 years. A.G.M. 1969.
　　I. × a. 'Lawsoniana' 222, 326 Female form of *I. a.* 'Hendersonii' with large, sparsely spined leaves, medium length, yellow edge, marbled centre, deep and pale greens. May revert to plain green. 20ft (6m) in 20 years.

I. × *a.* **'Purple Shaft' 222** Very vigorous purple-shooting form. Masses of berries. 20ft (6m) in 20 years.

I. × *a.* **'Silver Sentinel' 222**, 326 Female form. Leaves dark green, mottled pale green and grey, margins pale yellow or whitish, flat, sparsely spined. 20ft (6m) in 20 years.

I. aquifolium* 220–2, 326, 327 English holly. S. Europe, N. Africa, W. Asia to China. Zone 6. To 45 or 70ft (13.5 or 21.5m), short spreading branches, dense, pyramidal. Leaves oval, spiny, shiny green, evergreen. Flowers small, white, fragrant, May–June. Fruit, red berries, Sept. through winter. Suited to industrial and coastal areas. 15ft (4.5m) in 20 years.

I.a. **'Argenteomarginata Pendula' 222**, 326 Perry's weeping silver holly. Silver foliage on drooping branches. Berries profuse. 10 to 15ft (3 to 4.5m) in 20 years.

I.a. **'Argenteo-Medio Picta' 222** Silver Milkboy. To 30ft (9m), pyramidal. Leaves spiny, dark green, with central creamy spot. Flowers negligible, male. Most soils. Holly leaf miner. 10 to 15ft (3 to 4.5m) in 20 years.

I.a. **'Aurea Regina' 222** Golden Queen. Leaves broad, dark green, shaded pale green and grey, wide yellow edge. Male plants only. 10 to 15ft (3 to 4.5m) in 20 years. A.G.M. 1969.

I.a. **'Bacciflava' 222**, 327 Profuse yellow berries. 10 to 15ft (3 to 4.5m) in 20 years.

I.a. **'Crispa' 222** Leaves twisted and curled, thick, leathery; spine curved back on itself at tip. 10 to 15ft (3 to 4.5m) in 20 years.

I.a. **'Elegantissima' 221** Green stems. Leaves spiny, wavy edges, creamy-white margins. 10 to 15ft (3 to 4.5m) in 20 years.

I.a. **'Ferox' 221**, 222 Hedgehog holly. Leaves with clusters of short, sharp spines. Male form, no berries. 10 to 15ft (3 to 4.5m) in 20 years.

I.a. **'Ferox Argentea' 221** Silver hedgehog holly. Male form with purple twigs. Leaves with creamy-white spines and margins. 10 to 15ft (3 to 4.5m) in 20 years.

I.a. **'Fructoluteo'** One of the best yellow-berried hollies.

I.a. **'Golden Milkboy' 222**, 326 Male. Leaves big, spiny, green, centre marked with gold. 10 to 15ft (3 to 4.5m) in 20 years.

I.a. **'Golden Queen' 222**, 326 Male. Young shoots green or reddish. Leaves broad, dark shiny green with pale green shading, yellow margin. 10 to 15ft (3 to 4.5m) in 20 years. A.G.M. 1969.

I.a. **'Hastata' 221** Dense form with deep purple shoots. Leaves small, rigid, wavy; sometimes single spine. 10ft (3m) in 20 years.

I.a. **'Pyramidalis'** A bright green, tall-growing form which usually flowers well. A.G.M. 1969.

I.a. **'Silver Milkboy' 222**, 326 Male. Leaves spiny, dark green with central blotch of creamy-white. 10 to 15ft (3 to 4.5m) in 20 years.

I.a. **'Silver Queen' 221**, 222, 326 Male. Leaves broad oval, dark green, creamy-white margin. 10 to 15ft (3 to 4.5m) in 20 years.

I. cassine 223 Dahoon holly. S.E. United States. Zone 7. To 35ft (10.5m), rounded. Leaves evergreen, lance-shaped, spineless. Fruits red, profuse clusters. Dislikes chalky soils.

I. decidua 220 Possumhaw. S.E. United States. Zone 6. To 25ft (7.5m). Deciduous blunt-toothed leaves. Fruit orange-red. Likes moist lime-free soil.

I. latifolia 223, 326, 327 Tarajo, Lustreleaf holly. Japan. Zone 7. To 60ft (18m). Biggest leaves of any holly, oblong, evergreen, serrated edges, dark green above, yellow beneath, stalked. Fruit round, orange red, profuse clusters. Shade-tolerant; best in shelter. 25 to 30ft (7.5 to 9m) in 20 years.

I. opaca* 220, 222, 317, 326 American holly. E. and C. United States. Zone 5. To 50ft (15m), pyramidal. Leaves evergreen, spiny, dull green above, yellowish beneath, stalk grooved. Male flowers in slender heads, female flowers solitary, white. Fruits, red. Dislikes chalky soils. 8ft (2.5m) in 20 years.

I.o. **'Xanthocarpa' 220**, 327 As *I. opaca*, but berries yellow.

I. pedunculosa 223, 326 Longstalk holly. Japan. Zone 5. To 30ft (9m), small tree or shrub, pyramidal. Leaves evergreen. Fruits small, red, on stalks. Dislikes chalky soils.

I. perado 222 Azorean holly. Azores, Canary Islands. Zone 8. Evergreen tree, small. Leaves dark green, sometimes spiny, winged stalks. Berries deep red, clustered in leaf axils.

I. pernyi* 223, 326, 327 C. and W. China. Zone 6. To 30ft (9m), narrow-pyramidal. Tiny leaves evergreen, triangular, with 2 big, lateral spines, leathery, dark shiny green. Flowers yellow, tiny clusters. Fruit small, red, clustered berries. 15ft (4.5m) in 20 years.

I. verticilluta N.E. America. Zone 3. Bushy deciduous holly with red fruit and yellow autumn leaves. Lime-free soil.

I. vomitorea* Yaupon, S.E. United States. Zone 7. To 26ft (8m). Leaves dark green, flowers profuse, fruit red, abundant.

Ilex x altaclarensis
Highclere hybrid hollies

'Hodginsii', Hodgin's holly. Male form, to 55ft (17m). Leaves broad, 4 × 3½in (9 × 8cm). Dark green, with a dull sheen. Vary from having no spines to many.

'Camelliifolia' Female cultivar, to 50ft (15m). Leaves dark green, glossy, with very few, if any, spines.

Ilex opaca
American holly

Shoots densely hairy at first, red-brown, later smooth, brown.

Leaves 4in (10cm), thick, leathery, glossy, dark green above, yellowish below with prominent veins, persist 3 years.

Buds small, green, sharply pointed.

Male flowers in cymes of 3-9. Female flowers usually single.

To 50ft (15m). Crown narrow, dense, conical. Leaves more spiny on lower branches within reach of animals. Crown of wild trees more open. Branches upswept at tips. Bark light grey, thin, smooth but warty.

Fruit ⅓in (8mm), ovoid, in clusters. Skin tough. Flesh yellow, holds 4 ribbed yellow seeds. Ripens autumn, persistent.

Ilex pernyi
Perny's holly

From China. Forms a neat, narrow pyramid, to 30ft (9m).

Leaves spiny, very small, 1¼in (3cm). Set densely. Dark green, glossy.

Ilex vomitoria
Yaupon

Leaves elliptic to oblong.

Fruit ⅓in (8mm), in great abundance on previous year's shoots, short-stalked, soon falls.

Leaves 2in (5cm). Apex obtuse.

Margins serrate. Petioles grooved.

Leaves shiny dark green above, pale opaque below. Buds obtuse, very dark.

Bark very thin, only ⅓in (8mm), light red-brown, developing small scales.

Juglans cinerea
Butternut

Fruit *in racemes of 1-5.*

Fruit *2½in (6cm), ovoid, pointed, husks with clammy matted hairs and 2 or 4 sutures.* **Seeds** *2½in (6cm), oily, deeply ribbed.*

Leaves *30in (75cm).* **Leaflets,** *7-19, pointed, toothed.*

To 60ft (18m). Crown *broad, with open dome.* **Bole** *short.* **Bark** *thick, light grey, furrowed.*

Rachis *stout, downy.*

Leaflets *finely pubescent below.* **Pith** *chambered.*

Shoots *stout, with reddish hairs at first; ridge of hairs remains above leaf.* **Terminal bud** *¾in (2cm), flattened.*

Juglans regia
English or Persian walnut

Leaves *18in (45cm), pinnate, highly aromatic when rubbed.* **Leaflets** *(5-7) to 7in (18cm).*

Leaf margins *entire.*

Leaflets *subsessile, except terminal.*

Fruit *2in (5cm).* **Seeds** *wrinkled.*

Fruit *ripe by September, the husk withering to expose hardened nut.*

Catkins *before leaves.*

Shoots *stout.* **Pith** *chambered.* **Buds** *⅓in (8mm), aromatic when rubbed.*

To 90ft (27.5m). Crown *wide, rounded.* **Branches** *low, very sinuous, heavy.* **Bark** *in smooth plates between wide fissures.* **Bole** *upright, pale ghostly grey.*

J

***JACARANDA acutifolia* 244, 245**
Jacaranda, Sharpleaf jacaranda. Brazil. Zone 10. To 50ft (15m). Foliage fine, fern-like. Flowers blue, numerous. Hot, dry position.

JUBAEA chilensis See *Jubaea spectabilis*
Jubaea spectabilis **123** Chilean wine palm. Chile. Zone 8. To 80ft (24.5m), trunk 4 to 6ft (1.2 to 1.8m) thick, covered with leaf-base scars. Pinnate leaves to 12ft (3.5m) long on stalks. Flowerstalks in axils of lower leaves. Yellow oval fruit.

***JUGLANS* 132, 144–7, 327**
Deciduous trees, sometimes shrubs. Big, pinnate leaves, toothed or entire. Male flowers in slender hanging catkins, female flowers sparse, sexes separate on same tree. Fruit is hard-shelled nut, autumn. Subject to honey fungus, crown rot, twig dieback, bacterial blight; leaf blotch in Britain. Any soil.
J. cathayensis **318** Chinese walnut, long leaves with many leaflets.
*J. cinerea** **319** Butternut. E. United States. Zone 3. To 60ft (18m) or more, wide-spreading head. 7 to 19 pointed, toothed leaflets, hairy below. Male catkins. Fruits covered with sticky hairs. 25ft (7.5m) in 20 years.
J. mandshurica **319** Manchurian walnut with very long leaves.
J. nigra 42, **144, 145,** 319, 326 Eastern black walnut. E. and C. United States. Zone 4. To 150ft (45m), rounded, spreading to upright. Leaves to 2ft (60cm) long. 11 to 23 leaflets, downy beneath. Fruit roundish, solitary or paired. 35ft (10.5m) in 20 years.
*J. regia** **144, 145,** 318, 326, 327 English or Persian walnut. S.E. Europe, Himalaya, China. Zone 5–6. To 90ft (27.5m), broad, rounded head. Leaves long. 5 to 7 oval leaflets. 25ft (7.5m) in 20 years.
   J.r. '**Laciniata**' **326** Cut-leaved walnut. Pendulous branchlets. Leaves compound, leaflets deeply lobed. 20ft (6m) in 20 years.
J. rupestris **145** Texan walnut. Texas. New Mexico. Zone 5. To 40ft (12m). Leaves long, 13 to 20 narrow, toothed leaflets. 25ft (7.5m) in 20 years.

***JUNIPERUS* 65, 91, 94, 98, 105–7, 326, 327**
Evergreen trees or shrubs. Leaves initially awl-shaped, adult leaves scale-like. 'Flowers' usually with sexes on separate trees. Fruit berry-like. Good on lime. Susceptible to fungal attacks. Generally slow-growing.
J. ashei **319** Large shrub, sometimes small tree. Young foliage sage green; adult dark green. Fruits deep blue, sweet. Needs shelter.
*J. chinensis** **105, 106,** 118, 119, 318 Chinese juniper. Himalaya, China, Japan. Zone 4. To 75ft (23m), conical. Juvenile leaves prickly, dark green, mixed with or at base of shoots of adult scale leaves. Male 'flowers' crowded on crown, spring. Cones ⅓in (7mm) across, waxy green becoming dark purple. Almost any soil. 20ft (6m) in 20 years.
   J.c. '**Aurea**' **106,** 326, 327 Young's golden juniper. To 35ft (10.5m), narrow, flat-topped column. Leaves bright gold. Male. Good in towns. 12ft (3.5m) in 20 years.
   J.c. '**Columnaris Glauca**' **326** Small, columnar, dense. Leaves awl-shaped.
   J.c. femina **106** Leaves crowded, sometimes lance-shaped, overlapping. 'Flowers' entirely female.
   J.c. '**Hetzii**' **106** Slightly taller than *J. chinensis* 'Pfitzeriana'. Leaves waxy blue.
   J.c. '**Kaizuka**' **106, 119,** 326 Small, branches wide-spreading at all angles. Leaves crowded, lustrous green. 'Hollywood' juniper.
   J.c. '**Keteleeri**' **106** Narrow, conical. Adult leaves dark, shiny grey-green. Cones ½in (1cm) wide, waxy, blue-green. 15ft (4.5m) in 20 years.
   J.c. '**Pfitzeriana**' **106** Small-medium, wide-spreading shrub. Leaves green, some sprays of juvenile leaves with waxy surfaces. Shade-tolerant. A.G.M. 1969.
   J.c. '**Pyramidalis**' **106** Conical. Leaves mostly juvenile, prickly, waxy blue.
   J.c. '**San Jose**' **118** Dwarf shrub with prostrate branches. Leaves usually juvenile, grey-green.
   J.c. '**Variegata**' **118** Pyramidal bush with dense ascending branches and erect branchlets. Leaves bloomed above, green beneath. Scattered sprays of white foliage.
*J. communis** **105,** 325 Common juniper. N. America, Europe, Asia, Korea, Japan. Zone 2. Small, rarely to 15ft (4.5m), sprawling or erect, conical. Cones small, blue, waxy. Tolerates high chalk content. 8ft (2.5m) in 20 years.
   J.c. '**Compressa**' **105** Dwarf form, 18in (45cm) high, narrow, columnar, shapely. Leaves small, crowded. Cones small. Very slow.

J.c. 'Hibernica' 105, 318, 326 Irish juniper. To 20ft (6m), narrow, smooth, conic-topped column, showing much blue from inner surfaces of leaves. 12ft (3.5m) in 20 years.

J.c. 'Hornibrookii' 119 Dense prostrate shrub to 18in (45cm), creeping branches with irregular sprays of foliage. Leaves small, pointed, dull dark green below, broad white band above.

J.c. 'Suecica' 105, 318 Medium, columnar. Branches ascending, weeping at tips. Leaves blue-green. Fruits oblong.

J. deppeana 319 Small conical tree. Leaves waxy-blue. Fruits globular, reddish-brown.

J.d. pachyphlaea 105, 106 Alligator juniper. Mexico. Zone 7. To 10 or 35ft (3 or 10.5m) conical. Leaves with gland underneath containing white resin, small. 'Flowers', sexes separate on same tree. Fruit round. Bark attractive, flaky. 10ft (3m) in 20 years.

J. distans 318 Small Chinese juniper, grey-green.

J. drupacea 106, 318, 326 Syrian juniper. Asia Minor, Syria, Greece. Zone 7. To 60ft (18m), narrowly columnar. Leaves narrow, in whorls of 3, biggest juniper leaf; midrib, broad, green, white banded. Fruits blue-black, waxy; edible when ripe. 15ft (4.5m) in 20 years.

J. excelsa 318 'Greek juniper'. Small conical juniper, grey-green.

J. formosana 318 'Prickly cypress'. Pretty, small, drooping; tender in Britain.

J. monosperma 105 Cherrystone juniper. S. United States. Zone 7. 30 to 50ft (9 to 15m), dense, erect branches. Leaves pressed to shoot, glossy grey-blue. Cones round, ¼ in (6mm) across, dark blue or copper-coloured.

J. occidentalis 105, 106 Western juniper. California. Zone 7. To 20 or 60ft (6 or 18m), upright. Leaves in 6 ranks, and whorls of 3, pointed, short, closely pressed to shoot, resin gland on reverse. Fruits oblong, waxy, blue-black. Flourishes in full sunlight. Main pests are heartwood rot and juniper bark beetle.

J. osteosperma 105 Utah juniper. S.W. United States. Zone 7. Small conical tree with slender, light green branchlets. Male and female 'flowers' on same tree. Round cones ¼ to ½ in (6mm to 1cm) across, reddish brown.

J. oxycedrus 106, 318 'Prickly juniper'. Mediterranean equivalent of *J. communis.*

J. phoenicea 107, 318 Phoenician juniper' from eastern Mediterranean.

J. procumbens 'Nana' 119 Dwarf, smaller than type, forming a compact mat of foliage. Leaves small, bluish-green.

J. recurva 318, 326 Drooping juniper. S.W. China, Nepal. Zone 7. To 30ft (9m), broad-pyramidal, spreading branches with hanging branchlets. Leaves dull green or greyish-green. Fruit glossy olive-brown.

J.r. coxii 106, 318, 326 Upper Burma. Zone 7. To 35ft (10.5m), pendulous. Leaves small, sage green above, midrib dark, in whorls of 3. 'Flowers', sexes may be separate on same tree; males at ends of branchlets, in tiny heads. Fruits purple-brown or black, ovallish, small.

J. rigida 106, 318 Japan, Korea, N. China. Zone 5. 20 to 40ft (6 to 12m), tree or shrub. Leaves in whorls of 3, pointed, short, grey-green to green, white bands above. Fruit black, round, waxy, ripens 2nd year. 15ft (4.5m) in 20 years.

J. sabina 106 Low-spreading juniper from central Europe.

J. scopulorum 105 Rocky Mountain juniper. Rocky Mts. Zone 5. To 50ft (15m), spreading. Leaves dark or yellowish green. Cones small, blue, waxy.

J.s. 'Columnaris' 105 To 30ft (9m), columnar, very slow growing.

J. squamata 106 W. and C. China, Formosa. Zone 4. Varies from prostrate shrub to small bushy tree with drooping branches. Leaves short, white or pale green above; old leaves often persist, brown. Fruit ⅓ in (7mm) long, reddish-brown turning black.

J.s. 'Meyeri' 106 To 20ft (6m), spreading. Leaves crowded, waxy, bluish. Vigorous.

J. thurifera 318 'Spanish juniper'. Columnar, rather tender.

J. virginiana* 42, 90, **105, 106,** 319 Pencil cedar. E. and C. United States. Zone 2. To 100ft (30m), broadly conical. Leaves small, paired, pointed, waxy above on juvenile branches; leaves on older branches becoming brown. Fruits small, waxy, brown-purple, ripening in 1st year. 18ft (5.5m) in 20 years.

J.v. 'Canaertii' 105 Small, conical. Leaves bright green. Fruits cobalt blue to violet, waxy. Free-fruiting.

J.v. 'Glauca' 105 Small-medium, columnar. Leaves silver-grey, waxy, colour best spring and autumn.

J.v. 'Pendula' 326 35 to 45ft (10.5 to 13.5m) open crown, hanging branchlets. Leaves light green.

J.v. 'Pseudocupressus' 106, 319 Narrow columnar form.

J.v. 'Skyrocket' 319, 326 Very narrow, conical, upright, slender-branched. Pale grey foliage. Becomes thin, leaning. 10ft (3m) in 20 years.

Juniperus chinensis
Chinese juniper

To 75ft (23m). Crown of best trees (such as 'Aurea' shown here) dense and conic, one-stemmed.

Branches ascend gently.

Bole often deeply fluted. **Bark** peels in narrow, stringy strips.

Male flowers.

Scale leaves small, blunt. **Awl leaves** ½in (1cm), prickly, set in both twos and threes. Juvenile leaves dark green, mixed with or at base of shoots of adult scale leaves.

Cones ⅓in (8mm), waxy green becoming dark purple.

Juniperus communis
Common juniper

To 15ft (4.5m). Crown small, usually spreading, shrubby, scruffy, but cultivars very variable. All common juniper have only juvenile foliage.

Leaves glaucous white on inner surfaces. **Berries** ½in (1cm), green for 2-3 years, bluish when ripe. The berries are used for flavouring gin.

Shoots very slender. **Leaves** short, ½in (1cm), sharp, concave, set in whorls of 3.

Juniperus virginiana
Pencil cedar, Eastern red cedar

To 100ft (30m). Crown ragged, open, conic when tree young.

Cones ¼in (6mm), rounded or ovoid, glaucous, ripening in first year.

Shoots very slender, 4-angled. **Leaves** mainly scale-like, pointed in opposite pairs. **Juvenile leaves** set at tips and bases of sprays.

Bole is often fluted.

Branches upswept or spreading. **Bark** peels in strips.

Juvenile leaves ¾in (2cm).

Koelreuteria paniculata
Gold-rain tree, Pride of India

Leaves *huge, 8-16in (20-40cm), pinnate with 11-13 leaflets or bipinnate.* **Leaflets** *1¼-3½in (3-8cm), coarsely toothed, paler below.* **Petioles** *grooved above.* **Shoots** *irregular.* **Buds** *small, ¹⁄₆in (4mm).*

Flowers *½in (1cm), in large panicles.*

Veins *pubescent below.*

Laburnum watereri
Waterer's laburnum

To 30ft (9m). Crown *spreading on arching, ascending branches.*

Bark *smoothish, with columns of buff-brown lenticels.*

Leaves *compound, comprising 3 leaflets.*

Leaflets *to 2½-3½in (6-8cm), entire, elliptic or oval with cuneate base, matt above, glaucous and glabrous below, often cupped.*

Buds *grey-brown, ovoid, with silky white hairs.*

Flowers *¾in (2cm), with 5 petals, 2 upper petals having brown markings, borne in dense racemes, 10-20in (25-50cm) long, in late May-June.*

Shoots *grey-green at first, with adpressed hairs.*

Fruit pods *1½-2½in (4-6cm), sparsely haired, 1-3 from each raceme.* **Seeds** *poisonous.*

K

KALOPANAX *pictus* **245,** 319, 327
Castor aralia. Zone 4. To 100ft (30m). resembles *Acer*, but leaves alternate and stems prickly. Leaves 12in (30cm) across in young plants. Small white flowers in large, flattish heads. Tolerates alkaline conditions; does best on deep, rich, moist soil. Black fruits. 25ft (7.5m) in 20 years.
  K.p. *maximowiczii* **319** Leaves deeply lobed.

KETELEERIA *davidiana* **318**
Small handsome relation of silver firs. China. Zone 8.

KOELREUTERIA *paniculata** **225,** 317, 318, 327
Golden-rain tree, Pride of India. China. Zone 5. To 35ft (10.5m), flat-topped. Leaves pinnate, deciduous; leaflets ovallish, coarsely toothed, short-stalked. Flowers small, yellow, in clusters, to 18in (45cm) long. Fruit, capsules, bladder-like, yellow-brown. Sun-loving. Tolerant of dryness. Susceptible to coral-spot fungus. 18ft (5.5m) in 20 years.

L

LABURNUM 208, **210,** 326, 327
Deciduous trees or shrubs. Compound leaves of 3 leaflets. Yellow flowers, usually clustered. Straight pods, slightly winged margins.
Laburnum *alpinum* **210,** 318 Scotch laburnum. C. and S. Europe. Zone 4. To 25 (7.5m), short, sturdy trunk, stiff upright branching. Leaves medium length, deep green, shiny, stalked; few hairs on pale underside. Flowers pea-shaped, June. Many soils, good in polluted areas. Subject to wood-rot fungi, leaf-rot, mildew, fungi. 25ft (7.5m) in 20 years.
L. *anagyroides* **210,** 318 Common laburnum, Goldenchain. C. and S. Europe. Zone 5. To 20ft (6m), upright, often branching near ground. Leaves medium length, oval, downy beneath, dull green. Flowers on thin, hairy stalks. May–June. 20ft (6m) in 20 years.
  L.a. 'Aureum' 326 Golden-leaved laburnum. Yellow in summer.
L. × vossii See *L.* × *watereri*
L. × watereri* **210** Waterer's laburnum. Zone 5. Hybrid between *L. alpinum* and *L. anagyroides*. To 30ft (9m), stiffly upright. Leaves glossy green, hairy beneath, elliptic or oval. Flowers pea-like. Pods usually only partially developed, sometimes sterile. 30ft (9m) in 20 years. A.G.M. 1928.

LAGERSTROEMIA *indica*
Crape myrtle. China. Zone 8. A lightweight ornamental tree to 20ft (6m). Smooth mottle-grey bark, privet-like leaves and panicles of pink or red flowers in summer to autumn. Much grown in streets in parts of southern Europe.

LARIX 42, 70, **92–3,** 112, 326, 327
Larches. Deciduous, conical. Leaves flat, narrow, needle-like, bright green, in rosettes on old shoots, singly on new. Male 'flowers' yellow, females variously coloured. Cone upright, sheds seed in autumn of 1st year, but persists on tree. Successful on many soils except dry, shallow chalk. Sun-loving. Susceptible to 'larch blight' caused by woolly aphid (*Chermes* sp.), also 'larch canker' caused by fungus *Dasyscypha calycina*; leaf-cast and rust in Europe, leaf-cast in U.S.A.
L. *decidua** **92–3,** 318, 325, 326 European larch. European Alps and Carpathians. Zone 2. To 180ft (55m), narrowly conical. Leaves darken in summer, turn gold in autumn, soft, thin. Shoots buff-coloured. Male 'flowers' on weak, pendulous shoots. 50ft (15m) in 20 years.
  L.d. *polonica* **318** A North European form of common larch.
L. × eurolepis* **93** Dunkeld hybrid larch. Scotland. Zone 4. To 100ft (30m). Leaves small, dull dark grey-green above, 2 grey bands beneath. Female 'flowers' pink as *L. decidua*. Cones as *L. decidua* but bigger. More resistant to insect and fungal attack than other forms. Vigorous. 55 to 65ft (17 to 20m) in 20 years.
L. *gmelini* **319** 'Dahurian larch' from Siberia.
  L.g. *olgensis* **319** Siberian larch with red, hairy shoots.
L. *griffithiana* **93,** 318 Sikkim larch. E. Nepal, Sikkim. Tibet. Zone 7. To 70ft (21.5m), broadly conic with wide-spreading, low branches, hanging shoots. Leaves in whorls, shiny, 2 narrow green-white bands beneath. Cones abundant, dark purple at first, slightly tapered cylinders to 5in (13cm). Needs mild area. 25ft (7.5m) in 20 years.
L. *kaempferi* **93,** 319, 326 Japanese larch, Red larch. Japan. Zone 7. To 100ft (30m), broadly conical. Leaves dark grey-green above, 2 broad greenish

grey bands beneath, becoming pale yellow, then orange. Male 'flowers' widely spread over crown. 50ft (15m) in 20 years.
L. laricina **93**, 319, 327 Tamarack, Eastern larch. E. United States. Zone 1. 40 to 80ft (12 to 24.5m), pyramidal. Leaves 3-angled, bright blue-green, yellowing to fall in early winter. Cones very small, ovallish. Tolerates wet, peaty soils. 40ft (12m) in 20 years.
L. occidentalis **92, 93,** 319 Western larch. United States. Zone 5. 140 to 180ft (42 to 55m), open and rather narrowly conical. Leaves similar to *L. laricina,* but slightly longer. Cones to 1½in (4cm) long. 35ft (10.5m) in 20 years.
L. sibirica 319 Siberian larch, medium-sized, not hardy in Britain.

LAURELIA serrata
Chilean laurel. Chile. Zone 8. A dark green, bushy small tree with aromatic leaves. Can be a beautiful pendulous tree. Any soil.

LAURUS 130–1
Evergreen shrubs or small trees. Flowers small, yellowish-green in clusters, separate trees, April. Fruits on female trees, black, shining. Likes well-drained soil.
L. nobilis **130**, 318, 326, 327 Laurel, Sweet bay. Mediterranean. Zone 6. To 35ft (10.5m), dense, often pyramidal. Narrow or oval aromatic leaves, medium length, dark glossy green, simple. Flowers on spikes. Fruit oval, dark green berry. 15 to 20ft (4.5 to 6m) in 20 years.
   L.n. angustifolia **130** Willow-leaf bay. Leaves long, narrow, leathery, pale green, wavy-edged. Hardier than the type.
   L.n. **'Aurea'** **130**, 326 Golden-yellow leaves.

LIBOCEDRUS decurrens See *Calocedrus decurrens*

LIGUSTRUM lucidum **240–1**, 317, 318, 326, 327
China. Zone 7. To 30ft (9m), occasionally to 50ft (15m) erect shrub or tree, dense branching. Leaves narrow, oval, medium length, glossy dark green above, simple, evergreen. Flowers small, white, bisexual, in clusters to 8in (20.5cm) long. Aug.–Sept. Fruit oblong, blue-black, Sept.–Oct. Sun-loving; tolerant of shade and dryness; requires shelter. Most soils. Pest-free. 15ft (4.5m) in 20 years. 'Glossy privet.'
   L.l. **'Excelsum Superbum'** A good yellow and cream variegated form, but the name is a hyperbole.
   L.l. **'Tricolor'** is variegated white and faint pink.

LINDERA obtusiloba
Japan, China. Zone 7. To 25ft (7.5m). A deciduous relation of the bay with broad three-lobed leaves, notable for mustard-coloured spring flowers and beautiful buttery autumn colour. Always handsome-looking but needs lime-free soil.

LIQUIDAMBAR **132–3**, 219, 326, 327
Small deciduous group. Leaves maple-like, toothed, good autumn colour. Flowers green-yellow in small round heads, male and female separate, petalless. Round fruiting heads of capsules. Dislike shallow chalky soil. Young plants liable to frost damage in late spring. No diseases in Britain; sweetgum blight in America.
L. formosana **133**, 318 Zone 7. To 120ft (36m). Leaves medium length, 3-lobed, often hairy beneath. Fruiting heads bristly. Fruits as in *L. styraciflua.* Not lime-tolerant. 35ft (10.5m) in 20 years.
L. orientalis **133**, 318 Oriental sweet gum. Asia Minor. Zone 6. To 100ft (30m). Leaves 5-lobed, simple, smooth, lobed or coarsely toothed, stalked. Flowers greenish, spring. Fruit woody.
L. styraciflua* **133** Sweet gum. E. United States. Zone 5. To 140ft (42m), broad dome, conic when young, small branches. Leaves alternate, medium length, 5 to 7 lobes, pointed, smooth and glossy above, hairy below, slender stalk. Male flowers on 3in (7.5cm) stalk; female flowers on the same tree in larger clusters. 20ft (6m) in 20 years. Usually pest-free. A.G.M. 1969.
   L.s. **'Aurea'** 326 Leaves striped and mottled with yellow.

LIRIODENDRON 42, 126, 130
Deciduous, alternate leaves, solitary flowers. Brown cone-like fruit, a cluster of husks each with 1- or 2-seed, winged nut. Prefer deep soil.
L. chinense 318 Chinese tulip-tree. China. Zone 7. To 50ft (15m), similar to *L. tulipifera.* Leaves with deeper lobes; turn bright yellow in autumn. Flowers smaller, green outside, yellowish inside. Best in a sheltered position. 45ft (13.5m) in 20 years.

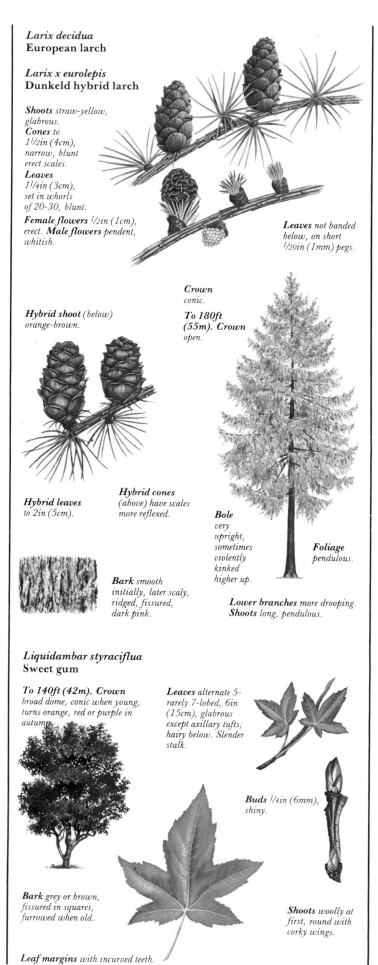

Larix decidua
European larch

Larix x eurolepis
Dunkeld hybrid larch

Shoots *straw-yellow, glabrous.*
Cones *to 1½in (4cm), narrow, blunt erect scales.*
Leaves *1¼in (3cm), set in whorls of 20-30, blunt.*
Female flowers *½in (1cm), erect.* **Male flowers** *pendent, whitish.*

Leaves *not banded below, on short 1/20in (1mm) pegs.*

Crown *conic.*

Hybrid shoot *(below) orange-brown.*

To 180ft (55m). Crown *open.*

Hybrid leaves *to 2in (5cm).*

Hybrid cones *(above) have scales more reflexed.*

Bole *very upright, sometimes violently kinked higher up.*

Foliage *pendulous.*

Bark *smooth initially, later scaly, ridged, fissured, dark pink.*

Lower branches *more drooping.* **Shoots** *long, pendulous.*

Liquidambar styraciflua
Sweet gum

To 140ft (42m). Crown *broad dome, conic when young, turns orange, red or purple in autumn*

Leaves *alternate 5-rarely 7-lobed, 6in (15cm), glabrous except axillary tufts; hairy below. Slender stalk.*

Buds *¼in (6mm), shiny.*

Bark *grey or brown, fissured in squares, furrowed when old.*

Shoots *woolly at first, round with corky wings.*

Leaf margins *with incurved teeth.*

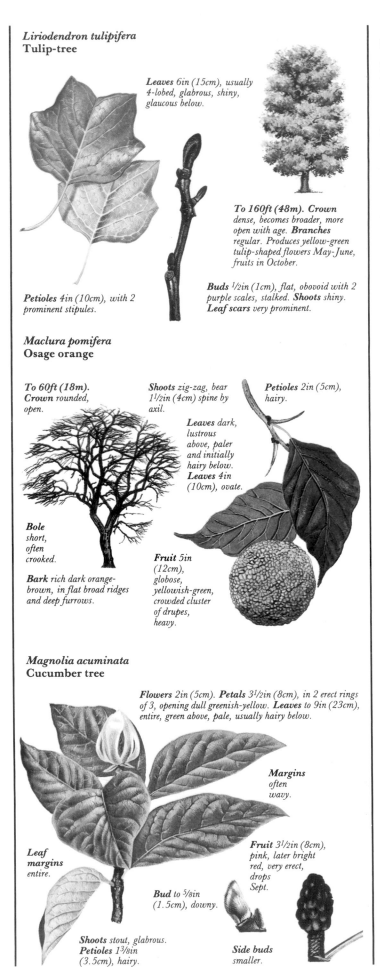

Liriodendron tulipifera
Tulip-tree

Leaves 6in (15cm), usually 4-lobed, glabrous, shiny, glaucous below.

To 160ft (48m). Crown dense, becomes broader, more open with age. **Branches** regular. Produces yellow-green tulip-shaped flowers May-June, fruits in October.

Petioles 4in (10cm), with 2 prominent stipules.

Buds ½in (1cm), flat, obovoid with 2 purple scales, stalked. **Shoots** shiny. **Leaf scars** very prominent.

Maclura pomifera
Osage orange

To 60ft (18m). Crown rounded, open.

Shoots zig-zag, bear 1½in (4cm) spine by axil.

Petioles 2in (5cm), hairy.

Leaves dark, lustrous above, paler and initially hairy below. **Leaves** 4in (10cm), ovate.

Bole short, often crooked.

Bark rich dark orange-brown, in flat broad ridges and deep furrows.

Fruit 5in (12cm), globose, yellowish-green, crowded cluster of drupes, heavy.

Magnolia acuminata
Cucumber tree

Flowers 2in (5cm). **Petals** 3½in (8cm), in 2 erect rings of 3, opening dull greenish-yellow. **Leaves** to 9in (23cm), entire, green above, pale, usually hairy below.

Margins often wavy.

Leaf margins entire.

Fruit 3½in (8cm), pink, later bright red, very erect, drops Sept.

Bud to ⅝in (1.5cm), downy.

Shoots stout, glabrous. **Petioles** 1⅜in (3.5cm), hairy.

Side buds smaller.

L. tulipifera * **126–7**, 317, 319, 326, 327 Tulip-tree. N. America. Zone 4. To 160ft (48m). Saddle-shaped leaves, medium length, rich yellow in autumn. Flowers tulip-shaped, yellow-green, orange markings inside. Flowers May–June, fruit October. 40ft (12m) in 20 years.
  L.t. '**Aureomarginatum**' **326** Leaves bordered with yellow.
  L.t. '**Fastigiatum**' **326** Broadly columnar, erect.

LITHOCARPUS densiflorus **162, 163,** 326
Tanbark oak. California, Oregon. Zone 7. To 100ft (30m), closely related to oak. Pyramidal when young, becoming open. Leaves evergreen, substantial, leathery, oval, pointed, toothed; woolly down at first. Flowers unisexual, males on erect spikes. Fruit acorn-like. Requires sun, sheltered site in moist soil, preferably neutral to acid. Not lime-tolerant. 15ft (4.5m) in 20 years.

LIVISTONA australis **122–3**
Australia. Zone 8. To 60ft (18m), trunk covered with leaf-bases and fibres. Palmate leaves to 4ft (1.2m) across, on 6ft (1.8m) stalk; leaflets glossy green, yellow stripe. Unisexual flowers on same tree. Tiny red-brown fruit clusters.

LYONOTHAMNUS floribundus aspleniifolius
California. Zone 8. Slender evergreen from Santa Catalina island. Fern-like leaves, creamy spiraea-like flowers in summer, red-brown bark that shreds in maturity. To 40ft (12m) in 25 years (with shelter).

M

MAACKIA **209**
Hardy, deciduous. Leaves pinnate. Flowers white, pea-like, in dense upright clusters. Pods oblong, up to 5 seeds. Slow-growing. Most soils. Full sun.
M. amurensis **209** Manchuria. Zone 4. To 20ft (6m). Leaves dark green above, paler beneath, very pretty at bud-break, shoots silvery-hairy. Flowers July–Aug. Pods Sept.–Oct. Prefers light loam. 12ft (3.5m) in 20 years.
M. sinensis **209** C. China. Zone 5. To 70ft (21.5m), broad-headed. Leaves with 11 or 13 leaflets, downy beneath. Flowers July–August.

MACLURA pomifera * **142–3,** 317, 319, 327
Osage orange. S. and C. United States. Zone 5. To 60ft (18m), rounded top, open and irregular, thorny. Leaves alternate, medium length, oval, pointed, dark green and hairless above, paler and downy beneath, yellow in autumn, deciduous. Flowers, sexes on separate trees. Fruit orange-shaped, yellowish-green, inedible. 20ft (6m) in 20 years.

MAGNOLIA 15, 125, **126–30,** 173, 327
Deciduous or evergreen trees or shrubs. Big simple leaves. Bisexual flowers borne singly. Cone-like fruit, red or pink, a cluster of seed capsules which split open to reveal shiny seeds. Neutral to acid soil; some species lime-tolerant. Subject to leaf-spot in Europe and America, canker and die-back in America.
M. acuminata * **128,** 319, 326, 327 Cucumber tree. E. United States. Zone 4. To 100ft (30m), upright, pyramidal, spreading with age. Leaves oval to oblong, medium to long, pointed, green, downy beneath, deciduous. Flowers inconspicuous, early summer. 35ft (10.5m) in 20 years. Usually pest-free.
M. campbellii **128, 129,** 316, 318, 327 Pink tulip tree. Sikkim. Zone 8–9. To 100ft (30m), open, few branches. Leaves oval, tapering, long, smooth above, hairy beneath. Flowers cup-shaped, spreading later, shell-pink, to 10in (26cm) across, early spring. Not lime-tolerant. Sheltered position; flowers frosted in cold, exposed areas. 30ft (9m) in 20 years.
  M.c. mollicomata **128,** 327 Slightly hardier than the type; flowers at earlier age.
M. cordata **127, 128** Yellow cucumber tree. S.E. United States. Zone 5. To 35ft (10.5m), upright, compact. Leaves medium length, deciduous. Flowers cup-shaped, yellow, summer and early autumn. 25ft (7.5m) in 20 years.
M. delavayi **127, 128,** 317, 326 China. Zone 7. To 35ft (10.5m), spreading, flat-topped. Leaves twice size of *M. grandiflora,* dull greyish-green above, downy beneath, evergreen. Flowers creamy-white, to 8in (20.5cm) across, fragrant, late summer. Buff-white bark. Likes chalk. 20ft (6m) in 20 years.
M. denudata **129,** 318, 327 Yulan, Lily tree. China. Zone 5. To 50ft (15m), rounded, many branches. Leaves medium length, oval, downy beneath. Flower buds conspicuous for grey, shaggy hairs in winter. Flowers pure white, early spring. Orange seeds. 20ft (6m) in 20 years. A.G.M. 1936.
M. fraseri **319** Similar to *M. macrophylla,* from S.E. United States.
M. grandiflora * 43, **126–7,** 173, 317, 319, 326, 327 Bull bay, Laurel magnolia, Southern magnolia. S.E. United States. Zone 7. To 100ft (30m), dense, pyramidal. Leaves oval to oblong, long, glossy green above, often

reddish-brown beneath, evergreen. Flowers creamy-white, fragrant, 8in (20.5cm) across, late spring and summer. 20ft (6m) in 20 years.

M.g. **'Exmouth' 127** Exmouth magnolia. Narrowly pyramidal. Leaves narrow, lance-shaped, furry beneath, hairs rust red. Flowers big, fragrant. A.G.M. 1969.

M.g. **'Goliath' 127** Leaves broad, dark shiny green. Flowers to 12in (30cm) across. A.G.M. 1969.

M. × *highdownensis* **128** Small tree, a hybrid between *M. sinensis* and *M. wilsonii*. Flowers big, white petals, purple core, early summer. Succeeds on chalk. 15ft (4.5m) in 20 years.

M. kobus* **128,** 319, 327 Japan. Zone 5. To 40ft (12m), pyramidal, becoming round-headed. Leaves obovate, medium length, leaf-buds downy. Flowers small, white, slightly fragrant, mid-spring, not flowering for 12/15 years. All soils. 20ft (6m) in 20 years. A.G.M. 1936.

M. liliiflora **129,** 327 C. China. Zone 5. To 12ft (3.5m), straggling. Leaves oval, deciduous, shiny, dark green above, furry beneath. Erect flowers 8in (20.5cm) wide, purple-tinted outside, creamy-white inside, late spring/early summer. Fruit brown, oblong. Dislikes chalk. 10ft (3m) in 20 years.

M.l. **'Nigra' 129,** 327 Japan. Zone 5. Form with slightly larger flowers, purple-flushed, spring/summer. A.G.M. 1969.

M. × *loebneri* **128–9,** 316 Zone 4. To 50ft (15m), variable hybrid, pyramidal, open. Flowers, numerous white petals, fragrant, early spring. All soils. A.G.M. 1969.

M. × *l.* **'Leonard Messel'** A form with deep pink buds opening to lilac-pink flowers.

M. macrophylla **127–8,** 319, 326, 327 Bigleaf magnolia. S.E. United States. Zone 5. To 60ft (18m), open, spreading head. Leaves to 25in (64cm) long, bright shiny green above, bloomed beneath, deciduous. Flowers creamy white, fragrant, to 12in (30cm) across, summer. Orange seeds. Not lime-tolerant. 25ft (7.5m) in 20 years.

M. obovata **128,** 316, 319, 327 Whiteleaf Japanese magnolia. Japan. Zone 5. To 100ft (30m), pyramidal and open. Leaves wedge-shaped, to 18in (45cm) long, green and bloomed above, blue-white, slightly downy beneath, deciduous. Flowers fragrant, white petals, stamens purple, yellow anthers, early summer. Orange seeds. Not lime-tolerant. 25ft (7.5m) in 20 years.

M. salicifolia **129,** 319, 327 Anise magnolia. Japan. Zone 5. To 30ft (9m), pyramidal. Leaves lance-shaped, deciduous, smooth, dull green above, waxy, slightly downy beneath. Flowers white, fragrant, early spring. Fruit cucumber-like, early autumn. 25ft (7.5m) in 20 years. A.G.M. 1941.

M. sargentiana **318** Tree-size magnolia from W. China; very big pink flowers.

M. sieboldii **128** Oyama magnolia. Japan, Korea. Zone 5–6. To 30ft (9m), rounded. Leaves broadly oval, deciduous, hairy and waxy beneath, dark green above. Flowers cup-shaped, white, fragrant, summer. 15ft (4.5m) in 20 years. A.G.M. 1935.

M. sinensis **128** W. China. Zone 7. To 20ft (6m), wide-spreading. Leaves oval to round, deciduous, shiny, bright green above, furry beneath. Nodding flowers to 5in (13cm) wide, white, saucer-shaped, lemon-smelling, summer. 15ft (4.5m) in 20 years. A.G.M. 1969.

M. × *soulangiana** **28–9, 128, 129,** 318, 327 Saucer magnolia. Zone 5. To 25ft (7.5m), hybrid between *M. denudata* and *M. liliiflora,* often many-stemmed, low and spreading. Leaves medium length, downy beneath. Flowers tulip-shaped, white, stained rose-purple at base, spring. Other clones have coloured flowers. Tolerates poor soils, pollution; moderately lime-tolerant. Best in full sun. 10ft (3m) in 20 years. Scale pest. A.G.M. 1932.

M. × *s.* **'Alba Superba'** A splendid, rather erect, white-flowered form. The flowers are fragrant. A.G.M. 1969.

M. × *s.* **'Brozzonii'** The largest-flowered, white with purple shading at the base. Needs shelter. Flowers late. A.G.M. 1969.

M. × *s.* **'Lennei' 128** A vigorous clone with purple flowers, dark outside and pale within.

M. × *s.* **'Rustica Rubra'** An outstanding vigorous sport of 'Lennei'. Flowers cup-shaped and rich red. A.G.M. 1969.

M. stellata **128** Star magnolia. Japan. Zone 5. To 10ft (3m), rounded, spreading shrub. Leaves small, dark green. Flowers double, white, fragrant, April. Slow-growing.

M. tripetala **319** Umbrella tree; big spreading magnolia from E. United States. Flowers late spring.

M. × *veitchii* **129,** 316, 327 Veitch magnolia. Zone 7. To 70ft (21.5m), vigorous, open. Leaves oblong, long, dark green. Flowers 6in (15cm) across, white, flushed purple-pink, spring. Flowers earlier in life than *M. campbellii*. Not lime-tolerant. 35ft (10.5m) in 20 years.

M. virginiana **42, 127,** 327 Swamp bay, Sweet bay. E. United States. Zone 5. To 65ft (20m) but more shrub-like in colder areas. Leaves oval or oblong,

Magnolia grandiflora
Bull bay, Laurel magnolia, Southern magnolia

Fruit *4in (10cm), on stout,* ⅝*in (1.5cm) stalk, hairy.*

Petioles *1in (2.5cm), stout, hairy.*

Leaves *8in (20cm), thick, leathery, shiny, laurel-like, rufously pubescent beneath.*

Flowers *8in (20cm) across, creamy-white, from May to August.*

Magnolia kobus
Japanese magnolia

To 40ft (12m). Crown *of young trees broad and conic, becoming domed.* **Branches** *level.* **Bare branches** *regularly clothed in white flowers on older trees; younger trees shy to flower.*

Leaves *6in (15cm).* **Shoots** *shiny, greenish-brown.*

Leaves *crinkled, shiny below.* **Veins** *impressed.* **Petioles** ⅝*in (1.5cm).*

Flowers *5in (12cm), carried profusely, appear mid-spring before leaves.*

Magnolia x soulangiana
Saucer magnolia

Fruit *comprises spirally set carpels, each splitting to release 1 or 2 seeds.*

To 25ft (7.5m). Crown *low.*

Leaves *6in (15cm) (larger in some forms), downy below. Tapered at both base and apex. Russet in autumn.*

Bole *short.* **Bark** *smooth, grey.* **Flowers** *before or with new leaves.*

Flowers *to 8in (20cm).* **Petals** *(6-9) each 4in (10cm).*

Malus baccata
Siberian crab apple

*Fruit ¹/₂in (1cm), green, ripening to clear red. **Pedicels** up to 2¹/₂in (6cm), very slender.*

*Leaves to 3in (7cm), narrow, sharply serrate. **Petioles** 2in (5cm).*

*To 50ft (15m). **Crown** upright, narrow when young, becoming domed. **Branches** arched, dense.*

Flowers to 1¹/₂in (4cm) wide, profuse, ivory white with spaced narrow petals. Fragrant, May.

Malus floribunda
Japanese flowering crab apple

Fruit ³/₄in (2cm), ripens red or yellow.

*To 35ft (10.5m). **Crown** dense. **Leaves** to 3¹/₂in (8cm), paler and pubescent below, sometimes lobed on vigorous shoots.*

Teeth coarse.

*Flowers open in May. **Flowers** 1¹/₂in ((4cm), red in bud, fading to pink, then whitish, in umbels of 4-7.*

Shoots hairy, becoming almost glabrous.

Malus x purpurea
Purple crab apple

*Flowers 1¹/₂in (4cm) wide, open in early May in sixes and sevens. **Petals** obovate, darker in bud.*

Fruit small, ³/₄in (2cm), red-purple.

medium length, glossy green above, blue-white and downy beneath, partially evergreen. Flowers to 3in (7.5cm) wide, white, very fragrant, early summer.
M. wilsonii **128,** 316 Wilson's magnolia. W. China. Zone 6. To 24ft (7m), wide-spreading, often shrubby and open. Small, pointed leaves. Flowers white, crimson stamens, fragrant, hanging, May and June. Partial shade.

MALUS 64, 190, **194–7,** 327
Mostly small to medium deciduous trees. Leaves simple, toothed, fragrant if crushed. Flowers in small clusters, often profuse, widely ranging in colour, often fragrant, spring. Fruit varies from round to oval, up to 2in (5cm) wide, usually ornamental, autumn. Many species do not bear flowers and fruit annually. All fertile soils. Hardy. Sun-loving. Susceptible to borers, white woolly aphids, scale insects, apple-scab, fire-blight, rusts.
M. baccata* **195, 196, 197,** 318 Siberian crab apple. N.E. Asia. Zone 2. To 50ft (15m), upright, narrow when young, becoming domed, dense branching. Flowers white, very fragrant, May. Fruit tiny, red or yellow, Aug.–Oct. Flowers and fruits very variable. Resistant to apple scab.
　　M.b. **'Columnaris'** 326 Columnar, fruiting annually. Subject to fire-blight.
　　M.b. **'Mandshurica'** **197,** 316 Zone 2. To 50ft (15m), upright. Leaves ovallish, narrow, pointed, smooth above, possibly downy below, stalked. Flowers white, fragrant. Fruits small, red or yellow. Prefers slightly alkaline soil. Resistant to apple-scab.
M. coronaria **'Charlottae'** **196, 197,** 316 Zone 4. To 30ft (9m), wide-spreading. Leaves oval to 3-lobed, smooth, mellow autumn colours, stalked. Flowers shell-pink, violet scented, spring or early summer. Fruit green-yellow, acid-tasting. Prefers slightly alkaline soil.
M. domestica 64, **195** Orchard apple. Differs from crab apple trees in that fruit is larger, often sweeter. Possibly 1,000 varieties.
M. **'Dorothea'** **197** Zone 4. To 25ft (7.5m), spreading, hybrid. Leaves ovallish, pointed, blunt at base, stalked. Flowers crimson to rose, many-petalled, spring. Fruits yellow. Fruit and flowers annually. Resists scab.
M. **'Echtermeyer'** **197** Zone 4. 12 to 15ft (3.5 to 4.5m), wide-spreading, some branches pendulous. Leaves bronze-green to purple. Flowers pink-red, fruits crimson-purple.
M. floribunda* **196, 197,** 316, 326 Japanese flowering crab apple. Zone 4. To 35ft (10.5m), spreading. Leaves vary from oval to 3- or 5-lobed, upper side smooth, dull green, under side downy, paler. Flowers pink-red, fragrant, spring. Fruit small, red or yellow.
M. **'Golden Hornet'** **197,** 317 Zone 4. To 25ft (7.5m), upright, soon pendulous. Flowers white. Heavy crops of yellow, persistent fruits. A.G.M. 1969.
M. halliana **'Parkmanii'** **197** Parkman crab apple. Zone 5. To 15ft (4.5m), upright. Leaves oval, long-pointed, leathery, glossy, dark green, possibly purple-tinted, stalked. Flowers deep rose-pink, on purplish stalks. Fruit round, pea-sized, red-purple, autumn–winter.
M. hupehensis **197** China, Japan. Zone 4. To 25ft (7.5m), upright, narrow. Leaves oval, pointed, smooth on top, downy on midrib beneath, dark green, purplish at first, stalked. Flowers, pink petals fading to white, fragrant, spring. Fruit round, green-yellow to red, small, autumn. A.G.M. 1930.
M. ioensis **'Plena'** **197** Bechtel's crab apple. Zone 2. To 30ft (9m), spreading. Leaves oval, woolly beneath. Flowers in flat heads, white or rose-tinted, fragrant, late spring. Fruit sparse, yellow-green. Dislikes chalk. Leaves susceptible to Juniper rust.
M. **'Lemoinei'** **196, 197,** 326 Zone 4. To 25ft (7.5m), erect. Leaves ovallish, purple-red to dark green. Flowers red to purple, spring. Fruits purple-red, small, late summer or autumn. Resistant to scab. A.G.M. 1937.
M. **'niedzwetzkyana'** **197** S.W. Siberia, Turkestan. Zone 3. To 20ft (6m), spreading. Leaves ovallish, undersurface downy, red-tinted at first, turning purplish later, stalk and midrib red. Flowers deep-red to purple. Fruit cone-shaped, red, furrowed, waxy.
M. **'Profusion'** **197,** 316 Zone 4. To 20ft (6m). Young leaves crimson-copper. Flowers profuse, purple-red, slightly fragrant, early summer. Fruits small, dark red. A.G.M. 1969.
M. × *purpurea** **196,** 326 Zone 4. To 25ft (7.5m), dense. Dark purple-green leaves and shoots. Flowers crimson, May. Fruit red-purple. A.G.M. 1923.
M. **'Red Jade'** **197,** 317 Zone 4. To 20ft (6m), pendulous. Leaves bright green. Flowers small, single, white or pale pink, spring. Fruits small, crimson, autumn, persisting into winter. Fruit every other year.
M. **'Red Sentinel'** **197,** 317 Zone 4. To 15ft (4.5m), upright. Flowers White. Fruit in large clusters, blood red, persists through winter.
M. **'Red Tip'** **197** Leaves broad, slightly lobed, bright red initially. Flowers red-purple. Fruit tinted red.

M. × *robusta* **197** Cherry crab apple. Zone 3. To 40ft (12m), upright, hybrid. Leaves oval, possibly tapering. Flowers white or white-pink, fragrant, spring. Fruits cherry-red or yellow, every other year. A.G.M. 1958.

M. sargentii **197** Sargent crab apple. Japan. Zone 5. To 6ft (1.8m), shrubby, spreading. Leaves often 3-lobed, hairy at first, smooth later, stalked, orange-yellow in autumn. Flowers fragrant, spring. Fruit round, small, cherry-red, autumn. A.G.M. 1927.

M. spectabilis **318** Erect small crab. Flowers pink, large.

　M.s. **'Riversii' 197** Rivers' crab apple. Zone 4. To 24ft (7m), open. Flowers semi-double, rose-pink, every other year, late spring. Fruit green.

M. sylvestris **197** Common crab apple. Europe. Zone 3. Small tree or shrub. Leaves oval, becoming smooth. Flowers pale pink or white. Fruit greenish or red-tinted. Often bears a few thorns.

　M.s. **'John Downie' 197,** **317** Zone 4. To 20ft (6m), upright. Flowers white. Fruits large, cone-shaped, orange to red, pleasantly flavoured. A.G.M. 1969.

M. toringoides **197** Cutleaf crab apple. W. China. Zone 5. To 25ft (7.5m), spreading. Leaves oval to lance-shaped, deeply lobed, hairy at first, becoming smooth above, stalked. Flowers in flat heads, small, white, fragrant, spring, in alternate years. Fruits yellow and red, autumn to early winter. A.G.M. 1929.

M. trilobata **318** Tall erect crab from Greece with maple-like leaves.

M. tschonoskii **197,** **326** Japan. Zone 5. To 40ft (12m), pyramidal, upright. Leaves oval to round, pointed, downy at first, smooth later, permanently downy beneath; red, orange, yellow and purple in autumn. Flowers, rose-pink becoming white, in flat heads. Fruits dirty yellow, tinged purple.

　M.t. **'Van Eseltine' 326** Hybrid between *M. arnoldiana* and *M. spectabilis*. Zone 4. To 20ft (6m), narrow, upright. Flowers double, pink, May. Fruit yellow and red, early autumn.

MANGLIETIA **insignis 318**
Evergreen relation of *Magnolia*; tender in Britain.

MAYTENUS **boaria 177,** **319**
Mayten tree. Chile. Zone 8 or 9. To 30ft (9m), evergreen shrub or small tree, pendulous, spreading. Leaves shiny green, narrow, oval, pointed, toothed. Flowers insignificant. Fruit orange-red, tiny. 15ft (4.5m) in 20 years.

MELIA **azedarach* 242, 243,** 316, 327
Bead tree, Chinaberry. N. India, C. and W. China. Zone 7. To 45ft (13.5m), round-headed, dense-branching. Leaves alternate, doubly pinnate to 2ft (60cm) long, ovallish, toothed leaflets, light green, deciduous. Flowers small, lilac-coloured, clustered, April–May. Fruit small, egg-shaped, yellow; remains after leaves. Needs hot summers.

MELIOSMA **veitchiorum**
W. China. Zone 7. A rare but notably eye-catching deciduous tree to about 40ft (12m). Short, stiff branches are luxuriantly clad in big pinnate leaves with red stems, each of 9 or 11 oblong leaflets being up to 7in (17.5cm) long. Broad panicles of creamy honey-scented flowers, up to 18in (45cm) long in May. Fruit blue. Likes deep neutral soil.

MESPILUS **germanica 194–5,** 317, 327
Medlar. S.E. Europe, Asia Minor. Zone 5. To 15ft (4.5m), wide-spreading, closely related to *Crataegus*. Leaves oval to lance-shaped, simple, deciduous, hairy, red-brown in autumn. Flowers single, white, possibly pink-tinged, early summer. Fruits rounded, brown, edible if picked after frost.

METASEQUOIA **glyptostroboides* 113,** 318, 326, 327
Water larch, Dawn redwood. C. China. Zone 5. To 110ft (33m), conical, branches often upswept, deciduous. Leaves opposite, down-curved at tips, short. Tiny male 'flowers'. Cones green, maturing to dark brown. Bark bright orange-or red-brown, peeling away in narrow strips, later deeply fissured. Slower in chalk soils. Water-loving. 50ft (15m) in 20 years.

METROSIDEROS **robusta**
Rata. New Zealand. Zone 9. A tender, acid-loving evergreen, to 40ft (12m). Dark, leathery, roundish leaves; reddish new shoots; scarlet flowers in mid to late summer.

MICHELIA **doltsopa**
W. China. Zone 9. A tender relation of the magnolia. Evergreen, to 40ft (12m), with dark magnolia-like leaves, paler beneath. Fragrant, creamy, many-petalled flowers in the leaf axils in spring.

Melia azedarach
Bead tree, Chinaberry

To 45ft (13.5m). Crown *rounded, dense and spreading.* **Bark** *brown or red-brown, furrowed.* **Leaves** *deciduous but semi-evergreen in extreme south of range.*

Fruit *¹/₂in (1cm), a yellow drupe, becoming wrinkled. Flesh thin, odorous. Poisonous.*

Leaves *24in (60cm), bipinnate, about 5 pinnae. Hairy, soon glabrous.* **Leaflets** *have 5-9 ovate or oval 2in (5cm) pinnules.* **Apex** *acuminate.* **Margins** *serrate or entire and lobed.*

Flowers *³/₄in (2cm), fragrant, in axillary panicles, with 5 mauve petals and narrow violet tube.*

Metasequoia glyptostroboides
Water larch, Dawn redwood

Leaves *³/₄-1¹/₂in × ¹/₁₀in (2-4cm × 2mm), opposite, soft, curved in flat sprays.* **Shoots** *opposite, deciduous when not bearing buds.*

Bole, *shown in cross-section left, very deeply fluted, tapering.*

Bark *bright orange- or red-brown, stringy, flaking away, later deeply fissured.*

Foliage *fern-like, bright yellow-green then darkening*

To 110ft (33m). Crown *sparse, narrow conic becoming columnar.*

Branches *ascend, then hang.* **Foliage** *turns yellow and brown in autumn.*

Morus alba
White mulberry

Leaves 8in (20cm), heart-shaped or oval, frequently lobed on strong shoots. Bright, shiny green, smooth; finely haired below. Petioles 1in (2.5cm). Bases cordate. Apexes acute or rounded. Margins coarsely toothed.

Shoots initially hairy, soon glabrous, slender. Buds small, conical.

Fruit 1in (2.5cm), sweet/acid, white to pink.

Nothofagus obliqua
Roblé beech

Margins irregularly serrate. Teeth sharp.

Leaves 3¹/₂in (8cm), ovate-oblong, slanted at base, deep green; pale, glaucous below. Sometimes develop lobes. Veins in 7-11 pairs, impressed, extend to tips of teeth.

Petiole ¹/₄in (6mm), red.

Shoots slender, hairy, dark red above and paler below. Buds ¹/₄in (6mm), ovoid, spreading. Fruit 3¹/₂in (8cm), set singly, 4-ribbed. Bears small scales.

To 110ft (33m). Crown ovoid, open, spreading, eventually pendulous. Lower branches pendulous.

Bark fissured.

Olea europaea
Olive

Shoots downy. Flowers ¹/₄in (6mm), set densely in 2in (5cm) axillary racemes.

Leaves 3¹/₂in (8cm).

Leaves narrow, leathery, shiny or silvery beneath.

Bark ridged, plated in small squares. Bole gnarled, dimpled, can be immense, then often hollow.

Fruit a 1¹/₄in (3cm) drupe, purple.

MORUS 142–3
Deciduous trees or shrubs. Leaves toothed, sometimes lobed. Sexes on the same or different trees, hanging catkins. Fruits tiny, clustered (blackberry-like) white, red or black, late summer. All soils. Suited to urban and seaside areas.
M. alba* 143, 318 White mulberry. China. Zone 4. To 45ft (13.5m), round-topped, dense. Leaves heart-shaped or oval, bright green. Fruit white to pink. 10 to 15ft (3 to 4.5m) in 20 years.
M. nigra 142–3, 318, 326, 327 Black mulberry. W. Asia. Zone 6. To 30ft (9m), dense, spreading head. Leaves broad, oval, medium length, 2 to 5 toothed lobes, rough and deep glossy above, pale and downy below. Flowers small, sexes separate in small clusters on same tree, spring. 10ft (3m) in 20 years.

MYRTUS apiculata 214, 317, 319
Myrtle. Chile. Zone 8. To 20ft (6m), broad. Leaves small, oval, dull green above, paler beneath, evergreen. Flowers small, solitary, white, Aug.–Sept. Fruits small, black, edible. Pretty peeling bark. Tolerant of lime. Best in full sun.

N

NOTHOFAGUS 152–3, 327
Evergreen or deciduous trees or shrubs from southern hemisphere. Leaves usually small. Male flowers usually solitary, females often in threes. Nuts similar to *Fagus* sp. Prefers neutral soil. Fast-growing, sun or shade; requires shelter from wind.
N. antarctica 152, 153, 319, 326 Antarctic beech. Chile. Zone 7. To 100ft (30m) but often many-stemmed and spreading. Leaves short with rounded tip, toothed, hairless except for midrib beneath, on short, downy stalk, dark green and glossy. Flowers unisexual on same tree, small, early summer. Fruit, 4-lobed husk with 3 nuts. 35ft (10.5m) in 20 years.
N. betuloides 319 Very leafy evergreen from Chile.
N. cliffortioides 153, 319, 326 Mountain beech. New Zealand. Zone 7. To 50ft (15m). Leaves oval with curled edges, short, alternate, hairless, on a short, very downy stalk. Evergreen. 40ft (12m) in 20 years.
N. dombeyi 153, 319 Coigue. Chile, Argentina. Zone 7. To 85ft (27m), wide-spreading. Leaves oval, evergreen or semi-evergreen, simple, dark, toothed, shiny green above, paler beneath, occasional black speckling on older leaves. 35ft (10.5m) in 20 years.
N. fusca 319 Red beech; an evergreen southern beech from New Zealand. Vigorous.
N. moorei 319 Australian beech; evergreen, from New South Wales. Rather tender.
N. obliqua* 153, 319, 325, 326 Roblé beech. Chile. Zone 7. To 110ft (33m). Leaves alternate, oval with blunt tip, medium length, toothed, dark green above, paler beneath, stalked. Flowers unisexual, small, usually single. Lime tolerant. 60 to 80ft (18 to 24.5m) in 20 years.
N. procera 153, 319, 327 Chile. Zone 7. To 80ft (24.5m). Leaves oblong with rounded tip, finely toothed, small to medium length, yellowish-green above, downy, paler beneath, conspicuously veined, like hornbeam, deciduous, often with good autumn colour. Buds stand out from twigs at an angle. 50 to 80ft (15 to 24.5m) in 20 years.
N. pumila 319 Fast-growing species from Chile, similar to *N. procera* but with small wrinkled leaves.
N. solandri 152, 153, 326 Black beech. New Zealand. Zone 7. To 80ft (24.5m). Slender, with ascending branches, evergreen. Leaves tiny, oval, glossy above, downy beneath. Flowers unisexual, small. 45ft (13.5m) in 20 years.

NYSSA
N. sinensis China. Zone 7. The little-known oriental form of *N. sylvatica*, smaller but even more colourful, with red new leaves and brilliant autumn colour. To 45ft (13.5m).
N. sylvatica 219, 319, 326, 327 Sour gum, Black gum, Tupelo. S. Canada, E. United States, C. and S. Mexico. Zone 4. To 100ft (30m), pyramidal. Leaves usually oval with tapering base, simple, deciduous, leathery, shiny, dark green above, dull below; orange to scarlet in autumn, stalk reddish. Sexes in separate heads, female heads sparser, spring. Fruits in clusters, egg-shaped, fleshy single seeds, bluish-black, autumn. Prefers moist, lime-free soils. Sun or semi-shade. Requires shelter. Resents transplanting. Subject to leaf blotch in America. 15ft (4.5m) in 20 years. A.G.M. 1969.

O

OLEA europaea* 240–1, 326
Olive. Mediterranean. Zone 9. 20 to 40ft (6 to 12m), spreading. Leaves oval or narrowly oval, simple, evergreen, leathery, shiny or silvery beneath. Flowers small, whitish, clustered, fragrant, late summer. Olives green, becoming purple and wrinkled. Requires shelter; tolerant of dryness; tender. Slow-growing.
O. excelsa (Notelea excelsa) 318 A hardier cousin of the olive. Zone 8.

OSTRYA 170–1
Hop-hornbeams. Medium to large deciduous trees. Leaves oval, toothed. Upright female catkins, drooping male catkins. Flowers in spring with leaves. Fruit is a nutlet in a husk, clusters, ripe in autumn. Any fertile soil. Of easy cultivation.
O. carpinifolia 171, 318 Hop hornbeam. S. Europe, Asia Minor. Zone 5. To 65ft (20m), round-headed. Leaves alternate, pointed, medium length, doubly toothed, dark green above, sparsely hairy below, clear yellow in autumn. Male catkins 1½ to 3in (4 to 7.5cm) long. Fruiting clusters to 2in (5cm) long. 30ft (9m) in 20 years.
O. japonica Japanese hop hornbeam. Japan. Zone 6. Smaller, spreading, with softer, less-veined leaves; pretty green fruit and attractive yellow autumn colour.
O. virginiana* Ironwood. E. United States. Zone 6. An American species with very hard timber. Leaves have fewer veins than *O. carpinifolia* and shoots are hairier. Good warm yellow in autumn. To 40ft (12m).

OXYDENDRUM arboreum* 185, 317, 326, 327
Sorrel tree. E. United States. Zone 5. To 75ft (23m), slender trunk. Leaves narrow, oblong, medium to long, tapering, dark green above, paler beneath, red in autumn. Small cylindrical white flowers clustered along spike 5 to 10in (13 to 26cm) long. July, August. Fruit greyish, hairy, woody capsule. Lime-free soil. 25ft (7.5m) in 20 years. A.G.M. 1947.

P

PARROTIA persica* 132, 133, 318, 326, 327
Persian parrotia, Ironwood. N. Persia to Caucasus. Zone 5. To 50ft (15m), widely spreading in cultivation, with rounded head and usually several trunks; tall, erect tree in the wild. Leaves ovate, medium length, coarsely toothed, almost hairless above, slightly hairy beneath, deciduous. Flowers, clusters of crimson stamens, early spring. Fruit, nut-like seed-vessel. Bark flaking. Thrives on chalk soils, but does not always colour well. Usually pest-free. A.G.M. 1969.

PAULOWNIA 244–5
Small genus of Chinese trees. Leaves large. Flowers foxglove-shaped, carried in erect panicles, formed in autumn, open next spring. Sun-loving; needs shelter from gales. Deep, well-drained soils.
P. fargesii 245 W. China. Zone 7. To 65ft (20m), spreading. Leaves deciduous, simple. Flowers absent on young trees, fragrant, dark purple-speckled, cream at base. Tolerates dryness. 40ft (12m) in 20 years.
P. tomentosa 244, 245, 316, 318, 326 Empress tree, Royal paulownia. China. Zone 5. To 50ft (15m), spreading, thick, stiff branches. Leaves oval to 5-lobed, simple, deciduous, to 3ft (1m) wide, dark green above, grey beneath, hairy, long-stalked. Flowers similar to those of *P. fargesii,* violet-scented, yellow-striped inside, open in spring. Fruit, oval, pointed capsule, holding winged seeds. 40ft (12m) in 20 years. The flowers are susceptible to late frost.

PHELLODENDRON amurense 237, 316, 326, 327
Amur cork tree. Japan, Korea, N. China, Ussuri, Amur, Manchuria. Zone 3. To 50ft (15m), wide-spreading branches. Leaves pinnate, medium length, deciduous; leaflets ovallish, bright green, golden in autumn. Flowers small, off-white, in small clusters, smell of turpentine, late spring. Fruits black, shiny, clustered, autumn. Bark deeply fissured, like black cork. Likes chalk. Sun-loving. 20ft (6m) in 20 years.

PHILLYREA latifolia 240, 318, 327
S. Europe, W. Asia. Zone 7. To 30ft (9m), spreading shrub or tree, densely branched. Leaves variable, ovallish, toothed, dark shiny green above, paler beneath, evergreen. Flowers small, greenish white. Fruit small, round, blue-black. All soils. Slow.

Ostrya virginiana
Ironwood

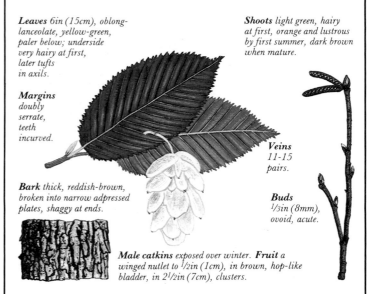

Leaves 6in (15cm), oblong-lanceolate, yellow-green, paler below; underside very hairy at first, later tufts in axils.

Margins doubly serrate, teeth incurved.

Shoots light green, hairy at first, orange and lustrous by first summer, dark brown when mature.

Veins 11-15 pairs.

Bark thick, reddish-brown, broken into narrow adpressed plates, shaggy at ends.

Buds 1/3in (8mm), ovoid, acute.

Male catkins exposed over winter. **Fruit** a winged nutlet to 1/2in (1cm), in brown, hop-like bladder, in 2 1/2in (7cm), clusters.

Oxydendrum arboreum
Sorrel tree

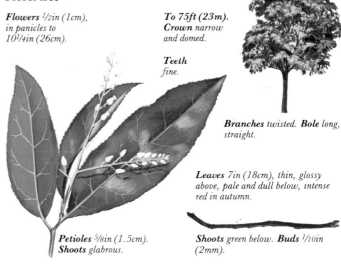

Flowers 1/2in (1cm), in panicles to 10 1/4in (26cm).

To 75ft (23m). **Crown** narrow and domed.

Teeth fine.

Branches twisted. **Bole** long, straight.

Leaves 7in (18cm), thin, glossy above, pale and dull below, intense red in autumn.

Petioles 5/8in (1.5cm). **Shoots** glabrous.

Shoots green below. **Buds** 1/10in (2mm).

Parrotia persica
Persian parrotia, Ironwood

Crown usually a huge spreading bush in cultivation, rounded head and usually several trunks.

Leaves with 6-9 pairs impressed veins, brown hairs below.

Buds downy, brown or black-purple.

Shoots green-brown, with star-shaped stiff hairs. **Flowers** have rich red stamens. Appear before leaves, early spring.

Bark similar to that of London plane, peels to expose brown or yellow beneath.

Leaf margins waved, glossy.

Picea brewerana
Brewer's spruce

To 100ft (30m). Crown broad conic, or columnar. Cones on upper branches pendulous.

Cones 5in (12cm), cylindrical, often patched with resin. Scales round, woody, flexible.

Shoots hairy, slender.

Buds ¹⁄₃in (8mm), blunt.

Branches initially ascending, later down-curving; side branches droop in blackish curtains. Leaves 1¹⁄₂in (3.5cm), radial on pendulous shoots, flat, apex blunt, 2 blue-white lines below.

Picea glauca
White spruce

Buds ¹⁄₄in (6mm), ovoid, smooth, shiny pale brown. Crushed foliage very fragrant.

Cones 2¹⁄₂in (6cm), ovoid. Scales smooth, round, thin but woody.

Foliage assurgent, all above shoot. Needles even length, ⁵⁄₈in (1.5cm), round, grey or blue-green with narrow white bands.

Shoots glabrous, white, later orange-brown.

Picea mariana
Black spruce

To 100ft (30m). Crown conic, sometimes very narrow, appears dark blue-grey from distance. Branches horizontal or slightly pendent, reach to ground; when pressed there by snow for long periods they frequently layer.

Cones 1¹⁄₂in (3.5cm), ovoid, pendent, often curved, grow profusely even on young trees.

Leaves ⁵⁄₈in (1.5cm), dark blue-green with 2 bluish-white bands below; spreading around shoot, looser below and pressed down above.

Bark grey, flaky. Buds ovoid, hairy, red-brown. Cones persistent, clustered in crown.

Shoots densely hairy. Leaves stiff, 4-sided.

PHOENIX *canariensis* **123**
Canary Island palm. Canary Islands. Zone 8. To 60ft (18m), very thick trunk covered with old leaf bases. Dense crown. Pinnate leaves 17 to 20ft (5–6m) long, short pointed light green leaflets. Flowerstalk 6ft (1.8m) long. Roundish orange fruit 1in (2.5cm) across, hangs in heavy clusters.
P. dactylifera **123** Date palm. N. Africa. Zone 9. To 100ft (30m), slender, suckering at base. Leaf bases persist for years, later leaving scars. Pinnate leaves 20ft (6m) long, grey-green leaflets. Sexes on separate trees, flowers white, fragrant, on 4ft (1.2m) stalk. Oblong fruit, 1 to 2in (2.5 to 5cm) long, deep orange, edible. Not as hardy as *P. canariensis*. Not shade-tolerant, requires warm, dry climate.

PHOTINIA *serrulata* **203,** 326, 327
Chinese photinia. China. Zone 7. To 40ft (12m), spreading. Leaves oblong to oval, simple, evergreen, leathery, dark, shiny green, roughly-toothed; young leaves red copper. Flowers small, in large flat heads, white, spring. Fruits small, red, fleshy berries, autumn and early winter. Lime-tolerant. Most soils. Sun-loving. No diseases in Britain; fungal leaf-spot and fire-blight in America.

PICEA 69, 70, 73, 78, **84–7,** 93, 98, 327
Spruces. Very hardy evergreen trees, often conical. Leaves needle-like, short, 4-sided, in 2 ranks. Male and female 'flowers' on different branches of same tree; male 'flowers' oval, yellow or red, females purple. Cones hanging, cylindrical to oval. Seeds winged. Many soils. Subject to aphid attack, honey fungus, stem canker in Europe; rusts in Europe and America.
P. abies **86–7,** 93, 318 Norway spruce. N. Europe. Zone 5. To 200ft (60m), narrowly conical, except very old trees, which are columnar or irregular. Leaves forward pointing, lower leaves spreading, small. Male 'flowers' infrequent, round, female 'flowers' spread on crowns of older trees, pink-red. Cones 8in (20.5cm) long. 40ft (12m) in 20 years.
   P.a. **'Procumbens' 119** Dwarf, to 3ft (1m), broad. Horizontal branches. Foliage in flat, yellow-green sprays.
P. asperata **86** Chinese spruce. Dragon spruce. W. China. Zone 5. To 100ft (30m), similar to *P. abies* in habit, but more broadly conical. Male 'flowers' round, shedding pollen in spring; female 'flowers' scarlet. Branches very rough. Cones dull brown, 5in (13cm) long. Not for chalky soils. 30ft (9m) in 20 years.
P. brachytyla **86** Sargent spruce. W. and C. China. Zone 5. To 80ft (24.5m), conical, becoming round-headed. Leaves crowded, firm, yellow to green, whitish beneath, flattened. Cones, to 3½in (8.5cm) long, green, ripening dull brown.
P. brewerana* 83, **85, 87,** 98, 319, 326 Brewer's spruce, Weeping spruce. N.W. California and S.W. Oregon. Zone 5. 80 to 100ft (24.5 to 30m), weeping with curving branches trailing vertically-hanging branchlets. Leaves all round shoot, slender, dark green. 15ft (4.5m) in 20 years.
P. engelmannii **85** Engelmann spruce. W. United States. Zone 2. To 120ft (36m). Leaves 4-sided, grey-green, small, rank smell. Cones oblong-cylindrical, to 2in (5cm) long. Dislikes dry or shallow chalk soil. 20ft (6m) in 20 years.
   P.e. **'Glauca' 85** Foliage more blue-grey.
P. glauca* 42, **84–5,** 319 White spruce. Canada, N.E. United States. Zone 2. 60 to 70ft (18 to 20m), conical. Leaves small, blue-green, pungent when crushed. Cones small, narrow, oblong. 35ft (10.5m) in 20 years.
   P.g. albertiana **'Conica' 85,** 319 Ovoid-conical bush. Leaves soft, grassy-green, curved, pointed, susceptible to frost in bad winters and to red spider mite. A.G.M. 1969.
P. glehnii 319 'Sakhalin spruce'; small narrow Japanese spruce, rather like *P. abies*.
P. jezoensis 319 Yezo spruce. N.E. Asia, Japan. Zone 4. To 100 or 150ft (30 or 45m), spire-like, branch ends upturned. Leaves flattened, shining rich green above, silver white beneath with 2 white bands crowded and overlapped on upper part of shoot, those below curving upwards. Cones crimson, becoming leathery-brown, to 3in (7.5cm) long; scales toothed. Can be frost-damaged in spring in Europe.
P. koyamai 319 Narrow-growing mountain spruce from Japan.
P. likiangensis **86–7,** 318, 327 Likiang spruce. W. China. Zone 5. 50 to 65ft 15 to 20m), conical. Leaves forward pointing on upper side of shoot, on lower side in 2 opposite ranks. Upper leaves blue-grey, lower with 2 broad white bands. 'Flowers' profuse; male 'flowers' large, round, crimson; females scarlet, small. Cones to 5in (13cm) long, slightly tapered. Vigorous and adaptable. 35ft (10.5m) in 20 years.
P. mariana* 42, **84–5,** 319 Black spruce. N.W. America. Zone 2. To 100ft (30m), dense, pyramidal. Leaves small, blue-green, blunt-pointed. Cones

small, purplish, becoming brown, persist up to 30 years. 15ft (4.5m) in 20 years.

P.m. 'Doumetii' 85 Zone 2. Small, dense, conical, becoming rounded, irregular. Leaves thin, sharp-pointed, crowded, pale grey.

P. obovata 319 Siberian spruce, similar to Norway spruce.

P. omorika* 86, 318, 326 Yugoslavia. Zone 4. To 100ft (30m), narrowly conical. Leaves more or less horizontally arranged, flattened, small, glossy greyish green with two white lines beneath. Cones egg-shaped. Grows on limestone, very acid peats. Resists frost, town air. 35ft (10.5m) in 20 years. A.G.M. 1969.

P. orientalis 69, **86, 87,** 318, 326 Oriental spruce. Caucasian spruce. Asia Minor, Caucasus. Zone 4. To 180ft (55m), conical. Leaves shortest amongst spruces, growing all round shoot, to ⅓in (7mm) long, deep shining green. Male 'flowers' deep red. Cones freely borne over upper crowns of older trees, purple at first, brown at maturity. 40ft (12m) in 20 years.

P.o. 'Aurea' 86, 326 Small. Leaves pale yellow, then golden-yellow, finally green. Beautiful for 3 weeks in spring.

P. polita 86, 319 Tiger-tail spruce. Japan. Zone 5. To 100ft (30m), pyramidal. Leaves dark-shiny green, rigid-spined, very sharp. Cones ovallish, shining yellow-brown, to 4in (10cm) long, brown at maturity. 20ft (6m) in 20 years.

P. pungens 85, 327 Colorado spruce. S.W. United States. Zone 2. To 100ft (30m), stout horizontal branches. Rigid leaves, small, pointed, bluish-green. Oblong cones to 4in (10cm). Tolerates drought. 25 to 30ft (7.5 to 9m) in 20 years.

P.p. 'Glauca' 85, 326 Blue spruce. Zone 5. To 75ft (23m), narrowly conical, columnar at bottom. Leaves waxy, grey-green or green with age. 25ft (7.5m) in 20 years.

P.p. 'Koster' 85 Small-medium, conical. Leaves silver-blue.

P.p. 'Moerheimii' 85 To 30ft (9m), conical, dense. Leaves pale waxy blue. 15ft (4.5m) in 20 years.

P. rubens 84–5 Red spruce. N.E. United States. Zone 2. 60 to 70ft (18 to 21.5m) narrowly conical. Leaves dark yellow-green, wiry, curved. Cones to 2in (5cm) long, brown at maturity, falling during first winter or following spring. Likes moisture, not chalk. 30ft (9m) in 20 years.

P. schrenkiana 225 Schrenk's spruce from central Asia; similar to *P. smithiana.*

P.s. 'Globosa' 119 Miniature form; broad, low, cone shape.

P. sitchensis 73, 83, **84, 85, 86,** 100, 319, 327 Sitka spruce. W. United States. Zone 6. To 180 or 200ft (55 or 60m), conical. Leaves flattened, bright blue-green above, blue-white beneath, sharp-pointed. Cones to 4in (10cm) long, falling by winter of first year. Pale trunk of big trees splays out at base. Likes cool, damp summers; acid or any soils. 55 to 65ft (17 to 20m) in 20 years.

P. smithiana 86, 87, 318, 326 West Himalayan spruce. W. Himalaya. Zone 6. To 200ft (60m), pendulous. Leaves slender, curving, medium length, dark green. Male 'flowers' small, end of shoots. Cones green becoming brown, to 7in (17.5cm) long. 35ft (10.5m) in 20 years.

P. spinulosa 318 Eastern Himalayan weeping spruce, similar to *P. smithiana* but with sharp prickly needles.

PICRASMA quassioides 318

Small attractive relation of *Ailanthus.* Good autumn colour.

PINUS 70–7, 327

Evergreen trees, conical, becoming flat-topped or bushy. Leaves in groups of 2 to 5 usually, needle-like, long, minutely toothed in cross-section, semi-circular or 3-sided. Male and female 'flowers' on same tree; males red or yellow, cylindrical; females scaly, woody. Cones open when ripe or remain closed. Seeds may be wingless. Dislikes shallow chalk soils. Sun-loving. Susceptible to insect attack, dry-rot fungi, honey-fungus, white-pine blister rust.

P. albicaulis 73 White-bark pine. W. United States. Zone 3. Usually shrubby, sometimes to 50ft (15m), trunk and branches silvery, twisted. Leaves medium length, in fives, green or grey-green. Cones to 3in (7.5cm) long, oval, purple, maturing light brown. Seeds edible.

P. aristata* 72, 319 Bristle-cone pine. S.W. United States. Zone 5. 15 to 40ft (4.5 to 12m). Leaves short, in fives, deep green, often white speckled with resin; persist up to 17 years. Cones to 3½in (9cm) long, scales spiny. Very slow-growing.

P. armandii 75, 318 Armand's pine. W. China, Formosa, Korea. Zone 5. To 60ft (18m), spreading. Leaves drooping in fives, soon shed, medium-length, pointed, waxy, green above, inner faces white. Cones in pairs or threes, to 7in (17.5cm) long, becoming pendulous.

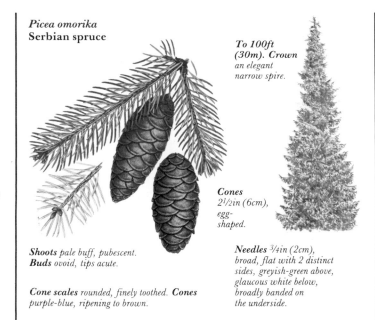

Picea omorika
Serbian spruce

To 100ft (30m). Crown an elegant narrow spire.

Cones 2½in (6cm), egg-shaped.

Shoots *pale buff, pubescent.*
Buds *ovoid, tips acute.*

Cone scales *rounded, finely toothed.* **Cones** *purple-blue, ripening to brown.*

Needles *¾in (2cm), broad, flat with 2 distinct sides, greyish-green above, glaucous white below, broadly banded on the underside.*

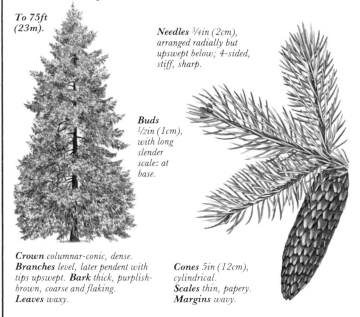

Picea pungens 'Glauca'
Colorado blue spruce

To 75ft (23m).

Needles *¾in (2cm), arranged radially but upswept below; 4-sided, stiff, sharp.*

Buds *½in (1cm), with long slender scales at base.*

Crown *columnar-conic, dense.*
Branches *level, later pendent with tips upswept.* **Bark** *thick, purplish-brown, coarse and flaking.*
Leaves *waxy.*

Cones *5in (12cm), cylindrical.*
Scales *thin, papery.*
Margins *wavy.*

Pinus aristata
Bristle-cone pine

Buds *⅓in (8mm), pointed, scales free at base.*

Leaves *1½in (4cm), deep green, thick and stiff, dotted with whitish resin spots.*
Foliage *very dense, persistent, curving forwards on stout orange shoot.*

Margins *entire.*

Cones *4in (9cm), spreading, with short stalk. Raised centre of the scale has a small spreading or curved prickle.*

Pinus contorta
Shore pine

P. c. latifolia
Lodgepole pine

Shore pine foliage dense.

Shore pine to 80ft (24.5m). *Lodgepole crown more open.* **Bark** *finely scaled.*

Lodgepole leaves to 4in (10cm).

Cones *(both trees) 2in (5cm), prickled.*

Shore pine leaves *2in (5cm), straight.*

Lodgepole foliage less dense, splayed, twisted.

Male flowers *at base of new shoots, shed pollen in April.*

Pinus coulteri
Big-cone pine, Coulter pine

Foliage *stout, rigid, spaced, not densely set, becomes crinkled in 2nd year.* **Shoots** *stout, glabrous.*

Cones *huge, 10¼in (26cm), weighing up to 6lb (2.5kg).* **Seeds** *⅔in (1.7cm).* **Scales** *thick.* **Umbos** *sharp.*

Leaves *10¼in (26cm), light grey-green, stiff.* **Sheath** *1in (2.5cm).*

Pinus jeffreyi
Jeffrey's pine

Buds *1¼in (3cm), pointed.* **Scale tips** *free, non-resinous.*

Cones *10¼in (26cm), deltoid when open.*

Umbos *recurved.* **Shoots** *bloomed blue-grey.*

Foliage *dense, persisting 5-8 years.*

Leaves *10in (25cm), stiff, spreading, bluish-green or grey.*

P. attenuata **72** Knobcone pine. S.W. United States. Zone 7. To 80ft (24.5m), upsweeping crown of branches. Leaves medium to long, persistent, grey-green, pointed. Cones to 5in (13cm) long, single or in whorls, sharp prickled; remain closed for several years, often opened by forest fires. Short-lived in cultivation, and much less bright green than in California.

P. ayacahuite **73, 319** Mexican white pine. Mexico and Central America. Zone 8. 100 to 160ft (30 to 48m), spreading. Leaves medium to long, slender, persistent, waxy green. Cones to 8in (20.5cm) long, cylindrical.

P. banksiana **71, 319** Jack pine. N. United States, Canada. Zone 2. 25 to 60ft (7.5 to 18m), branches crooked, sometimes bushy. Leaves short, rigid, paired, olive-green. Cones small, oval, often closed for several years. 30ft (9m) in 20 years.

P. bungeana **75, 318, 326, 327** Lace-bark pine. China. Zone 4. 80 to 100ft (24.5 to 30m), possibly a small bush, often with several stems, conical. Leaves medium length, smooth, rigid, flattened. Bark pale, flaking. Cones solitary or paired, oval. Likes limestone. 25ft (7.5m) in 20 years.

P. canariensis Canary Island pine. Canary Islands. Zone 9. Magnificent but tender tree with slender 9in (23cm) needles in threes, long branches and drooping sprays. To 90ft (27.5m) in sub-tropical conditions. Tolerates alkaline soil.

P. cembra **75, 76, 77, 318, 326** Arolla pine. Mts of C. Europe and N. Asia. Zone 4. 60 to 80ft (18 to 24.5m), narrow, densely columnar, becoming more open. Leaves in fives, crowded, dark shining green, medium length. Male 'flowers' crowded at base of weak shoots. Cones 3in (7.5cm) long, deep blue to purple, erect; scales never open on tree. Susceptible to honey-fungus. 25ft (7.5m) in 20 years.

P. cembroides **73** Mexican nut pine. S. Arizona to Mexico. Zone 7. 15 to 25ft (4.5 to 7.5m), rounded, bushy head. Leaves in threes or fives, short, curved, pointed. Cones round to oval, small. Seeds edible.

*P. contorta** **72, 73, 327** Shore pine. W. United States. Zone 7. To 80ft (24.5m), occasionally bushy. Leaves in pairs, medium length, characteristically twisted, yellow green. Cones ovallish, small, paired or clustered. Much planted on light, stony or sandy land. 50ft (15m) in 20 years.

*P.c. latifolia** **73** Lodgepole pine. W. United States. Zone 7. To 60ft (18m). Leaves slightly broader, medium length. Cones larger than for above. Not lime-tolerant. Susceptible to pine-shoot moths in Britain.

P. cooperi **319** Like a shorter-leaved *P. montezumae*; Mexico.

*P. coulteri** **72, 73** Big-cone pine. Coulter pine. S. California, N. Mexico. Zone 7. 40 to 50ft (12 to 15m). Leaves in clusters of 3, 10in (26cm) long, blue-grey. Cones ovallish, very heavy, 10in (26cm) long (biggest of any pine), scales clawed, light brown. 40ft (12m) in 20 years.

P. densiflora **74–5, 319** Japanese red pine. Japan. Zone 4. 70 to 120ft (21.5 to 36m), often twisted or crooked, broad and irregularly conical. Leaves paired, medium length, bright green, sharply pointed. Female 'flower' turns purple-brown, becomes a cone 2in (5cm) long; pink-brown or purplish, persists many years. 30ft (9m) in 20 years.

P.d. 'Oculus-draconis' **74, 75** Dragon's eye. When viewed from above leaves show alternate rings of yellow and green.

P.d. 'Umbraculifera' **74, 326** Small tree, to 12ft (3.5m), numerous stems radiating upwards, with umbrella-like crown. Leaves slender, dull green. Cones slightly larger than *P. sylvestris*. Extremely slow-growth.

P. echinata **43, 71, 319** Short-leaf pine. E. and S.E. United States. Zone 5. To 120ft (36m), narrow, possibly drooping. Leaves usually paired, persistent, medium length, slender, flexible, grey-green. Cones small, clustered, persist after seeds shed. Needs some lime.

P. elliottii **71, 73** Slash pine. S.E. United States. Small tree. Leaves in twos or threes, long. Cones conical, 5½in (14cm). Tender. Needs lime-free soil.

P. flexilis Limber pine. Rocky Mts. Zone 3. Conical, to 50ft (15m). 5 needles, grey-green, tend to be bunched at the ends of very pliable branches. Cones up to 10in (26cm) long.

P. gerardiana Gerard's pine. Afghanistan. Zone 7. Very rare slow-growing three-needled pine remarkable chiefly for flaking bark, making the trunk a pattern of pale colours.

P. halepensis **77, 318, 327** Aleppo pine. Mediterranean, W. Asia. Zone 7. 50 to 60ft (15 to 18m), irregularly branched. Leaves paired, medium length, slender, pointed, hard, green. Cones in groups of 1 to 3, drooping, to 4½in (11.5cm), often persist many years. Tolerates chalk. 30ft (9m) in 20 years.

P. × holfordiana (*P. ayacahuite × wallichiana*). A vigorous hybrid named for the founder of Westonbirt Arboretum, England, where it originated. A fast-growing, long-branched, beautifully glaucous and soft-needled tree, producing many curving resinous cones. To 60ft (18m) in 40 years.

*P. jeffreyi** **71, 72** Jeffrey's pine. S.W. United States. Zone 5. To 200ft (60m), conical. Leaves long, stout, blue-green to grey; crushed leaves smell of pineapple. Cones to 10in (26cm) long. 35ft (10.5m) in 20 years.

P. koraiensis **75** Korean pine. E. Asia. Zone 3. 100 to 150ft (30 to 45m), open, conical. Leaves medium length, rough-textured, waxy, deep blue-green. Cones conical to oblong, to 6in (15cm), yellow-brown.

P. lambertiana **72, 73** Sugar pine. Oregon and California. Largest member of genus, 220 to 250ft (66 to 76m), with very long branches. Leaves medium length, spiralled, in fives, blue- to grey-green. Cones to 26in (66cm) long, narrow. Susceptible to white-pine blister rust. 40ft (12m) in 20 years.

P. leucodermis **76, 77,** 318 Bosnian pine. Italy, Balkan Peninsula. Zone 5. To 90ft (27.5m), narrow, oval. Leaves paired, dense, rigid, medium length, dark green, pointed. Cones oval, blue in summer, dull brown. Found on driest limestone; also likes acid soil. 30ft (9m) in 20 years.

P. massoniana **319** S.E. China. Similar to *P. densiflora*, but with longer leaves and shiny, nut-brown cones. Tender.

P. montezumae **70, 73,** 326 Montezuma pine. Mts of Mexico. Zone 8. 70ft (21.5m), rounded and spreading. Leaves long, grey-green. Cones to 10in (26cm) long. Susceptible to late spring frosts. 25ft (7.5m) in 20 years.

P. monticola **72, 73** Western white pine. W. United States. Zone 5. 150 to 180ft (45 to 55m), slender, columnar crown. Leaves to 4in (10cm) long, blue-green. Cones to 15in (38cm) long, often curved, pale brown. Susceptible to white-pine blister rust. 40ft (12m) in 20 years.

P. mugo **77,** 326 Dwarf mountain pine. Mts of Central Europe. Zone 2. Small, bushy, with numerous crooked, irregularly spreading branches. Leaves paired, short, dark green. Cones small. 8ft (2.5m) in 20 years.

P. muricata **71, 73,** 327 Bishop pine. California. Zone 7. Usually broadly domed, with end branches upturned, descending with age; can also be tall, narrow and domed. Leaves paired, medium length. Cones small, clustered; persist up to 70 years. Very vigorous on poorest acid, sandy soils and in fierce maritime exposure. 40 to 60ft (12 to 18m) in 20 years.

P. nigra caramanica **77,** 318 Crimean pine. S.E. Europe, W. Asia. To 135ft (41m), wide, conical. Leaves stiff, twisted, medium length. Cones usually larger than *P. nigra nigra*.

P.n. maritima* **75, 76, 77,** 318 Corsican pine. S. Italy, Corsica, Sicily. 40 to 140ft (12 to 42m). Crown more open, branches fewer, shorter, more level than *P. n. nigra*. Leaves grey-green. Most soils. 25ft (7.5m) in 20 years.

P.n. nigra* **75, 76–7,** 318, 327 Austrian pine. S. and E. Europe. Zone 4. 120 to 150ft (36 to 45m), conical, spreading, becoming flat-topped. Leaves paired, persistent, medium length, rigid, densely crowned, dark green. Cones small, golden yellow. Grows on clay, chalk, limestone. 30ft (9m) in 20 years after a slow start.

P. palustris **43, 71, 73,** 319, 326 Longleaf pine, Pitch-pine. E. United States. Zone 7. 80 to 120ft (24.5 to 36m), few stout branches, level, then ascending. Leaves in threes to 18in (45cm), light grassy-green. Cones to 10in (26cm), narrow, dull-brown; scales at base remain when cone is shed.

P. parviflora **74, 75,** 326 Japanese white pine. Zone 5. 20 to 50ft (6 to 15m), young trees conical, mature trees with flat heads of stout, spreading branches. Leaves in fives, curved blunt-tipped, small. Cones solitary or in clusters, upright, ovallish, small with few scales. 20ft (6m) in 20 years.

P. patula **73,** 326 Jelecote or spreading-leaf pine. Mexico. Zone 9. Broadly conical, spreading, then upturned branches. Leaves in threes, slender, to 1ft (30cm) long, bright grassy-green. Cones in whorls of 2 to 5, pale brown, persistent. 40ft (12m) in 20 years.

P. peuce **77,** 318 Macedonian pine. Balkan Peninsula. Zone 4. To 100ft (30m), columnar-conical. Leaves in fives, medium length, sharp pointed, blue-green, white beneath. Cones cylindrical, 6in (15cm) long, in clusters spreading or drooping. Exceedingly healthy and hardy on severe sites. Disease-free.

P. pinaster **77,** 318, 327 Maritime pine. W. Mediterranean. Zone 7. 90 to 120ft (27.5 to 36m), branches upsweeping; old trees with bare trunk and flat-domed head. Leaves paired, stiff, medium length, short-pointed. Male 'flowers' abundant; female 'flowers' on tips of expanding shoots, dull red. Cone small, dark olive-green ripening to orange-brown. Grows on sand. 50ft (15m) in 20 years.

P. pinea* **77,** 318, 326 Stone pine, Umbrella pine. Mediterranean. Zone 8. To 80ft (24.5m), flat-topped or umbrella-shaped. Leaves paired, slightly twisted, medium length, sharp-pointed. Cones symmetrical, small, pale brown, smooth, closed for 3 years.

P. ponderosa **71, 72, 73,** 114, 319 Ponderosa pine, Western yellow pine. W. United States. Zone 5. To 235ft (72m), narrowly conical, variable when older. Leaves in threes, medium to long, dark grey- to yellow-green. Cones to 6in (15cm) long, solitary or clustered, dark brown. Tolerates many soil types, drought. 35ft (10.5m) in 20 years.

P. pumila **319** Dwarf Siberian pine; like dwarf cembran pine.

P. pungens **319** Prickle pine, Hickory pine. E. United States. Small- to medium-sized tree, often bushy.

Pinus nigra var. *nigra*
Austrian pine

P. nigra var. *maritima*
Corsican pine

Austrian pine: *heavily branched, bushy crown.* **Foliage** *dense, in forward-pointing bunches.* **Shoots** *ridged and shiny.*

Buds *long, ²/₃in (1.7cm).*

Leaves *6in (15cm), stiff, curved in 2nd year.* **Sheaths** *¹/₂in (1cm), persistent.*

Bark *coarse, deeply furrowed.*
Corsican pine *(below):* **140ft (42m). Crown** *lighter than Austrian pine.*

Cones *(both trees)* *3¹/₂in (8cm).*

Corsican pine foliage *slender, spreading, twisted. Grey-green.*

Leaves *7in (18cm), in spaced fascicles.*

Buds *resinous.*

Pinus pinea
Stone pine, Umbrella pine

To 80ft (24.5m). Crown *wide.*

Cones *4in (10cm), pale, glossy, ripening over 3 years.* **Scales** *smooth.* **Umbo** *'rings' show 2 years' growth.*

Leaves *5¹/₂in (14cm). Paired, slightly twisted, sharp-pointed.*

Easily recognizable *by distinctive umbrella shape.* **Branches** *radiate from short bole.* **Foliage** *sparse.* **Bark** *very fissured.*

Pinus sylvestris
Scots pine

To 150ft (45m).
Crown *broad*
on old trees,
conical when
young.

Buds *resinous,*
short-pointed,
cylindrical.

Branches
short,
horizontal
or slightly
ascending.

Bark *in upper crown*
pinky-orange, flaking;
deeply fissured at base.

Cones *3½in*
(8cm), ovoid, green
in 1st year. Later
greyish or dull
brown. **Scales** *not*
spined.
Shoots *glabrous, ridged.*

Leaves *3½in (8cm) 6in (15cm) on*
young trees, bluish, broad, stout, twisted.

Pistacia vera
Pistachio

Leaves *pinnate, with 3-11*
leaflets, on long petiole.

Leaflets *sessile, at*
first downy,
later leathery.

Fruit *1in (2.5cm), an*
ovoid drupe, in
erect panicles to 4in
(10cm), reddish,
develops from
flowers on
female trees
only.
Stone
bony.
Seeds
green or
yellow.

Leaflets
2½in (6cm),
ovate.

Pittosporum tenuifolium
Pittosporum

Shoots *slender, dark*
chocolate-purple.

To 50ft
(15m).
Crown
small,
ovoid bushy.

Leaves *2in (5cm), alternate,*
well spaced, elliptic-oblong;
glossy above, whitish below.
Margins *entire but wavy.* **Leaf**
stalks *½-2in (1-5cm).*

Fruit *capsules ⅝in (1.5cm),*
ripening black.

P. radiata **72, 73,** 319, 327 Monterey pine. California. Zone 7. 110 to 120ft (33 to 36m), domed. Leaves in threes, wide-spreading, medium length, deep green, slender, flexible. Cones asymmetrical at base, tawny yellow, to 7in (17.5cm) long, persist for many years. Many soils. Immensely vigorous. 45 to 65ft (13.5 to 20m) in 20 years.

P. resinosa **71, 73,** 319 Red pine, Norway pine. E. Canada, N.E. United States. Zone 2. To 80ft (24.5m), symmetrical oval crown. Leaves medium length, paired, dark yellow-green, snap cleanly when doubled over. Cones small. Susceptible to buff-tip moth. 30ft (9m) in 20 years.

P. rigida **71, 73,** 319 Pitch pine, Northern pitch pine. E. United States. Zone 4. In north, small, where on poorest soils; farther south, 50 to 60ft (15 to 18m), shape irregular when exposed, otherwise small and open. Leaves medium length, in threes, yellow-green, usually twisted. Cones small. 25ft (7.5m) in 20 years.

P. roxburghii **318** 'Long-leaved Indian pine'. Long pale leaves. Himalayas.

P. sabiniana Digger pine. California. Zone 7. Long-branched, often thin and less impressive relation of *P. coulteri.* Three-needled, slender grey-green, to 12in (30cm). The scales of cones have claw-like hooks. 50ft (15m) in 40 years.

P. strobus **70–1, 73,** 111, 319, 326 Eastern white pine, Weymouth pine. E. United States. Zone 3. 150 to 200ft (45 to 60m), narrow conical crown at first, under forest competition branches plume-like, open. Leaves medium length, dark blue-green, in fives, flexible. Cones to 8in (20.5cm) long, curved, usually fall first winter. Susceptible to white pine blister rust and white pine weevil. 40ft (12m) in 20 years.

P. sylvestris* **76, 77,** 112, 119, 324, 326, 327 Scots pine. N. Europe, Siberia. Zone 2. To 150ft (45m), conical at first, older trees flat-crowned. Leaves paired, stiff, twisted, short to medium length, waxy blue-green or yellowish grey-green. Male 'flowers' on weak hanging shoots, female 'flowers' on tips of expanding strong shoots, in whorls of 2 to 5. Cones greyish or dull brown, small. Many soils. Bark flakes pink and orange. 40ft (12m) in 20 years. A.G.M. 1969.

    P.s. **'Aurea' 326** Leaves yellowish grey-green summer and autumn; golden in winter. Slow.

    P.s. **'Fastigiata' 326** Slender columnar form with long erect branches.

    P.s. **'Globosa Viridis' 119** Dwarf, to 3ft (1m), round, dense. Leaves curved, green. Slow.

P. tabulaeformis **318** 'Chinese pine'; short with long level branches.

P. taeda **71, 73,** 319 Loblolly pine. S. and E. United States. Zone 6. 90 to 110ft (27.5 to 33m), open-crowned. Leaves medium to long, yellow-green, slender. Cones to 6in (15cm) long, narrow to oval. 35ft (10.5m) in 20 years.

P. thunbergii **74, 75,** 319, 326, 327 Japanese black pine. Japan, Korea. Zone 5. To 130ft (40m) long, projecting, twisted branches forming an irregular crown, often leaning when mature; old trees with long, wandering branches. Leaves paired, sharply pointed, densely crowded, to 4in (10cm), grey-green. Winter buds long and shining white. 25ft (7.5m) in 20 years.

P. torreyana **73** Soledad pine. California. Zone 7. 30 to 40ft (9 to 12m), low bush in exposed positions. Leaves in fives, crowded at ends of branchlets, dark green. Cones oval, to 5½in (14cm) long, mature after 3 years. Seeds edible.

P. virginiana **319** Scrub pine. E. United States. Zone 4. To 45ft (13.5m), bushy. Buds resinous. Leaves paired, short, twisted. Dislikes shallow chalk soils.

P. wallichiana **75,** 318, 326 Bhutan pine. Temperate Himalayas. Zone 5. 50 to 150ft (15 to 45m), elegant. Leaves in fives, slender, medium length, grey-green. Cones erect at first, becoming pendulous, to 1ft (30cm) long, light brown. 50 to 60ft (15 to 18m) in 20 years. Formerly known as *P. excelsa.*

PISTACIA 234–5

Evergreen or deciduous shrubs or small trees. Alternate compound leaves. Inconspicuous flowers, sexes sometimes on separate trees. Fruits are oval nuts. Mostly tender. Sun-loving.

P. chinensis **234** Chinese pistachio. Central W. China. Zone 7. To 80ft (24.5m), in China, smaller, often shrubby in America and Britain. Leaves pinnate, medium length, deciduous; good autumn colour. Flowers unisexual. Fruit the size of peppercorns, red, turning blue. Any soil. Mainly pest-free.

P. vera* **234** Pistachio. W. Asia. Zone 9. Small tree. Leaves pinnate, 5 leaflets, downy. Flowers unisexual. Fruits (pistachio nuts) oval, reddish. Best in sheltered, dry position.

PITTOSPORUM 132, 133, 327

Evergreen shrubs or small trees. Leaves simple. Flowers fragrant. Fruit, round to angular capsules holding many sticky seeds. Well-drained soils, sheltered sites.

P. tenuifolium * New Zealand. Zone 8. Small tree much used by florists for its pale, undulating, grey-green leaves on near-black twigs. Dark but sweet-scented little flowers in spring. Any dry soil.

P. tobira **133** Japan, China. Zone 9. Shrubby. Leaves ovallish, glossy green. Flowers cream-coloured, fragrant, summer. Very drought-resistant.

PLATANUS 134–5

Big deciduous trees. Leaves maple-like, lobes of varying size. Flowers small, insignificant, in globular clusters; sexes separate on same tree. Fruits in spherical heads, singly or several, stalked. Sun-loving. Young of some species susceptible to frosts. Tolerate city conditions.

P. × *hispanica* * 65, **134**, 318, 324, 326, 327 London plane. Zone 5. To 140ft (42m), spreading, tall, broad round head, outer branches drooping. Leaves 5-lobed, large, simple, roughly toothed, stalked. Fruit-heads usually paired, holding small nuts, early summer through to spring. Excellent in industrial areas. 35ft (10.5m) in 20 years.

P. occidentalis * **134, 135**, 319, 327 American plane, Buttonwood, Sycamore. S. Ontario, E. United States, N.E. Mexico. Zone 4. To 150ft (45m), spreading, tall trunk, rounded head. Leaves large, 3- to 5-lobed, simple, roughly toothed, long-stalked. Flowers greenish, May. Fruit clusters usually solitary, holding small nuts, persist until winter. Creamy-white new bark. Young plants prone to spring frost. Subject to anthracnose, canker in America.

P. orientalis **134**, 318, 326 Oriental plane. S.E. Europe. Zone 6. To 100ft (30m), spreading, short, thick trunk, broad round head. Leaves 5-lobed, simple, downy at first, shiny above, stalked, large. Flowers greenish. Fruits bristly, autumn and winter. Excellent in dry soils including chalk. 25ft (7.5m) in 20 years.

P. racemosa **134** California plane tree. California, N.W. Mexico. Zone 7. To 120ft (36m), spreading irregularly. Leaves 3- or 5-lobed, simple, thickly downy beneath, broad, often toothed. Flowers ball-like, hanging. Fruits also in clusters. Susceptible to blight.

PODOCARPUS 110, 111, 327

Evergreen trees and shrubs. Leaves spirally arranged, vary from scale-like to 1ft (30cm) long. Male and female 'flowers' on separate trees. Fruit, a single seed in brightly-coloured cup. Acid or alkaline soils. Some species hardy.

P. andinus * **111**, 319 Plum-fruited yew. Andes of S. Chile. Zone 7. Pointed, upswept bush, often on many stems, rarely a conical tree. Leaves pointing forwards, short, with acute tips. Male 'flowers' stalked, emerging where branches and leaves join. Fruit yellow-white, plum-shaped. 18ft (5.5m) in 20 years.

P. dacrydioides **111** New Zealand. Zone 9. To 150ft (45m), branchlets drooping. Leaves on young trees, small, pointed, in a single row, bronze to bronze-green, scale-like; smaller, green or bronze-tinted, spiralled or overlapped on older trees. Seed cup red, waxy.

P. latifolius **111** Real yellow-wood. S. Africa. Zone 9. To 100ft (30m). Leaves oblong to lance-shaped, short. Male 'flowers' small, single. Seed-cups green.

P. macrophyllus **110, 111**, 319 Kusamaki. China, Japan. Zone 7. Small tree or upright, narrow bush. Leaves medium length, dark glossy green, often yellowish above, leathery, pliant. Seed cup purple. 8ft (2.5m) in 20 years.

P. salignus **111**, 319 Willow-leaf podocarp. Chile. Zone 7. Usually many-stemmed, bushy tree; occasionally single, irregularly conical, narrow crown and single stem. Leaves medium length, blunt-tipped, shiny deep green above, pale beneath. 20ft (6m) in 20 years.

PONCIRUS 237

P. trifoliata Japanese bitter orange, Hardy orange. N. China. Zone 5. Large shrub or small tree to 15ft (4.5m). Attractive spiny green stems with 3-part deciduous leaves. Fragrant blossom, small fruit edible but bitter. The hardiest 'orange tree'.

P. trifoliata × *Citrus sinensis* **237** Citrange. Zone 6. Bushy, somewhat erect tree, stiff, angular, often spiny branches, dense foliage. Leaves usually in threes. Fruits very variable, mostly acid and bitter. Flowers fragrant, differ from either parent. Many named cultivars.

P.t. × *Fortunella* **237** Citrangequat. Zone 10. Vigorous evergreen trees, upright; old wood spiny. Leaves singly, paired or in threes, medium length, thick, stiff, dark green. Flowers small, white. Fruit small, yellow or orange-yellow, with thin roughened rind.

POPULUS 180–3, 327

Hardy, deciduous trees. Leaves simple, alternate, usually toothed, fairly long-stalked. Flowers usually catkins, sexes on separate trees, before leaves.

Platanus x hispanica (Platanus x acerifolia)
London plane

To 140ft (42m). Crown high, domed, spreading.

Bark flakes to give a dappled effect.

Branches large, mostly ascending, later gracefully pendulous.

Leaves to 8in (20cm) but very variable; downy initially but soon glossy, glabrous except on veins below. Petiole 2in (5cm), enlarged base hides bud. Leaf base variable.

Platanus occidentalis
American plane, American sycamore

Bark at first smooth, pale, but more characteristic where it peels, revealing yellow, white or green underbark.

To 150ft (45m). Crown broad, open. Bole straight, single. To 13ft (4m) diameter at base.

Mature leaves 7in (18cm), broad ovate, thin, bright green above, paler below.

Sinuses rounded.

Lobes (3-5) variable in depth, usually shallow.

Podocarpus andinus
Plum-fruited yew, Chile yew

Foliage dense; bunched at shoot tips, elsewhere irregularly pectinate.

To 50ft (15m). Bark smooth.

Fruit ³/4in (2cm), up to 6 in a bunch, plum-like edible flesh.

Leaves to ³/4in (2cm) with 2 light bands on underside. Acute tips.

Fruit yellow-green when ripe.

Populus alba
White poplar

Shoots slender, cottony, green in first year. Buds ovoid. Male catkin, 1¹/₂-3in (4-8cm), appears March, before leaves.

Blade woolly both above and below when opens.

To 100ft (30m). Crown often leans. Weak wood, breaks. Branches twist, drooping at tips. Bark smooth cream-grey with black, rhomboid lenticels. Bole surrounded by suckers.

Leaves variable, 4in (9cm), 5-lobed on strong shoots, 2in (5cm), rounded on weak shoots. Petiole 1¹/₂in (4cm), flattened. Leaf pubescence only retained below and on petiole; new midsummer leaves open snow-white.

Populus nigra
Black poplars

P. nigra 'Italica' leaf broad at base, glabrous, simple.

P. nigra 'Italica': Lombardy poplar. 90ft (27.5m). Crown fastigiate. Bole burred, often with epicormic shoots.

Leaves (of both trees) 3¹/₂in (8cm), yellow in autumn. Teeth forward curved. Margins thick, translucent.

Buds (of both trees) to ¹/₃in (8mm).

Shoots smooth; grey by 3rd year.

Male catkins (of both trees) 2in (5cm), opening in March.

P. nigra betulifolia: 130ft (40m). Crown spreading and densely leaved, twiggy in winter. Bole often burred.

Seeds, each with long tuft of hairs, in a capsule. Often on wet sites; prefer full sun; many tolerant of exposure. Majority dislike shallow, chalky soils. Fast-growing. Some species subject to canker, leaf rusts, leaf blister, leaf blight.

P. alba* 180, 181, 183, 326, 327 White poplar. C. and S. Europe to W. Siberia and W. Asia. Zone 3. To 100ft (30m), spreading. Leaves variable, oval to 5-lobed, simple, at first hairy, later upper surface smooth, dark green, underside white. Tolerates dryness. Suckers. 40ft (12m) in 20 years.

P.a. 'Pyramidalis' 180, 183, 326 Bolle's poplar. To 70ft (21.5m), pyramidal form as Lombardy poplar. Leaves, under-surfaces white, flashing in wind.

P.a. 'Richardii' 183, 326 Slightly smaller than *P. alba.* Leaves golden yellow, with white wool on underside.

P. balsamifera 42, 180, 183 Balsam poplar. United States. Zone 5. To 100ft (30m), upright. Leaves broad, oval, simple, dark green above, smooth; possibly slightly downy, paler beneath. Smells of balsam. Short-lived on dry, chalky soils. Suckers. Prone to canker. 50ft (15m) in 20 years.

P. × canadensis (hybrids of *P. deltoides* with *P. nigra*)

P. × 'Eugenei' 183 Zone 2. To 150ft (45m), hybrid, columnar. Leaves roughly triangular, short-haired, rough. Male catkins only. Canker-resistant.

P. × 'Marilandica' 183 Wide-spreading. Leaves green. Female catkins only. 2½in (6.5cm) long. Likes chalk.

P. × 'Regenerata' 183 Hybrid. Leaves long, triangular. Female catkins only. 2½in (6.5cm).

P. × 'Serotina' 183, 318 Black Italian poplar. To 100ft (30m), spreading. Leaves oval to triangular, simple, edges hairy at first, leaf-stalk flattened. Only male trees of this hybrid known. Very hardy. 65ft (20m) in 20 years.

P. × s. 'Aurea' 183, 326 Golden poplar. As *P. serotina* but leaves rich yellow, becoming greenish, then rich yellow again.

P. × candicans 180, 183 Balm of Gilead, Ontario poplar. United States. Zone 4. To 100ft (30m), wide-spreading. Leaves triangular or broadly oval, simple, furry beneath, underside whitish, balsam-scented. Only female trees known. 50ft (15m), in 20 years.

P. × c. 'Aurora' 180, 183 Variegated form. Leaves at first creamy-white, pink tinted; older leaves green.

P. × canescens 181, 183, 327 Grey poplar. W., C. and S. Europe. Zone 4. To 100ft (30m). Leaves roundish, simple, grey and matted on underside, red and yellow in autumn. Catkins late winter, red. Likes chalk, tolerates exposure and drought. 50ft (15m) in 20 years.

P. deltoides 180, 183 Cottonwood, Necklace poplar. E. United States. Zone 2. To 100ft (30m), wide-spreading. Leaves heart-shaped, simple, smooth, dark green above, lighter beneath, edges hairy, stalk flattened. Male catkins densely-flowered, females twice as long, 8in (20.5cm). 80ft (24.5m) in 20 years.

P. grandidentata 183 Big-toothed aspen. E. United States. Zone 3. To 60ft (18m). Leaves round or oval, grey and furry at first, later dark green above, stalk partly compressed. Catkins to 2½in (6.5cm) long. 65ft (20m) in 20 years.

P. lasiocarpa 183, 326 Chinese poplar. C. China. Zone 5. To 65ft (20m), spreading. Very big leaves, heart-shaped, broad, simple, at first hairy, upper surface becoming smooth, veins, midrib and stalk red, otherwise light green. Female catkins to 8in (20.5cm) long, twice as long as males. 35ft (10.5m) in 20 years.

P. maximowiczii 182 Japanese poplar. Japan, Korea. Zone 4. To 90ft (27.5m), wide, open. Leaves roundish, leathery, dull dark green above, whitish beneath, twisted tip. Male catkins to 4in (10cm), females to 10in (26cm). Fruit, July.

P. nigra* 181, 182, 183, 326 Black poplar. C. and S. Europe, W. Asia. Zone 2. To 130ft (40m), upright, broad. Leaves diamond-shaped to oval, simple, smooth, green. Flowers, red catkins. 60 to 70ft (18 to 21.5m) in 20 years.

P.n. 'Italica'* 180, 182, 183, 323, 326, 327 Lombardy poplar. Zone 2. To 90ft (27.5m), narrow erect. Leaves broad at base, simple. Most specimens are male trees, bearing male catkins only; female trees are broader. Mature trees susceptible to canker of upper branches. 40ft (12m) in 20 years.

P.n. 'Plantierensis' 183 Similar to *P. n.* 'Italica' but broader with more bushy head.

P. 'Robusta' 181, 183, 327 Big, upright, narrow at first, broadening later. Leaves triangular to oval, simple, copper-coloured at first. Only male trees of this hybrid known. Very fast. 90ft (27.5m) in 20 years.

P. simonii 180, 183 N. China. Zone 2. To 40ft (12m), narrow. Leaves diamond-shaped or ovallish, smooth, dark green above, paler beneath, short-stalked. Liable to canker.

P. tacamahaca 319 Old name for *P. balsamifera.*

P. tremula **181, 182, 183,** 326, 327 Aspen. Europe, Asia, N. Africa. Zone 2. To 100ft (30m), usually less, upright, narrow. Leaves roundish, simple, woolly at first, later almost smooth, grey-green. Long stalk flattened, so leaves tremble in wind, yellow in autumn. Suckers. 25ft (7.5m) in 20 years.
P. tremuloides **182, 183,** 326 American aspen. Quaking aspen. From N. Mexico to Alaska. Zone 1. To 100ft (30m), wide-spreading. Leaves roundish, simple, smooth, dark green above, paler beneath, quake in breeze. Short catkins. Larger trees more susceptible to pests.
P. trichocarpa **180, 183,** 326, 327 Black cottonwood. From Alaska to Mexico. Zone 4. To 200ft (60m), pyramidal. Leaves oval, slender-tipped, simple, shiny, dark green above, whitish beneath, balsam-scented. Liable to canker. 65 to 85ft (20 to 27m) in 20 years.
P. wilsonii China. Zone 7. Striking huge-leaved poplar like *P. lasiocarpa.*

PRUNUS **198–203,** 327

Big group of deciduous or evergreen trees. Leaves simple, edges toothed, crushed leaves often fragrant. Flowers 5-petalled, white or pink; in doubled forms number of petals is increased; spring. Fruit has one cell and one seed, fleshy; reduced and inedible in certain ornamental species. Most thrive on lime or chalk. Sun-loving. Usually very hardy. Susceptible to borers, scale and leaf-eating insects and virus diseases.
P. 'Accolade' (*sargentii* × *subhirtella*) Small spreading flowering cherry, pink, semi-double, profuse in early spring. A.G.M. 1961.
P. × *amygdalo-persica* '*Pollardii*' **202, 203,** 316 Similar to almond, but flowers richer pink. Fruit between peach and almond. A.G.M. 1937.
P. armeniaca **202, 203** Apricot. C. Asia, China. Zone 5. To 35ft (10.5m), spreading. Leaves roundish, pointed, deciduous, smooth, shiny green, stalked. Flowers solitary, small. Fruits 1¼ in (3cm) wide, larger in cultivation, yellow-orange, red-tinged, early summer, edible.
P. avium* **200,** 327 Gean, Mazzard, Wild cherry. W. Asia. Zone 3. To 70ft (21.5m), pyramidal. Leaves oval, long-pointed, deciduous, red in autumn, stalked. Flowers clustered, white, small. Fruit small, round, red-black, bitter or sweet. 45ft (13.5m) in 20 years.
　P.a. '*Plena*' **200,** 316 Double Gean. Europe. Zone 3. To 60ft (18m). Flowers profuse, small, double-petalled, drooping masses. Fruits rare. Hardier than oriental cherries. As large as type and longer-lasting. A.G.M. 1924.
P. campanulata **201** Formosan cherry, Bell-flowered cherry. Formosa, S. Japan. Zone 7. To 30ft (9m), bushy. Leaves roughly oval, deciduous, shiny, stalked. Flowers small, rose-pink, bell-shaped at first, opening later.
P. cerasifera* **202,** 318 Cherry plum, Myrobalan. W. Asia. Zone 3. To 25ft (7.5m), sometimes thorny, slender branches. Leaves ovallish, toothed, light green. Flowers solitary white, March. Fruit round, 1in (2.5cm) across, red or yellow, on mature trees.
　P.c. '*Pissardii*'* **202, 203,** 326, 327 Pissard plum, Purple-leaved plum. Persia. Zone 4. To 35ft (10.5m), upright, spreading. Leaves ovallish, deciduous, ruby at first, becoming claret then purple. Flowers single, small, profuse. Fruit purple, rarely produced. 25ft (7.5m) in 20 years. A.G.M. 1928.
P. cerasus **200, 201** Sour cherry, Wild dwarf cherry. S.W. Asia. Zone 3. To 35ft (10.5m), spreading. Leaves oval, abruptly pointed, deciduous, smooth, shiny, pale green, stalked. Flowers dense-clustered, white. Fruits roundish, red-black, acid-tasting, summer.
　P.c. '*Rhexii*' **201,** 318 As *P. cerasus* but flowers doubled, hardier. Last in flower.
P. conradinae **201** C. China. Zone 6. To 25ft (7.5m), elegant. Leaves ovallish, medium length, toothed. Flowers white or pinkish, profuse, Feb., before leaves. Fruit oval, red.
　P.c. '*Semiplena*' **201,** 316 Double Conradine cherry. Zone 6. To 35ft (10.5m), spreading. Leaves oval, slender-pointed, deciduous, smooth or virtually so above, downy below, short-stalked. Flowers doubled, white or pale pink, profuse, fragrant, long-lasting, late winter or early spring. Fruit small, ovoid, red.
P. cornuta **318** Himalayan bird cherry; bigger leaves than *P. padus.*
P. dulcis **200, 202,** 316, 318, 327 Common almond. N. Africa to W. Asia. Zone 4. 20 to 30ft (6 to 9m), spreading. Leaves lance-shaped, deciduous, smooth, stalked. Flowers 2in (5cm) across, single or paired, early spring. Fruit to 2½ in (6.5cm), velvety. Tolerates dryness. 25ft (7.5m) in 20 years.
　P.d. '*Roseoplena*' **202** Double almond. Flowers pale pink, double, numerous petals.
P. × *hillieri* '*Spire*' **201,** 316 Zone 5. To 25ft (7.5m), narrow, pyramidal. Leaves turning red in autumn. Flowers profuse, soft pink.
P. 'Kursar' (*kurilensis* × *sargentii*) Pretty March-flowering cherry bred by Captain Collingwood Ingram. Dense deep-pink flowers, bronze new leaves.

Prunus avium
Gean, Wild cherry, Sweet cherry

To 70ft (21.5m). Crown *open, conic when young.* ***Branches*** *whorled.*

Bole *straight.* *Bark* *smooth with horizontal lenticels, fissures with age.*

Flowers *to 1½in (3.5cm) wide, in umbels of 2-5 in 1¼-2in (3-5cm) pedicels, appear with or before leaves in April.* ***Shoots*** *shiny, purple-brown above, grey-brown on underside.*

Fruit *½in (1cm), red-black, ripens July.* ***Petioles*** *1½in (4cm), grooved, yellow below, with glands (circled) at leaf base.*

'Plena' flowers *double, globose, with 30-40 petals, open in May, last much longer than type.*

Leaves *5in (12cm), ovate or oblong-ovate.* *Underside veins* *hairy.*

Prunus cerasifera
Cherry plum, Myrobalan

P. cerasifera 'Pissardii'
Pissard plum, Purple-leaved plum

Cherry plum, Myrobalan (right): *Flowers 1-5, ¾in (2cm) across, borne on previous year's wood and spur shoots, purest white, open with fresh green leaves in March.* *Petioles ½in (1cm).*

To 25ft. *(7.5m).*

Fruit 1in (2.5cm), globose, red or yellow. *Leaves downy below, toothed, to 3in (7cm).*

Pissard plum, Purple-leaved plum (left): *Crown ovoid, more open in type, densely wreathed with small pale pink flowers. To 35ft (10.5m).* *Bark purplish.*

Prunus padus
Bird cherry

Flowers ¹/₂-⁵/₈in
*(1-1.5cm), on crowded,
irregular racemes, open in
late May, almond scented.*
*Racemes 6in (15cm),
glabrous, semi-erect or
drooping, leaves set at base.*

Petiole
³/₄in (2cm),
*stout,
grooved.*

Leaves to 5in (12cm), stout and leathery, grey-green
below, with axil tufts. *Teeth* fine. *Veins* impressed.

Fruit ¹/₃in (8mm), globular, green ripening
red to black, bitter. Not, in fact,. attractive to birds.

Prunus persica
Peach

*Leaves 7in (18cm), narrow elliptic,
finely serrate, matt green, paler
below with raised midrib. Do not
have basal glands.*

*Flowers pure pink,
1¹/₂in (4cm), singly
or in pairs.*

*Shoots glabrous,
angular, green or
red-purple.* *Buds*
¹/₁₀in (2mm), green
and brown.

*Fruit round, fleshy, to 3in (7.5cm),
stone deeply furrowed, clings to flesh.*

Prunus sargentii
Sargent's cherry

*To 40ft
(12m).*

*Flowers
appear in
April.*

*Branches
radiate
from 7ft
(2m) bole.*
*Bark
purplish-
brown.*

*Leaves 6in (15cm),
unfold reddish, turn
orange and scarlet
in early autumn.*

*Fruit ¹/₂in (1cm),
ripens green to red,
then black by June.*

*Flowers 1¹/₂in (4cm),
clear pink, single, in
clusters of 4-6. One of
the first cherries to flower
in the spring.*

P. laurocerasus 202–3, 318, 327 Cherry laurel, Common laurel. Europe, Asia Minor. Zone 6–7. To 40ft (12m), wide-spreading. Leaves lance-shaped or oblong, tapering, evergreen, leathery, glossy, dark green, short-stalked. Flowers tiny, dull white, upright clusters. Fruit small, conical, red, turning black. Shade-tolerant. 30ft (9m) in 20 years.

P.l. 'Camelliifolia' 202–3, 326 Shrub or small tree. Leaves dark green, contorted.

P.l. 'Magnoliifolia' The biggest-leaved laurel, pale, very shiny, very vigorous and imposing. 20ft (6m) in 10 years.

P.l. 'Rotundifolia' A short-leaved form making a good dense bush.

P. lusitanica 203, 318, 326, 327 Portugal laurel. Spain, Portugal. Zone 6–7. To 60ft (18m), often shrubby. Leaves oblong, medium length, finely toothed, dark shiny green above, paler beneath, evergreen. Flowers tiny, cup-shaped; in slender clusters to 10in (26cm) long. Fruit purple, oval, ¹/₂ in (1cm) long. 25ft (7.5m) in 20 years.

P.l. 'Angustifolia' 203 To 15ft (4.5m), conical, dense. Leaves smaller than *P. lusitanica*, shiny deep green.

P.l. azorica 203 Azores. Shrub or small tree. Leaves bigger than the type, bright green.

P.l. 'Variegata' 203 Leaves variegated white, often with pink flush in winter.

P. maackii 201, 319, 327 Manchurian cherry, Amur chokecherry. Manchuria, Korea. Zone 2. To 50ft (15m), spreading. Leaves oval, pointed, deciduous, hairy on veins and midrib. Flowers small, white, in downy clusters. Fruit small, black. Shiny amber bark. 30ft (9m) in 20 years.

P. mahaleb 318 'St. Lucie cherry' from southern Europe; fragrant white flowers; small spreading tree.

P. mume 202 Japanese apricot. China, Korea. Zone 6. To 20ft (6m), spreading. Leaves round to oval, long-pointed, deciduous, becoming smooth, short-stalked. Flowers single or paired, early spring, occasionally winter or late spring, almond-scented. Fruit to 1¼ in (3cm), across, round, yellow, hardly edible. Best against a wall in cold, exposed areas.

P.m. 'Alphandii' 202 Flowers semi-double, pink, March or earlier.

P. padus* 201, 327 Bird cherry. Europe, N. Asia to Japan. Zone 3. To 50ft (15m), spreading. Leaves oval, pointed, rounded at base, deciduous, smooth, dull green above, greyish beneath, short-stalked. Flowers small, in spreading spikes, almond-scented. Fruit small, round, black, harsh, bitter-tasting, summer. Less susceptible to tent caterpillar than other species. 30ft (9m) in 20 years.

P.p. 'Colorata' 201 Leaves initially purplish-brown, purple coloration retained in veins and on undersides. Shoots dark purple.

P.p. commutata 201, 326 Leaves bright green. Flowers several weeks before other varieties, early spring. One of the first trees into leaf.

P.p. 'Watereri' 201 Flowers in extra long clusters, up to 8in (20.5cm) long standing out with great vigour from all over tree. A.G.M. 1930.

P. pensylvanica 201 Wild red cherry. Pin cherry. United States. Zone 2. To 40ft (12m), spreading. Leaves oval, pointed, deciduous, smooth, bright green. Flowers in flat heads, small. Fruit small, red, round, late autumn.

P. persica* 202, 316, 318 Peach. China. Zone 4. To 25ft (7.5m), spreading. Leaves lance-shaped, deciduous, smooth, short-stalked. Flowers usually single, to 1½ in (4cm) across, pink. Fruits to 3in (7.5cm) wide, slightly furry, round, yellow-orange, red-tinged on sunny side, juicy. Susceptible to trunk borers and peach leaf curl. Dry soils.

P.p. 'Klara Meyer' 202 Flowers many-petalled, deep, bright pink. A.G.M. 1939.

P.p. 'Laevis' 202 Nectarine. Fruit smooth-skinned, otherwise identical to the type.

P. sargentii* 198, 199, 326 Sargent's cherry. Japan, Sakhalin, Korea. Zone 4. To 40ft (12m), upright, spreading. Leaves oval, slender-pointed, deciduous, smooth, bronze-red, orange and red in autumn, stalked. Flowers clear pink, in small clusters; one of first cherries to flower and to colour in autumn. Fruits tiny. 30ft (9m) in 20 years.

P. serotina 201, 317, 319 Black cherry, Rum cherry. E. United States, E. and S. Mexico, Guatemala. Zone 3. To 100ft (30m), spreading. Leaves oval to lance-shaped, tapered both ends, deciduous, smooth, glossy above, lighter beneath, pale yellow in autumn, stalked. Flowers in hanging cylindrical clusters, white, small, early summer. Fruit small, shining, black, late summer, sparse. 40 to 50ft (12 to 15m) in 20 years.

P. serrula 201, 327 W. China. Zone 5. To 35ft (10.5m), wide-spreading. Leaves lance-shaped, deciduous, downy beneath, sometimes becoming smooth. Flowers small, white, in small groups. Fruit oval, red, small. Bark glossy, dark red, peeling. Most soils. 25ft (7.5m) in 20 years.

P. serrulata 198 Japanese cherry. Zones 5–6. To 80ft (24.5m), wide-spreading, flat-topped. Leaves oval to lance-shaped, smooth, waxy beneath, deciduous, short, possibly double-toothed. Flowers to 2½ in (6.5cm) across, single or paired. Fruit small, black.

P. 'Amanogawa' 198, 199, 326 To 30ft (9m), upright, narrow. Leaves greenish-bronze. Flowers double, fringed, pink, profuse, fragrant. Fruits small, black. Most soils; especially floriferous on chalky soils.

P. 'Hokusai' 198 Vigorous, wide-spreading. Young leaves brown. Flowers big, semi-double, pale pink, spring.

P. 'Kanzan' 198, 199 To 35ft (10.5m), upright at first, later spreading. Leaves at first red-brown. Flowers doubled, purply-pink, large. Most soils; especially floriferous on chalky soils. A.G.M. 1930.

P. 'Kiku-shidare Sakura' 326 Small, spreading with drooping branches. Flowers very double, deep pink, early spring.

P. 'Pink Perfection' Like a more delicate, paler and less vigorous version of 'Kanzan'.

P. 'Shimidsu Sakura'* 199, 316 18 to 25ft (5.5 to 7.5m), wide-spreading. Young leaves green. Flowers double, big, fringed, draped in long clusters. Most soils. A.G.M. 1933.

P. 'Shirofugen' 199, 316, 326 18 to 25ft (5.5 to 7.5m), wide-spreading with long horizontal branches. Young leaves coppery. Flowers doubled, purplish in bud, white when opening, later pinkish, in long clusters, long-lasting, early summer. Most soils. A.G.M. 1959.

P. 'Shirotae' 199 18 to 25ft (5.5 to 7.5m), wide-spreading to hanging. Leaves pale green, fringed. Flowers usually single, very big, fragrant, white. Most soils.

P.s. spontanea 198–9 Hill cherry. Japan. Zone 6. 60 to 80ft (18 to 24.5m) spreading. Leaves bronze-tinted, initially. Flowers small, white or pink, spring. Fruit purple, October.

P. 'Tai Haku'* 199 Great white cherry. To 35ft (10.5m), spreading. Leaves at first red-brown, deciduous. Flowers single, very big, bright white. Most soils. A.G.M. 1964.

'Ukon' 198 18 to 25ft (5.5 to 7.5m), spreading. Leaves copper brown turning rusty red or purplish. Flowers pale yellow, tinged green, possibly pink. Most soils.

Sato Zakura 198, 199 refers to Japanese cherries of garden origin.

P. spinosa 202, 203, 327 Sloe, Blackthorn. Europe. N. Africa, W. Asia. Zone 4. 10 to 15ft (3 to 4.5m), spreading and suckering to form thickets. Leaves oval, deciduous, becoming smooth. Flowers small, single or pairs. Fruit blue-black, waxy, later shiny, round. Tolerates exposure.

P. subhirtella 198–9 Spring cherry. Japan. Zone 5. To 30ft (9m), densely branched. Leaves small, toothed. Flowers small, light pink. March–April. Fruit small, black. A.G.M. 1927.

P.s. 'Autumnalis'* 198, 317 Autumn cherry. Zone 5. To 30ft (9m). Leaves ovallish, long, pointed, deciduous, hairy beneath. Tiny flowers doubled, pink or white, profuse, autumn and intermittently through winter to spring. Fruits tiny, shiny, black. A.G.M. 1924.

P.s. 'Fukubana' 198 Small. Flowers numerous, rose-pink with many petals, spring. Fruit unlikely.

P.s. 'Pendula' 198, 326 15 to 30ft (4.5 to 9m), weeping. Flowers single or double, pink, tiny.

P. virginiana 201, 327 Virginian bird cherry. Choke cherry. E. United States. Zone 2. To 35ft (10.5m), pyramidal. Leaves ovallish with abrupt point, deciduous, smooth, shiny, dark green above, lighter beneath, becoming red-purple, stalked. Flowers in small clusters, white. Fruits small, round, dark red, bitter.

P. × yedoensis* 198, 316, 319 Flowering cherry, Yoshino cherry, Tokyo cherry. Zone 5. To 25ft (7.5m), flat-topped. Leaves oval to wedge-shaped, deciduous, smooth above, furry below, dark green. Flowers in clusters, usually before leaves, small, slightly fragrant. Fruit small, black, shining, acid. A.G.M. 1930.

PSEUDOLARIX amabilis 93, 318, 326
Golden larch. E. China. Zone 5. 100 to 130ft (30 to 40m), but often short and wide, deciduous. Leaves spirally arranged on long shoots, or clustered on short shoots. Male 'flowers' in clustered heads; female 'flowers' on separate branches of same tree. Dislikes lime. First few years main shoots often cut by late frost. Beautiful autumn yellow-gold. Subject to die-back and canker. 20ft (6m) in 20 years.

PSEUDOTSUGA 82–3
Douglas firs. Evergreen trees, broadly conical. Leaves needle-like, in 2 spiralling ranks. Male and female 'flowers' separate on same tree. Cones pendulous, oblong. Seeds winged. Dislikes chalk. Susceptible to dwarf-mistletoe in America, fungal root rot and needle cast in America and Europe.
P. japonica 319 Japanese Douglas fir. Small, bushy. Leaves pale green.

Prunus 'Shimidsu Sakura'

Crown *low, spreads.* **Branches** *often pendent.*
Flowers *2½in (6cm), pink in bud, opening to white.*
Peduncle *2½in (6cm).* **Young leaves** *green.*

Prunus 'Tai-Haku'

Flowers *2½in (6cm), largest in genus, hang outwards in threes or fours on 1¼in (3cm) stalk.*

To 35ft (10.5m). Leaves *8in (20cm), open golden coppery.*

Prunus subhirtella 'Autumnalis'
Autumn cherry

Leaves *2½in (6cm).* **Veins** *hairy below.* **Leaf stalk** *½in (1cm), dark red, hairy.*

To 30ft (9m). Crown *open.*

Flowers *¾in (2cm), in umbels of 2-5, pink or white.*

Buds *⅙in (4mm).*

Shoots *very hairy.*
Branches *densely twigged when older.*

Prunus x yedoensis
Flowering cherry, Yoshino cherry, Tokyo cherry

Flowers *1½in (3.5cm) set densely in umbels of 5-6, appear before the leaves. Deep pink in bud, soon fade whitish. Almond scented.*

To 25ft (7.5m). Crown *low, very spreading.*

Leaves *to 6in (15cm), finely pubescent below.*
Fruit *½in (1cm).*

Pseudotsuga menziesii
Oregon Douglas fir, Grey Douglas fir

P. m. glauca
Blue Douglas fir

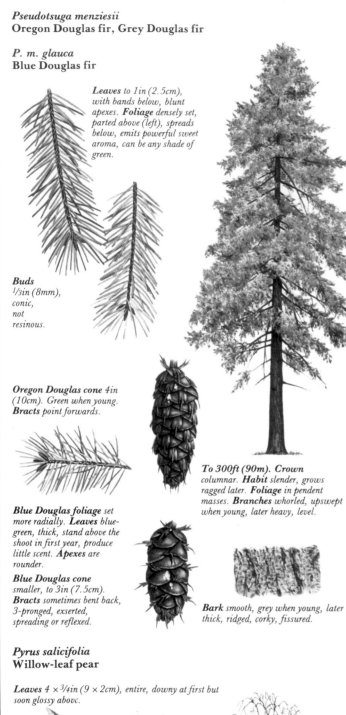

Leaves to 1in (2.5cm), with bands below, blunt apexes. **Foliage** *densely set, parted above (left), spreads below, emits powerful sweet aroma, can be any shade of green.*

Buds
⅓in (8mm), conic, not resinous.

Oregon Douglas cone 4in (10cm). Green when young. **Bracts** *point forwards.*

To 300ft (90m). **Crown** *columnar.* **Habit** *slender, grows ragged later.* **Foliage** *in pendent masses.* **Branches** *whorled, upswept when young, later heavy, level.*

Blue Douglas foliage *set more radially.* **Leaves** *blue-green, thick, stand above the shoot in first year, produce little scent.* **Apexes** *are rounder.*

Blue Douglas cone
smaller, to 3in (7.5cm). **Bracts** *sometimes bent back, 3-pronged, exserted, spreading or reflexed.*

Bark *smooth, grey when young, later thick, ridged, corky, fissured.*

Pyrus salicifolia
Willow-leaf pear

Leaves 4 × ¾in (9 × 2cm), entire, downy at first but soon glossy above.

Fruit ¾–1¼in (2–3cm), lenticelled.

To 25ft (7.5m). **Crown** *domed.* **Branches** *slender, pendulous.*

Flowers ¾in (2cm), opening April, in dense corymbs. **Petioles** *⅝in (1.5cm), slender.*

P. macrocarpa 319 Large-coned Douglas fir. S.W. California. Zone 9. Broad crown with level branches. Cones to 7in (17.5cm) long, biggest in the genus.

P. menziesii* 80, **82–3**, 85, 88, 319 Oregon Douglas fir, Grey Douglas fir. W. United States. Zone 6. To 300ft (90m), upper branches horizontal, lower branches down-curved, often almost to ground. Leaves small, deep green. Female 'flowers' pink or cream. Cone 4in (10cm) long, light brown; three-pronged bracts protrude from cone, pointing forwards. Most soils except chalk. 55ft (17m) in 20 years.

P. m. glauca* 83 Blue Douglas fir, Rocky Mountain Douglas fir, Colorado Douglas fir. Rocky Mts, Montana to Mexico. Zone 4. To 130ft (40m) more compact, with ascending young branches. Leaves waxy, blue-green, upstanding. Cones smaller, to 3in (7.5cm) long; bracts on cone spread widely or bend backwards. Hardier, less susceptible to frost than *P. menziesii.* 30ft (9m) in 20 years.

PTELEA trifoliata 236, 237, 317
Hop-tree. E. United States, Mexico. Zone 4. To 25ft (7.5m), shrub or small round-headed tree. 3-part leaves, deciduous, oblong leaflets, faintly dotted with tiny oily glands, shiny dark-green above, pale below. Flowers small, greenish-white; in flat-topped clusters to 3in (7.5cm) across; June, fragrant. Fruits clustered, winged, greenish. Prefers some shade. Fast.

PTEROCARYA 144, 145, 146, 174, 327
Deciduous trees, big, alternate, pinnate leaves with toothed leaflets. Unisexual flowers in separate catkins on same tree, summer. Fruits small winged nuts on long hanging spikes, late summer. Fast-growing on any moist soil.

P. fraxinifolia 147, 317, 318, 326, 327 Caucasian wing-nut. Caucasus to N. Persia. Zone 5. To 100ft (30m), broad, spreading. Leaves 8 to 24in (20.5 to 60cm) long, oblong, leaflets deciduous, shiny, with hairs along midrib, dark green, leaflets unstalked. Flowers greenish, male catkins cylindrical, to 5in (13cm) long; female catkins to 20in (52cm) both pendulous. Prefers sunshine. 35ft (10.5m) in 20 years.

P. × rehderana 147 Zone 5. Hybrid between species above and below. To 70ft (21.5m), a broad dome. Leaves with winged stalk, leaflets untoothed. Catkins long, drooping, persist for several months. Fruit short, round. All soils, even chalk. 45 to 60ft (13.5 to 18m) in 20 years.

P. stenoptera 147, 318 China. Zone 6. To 100ft (30m), spreading. Leaves deciduous, oblong or narrowly oval leaflets, tapering at both ends, leaf stalk prominently winged. Male catkins 2½in (6.5cm), female catkins 8in (20.5cm) long, summer. Fruits with narrow, erect wings. Best in moist loam. 35ft (10.5m) in 20 years.

PTEROSTYRAX hispida 189, 316, 318
Fragrant epaulette tree. Japan. Zone 5. To 45ft (13.5m), slender spreading branches, open crown. Leaves oblong, medium size, toothed, deciduous. Flowers small, creamy-white, in hanging clusters 10in (26cm) long, June. Fruit tiny, bristly. Dislikes shallow, chalky soils. 30ft (9m) in 30 years.

PYRUS 190, 204
Pears. Deciduous trees, sometimes shrubs. Leaves simple, toothed, sometimes lobed. Flowers white, spring. Fruits pear-shaped or round, usually distinguished by fleshy stalk joining fruit on a bump, not in a depression as in apples. Hardy. Susceptible to fire blight, apple scab, rusts.

P. calleryana 204 China. Zone 5. Medium-sized tree, thorny branches. Leaves broad oval, glossy green. Flowers white. Fruits round, small, brown, on slender stalks.

P. c. 'Bradford' 204 To 45ft (13.5m), pyramidal. Leaves red or bright red in the autumn. Flowers small, profuse. Fruits pea-shaped. Less hardy than *P. ussuriensis,* but less vulnerable to fire blight. Sun-loving. Will tolerate dryness.

P. communis 204, 327 Common pear, Garden pear. Zone 4. 30 to 40ft (9 to 12m). Leaves glossy green, red-brown in autumn. Flowers profuse. Fruits sweet-tasting, pleasant. Over 1,000 cultivated varieties. Sun-loving. Tolerates dryness. Medium growth.

P. nivalis 204 S. Europe. Zone 5. To 50ft (15m), upright, narrow. Leaves oval, furry, especially at first, silvery-grey. Flowers 1½in (4cm) across, profuse in showy clusters. Fruits rounded, yellow-green, sweeten when over-ripe. Sun-loving. Medium growth.

P. salicifolia* 204, 318, 326 Willow-leaf pear, Weeping silver pear. Caucasus. Zone 4. To 25ft (7.5m), often pendulous. Leaves lance-shaped, tapered, at first furry, later glossy grey-green above. Tiny flowers in tight flat heads. Fruits brown, 1in (2.5cm) long, not pleasant-tasting. Sun-loving.

P.s. **'Pendula' 327** Weeping branches, silver-grey foliage. A.G.M. 1969.

P. ussuriensis **204, 316** Ussurian pear. N.E. Asia. Zone 4. To 50ft (15m), roughly pyramidal. Leaves roundish, slender-pointed, smooth, becoming red-brown, stalked. Flowers profuse. Fruit 1½ in (4cm) long, round, green-yellow, hard, not edible. Less susceptible to fire-blight than other species. Sun or semi-shade.

Q

QUERCUS 154–161

Oaks. Deciduous and evergreen trees and shrubs. Simple leaves, often lobed. Male catkins profuse, hanging; females sparse on same tree. Fruit acorn partly enclosed in cup. Mostly lime-tolerant, but not on shallow, chalky soil. Hardy. Subject to leaf mildew, honey fungus, borers, galls, Europe and America; oak wilt, America.

Q. acuta **157,** 319, 326 Japan. Zone 5. Bushy tree, to 40ft (12m). Leaves oval, evergreen, leathery, shiny green, margin waxy. Acorns clustered, downy cup. Needs lime-free soil.

Q. acutissima **157,** 318 Sawtooth oak. China, Korea, Japan. Zone 6. To 45ft (13.5m), round-headed, very wide-spreading. Leaves oblong, bristle-toothed, shiny, chestnut-like; persist into winter. Fruit stalkless.

Q. agrifolia **159, 161,** 326 California/Coast live oak. California, Mexico. Zone 9. To 100ft (30m) in America, smaller in Europe; spreading branches, round-headed. Leaves hard, oval or rounded with spiny marginal teeth, smooth, shiny green above, paler beneath; short, evergreen. Acorns stalkless, cone-shaped, 1in (2.5cm) long. Bark smooth, black, rough when older. Tolerates dryness, prefers sun. 20ft (6m) in 20 years.

Q. alba* 43, **158, 159, 160, 161,** 319, 326, 327 White oak. S.E. Canada, E. United States. Zone 4. To 100ft (30m), spreading branches, round head. Leaves lobed, soft-green, purple-crimson in autumn, deciduous. Acorns ¾ in (2cm) long, mature in one season. Pale grey fissured bark. Not lime-tolerant or successful in Europe. 20ft (6m) in 20 years.

Q. aliena 319 Small Japanese oak with big toothed leaves.

Q. alnifolia 318 Golden oak from Cyprus, shrubby evergreen with gold felt under leaves.

Q. bicolor **159, 161,** 319, 327 Swamp white oak. S.E. Canada, E. United States. Zone 3. To 100ft (30m), narrow, round-topped head. Leaves medium length, lobed, dark, shiny green above, pale grey beneath, downy, deciduous. Acorns 1in (2.5cm) long, usually paired on downy stalk. Bark loose, scaly. Not lime-tolerant, suited to moist soils. 15ft (4.5m) in 20 years.

Q. canariensis **156,** 318, 326 Algerian oak. N. Africa, S. Portugal, Spain. Zone 7. To 120ft (36m). Leaves oval, coarsely toothed or lobed, medium length, dark green and hairless above, paler with faint bloom beneath, deciduous. Acorns 1in (2.5cm) long, in twos or threes on short stalk, cups scaly. Tolerates heavy clay or shallow chalky soil. 35ft (10.5m) in 20 years.

Q. castaneifolia **157,** 318, 326 Chestnut-leaved oak. Caucasus, Persia. Zone 7. To 100ft (30m), wide-spreading. Leaves oval to oblong, medium length, deciduous, shiny, dark green above, downy beneath, coarsely toothed. Acorns flat-topped, half-enclosed in spiny cup. 45ft (13.5m) in 20 years.

Q. cerris* 155, 156, **157,** 318, 326 Turkey oak. S. Europe, Asia Minor. Zone 6. To 110ft (33m), broad, pyramidal or spreading. Leaves oval, hard, toothed or lobed, medium length, dark green above, greyish green below, downy, deciduous. Acorns single, paired or in fours. 1¼ in (3cm) long, with short-stalked, downy cup. Good on chalk soil and in exposed positions. 40ft (12m) in 20 years.

   Q.c. **'Variegata'** A brilliantly white-variegated form. Irresistible when small.

Q. chrysolepis **159, 160, 161** California live oak, Golden-cup oak, Maul oak. S.W. United States, Mexico. Zone 7. To 65ft (20m), spreading, short, thick trunk. Leaves oval, short to medium, spine toothed on young trees, downy at first, later dark shiny green, dull beneath, evergreen. Acorns to 1in (2.5cm) long, downy cup. Thrives in sun. Tolerates dryness. 10ft (3m) in 20 years.

Q. coccinea* **159, 160, 161,** 319, 324, 326, 327 Scarlet oak. S.E. Canada, E. United States. Zone 4. To 80ft (24.5m), round-topped, open head. Deciduous leaves medium length, oval, deeply lobed and toothed, glossy green on both sides, scarlet in autumn. Acorns to 1in (2.5cm) long. Not very lime-tolerant. 30 to 50ft (9 to 15m) in 20 years.

Q. dentata **157,** 326 Daimyo oak. Japan, Korea, N. and W. China. Zone 5. To 75ft (23m), round-headed, often shrubby in Europe. Leaves to 1ft (30cm) long, big lobes, dark green above, downy below. Fruits small.

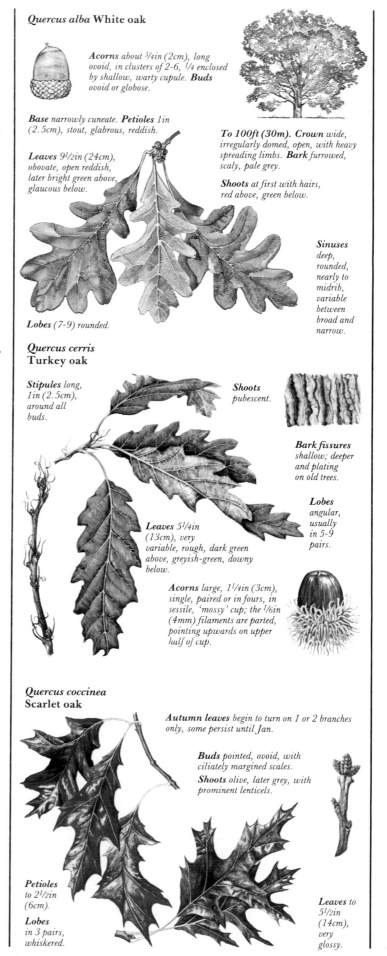

Quercus alba White oak

Acorns about ¾in (2cm), long ovoid, in clusters of 2-6, ¼ enclosed by shallow, warty cupule. *Buds* ovoid or globose.

Base narrowly cuneate. *Petioles* 1in (2.5cm), stout, glabrous, reddish.

Leaves 9½in (24cm), obovate, open reddish, later bright green above, glaucous below.

To 100ft (30m). Crown wide, irregularly domed, open, with heavy spreading limbs. *Bark* furrowed, scaly, pale grey.

Shoots at first with hairs, red above, green below.

Sinuses deep, rounded, nearly to midrib, variable between broad and narrow.

Lobes (7-9) rounded.

Quercus cerris
Turkey oak

Stipules long, 1in (2.5cm), around all buds.

Shoots pubescent.

Bark fissures shallow; deeper and plating on old trees.

Leaves 5¼in (13cm), very variable, rough, dark green above, greyish-green, downy below.

Lobes angular, usually in 5-9 pairs.

Acorns large, 1¼in (3cm), single, paired or in fours, in sessile, 'mossy' cup; the ⅙in (4mm) filaments are parted, pointing upwards on upper half of cup.

Quercus coccinea
Scarlet oak

Autumn leaves begin to turn on 1 or 2 branches only, some persist until Jan.

Buds pointed, ovoid, with ciliately margined scales.

Shoots olive, later grey, with prominent lenticels.

Petioles to 2½in (6cm).

Lobes in 3 pairs, whiskered.

Leaves to 5½in (14cm), very glossy.

Quercus frainetto
Hungarian oak

Lobes *large, in 7-11 pairs, with lobulate margins.* **Sinuses** *the most deeply cut of any oak.*

To 130ft (40m). Crown *strongly domed.* **Branches** *radiate.* **Bole** *stout.* **Bark** *dark, fissured.*

Leaves *large, to 10in (25cm), with basal auricles.* **Blade** *sub-glossy above, hairy below.* **Petiole** *¹/₂in (1cm), pubescent.*

Buds *large, to ¹/₂in (1cm), with many downy scales.*

Shoots *downy becoming glabrous; ridged when tree young.*

Quercus garryana
Oregon oak, Oregon white oak

Sinuses *very deep.*

Acorns *1¹/₄in (3cm), ovoid, sessile or short-stalked.* **Cupule** *up to ¹/₃ encloses acorn, very thin, loose, scaly, hairy outside, inside glabrous, pale.*

Apex *toothed or blunt.*

Petioles *1in (2.5cm), stout, hairy.*

Buds *¹/₂in (1cm), acute, hairy.*

Base *cuneate or rounded.* **Margin** *down-turned.*

Leaves *6 × 2-5in (15 × 5-12cm), thick, leathery, hairy below.* **Lobes** *(5-9) may be slightly toothed.*

Quercus lyrata
Overcup oak

Leaves *9¹/₂in (24cm), irregular, usually narrow oblong.*

Lobes *(5-9) rounded or short-pointed, longest at tip.*

Sinuses *broad, rounded.*

To 90ft (27.5m). Crown *rounded, open.* **Branches** *small, often droop.* **Bark** *grey, with thin scaly plates.*

Acorns *1in (2.5cm), ovoid or spherical, sessile or on 1¹/₄in (3cm) hairy stalk.* **Cupules** *thin, hairy, with fused ovoid scales; usually enclose acorn, splitting the first year.*

Leaves *hairy at first, later glabrous, although possibly slightly downy on paler underside.* **Shoots** *medium-stout, initially pubescent.* **Buds** *¹/₆in (4mm), downy.*

Leaf base *cuneate.* **Petiole** *1in (2.5cm).*

Q. douglasii 160 Blue oak. California. Zone 8. Small tree or shrub. 20 to 60ft (6 to 18m), rounded crown. Leaves deciduous, sea-blue, paler beneath. Withstands drought.

Q. frainetto* 156, 318, 326 Hungarian oak. S.E. Europe. Zone 5. To 130ft (40m). Leaves roughly triangular, medium length, deeply lobed, short stalk, deciduous; dark green and smooth above, greyish-green, downy beneath. Acorns to ¾ in (2cm) long, cup with downy scales, short stalk. All soils. 35ft (10.5m) in 20 years.

Q. garryana* 159, 160, 161, 319 Oregon oak. Oregon white oak. W. United States. Zone 6. To 100ft (30m), spreading, dense foliage. Deciduous leaves medium length, shiny green, lobed, hairless above, slightly downy beneath, downy stalk. Acorns stalkless, usually solitary, downy cup.

Q. glandulifera 318 Small deciduous oak with long narrow leaves. China.

Q. glauca 327 Small, evergreen, often a bushy shrub; from Japan, Formosa. China. Zone 8.

Q. × heterophylla 319 E. United States. Zone 5. Hybrid between *Q. phellos* and *Q. rubra*. Leaves oblong or oval, entire or toothed, smooth.

Q. × hispanica 326 S. Europe. Variable hybrid between *Q. cerris* and *Q. suber*. Occasionally evergreen. Hardy. Very lime-tolerant.

Q. × h. 'Fulhamensis' 155 Fulham oak. Dense head, slender branches, drooping branchlets. Leaves broad, rounded, grey beneath, coarsely toothed. Bark corky.

Q. × h. 'Lucombeana' 155, 326, 327 Lucombe oak. Zone 7. To 100ft (30m), big rounded head. Leaves oval, sometimes slightly lobed, tapering, toothed, medium length, glossy green above, downy below, short stalk, may be evergreen in mild areas. Acorns single or paired on short stalks, cup with downy scales. Bark corrugated, trunk buttressed at base. Any soil. 30ft (9m) in 20 years.

Q. ilex 156, 157, 318, 322, 326, 327 Evergreen oak, Holm oak, Holly oak. Mediterranean, S.W. Europe. Zone 7–8. To 80ft (24.5m); broad, spreading, rounded head. Leaves usually narrow-oval, short to medium, pointed, sometimes entire, leathery, glossy green above, greyish, downy beneath, short stalk, evergreen. Acorns to ¾ in (2cm) long, 1 to 3 on short, downy stalk. Tolerates shade and any well-drained soil. 15ft (4.5m) in 20 years.

Q. imbricaria 159, 160, 319 Shingle oak, Northern laurel oak. E. United States. Zone 5. To 100ft (30m), pyramidal, round-topped when older. Leaves narrowly oval, medium length, tapering at both ends, usually unlobed, dark, shiny green above, downy beneath, deciduous, rich autumn colours. Acorns usually solitary, to ⅔in (1.6cm) long, short-stalked cup. Not lime-tolerant. 20ft (6m) in 20 years.

Q. incana 318 Small, tender evergreen oak. Leaves narrow, toothed, white below. Himalayas.

Q. infectoria 318 Small semi-evergreen oak with shiny leaves, from Greece and Turkey.

Q. kelloggii 159, 160, 319 California black oak. California and Oregon. Zone 7. To 90ft (27.5m) rounded, open; stout, spreading branches. Leaves medium length, bristle-toothed, deeply lobed, shiny green. Tolerates dry sandy soils.

Q. × kewensis 155 Kew oak. Zone 7. Small to medium-sized, dense compact head. Leaves small, dull green above, shiny below, evergreen.

Q. laurifolia 159, 160, 326 Laurel oak. E. United States. Zone 7. To 100ft (30m), dense rounded head. Leaves glossy green, oblong, sometimes lobed, deciduous. Small acorns on short stalk. Not lime-tolerant.

Q. × leana 319 Hybrid between *Q. imbricaria* and *Q. velutina*.

Q. libani 157, 318, 327 Lebanon oak. Syria, Asia Minor. Zone 5. To 35ft (10.5m), rounded head, slender branches. Leaves oblong and tapered, sharply toothed, dark glossy green above, paler green beneath, stalked, deciduous. Acorns 1in (2.5cm) long, single or paired on thick stalk. 25ft (7.5m) in 20 years.

Q. × ludoviciana 319 Hybrid between *Q. phellos* and *Q. falcata* from S.E. United States.

Q. lusitanica Portuguese oak. Portugal and Spain. Zone 6. Variable but attractive spreading mid-sized tree with leathery, downy, felty leaves, often persistent all winter.

Q. lyrata* 159, 160, 161 Overcup oak. S.E. United States. Zone 5. To 90ft (27.5m), round-headed, often hanging branches. Leaves oblong, medium to long, lobed, smooth dark green above, downy beneath. Acorns round, sometimes not stalked, to 1in (2.5cm) long.

Q. macedonica 318 'Macedonian oak', similar to a small holm oak, but deciduous.

Q. macranthera 156, 318 Caucasus, N. Persia. Zone 5. To 65ft (20m). Leaves long, oval, lobed, green above, pale and downy beneath, deciduous. Acorns 1in (2.5cm) long on short stalk, cup with downy scales. May be grown in deep soils over chalk. 35ft (10.5m) in 20 years.

Q. macrocarpa **159, 160, 161,** 319 Burr oak, Mossy-cup oak. N.E. and N.C. United States. Zone 2. To 130ft (40m), spreading. Leaves roughly triangular, medium to long, dark glossy green above, downy beneath, downy stalk, deciduous. Twigs corky, bark like white oak. Acorns to 1 ½ in (4cm) long, usually solitary, with a fringed cup. Not lime-tolerant. 15ft (4.5m) in 20 years.

Q. marilandica **160** Blackjack oak. E. United States. Zone 6. To 30ft (9m), spreading. Leaves roughly triangular, deciduous, wide and 3-lobed at tip, medium length, shiny, dark green, yellow-brown beneath. Acorns ¾ in (2cm) long, solitary or in pairs. Good on poor, dry soil.

Q. michauxii **159, 161** Basket oak, Swamp chestnut oak. E. United States. Zone 5. To 100ft (30m), round-headed, compact. Leaves roughly triangular, coarsely toothed, bright green, rich autumn colour, deciduous. Acorns stalked, to 1 ½ in (4cm) long. Not lime-tolerant; prefers moist soil.

Q. muehlenbergii **159, 161** Chinkapin oak, Yellow chestnut oak. S. Canada, E. United States, N.E. Mexico. Zone 5. To 80ft (24.5m). Leaves oblong, coarsely toothed, yellow-green above, pale and downy beneath with yellow midrib and stalk; rich autumn colour, deciduous. Roundish acorns. ¾ in (2cm) long. Not lime-tolerant.

Q. myrsinifolia **318** Small evergreen oak with pointed leaves and reddish shoots.

Q. nigra **159, 160, 161,** 319, 326 Water oak. S. United States. Zone 6. To 80ft (24.5m), conical or round-topped, fine-textured foliage. Leaves roughly triangular, sometimes lobed, sometimes entire, medium length, smooth shiny green, short stalk. Acorns usually single, ½ in (1cm) long. Not lime-tolerant, likes moist ground.

Q. nuttallii **159, 160** Nuttall oak. Central S. United States. Zone 5. To 80ft (24.5m). Leaves medium size, deeply lobed with sharp points, deciduous. Roundish acorns.

Q. palustris **159, 160, 161,** 319, 326, 327 Pin oak. S.E. Canada, E. United States. Zone 4. To 120ft (36m), dense pyramidal head, branch ends drooping. Leaves medium length, lobed, toothed near tip, glossy green, hairless except where veins join beneath, slender stalk, deciduous. Acorn about ½ in (1cm) long, shallow, saucer-shaped cup. Not lime-tolerant, likes moist soil. 30ft (9m) in 20 years.

Q. petraea **154, 156,** 327 Sessile oak, Durmast oak. W., C. and S.E. Europe, Asia Minor. Zone 4. To 100ft (30m). Leaves medium length, stalked, oval, deeply lobed, dark glossy green above, greyish, downy beneath, deciduous. Acorns to 1 ¼ in (3cm) long, solitary or clustered, stalkless on twig. 30ft (9m) in 20 years.

Q. phellos **159, 160, 161,** 319, 326, 327 Willow oak. E. United States. Zone 5. To 100ft (30m), conical or round-topped head, slender branches. Leaves medium length, narrow, pointed at both ends, entire, pale green, yellow in autumn, deciduous. Acorns tiny. Not lime-tolerant. 30ft (9m) in 20 years.

Q. pontica **318** 'Armenian oak'; small deciduous oak with huge yellow-stalked leaves.

Q. prinus* **159, 161,** 319 Chestnut oak, Basket oak. S.E. Canada, E. United States. Zone 5. To 90ft (27.5m), open, spreading crown. Leaves medium length, toothed, upper surface dark glossy green and hairless, midrib yellow, lower surface pale grey, downy, rich yellow in autumn, deciduous. Acorns oval, 1 ¼ in (3cm) long, single or paired in thin, stalked cup. Not lime-tolerant, likes dry soils. 15ft (4.5m) in 20 years.

Q. pyrenaica **318** 'Pyrenean oak'; big, often pendulous Mediterranean relation of *Q. robur*.

Q. robur* **41,** **154, 156,** 326, 327 Common oak, English oak. Europe, Caucasus, Asia Minor, N. Africa. Zone 5. To 100ft (30m), broad open head, short trunk. Leaves oblong, medium length, lobed, dark green above, greyish, hairless below, deciduous. Acorns to 1 ¼ in (3cm) long, ovoid, one or more on long stalk. 30 to 45ft (9 to 13.5m) in 20 years.

Q.r. **'Atropurpurea' 154, 156,** 326 Purple English oak. Small to medium. Leaves and shoots rich purple. Slow-growing.

Q.r. **'Concordia' 154,** 326 Golden oak. Small, rounded tree. Leaves golden-yellow, scorched in hot sunshine. Very slow.

Q.r. **'Fastigiata'* 154** Cypress oak. Big columnar head, upright branches.

Q.r. **'Pendula' 326** Weeping oak. Small to medium-sized, pendular branches.

Q.r. **Variegata 154,** 326 Leaves with white or yellow markings. Leaves of a tree at Kew initially green, variegated later.

Q. × *rosacea* **'Filicifolia' 154** Leaves divided pinnately into narrow segments. Fruit stalked.

Q. rubra **43,** **158, 159, 160,** 326, 327 Red oak. E. United States. Zone 4. To 80ft (24.5m), becoming broad and round-topped. Leaves oval, medium to long, lobed, smooth, dark green above, greyish beneath with tufts of hair,

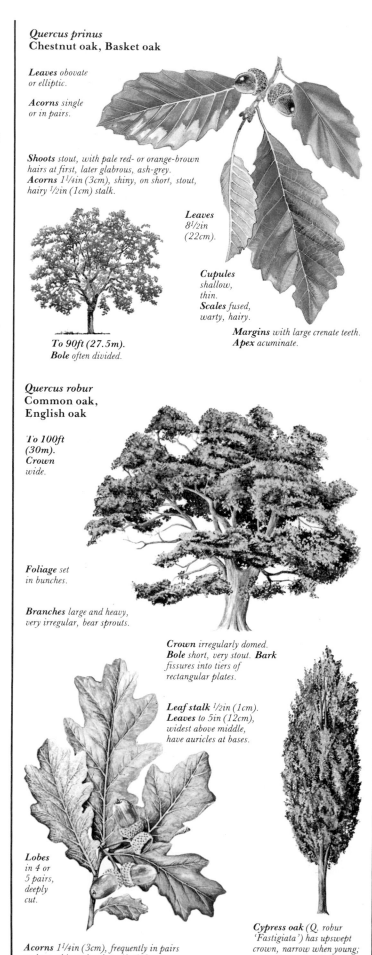

Quercus prinus
Chestnut oak, Basket oak

Leaves *obovate or elliptic.*

Acorns *single or in pairs.*

Shoots *stout, with pale red- or orange-brown hairs at first, later glabrous, ash-grey.*
Acorns *1¼in (3cm), shiny, on short, stout, hairy ½in (1cm) stalk.*

Leaves *8½in (22cm).*

Cupules *shallow, thin.*
Scales *fused, warty, hairy.*

Margins *with large crenate teeth.*
Apex *acuminate.*

To 90ft (27.5m).
Bole *often divided.*

Quercus robur
Common oak, English oak

To 100ft (30m). Crown *wide.*

Foliage *set in bunches.*

Branches *large and heavy, very irregular, bear sprouts.*

Crown *irregularly domed.*
Bole *short, very stout.* **Bark** *fissures into tiers of rectangular plates.*

Leaf stalk *½in (1cm).*
Leaves *to 5in (12cm), widest above middle, have auricles at bases.*

Lobes *in 4 or 5 pairs, deeply cut.*

Acorns *1¼in (3cm), frequently in pairs on long, thin peduncle to 4in (10cm).*

Cypress oak (Q. robur 'Fastigiata') has upswept crown, narrow when young; grows in central Europe.

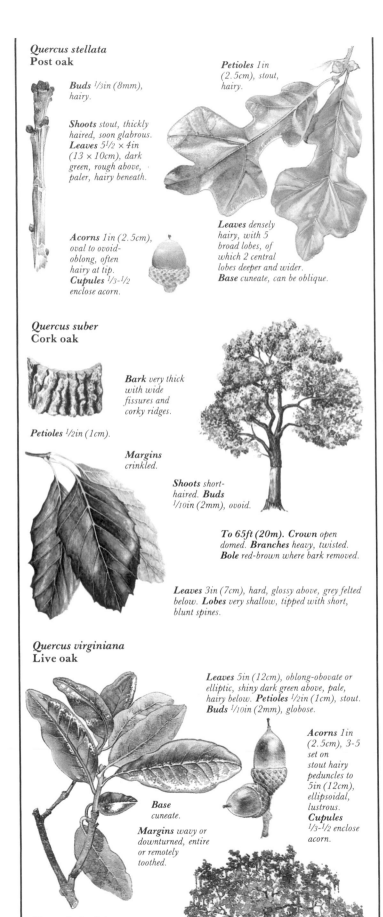

Quercus stellata
Post oak

Buds *1/3in (8mm), hairy.*

Shoots *stout, thickly haired, soon glabrous.* **Leaves** *5 1/2 × 4in (13 × 10cm), dark green, rough above, paler, hairy beneath.*

Acorns *1in (2.5cm), oval to ovoid-oblong, often hairy at tip.* **Cupules** *1/3-1/2 enclose acorn.*

Petioles *1in (2.5cm), stout, hairy.*

Leaves *densely hairy, with 5 broad lobes, of which 2 central lobes deeper and wider.* **Base** *cuneate, can be oblique.*

Quercus suber
Cork oak

Bark *very thick with wide fissures and corky ridges.*

Petioles *1/2in (1cm).*

Margins *crinkled.*

Shoots *short-haired.* **Buds** *1/10in (2mm), ovoid.*

To 65ft (20m). Crown *open domed.* **Branches** *heavy, twisted.* **Bole** *red-brown where bark removed.*

Leaves *3in (7cm), hard, glossy above, grey felted below.* **Lobes** *very shallow, tipped with short, blunt spines.*

Quercus virginiana
Live oak

Leaves *5in (12cm), oblong-obovate or elliptic, shiny dark green above, pale, hairy below.* **Petioles** *1/2in (1cm), stout.* **Buds** *1/10in (2mm), globose.*

Base *cuneate.*

Margins *wavy or downturned, entire or remotely toothed.*

Acorns *1in (2.5cm), 3-5 set on stout hairy peduncles to 5in (12cm), ellipsoidal, lustrous.* **Cupules** *1/3-1/2 enclose acorn.*

Shoots *slender, hairy.*

To 60ft (18m). Crown *very broad, branches nearly horizontal to 160ft (50m).* **Bark** *rough, deeply furrowed.*

stalk yellow, deciduous, red or red-brown in autumn. Acorns to 1 1/4 in (3cm) long. Fast when young. Not very lime-tolerant.

Q. × *schochiana* **319** Hybrid between *Q. palustris* and *Q. phellos.*

Q. shumardii **159, 160,** 319, 327 Shumard oak. S. and C. United States. Zone 5. To 120ft (36m), open, round head. Leaves medium length, obovate with sharp-pointed toothed lobes, smooth, dark glossy green above, red or golden-brown in autumn. Acorns 1in (2.5cm) long. Not lime-tolerant.

Q. stellata* **161** Post oak. W. and C. United States. Zone 5. To 60ft (18m). Leaves roughly triangular, lobed at tip, medium to long, deciduous, dark green and rough, paler, hairy beneath. Acorns single or paired, downy cups. An important timber tree, producing a tough wood.

Q. suber* **155, 156,** 318, 326, 327 Cork oak. S. Europe, N. Africa. Zone 7. To 65ft (20m), wide-spreading and rounded large branches. Leaves oval to oblong, short to medium, toothed, dark glossy green above, downy beneath, evergreen. Acorns 3/4 in (2cm) long, single or paired on short downy stalk. Bark thick, rugged, corky. Needs full sun, dislikes cold exposure. 12ft (3.5m) in 20 years.

Q. variabilis **157,** 318 Oriental cork oak. Japan, China, Korea. Zone 5. To 80ft (24.5m), spreading. Leaves oval to oblong, dull green, bristly margin, hairy beneath, deciduous. Bark corky.

Q. velutina 43, **158, 160,** 319 Black oak, Yellow-bark oak. E. and C. United States. Zone 4. To 100ft (30m) or more, dense rounded head. Leaves oval, medium to long, deeply lobed, glossy green above, downy beneath, rich autumn colours, deciduous. Acorns usually solitary on short stalk, to 3/4 in (2cm) long. Inner bark bright yellow. Not lime-tolerant. 30ft (9m) in 20 years.

    Q.v. 'Rubrifolia' Very striking, with leaves up to 16in (40cm) long.

Q. virginiana* **160, 161,** 326 Live oak. S.E. United States, N.E. Mexico, W. Cuba. Zone 7. To 60ft (18m), very wide-spreading, branches nearly horizontal. Leaves oblong, medium length, leathery, glossy green above, pale downy beneath, evergreen. Acorns oval, 1in (2.5cm) long.

Q. warburgii Cambridge oak. A beautiful hybrid of unknown origin. Spectacular in the Cambridge Botanic Garden, England, where new leaves and catkins are both reddish. A broad dome, almost evergreen.

Q. wislizenii 319 Small evergreen oak from California.

R

RHAMNUS *frangula*

Alder buckthorn. Europe. Zone 4. A tough alder-like shrubby tree with yellow autumn colour and red fruits, turning black. 'Tall Hedge' is a useful American nursery form.

RHODODENDRON 184, 185, 186, 187, 326, 327

Evergreen or deciduous, some trees, usually shrubs. Simple, entire leaves. Flowers usually in clusters on shoot ends, often funnel-like. Fruit, capsule, usually oval or oblong, minute seeds. Not lime-tolerant.

R. arboreum 48, **187,** 316, 326 Temperate Himalaya, Kashmir to Bhutan, Khasia Hills, Ceylon. Zone 6. 30 to 40ft (9 to 12m) in cultivation; evergreen, thick trunk, wide head. Narrow, oblong leaves, medium to long, dark green above, scaly beneath. Dark red, bell-shaped flowers, spring.

R. barbatum **187,** 326, 327 Nepal, Sikkim, Bhutan. Zone 7. Shrub or small tree, to 40ft (12m), evergreen, smooth blue-grey branches. Oblong leaves, pointed, medium length, dark dull green above, paler beneath. Dark red bell-shaped flowers 4in (10cm) across. Peeling bark.

R. calophytum **326** W. China. Zone 7. To 35ft (10.5m), often shrubby. Leaves long, narrow. Flowers bell-shaped, white or rose-pink with a maroon blotch.

R. falconeri **187,** 326 Sikkim, Nepal, Bhutan. Zone 7. To 30ft (9m). Thick, sparse branches. Oval to oblong evergreen leaves, long, dark green above, rust-coloured felt beneath. Creamy-white flowers shaded with lilac, dark purple blotch at base.

R. giganteum 49 Yunnan. Zone 9. 40 to 80ft (12 to 24.5m). Leaves long, evergreen; green above, reddish-brown felt beneath. Flowers bell-shaped, deep rose-crimson.

R. maximum **187,** 326 Great laurel, Rose bay. E. United States. Zone 3. To 40ft (12m). Narrow, oblong leaves, medium to long, dark green above, paler beneath. Rose-purple to pink flowers spotted with olive-green to orange, small, June/July.

R. sinogrande 49, 326 Yunnan, Upper Burma, S.E. Tibet. Zone 7. To 45ft (13.5m). Evergreen oval or oblong leaves, rounded ends, to 20in (52cm) long; dark green above, silvery grey beneath. Creamy white to yellow bell-shaped flowers, large.

RHUS 235

Deciduous or evergreen shrubs, sometimes trees or climbers. Compound, alternate leaves. Uni- or bi-sexual flowers on same or different trees. Fruits roundish, fleshy, hard stones. Any fertile soil. Subject to coral spot fungus, fungal wilt in America; few diseases in Britain.

R. typhina * **235**, 326 Staghorn sumach. E. United States. Zone 5. Small tree or shrub, to 35ft (10.5m), wide-spreading; sparse branches thick and pithy, yielding thick white juice when cut. Leaves downy at first, large, turning orange, red, purple in autumn. Male and female flowers clustered on separate trees. Fruits closely packed, hairy, decorative. Good in built-up areas. A.G.M. 1969.

R. verniciflua **235** Varnish tree. Japan, China, Himalaya. Zone 5. To 65ft (20m). Large leaves, downy beneath. Flowers inconspicuous, separate trees. Fruits small, yellowish.

ROBINIA 42, 208, 209, 327

Deciduous trees or shrubs. Leaves pinnate. Flowers white to pink or pale purple, pea-like, hanging clusters, summer. Fruits a flattened brown pod, several seeds. Many soils. Hardy. Sun-loving.

R. × ambigua **'Bella-rosea' 208** Shoots sticky. Flowers bigger and deeper pink than the type.

R. × hillieri (*R. kelseyi × pseudoacacia*) A very pretty hybrid, medium-sized with apple-blossom pink flowers among the delicate pale leaves.

R. hispida **319** Rose acacia. S.E. United States. Zone 5. Scandent shrub. Flowers big, rose-coloured or pale purple, May and June. Needs shelter.

R. pseudoacacia * **208**, 316, 319 Black locust, Common acacia, False acacia. E. United States. Zone 3. To 80ft (24.5m), upright, open, few branches. Leaflets opposite, oval, hairy at first. Flowers white, fragrant, June. Pod to 3½ in (9cm) long, upper edge winged. Bark rough, furrowed. Tolerates dryness. Good in industrial areas. Subject to locust borer, locust leaf miner, witches' broom, virus growths. 40ft (12m) in 20 years.

R.p. **'Frisia' 208, 209,** 326 Small-medium. Leaves golden yellow all summer. A.G.M. 1969.

R.p. **'Inermis' 209** Mop-head acacia. Small, compact round head, branches spineless. Flowers rare. A.G.M. 1969.

R. viscosa **208** Clammy locust. S.E. United States. Zone 3. To 35ft (10.5m), branchlets dark red-brown. Young shoots and leaf-stalks sticky. Flowers pink with yellow blotch, May and June. Pod narrow, to 3in (7.5cm) long.

ROSA 190, 327

Deciduous shrubs, stems thorny. Leaves pinnate. Flowers 5-petalled. Fruit, rose 'hip', a fleshy covering of the true fruit which is bony, seedlike. Succeeds in most except acid soils. Sun-loving. Subject to black spot, mildew, etc.

R. brunonii **190** Himalayan musk rose. Himalaya. Zone 7. Climbing form, to 35ft (10.5m). Leaves limp, sea green. Flowers white, densely clustered, very fragrant.

R. filipes **'Kiftsgate' 190** Climbing form, to 60ft (18m). Leaves pale green, brown initially. Flowers white, profuse, large clusters. Fragrant. Fruits small, red, numerous.

ROYSTONIA regia* 123

Royal palm. Cuba. Zone 10. To 70ft (21.5m). Pinnate leaves to 10ft (3m) long, four rows of leaflets. Flowerstalk develops below smooth glossy crownshaft. Purplish fruit, ½ in (1cm) long.

S

SABAL palmetto 122–3

Caribbean cabbage palm. Caribbean, Central America. Zone 9. 20 to 90ft (6 to 27.5m), very variable. Trunk bare or covered with leaf bases. Palmate leaves 12ft (3.5m) long, green or blue-green. Unisexual flowers on same tree, flowerstalk to 3ft (1m) long. Roundish shiny black fruit ⅓ in (8mm) across.

SALIX 176–9, 327

Mostly deciduous trees and shrubs. Leaves simple, typically alternate, long and narrow, pointed, toothed, but other shapes occur. Flowers, sexes usually on separate trees, without petals, in upright silky or hairy catkins, spring, before or after leaves. Seeds in small capsules. Tolerant of moisture; prefer full sun. Very hardy. Fast-growing. Subject to watermark disease, rusts, twig blights, cankers, aphids.

S. alba * **176, 177, 178, 179,** 326, 327 White willow. Europe, N. Asia, N. Africa. Zone 2. To 80ft (24.5m), rather upright. Leaves lance-shaped, deciduous, white-furred, yellow in autumn, short-stalked. Flowers, spring.

Rhus typhina
Staghorn sumach

To 35ft (10.5m). Crown *low, broad and shrubby.* **Bark** *thin, becoming scaly.* **Leaves** *24in (60cm), with 15-31 leaflets.*

Fruit *a panicle of densely haired drupes, persistent.*

Leaflets *to 5in (12cm), hairy at first, toothed, orange, red, purple in autumn.*

Flowers *(right) in dense, hairy panicles to 8in (20cm).*

Robinia pseudoacacia
Black locust, Common acacia

To 80ft (24.5m). Crown *light, open.*

Flowers *in racemes up to 8in (20cm) long, fragrant, appear mid to late June.* **Leaves** *8in (20cm), 9-17 leaflets.* **Buds** *naked, hidden in petiole.*

Bole *short, fluted.* **Bark** *rough, furrowed.*

Shoots *ribbed.* **Spines** *paired, by most buds.*

Roystonia regia
Royal palm

Leaflets *3ft (1m), up to 1¼in (3cm) wide at base but tapering towards apex, numerous, with glandular spots below and many parallel veins.*

To 70ft (21.5m). Crown *an apical cluster of foliage.*

Bole *long, often swollen at middle.*

Bark *blotchy in colour, broken into small, irregular plates.* **Leaf rachis** *hemispherical, unarmed, scaly, clasping stem at base.*

Leaves *3ft (1m), closely pinnate, arched.*

Fruit *½in (1cm) long, blue-black, subsessile, with thin loose outer coat.*

Salix alba
White willow

White willow (above): 80ft (24.5m).
Branches spread. Bole stout.
Bark cross-ridged, fissured.

Leaves (right) 3¹/₂in
(8cm), open light green.
Blades have long,
white, silky hairs above,
densely tomentose on
undersides. Crown
rounded, densely leaved.

Buds
¹/₁₀in (2mm),
flattened.

Teeth
fine.

Leaf stalk
short, ¹/₄in (5mm).

Shoots
fine, densely
haired, not
brittle at base.

Salix x chrysocoma

To 50ft (15m). Crown broad.
Branches arching. Shoots very
pendulous, long, slender, yellow,
becoming brighter in late winter.
A hybrid of the Weeping willow,
S. hahylonica, and the golden-
stemmed form of the White willow,
S. alba 'Vitellina'.

S. alba 'Sericea'
Silver willow

Male catkin (of both willows)
2in (5cm).

Silver willow (above): 50ft (15m).
Crown conic. Branches ascend.
Branchlets pendulous. Shoots and buds
are also hairy and appear silvery white.

Leaves (below) similar to White
willow but slightly wider and
more hairy.

Leaves 4 × ⁵/₈in (10 × 1.5cm),
glossy, glaucous below, finely
haired on both surfaces, opening
in early April.

Catkins
3¹/₂in (8cm),
often
curving up,
usually
male.

Dislikes shallow chalky soils. Susceptible to leaf-eating insects and other pests and diseases. 70ft (21.5m) in 20 years.

S.a. 'Chermesina' 177, 178, 179 Scarlet willow. Bark striking orange-scarlet colour, most obvious in winter.

S.a. 'Sericea'* 326 Very effective smaller form, silvery-white leaves.

S.a. 'Vitellina' 177, 178 Golden-stemmed willow. Similar to *S. alba*; only male trees known. Shoots bright yellow. 50ft (15m) in 20 years. A.G.M. 1969.

S. amygdaloides 179 Peach-leafed willow. Canada, E. and W. United States. Zone 4. To 60ft (18m) but usually smaller. Ascending branches, branchlets shiny red-brown or orange. Leaves lance-shaped, toothed, pale beneath. Male catkins to 2in (5cm), female 4in (10cm).

S. babylonica 176–7, 178, 179, 180, 318, 324, 326 Weeping willow. China. Zone 6. To 40ft (12m), weeping. Leaves lance-shaped, deciduous, smooth, except at first, dark green above, paler beneath, short-stalked. Flowers early spring. Pests as *S. alba*.

S.b. 'Annularis' 179 Form with spirally curled leaves; not easy to grow.

S. × blanda 177 Wisconsin weeping willow. Europe. Zone 4. 40 to 70ft (12 to 21.5m), hybrid, wide-spreading, weeping. Leaves lance-shaped, smooth, sea green beneath. 45ft (13.5m) in 20 years.

S. 'Caerulea' 179, 326, 327 Cricket-bat willow. British Isles. Zone 2. To 100ft (30m), pyramidal. Leaves lance-shaped, deciduous, downy at first, smooth later, blue-green. Flowers, only female catkins known. 85ft (27m) in 20 years.

S. caprea 177, 178, 327 Goat willow, Common Sallow. Europe, W. Asia. Zone 4. To 30ft (9m), spreading. Leaves broad, oblong, deciduous, downy at first, woolly beneath, wrinkled above, grey-green, short-stalked. Flowers, sexes on separate trees, spring; male catkins large, yellow; females silver-grey. 35ft (10.5m) in 20 years.

S. × chrysocoma* 177, 326 Weeping willow. Zone 2. To 50ft (15m), hybrid, weeping. Leaves lance-like, branchlets very long, rich yellow. Flowers occasionally separate, usually both male and female in same catkin. Susceptible to scab and canker. 45ft (13.5m) in 20 years. A.G.M. 1931.

S. cinerea 177 Grey sallow. Europe. W. Asia. Zone 2. To 15ft (4.5m), often shrubby. Leaves ovallish, dull green above, grey, woolly beneath. Catkins before the leaves, early spring.

S. daphnoides 178, 316, 318, 327 Violet willow. N. Europe, C. Asia, Himalaya. Zone 4. To 30ft (9m), upright. Leaves oval to lance-shaped, shiny, dark green, short-stalked. Stems dark purple with white blossom. Flowers late winter. Pests as *S. alba*. 35ft (10.5m) in 20 years. A.G.M. 1969.

S. discolor 177, 178 E. United States. Zone 2. To 35ft (10.5m), shrub or small tree. Leaves oval to oblong, grey furry beneath, bright green above, stalked. Catkins in spring, before leaves.

S. elaeagnos 326 Hoary willow. C. and S. Europe, W. Asia. Zone 4. Dense bushy shrub. Slender reddish-brown stems. Leaves narrow, green above, white beneath, rosemary-like.

S. × 'Elegantissima' 177 Thurlow weeping willow. Zone 4. To 70ft (21.5m). Female form, similar to *S. blanda*; long, pendulous branches. Leaves medium length, bright green above, bluish-green below. Female catkins 2in (5cm) long. 40ft (12m) in 20 years.

S. × erythroflexuosa 179, 326 Zone 4. 20 to 30ft (6 to 9m), hybrid. Shoots orange-yellow, weeping, twisted in corkscrew fashion, as are narrow leaves.

S. exigua Coyote willow. S.W. United States. Zone 7. A slender silvery little tree or big bush. Very narrow pale silky leaves on thin stems. To 20ft (6m).

S. fragilis 177, 179, 327 Crack willow. Europe, N. Asia. Zone 4. To 100ft (30m), wide-spreading. Leaves lance-shaped to narrow-oblong, deciduous, smooth, dark green above, blue-green beneath, stalked. Flowers, spring. Fruit stalked. Bark roughly channelled, twigs liable to break off. 40ft (12m) in 20 years.

S. gracilistyla 178, 319 Japan, Korea, Manchuria. Zone 5. To 10ft (3m), bushy shrub. Leaves oval to oblong, downy at first, shiny green, short-stalked, persist into late autumn. Red catkins before leaves; males grey becoming yellow. 15ft (4.5m) in 20 years. A.G.M. 1969.

S. lanata 179 Woolly willow. N. Europe, N. Asia. Zone 3. Small shrub, buds and young branches woolly. Leaves ovallish, dull green above, silky-hairy beneath. Catkins with leaves, spring, yellow, silky.

S. magnifica 179 W. China. Zone 6. To 18ft (5.5m), often shrubby. Young shoots purple. Leaves big, oval; dull bluish green above, waxy beneath. Catkins very long, females to 1ft (30cm), spring.

S. matsudana 'Tortuosa' 177, 179, 318, 326 Corkscrew willow, Contorted willow. N. China, Manchuria, Korea. Zone 4. To 40ft (12m), branches twisted in corkscrew fashion. Leaves lance-shaped, deciduous, smooth, waxy above, bright green. Flowers spring. 55ft (17m) in 20 years.

S. moupinensis **179** W. China. Zone 5. To 18ft (5.5m), often shrubby. Shoots orange and buds shiny red-brown. Leaves big, smooth bright green. Catkins to 6in (15cm) long.

S. pentandra **179** Bay willow, Laurel willow. Europe, N. Asia. Zone 4. To 65ft (20m), spreading. Leaves ovallish, deciduous, smooth, shiny, dark green above, paler beneath, midrib yellow, short-stalked, aromatic when crushed. Flowers, late spring; male catkins bright yellow. Susceptible to insect pests. 45ft (13.5m) in 20 years.

S. **'Sepulcralis'** 177, 326 Zone 4. To 40ft (12m), pendulous. Leaves narrow, lance-shaped, deciduous, shiny, waxy beneath at first, bright green. Pests as *S. alba*. 40ft (12m) in 20 years.

S. triandra **179** Almond-leaved willow. Europe to E. Asia. Zone 4. To 30ft (9m), shrub or small tree. Leaves lance-shaped, founded at base, smooth. Male catkins upright, fragrant. Bark flaky.

S. viminalis Common Osier. Europe, N.E. Asia. Zone 3. Usually many-stemmed, and often cropped for wickerwork. Long narrow leaves, silky-haired beneath.

SAMBUCUS 246–7, 327

Hardy deciduous trees or shrubs. Compound leaves with 3 to 11 toothed leaflets. White flowers in clusters. Fruits are small round berries. Most soils and situations. Subject to leaf-spot.

S. canadensis 'Maxima' American elderberry. Canada and E. United States. Zone 3. Very vigorous big-leaved and big-flowered elder, worth growing for jungle effect. Leaves grow monstrous if stems are coppiced every winter and the stool well fed.

S. coerulea **246,** 327 Blue elderberry. Zone 5. Small tree or shrub to 50ft (15m). Leaves medium to long. Flowers yellowish-white. June and July. Berries black with pale bloom, edible. Vigorous growth.

S. nigra **246,** 327 Common elder. Europe, N. Africa, W. Asia. Zone 5. Large shrub or small tree, to 35ft (10.5m). Flowers yellowish or dull white with heavy odour, June, followed by heavy bunches of shining black fruits. Fissured, rugged bark. Very chalk-tolerant.

  S.n. **'Albovariegata'** A brightly variegated, vigorous and attractive form.

  S.n. **'Laciniata'** Very finely dissected dull green leaves give an unusual parsley-like texture.

  S.n. **'Purpurea'** A deep purple flush in the leaves extends to the flowerheads, which are pink.

SASSAFRAS *albidum* * 130–1, 319, 326

Sassafras. E. United States. Zone 4. To 125ft (38m), aromatic. Very various, ovallish or lobed leaves, medium length, bright green above, bloomed beneath, deciduous. Unisexual flowers on separate trees. April/May; males insignificant, females small, yellow, clustered, before leaves. Oval fruit, fleshy, ⅓in (8mm) long, bluish-black. Sept. Bark deeply furrowed. Warm, loamy, lime-free soil. 25ft (7.5m) in 20 years.

SAXEGOTHAEA *conspicua* * 111, 319, 326

Prince Albert's Yew, Chile. Zone 7. Often bushy, possibly a slender, conical, slightly bent tree, evergreen with hanging branches and shoots. Leaves sparse, irregular, characteristically curved with white bands beneath. Male 'flowers' paired. Cones on same tree, bright powdery blue-grey, short. Bark purple-brown, smooth, scales falling to leave red-brown areas. 15ft (4.5m) in 20 years.

SCHINUS *molle* 234–5

'California' Pepper tree. S. America. Zone 9. Small evergreen tree, to 30ft (9m). Drooping branches. Much-divided compound leaves. Female flowers small, yellowish-white. Fruit, clusters of pea-sized red berries.

SCIADOPITYS *verticillata* 75, 327

Japanese umbrella pine. Japan. Zone 5. Many-stemmed, broadly conical, or single-stemmed, irregular, narrowly conical, evergreen. Leaves in characteristic united pairs, medium length, glossy green above, yellow-green beneath, arranged in whorls. Male 'flowers' in terminal clusters on small shoots; cones green, ripening to brown, scaly. Bark dark red-brown, peeling. Prefers lime-free soils. 15 to 25ft (4.5 to 7.5m) in 20 years.

SEQUOIA *sempervirens* * 112, **114–15,** 118, 319, 327

Coast redwood. California, Oregon. Zone 7. Up to 350ft (107m), narrow, irregularly conical. Leaves small, spirally arranged, in ranks. 'Flowers', sexes on same tree, solitary; male 'flowers' clustered at shoot tips, with spirally arranged filaments; female 'flowers' consist of 15 to 20 pointed scales. Cones small, red-brown, mature after one season. Bark deeply furrowed, to

---

Sassafras albidum
Sassafras

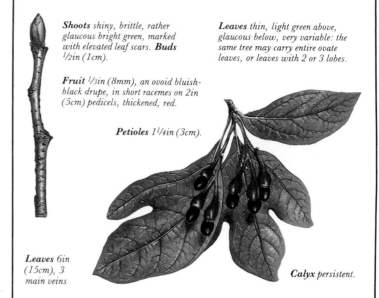

Shoots *shiny, brittle, rather glaucous bright green, marked with elevated leaf scars.* **Buds** *½in (1cm).*

Fruit *⅓in (8mm), an ovoid bluish-black drupe, in short racemes on 2in (5cm) pedicels, thickened, red.*

Petioles *1¼in (3cm).*

Leaves *thin, light green above, glaucous below, very variable: the same tree may carry entire ovate leaves, or leaves with 2 or 3 lobes.*

Leaves *6in (15cm), 3 main veins.*

Calyx *persistent.*

Saxegothaea conspicua
Prince Albert's yew

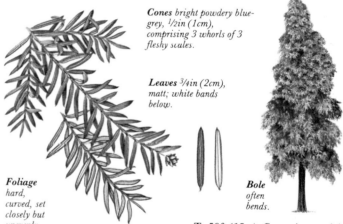

Cones *bright powdery blue-grey, ½in (1cm), comprising 3 whorls of 3 fleshy scales.*

Leaves *¾in (2cm), matt; white bands below.*

Foliage *hard, curved, set closely but unevenly.*
Leaf tips *abruptly pointed.*

Bole *often bends.*

To 50ft (15m), **Crown** *has rounded apex.* **Branches** *droop.*

Sequoia sempervirens
Coast or California redwood

Cones *1¼in (3cm).* **Scales** *(15-20) ripen in first season when cones become red-brown.*

Strong shoot leaves *small, ¼-⅓in (6-8mm), scale-like, awl-shaped, adpressed around stem with tips incurved.*

Side-shoot leaves *½-¾in (1-2cm), tapering to hard apexes with 2 white bands below, set in flat sprays.*

Shoots *green.*

To 367ft (110m) — the *tallest tree in the world.* **Crown** *thin, columnar conic, becoming flat-topped.* **Bole** *straight, tapering, sometimes accompanied by suckers.*

Bark *thick, very soft, fibrous; bright red-brown on young trees, darker and fissured on old ones.*

Sequoiadendron giganteum
Giant sequoia, Wellingtonia

Leaves small, to ¹/₃in (8mm), awl-shaped, hard, dotted with white stomata. Foliage blue-green when young.

Shoots stout, initially covered by leaves, later developing grey-brown fissures.

Cones large, up to 4in (9cm), 35-40 scales, green for 2 years, then brown.

Bark very thick, to 24in (60cm), soft and resilient, often dimpled by tree-creepers using it for winter roosting.

To 285ft (86m). Not as tall as Sequoia sempervirens but far wider. Crown often has rounded apex. Bole tapers, fluted. Branches have tips upswept.

Sophora japonica
Pagoda tree

Leaves 10in (25cm), pinnate, up to 15 leaflets, whitish below.

To 80ft (25m). Crown uneven, low-spreading.

Flowers ⁵/₈in (1.5cm), in 10in (25cm) panicles. Mostly in September.

Bark has long, coarse ridges. Branches very contorted.

Shoots initially hairy.

Sorbus americana
American mountain ash

Shoots hairy at first. Buds ³/₄in (2cm), glabrous or nearly so, sticky.

Leaves 8in (20cm).

Leaflets (7-17) 4in (10cm), lanceolate. Rachis grooved.

Fruit 4in (10cm), in dense broad heads, ripening to scarlet.

1ft (30cm) thick. Tolerant of most soil conditions, but not of exposure. World's tallest tree. 45 to 60ft (13.5 to 18m) in 20 years.

    S.s. 'Adpressa' 118 Shoot tips cream-coloured. Leaves shorter than the type. Often grown as a dwarf but reverts to normal size.

SEQUOIADENDRON *giganteum* * 112, **114–15**, 319, 326
Giant sequoia, Wellingtonia, California. Zone 6. 250 to 285ft (76 to 86m). Shorter than redwood or Douglas fir, but far wider. Evergreen. Leaves short, blue-green, turning brown after 2 to 3 seasons, triangular. Cones to 3½ in (9cm) long, maturing in 2 years, usually closed for 20 years. Bark to 2ft (60cm) thick on old trunks, cinnamon-red, fissured. Immensely long-lived. Distinct from *Sequoia* because of larger cones and awl-shaped leaves. Lime-tolerant, but dislikes shallow chalky soil. 40 to 55ft (12 to 17m) in 20 years.

    S.g. 'Pendulum' 326 Columnar, long branches hang against trunk.

SOPHORA 210–11
Deciduous or evergreen trees or shrubs. Leaves pinnate, 7 or more leaflets. Flowers pea-shaped, clustered along spike, mostly Sept. Fruit, cylindrical pod. Likes loamy, well-drained soil. Sun-loving. Some species hardy.
S. japonica * **211**, 326 Japanese pagoda tree. China. Zone 5. Spreading, zig-zaggy tree to 75ft (23m). Leaves to 10in (25cm), up to 15 leaflets. White flowers in 10in (25cm) terminal panicles in late summer, but not on young trees or in cold summers. 20ft (6m) in 10 years.
    S.j. 'Pendula' 211, 326 Small weeping form, seldom flowers.
***S. tetraptera* 211**, 319, 326 New Zealand sophora, Kowhai. Zone 8. To 40ft (12m), shrub or small tree. Leaves semi-deciduous to evergreen, tiny leaflets, oblong to round. Flowers golden yellow, to 2in (5cm) long, spring. Fruits seldom appear. 15ft (4.5m) in 20 years.

SORBUS 190, **205–7**, 327
Deciduous trees or shrubs. Leaves simple or compound. Flowers small, white or pink, in large flat clusters, late spring or early summer. Fruits small, round or oval, usually bright-coloured. Most soils. Sun-loving. Susceptible to pests such as borers, San Jose scale and sun scald of the trunk. Divided here into 'Whitebeam' and 'Mountain ash' types according to leaf character.
***S. alnifolia* 206**, 326, 327 Whitebeam. Japan. Zone 5. 30 to 40ft (9 to 12m). Leaves ovallish, simple, pointed, hairy beneath at first, autumn colours red and orange, double-toothed, stalked. Flowers white, late spring. Fruits oval, crimson, persistent. 25ft (7.5m) in 20 years.
S. americana * **207**, 319, 326 American mountain ash. E. United States. Zone 2. 15 to 30ft (4.5 to 9m), narrow, round-headed. Leaves pinnate, leaflets narrow, oblong, smooth, serrated edges. Flowers, pointed petals, white. Fruits red, round, persist into winter. Prefers acid soil.
***S. aria* 205**, 326, 327 Whitebeam. Europe. Zone 5. 30 to 45ft (9 to 13.5m), spreading. Leaves oval, simple, upper surface smooth, pale green, golden brown in autumn, lower surface white, hairy, double-toothed, stalked. Flowers dull white, heavily scented. Fruits red, speckled brown, autumn. Likes chalk. 30ft (9m) in 20 years. A.G.M. 1969.
    S.a. 'Chrysophylla' 205 Whitebeam. Yellow-leaved form.
    S.a. 'Decaisneana' ('Majestica') 205 Majestic Whitebeam. Leaves large, 7in (17.5cm) long, oval, simple, underside white and hairy. Fruits large, scarlet, brown-spotted. Prefers alkaline soils, but successful in acid soils. 30ft (9m) in 20 years. A.G.M. 1969.
    S.a. 'Lutescens' 205 Whitebeam. Upper leaf surfaces off-white, hairy, spectacular in spring, grey-green later. A.G.M. 1969.
    S.a. 'Pendula' 205 To 9ft (2.7m) weeping. Leaves narrow, small.
S. aucuparia * 190, **206–7**, 326, 327 European mountain ash, rowan. Europe. Zone 2. To 65ft (20m), spreading. Leaves pinnate, leaflets oval to oblong, waxy beneath, red in autumn, toothed. Flowers white, numerous. Fruit, red berries, large clusters, persist into early winter. Short-lived on chalky soils; acid-tolerant; can be scorched in hot summers. Very susceptible to borers in America, especially near base of trunk. 25ft (7.5m) in 20 years. A.G.M. 1969.
    S.a. 'Asplenifolia' 207, 326 Cutleaf European mountain ash. Elegant tree. Leaflets doubly-toothed, cut deeper, fern-like. Otherwise as *S. aucuparia*. A.G.M. 1969.
    S.a. 'Beissneri' An erect rowan with yellow-green leaves and shiny dark-orange bark.
    S.a. 'Edulis' 207 (Mountain ash), Moravian rowan. Leaves larger, leaflets toothed near tip. Fruits large, edible.
    S.a. 'Sheerwater Seedling' 207 (Mountain ash). Small, erect tree; compact, oval-headed. Fruit profuse, orange-red.
    S.a. 'Xanthocarpa' 207 (Mountain ash). As *S. aucuparia,* but fruits orange-yellow. A.G.M. 1969.

S. cashmiriana **207,** 316 Kashmir mountain ash. Kashmir. Zone 4. 15 to 25ft (4.5 to 7.5m), wide-spreading, pyramidal. Leaves pinnate. Flowers blush-pink at first, becoming paler. Fruits in hanging clusters, white, stalks pink-red, early autumn, persistent. Medium-growth.

S. cuspidata **205,** 318, 326 Himalayan whitebeam. Himalaya. Zone 3. To 35ft (10.5m), upright at first, later spreading. Leaves ovallish, large, to 9in (23cm) across, simple; green above, lower surface covered with close felt, white becoming grey. Flowers white. Fruits ⅝in (1.5cm) across, roundish, green, brown speckled, clustered. 40ft (12m) in 20 years.

S. commixta **317** (Mountain ash). Japan. Zone 5. To 25ft (7.5m), narrow, upright. Leaves pinnate, leaflets slender, pointed, shiny, dark green, coppery at first, red in autumn, saw-toothed. Flowers tiny, white, spring. Fruits small, round, red or red-orange, clustered.

S. discolor **207** (*S.* **'Embley'**) (Mountain ash). N. China. Zone 5. To 35ft (10.5m), upright, spreading. Leaves pinnate, leaflets narrow, pointed, waxy; dark green above, paler beneath, red in autumn, partly toothed. Flowers white. Fruits oval, clustered, cream-white, possibly pinkish.

S. domestica **318** Service tree. S. Europe, N. Africa, W. Asia. Zone 5. To 60ft (18m), open spreading branches. Leaves pinnate 11 to 21 narrow leaflets, smooth above, hairy beneath. Flowers small, May. Fruits apple- or pear-shaped, 1in (2.5cm) long, yellow-green or brownish, Oct. and Nov.

S. **'Embley'** See *Sorbus discolor*

S. esserteauana **318** A Chinese mountain ash. Excellent for dense deep-green foliage and big fruit-clusters. 'Flava' is a good yellow-berried form.

S. folgneri **318** Folgner mountain ash. C. China. Zone 5. 20 or 30ft (6 or 9m), usually spreading. Leaves lance-shaped, simple, silver down beneath, dark green, smooth above, becoming brown-red, stalked. Flowers inconspicuous, white. Fruits oval, dark red or purplish. 'Lemon Drop' is a very pretty yellow-fruited form. Susceptible to red spider mite and other insects. 25ft (7.5m) in 20 years.

S. harrowiana **207** (Mountain ash). Yunnan. Zone 7. 20 to 40ft (6 to 12m), broad, upright. Leaves pinnate, leaflets to 8in (20.5cm) long, shiny green above, pale waxy beneath, oblong, leathery, minutely toothed, short-stalked. Flowers off-white. Fruit tiny, pinkish, oval. Fairly tender. *S. insignis* is very similar, but hardier.

S. hupehensis *** 207,** 318 (Mountain ash). W. China. Zone 5. 30 to 40ft (9 to 12m), upright, narrow. Leaves pinnate, leaflets narrow, oblong, blue-green above, paler beneath, downy on midrib, partly toothed. Flowers off-white. Fruits round, white or pink, clustered, persist into winter. 30ft (9m) in 20 years. A.G.M. 1969.

S. hybrida **205, 206** (Whitebeam). Bastard service tree. Scandinavia. Zone 4. 20 to 40ft (6 to 12m), compact. Leaves semi-compound, 1 or 2 pairs of long leaflets towards base, lobed, toothed, underside grey downy. Flowers off-white. Fruits scarlet, round.

S. insignis **207,** 318 (Mountain ash). Assam. Zone 6. Small, narrow. Leaves 10in (26cm) long, pinnate, leaflets oblong to lance-shaped, shiny, dark green, waxy beneath. Fruit oval, pink, clustered, persists through winter.

S. intermedia *** 205** Swedish whitebeam. N.W. Europe. Zone 5. To 35ft (10.5m), upright, broad. Leaves oval, pointed, lobed halfway towards base, simple, smooth, shiny green above, lower surface pale grey, felty, roughly toothed. Flowers off white. Fruits oval, clustered, ripening from green to scarlet. 20ft (6m) in 20 years.

S. **'Joseph Rock'** China? Zone 6. A conspicuous erect-branched rowan up to 40ft (12m) high, colouring like flames in autumn, while heavy with amber fruit. A.G.M. 1969.

S. lanata **326** (Whitebeam). Himalaya. Zone 7. Shrub or small tree. Leaves medium length, oval, toothed; olive-green above, greyish below. Fruits round, green, in loose clusters.

S. latifolia **206** (Whitebeam). Service tree of Fontainebleau. E.C. Portugal to S.W. Germany. Zone 4. To 60ft (18m). Leaves oval, simple, shiny, dark green above, grey, furry beneath, sharply lobed, stalked. Flowers white, furry stalks, late spring. Fruits round, brownish, speckled, can be grown from unfertilized seeds. Bark peeling, shaggy.

S. **'Mitchellii'** **205, 206,** 326 (Whitebeam). A form of *S. cuspidata.* Very big mature leaves, almost exactly round, dark green above, white matted hairs below. 40ft (12m) in 20 years.

S. pohuashanensis **207,** 317, 318 (Mountain ash). N. China. Zone 4–5. To 35ft (10.5m), spreading, upright. Leaves pinnate, leaflets smooth, green above, downy, greyish beneath. Fruits orange-red, clusters weigh down branches, autumn.

S. sargentiana **207,** 317, 326 Sargent's mountain ash. W. China. Zone 6. To 35ft (10.5m), broad, pyramidal. Leaves pinnate, leaflets oblong to lance-shaped, smooth, leafstalks red. Buds red and sticky. Flowers, white, hairy stalks. Fruit red, round. 20ft (6m) in 20 years. A.G.M. 1969.

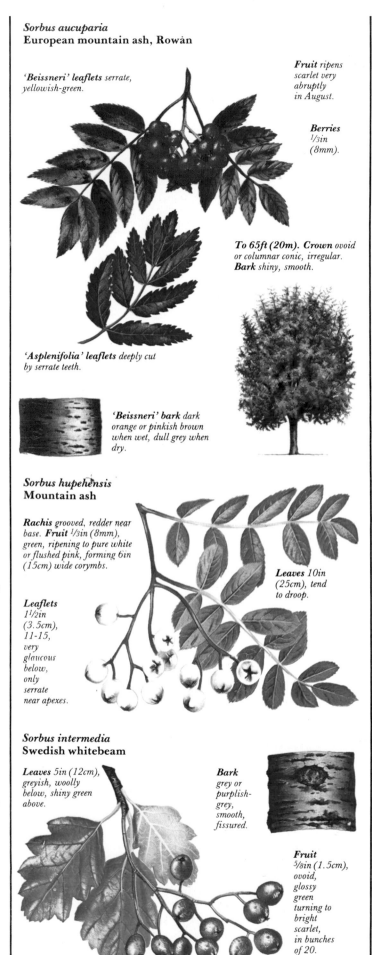

Sorbus aucuparia
European mountain ash, Rowan

'Beissneri' leaflets serrate, yellowish-green.

Fruit ripens scarlet very abruptly in August.

Berries ⅓in (8mm).

'Asplenifolia' leaflets deeply cut by serrate teeth.

To 65ft (20m). Crown ovoid or columnar conic, irregular. Bark shiny, smooth.

'Beissneri' bark dark orange or pinkish brown when wet, dull grey when dry.

Sorbus hupehensis
Mountain ash

Rachis grooved, redder near base. Fruit ⅓in (8mm), green, ripening to pure white or flushed pink, forming 6in (15cm) wide corymbs.

Leaves 10in (25cm), tend to droop.

Leaflets 1½in (3.5cm), 11-15, very glaucous below, only serrate near apexes.

Sorbus intermedia
Swedish whitebeam

Leaves 5in (12cm), greyish, woolly below, shiny green above.

Bark grey or purplish-grey, smooth, fissured.

Fruit ⅝in (1.5cm), ovoid, glossy green turning to bright scarlet, in bunches of 20.

Stewartia (Stuartia) pseudocamellia
Japanese stewartia

Bark *brown with purple-grey scales; reddish where flaking has occurred.*

Leaves *4in (9cm), unusual in being dull above, glossy underneath. Turn brilliant colour before they fall in autumn.*

Buds *¼in (6mm), shiny.*

Flowers *2in (5cm) across, cup-shaped, single, camellia-like, on ½in (1cm) pedicel. July. Remains in bloom over several weeks.*

Shoots *glabrous, slender.*

Veins *impressed.*

Styrax japonica
Japanese snowbell

Buds *⅙in (4mm), hairy, adpressed, conic, pale greenish-brown.*

Leaf margins *waved.* **Serration** *remote.*

Pedicels *¾-1½in (2-4cm).*

Petioles *⅓in (8mm).*

Flowers *small, 1in (2.5cm). Bell-shaped. Waxy. June. Hang in clusters.*

Leaves *3½in (8cm), taper both ends, cupped, glossier and paler below.* **Apex** *often droops.*

Shoots *slightly hairy, zig-zagged, speckled black.*

Fruit *small, to ⅝in (1.5cm), obovoid, in 5-lobed calyx.*

Styrax obassia
Fragrant snowbell

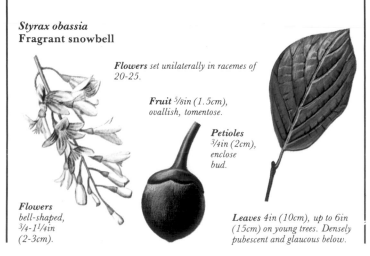

Flowers *set unilaterally in racemes of 20-25.*

Fruit *⅝in (1.5cm), ovallish, tomentose.*

Petioles *¾in (2cm), enclose bud.*

Flowers *bell-shaped, ¾-1¼in (2-3cm).*

Leaves *4in (10cm), up to 6in (15cm) on young trees. Densely pubescent and glaucous below.*

S. scalaris W. China. Zone 6. A small rowan with most distinct pinnate leaves made up of up to 33 dark, shiny leaflets. Very ornamental, with small red fruit and purplish autumn colour. 15ft (4.5m) in 10 years.

S. scopulina **207** (Mountain ash). W. United States. Zone 5. To 15ft (4.5m), shrub or small tree, columnar. Leaves pinnate, leaflets dark green. Fruits bright red, large, clustered. A.G.M. 1969.

S. thibetica **326** (Whitebeam). Tibet, Bhutan. Small, columnar, upright branches. Leaves oval, green and ribbed above, hairy beneath. Fruit small, round, amber-coloured, in loose clusters.

S. × *thuringiaca* **206** To 30ft (9m), compact, hybrid. Leaves semi-compound, 1 to 3 pairs of leaflets, oblong, grey, furry beneath, dull green above, lobed, toothed. Fruit round, red, few brown dots. Similar to *S. hybrida*, but more compact.

S. × *t.* 'Fastigiata' **206, 326** Europe. Small, upright, narrow, hybrid. Leaves broadly oval, often divided into two leaflets, variously toothed and lobed, green upperside, grey matted hairs on underside. Fruits, round berries, in large heads.

S. torminalis **206** (Whitebeam). Wild service tree. Europe, Asia Minor, N. Africa. Zone 5. To 80ft (24.5m), spreading. Leaves oval, lobed, simple, double-toothed, upper side smooth, shiny, dark green, underside paler, in autumn yellow-brown. Flowers white. Fruits oval, edible. Bark scaly. 20ft (6m) in 20 years.

S. vilmorinii **207, 318** Vilmorin's mountain ash. W. China. Zone 5. 15 to 18ft (4.4 to 5.5m), spreading. Leaves pinnate, leaflets numerous, oval or narrowed, small, smooth, stalkless, partly toothed, purple-red in autumn. Flowers tiny, white. Fruits tiny, pink red, becoming paler, early autumn. 15ft (4.5m) in 20 years. A.G.M. 1953.

STEWARTIA (STUARTIA) 173, 326, 327

Deciduous shrubs or trees related to camellias. Leaves alternate, finely-toothed, rich autumn colour. Flowers white, cup-shaped, bisexual, often big, July and autumn. Fruit, woody capsule, flattened, usually winged seeds. Warm, lime-free soil; semi-shade.

S. koreana **173, 326, 327** Korea. Zone 5. To 50ft (15m). Leaves ovallish, simple, hairy at first, orange-red in autumn, stalked. Flowers 3in (7.5cm) across, solitary, summer. Fruit, oval, hairy, small. Bark flaking. 10 to 15ft (3 to 4.5m) in 20 years.

S. monadelpha **319** Small Japanese stewartia.

*S. pseudocamellia** **173, 317, 326, 327** Japanese stewartia. Japan. Zone 5. To 65ft (20m). Leaves ovallish, simple, bright green, red and yellow in autumn. Flowers 2in (5cm) across, single, hairy, summer. Bark reddish, flaking. 25ft (7.5m) in 20 years.

S. serrata **319** Small Japanese stewartia.

STYRAX 188−9, 326, 327

Deciduous or evergreen trees and shrubs. Leaves alternate, often downy. Flowers white, clustered in spikes on short side-branches, late spring and summer. Fruit dry or fleshy with 1 or 2 seeds. Needs moist, loamy, lime-free soil. Sun or semi-shade.

*S. japonica** **189, 316, 326, 327** Japanese snowbell. Japan, Korea. Zone 5. To 35ft (10.5m), wide-spreading. Leaves oval to oblong, simple, deciduous, almost smooth, shiny, dark green above, minutely toothed, stalked. Flowers small, bell-shaped, waxy. Fruit small, ovallish. 20ft (6m) in 20 years. A.G.M. 1969.

*S. obassia** **189, 327** Fragrant snowbell. Japan. Zone 5. To 35ft (10.5m), upright. Leaves round to oval, long, simple, deciduous, upper surface dark green, minutely toothed, downy beneath, stalked. Flowers bell-shaped. Fruit small, ovallish, downy. 30ft (9m) in 20 years.

T

TAXODIUM 112−13, 327

Deciduous trees, usually pyramidal. Leaves narrow, flat or awl-shaped, in 2 ranks, soft, bright green. Male and female 'flowers' separate on same tree; male 'flowers' in drooping clusters. 4 to 5in (10 to 13cm) long. Cones round or oval, small. Seeds winged. Dislikes chalk. Sun-loving. Hardy.

T. ascendens **112−13, 326, 327** Pond cypress. S.E. United States. Zone 4. 70 to 80ft (21.5 to 24.5m), narrowly conical or columnar; base of trunk swollen in wet areas. Leaves lance-shaped, small, deciduous, turn rich brown in autumn. Cones upright, purple-tinted. Not as hardy as *T. distichum*. 18ft (5.5m) in 20 years.

*T. distichum** **42, 112, 113, 325, 326, 327** Bald cypress, Southern cypress, Swamp cypress. S. United States. Zone 4. 100 to 120ft (30 to 36m), narrowly

pyramidal, flattening later; buttressed roots which, by water, produce woody humps called 'cypress knees'. Leaves deciduous, short, yellow-green. Cones persist after first season. 25ft (7.5m) in 20 years.
T. mucronatum 113 Mexican cypress. Mexico. Zone 8. Leaves semi-evergreen or evergreen occasionally. 'Flowers' open in autumn.

TAXUS 64–5, **108–11**, 327
Evergreen shrubs and trees. Leaves needle-like, with 2 yellow bands beneath. Male and female 'flowers' on separate trees, both small, hardly noticeable. Fruit, seed in brightly coloured cup. Good on most soils; chalk-tolerant. Very hardy. Subject to shoot dieback in Europe and America.
T. baccata* 108, 109, 323, 327 Common yew. Europe, N. Persia, Algeria. Zone 6. To 80ft (24.5m), young trees broadly conical, open with level, wide-spreading branches; old trees irregular, broadly domed, often many-stemmed. Leaves short, deep shiny green above, pale, yellowish-green beneath. Male 'flowers' beneath new shoots; female 'flowers' on separate trees, dark green. Red, fleshy seed-cup. Survives drought. 20ft (6m) in 20 years. A.G.M. 1969.
    T.b. 'Aurea' 326 Golden yew. Compact shrub. Leaves golden-yellow for one year, turning green.
    T.b. 'Dovastoniana' 108, 326 Westfelton yew. British Isles. Upright with wide-spreading branches, long weeping branchlets. Male and female 'flowers' have appeared on same tree. A.G.M. 1969.
    T.b. 'Fastigiata' 108–9, 326 Irish yew. Ireland. Columnar, compact. Almost all existng trees female, obtained by cuttings or grafts from 2 originals discovered in 1780. A.G.M. 1969.
    T.b. 'Fastigiata Aurea' 109 Sub-variety, initially with golden leaves. Small, good golden form is male.
    T.b. 'Semperaurea' The best bushy yew for yellow leaves in winter. It becomes immensely wide in time.
    T.b. 'Standishii' 326, 327 Female. Dense, columnar. Leaves golden yellow on tightly-packed upright branches.
T. canadensis 108 Canadian yew. Canada, N.E. United States. Zone 2. Small, straggling shrub. Leaves short, curved, thin, pointed. 'Flowers', sexes separate on same shrub. Seed-cup bright red. 20ft (6m) in 20 years.
T. cuspidata 108, 109 Japanese yew. Japan. Zone 4. To 50ft (15m), may be bushy. Leaves short, curved or straight, dark green above, golden-green beneath. Red seed-cup. Bark red to grey-brown, slightly fissured. 20ft (6m) in 20 years.
T. × media 109 Hybrid between *T. baccata* and *T. cuspidata*. Zone 4. Upright shrub. Leaves short, spines, pale green underneath. Fruit abundant, big, shiny, bright scarlet.

TETRACENTRON *sinense* 318
China. Zone 6. Rare, small, wide-spreading summer-flowering tree with yellow catkins. Leaves heartshaped, pointed, red at first.

TETRACLINIS *articulata* 97
Algeria, Morocco, Malta, S.E. Spain. Zone 8. 40 to 50ft (12 to 15m), conical, branches ascending, evergreen. Leaves in fours, flattened, scale-like, pointed, lateral ones larger. 'Flowers' separate, but on same tree. Cones small, round, waxy, 4 woody scales.

THUJA 102–3, 326
Evergreen trees and shrubs, mostly conical. Leaves small, scale-like, pressed closely to branches, sometimes needle-like. Male and female 'flowers' separate on same tree; males round, red; females small, green, purple tinged. Cones small, single. Seeds winged. Succeeds in many soils. Hardy. Susceptible to scale insects, honey-fungus, needle blight.
T. koraiensis 318 Korean arborvitae. Sprays are white underneath; bark peeling.
T. occidentalis* 102, 103 White cedar, American arborvitae, Tree of life. E. United States. Zone 2. 40 to 50ft (12 to 15m), pyramidal, later more oblong, columnar. Leaves in fan-like sprays, dark green on top, pale underneath. Cones small, persist in winter. Bark thin, furrowed, red to grey-brown. Thrives on limestone outcrops; useful on poorly drained ground and heavy clays. 25ft (7.5m) in 20 years.
    T.o. 'Lutea' 102, 103 Conical. Young branchlets yellow-green in winter, become greener during second spring. Strongest-growing cultivar of *T. occidentalis.*
    T.o. 'Rheingold' 102, 119, 326, 327 Small, rarely to 12ft (3.5m), broadly conical, rounded top. Leaves gold in summer, copper-gold in winter. Male 'flowers' open in spring. Cones rare, green becoming purple, small. Seeds sometimes wingless. Bark thin, scaling. A.G.M. 1969.

Taxodium distichum
Bald cypress, Southern cypress, Swamp cypress

Winter twig has scars left by fallen deciduous shoots.

Leaves ¹/₂-⁵/₈in (1-1.5cm), set in 2 flat rows.

Foliage on side-shoots falls in November.

To 120ft (36m). **Crown** has domed apex. **Bark** fibrous. **Aerial roots** (pneumatophores) may be a way of supplying oxygen to the roots of trees growing in water-logged sites.

Cones 1¹/₄in (3cm), globular, green, ripening brown in first season.

Taxus baccata
Common yew, English yew

Leaves 1¹/₂ × ¹/₆in (4cm × 4mm), short-pointed.

Foliage spreading, glossy; dull and paler below.

Aril ¹/₂in (1cm), red, fleshy, encloses hard seed.

To 80ft (24.5m). **Crown** dense, often on several stems. **Bark** scaly.

Irish yew (T. baccata 'Fastigiata') usually female. Compact, columner.

Thuja occidentalis
White cedar, American arborvitae, Tree of Life

Cones ¹/₂in (1cm), upright, on stronger shoots, often very frequent, with rounded scale tips, ripening brown by autumn.

Foliage smells of apples.

Glands *translucent.*

Foliage in twisted, erect sprays when young, otherwise hanging. Fan-like. Can be rather drab.

Leaves *acutely tipped.*

Leaves *small, ¹/₈in (2.5mm), thick, dark green on top, uniformly paler and glandular below.*

Thuja plicata
Western red cedar, Giant arborvitae

To 180ft (55m).

Crown *conic, broadening with age.* **Tip** *erect.*

Seeds *¹/₄in (6mm), winged, notched.*

Cones *¹/₂in (1cm), with 10–12 scales, have hooked tip, flask-shaped when closed.*

Foliage *flattened, overlapping.* **Leaves** *incurved, glossy, paler below with whitish streaks.*

Branches *light, even, upswept at ends, can layer in old trees.*

Foliage *highly aromatic.*

Bark *red-brown, grey with age, ridged.* **Bole** *fluted. The timber is light, durable, fragrant, much used in building.*

Thujopsis dolabrata
Hiba

Foliage hard, glossy, growing slowly in erect shoots, the widest of any scale-leaved species. The underside is most useful recognition feature; glaucous, silver-white, edged with green.

Leaves *large, broad, to ¹/₃ × ¹/₆in (8 × 4mm).*

Leaf tips *incurved.*

To 45ft (13.5m). **Crown** *usually conic on several stems. Sometimes single-boled.* **Bark** *finely shredded.*

'Variegata' has some cream-green shoots.

Tilia petiolaris
Weeping silver lime, Pendent silver linden

Leaf blade *to 5in (12cm), very cordate, serrate, densely pubescent below.*

Petiole *more than half blade length.*

80ft (24.5m). **Crown** *dense, narrow.* **Branchlets** *pendent.* **Bark** *has shallow ridges. Flowers heavily scented, summer.*

T.o. 'Spiralis' 102 Narrowly columnar small tree, densely branched. Short sprays of dark-green foliage. Very pretty.

T.o. 'Wintergreen' 102, 103 Small-medium, columnar. Foliage green throughout year.

T. orientalis 102, 103 Chinese thuja. N. and W. China. Zone 6. Roughly conical, branches upsweeping. Leaves triangular, blunt-pointed, in vertical plates, mid-green. Cones numerous, often crowded. Prefers limestone; short-lived on very acid soils. Tolerates drought. 15ft (4.5m) in 20 years.

T.o. 'Conspicua' 103 Narrow and dense; golden leaves have greenish tinge.

T.o. 'Elegantissima' 103, 119, 326, 327 Narrow, flame-shaped, gold outer foliage in summer, dull yellow turning green and brown in winter. Broad with age.

T. plicata* 102–3, 324, 326, 327 Western red cedar, Giant arborvitae. W. United States. Zone 5. To 180ft (55m), wide spreading. Foliage in long, flat, fragrant sprays. Cones green, turning brown, ovallish. Bark red-brown, grey with age, ridged. Tolerates chalk, shade. 45ft (13.5m) in 20 years.

T.p. 'Fastigiata' 326 Tall, narrow, columnar form; slender ascending branches.

T.p. 'Zebrina' 103, 326 To 60ft (18m), conical. Leaves green, variously barred yellow.

T. standishii 103 Japanese thuja. Central Japan. Zone 5. To 60ft (18m), broadly cone-shaped. Leaves in dense sprays, dark grey-green or yellow-green, scented when crushed. Bark deep red. 18ft (5.5m) in 20 years.

THUJOPSIS dolabrata* 103, 327
Hiba. False arborvitae. Japan. Zone 6. Form allied to *Thuja* sp. To 45ft (13.5m), usually many-stemmed bush, but sometimes single-boled tree with branches sharply down-curved from bole, then upswept. Leaves broad, scaly, shiny green margin, vividly white on underside. 'Flowers', sexes on separate trees; male 'flowers' ovallish, green-black, down-curving on side shoots, females clustered on tips of sprays. Needs cool summer, plenty of moisture. Any soil. 15ft (4.5m) in 20 years.

TILIA 174–5
Deciduous trees. Leaves alternate, toothed. Flowers small, fragrant, creamy-white, in drooping clusters. Fruit pea-sized, usually one-seeded. Prefer full sun, but tolerate semi-shade. Hardy. Fast-growing when young. Subject to bark fungi, leaf fungi, leaf-eating insects.

T. americana 175, 326 Basswood, American lime, Linden. E. and C. United States. Zone 2. To 135ft (41m), spreading. Leaves roundish, simple, to 15in (38cm) across, virtually smooth, dark green above, paler beneath, stalked. Flowers early summer. Fruit small and nut-like. 25ft (7.5m) in 20 years.

T. chinensis 318 Small lime with shiny, toothed leaves.

T. cordata 174, 317 Small-leaved linden, Small-leaved lime. Europe. Zone 3. To 100ft (30m), pyramidal. Leaves small, heart-shaped, simple, smooth above, red-brown hair beneath, dark green, paler beneath, stalked. Flowers very fragrant, summer. Fruit round, thin-shelled, felt-covered. 30ft (9m) in 20 years.

T.c. 'Swedish Upright' 174, 326 Narrow and upright form.

T. dasystyla 318 Smallish lime with toothed leaves and red twigs, from Caucasus.

T. × euchlora 174, 326, 327 Crimean linden. Zone 5. To 65ft (20m), slightly pendulous. Leaves roundish, simple, few hairs beneath, otherwise smooth, glossy, dark green above, paler beneath, stalked. Flowers inconspicuous, narcotic to bees, summer. Fruit oval, pointed, covered with brown wool. Freer from insect pests, such as aphids, than other limes. 20ft (6m) in 20 years. A.G.M. 1969.

T. × europaea 174, 326, 327 Common lime, European linden. Hybrid between *T. cordata* and *T. platyphyllos*. Zone 3. To 130ft (40m), upright to spreading. Leaves ovallish, simple, smooth except for a few hairs beneath, bright green. Suckers badly, causing unsightly burrs. Often pollarded. 30ft (9m) in 20 years.

T. henryana 175 C. China. Zone 6. To 50ft (15m). A rare tree, distinguished by leaves with a fringe of conspicuous teeth, silver-downy on both sides. 25ft (7.5m) in 20 years.

T. insularis 318 Large Korean lime with toothed leaves.

T. kiusiana 319 Shrubby lime with small oval leaves. From Japan.

T. mandshurica 319 Small Siberian lime with big leaves like American basswood.

T. oliveri 175 C. China. Zone 5. To 40ft (12m); shoots tend to weep. Leaves oval or round, tapering, smooth above, silver-white felted beneath, rich green above. 25ft (7.5m) in 20 years.

T. petiolaris * **175,** 326 Weeping silver lime, Pendent silver linden. Zone 5. To 80ft (24.5m), slightly weeping. Leaves roundish, simple, few hairs above, dark green, silver furry beneath, stalked. Flowers extremely fragrant, narcotic to bees, summer. Fruit round, grooved, warty. 35ft (10.5m) in 20 years. A.G.M. 1969.
T. platyphyllos **174, 175,** 324, 326 Big-leafed lime, Big-leaf linden. C. and S. Europe, British Isles. Zone 3. To 135ft (41m), pyramidal. Leaves roundish, largest of European forms, up to 5in (13cm) wide; simple, slightly downy above, thicker down below, dark green, stalked. Flowers, summer. Fruit pear-shaped, downy, ribbed. 35ft (10.5m) in 20 years.
　　T.p. **'Rubra'** **174,** 327 Red-twigged lime. Large, vigorous tree, twigs red, conspicuous in winter. Leaves unequally heart-shaped, densely downy beneath. Flowers June, early July.
T. tomentosa **175,** 326 Silver linden, Silver lime. S.E. and E.C. Europe. Zone 4. To 100ft (30m), pyramidal. Leaves ovallish, simple, silver-downy beneath. Flowers inconspicuous, narcotic to bees, summer. Fruit oval, pointed, downy, warty. 30ft (9m) in 20 years.

TORREYA 110
Trees or shrubs with whorled branches. Leaves narrow, spiny tips, pungent. Sexes on same or different trees. Fruit plum-like, thin fleshy coat. Tolerates shade and chalk.
Torreya californica * **110** California nutmeg. California. Zone 7. 50 to 70ft (15 to 21.5m). Leaves spirally arranged, persistent; commonly 2-ranked, tapering, dark yellow-green above, two white bands and bright yellow margin below. 'Flowers', sexes separate on same tree, males solitary, female paired. Fruits fleshy, single large seed. Bark red-brown, finely latticed. 18ft (5.5m) in 20 years.
T. grandis **318** Small Japanese torreya.
T. nucifera **110** Kaya. Japan. Zone 5. 20 to 80ft (6 to 24.5m), slender tree or large bush. Leaves narrow, pointed, stiff, curved, pungent if rubbed, shiny, dark green above. Fruit green, tinted purple, edible. Bark reddish, smooth. Likes chalk. Shade-tolerant.

TRACHYCARPUS *fortunei* 122
Chinese windmill palm. Asia. Zone 7. To 40ft (12m), trunk covered by mat of fibres. Palmate leaves 3ft (1m), across, dark green above, waxy bloom below. Unisexual flowers on same tree, yellow, fragrant. Fruit small, ripens blue.

TSUGA 88-9
Hemlocks, Hemlock spruces, Hemlock firs. Evergreen trees, broadly conical. Leaves needle-like, short, usually in 2 ranks. Male and female 'flowers' separate on same tree. Cones small, pendulous, leathery-scaled. Seeds winged. Shade-tolerant. Virtually disease-free, except for decay.
T. canadensis **89,** 326 Eastern hemlock, Canadian hemlock. E. United States. Zone 4. 60 to 100ft (18 to 30m), often many-stemmed, broadly conical. Bark brown to black, deeply furrowed when old. Any soil. 30ft (9m) in 20 years.
　　T.c. **'Pendula'** **89,** 326 Irregularly dome-shaped, flat-topped bush with branches drooping to ground. Slow.
T. caroliniana **89** Carolina hemlock. S.E. United States. Zone 4. To 75ft (23m), irregularly conical. Leaves sparse, slightly larger than *T. canadensis*. Bark dark red-brown with large yellow pores, becoming purple-grey, fissured. Dislikes chalk. 20ft (6m) in 20 years.
T. diversifolia **89** Northern Japanese hemlock. Japan. Zone 5. To 45ft (13.5m), usually with many stems, forming a low-domed crown. Leaves regular, oblong with broad, rounded and notched tip, deep glossy green above, two white bands beneath. Male 'flowers' bright rusty red. Cones oval, shiny brown. Bark orange-brown, pink fissures. Dislikes chalk. 15ft (4.5m) in 20 years.
T. Dumosa **318** Himalayan hemlock, graceful but frost-prone.
T. formosana **318** Formosan hemlock; small tree. Rarely seen in cultivation.
T. heterophylla * 85, **88-9,** 326, 327 Western hemlock. W. United States. Zone 6. 200 to 270ft (60 to 82m), largest of the hemlocks; regularly broad-conical. Leaves flattened, dark shiny green. Cones long, light brown, numerous. Bark thin, narrowly fissured, russet-brown. Any soil, but growth soon poor on chalk. Likes moisture, shelter; tolerates shade. 50 to 65ft (15 to 20m) in 20 years.
T. mertensiana **88-9** Mountain hemlock, Black hemlock. W. United States. Zone 5. 75 to 100ft (23 to 30m), columnar to conical, slightly pendulous. Leaves thick, grey-green, all round shoot, pointing forward, distinctive amongst hemlocks. Cone 2in (5cm) long, fawn-pink, becoming dark brown

Torreya californica
California nutmeg

Fruit aril *fleshy with purple stripes when ripe.*
Fruit *1¹/₂in (4cm), obovoid, contains hard seed similar to that of the true nutmeg.*

Shoots *ridged behind leaves.*

Foliage *irregularly spaced and ranked. Pungent.*

Leaf tips *hard, spiky and sharp.*

Leaves *often curve upwards.*

Leaves *3in (7cm), glossy, dark yellow-green above; undersides with 2 sunken white bands.*

Tsuga heterophylla
Western hemlock

Needles *³/₄in (2cm) at side but only ¹/₂in (1cm) above, tip rounded.*

Shoots *slender, ribbed, cream-brown, hairs brown.*

Leaves *dark, shiny green with white bands below.*

To 270ft (82m). *Largest of the hemlocks.* **Crown** *conic, broader on old trees, dense, pendulous tips to straight branches ascending at 45°, low branches droop.* **Foliage** *irregularly arranged — hence* heterophylla.

Cones *1¹/₄in (3cm), pendulous, ovoid, scales rounded, entire.*

Buds *small, ovoid, non-resinous.*

Young tree *(right) has leading shoot which arches over.*

Foliage *spreading below, parted above.*

Bark *thin, smooth, fissured and ridged in older trees. Russet-brown.* **Bole** *straight, fluted; single stem straight from ground to tip of tree.*

Ulmus procera
English elm

To 150ft (45m).
Crown *broadest at top, fan-shaped, billowing, in leaf the most dense of all the elms.*

Branches *heavy, large, ascending.*

Bark *finely cracked into small plates, dark brown.*

Bole *straight, massive, burred, grows through to top of crown. Elm is the traditional wood for making coffins.*

Leaves *short-tipped.*
Veins *in 10-12 pairs.*

Shoots *slender, zig-zag, hairy.* **Buds** *¹/₆in (4mm), slightly hairy.*

Leaves *to 4in (10cm), thick, rounded, obliquely based. Rough above, densely hairy below. Remain green until November.* **Petioles** *¹/₄in (6mm), downy.*

Flowers *bisexual, open February-March, before the leaves appear.*

Shoots *densely hairy.*

Teeth *double, sharp.*

Fruit *¹/₂in (1cm).* **Seeds** *not set centrally. Infertile, Reproduction is by root-suckering.*

Ulmus thomasii
Rock elm

Scales *ciliate, downy, chestnut-brown, marked with white at apex.*
Shoots *slender, hairy in first year, often develop thick, corky ⁵/₈in (1.5cm) wings after 3-4 years.*

Fruit *1in (2.5cm), in threes, sometimes twos or fours. Very hairy, ciliate.* **Apex** *shallowly notched.*

Buds *¹/₃in (8mm), ovoid.*

Apex *acuminate.*

Leaves *5in (13cm), obovate or oval, hairy below.*
Margins *doubly serrate.*
Base *rounded.*

Bark *thick, irregularly deeply fissured, scaly, dark grey and red-brown.*

---

then nearly black and spruce-like. Tolerates drought, lime. 25ft (7.5m) in 20 years.
    T.m. 'Glauca' 326 Leaves waxy blue-grey.
T. sieboldii 89 Southern Japanese hemlock. S. Japan. Zone 5. To 100ft (30m), possibly bushy. Leaves grooved above, shiny, dark green, white bands beneath. Cones oval, shiny.

U

ULMUS 136–9, 327
Big deciduous trees. Leaves simple, edges serrated, sometimes doubly so. Flowers tiny, in dense clusters, petalless, bisexual. Fruit, small nut with disk-like papery wing. Hardy. Best in full sun. Fast-growing. Tolerates exposure. Any fertile, moist soil. Subject to Dutch elm disease.
U. americana 43, **136, 138, 139,** 326, 327 American elm, White elm. E. and C. United States. Zone 2. To 130ft (40m), upright. Forming wide fountain-like crown with pendulous branchlets. Leaves ovallish, hairy, upper surface becoming smoother, short-stalked. Flowers green-white, hairy nuts. Bark ash grey. 30ft (9m) in 20 years.
U. angustifolia cornubiensis 139, 326 Cornish elm. British Isles, France. To 100ft (30m), pyramidal. Leaves ovallish, smooth, shiny dark green above, lighter underneath, short-stalked. Flowers and fruit rare. 25ft (7.5m) in 20 years.
U. carpinifolia 137, 138, 139, 326 Smooth-leaved elm. Europe, N. Africa. Zone 4. To 110ft (33m), spreading, branchlets drooping. Leaves narrow, ovallish, smooth, lower side downy, shiny green above, short-stalked. Fruits ovallish, smooth.
U. glabra 136, 138, 139, 326, 327 Wych elm, Scotch elm. Europe, N. and W. Asia. Zone 4. To 130ft (40m), wide-spreading. Leaves ovallish, under-surface downy, upper surface rough, dull green, short-stalked. Flowers greenish, early spring. Fruits downy at tip. Susceptible to elm leaf miner. 35ft (10.5m) in 20 years.
    U.g. 'Camperdownii' 139, 326 Camperdown elm. Weeping form of *U. glabra,* with mushroom-shaped head.
    U.g. 'Pendula' 139, 326 Tabletop elm, Weeping wych elm. To 30ft (9m), flat-topped, weeping. Otherwise as *U. glabra.*
U. × hollandica 139 Dutch elm. Zone 4. To 120ft (36m), spreading. Leaves ovallish, upper surface smooth, dark green, lower surface bright green, downy. Flowers as *U. glabra.* Fruit ovallish. Relatively disease-free. 40ft (12m) in 20 years.
    U. × h. 'Bea Schwarz' 139 Dutch elm. Disease-resistant.
    U. × h. 'Belgica' 139 Belgian elm. Netherlands. Broad-crowned tree, straight stems. Leaves oblong to oval. Rough bark.
    U. × h. 'Christine Buisman' 139 Dutch elm. Large, spreading. Disease-resistant.
    U. × h. 'Major' 139 Dutch elm. To 120ft (36m), short-trunked, wide-spreading tree. Leaves oval, dark green above, slightly hairy beneath.
    U. × h. 'Wredei' Upright golden form, also called 'Dampieri Aurea'.
U. × hybrida 'Sapporo Autumn Gold' A recent American introduction, so far resistant to elm disease, making a medium-sized tree with a fan-shaped branch formation. Clear yellow in autumn. 30ft (9m) in 15 years.
U. parvifolia 139, 326 Chinese elm. N. and C. China, Korea, Formosa, Japan. Zone 5. To 80ft (24.5m), spreading. Leaves very small, oval, pointed, upper surface bright green, lower surface paler, short-stalked. Flowers green-white, Aug. and Sept. Fruit smooth. Bark flaking, mottled. Resistant to disease. 18ft (5.5m) in 20 years.
U. procera* 136, 138, 139, 323, 326, 327 English elm. British Isles. Zone 5. To 150ft (45m). Narrow-waisted above broad skirts and below stiff fan-shaped crown. Leaves rounded, rough-textured, dark green, paler, downy beneath. Flowers greenish, spring. Seeds infertile, spreads extensively by suckers. Fruit round, smooth. 35ft (10.5m) in 20 years.
    U.p. 'Louis van Houtte' 327 Leaves golden yellow throughout the summer.
U. pumila 139, 328 Dwarf elm, Siberian elm. N. Asia. Zone 4. To 40ft (12m), small tree or bush. Leaves broadly lance-shaped, thin, smooth. Flowers, spring. Fruit smooth. 25 to 35ft (7.5 to 10.5m) in 20 years.
U. rubra 139 Slippery elm, Red elm. C. and E. United States. Zone 3. To 70ft (21.5m), spreading. Leaves ovallish, lower side downy, upper surface rough, short-stalked. Fruit red-brown, ovallish, hairy at top. Bark slippery. Relatively disease-resistant. 15ft (4.5m) in 20 years.
U. × sarniensis 139, 326, 327 Jersey elm, Wheatley elm. Zone 5. To 100ft (30m), conical. Leaves oval, small. Fruits smooth. 30ft (9m) in 20 years. A.G.M. 1969.

U. serotina 319 Big pendulous elm, S.E. United States.
U. thomasii* 319 Rock elm; medium-sized upright elm from Great Lakes.
U. × vegeta 139 Huntingdon elm, Chichester elm. Zone 5. To 140ft (42m), upright. Leaves ovallish, smooth above, slightly hairy beneath, shiny, dark green. Flowers greenish, dense, early spring. Fruit oval. 40ft (12m) in 20 years.
   U. ×v. 'Commelin' 139 Commelin elm. Leaves compact, small. Disease-resistant.

UMBELLULARIA *californica** 130–1, 326
Oregon myrtle, California laurel. California, Oregon. Zone 7. To 80ft (24.5m), spreading. Leaves alternate, narrowly oval or oblong, tapered both ends, simple, evergreen, leathery, glossy above, paler beneath, dark green, pungently fragrant. Bisexual flowers, yellowish-green, spring. Fruit roundish, pear-shaped, green changing to purple. Sept.–Oct. Scaly bark. Occasionally injured by severe frost. 20ft (6m) in 20 years.

V

VIBURNUM 246
Deciduous or evergreen trees and shrubs. Most deciduous species colour well in autumn. Flowers usually white, fragrant, clustered. Fruits brightly coloured, fleshy, with single flat stone. Easily cultivated.
V. lantana 246 Wayfaring tree. C. and S. Europe, W. Asia, N. Africa. Zone 3. Upright shrub or small tree to 15ft (4.5m). Leaves broad oval, toothed, with a whitish down underneath; turn crimson in autumn. Flowers creamy-white, May and June. Fruit oblong, red turning black, July to Sept. Thrives on chalk.
V. opulus 246 Guelder rose. Europe, N. Africa, N. Asia. Zone 3. Shrub to 12ft (3.5m), spreading. Leaves maple-like. Flowers white, in flat heads, June and July. Fruits small, round, red, Aug. and Sept., persist through winter. Thrives in wet areas.

W

WASHINGTONIA *filifera** 123
Petticoat palm. California. Zone 8. To 50ft (15m); trunk to 3ft (1m) across, usually covered with dead hanging leaves. Palmate leaves 6ft (1.8m) across on 6ft (1.8m) long toothed stalk. White flowers on 9 to 12ft (2.7 to 3.5m) long stalk. Oval fruit ½ in (1cm) long.

Y

YUCCA *brevifolia* 123
Joshua tree. S.W. United States. Zone 8. Erect stem, fibrous and fleshy, scarred by fallen leaves, several stout branches. Leaves long, narrow, pointed, crowded in a round head, evergreen. Flowers lily-like, cream to greenish-white, clustered on erect stalk, to 6ft (1.8m) tall, late summer. Fruit, oval capsule to 3in (7.5cm) long, black seeds.

Z

ZELKOVA 140, 141, 147
Deciduous trees or shrubs with smooth trunks, related to elms. Leaves like those of the elm but singly toothed; alternate, coarsely-toothed. Sexes separate on same tree, small, green; males clustered, females solitary, spring. Fruits small, roundish, autumn.
Z. carpinifolia 140, 141, 326, 327 Elm zelkova. Caucasus. Zone 6. To 80ft (24.5m), often with many upright branches from short trunk. Leaves oval, simple, hairy beneath, slightly hairy above, dark green, short-stalked. Flowers green; males at base of twigs, females on tip. Fruits ridged above. Bark smooth at first, flaking later. Long-lived. Shade-tolerant. 30ft (9m) in 20 years.
Z. cretica 318 Shrubby zelkova from Crete.
Z. serrata* 140, 141, 326 Japanese zelkova. Japan, Korea, China. Zone 5. To 100ft (30m), upright. Trunk short, branches long and spreading. Leaves ovallish, simple, dark green, slightly hairy above, paler beneath, yellow-brown in autumn, short-stalked. Flowers similar to *Z. carpinifolia*, spring. Fruits woody, pea-like. Bark smooth, grey, becoming flaky. Shade-tolerant; young trees susceptible to frost. 25ft (7.5m) in 20 years.

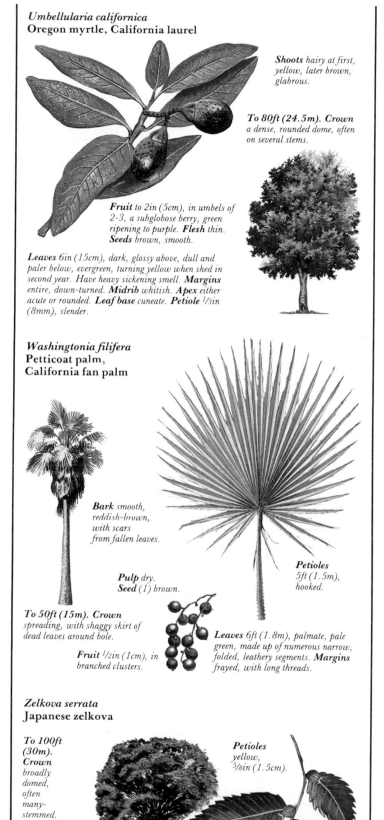

Umbellularia californica
Oregon myrtle, California laurel

Shoots *hairy at first, yellow, later brown, glabrous.*

To 80ft (24.5m). Crown *a dense, rounded dome, often on several stems.*

Fruit *to 2in (5cm), in umbels of 2-3, a subglobose berry, green ripening to purple.* **Flesh** *thin.* **Seeds** *brown, smooth.*

Leaves *6in (15cm), dark, glossy above, dull and paler below, evergreen, turning yellow when shed in second year. Have heavy sickening smell.* **Margins** *entire, down-turned.* **Midrib** *whitish.* **Apex** *either acute or rounded.* **Leaf base** *cuneate.* **Petiole** *⅓in (8mm), slender.*

Washingtonia filifera
Petticoat palm, California fan palm

Bark *smooth, reddish-brown, with scars from fallen leaves.*

Pulp *dry.* **Seed** *(1) brown.*

To 50ft (15m). Crown *spreading, with shaggy skirt of dead leaves around bole.*

Fruit *½in (1cm), in branched clusters.*

Petioles *5ft (1.5m), hooked.*

Leaves *6ft (1.8m), palmate, pale green, made up of numerous narrow, folded, leathery segments.* **Margins** *frayed, with long threads.*

Zelkova serrata
Japanese zelkova

To 100ft (30m). Crown *broadly domed, often many-stemmed.*

Bark *smooth, pale grey, with orange lenticels.*

Leaves *long, 4in (10cm), pointed, serrated often cupped. Dark green. Slightly hairy above. Turn yellow and bronze in autumn.* **Shoots** *carry tiny buds.*

Petioles *yellow, ⅝in (1.5cm).*

Teeth *large, sharp.*

Underside veins *finely pubescent.*

Urban, Pastoral, Classical, Romantic...

Four very different entirely man-made tree-settings,
all photographed in spring, illustrate
the power of trees to create an atmosphere.
The species in the pictures are detailed
in the diagrams opposite.

The urban *On the East River in downtown Manhattan flourishing trees in private gardens make a bizarre contrast to the city skyline. Most surprising are the firs (above the footbridge). Polluted air can kill conifers more quickly than most trees, yet these seem healthy.*

The classical *Stourhead in Wiltshire, one of the great English 18th-century landscape gardens has been en-riched (some say over-enriched) with 19th-century tree-planting.*

The pastoral *The simplest native ingredients give the most powerful effect of Elysean peace at Olantigh in Kent.*

The urban
Right

1 Honey locust
Gleditsia triacanthos

2 Tree of Heaven
Ailanthus altissima

3 Maidenhair tree
Ginkgo biloba

4 Colorado white fir
Abies concolor

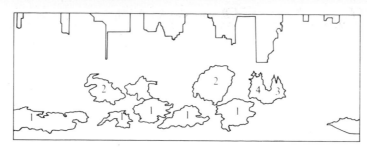

The classical
Below

1 and 9 Caucasian fir
Abies nordmanniana

2 Monkey puzzle
Araucaria araucana

3 and 5 Weeping ash
Fraxinus excelsior
'Pendula'

4 Cedar of Lebanon
Cedrus libani

6 Copper beech
Fagus sylvatica
'Purpurea'

7 *Chamaecyparis pisifera*
'Filifera aurea'

8 Tigertail spruce
Picea polita

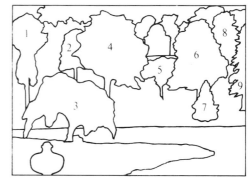

The pastoral
Below

1 Silver birch
Betula pendula

2 Weeping silver pear
Pyrus salicifolia
'Pendula'

3 English yew

Taxus baccata

4 Silver white willow
Salix alba 'Sericea'

5 *Gunnera manicata*
not a tree

6 Weeping willow
Salix × chrysocoma

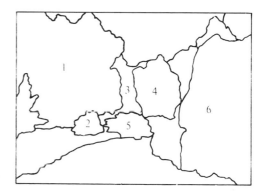

The romantic
Below

1 European beech
Fagus sylvatica

2 *Magnolia ×
soulangiana*

3 Irish yew
Taxus baccata

'Fastigiata'.

4 *Magnolia obovata*

5 *Thuja occidentalis*
'Elegantissima'

6 Paper-bark maple
Acer griseum

The romantic *A very
private paradise-garden
in the South of England
uses exotic trees and the
sense of enclosure to
create a fantasy world
entirely removed from the
surrounding country.*

Right

7 Tree of Heaven
Ailanthus altissima

8 Weeping silver pear
Pyrus salicifolia
'Pendula'

9 Weeping willow
Salix × chrysocoma

10 Rhododendron

11 Coast redwood
Sequoia sempervirens

Natural Forest Vegetation

The climate (both prehistoric and modern), the soil, the mountains, the rainfall, the length of nights and angle of the sun are factors that shape natural forest vegetation. On these pages are maps of its outlines in North America and Europe.

The European pattern is relatively simple. Starting in the north, after tundra (where trees, if any, are stunted dwarfs) comes the vast northern coniferous forest of pine and spruce, sprinkled with birch and, further east, fir, larch and spruce.

South of a line on about the latitude of northern Scotland deciduous trees come into the picture in greater numbers. The northern limit of the oak is roughly along this line. All northern Europe comes into the mixed coniferous/deciduous belt with oak, beech, fir, pine etc. as the principal trees, except where mountains make islands of coniferous forest or where heath (Scotland, North Germany) or grassland (Hungary, S.W. Russia) occupies very poor soil.

The Mediterranean zone is approximately marked by the northern limit of the olive. Its forest is largely evergreen (pine, oak, cork oak, carob) alternating with areas of aromatic shrubs and herbs (myrtle, thyme) dotted with olive, juniper and cypress.

North America is much more complex.

The forest zones of the east, compared with the hardiness zones on page 30, show the same strong continental influence, modified by river-valleys and mountains. In the west the ocean and the mountains are dominant, largely through their effect on rainfall (see page 31).

The overriding factor in Europe is less one of temperature zones (the vegetation bears little relation to the hardiness zones on page 31) than of daylength. Northern Scotland is on the same latitude as southern Alaska. At these latitudes conifers with their relatively small but permanent leaf-area begin to have marked advantages.

USA Vegetation Zones

1. Pine, fir, spruce, larch, poplar.

2. Pine, spruce, tamarack, balsam fir, poplar, birch.

3. Oak, hickory.

4. Oak, chestnut, yellow poplar.

5. Oak, pine.

6. Beech, maple, birch, hemlock.

7. Beech, chestnut, maple, oak.

8. Hemlock, pine, fir, spruce.

9. Longleaf and loblolly pines.

10. Atlantic pine barrens.

11. Cypress, magnolia, white cedar.

12. Spruce, hemlock.

13. Douglas fir, hemlock.

14. Douglas fir, oak, redwood, cypress.

15. Yellow pine, Douglas fir.

16. Lodgepole, yellow and sugar pine.

17. Piñon, pine and juniper.

18. Californian chaparral.

19. Temperate and semi-desert mesquite grasslands.

20. Yucca, sage brush, cactus, agave.

21. Dwarf willow, birch and alder.

Europe: Vegetation Zones

1. *Pine, spruce, Siberian larch, fir, birch.*

2. *Fir, pine, spruce, sometimes with oak, beech, chestnut.*

3. *Mixed forest and meadow: oak, beech, fir.*

4. *Holm oak, cork oak, stone pine, carob.*

5. *Evergreen maquis and meadow: myrtle, olive, aromatic shrubs.*

6. *Grassland.*

7. *Steppe.*

8. *Heath, moor, sandy coastal wastes.*

9. *Alpine.*

A Twelve-Month Succession of Ornamental Flowers, Fruit and Foliage

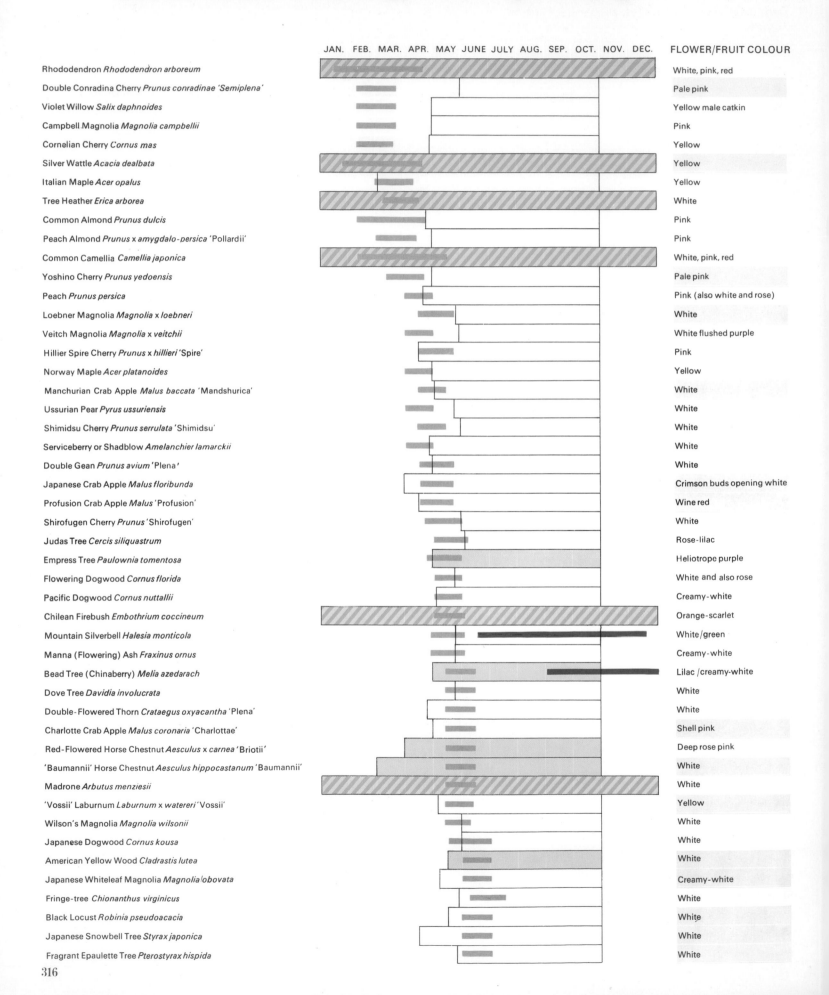

	JAN.	FEB.	MAR.	APR.	MAY	JUNE	JULY	AUG.	SEP.	OCT.	NOV.	DEC.	FLOWER/FRUIT COLOUR
Rhododendron *Rhododendron arboreum*													White, pink, red
Double Conradina Cherry *Prunus conradinae* 'Semiplena'													Pale pink
Violet Willow *Salix daphnoides*													Yellow male catkin
Campbell Magnolia *Magnolia campbellii*													Pink
Cornelian Cherry *Cornus mas*													Yellow
Silver Wattle *Acacia dealbata*													Yellow
Italian Maple *Acer opalus*													Yellow
Tree Heather *Erica arborea*													White
Common Almond *Prunus dulcis*													Pink
Peach Almond *Prunus* x *amygdalo-persica* 'Pollardii'													Pink
Common Camellia *Camellia japonica*													White, pink, red
Yoshino Cherry *Prunus yedoensis*													Pale pink
Peach *Prunus persica*													Pink (also white and rose)
Loebner Magnolia *Magnolia* x *loebneri*													White
Veitch Magnolia *Magnolia* x *veitchii*													White flushed purple
Hillier Spire Cherry *Prunus* x *hillieri* 'Spire'													Pink
Norway Maple *Acer platanoides*													Yellow
Manchurian Crab Apple *Malus baccata* 'Mandshurica'													White
Ussurian Pear *Pyrus ussuriensis*													White
Shimidsu Cherry *Prunus serrulata* 'Shimidsu'													White
Serviceberry or Shadblow *Amelanchier lamarckii*													White
Double Gean *Prunus avium* 'Plena'													White
Japanese Crab Apple *Malus floribunda*													Crimson buds opening white
Profusion Crab Apple *Malus* 'Profusion'													Wine red
Shirofugen Cherry *Prunus* 'Shirofugen'													White
Judas Tree *Cercis siliquastrum*													Rose-lilac
Empress Tree *Paulownia tomentosa*													Heliotrope purple
Flowering Dogwood *Cornus florida*													White and also rose
Pacific Dogwood *Cornus nuttallii*													Creamy-white
Chilean Firebush *Embothrium coccineum*													Orange-scarlet
Mountain Silverbell *Halesia monticola*													White/green
Manna (Flowering) Ash *Fraxinus ornus*													Creamy-white
Bead Tree (Chinaberry) *Melia azedarach*													Lilac/creamy-white
Dove Tree *Davidia involucrata*													White
Double-Flowered Thorn *Crataegus oxyacantha* 'Plena'													White
Charlotte Crab Apple *Malus coronaria* 'Charlottae'													Shell pink
Red-Flowered Horse Chestnut *Aesculus* x *carnea* 'Briotii'													Deep rose pink
'Baumannii' Horse Chestnut *Aesculus hippocastanum* 'Baumannii'													White
Madrone *Arbutus menziesii*													White
'Vossii' Laburnum *Laburnum* x *watereri* 'Vossii'													Yellow
Wilson's Magnolia *Magnolia wilsonii*													White
Japanese Dogwood *Cornus kousa*													White
American Yellow Wood *Cladrastis lutea*													White
Japanese Whiteleaf Magnolia *Magnolia obovata*													Creamy-white
Fringe-tree *Chionanthus virginicus*													White
Black Locust *Robinia pseudoacacia*													White
Japanese Snowbell Tree *Styrax japonica*													White
Fragrant Epaulette Tree *Pterostyrax hispida*													White

There is no difficulty in having beauty and interest in garden trees in the spring. This chart suggests trees to carry on the interest, with either flowers, ornamental fruit or eye-catching leaves, all the year round.

	Legend
	Foliage
	Striking foliage
	Evergreen foliage
	Flowering time
	Fruiting time
	Scented flowers

JAN. FEB. MAR. APR. MAY JUNE JULY AUG. SEP. OCT. NOV. DEC.

Tree	FLOWER/FRUIT COLOUR
Moroccan Broom *Cytisus battandieri*	Yellow
Tulip tree *Liriodendron tulipifera*	Green and orange
Washington Thorn *Crataegus phaenopyrum*	White
Silk Tree *Albizia julibrissin*	Pink
Western Catalpa *Catalpa speciosa*	White
Bull Bay Magnolia *Magnolia grandiflora*	Creamy-white
Delavay Magnolia *Magnolia delavayi*	Parchment white
Small-Leaved Lime *Tilia cordata*	Ivory white
Japanese Hornbeam *Carpinus japonica*	Green turning brown
Sweet or Spanish Chestnut *Castanea sativa*	Yellow-green/green turning brown
Chinese Yellow Wood *Cladrastis sinensis*	White
Golden-Rain Tree *Koelreuteria paniculata*	Yellow
Amur Cork Tree *Phellodendron amurense*	Green turning black
Japanese Stewartia *Stewartia pseudocamellia*	White
Tree of Heaven *Ailanthus altissima*	Green turning reddish
Indian Bean *Catalpa bignonioides*	White
Japanese Dogwood *Cornus kousa*	Red
Sorrel Tree (Sourwood) *Oxydendrum arboreum*	White
Caucasian Wingnut *Pterocarya fraxinifolia*	Green
Japanese Angelica Tree *Aralia elata*	Creamy-white
Red Flowering Gum *Eucalyptus ficifolia*	Scarlet
Lily-of-the-Valley Clethra *Clethra arborea*	White
Glossy Privet *Ligustrum lucidum*	Creamy-white
Myrtle *Myrtus apiculata*	White
Hop Tree *Ptelea trifoliata*	Green turning brown
Rum Cherry *Prunus serotina*	Black
Kashmir Mountain Ash *Sorbus cashmiriana*	White
'Commixta' Mountain Ash *Sorbus commixta*	Red or orange-red
'Pohuashanensis' Mountain Ash *Sorbus pohuashanensis*	Orange-red
Wilson's Magnolia *Magnolia wilsonii*	Crimson
Golden Hornet Apple *Malus* 'Golden Hornet'	Yellow
John Downie Apple *Malus* 'John Downie'	Orange and red
Red Jade Apple *Malus* 'Red Jade'	Red
Red Sentinel Apple *Malus* 'Red Sentinel'	Red
'Cornubia' Cotoneaster *Cotoneaster* 'Cornubia'	Red
J.C. van Tol Holly *Ilex aquifolium* 'J.C. van Tol'	Red
'Camelliifolia' Holly *Ilex x altaclarensis* 'Camelliifolia'	Red
American Holly *Ilex opaca*	Red
Chinese Persimmon *Diospyros kaki*	Orange-red
Idesia *Idesia polycarpa*	Red
Korean Euodia *Euodia daniellii*	Black
Pagoda Tree *Sophora japonica*	Creamy-white
Sea Buckthorn *Hippophae rhamnoides*	Orange
Osage Orange *Maclura pomifera*	Green
Sargent Mountain Ash *Sorbus sargentiana*	Scarlet
Cockspur Thorn *Crataegus crus-galli*	Red
Medlar *Mespilus germanica*	Brown
Autumn Cherry *Prunus subhirtella* 'Autumnalis'	Pale pink

A Chart of Tree Discoveries

The chart on these pages relates our knowledge of the trees of the world to an historical time-scale. It gives the date of introduction to the British Isles of 300 tree species. This can be taken in most cases to be the approximate date of their identification and naming. In a few instances where the exact date of introduction is not known (e.g. *Fraxinus ornus*), the approximate date is indicated by an arrow.

The astonishing acceleration of botanical knowledge in the 18th century, with the exploration of North America, can clearly be seen. The climax came at the end of the 19th century, with the introduction to the western world of the trees of Japan and China.

For reasons of space (and since many of the trees have no real common names) all names are given in their botanical Latin form, which can be translated by referring to the Index.

The chart is the work of Alan Mitchell, and is reproduced here for the first time with his kind permission.

Date	NORTH EUROPE	SOUTH EUROPE & MEDITERRANEAN	CAUCASUS & SOUTHWEST ASIA	INDIA & BURMA	CHINA	KOREA	FORMOSA
Ancient	U. carpinifolia, A. pseudoplatanus	U. procera, C. sativa, Lau. nobilis	Jug. regia, Fic. carica, Pr. dulcis		Pr. persica, Mo. alba		
1500	Pi. abies	Cup. sempervirens, Sor. domestica	P. cerasifera				
1520			Pr. cerasus 'Rhexii'				
1540							
1550		Pl. orientalis	Mo. nigra				
1560		Lab. anagyroides Q. ilex					
1580		Jun. sabina, Pr. laurocerasus, Cer. siliquastrum, Ph. latifolia, P. pinea Lab. alpinum	Dio. lotus		Mo. alba		
1600	Ab. alba	Ae. hippocastanum					
1620	L. decidua						
1640			Ced. libani				
1650		P. pinaster, Pr. lusitanica	Fr. ornus				
1660							
1680	A. platanoides	Pl. × hispanica P. halepensis					
		Jun. phoenicea					
		Q. suber					
1700							
		Pr. mahaleb					
1720		Os. carpinifolia, Arb. andrachne			Th. orientalis		
		Q. canariensis			S. babylonica		
		Q. cerris, A. monspessulanum	Cel. tournefourtii				
1740		Jun. oxycedrus	Carp. orientalis		Cam. japonica		
1750	P. cembra	A. opalus A. sempervirens, Jun. thurifera, A. tataricum P. nigra var. maritima	Liq. orientalis, Z. carpinifolia		Sop. japonica, Ai. altissima	G. biloba	
	Pop. 'Serotina'						
1760					Ko. paniculata, Jun. chinensis, Mal. spectabilis		
	Jun. communis suecica						
	Al. incana		Ti. tomentosa				
1780		Py. salicifolia	Pt. fraxinifolia		Mag. denudata	Mal. baccata	
		O. excelsa	Cra. tanacetifolia, P. nigra caramanica		U. parvifolia, Dio. kaki	Lig. lucidum	
		Cel. australis					
1800				P. roxburghii, Q. incana	Cun. lanceolata		
		Fr. angustifolia, Cra. orientalis sanguinea Q. alnifolia	Fr. oxycarpa	Pi. smithiana			
1820	Al. viridis	Al. cordata					
	Mag. × soulangiana	Q. pyrenaica Ab. cephalonica, Jun. excelsa	S. daphnoides	Ab. spectabilis, P. wallichiana, Cot. frigidus	Cup. torulosa, Jun. recurva, Cas. cuspidata	Q. dentata, Pau. tomentosa	
	Jun. communis 'Hibernica'	P. nigra nigra Ab. pinsapo, Q. frainetto Jun. excelsa, A. lobelii	Pi. orientalis Par. persica, A. cappadocicum	Ced. deodara			
1840		Ced. atlantica, Q. canariensis	Ti. petiolaris, Q. infectoria	A. villosum, Ab. pindrow	Cry. japonica v. sinensis, Cat. ovata	P. bungeana	Jun. formosana
1850		Ab. numidica	Q. castaneifolia Jun. drupacea, Ab. nordmanniana Ab. cilicica	Ts. dumosa, L. griffithiana, Ae. indica	Cup. funebris, Psl. amabilis, Pt. stenoptera	Tr. fortunei, Q. myrsinifolia, T. grandis	
1860		P. peuce	Al. subcordata Q. libani, Ti. euchlora A. hyrcanum	Pr. cornuta, Fr. xanthoxyloides	Cedrel. sinensis, P. tabulaeformis, I. polycarpa	Q. variabilis, Q. acutissima	
	A. heldreichii Mal. trilobata		Q. macranthera A. velutinum, A. velutinum vanvolxemii	Sor. cuspidata, Pi. spinulosa	Pts. hispida, Fr. mariesii	Liq. formosana	
1880		Pi. omorika Ced. brevifolia, Ab. borisii-regis, P. leucodermis, Q. macedonica	Ti. dasystyla, Q. pontica, B. medwediewii	Mag. campbellii, B. utilis, Q. semecarpifolia	Sor. pohuashanensis, A. truncatum, Ket. davidiana, P. armandii, D. vilmoriniana, Jug. cathayensis	Q. glandulifera, A. davidii, A. nikoense, Sor. vilmorinii, Euco. ulmoides, Cat. fargesii	Pic. quassioides, A. buergeranum, Ti. oliveri Dip. sinensis
1900					Lir. chinense, Sor. esserteauana	Te. sinense, Sor. folgneri	Carp. turczaninowii
		A. syriacum	F. orientalis	A. caudatum	B. albosinensis var. septentrionalis, Sor. hupehensis, F. englerana, Ab. delavayi	Ab. squamata Pi. asperata, Ab. sutchuenensis, Ti. insularis Th. koraiensis	Ch. formosensis, Mag. sargentiana, Ab. koreana, Pi. likiangensis
	L. decidua polonica			Man. insignis, Jun. recurva coxii			
1920		Z. cretica, Ab. nebrodensis	A. divergens	Ab. pindrow brevifolia, Sor. insignis, A. campbellii	S. matsudana 'Tortuosa', Jun. distans, A. amplum	A. hersii, Ti. chinensis	Ta. cryptomerioides, A. triflorum, Ab. kawakamii, Ts. formosana
1940					Met. glyptostroboides		
1950							
1960							
1970							

	JAPAN & MANCHURIA	NORTH ASIA	AUSTRALASIA	SOUTH AMERICA	EASTERN & CENTRAL NORTH AMERICA	WESTERN NORTH AMERICA & MEXICO

Key to abbreviations

Abbr.	Genus	Abbr.	Genus	Abbr.	Genus
A.	Acer	F.	Fagus	P.	Pinus
Ab.	Abies	Fic.	Ficus	Par.	Parrotia
Ac.	Acacia	Fitz.	Fitzroya	Pau.	Paulownia
Ae.	Aesculus	Fr.	Fraxinus	Ph.	Phillyrea
Ag.	Agathis			Pi.	Picea
Ai.	Ailanthus	G.	Ginkgo	Pic.	Picrasma
Al.	Alnus	Gle.	Gleditsia	Pl.	Platanus
Arau.	Araucaria	Gym.	Gymnocladus	Pod.	Podocarpus
Arb.	Arbutus			Pop.	Populus
Ath.	Athrotaxis	H.	Halesia	Pr.	Prunus
				Psl.	Pseudolarix
B.	Betula	I.	Idesia	Pst.	Pseudotsuga
				Pt.	Pterocarya
C.	Castanea	Jug.	Juglans	Pts.	Pterostyrax
Cam.	Camellia	Jun.	Juniperus	Py.	Pyrus
Car.	Carya				
Carp.	Carpinus	Kal.	Kalopanax	Q.	Quercus
Cas.	Castanopsis	Ket.	Keteleeria		
Cat.	Catalpa	Ko.	Koelreuteria	R.	Robinia
Ced.	Cedrus				
Cedrel.	Cedrela	L.	Larix	S.	Salix
Cel.	Celtis	Lab.	Laburnum	Sass.	Sassafras
Ceph.	Cephalotaxus	Lau.	Laurus	Sax.	Saxegothaea
Cer.	Cercis	Laur.	Laurelia	Seq.	Sequoia
Ch.	Chamaecyparis	Lig.	Ligustrum	Seqd.	Sequoiadendron
Cord.	Cordyline	Liq.	Liquidambar	Soph.	Sophora
Cot.	Cotoneaster	Lir.	Liriodendron	Sor.	Sorbus
Cra.	Crataegus			St.	Stewartia
Cry.	Cryptomeria	Mac.	Maclura		
Cun.	Cunninghamia	Mag.	Magnolia	T.	Torreya
Cup.	Cupressus	Mal.	Malus	Ta.	Taiwania
		Man.	Mangletia	Tax.	Taxodium
D.	Davidia	May.	Maytenus	Te.	Tetracentron
Dac.	Dacrydium	Met.	Metasequoia	Th.	Thuja
Dio.	Diospyros	Mo.	Morus	Ti.	Tilia
Dip.	Dipteronia	Myr.	Myrtus	Tr.	Trachycarpus
Dr.	Drimys			Ts.	Tsuga
		N.	Nyssa		
Euc.	Eucalyptus	Not.	Nothofagus	U.	Ulmus
Euco.	Eucommia				
Eucr.	Eucryphia	O.	Olea	Z.	Zelkova
		Os.	Ostrya		

Timeline (year scale at right: 1500 – 1970)

Eastern & Central North America

- ~1530 Th. occidentalis
- ~1545 P. strobus
- ~1615 Pr. serotina   Car. ovata / Sass. albidum / Jug. cinerea   Pl. occidentalis / R. pseudoacacia / Tax. distichum
- ~1645 A. rubrum / Cel. occidentalis
- ~1655 Lir. tulipifera
- ~1660 Jun. virginiana
- ~1680 Liq. styraciflua / Jug. nigra   Pop. tacamahaca / A. negundo   Q. prinus / Cra. crus-galli   Ab. balsamea / Q. coccinea / Gle. triacanthos   Pi. glauca
- ~1700 Pi. mariana / Ae. pavia
- ~1725 A. saccharinum   Fr. americana   Q. phellos / Cat. bignonioides   Q. alba   Q. nigra / Mag. grandiflora   Ts. canadensis   Q. borealis / A. saccharum   P. palustris   Ch. thyoides / Mag. acuminata   P. resinosa   B. nigra / L. laricina   P. echinata   P. virginiana
- ~1740 P. taeda   R. hispida / Gym. dioicus / A. spicatum   N. sylvatica   B. papyrifera / Mag. tripetala   Ti. americana   U. americana / H. carolina
- ~1755 A. pensylvanicum / B. lenta
- ~1760 P. rigida   Ae. flava / Car. cordiformis   Car. tomentosa / B. alleghaniensis
- ~1775 P. banksiana   Fr. pensylvanica / Sor. americana / Mag. fraseri   Q. imbricaria / Tax. ascendens / Car. glabra   Q. bicolor   Q. palustris
- ~1800 Mag. macrophylla   Q. velutina / Car. laciniosa   P. pungens / Ab. fraseri   Ae. glabra   Q. macrocarpa
- ~1815 Mac. pomifera
- ~1820 Q. heterophylla / U. rubra
- ~1840 Q. × leana
- ~1860 Cat × erubescens / U. thomasii / Q. × ludoviciana
- ~1880 Cat. speciosa / Ts. caroliniana / Q. × schochiana / H. monticola   Q. shumardii
- ~1900 U. serotina   Pi. glauca albertiana / Fr. tomentosa
- ~1925 Jun. virginiana 'Pseudocupressus'
- ~1945 Jun. virginiana 'Skyrocket'

Western North America & Mexico

- ~1690 Cup. lusitanica
- ~1820 A. macrophyllum / A. circinatum / P. ponderosa   Ab. amabilis / Pst. menziesii   Ab. procera / Ab. grandis   P. radiata / Pi. sitchensis / Cup. macrocarpa   Ab. religiosa
- ~1840 Ab. concolor lowiana   P. ayacahuite / Th. plicata   Seq. sempervirens / Ch. nootkatensis / Ab. magnifica   Seqd. giganteum / Ab. bracteata   Ts. heterophylla
- ~1860 Pi. engelmanii / P. aristata   Q. wislizenii / Fr. latifolia / Q. garryana   Q. lobata / Ab. concolor   Q. kelloggii / Cup. guadalupensis
- ~1880 Cup. arizonica   L. occidentalis / Al. rubra / Pi. brewerana   Fr. velutina / Pop. trichocarpa
- ~1900 Jun. deppeana / Cup. glabra / Cup. sargentii   Pst. macrocarpa
- ~1925 Cup. forbesii   Jun. ashei / Cup. bakeri / Cup. abramsiana
- ~1955 Ab. vejari
- ~1960 P. cooperi

Japan & Manchuria

- ~1770 T. nucifera
- ~1800 Pod. macrophyllus
- ~1818 A. palmatum / Cep. harringtonia drupacea / P. massoniana
- ~1840 Cry. japonica 'Lobbii'
- ~1848 Ts. sieboldii   Jug. mandshurica / P. densiflora   P. thunbergii / Th. standishii   Pi. polita   Ch. obtusa
- ~1855 Ab. firma   Ts. diversifolia   L. kaempferi / Mag. obovata   Mag. kobus / Kal. pictus   A. japonicum / A. rufinerve albolimbatum   A. cissifolium / Pi. glehnii   Q. acuta / Kal. pictus maximowiczii   A. argutum
- ~1875 Pi. jezoensis   A. crataegifolium / A. mono   A. distylum   A. rufinerve / A. carpinifolium   A. diabolicum / B. maximowicziana   A. capillipes / A. miyabei   Mag. salicifolia / Pst. japonica   B. grossa
- ~1895 S. gracilistyla   Pr. yedoensis / A. mandshuricum / Ab. holophylla / St. monodelpha / Pi. koyamai   Q. aliena   Pr. maackii / Carp. laxiflora / St. serrata
- ~1930 Ti. kiusiana

North Asia

- ~1795 L. sibirica / P. pumila
- ~1818 Ab. sibirica / L. gmelini
- ~1848 Pi. obovata
- ~1855 Ti. mandshurica / Pi. schrenkiana
- ~1858 U. pumila
- ~1880 B. costata
- ~1910 L. gmelini olgensis

Australasia

- ~1770 Soph. tetraptera
- ~1775 Euc. obliqua
- ~1805 Ac. dealbata
- ~1818 Ag. australis / Cord. australis / Euc. globulus
- ~1845 Euc. coccifera / Euc. gunnii / Dac. franklinii
- ~1858 Ath. spp. / Laur. serrata

South America

- ~1790 Arau. araucana
- ~1815 May. boaria
- ~1820 Dr. winteri / Not. betuloides / Not. antarctica
- ~1840 Myr. apiculata / Sax. conspicua / Fitz. cupressoides / Eucr. cordifolia / Pod. salignus
- ~1858 Pod. andinus
- ~1880 Not. fusca / Not. cliffortioides / Not. moorei
- ~1900 Not. obliqua / Not. procera / Not. dombeyi
- ~1965 Not. pumila

A mighty army of insects, fungi and bacteria relies on trees for food. Most of them are harmless. But a great number can also maim, disfigure and kill when they really take hold.

The list that follows describes some of the commonest pests and diseases, but it is not intended to be an arboricultural medical dictionary. Unless the trouble is obvious it is always worth talking to a qualified tree surgeon before taking action.

Aphids

Aphids are small, generally wingless insects (29). Many secrete honeydew which can act as a germination site for mould. Some can cause galls. Aphids are found mainly on broadleaves; they deform foliage and can deform branches.

Commonest species:

Craphalodes–attacks spruce, causing distortion of the twigs, and pineapple-like galls (27).

Eriosoma lanuginosum–attacks elms, causing irregular, blister-like galls.

Pemphigus bursarius–attacks poplars, causing small oblong galls on the leafstalks and leaves (28).

Tetraneura ulmifoliae–attacks elms, causing club-shaped galls on the leaves.

Control: Tar-oil washes in winter; systemic insecticides; nicotine or malathion. Birds also help to keep numbers down.

Beetles

Beetles attack both conifers and broadleaves; leaf eaters are not serious pests; borers can transmit disease and destroy trees by 'ringing'.

Commonest species include:

Copper beech leaf miner *(Rhynchuenus fagi)*–larvae chew winding galleries in leaves of common and copper beech, causing them to turn brown in summer.

Elm bark beetle *(Scolytus scolytus* (16) in Britain, and *Hylurgopinus rufipes* (15) in America)–see Dutch elm disease.

Large pine weevil *(Hylobius abietis)* (17)–feeds on bark of young conifers (and on broadleaves if no conifers available).

Control: Sprays, burning of infested wood; predatory animals give some control.

Mites

Mites are minature spider-like creatures; their longish, hard mouthparts are specially adapted for penetrating woody substances. They can cause defoliation.

Commonest species:

Red spider mite *(Paratetranychus pilosus)* (18)–larvae attack mainly apple, pear and cherry tree leaves, leaving a fine web. The leaves eventually die.

Moths

The larvae of various moths, if they occur in large enough numbers, can cause serious defoliation and damage to leader shoots of conifers and broadleaves.

Commonest species:

Bagworm *(Thyridopteryx ephemeraeformis)* – winged male moths (24) are harmless. The wingless females live in a bag made of silk and covered by leaves and leaf-stalks (26). They can cause partial defoliation of young trees.

Buff-tip moth *(Phalera bucephala)*–larvae defoliate a number of small broadleaved species.

Larch case-bearer *(Coleophora laricella)* (25)–larvae hollow out larch needles, causing them to drop off eventually.

Tent caterpillar *(Malocosoma pluvialis)*–larvae live in communal web 'tent' on conifers, especially larch, and cause defoliation.

Control: Caterpillar-eating birds and various bacteria keep down larval populations. Caterpillars can also be picked off and destroyed by hand; use tar-oil washes and pesticides only as a last resort.

Sawflies

The adults (20) are harmless. The caterpillar-like larvae (21) attack both conifers and broadleaves, causing galls, and, in large numbers, serious defoliation.

Commonest species:

Larch sawfly *(Lygaenematus erichsoni)*–larvae eat larch needles causing severe defoliation.

Willow sawfly *(Pontania vesicator)* (19) and (22)–causes oblong galls on willow leaves.

Control: Various pesticides; smaller insect-eating birds such as tits and warblers.

Scale Insects

Scale insects secrete a waxy protective shield which makes them difficult to eliminate. Only the females are harmful. They mainly attack broadleaves, making leaves curl up and fall off; they also attack and damage fruit.

Commonest species:

Citrus scale *(Aspidiotus perniciosus)*–attacks foliage and fruit of apple and pear trees in Europe, orange and other citrus trees in the United States.

Felted beech scale *(Cryptococcus fagi)* – attacks beech, giving white-washed appearance to tree.

Oystershell scale *(Lepidosaphes ulmi)*–attacks bark of a number of trees and bushes.

Control: Coccinellid beetles will eat the young; otherwise tar-oil and malathion sprays. Some trees are damaged by tar-oil, however, and malathion is ecologically harmful.

Anthracnose

A fungus disease common to broadleaves, particularly willow and plane, which first attacks the foliage in damp seasons, giving it a white spotted appearance (1). It then spreads over the whole tree.

Control: Regular spraying with copper compounds (e.g. Bordeaux mixture). Burn infected leaves. Fertilizer helps.

Bark and Timber Fungi

Fungi can seriously damage wood and kill trees. The fruit of many fungi often appears as a 'bracket fungus' on the bark. Others produce spores which appear on the trunk as small coloured spots (some of which produce canker) (q.v.). Beefsteak fungus *(Fistulina hepatica)* 9, which attacks oak, can give a deep brown colour to the wood enhancing its market value. Other fungi attack the roots and show above ground as toadstools. Honey (or bootlace) fungus *(Armillaria mellea)* (6) is the deadliest.

Control: Felling and burning of infected trees and sterilisation of surrounding soil. Soaking the foot of the tree with creosote has destroyed honey fungus.

Canker

A term for several diseases common to conifers and broadleaves. They are caused by bacteria or fungi, whose spores enter open wounds on the tree. The bark usually swells around the wound (7). Balsam poplars are subject to a canker resisted by other poplars.

Control: Infected parts should be cut away or painted with antibiotic and tree paint. Badly infected trees must be burned.

Chestnut Blight *(Endothia)*

A fungal disease affecting bark and cambium of chestnuts. The trunk of infected trees is covered with small coloured dots (4). The disease is usually fatal to the top of the tree but new bark often develops beneath the wound.

Control: As for bark and timber fungi.

Dutch Elm Disease

A fungal disease affecting elms, spread mainly by elm bark beetles, but also by natural root grafts between healthy and infected trees. The foliage of infected trees turns yellow and wilts.

Adult beetles make breeding galleries in the bark. Those of the American beetle are horizontal (10, 12);

Key
1 *Anthracnose on plane*
2 *Rust fungus on lime*
3 *Mildew*
4 *Chestnut blight*
5 *Fireblight of Cotoneaster*
6 *Honey fungus on pine*
7 *Bacterial canker on poplar*
8 *White pine blister rust on timber pine*
9 *Beefsteak fungus on oak*
10/11 *American elm bark beetle gallery in elm bark/wood*
12/13 *European elm bark beetle galleries on elm wood/bark*
14 *Oystershell scale insects on elm*
15 *American elm bark beetle*
16 *European elm bark beetle*
17 *Pine weevil*
18 *Red spider mite*
19 *Willow sawfly*
20 *Sawfly*
21 *Sawfly larva*
22 *Willow sawfly larva*
23 *Tent caterpillar*
24 *Male bagworm moth*
25 *Larch case-bearer*
26 *Bagworm*
27 *Pineapple gall on spruce (see* Craphalodes*)*
28 *Aphid purse gall on poplar leaf stalk*
29 *Wingless female aphid*

those of the European are vertical (11, 13). These galleries and the winding ones made by emerging larvae, are ideal reproduction sites for fungi. Up to 1,000,000 sticky fungal spores are carried to healthy trees by each beetle.

Control: Infected bark should be burnt or sprayed with insecticide. Healthy trees can be sprayed to kill feeding beetles. Recently infected trees can often be saved by injection with fungicide. Localised injection into the soil of root-killing chemicals, or trenching, will combat the natural spread by root grafts. Fell only dead trees or those with more than half the crown affected.

Fireblight

A bacterial disease of many members of the Rose family, especially pears, which is spread by pollinating insects. It causes die-back in the flowers and leaves. The twigs of infected trees often exude a bacterial slime (5).

Control: Burning of infected foliage, or anti-biotic sprays such as streptomycin.

Mildew and Rusts

Fungal diseases which can seriously affect the growth of seedlings and young trees by causing defoliation. In trees affected by mildew the foliage has a whitish powdery coating (3); the foliage of rust-diseased trees is spotted with black, orange-brown or red (2).

White pine blister rust (8) attacks pines (both foliage and, here, shoots) and currant bushes during its life-cycle.

Control: As for Anthracnose.

Rates of Growth

No rate of growth holds good for any species of tree under all circumstances. A tree's performance is governed very much by the area in which it is planted: climate and soil are all-important. Soils vary considerably in depth, moisture content and nutrient supply. These factors in turn depend on temperature and rainfall. Trees, however, have their characteristic patterns of growth. The graphs on the right show how a selection of conifers and of broadleaves reach their maximum growth-rates at different ages: some holding back for the first ten years before putting on three feet a year; others racing away but soon slowing down. The trees illustrated below and on the following pages are chosen for the wide differences in their speed of growth.

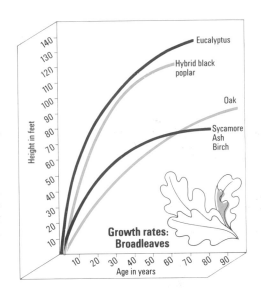

Growth rates: Broadleaves

Height in feet — Age in years

Eucalyptus
Hybrid black poplar
Oak
Sycamore
Ash
Birch

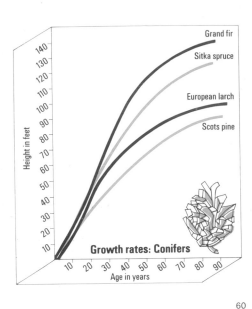

Growth rates: Conifers

Height in feet — Age in years

Grand fir
Sitka spruce
European larch
Scots pine

Holm oak

Wellingtonia

Cider gum

White willow

The holm oak starts slowly: it barely reaches ten feet in ten years. Then it speeds up to reach 35 feet in 30 years. In the next 70 years it only doubles its height, but spreads hugely.

Wellingtonia (or 'big tree') can be relied on to grow a steady two feet a year for 40 or 50 years, slowing down as it approaches 100 feet.

Cider gum is immensely vigorous from the start, reaching 40 feet in ten years but then slowing down, scarcely doubling its height in the following 20.

White willow makes a really big tree faster than almost any: its height and spread at 30 years make it look twice its age. Thereafter progress is very slow.

Monterey pine is one of the fastest of all conifers: in exceptional conditions it has grown 20 feet in one year: it can be relied on to do three or four.

Silver birch gets away quickly but settles down to a slow advance after 15 or 20 years—making it an excellent garden tree.

English yew is notoriously slow to start with, but grows as wide as it is high—and eventually much wider.

English elm is always vigorous, but most so in middle age: a 100-year-old tree looks 200 or 300 years old.

70 — 15 years
60
50
40
30
20
10
0

130 — 100 years
120
110
100
90
80
70
60
50
40
30
20
10
0

70 — 70
60 — 60
50 — 50
40 — 40
30 — 30
20 — 20
10 — 10
0 — 0

130 — 130
120 — 120
110 — 110
100 — 100
90 — 90
80 — 80
70 — 70
60 — 60
50 — 50
40 — 40
30 — 30
20 — 20
10 — 10
0 — 0

Monterey pine   Common silver birch   English yew   English elm

70 — 15 years
60
50
40
30
20
10
0

130 — 100 years
120
110
100
90
80
70
60
50
40
30
20
10
0 Feet

70 — 70
60 — 60
50 — 50
40 — 40
30 — 30
20 — 20
10 — 10
0 — 0

130 — 130
120 — 120
110 — 110
100 — 100
90 — 90
80 — 80
70 — 70
60 — 60
50 — 50
40 — 40
30 — 30
20 — 20
10 — 10
Feet 0

Douglas fir   European horse chestnut   Lombardy poplar   English holly

Douglas fir in good damp conditions is a three-feet-a-year tree for the 30 years from five to 35. It then slows down and thickens its stem.

Horse chestnut reaches its full height, like many broadleaf trees, in 50 or 60 years at about two feet a year. Thereafter it just spreads.

Lombardy poplar can grow between two and three feet a year for 25 years before it slows down. Planted at eight feet it should make a 20-foot screen in five years.

English holly starts as slowly as yew. Only after about 15 years does it put on 18-inch shoots in one season.

323

Rates of Growth

Scots pine grows surprisingly fast after the first three or four years: a three-foot shoot is normal. But it soon loses its upward vigour and spreads out.

Scarlet oak in the acid loam it likes is among the fastest of the oaks. The growth-rates shown here are about average for any oak.

Wingnut is in the championship class for high-speed broadleaves, growing 45 feet in only 15 years, then building a wide symmetrical dome.

Giant Thuja is one of the fastest conifers: a reliable two-feet-a-year tree in gardens, though much more in the Pacific north-west.

Weeping willows usually surprise their owners by their rapid spread: at 15 years 30 feet across as well as high.

15 years

70 60 50 40 30 20 10 0

Scots pine   Scarlet oak   Wingnut   Giant thuja   Weeping willow

70 60 50 40 30 20 10 0

100 years

130 120 110 100 90 80 70 60 50 40 30 20 10 0

130 120 110 100 90 80 70 60 50 40 30 20 10 0

15 years

70 60 50 40 30 20 10 0

European beech   Serbian spruce   Maidenhair tree   London plane   Big-leafed lime

70 60 50 40 30 20 10 0

100 years

130 120 110 100 90 80 70 60 50 40 30 20 10

0 Feet

130 120 110 100 90 80 70 60 50 40 30 20 10 0 Feet

European beech is rather slow in its early years but makes up for it in its second and third decades. At 100 years it is fully mature: as wide as it is high.

Serbian spruce is the best of the spruces for a confined space, never spreading but mounting at two feet a year in a trim spire.

The gingko or maidenhair tree is never a fast grower. A one-foot shoot is about normal for its formative years.

The London plane is slower than its American parent, but the estimate here is conservative: it should grow two feet a year in its early years.

The big-leafed lime (T. platyphyllos) is not exceptional for speed but keeps a narrow tower-like shape in maturity, unlike most broadleaves.

Spanish chestnut is relatively slow in its earlier years but immensely vigorous in middle age, when it will put out ten-foot shoots in one year if it is cut back hard.

Silver maple is among the fastest of the maples, but has a reputation for making weak wood which is liable to split. Its initial energy fades relatively early in life.

All larches are among the quicker-growing conifers. The speed of the European larch is typical: at 15 years it is growing three feet a year. A hundred years brings it to maturity.

The junipers are a slow-growing race—hence excellent for small gardens. Common European juniper scarcely reaches tree stature—even in 100 years.

70 60 50 40 30 20 10 0 — 15 years

70 60 50 40 30 20 10 0

130 — 100 years

Spanish chestnut

Silver maple

European larch

Common juniper

130 120 110 100 90 80 70 60 50 40 30 20 10 0

130 120 110 100 90 80 70 60 50 40 30 20 10 0

70 60 50 40 30 20 10 0 — 15 years

70 60 50 40 30 20 10 0

130 — 100 years

Roblé beech

Swamp cypress

European ash

Cedar of Lebanon

130 120 110 100 90 80 70 60 50 40 30 20 10 0 Feet

130 120 110 100 90 80 70 60 50 40 30 20 10 0 Feet

The southern beeches (Nothofagus) are among the fastest of all broadleaves: the Roblé beech's 60 feet in 15 years is comparable to the performance of much shorter-lived willows and poplars.

Swamp cypress grows fairly slowly but steadily to a great age. At 100 years it is still not fully grown.

American ash is one of the fastest-growing American hardwoods. European ash (**above**) is steadier but still vigorous, reaching 100 feet or so in well under 100 years.

Cedar of Lebanon grows and forms its venerable plateaux much faster than you might expect. A hundred years is enough to complete the picture of sublime old age.

A Guide to Choosing Trees

By their shape, colour, performance and preferences

The following lists classify a selection of trees from the Conifers and Broadleaves sections according to their outstanding characteristics.

SHAPE

Picturesque/romantic/irregular

Black mulberry *Morus nigra*
Japanese snowbell *Styrax japonica*
Judas tree *Cercis siliquastrum*
Strawberry tree *Arbutus unedo*

Araucaria *Araucaria* species
Nikko fir *Abies homolepis*
Pines – most with age, especially
Eastern white pine *Pinus strobus*
Japanese black pine *Pinus thunbergii*
Japanese white pine *Pinus parviflora*
Scots pine *Pinus sylvestris*
Umbrella pine *Pinus pinea*

Broad-domed

Algerian oak *Quercus canariensis*
American walnut *Juglans nigra*
Black poplar *Populus nigra*
Blue gum *Eucalyptus globulus*
Broad-leaved lime *Tilia platyphyllos*
California laurel *Umbellularia californica*
Caucasian wingnut *Pterocarya fraxinifolia*
Chestnut-leaved oak *Quercus castaneifolia*
Elm zelkova *Zelkova carpinifolia*
English oak *Quercus robur*
European beech *Fagus sylvatica*
European walnut *Juglans regia*
Hardy rubber tree *Eucommia ulmoides*
Holm oak *Quercus ilex*
Hungarian oak *Quercus frainetto*
Italian maple *Acer opalus*
Indian bean tree *Catalpa bignonioides*
Japanese crab *Malus floribunda* (and others)
Japanese zelkova *Zelkova serrata*
London plane *Platanus × hispanica*
Lucombe oak *Quercus × hispanica* 'Lucombeana'
Norway maple *Acer platanoides*
Red horse chestnut *Aesculus × carnea*
Red oak *Quercus rubra*
Silk tree *Albizia julibrissin*
Sweet chestnut *Castanea sativa*
Sycamore *Acer pseudoplatanus*
Turkey oak *Quercus cerris*

Cedar of Lebanon *Cedrus libani*
Monterey cypress *Cupressus macrocarpa*

Tower-like

Bat willow *Salix* 'Caerulea'
Bitternut *Carya cordiformis*
Common lime *Tilia × europaea*
Cucumber tree *Magnolia acuminata*
English elm *Ulmus procera*
Mockernut *Carya tomentosa*
Pecan *Carya illinoensis*
Pignut *Carya glabra*
Pin oak *Quercus palustris*
Roblé beech *Nothofagus obliqua*
Shagbark hickory *Carya ovata*
White willow *Salix alba*

Giant cone

Atlantic cedar *Cedrus atlantica*
Big tree *Sequoiadendron giganteum*
European larch *Larix decidua*
Japanese cedar *Cryptomeria japonica*
Japanese larch *Larix kaempferi*
Western hemlock *Tsuga heterophylla*
Western red cedar *Thuja plicata*

Globular-headed

Black locust *Robinia pseudoacacia* 'Inermis'
Cockspur thorn *Crataegus crus-galli*
Norway maple *Acer platanoides* 'Globosum' and 'Summershade'
Sugar maple *Acer saccharum* 'Globosum'

Horizontally spreading

Black mulberry *Morus nigra*
Chinese witch hazel *Hamamelis mollis*
Fig *Ficus carica*
Japanese cherry *Prunus* 'Kiku-shidare Sakura' and 'Shirofugen'
Japanese snowbell *Styrax japonica*
Laburnum *Laburnum* species
Persian parrotia *Parrotia persica*

Silk tree *Albizia julibrissin*
Witch hazel *Hamamelis virginiana*

Golden larch *Pseudolarix amabilis*

Pyramidal: broad

Dove (or handkerchief) tree *Davidia involucrata* and *D.i.* var. *vilmoriniana*
Silver lime *Tilia tomentosa*
Turkish hazel *Corylus colurna*

Golden larch *Pseudolarix amabilis*

Pyramidal: narrower

Alder *Alnus* species
Cornish elm *Ulmus angustifolia cornubiensis*
Jersey elm *Ulmus × sarniensis*
Sweetgum *Liquidambar styraciflua*

Caucasian fir *Abies nordmanniana*
Dawn redwood *Metasequoia glyptostroboides*
Serbian spruce *Picea omorika*

Upright, columnar or fastigiate

Common hawthorn *Crataegus monogyna* 'Stricta'
Crabs *Malus baccata* 'Columnaris' and *M.* 'Van Eseltine'
Dawyck beech *Fagus sylvatica* 'Dawyck' and *F.s.* 'Dawyck Purple'
English oak *Quercus robur*
Honey locust *Gleditsia triacanthos* 'Columnaris'
Japanese cherry *Prunus* 'Amanogawa'
Lombardy poplar *Populus nigra* 'Italica'
Norway maple *Acer platanoides* 'Columnare' and *A.p.* 'Erectum'
Red maple *Acer rubrum* 'Columnare'
Silver birch *Betula pendula* 'Fastigiata'
Small-leaved lime *Tilia cordata* 'Swedish Upright'
Sorbus *Sorbus × thuringiaca* 'Fastigiata'
Sugar maple *Acer saccharum* 'Temple's Upright'
Tulip tree *Liriodendron tulipifera* 'Fastigiatum'
Washington thorn *Crataegus phaenopyrum* 'Fastigiata'
White poplar *Populus alba* 'Pyramidalis'

Arolla pine *Pinus cembra*
Atlantic cedar *Cedrus atlantica* 'Fastigiata'
Chinese juniper *Juniperus chinensis* 'Aurea' and 'Columnaris Glauca'
Incense cedar *Calocedrus decurrens*
Irish juniper *Juniperus communis* 'Hibernica'
Irish yew *Taxus baccata* 'Fastigiata'
Italian cypress *Cupressus sempervirens*
Lawson cypress *Chamaecyparis lawsoniana* 'Columnaris', 'Erecta Viridis' and many others
Leyland cypress *× Cupressocyparis leylandii*
Maidenhair tree *Ginkgo biloba* 'Sentry'
Pencil cedar *Juniperus virginiana* 'Skyrocket'
Pond cypress *Taxodium ascendens*
Rocky mountain juniper *Juniperus scopulorum* 'Skyrocket'
Scots pine *Pinus sylvestris* 'Fastigiata'
Syrian juniper *Juniperus drupacea*
Western red cedar *Thuja plicata* 'Fastigiata'

Pendulous (not weeping)

Japanese crab *Malus floribunda*
Silver birch *Betula pendula*
Smooth-leaved elm *Ulmus carpinifolia*
Weeping silver lime *Tilia petiolaris*
White elm *Ulmus americana*
Wych elm *Ulmus glabra*

Brewer's spruce *Picea breweriana*
Deodar *Cedrus deodara*
Drooping juniper *Juniperus recurva* and *J.r. coxii*
European larch *Larix decidua*
Huon pine *Dacrydium franklinii*
Kashmir cypress *Cupressus cashmeriana*
Lawson cypress *Chamaecyparis lawsoniana* 'Intertexta'
Nootka cypress *Chamaecyparis nootkatensis* and *C.n.* 'Pendula'

Pencil cedar *Juniperus virginiana* 'Pendula'
Prince Albert's yew *Saxegothaea conspicua*
Westfelton yew *Taxus baccata* 'Dovastoniana'
West Himalayan spruce *Picea smithiana*

Weeping

Camperdown elm *Ulmus glabra* 'Camperdownii'
Perry's silver weeping holly *Ilex aquifolium* 'Argenteomarginata Pendula'
Silver birch *Betula pendula* 'Tristis'
Spring cherry *Prunus subhirtella* 'Pendula'
'Tortuosa' beech *Fagus sylvatica* 'Tortuosa'
Weeping beech *Fagus sylvatica* 'Pendula'
Weeping oak *Quercus robur* 'Pendula'
Weeping purple beech *Fagus sylvatica* 'Purpurea Pendula'
Weeping willow *Salix babylonica, S. × chrysocoma, S. sepulchralis*
Weeping wych elm *Ulmus glabra* 'Pendula'
Young's weeping birch *Betula pendula* 'Youngii'

Big tree *Sequoiadendron giganteum* 'Pendulum'
Eastern hemlock *Tsuga canadensis* 'Pendula'
Japanese red pine *Pinus densiflora* 'Umbraculifera'

Weeping–height depending on graft

Flowering dogwood *Cornus florida* 'Pendula'

Japanese pagoda tree *Sophora japonica* 'Pendula'
Weeping ash *Fraxinus excelsior* 'Pendula'
Young's weeping birch *Betula pendula* 'Youngii'

Atlantic cedar *Cedrus atlantica* 'Pendula'

Multistemmed

Caucasian wingnut *Pterocarya fraxinifolia*
Hazel *Corylus avellana*
Japanese maple *Acer japonicum, A. palmatum*
Oleaster *Elaeagnus angustifolia*
Olive *Olea europaea*
Rhododendron *Rhododendron* species
Sea buckthorn *Hippophae rhamnoides*
Stewartia *Stewartia* species
Vine maple *Acer circinatum*

Chinese juniper *Juniperus chinensis* 'Kaizuka'
Eastern hemlock *Tsuga canadensis*
Lace-bark pine *Pinus bungeana*
Mountain pine *Pinus mugo*

Contorted trees

Corkscrew hazel *Corylus avellana* 'Contorta'
Corkscrew willow *Salix matsudana* 'Tortuosa' and *S. × erythroflexuosa*
'Tortuosa' beech *Fagus sylvatica* 'Tortuosa'

LEAVES, FLOWERS, FRUIT AND BARK

Leaves–big

American lime *Tilia americana*
American walnut *Juglans nigra*
Bigleaf magnolia *Magnolia macrophylla*
Bigleaf maple *Acer macrophyllum*
Burr oak *Quercus macrocarpa*
Caucasian wingnut *Pterocarya fraxinifolia*
Chinese poplar *Populus lasiocarpa*
Chinese toon *Cedrela sinensis*
Daimyo oak *Quercus dentata*
'Delavay' magnolia *Magnolia delavayi*
Empress tree *Paulownia tomentosa*
Hercules club *Aralia spinosa*
Himalayan whitebeam *Sorbus cuspidata* and *S.* 'Mitchellii'
Idesia *Idesia polycarpa*
Japanese angelica tree *Aralia elata*
Japanese broadleaf holly *Ilex latifolia*
Japanese horse chestnut *Aesculus turbinata*
Kentucky coffee tree *Gymnocladus dioicus*

Mockernut *Carya tomentosa*
Palms All species
Rhododendron *Rhododendron calophytum, R. falconeri, R. sinogrande*
Southern catalpa *Catalpa bignonioides*
Tree of heaven *Ailanthus altissima*

Jelecote pine *Pinus patula*
Montezuma pine *Pinus montezumae*
Pitch pine *Pinus palustris*

Leaves–very small

Antarctic beech *Nothofagus antarctica*
Black beech *Nothofagus solandri*
Chinese elm *Ulmus parvifolia*
Mountain beech *Nothofagus cliffortioides*
New Zealand sophora *Sophora tetraptera*
Perny holly *Ilex pernyi*

Oriental spruce *Picea orientalis*

Evergreen trees (not conifers)

Acacia *Acacia* species
American holly *Ilex opaca*
Bull bay magnolia *Magnolia grandiflora*
California laurel *Umbellularia californica*
California live oak *Quercus agrifolia*
Camellia *Camellia* species
Carob *Ceratonia siliqua*
Chilean fire-bush *Embothrium* species
Chinese photinia *Photinia serrulata*
Citrus *Citrus* species
Cork oak *Quercus suber*
'Delavay' magnolia *Magnolia* 'Delavayi'
English holly *Ilex aquifolium*
Eucalyptus *Eucalyptus* species
Evergreen dogwood *Cornus capitata*
Glossy privet *Ligustrum lucidum*
Golden chestnut *Chrysolepis chrysophylla*
Heath *Erica* species
Highclere holly *Ilex × altaclerensis*
Holm oak *Quercus ilex*
Holly *Ilex latifolia, I. pedunculosa*
Laurel *Laurus nobilis*
Live oak *Quercus virginiana*
New Zealand sophora *Sophora tetraptera*
Oak *Quercus acuta, Q. glauca*
Olive *Olea europaea*
Palms All species
Perny holly *Ilex pernyi*
Portugal laurel *Prunus lusitanica*
Rhododendron *Rhododendron arboreum, R. barbatum, R. falconeri, R. maximum*
Silk oak *Grevillea robusta*
Strawberry tree *Arbutus* species
Tanbark oak *Lithocarpus* species

Leaves–red/purple

Crab *Malus* 'Lemoinei', *Malus × purpurea*
English oak *Quercus robur* 'Atropurpurea'
Japanese maple *Acer palmatum* 'Atropurpureum'
Norway maple *Acer platanoides* 'Goldsworth Purple' and 'Schwedleri'
Purple beech *Fagus sylvatica* 'Riversii'
Purple-leaf filbert *Corylus maxima* 'Purpurea'
Purple-leaved plum *Prunus cerasifera* 'Pissardii'
Smoke tree *Cotinus coggygria* 'Royal Purple'
Sycamore *Acer pseudoplatanus* 'Purpureum' and 'Spaethii'
Japanese cedar *Cryptomeria japonica* 'Elegans'

Leaves–silver/grey

English holly *Ilex aquifolium* 'Argenteomarginata Pendula', 'Silver Milkboy', 'Silver Queen', 'Silver Sentinel'
Olive *Olea europaea*
Russian olive *Elaeagnus angustifolia*
Sea buckthorn *Hippophae rhamnoides*
Silver maple *Acer saccharinum*
Weeping silver lime *Tilia petiolaris*
Whitebeam *Sorbus aria, S. lanata, S.* 'Mitchellii', *S. thibetica*
White poplar *Populus alba*
White willow *Salix alba* 'Sericea'
Willow-leaved pear *Pyrus salicifolia*

Arizona cypress *Cupressus glabra* 'Pyramidalis'
Blue spruce *Picea pungens glauca*
Colorado white fir *Abies concolor* 'Candicans'

Leaves–green and yellow

Box elder *Acer negundo* 'Elegans'
Chestnut *Castanea sativa* 'Aureomarginata'
English holly *Ilex aquifolium* 'Golden Milkboy' and 'Golden Queen'
English oak *Quercus robur* 'Variegata'
Highclere holly *Ilex × altaclerensis* 'Golden King' and 'Lawsoniana'
Japanese angelica tree *Aralia elata* 'Aureovariegata'
Sweetgum *Liquidambar styraciflua* 'Aurea'
Tulip tree *Liriodendron tulipifera* 'Aureomarginatum'

Chinese arborvitae *Thuja orientalis* 'Elegantissima'
Golden yew *Taxus baccata* 'Aurea'
Lawson cypress *Chamaecyparis lawsoniana* 'Lanei', 'Lutea'
Oriental spruce *Picea orientalis* 'Aurea'
Western red cedar *Thuja plicata* 'Zebrina'
Yew *Taxus baccata* 'Standishii'

Leaves–cream/yellow/gold

English elm *Ulmus procera* 'Louis van Houtte'
English oak *Quercus robur* 'Concordia'
European alder *Alnus glutinosa* 'Aurea'
European ash *Fraxinus excelsior* 'Jaspidea'
European beech *Fagus sylvatica* 'Zlatia'
False acacia *Robinia pseudoacacia* 'Frisia'
Golden-leaved laburnum *Laburnum anagyroides* 'Aureum'
Golden poplar *Populus* 'Serotina Aurea'
Honey locust *Gleditsia triacanthos* 'Sunburst'
Japanese maple *Acer japonicum* 'Aureum'
Laurel *Laurus nobilis* 'Aurea'
Southern catalpa *Catalpa bignonioides* 'Aurea'
Sycamore *Acer pseudoplatanus* 'Brilliantissimum' and 'Worlee'
White poplar *Populus alba* 'Richardii'

American arborvitae *Thuja occidentalis* 'Rheingold'
Atlantic cedar *Cedrus atlantica* 'Aurea'
Chinese juniper *Juniperus chinensis* 'Aurea'
Hinoki cypress *Chamaecyparis obtusa* 'Crippsii'
Lawson cypress *Chamaecyparis lawsoniana* 'Winston Churchill'
Scots pine *Pinus sylvestris* 'Aurea'

Leaves–blue-green

Eucalypt *Eucalyptus* species

Bhutan pine *Pinus wallichiana*
Blue Cedar *Cedrus atlantica glauca*
Hemlock *Tsuga mertensiana* 'Glauca'
Lawson cypress *Chamaecyparis lawsoniana* 'Columnaris', 'Pembury Blue', 'Triomf van Boskoop', 'Wisselii', etc
Scots pine *Pinus sylvestris*
Weymouth pine *Pinus strobus*

Leaves–unusual and attractive

Camellia *Camellia* species
Cherry laurel *Prunus laurocerasus* 'Camelliifolia'

Chinese persimmon *Diospyros kaki*

Chinese persimmon *Diospyros kaki*
European alder *Alnus glutinosa* 'Imperialis'
Fern-leaved beech *Fagus sylvatica heterophylla*
Golden chestnut *Chrysolepis chrysophylla*
Holly *Ilex* species
Hornbeam *Carpinus betulus* 'Incisa'
Hungarian oak *Quercus frainetto*
Japanese maple *Acer japonicum* 'Aconitifolium' and 'Vitifolium', *A. palmatum* 'Dissectum' and 'Linearilobum'
Katsura tree *Cercidiphyllum japonicum*
Oriental plane *Platanus orientalis*
Paper mulberry *Broussonetia papyrifera*
Scarlet oak *Quercus coccinea*
Swedish birch *Betula pendula* 'Dalecarlica'
Sweetgum *Liquidambar styraciflua*
Tulip tree *Liriodendron tulipifera*

Maidenhair tree *Ginkgo biloba*

Leaves–divided/cut

Cut-leaved walnut *Juglans regia* 'Laciniata'
European alder *Alnus glutinosa* 'Imperialis'
Fern-leaved beech *Fagus sylvatica heterophylla*
Hornbeam *Carpinus betulus* 'Incisa'
Japanese maple *Acer japonicum* 'Aconitifolium', *A. palmatum* 'Dissectum'
Mountain ash *Sorbus aucuparia* 'Asplenifolia'
Norway maple *Acer platanoides* 'Dissectum', 'Laciniatum', 'Lorbergii'
Swedish birch *Betula pendula* 'Dalecarlica'

Leaves–very early

Bird cherry *Prunus padus commutata*
Hawthorn *Crataegus oxyacantha*
Horse chestnut *Aesculus hippocastanum*
Japanese flowering crab *Malus floribunda*
Manchurian birch *Betula platyphylla*
Roblé beech *Nothofagus obliqua*
Southern beech *Nothofagus procera*

Dawn redwood *Metasequoia glyptostroboides*

Leaves–late to drop

Algerian oak *Quercus canariensis*
Chinese elm *Ulmus parvifolia*
English elm *Ulmus procera*
Hawthorn *Crataegus × lavallei*
Laurel oak *Quercus laurifolia*
Lucombe oak *Quercus × hispanica* 'Lucombeana'
Water oak *Quercus nigra*
White oak *Quercus alba*

Autumn colour

Amur cork tree *Phellodendron amurense*
Antarctic beech *Nothofagus antarctica*
Aspen *Populus tremula*
Beech *Fagus* (most species)
Birch *Betula* (most species)
Black cottonwood *Populus trichocarpa*
Black tupelo *Nyssa sylvatica*
Buckeye *Aesculus parviflora*
Caucasian wingnut *Pterocarya fraxinifolia*
Cercidiphyllum *Cercidiphyllum japonicum*
Chinese persimmon *Diospyros kaki*
Chinese toon *Cedrela sinensis*
Chinese witch hazel *Hamamelis mollis*
Crab *Malus tschonoskii*
Disanthus *Disanthus cercidifolius*
English elm *Ulmus procera*
Flowering dogwood *Cornus florida*
Franklinia *Franklinia* species
Giant dogwood *Cornus controversa*
Guelder rose *Viburnum opulus*
Hickory *Carya* species
Japanese cherry *Prunus sargentii*
Japanese dogwood *Cornus kousa*
Japanese maple *Acer palmatum* 'Ozakazuki'
Kentucky coffee tree *Gymnocladus dioicus*
Mountain ash *Sorbus alnifolia, S. americana, S. aucuparia, S. commixta, S.* 'Embley', *S. sargentiana*
Nikko maple *Acer nikoense*
Norway maple *Acer platanoides*
Ohio buckeye *Aesculus glabra*
Pacific dogwood *Cornus nuttallii*
Persian parrotia *Parrotia persica*
Pin oak *Quercus palustris*
Quaking aspen *Populus tremuloides*
Red maple *Acer rubrum*
Red oak *Quercus rubra*
Sassafras *Sassafras albidum*
Scarlet oak *Quercus coccinea*
Smoke tree *Cotinus* species
Snowy mespilus *Amelanchier* species
Sourwood *Oxydendrum arboreum*
Stag's horn sumach *Rhus typhina*
Stewartia *Stewartia koreana, S. pseudocamellia*
Sugar maple *Acer saccharum*
Sweetgum *Liquidambar styraciflua*
Trident maple *Acer buergeranum*
Tulip tree *Liriodendron tulipifera*
White oak *Quercus alba*
White poplar *Populus alba*
Willow oak *Quercus phellos*

Witch hazel *Hamamelis virginiana*
Yellow wood *Cladrastis* species
Zelkova *Zelkova serrata*

Dawn redwood *Metasequoia glyptostroboides*
Golden larch *Pseudolarix amabilis*
Larch *Larix* species
Maidenhair tree *Ginkgo biloba*
Pond cypress *Taxodium ascendens*
Swamp cypress *Taxodium distichum*

Flowers–early in spring
Alder *Alnus* species
Almond *Prunus dulcis*
Aspen *Populus tremula*
Birch *Betula* species
Camellia *Camellia* species
Cherry plum *Prunus cerasifera*
Elm *Ulmus* species
Goat willow *Salix caprea*
Hazel *Corylus* species
Italian maple *Acer opalus*
Magnolia *Magnolia campbellii*
Norway maple *Acer platanoides*
Silver wattle *Acacia dealbata*
Witch hazel *Hamamelis* species

Flowers–ornamental
Broom *Cytisus battandieri*
Camellia *Camellia* species
Carolina silverbell *Halesia carolina*
Cherry *Prunus* (most species)
Chilean fire bush *Embothrium lanceolatum*
Chinese witch hazel *Hamamelis mollis*
Cootamundra wattle *Acacia baileyana*
Crab *Malus* (most species)
Dogwood *Cornus* species
Dove (or handkerchief) tree *Davidia involucrata, D.i.* var. *vilmoriniana*
European pussy willow *Salix caprea*
Golden-rain tree *Koelreuteria paniculata*
Hawthorn *Crataegus* species
Horse chestnut *Aesculus hippocastanum, A.h.* 'Baumannii'
Indian horse chestnut *Aesculus indica*
Japanese witch hazel *Hamamelis japonica* 'Arborea'
Judas tree *Cercis siliquastrum*
Laburnum *Laburnum* species
Magnolia *Magnolia* species
Mountain silverbell *Halesia monticola*
Red buckeye *Aesculus pavia*
Redbud *Cercis canadensis*
Red horse chestnut *Aesculus × carnea*
Silk tree *Albizia julibrissin, A.j.* 'Rosea'
Silver wattle *Acacia dealbata, A. decurrens*
Stewartia *Stewartia koreana, S. pseudocamellia*
Sydney golden wattle *Acacia longifolia*
Violet willow *Salix daphnoides*
Willow *Salix gracilistyla*
Wingnut *Pterocarya* species
Witch hazel *Hamamelis virginiana*
Yellow wood *Cladrastis lutea*

Lawson cypress *Chamaecyparis lawsoniana*
Likiang spruce *Picea likiangensis*
Pine *Pinus* (many species)

Fruit–ornamental
American holly *Ilex opaca, I.o.* 'Xanthocarpa'
Black mulberry *Morus nigra*
Blackthorn *Prunus spinosa*
Blueberry elder *Sambucus caerulea*
Campbell's magnolia *Magnolia campbellii mollicomata*
Caucasian wingnut *Pterocarya fraxinifolia*
Chinaberry *Melia azedarach*
Chinese persimmon *Diospyros kaki*
Choke cherry *Prunus virginiana*
Cotoneaster *Cotoneaster × watereri*
Crab *Malus* (many species)
Dogwood *Cornus* (many species)
Elder *Sambucus nigra*
English holly *Ilex aquifolium* 'Bacciflava', *I.a.* 'J. C. van Tol'
Hawthorn *Crataegus* (most species)
Highclere holly *Ilex × altaclerensis* 'Camelliifolia', 'Golden King'
Italian alder *Alnus cordata*
Japanese broadleaf holly *Ilex latifolia*
Japanese hornbeam *Carpinus japonica*
Japanese whiteleaf magnolia *Magnolia obovata*
Judas tree *Cercis siliquastrum*
Medlar *Mespilus germanica*
Mountain ash *Sorbus* species
Osage orange *Maclura pomifera*
Perny holly *Ilex pernyi*
Persimmon *Diospyros virginiana*
Quince *Cydonia oblonga*
Sea buckthorn *Hippophae rhamnoides*
Strawberry tree *Arbutus unedo*
Tree of heaven *Ailanthus altissima*
Whitebeam *Sorbus* species

Cedar *Cedrus* species
Fir *Abies* species (late summer)
Pine *Pinus* species
Spruce *Picea* species (autumn/winter)
Yew *Taxus* species

Bark–ornamental
Amur cork tree *Phellodendron amurense*

Birch *Betula* (most species)
'Capillipes' maple *Acer capillipes*
Cherry *Prunus serrula*
Cork oak *Quercus suber*
David's maple *Acer davidii*
English walnut *Juglans regia*
Eucalypt *Eucalyptus* species
Hers's maple *Acer hersii*
Japanese maple *Acer palmatum* 'Senkaki'
London plane *Platanus × hispanica*
Manchurian cherry *Prunus maackii*
Paperbark maple *Acer griseum*
Persian parrotia *Parrotia persica*
Rhododendron *Rhododendron barbatum*
Shagbark hickory *Carya ovata*
Snakebark maple *Acer grosseri*
Snowgum *Eucalyptus niphophila*
Sorbus *Sorbus alnifolia*
Strawberry tree *Arbutus* species
Striped maple *Acer pensylvanicum*
Violet willow *Salix daphnoides*
White willow *Salix alba*
Zelkova *Zelkova carpinifolia*

Coast redwood *Sequoia sempervirens*
Lace-bark pine *Pinus bungeana*
Scots pine *Pinus sylvestris*

SOIL
Soil–able to grow in clay
Alder *Alnus* species
Ash *Fraxinus* (most species)
Birch *Betula* species
Cherry *Prunus* species
Cotoneaster *Cotoneaster* species
Crab *Malus* species
Dogwood *Cornus* species
Eucalypt *Eucalyptus* species
Hawthorn *Crataegus* species
Hazel *Corylus* species
Hornbeam *Carpinus* species
Horse chestnut *Aesculus* species
Laburnum *Laburnum* species
Lime *Tilia* species
Maple *Acer* species
Poplar *Populus* species
Rose *Rosa* species
Smoke tree *Cotinus* species
Sorbus *Sorbus* species
Willow *Salix* species
Witch hazel *Hamamelis* species

Arborvitae *Thuja* species
Fir *Abies* species
Larch *Larix* species
Swamp cypress *Taxodium distichum*

Soil–can be acid
Aspen *Populus tremula*
Birch *Betula* species
Chilean fire bush *Embothrium* species
Cotoneaster *Cotoneaster* species
Disanthus *Disanthus cercidifolius*
English oak *Quercus robur*
Franklinia *Franklinia* species
Grey poplar *Populus × canescens*
Heath *Erica* species
Holly *Ilex* species
Rhododendron *Rhododendron* species
Sourwood *Oxydendrum arboreum*
White poplar *Populus alba*

Juniper *Juniperus* species
Pine *Pinus* species
Yew *Taxus* species

Soil–can be alkaline
Ash *Fraxinus* species
Beech *Fagus* species
Birch *Betula* species
Cotoneaster *Cotoneaster* species
Crab *Malus* species
Dogwood *Cornus* species
English holly *Ilex aquifolium*
Hawthorn *Crataegus* species
Hedge maple *Acer campestre*
Highclere holly *Ilex × altaclerensis*
Hornbeam *Carpinus* species
Horse chestnut *Aesculus* species
Laurel *Laurus nobilis*
Phillyrea *Phillyrea* species
Whitebeam *Sorbus* species

American arborvitae *Thuja occidentalis*
Austrian pine *Pinus nigra*
English yew *Taxus baccata*
Hiba false arborvitae *Thujopsis dolabrata*
Juniper *Juniperus* species
Western red cedar *Thuja plicata*

Soil–must be lime-free (acid)
Bigleaf magnolia *Magnolia macrophylla*
Black tupelo *Nyssa sylvatica*
Camellia *Camellia* species
Campbell's magnolia *Magnolia campbellii, M.c. mollicomata*
Chilean fire bush *Embothrium* species
Clethra *Clethra arborea*
Gordonia *Gordonia* species
Japanese whiteleaf magnolia *Magnolia obovata*
Japanese willowleaf magnolia *Magnolia salicifolia*
Lily-flowered magnolia *Magnolia liliiflora, M.l.* 'Nigra'

Pin oak *Quercus palustris*
Red oak *Quercus rubra*
Rhododendron *Rhododendron* species
Scarlet oak *Quercus coccinea*
Shumard oak *Quercus shumardii*
Silverbell *Halesia* species
Snowbell *Styrax* species
Sourwood *Oxydendrum arboreum*
Southern beech *Nothofagus* species
Stewartia *Stewartia* species
Sweetgum *Liquidambar styraciflua*
Veitch magnolia *Magnolia × veitchii*
Willow oak *Quercus phellos*
Yulan magnolia *Magnolia denudata*

Soil–very dry, either acid or alkaline
Aspen *Populus tremula*
Chestnut *Castanea* species
Grey poplar *Populus × canescens*
Robinia *Robinia* species
Siberian elm *Ulmus pumila*
White poplar *Populus alba*

Cedar *Cedrus* species
Cypress *Cupresses* (some species)
Juniper *Juniperus*
Yew *Taxus* species

Soil–can be badly drained
Alder *Alnus* species
Black tupelo *Nyssa sylvatica*
Caucasian wingnut *Pterocarya fraxinifolia*
Elder *Sambucus* species
European birch *Betula pendula*
Hawthorn *Crataegus oxyacantha*
Medlar *Mespilus germanica*
Mountain ash *Sorbus aucuparia*
Pear *Pyrus communis*
Pin oak *Quercus palustris*
Poplar *Populus* species
Red maple *Acer rubrum*
River birch *Betula nigra*
Swamp bay magnolia *Magnolia virginiana*
Swamp white oak *Quercus bicolor*
Sweetgum *Liquidambar styraciflua*
White birch *Betula pubescens*
Willow *Salix* species

American arborvitae *Thuja occidentalis*
Dawn redwood *Metasequoia glyptostroboides*
Pond cypress *Taxodium ascendens*
Sitka spruce *Picea sitchensis*
Swamp cypress *Taxodium distichum*
Tamarack *Larix laricina*

SPECIAL SITES
Seaside/maritime areas
Aspen *Populus tremula*
Chamaerops *Chamaerops humilis*
English oak *Quercus robur*
Eucalypt *Eucalyptus* species
European ash *Fraxinus excelsior*
Grey poplar *Populus × canescens*
Hawthorn *Crataegus* (many species)
Holm oak *Quercus ilex*
Laurel *Laurus nobilis*
Mountain ash *Sorbus aucuparia*
Pittosporum *Pittosporum* species
Sea buckthorn *Hippophae rhamnoides*
Sessile oak *Quercus petraea*
Strawberry tree *Arbutus unedo*
Whitebeam *Sorbus aria*
White poplar *Populus alba*
Willow *Salix* species

Aleppo pine *Pinus halepensis*
Bishop pine *Pinus muricata*
Black pine *Pinus thunbergii*
Juniper *Juniperus* (many species)
Maritime pine *Pinus pinaster*
Monterey cypress *Cupressus macrocarpa*
Monterey pine *Pinus radiata*
Shore pine *Pinus contorta*
Sitka spruce *Picea sitchensis*

Trees which will tolerate industrial or urban atmosphere
Allegheny service-berry *Amelanchier laevis*
Almond *Prunus dulcis*
Ash *Fraxinus* (most species)
Birch *Betula platyphylla*
Bird cherry *Prunus padus*
Black mulberry *Morus nigra*
Box elder *Acer negundo*
Bull bay magnolia *Magnolia grandiflora*
Camellia *Camellia japonica*
Catalpa *Catalpa* species
Caucasian wingnut *Pterocarya fraxinifolia*
Cherry plum *Prunus cerasifera*
Chinaberry *Melia azedarach*
Chinese toon *Cedrela sinensis*
Clethra *Clethra arborea*
Cotoneaster *Cotoneaster × watereri*
Crab *Malus* species
Cucumber tree *Magnolia acuminata*
English elm *Ulmus procera*
English holly *Ilex aquifolium*
European birch *Betula pendula*
European hornbeam *Carpinus betulus*
European lime *Tilia × europaea*
False acacia *Robinia pseudoacacia*
Gean *Prunus avium*
Hackberry *Celtis* species

Hawthorn *Crataegus* species
Hedge maple *Acer campestre*
Highclere holly *Ilex × altaclerensis*
Holm oak *Quercus ilex*
Honey locust *Gleditsia triacanthos*
Horse chestnut *Aesculus* species
Japanese cherries *Prunus* species
Japanese pagoda tree *Sophora japonica*
Jersey elm *Ulmus × sarniensis*
Laburnum *Laburnum* species
Lime *Tilia × euchlora*
Lucombe oak *Quercus × hispanica* 'Lucombeana'
Magnolia *Magnolia kobus, M. × soulangiana*
Medlar *Mespilus germanica*
Norway maple *Acer platanoides*
Paper birch *Betula papyrifera*
Poplar *Populus* (most species)
Red-twigged lime *Tilia platyphyllos* 'Rubra'
Snowy mespilus *Amelanchier canadensis, A. lamarckii, A. ovalis*
Strawberry tree *Arbutus unedo*
Sycamore *Acer pseudoplatanus*
Tree of heaven *Ailanthus altissima*
Tulip tree *Liriodendron tulipifera*
White birch *Betula pubescens*
White elm *Ulmus americana*
Wych elm *Ulmus glabra*
Yulan magnolia *Magnolia denudata*

Colorado spruce *Picea pungens*
Maidenhair tree *Ginkgo biloba*
White fir *Abies concolor*

For small gardens
Carolina silverbell *Halesia carolina*
Cherry *Prunus* (most species)
Cotoneaster *Cotoneaster × watereri*
Crab *Malus* species
Dawyck beech *Fagus sylvatica* 'Dawyck'
Dogwood *Cornus* species
Eastern redbud *Cercis canadensis*
Flowering ash *Fraxinum ornus*
Fragrant snowbell *Styrax obassia*
Franklinia *Franklinia alatamaha*
Genista *Genista* species
Golden-rain tree *Koelreuteria paniculata*
Hawthorn *Crataegus* (most species)
Hazel *Corylus* species
Heath *Erica* species
Holly *Ilex* species
Japanese maple *Acer japonicum, A. palmatum*
Japanese snowbell *Styrax japonica*
Japanese willowleaf magnolia *Magnolia salicifolia*
Judas tree *Cercis siliquastrum*
Katsura tree *Cercidiphyllum japonicum*
Laburnum *Laburnum* species
Medlar *Mespilus germanica*
Ohio buckeye *Aesculus glabra*
Paperbark maple *Acer griseum*
Photinia *Photinia* species
Quince *Cydonia oblonga*
Rhododendron *Rhododendron* species
Russian olive *Elaeagnus angustifolia*
Sea buckthorn *Hippophae rhamnoides*
Silk oak *Grevillea* species
Snowy mespilus *Amelanchier* species
Sorbus *Sorbus* (most species)
Sourwood *Oxydendrum arboreum*
Stewartia *Stewartia* species
Willow *Salix* (some species)
Willow-leaf pear *Pyrus salicifolia* 'Pendula'
Witch hazel *Hamamelis* species

Dwarf conifers
Eastern hemlock *Tsuga canadensis*
Lace-bark pine *Pinus bungeana*

Street trees–big
Buttonwood *Platanus occidentalis*
Castor-aralia *Kalopanax pictus*
False acacia *Robinia pseudoacacia*
Green ash *Fraxinus pensylvanica lanceolata*
Honey locust *Gleditsia triacanthos*
London plane *Platanus × hispanica*
Norway maple *Acer platanoides*
Pin oak *Quercus palustris*
Red maple *Acer rubrum*
Red oak *Quercus rubra*
Scarlet oak *Quercus coccinea*
Velvet ash *Fraxinus velutina*
Willow oak *Quercus phellos*

Maidenhair tree *Ginkgo biloba*
Pine *Pinus* (many species)

For narrower streets
Any upright tree (see tables above)
'Capillipes' maple *Acer capillipes*
Cherry *Prunus* (most species)
Chinaberry *Melia azedarach*
Chinese toon *Cedrela sinensis*
Euodia *Euodia daniellii*
European hornbeam *Carpinus betulus* 'Columnaris'
Flowering ash *Fraxinus ornus*
Flowering dogwood *Cornus florida*
Hawthorn *Crataegus* species
Hedge maple *Acer campestre*
Japanese dogwood *Cornus kousa*
Japanese hornbeam *Carpinus japonica*

Lebanon oak *Quercus libani*
Montpelier maple *Acer monspessulanum*
Paperbark maple *Acer griseum*
Tatarian maple *Acer tataricum*

Screening–(very) fast
Bat willow *Salix × caerulea*
Black cottonwood *Populus trichocarpa*
Crack willow *Salix fragilis*
Eucalypt *Eucalyptus* species
Lombardy poplar *Populus nigra* 'Italica'
'Robusta' poplar *Populus* 'Robusta'

Leyland cypress × *Cupressocyparis leylandii*
Monterey cypress *Cupressus macrocarpa*
Monterey pine *Pinus radiata*
Western hemlock *Tsuga heterophylla*

Tolerant of heavy shade
Beech *Fagus* (some species)
Camellia *Camellia japonica*
Cherry laurel *Prunus laurocerasus*
Common elder *Sambucus nigra*
Holly *Ilex* (some species)
Holm oak *Quercus ilex*
Portugal laurel *Prunus lusitanica*
Sycamore *Acer pseudoplatanus*
Cephalotaxus *Cephalotaxus* species
Coast redwood *Sequoia sempervirens*
English yew *Taxus baccata*
Juniper *Juniperus* (most species)
Western hemlock *Tsuga heterophylla*
Western red cedar *Thuja plicata*

Suitable for tubs
Box *Buxus sempervirens*
Camellia *Camellia* species
Citrus *Citrus* (most species)
Holly *Ilex* (some species)
Laurel *Laurus nobilis*

Chinese arborvitae *Thuja orientalis* 'Elegantissima'
English yew *Taxus baccata* 'Standishii'
False cypress *Chamaecyparis thyoides* 'Andelyensis'
Lawson cypress *Chamaecyparis lawsoniana* 'Ellwoodii'

Resent moving–except when very small
Birch *Betula* species
Black tupelo *Nyssa sylvatica*
Castor-aralia *Kalopanax pictus*
Hickory *Carya* species
Holly *Ilex* species
Kentucky coffee tree *Gymnocladus dioicus*
Magnolia *Magnolia* species
Scarlet oak *Quercus coccinea*
Strawberry tree *Arbutus* species
Sweetgum *Liquidambar styraciflua*
Tulip tree *Liriodendron tulipifera*
Walnut *Juglans* species
White oak *Quercus alba*

Cedar *Cedrus* species
Fir *Abies* species
Monterey cypress *Cupressus macrocarpa*
Pine *Pinus* species (except five-needled pines)
Spruce *Picea* species

FEW PESTS OR DISEASES
Alder *Alnus* species
Amur cork tree *Phellodendron amurense*
Castor-aralia *Kalopanax pictus*
Dove tree *Davidia* species
English holly *Ilex aquifolium*
Eucalypt *Eucalyptus* species
Glossy privet *Ligustrum lucidum*
Golden-rain tree *Koelreuteria paniculata*
Highclere holly *Ilex × altaclerensis*
Honey locust *Gleditsia triacanthos*
Hornbeam *Carpinus* species
Japanese pagoda tree *Sophora japonica*
Katsura tree *Cercidiphyllum* species
Kentucky coffee tree *Gymnocladus dioicus*
Laburnum *Laburnum* species
Magnolia *Magnolia* species
Persian parrotia *Parrotia persica*
Russian olive *Elaeagnus angustifolia*
Snowbell *Styrax* species
Sweetgum *Liquidambar styraciflua*
Tree of heaven *Ailanthus altissima*
White poplar *Populus alba*

Araucaria *Araucaria* species
Coast redwood *Sequoia sempervirens*
Dawn redwood *Metasequoia glyptostroboides*
False cypress *Chamaecyparis* (most species)
Incense cedar *Calocedrus decurrens*
Japanese umbrella pine *Sciadopitys verticillata*
Juniper *Juniperus* species
Maidenhair tree *Ginkgo biloba*
Podocarpus *Podocarpus* species
Swamp cypress *Taxodium* species
Yew *Taxus* species

The Meanings of Botanical Names

Medieval botanical works used descriptive phrases in Latin to identify plants. Carl Linnaeus (1707–1778) did the same, but to each plant (or animal) he also gave a shorter, two-word Latin name: its genus followed by its species. So thorough and indispensable were his books that this convenient two-name system gradually took over completely. Today it is in universal use by all who deal professionally with living organisms.

Every known plant now has a Latin name which identifies it in every country. The advantages of the system are obvious. Most people, however, naturally stick to vernacular names for the few plants they know. For that matter only a minority of plants have vernacular names to stick to. In the United States strenuous efforts are made to give every exotic introduction an English name – but such productions as the Chinese fragrant epaulette tree can hardly be called true vernacular names. And the trouble with the old ones is that they mean different things to different people in different places. Sooner or later one is faced with the need to use, or at least with the value of understanding, the botanical Latin name. The list below demonstrates that for many trees it is a useful description, for others an interesting indication of where it comes from, for others a well-deserved memorial to the explorer who found it. The accent marks the syllable (if any) which is normally stressed. In this list 'ii' is normally pronounced as a long 'i' and 'ae' as a long 'e'.

A

Ábies Old Latin name for fir. From *abire*, to rise, alluding to the great height of some species.
abramsiana In honour of LeRoy Abrams (1874–1956). Professor of Botany at Stamford University, U.S.A.
Acácia Greek name for an African species of *Acacia*; from *akis*, a sharp point.
Ácer Old Latin name for maple; also means sharp; the wood was used for spears.
'Aconitifólium' Has leaves like an aconite.
acumináta Slender-pointed.
acúta Sharply pointed.
acutifólia With sharply pointed leaves or leaflets.
acutíssima Very acutely pointed.
adámii In honour of M. Adam, a nurseryman near Paris, France.
'Adpréssa' Closely pressed together (usually of leaves against shoots).
Áesculus Latin name for a kind of oak, but applied by Linnaeus to the horse chestnut.
aetnénsis From Mt. Etna, Sicily.
agrifólia With rough leaves.
Ailánthus Latinized version of the native Moluccan name *ailanto*, sky tree.
alátamaha From the North American Indian name *Altamaha* for the river where it was first found.
álba White.
albertiána Native of Alberta, Canada.
albicáulis White-stemmed (*albus*=white, *caulis*=stem).
álbidum Whitish.
Albízia In honour of F. del Albizzi, a Florentine nobleman who in 1749 introduced this (the 'silk tree') into cultivation.
'Álbolimbátum' Edged with white.
álbosinénsis *Albus*=white, and *sinensis*= China.
Aleurítes From the Greek *aleuron*, floury; in some species the young growth has a flour-dusted appearance.
alexándrae In honour of Queen Alexandra (1844–1925), wife of Edward VII.
alnifólia With leaves like those of alder.
Álnus Old Latin name for the alder.
alpínum From alpine regions.
altaclerénsis Raised at Highclere, a mansion in Hampshire, England.
altíssima Very tall.
amábilis Pleasant, but often used in the sense of lovely.
ambígua Uncertain or doubtful.
Amelánchier From the French Provençal name *amelanchier* for *A. ovalis*.
americánus, -a From the Americas.

amurénsis, -e From the region of the Amur River in Manchuria.
amýgdalo-pérsica A combination of *Prunus amygdalus* (*dulcis*), the almond, and *Prunus persica*, the peach.
amygdalóides Resembling almond.
amýgdalus The Greek name for the almond.
anagyróides Resembling *Anagyris*.
'Andelyénsis' From les Andelys, near Paris.
andínus From the Andes of South America.
andráchne Ancient Greek name.
andrachnóides Resembling *Arbutus andrachne* (ancient Greek name for the strawberry tree, used by Linnaeus).
angustifólia Narrow-leaved.
'Annuláris' Ring-shaped.
antárctica Literally from the South Polar region, but used in biology for plants and animals native to south of 45°S.
apiculáta Leaves abruptly tipped with a short point.
aquática Growing in or near water.
aquifólium Latin vernacular name for holly, meaning having leaves with points.
Arália From the Latinization of the French Canadian name *Aralie*.
araucána From the Araucani Indians of central Chile, in whose territory the first discovered species is native.
Araucária *See above.*
arbórea, -éscens, -um Tree-like.
Arbútus Latin name for strawberry tree.
Archonthophoénix From the Greek *archon*, a chieftain, and *phoenix*, the date palm; refers to the stately appearance of these palms.
Arecástrum '-astrum' indicates a resemblance to *Areca*, the Indian betelnut palm.
argéntea, -um Silvery.
'Argénteomargináta' With silver edges.
ária Old Latin name for whitebeam.
aristáta From the Latin *aristatus*, bearded; so, bear ed with awns like ears of barley.
arizónica From the state of Arizona, U.S.A.
armándii The Christian name of l'Abbé Armand David, the French missionary and naturalist who worked in China.
armeníaca From Armenia, on the Black Sea.
articuláta Articulated or jointed.
ascéndens From the Latin *ascendens*, rising upwards.
Asímina The Latinized version of the French form of the Indian vernacular *assimin*.
aspérata From the Greek *asperatus*, roughened.
'Aspleniifólia' With leaves like the spleenwort, i.e. fine, feathery, and fernlike.
Athrotáxis From the Greek *athroos*, crowded together, and *taxis*, arrangement; in reference to the crowded nature of the cone scales.
atlántica From the Atlas Mountains of North Africa (also from the shores of the Atlantic).

'Atropurpúrea', -um Dark purple.
attenuáta Narrowing to a point.
aucupária Old Latin name for rowan tree; from *aucupor*, bird catching, it being used as bait and as an ingredient of bird lime by bird catchers.
'Aúrea', -um, -us From *aurum*, the Latin for gold; literally, golden.
'Aúrea Nána' Golden-yellow, dwarf.
Aúreomarginátum With golden edges.
'Aúreospíca' With golden spikes.
'Aúreovariegáta' Gold-variegated.
'Auróra' A fanciful resemblance to the electrical phenomenon of the same name.
austrális Southern, in the sense of southern hemisphere or sometimes of southern Europe.
Aústrocédrus Literally, southern cedar.
'Autumnális' Flowering in the autumn.
avellána From Avella Vecchia in southern Italy.
ávium Of the birds (eaten by).
áyacahuíte The Mexican name for *Pinus ayacahuite*.
azédarach A contracted version of the Persian (Iranian) name *azaddhirakt* for *Melia azedarach*.
azórica From the Azores Islands.

B

babylónica From Babylon.
baccáta From the Latin *baccatus*, berry-like.
'Bacciflávа' Yellow-berried.
baileyána In honour of Frederick Manson Bailey (1827–1915), an Australian botanist.
bákeri In honour of John Gilbert Baker (1834–1920), the British botanist who was Keeper of Kew Herbarium from 1890–99.
balsaméa Balsam-like.
balsamifera Balsam-bearing.
banksiána In honour of Sir Joseph Banks (1743–1820), British naturalist who accompanied Captain Cook's round-the-world expedition of 1768–71 in the *Endeavour*.
barbátum Bearded.
battandiéri In honour of Jules Aimé Battandier (1848–1922), a French botanist and an authority on the flora of Algeria.
'Baumannii' In honour of E. N. Baumann of Bolivia.
'Bélgica' From Belgium or the Netherlands.
Bétula The old Latin name for the birch tree.
betulóides Resembling the birch tree, *Betula*.
bétulus Resembling the birch tree, *Betula*.
bícolor Two colours.
bídwillii In honour of J. C. Bidwill (1815–53). Director of the Botanic Garden, Sydney, who collected plants in New Zealand and Australia.
'Biflóra' Two-flowered.
bignonióides Resembling the trumpet creeper. *Bignonia*.
bilóba Two-lobed.
blánda Mild.
boária The Chilean vernacular name meaning loved by cattle (referring to the leaves of *Maytenus boaria*).
boreális Northern.
bracteáta Having conspicuous bracts.
brevifólia With short leaves.
brewerána In honour of William Henry Brewer (1828–1910), American pioneer botanist in California and professor of agriculture at Yale University.
'Brilliantíssimum' The most brilliant.
'Briótii' In honour of Pierre Louis Briot (1804–88), a French horticulturist.
Broussonétia In honour of Pierre Marie Auguste Broussonet (1761–1807), professor of botany at Montpellier, France.
brunónii In honour of the botanist Robert Bruon, F.R.S. (1773–1858).
buergeránum In honour of Heinrich Bürger (1804[6?]–58), German plant collector.
bungeána In honour of Alexander von Bunge (1803–90), a Russian botanist and professor of botany at Dorpat in Estonia.
Búxus The classical Latin name for the box tree.

C

caerúlea Dark blue.
cáesia Lavender blue.
califórnica From California, U.S.A.
calleryána In honour of J. M. Callery (1810–62), a Roman Catholic missionary and botanist in China and Korea.
Callitris From the Greek *kali*, beautiful, and *tris* indicating the arrangement in three of leaves, cone-scabs, etc.
Calocédrus From the Greek *kalos*, beautiful, and the Latin *cedrus*, cedar.
calophýtum From the Greek *kalos*, beautiful, and *phytum*, a plant.
camaldulénsis Named after Camaldule in Australia.
Caméllia In honour of Georg Joseph Kamel (1661–1706), a Jesuit pharmacist and botanist from Moravia who studied the plants of the Philippines and wrote an account of them.
'Camelliifólia' With leaves like a camellia.
campanuláta Bell-shaped.
campbéllii In honour of Dr. Archibald Campbell, Superintendent of Darjeeling and companion of Sir Joseph Hooker on his journey through the Sikkim Himalaya in 1849.

'Camperdównii' Castle in Angus, Scotland, where the elm *Ulmus glabra* 'Camperdownii' arose.
campéstre Of the fields.
cámphora Like camphor.
canadénsis From Canada.
'Canáertii' In honour of the late 19th-century Belgian nurseryman.
canariénsis From the Canary Islands.
cándicans Shining.
canéscens Off-white or ash-grey.
cápillípes With slender feet.
Capitáta With a dense knob-like head, meaning flowers, fruits, or whole plant.
cappadócicum From Cappadocia, an ancient province of Asia Minor.
cáprea Favoured by goats.
caramánica From Caramania (Karamania) in southern Asia Minor.
caribáea From the Caribbean area.
caríca From Caria, a district in Asia Minor.
cárnea Flesh or deep pink.
carolína, caroliniána From North or South Carolina, U.S.A.
carpinifólia, -um With leaves like those of *Carpinus* (hornbeam).
Carpínus The classical Latin name for the hornbeam.
Cárya From the Greek *karya*, walnut tree. Its fruit was known as *karyon*, which was also applied to other nuts.
cashmiriána From Kashmir.
cássine The North American Indian name for dahoon holly.
Castánea The Latin name for the sweet chestnut, from Kasanaia, a city in Asia Minor.
castaneifólia With leaves like those of *Castanea* (sweet chestnut).
Castanópsis Related to *Castanea*, the chestnut.
Casuarína The branches have been said to resemble cassowary (*Casuarinus*) feathers.
Catálpa The North American Indian name for *Catalpa bignonioides*, the first species in this genus to be cultivated in Europe.
Cedréla Diminutive of the Latin *cedrus*; from a similarity in the wood and its fragrance.
Cédrus The Latin name for the cedar, though originally the Latin *cedrus* and Greek *kedros* may have applied to species of juniper.
Céltis The Greek name of an unrelated tree, taken up for the hackberry by Linnaeus.
Cémbra The Italian name for the Swiss Arolla or stone pine.
cembróides Resembling *Pinus cembra*, the Swiss Arolla pine.
cephalónica From the island of Cephalonia in the Ionian Sea.
Cephalotáxus From the Greek *kephale*, a head, and *taxus*, the yew tree; referring to the relationship to the yew, and resemblance of some species.
cerasifera Cherry-like, referring to the fruits.
cérasus The Latin name for cherry.
Ceratónia The Greek name *keratonia* for the carob.
Cercidiphýllum With leaves like those of the Judas tree, *Cercis*.
Cércis From the Greek name *kerkis* used for the Judas tree.
cerífera Wax-bearing.
cérris A kind of oak, from the old Latin name.
Chámaecýparis From the Greek *chamai*, dwarf, and *kuparissos*, cypress. This now inapt name seems to have been derived from the dwarf juvenile forms formerly known as retinospora.
Chámaerops From the Greek *chamai*, dwarf, and *rhops*, a bush.
'Charles Raffill' In honour of C. P. Raffill (1876–1951), curator of Kew Gardens.
'Chermesína' *Salix alba* 'Chermesina' was named after the Chermes (*Adelges*) insect because of the similar reddish colour of the young shoots.
chilénsis From Chile.
chinénsis From China.
Chionánthus Having snow-white flowers; from the Greek *chión*, snow, and *anthos*, a flower.
chrysocóma With golden hairs.
chrysolépis With golden scales.
chrysophýlla Having golden leaves.
cinérea Ash-coloured.
Cinnamómum From the classical Greek name for cinnamon.
circinátum Rolled in a circular fashion.
citriodóra Citrus (lemon) scented.
Citrus The Latin name for the citron (*Citrus medica*).
Cladrástis From the Greek *klados*, branch, and *thraustos*, fragile; alluding to the brittle twigs.
Cléthra From the Greek *kléthra*, the white alder tree, which has similar leaves.
cliffortioídes Like *Cliffortia*, a South African shrub of the rose family.
coccífera Bearing red berries.
coccínea, -um Scarlet.
Cócos From the Portuguese for monkey (*Cocos*), referring to the nut which suggests a monkey's face.
coeruléa Blue.

coggýgria An inaccurate rendering of the Greek *kokkugia*, the vernacular name for the smoke tree (*Cotinus*).

'Colorata' Coloured.

'Columnáris', -e In the shape of a column.

colúrna Old Latin name for hazel nut or wood.

'Cómmelin' In honour of the Dutch botanists Johan (1629–92) and Caspar (1667–1731) Commelin.

commíxta Mixed together.

commúnis Growing in company, or common.

commutáta Changed or changing.

'Compréssa' Compressed or flattened.

concolór The same colour throughout.

conférta Crowded.

'Cónica' Cone-shaped.

conradinae In honour of Conradine, wife of the German botanist B. A. E. Koehne (1848–1918).

conspícua From the Latin *conspicuus*, conspicuous, distinctive, remarkable.

contórta From the Latin *contortus*, twisted or irregularly bent.

controvérsa Controversial, doubtful or questionable.

cordáta Heart-shaped.

cordifólia With heart-shaped leaves.

cordifórmis Heart-shaped.

Cordýline From the Greek *kordyle*, a club.

cornúbia Of Cornwall, England.

cornubiénsis Of Cornwall, England.

Córnus The old Latin name for the cornelian cherry, *Cornus mas*.

coronária Used for garlands.

Córylus The Greek name for the hazel bush, *Corylus avellana*.

Costáta Ribbed.

Cotínus From the Greek *kotinos*, a name for the wild olive and therefore of obscure meaning, though possibly used as a term for several bushes of no economic value.

Cotoneáster From the Latin *cotoneum*, a quince, and *aster*, superficial or incomplete resemblance; used to denote a wild or inferior species. Some species of *Cotoneaster* have leaves like those of quince.

cóulteri In honour of Thomas Coulter (1793–1843), an Irish botanist who travelled in the western States.

cóxii In honour of E. H. M. Cox, plant collector and author.

crataegifólium With leaves that resemble those of hawthorn, *Crataegus*.

Crataegoméspilus The combination of two generic names *Crataegus* and *Mespilus*, the fusion of their tissues forming this graft hybrid.

Crataégus The Greek name for hawthorn.

crenáta Cut in rounded scallops.

'Crippsii' In honour of the nurseryman Cripps of Tunbridge Wells, Kent, England.

'Críspa' Closely curled.

'Cristáta' Crested.

crus-gálli Cock's spur.

Cryptoméria From the Greek *krypto*, to hide, and *meris*, a part; all parts of the flowers (strobili) are concealed.

Cunninghámia In honour of James Cunningham, East India Company surgeon and plant collector.

Cunninghámia In honour of James Cunningham (see *Cunninghamia*).

'Cupréa' Copper-coloured.

cupressínum Resembling *Cupressus* or cypress.

Cupréssocýparis Compounded from *Cupressus* and *Chamaecyparis*, the parents of this bigeneric hybrid.

cúpressoides Resembling *Cupressus* or cypress.

Cupréssus The Latin name for *Cupressus sempervirens*, the Italian cypress tree.

cuspidáta From the Latin *cuspidatus*, bearing a stiff point.

Cyáthea From the Greek *kyatheion*, a little cup; the membrane covering the spore-cases on the underside of the leaves breaks at the top at maturity, forming a cup.

Cydónia The Latin name for this fruit tree, derived from Cydon, a town in Crete.

Cýtisus Broom, from the Greek *kytisos*, a name used for several shrubby members of the pea family (*Leguminosae*).

D

dacrydióides Resembling *Dacrydium*.

Dacrýdium From the Greek *dakrydion*, a small tear; some of these trees exude small drops of clear resin.

dactylífera Fingerlike.

Dáctylis From the Greek *daktylos*, a finger; the inflorescence appears fingerlike.

'Dalecárlica' From the Swedish province of Dalecarlia or Dalarna.

daniéllii After the surgeon-collector who toured Tientsin in 1860–62.

daphnóides Resembling *Daphne*, from the Greek name for the laurel.

dardárii In honour of M. Dardar of Bronvaux, Metz, in whose garden the graft hybrid *Crataegomespilus dardarii* arose.

Davídia In honour of l'Abbé Armand David (1826–1900), a French missionary and naturalist who worked and collected in China.

davídii In honour of l'Abbé Armand David (see *Davidia*).

'Dáwyck' From the famous Scottish garden on the banks of the River Tweed.

dealbáta Whitened, as with a powder.

'Decaisneána' In honour of Joseph Decaisne (1807–82), a director of the Jardin des Plantes, Paris, and a famous botanist and horticulturist.

decídua Deciduous (leafless in winter).

decóra, -um Decorative.

decúrrens Running down; used when leaf bases are extended down the stem in winglike tapering ridges.

delaváyi In honour of l'Abbé Jean Marie Delavay (1834–95), a missionary who collected plants in western China.

Délonix From the Greek *delos*, evident, and *onux*, a claw; referring to the long clawed (stalked) petals.

deltóides Triangular, like the Greek letter delta.

densiflóra, -us Densely flowered.

dentáta Toothed.

denudáta Bare or naked.

deodára From the native Indian name for the deodar cedar.

deppeáná pachyphláea Thick rinded.

diabólicum Devilish, applied to a plant with horned fruit.

Dicksónia In honour of James Dickson (1738–1822), a British nurseryman and botanist.

dicksónii In honour of James Dickson (see *Dicksonia*).

dioícus Dioecious; the separate-sexed flowers are borne on individual trees.

Diospýros From *dios*, divine, and *pyros*, wheat, a Greek name transferred to the persimmon, *Diospyros kaki*.

Disánthus Paired flowers; from *dis*, twice, and *anthos*, flower.

discólor Of two colours.

'Disséctum' Deeply cut, divided into segments.

distíchum From the Latin *distichus*, in two parallel ranks.

diversifólia From the Latin *diversus*, diverse, and *folium*, leaf, with diverse leaves.

dolabráta Hatchet-shaped.

dombeyi In honour of Joseph Dombey (1742–94), a French botanist.

doméstica Domesticated; much used in gardens.

'Donard Gold' From the Slieve Donard Nursery Co. Ltd., Ireland.

'Dovastónii', -iana *Cephalotaxus x media* 'Dovastonii' was 'found' by Mr John Dovaston of Westfelton, Shrewsbury, England.

'Drummóndii' In honour of Thomas Drummond (d 1835), nurseryman.

drupácea Bearing a fleshy fruit with a single seed within, like a cherry, an olive or a plum.

dúlcis Sweet.

E

ébenum Ebony-black.

echináta Prickly.

édulis Edible.

Ehrétia In honour of Georg Dionysius Ehret (1708–70), a German botanical artist.

Elaeágnus Said to be derived from the Greek *elaia*, the olive tree, and *agnos*, a name for the chaste-tree (*Vitex*), but more likely from *heleagnos—helodes*, marshy, and *hagnos*, pure (or white), in allusion to the white fruits.

eláta Tall.

'Elegáns' Elegant.

elegantíssima Italian word for 'very elegant'.

'Ellwóodii' In honour of Mr. Ellwood, who discovered *Chamaecyparis pisifera* 'Ellwoodii' c. 1920 as a chance seedling at Swanmore Park, Bishop's Waltham, England, where he was gardener.

Embóthrium From the Greek *en*, in, and *bothrion*, a little pit; the stamens are borne in recesses or pits in the petals.

engelmánnii In honour of Georg Engelmann (1809–84), a German-born American doctor, greatly interested in plants. He did some collecting, but did more by encouraging others.

'Erécta', -um Erect or upright.

'Erecta Viridis' Erect or upright, and green.

Érica From the Latin *erice*, heath.

'Ericóides' Resembling *Erica*.

ermánii In honour of G. A. Erman (1806–77) of Berlin, who collected in eastern Asia and elsewhere.

erubéscens Reddening.

'Erythrocládum' Red-branched; from the Greek *erythro-*, red, and *klados*, branch.

érythrofléxuosa Red, bent alternately, zigzag.

Eucalýptus From the Greek *eu*, well, and *kalypto*, to cover (as with a lid); alluding to the petals and sepals which are fused together to form a cap, shed when the flower opens.

euchlóra From the Greek *eu*, good, and *chloros*, green.

Eucómmia From the Greek *eu*, good, and *kommi*, gum; the name for the only hardy rubber-producing tree.

Eucrýphia From the Greek *eu*, well, and *kryphios*, covered; referring to the sepals which are joined at the tips to form a protective cap to the bud.

'Eugénei' In honour of the Prince Eugene of Savoy (1663–1736), said to have been a patron of botany.

Euódia From the Greek word meaning a sweet scent; the leaves are fragrant when bruised.

europáea From Europe.

excélsa Tall or high.

excélsior Taller.

F

Fágus The Latin name for the beech tree (*F. sylvatica*).

falcáta The Latin word for sickle-shaped.

falconéri In honour of Hugh Falconer (1808–65), a Scottish doctor, geologist and botanist in India (1830–55).

fargésii In honour of Paul Guillaume Farges (1844–1912), a French missionary and naturalist who worked in central China.

'Fastigiáta', -um Having erect growth and a columnar habit, from the Latin for a gable (which it does not resemble).

'Férox' Ferocious, very thorny.

'Fémina' A female.

ficifólia With leaves like those of a fig (but not the edible fig, *Ficus carica*).

fictolácteum From the Latin *fictus*, false, and *Rhododendron lacteum*, a species with which *Rhododendron fictolacteum* was at one time confused.

Fícus The Latin name for the fig.

'Filicifólia' Fern-leaved.

'Filicóides' Resembling fern, Latin *filix*, a fern.

filífera Thread-bearing.

'Filifórmis' Thread-like.

filípes With thread-like stalks.

Fitzróya In honour of Vice-Admiral Robert Fitzroy (1805–65), who commanded the five-year surveying expedition in H.M.S. *Beagle*. (Charles Darwin was the naturalist aboard.)

fláva Yellow.

'Flétcheri' Named after Fletcher's Nursery, Kent. Fletcher first distributed the branch mutant *Chamaecyparis lawsoniana* 'Fletcheri', which originally arose in 1913 in the Ottershaw Nursery, Chertsey, Surrey, England.

floribúnda Profusely flowering.

flórida Flowery.

fórdii In honour of Charles Ford (1844–1927), Superintendent of the Hong Kong Botanical Garden.

formosána From the island of Formosa (Taiwan).

forréstii In honour of George Forrest (1873–1932), from Scotland, who collected large numbers of seeds and specimens in western China.

fortúnei In honour of Robert Fortune (1812–80), Scottish horticulturist who collected plants in China and Japan (and introduced tea to India).

Fortunélla The Kumquat, an evergreen shrub, named after Robert Fortune (see *fortunei*).

frágilis Brittle or fragile and easily broken.

fraínetto The native name of the Hungarian oak.

Franklínia In honour of Benjamin Franklin (1706–90), American scholar and statesman.

franklínii In honour of Sir John Franklin (1786–1847), naval captain and arctic explorer (discovered the North West Passage), also governor of Tasmania 1836–43.

fráseri In honour of John Fraser (1750–1811).

fraxinifólia With leaves like *Fraxinus* (ash).

Fráxinus The old Latin name for the ash tree (*Fraxinus excelsior*).

frígidus Coming from cold regions.

'Frísia' From Friesland, W. Germany and E. Netherlands.

'Frúctu-lutéo' Yellow-fruited.

fúlvum Tawny-orange.

funébris Funereal, grown in graveyards.

fúsca Dusky brown.

G

garryána In honour of Nicholas Garry, Secretary of the Hudson's Bay Company, who between 1820–30 helped David Douglas in western North America.

'Generósa' Of noble appearance.

Genísta The Latin name for dyer's greenweed, but said to have come from the Celtic *gen*, a bush.

germánica From Germany.

gigánteum From the Latin *giganteus*, gigantic.

Gínkgo A misrendering of the ancient (and now obsolete) Japanese name *gin-kyo* (silver apricot).

gínnala The native vernacular name for this Asiatic maple.

giráldii In honour of Giuseppe Giraldi, an Italian missionary in China, who from 1890–95 collected plants in Shensi Province.

glábra, -áta Smooth, without hairs.

gláuca Blue-grey or blue-white.

Gledítsia In honour of Johann Gottlieb Gleditsch (1714–86), Director of the Berlin Botanic Garden.

'Globósa', -um Round, or spherical.

glóbulus Rounded or globular.

glutinósa Gluey or sticky (the buds and young leaves).

glyptostrobóides Resembling *Glyptostrobus*.

Glyptostróbus From the Greek *glypto*, to carve, and *strobilos*, a cone; referring to the depressions on the cone scales of *Glyptostrobus*, the deciduous Chinese cypress.

gmelínii In honour of Gottlieb Gmelin (1709–55), a German naturalist who travelled extensively in Siberia and Kamchatka.

'Goldsworth Purple' From the Goldsworth Old Nursery, Surrey.

Gordónia Named in honour of James Gordon (d. 1781), a correspondent of Linnaeus and a nurseryman of Mile End, London.

goveniána In honour of J. R. Gowen, of Highclere, Secretary of the Royal Horticultural Society 1845–50.

gracilistýla With a slender style.

grandidentáta With large teeth.

grandiflóra Large-flowered.

grandifólia Big-leaved.

grándis, -e Big or showy.

Grevíllea In honour of Charles Francis Greville (1749–1809), a founder of the Horticultural Society of London and a Vice-President of the Royal Society.

griffithiána, -um In honour of William Griffith (1810–45), a British doctor and botanist who collected plants in India and Afghanistan.

griffíthii In honour of William Griffith (see *griffithiana*).

grignonénsis Town in France where *Crataegus grignonensis* was first discovered.

griséum Grey.

grósseri *Acer grosseri* was discovered by Giraldi (see *giraldii*) in Shensa, China, and brought to England in 1927. Probably from *grossus*, very big.

gúnnii In honour of R. C. Gunn (1808–81) of Tasmania.

Gymnocládus From the Greek *gymnos*, naked, and *klados*, a branch; the tree is leafless in winter.

H

Hákea In honour of Baron Christian von Hake (1745–1818), German patron of botany.

halapénsis From Aleppo (Halep) in Syria.

Halésia In honour of the Rev. Stephen Hales (1677–1761), curate of Teddington, England, and a physiologist, chemist and inventor.

halliána In honour of George Rogers Hall (1820–99), an American doctor who introduced many plants from Japan to the U.S.A.

Hamamélis A Greek name, possibly for the medlar.

harrowiána In honour of George Harrow, manager of Veitch's Coombe Wood Nursery where many of E. H. Wilson's Chinese plants were raised from seeds.

'Hastáta' Spear-shaped.

Hébe Evergreen shrubs from South America and Australasia, named after the Greek goddess of youth.

hénryae In honour of the wife of Augustine Henry (see *henryi*).

hénryi, -ana In honour of Augustine Henry (1857–1930), Irish doctor and plant collector who travelled in China and Formosa (Taiwan), later professor of forestry.

'Heptalóbum' Seven-lobed.

hérsii In honour of Joseph Hers, who, whilst in China, sent back plants to the Arnold Arboretum during the 1920s.

heterophýlla From the Greek *heter* or *hetero*, various or diverse, and *phyllum*, leaf.

'Hibérnica' From Ireland.

highdownénsis After Sir Frederick Stern's garden at Highdown Towers, Sussex.

híllieri After the tree and shrub specialist nurserymen, Hillier & Sons, Winchester, Hampshire.

hippocastánum The Latin name for the horse chestnut; there are horseshoe-shaped leaf scars on the twigs.

Híppophae An old Greek name for a spiny spurge, later transferred to this shrub.

hispánica From Spain.

híspida Bristly.

Hohéria Latinized version of the New Zealand Maori name for these evergreen trees and shrubs, *houhere*.

hollándica From the Netherlands (Holland).

holophýlla From the Greek *holo*, entire, and *phyllum*, leaf.

homolépis From the Greek *homo*, same, one kind of, and *lepis*, scale.

horizontális Horizontal.

'Hudsónia' In honour of William Hudson (1730–93), a London apothecary.

húmilis Low-growing, or relatively so.

hupehénsis From Hupeh, China.

hýbrida Of hybrid origin, or appearing so. ▶

The Meanings of Botanical Names

I

Idésia In honour of Eberhard (or Evert) Ides (d. c. 1720), a Dutch (or German) explorer of northern Asia.

I'lex From the Latin name for the evergreen holm oak, the more toothed-leaved forms of which it resembles.

illinoénsis From the state of Illinois, U.S.A.

imbricária Overlapping in regular order, like the tiles on a roof.

'Imperiális' Imperial or showy.

incána Hoary or grey.

'Incísa' Deeply cut.

índica From India.

'Inérmis' Unarmed, i.e. having no prickles.

insígnis Remarkable.

intermedia Intermediate.

'Intertexta' Intertwined.

involucráta Surrounded or enclosed by an involucro (loaf, scale or petal-like bracts).

ioénsis From the state of Iowa, U.S.A.

irrorátum From the Latin *irroro*, to wet with dew or to besprinkle.

'Itálica' From Italy.

J

Jacaránda The Latinized form of the Brazilian name for these flowering trees.

jacquemóntii In honour of Victor Jacquemont (1801–32), a French naturalist who visited Asia.

japónica, -um From Japan.

'Jaspidea' Like jasper.

jeffréyi In honour of J. Jeffrey, a Scottish gardener who collected in Oregon, U.S.A., between 1850 and 1853.

jessoénsis, jezoénsis From Jezo, Japan.

'John Downie' In honour of the Scottish nurseryman and florist.

Jubaéa Named for King Juba of Numidia who killed himself when his kingdom was taken over by the Romans in 46 B.C.

Júglans The Latin name, from *jovis*, of Jupiter, and *glans*, acorn.

julibríssin The Persian (Iranian) name for the silk tree.

Juníperus Old Latin name for juniper tree.

K

kaémpferi In honour of Engelbert Kaempfer (1651–1716), a German physician who travelled widely in the East and lived for two years in Japan.

káki An abbreviation of the Japanese name *kaki-no-ki* for this fruit.

Kalópanax From the Greek *kalos*, beautiful, and *Panax*, a related genus.

kellóggii In honour of Albert Kellogg (1813–87), American doctor and botanist.

'Kiftsgate' After the garden at Kiftsgate Court, Gloucestershire.

'Kilmacúrragh' From the Irish garden of this name.

kóbus Latinization of the Japanese name *kobushi*.

Koelreutéria In honour of Joseph Gottlieb Koelreuter (1733–1806), natural history professor and pioneer in plant hybridization.

koraiénsis, koreána From Korea.

koúsa The Japanese name for this *Cornus*.

L

Laburnocýtisus A combination of *Laburnum* and *Cytisus*, parents of this unique graft hybrid.

Labúrnum Old Roman name for laburnum trees.

laciniáta, -um Deeply cut or slashed.

laéta Bright or vivid or pleasing.

laevigáta Smooth.

laévis Smooth or hairless.

lamárckii In honour of Jean Baptiste Antoine Pierre Monet, Chevalier de la Marck (1744–1829), a distinguished French biologist whose work on evolution foreshadowed that of Darwin.

lambertiána In honour of Aylmer Bourke Lambert (1761–1842), English botanist and author of *The Genus Pinus*.

lanáta Woolly.

lanceoláta, -um Lance-shaped.

'Lanei' Named after Lane's Nursery, Berkhamsted, Hertfordshire.

lantána The Latin name for *Viburnum*.

laricína Resembling (common or European) larch.

Lárix The old Latin name for the common larch, *L. decidua*.

lasiánthus With woolly anthers.

lasiocárpa Woolly fruited.

latifólius, -a Broad-leaved; from the Latin *latus*, broad, and *folium*, leaf.

Laurélia From the Spanish name for *Laurus*, the laurel or bay, referring to fragrant leaves.

laurifólia With leaves like those of *Laurus nobilis* (bay laurel).

laurína Resembling *Laurus*.

laurocerásus A combination of the Latin for laurel and cherry, hence 'cherry laurel'.

Laúrus Latin name for the bay laurel.

lavállei In honour of M. Lavalle, a French nurseryman, c. 1870.

lawsoniána In honour of Charles Lawson (1794–1873), nurseryman and author of *Pinetum Britannicum*, whose Edinburgh nursery received the first *Chamaecyparis lawsoniana* seeds from Oregon in 1854.

laxifólia Loose or open; from the Latin *laxus*, loose, and *folium*, leaf.

'Lemóinei' In honour of Victor Lemoine (1823–1911) and his son Emile (1862–1942), French nurserymen and plant breeders who introduced many new garden plants.

'Lénnei' In honour of M. Lanné, Director of Royal Gardens of Prussia.

lénta Tough but flexible.

leucodérmis White-skinned; from the Greek *leukos*, white, and *dermis*, skin.

leucoxyla, -on White-wooded.

leylándii In honour of C. J. Leyland, of Haggerston Hall, Northumberland (see page 101).

libáni From Mount Lebanon.

Libocédrus From the Greek *libos*, a tear, and *cedrus*, cedar; referring to drops of resin exuded by the incense cedar.

Ligústrum The Latin name for privet.

likiangénsis From the Lichiang range, Yunnan, western China.

liliiflóra Lily-flowered.

'Linearilobum' From the Latin *linear* and *lobum*, lobed.

lineáris Narrow, with nearly parallel sides.

Líquidámbar From the Latin *liquidus*, fluid or liquid, and the Arabic *ambar*, amber, alluding to the fragrant gum which exudes from this tree.

Liriodéndron Derived from the Greek *leirion*, a lily, and *dendron*, a tree.

Lithocárpus From the Greek *lithos*, stone, and *karpos*, fruit; a reference to the hard nuts (acorns).

Litséa Latinization of an old Japanese name.

Livistóna In honour of Baron of Livinstone, founder of Botanic Garden, Edinburgh.

'Lóbbii' In honour of Thomas Lobb (d. 1894) who collected plants for the nursery firm of James Veitch (from 1843 to 1860) in Java, India, Malaya, Borneo and Singapore.

lóebneri After Max Loebner, Prussian nurseryman.

longáeva Of great age.

longifólia With long leaves.

lowiána In honour of Henry Stuart Lowe (1926–90), a nurseryman of Clapton, London.

lúcidum Shining.

'Lucombeána' Originating in the nursery of Lucombe & Pince, Exeter, Devon.

lusitánica From Lusitania—better known as Portugal.

lútea Yellow.

'Lutéscens' Yellowish.

lyállii In honour of Dr. David Lyall (1817–95), botanist on H.M.S. *Terror* and other ships, and who collected plants in New Zealand.

lycopodióides Resembling *Lycopodium* (ground pine).

lyráta Lyre-shaped.

M

Máackia In honour of Richard Maack (1825–86), a Russian naturalist who explored the Ussuri River region in eastern Asia.

máackii (*as above*).

Maclúra In honour of William Maclure (1763–1840), an American geologist.

macranthéra Having large anthers.

macrocárpa With large fruits.

macrophýllus, -a, -um Large-leaved.

magnífica Splendid, magnificent or great.

Magnólia In honour of Pierre Magnol (1638–1751), professor of botany and director of the Montpellier Botanic Garden, France.

'Majestica' Majestic.

május Bigger or larger.

Málus The Latin name for the apple.

mandshúrica From Manchuria.

margaríta Pearl-like.

mariána Of Maryland, U.S.A.

mariésii In honour of Charles Maries (d. 1902), a plant collector who worked for the nursery firm of Veitch in China and Japan.

'Marilándica' From Maryland, U.S.A.

marítima From the Latin *maritimus*, maritime, by or near the sea.

más Male or masculine, formerly used to distinguish delicate species from robust ones.

matsudána In honour of Sadahisa Matsúdo (1857–1921), a Japanese botanist who wrote a flora of China.

máxima, -um Largest.

maximowícziána, -ii In honour of Carl Ivanovitch Maximowicz (1827–91), a Russian botanist who specialized in the plants of eastern Asia.

Máytenus From the Chilean name *maitèn* for *M. boaria*.

média Intermediate between two types.

medulláris Pithy.

Mélia The Greek name for an ash tree, in allusion to the similarity of the leaves.

menziésii In honour of Archibald Menzies (1754–1842), a Scottish naval doctor who sailed with Vancouver on his 1790–95 expedition to the northwest Pacific.

mertensiána In honour of Franz Carl Mertens (1764–1831), professor of botany at Bremen, Germany.

Méspilus The Latin name for medlar, the fruit.

Metasequóia From the Greek *meta*, meaning 'with', 'after', 'sharing' or 'changed in nature'; alluding to its ancient relationship with *Sequoia*.

'Meyen' In honour of Franz Julius Meyen (1804–40), German physician and plant collector.

'Meyeri' In honour of Frank N. Meyer (d. 1918), a Dutch-American plant collector.

micháuxii In honour of André Michaux (1746–1803), French explorer and plant collector who visited North America, Persia and Madagascar.

microphýlla With small leaves.

mimosifólia With leaves resembling those of *Mimosa*.

miniáta Vermilion-coloured.

'Minima' Smallest.

mitchellii In honour of Dr. John Mitchell (1711–68), American physician.

'Moorheim', -ii Named after a Dutch nursery firm.

mólle As *Rhus molle*, the Peruvian vernacular name for this tree. (*Molle* in Latin means soft, usually in the sense of hairy.)

móllicomáta With soft hairs.

móllis Softly hairy.

mollíssima Very soft, or velvety hairy.

monógyna Having one pistil.

monophýlla One leaved.

monospérma Having one seed.

monspessulánum From Montpellier in France.

montezúmae To honour Montezuma, emperor of Mexico in the 16th century.

montícola Growing on mountains.

Mórus The Latin name for mulberry.

moupinénsis From Mupin, western China (now Pooksing).

múcronátum Mucronate, ending with a spiny tip.

múgo Or *mugho*, the old Tyrolese name for *Pinus mugo*.

muhlenbérgii In honour of Gotthilf Henry Ernest Muhlenberg (1753–1815), Lutheran minister in Pennsylvania, U.S.A., and a noted amateur botanist.

múme From the Japanese name *ume* for the species *Prunus mume*.

muricáta (The cone) roughened with hard points, like the seashell *Murex*.

Mýrtus The Latin name for myrtle (*Myrtus communis*), a plant sacred to Aphrodite and later associated with the Virgin Mary.

N

'Nána' From the Latin *nanus*, dwarf.

'Nána Grácilis' Dwarf (*see above*), and *gracilis*, slender; very dwarf and graceful.

negúndo From the Sanskrit and Bengali *nirgundi*, used for a tree with a similar leaf to *Acer negundo*.

'Nidiformis' Nest-shaped.

niedzwetzkyana In honour of the Russian judge Niedzwetzky.

nígra, -um Black.

nikoénse From the mountains near Nikko in Honshu, Japan.

niphophíla Snow-loving, from the Greek *niphas*, snow and *phileo*, to love.

nítida Shining.

nivális Snow-white, or growing near snow.

nóbilis Notable, renowned, famous, stately or noble.

nootkaténsis From the Nootka Sound, Vancouver Island, British Columbia.

nordmanniána In honour of Alexander von Nordmann, professor of zoology at Odessa and Helsinki.

Nothofágus From the Greek *nothos*, false, and *fagus*, beech.

nucífera Nut-bearing.

numídica From Algeria.

núttallii In honour of Thomas Nuttall (1786–1859), an English botanist who collected in North America during 1811–34.

nymansénsis From Nymans, a famous garden in Sussex.

Nýssa Named from Nysa or Nyssa, a water nymph.

O

obássia Said to be from the Japanese name for *Styrax obassia*, but not mentioned in the standard *Flora of Japan*, by Chwi.

oblíqua Oblique or unequal.

oblónga Oblong.

óbovatus, -a An inverted egg-shape.

obtúsa Blunted.

occidentális From the Occident or western world.

odoráta Fragrant.

Oléa The Latin name for the olive.

olerácea Of the vegetable garden.

olivéri In honour of David Oliver (1830–1916), who was Keeper of Kew Herbarium from 1864 to 1890.

omórika The local name of the Serbian spruce.

opáca Dark or dull.

ópalus Probably from *opulus*, an old Latin name for maple, also given to the guelder rose (*Viburnum opulus*) with its maple-like leaves.

ópulus See **ópalus**.

orientális From the Orient, or eastern world (eastwards of Europe and Africa).

órnus The old Latin name for the manna ash.

ósteospérma With hard seeds; from the Greek *osteon*, a bone, and *sperma*, a seed.

óstrya From the Greek name *ostrys* for the hop-hornbeam tree.

ovális Oval.

ováta Egg-shaped.

oxyacántha Having sharp thorns.

oxycárpa Bearing pointed fruits.

oxyoédrue Ancient Greek name for a juniper.

Oxydéndrum From the Greek *oxys*, sharp (tasting), and *dendron*, a tree; the leaves are bitter.

P

pádus The Greek name for a wild cherry.

palmátum Having hand-like leaves with outspread finger-like lobes.

palmetto The Spanish name for the cabbage palm.

palústris Growing in marshes or liking wet places.

paniculata Having flowers in panicles.

papyrífera Paper-bearing.

paradísi From Paradise.

'Parkmanii' In honour of Francis Parkman, American horticulturist.

Parrótia In honour of F. W. Parrot (1792–1841), a Russian naturalist who climbed Mt. Ararat in 1834.

parviflóra Bearing small flowers.

parvifólia Small leaved.

pátula Spreading.

Paulównia In honour of the Princess Anna Paulowna (1795–1865), the daughter of Czar Paul I of Russia.

pávia From an old generic name in honour of Peter Paaw (d. 1617).

pedunculósa With well-developed flower stalks (peduncles).

'Pembury Blue' From the estate of this name in Kent, England.

péndula, -um Hanging down.

pensylvánica, -um From Pennsylvania, U.S.A.

pentándra Each flower having five stamens.

perádo The native (Azores) name for *Ilex perado*.

pérnyi In honour of Paul Hubert Perny (1818–1907), a French missionary in China.

pérsica From Persia (now Iran).

petioláris With a leaf stalk.

petraéa Rock-loving, growing in stony places.

peúce The Greek name for *Pinus peuce*.

'Pfitzeriana' In honour of Ernst Hugo Heinrich Pfitzer (1846–1906), a Stuttgart nurseryman.

phaenopýrum Having the appearance of a pear.

Phellodéndron From the Greek *phellos*, cork, and *dendron*, a tree; these trees have a corky bark.

phéllos The Greek name for the cork oak (*Quercus suber*), which Linnaeus used for *Quercus phellos*.

Phillýrea The classical Greek name.

Phoénix The Greek name for the date palm.

Photínia Said to be from the Greek *phos* or *photos*, light, in allusion to the glossy shining leaves of some species.

Picea From the old Latin name for pitch pine, now used for spruce.

Picrásma From the Greek *picrazein*, bitter.

pictus Painted or coloured.

pináster The old Latin name for a wild pine—as distinct from one (*Pinus pinea*) that was cultivated.

píndrow The native Himalayan name for *Abies pindrow*.

pínea Of the pines or growing on pines (as a parasite).

pinnatífida With leaves pinnately lobed.

pinsápo The Spanish name for *Abies pinsapo*.

Pínus The old Latin name for a pine tree, in particular the stone pine (*Pinus pinea*).

pisífera Pea-bearing.

'Pissardii' In honour of M. Pissard, the Shah of Persia's French gardener 100 years ago.

Pistácia From the Greek *pistake* (in turn probably derived from a Persian name) for the pistachio nut.

Pittospórum From the Greek *pitta*, pitch, and *spora*, seed; the seeds of this genus are embedded in a sticky, resinous substance.

plantierénsis Named after the Plantier nursery near Metz, France.

platanoídes Resembling the plane tree, *Platanus*.

Plátanus The Greek name for the oriental plane tree.

platyphýlla, -os With broad leaves.

'Pléna' Full or double flowered.

plicáta Pleated or folded.

'Plumósa' Feathery.

Podocárpus From the Greek *podos*, a foot, and *karpos*, a fruit; the fruits of these trees (some species, not all) are borne at the summit of a broad, fleshy stalk or receptacle.

pohuashanénsis From Po hua shan, China.

pólita Elegant or neat.

polycárpa Many fruited.

pomífera Bearing pomes or apples.

Poncírus From the French *poncire*, a kind of citrus.

ponderósa Heavy or weighty.

populifólia Having leaves like those of poplar (*Populus*).

Pópulus The Latin name for the poplar tree.

postelense Named after town in Silesia.

potaninii In honour of Grigori Potanin (1835–1920), a Russian who explored and collected in Asia and China.

praécox Developing or flowering earlier than most of its genus.

práttii In honour of Antwerp E. Pratt, an English zoologist who travelled in China in the 1880s.

prínus The Greek name for the common oak (*Quercus robur*), which Linnaeus used for *Quercus prinus*.

prócera Tall or slender.

procúmbens Prostrate.

prunifólia, -um With leaves like those of the cherry (*Prunus*).

Prúnus The Latin name for the cherry tree.

pseudoacácia False acacia.

pseudocaméllia False camellia.

Pseudolárix Literally, false larch; the tree resembles true larch (*Larix*).

pseudoplátanus The false plane tree.

Pseudotsúga False *Tsuga* (the hemlock); Douglas fir is not related to tsuga (nor does it look like one).

Ptélea The Greek name for an elm tree; possibly so named because of the somewhat flattened, circular, winged fruits.

Pterocárya From the Greek *pteron*, a wing, and *karyon*, a nut.

Pterostýrax From the Greek *pteron*, a wing, and the genus *Styrax*; this genus is distinguished by its winged fruits.

pubéscens Covered with soft, downy hairs.

púmila Dwarf.

punctáta Marked with dots.

púngens From the Latin *pungens*, piercing, so sharp-pointed.

púrpurascens Purplish.

purpúrea, -um Purple.

'Pygmáea' Pygmy.

'Pyramidális' Pyramidal.

pyráster The wild pear; from the Latin *pyrus*, pear and *aster*, superficial or incomplete resemblance to; used to denote a wild or inferior species.

Pýrus The Latin name for the pear.

Q

quadranguláta With four angles.

Quássia In honour of Graman Quasi, a Negro slave who used this tree bark as a remedy for fever.

quercifólia With leaves like *Quercus* (oak).

Quércus The Latin name for the oak.

R

racemósa The flowers are borne in a raceme.

radiáta Emitting or having rays.

reclináta Bent backward.

recúrva Curved backward.

régia Royal in appearance.

rehderána In honour of Alfred Rehder (1863–1949), a German American dendrologist, Curator of the Herbarium at the Arnold Arboretum, and author of the classic *Manual of Cultivated Trees and Shrubs*.

resinósa Bearing resin.

reticuláta Having a net-like pattern.

retúsus With a rounded or slightly notched tip.

rhamnoídes Resembling *Rhamnus*, the buckthorn.

Rhododéndron From the Greek *rhodon*, a rose, and *dendron*, a tree.

rhombifólium Rhomboid-leaved.

Rhus The Greek vernacular name for a species of sumach (probably *Rhus coriaria*) and now used as the scientific generic name.

'Richardii' In honour of I. C. Richard (1754–1821), a French botanist.

rígida Stiff or rigid.

'Rivérsii' Raised at England's oldest nursery firm of Thomas Rivers in Hertfordshire, England.

'Rivers Purple' A beech from the Rivers nursery (*see* 'Riversii').

Robínia In honour of Jean Robin (1550–1629), herbalist to Henri IV and Louis XIII of France, and his son Vespasian Robin, who first grew this tree in Europe.

róbur Latin name for any hard wood, especially oak.

robústa Robust, strong in growth.

romanzoffiána In honour of the Russian, M. P. Romanzoff (1754–1826).

Rósa The Latin name for the rose.

rosácea Rose-like.

'Rósea', -um Rose-coloured.

'Roseoplena' Rosy in colour and double.

Roystónea In honour of General Roy Stone (1836–1905), American army engineer in Puerto Rico.

rúbens From the Latin *rubens*, red or reddish.

rúbra, -um Red.

'Rubrifólia' Red-leaved.

rufinérve Red veined when leaves first emerge.

rugósa Wrinkled.

rupéstris Liking a rocky habitat.

'Rústica Rúbra' From the Latin *rusticus*, relating to the country, and *ruber*, red.

S

Sábal Possibly derived from the South American name for these palms.

sacchárinum Sugary.

sacchárum Sugarcane (from the Greek *sakcharon*, in turn probably derived from the Malay word for the sweet juice of the sugarcane, *singkara*).

salicifólia With leaves like those of *Salix*, the willow.

salígnus Resembling willow (*Salix*).

Sálix The Latin name for the willow.

Sambúcus The old Latin name for these shrubs and small trees, perhaps connected with *sambuca*, the Biblical sackbut.

Sápium The Latin name for a resinous pine; presumably applied here because of the sticky sap which is exuded.

sargentiána, -ii In honour of Charles Sprague Sargent (1841–1927), American botanist and dendrologist, first director of the Arnold Arboretum.

sarniénsis From Guernsey (once Sarnia) in the Channel Islands.

sasánqua From the Japanese name *sasankwa* (more correctly *sazanka*) for the species *Camellia sasanqua*.

Sássafras Probably from a North American Indian name used in Florida.

satíva Cultivated.

Saxegothǽa In honour of Prince Albert of Saxe-Coburg-Gotha (1819–61), Consort of Queen Victoria.

Schínus From the Greek *schinos*, a name for the mastic tree, which this genus resembles in its production of resin and a mastic-like juice.

schrenkiána After the Russian botanist, Schrenk (1816–76).

Sciadopítys From the Greek *skiados*, an umbel, and *pitys*, a fir tree; the whorls of spreading, straight, needle-like leaves resemble the spokes of an umbrella.

Scindápsus Ivy arum; from the Greek for an ivy-like plant.

scopulína Bearing small brushes.

scopulórum Growing on cliffs, crags or rocky outcrops.

seláginoides Resembling club-moss.

'Semipléna' Semi or partly double flowered.

sempervírens Evergreen.

septentrionális Northern.

sepulcrális Growing in burial places.

Sequóia Sequoia or Sequoiah was the Cherokee Indian name (meaning opossum) of the halfcaste George Gist (1770–1843), who had a German American father. He invented the Cherokee alphabet.

Sequoiadéndron From *Sequoia* and the Greek *dendron*, a tree.

'Sericea' Silky.

serotína Late flowering or ripening.

serráta Saw-toothed.

sérrula, -ata With small saw-like teeth.

shasténsis From Shasta in California, U.S.A.

shumárdii In honour of Benjamin Franklin Shumard (1820–69), State Geologist of Texas in 1860.

'Sibírica' From Siberia.

siebóldii In honour of Philipp Franz von Siebold (1796–1866), a German doctor who collected in Japan.

síliqua, -astrum Bearing pods with partitions like the fruits (siliquae) of certain members of the cabbage family (*Cruciferae*).

simónii In honour of Gabriel Eugene Simon (b. 1829), French consul and plant collector.

sinénsis From China.

sinogránde A species allied to *Rhododendron grande* from China.

sitchénsis Of Sitka, Alaska.

smithiána In honour of James Edward Smith (1759–1828), founder and first president of the Linnean Society of London.

smíthii In honour of John Smith (1798–1888), Scottish gardener and fern specialist at the Royal Botanical Gardens, Kew.

solándri In honour of Daniel Carl Solander (1736–82), a pupil of Linnaeus and botanist with Sir Joseph Banks on Captain Cook's first voyage to the Pacific.

Sóphora From the Arabic name for these shrubs and trees.

Sórbus From the Latin *sorbum*, for the fruit of the service tree (*Sorbus domestica*).

soulangiána In honour of the Chevalier Etienne Soulange-Bodin (1774–1846), a French horticulturist.

'Spaethii' After the Späth Nursery, Berlin.

speciósa Showy.

spectábilis, -e Showy or spectacular.

'Spek' After the Dutch nurseryman.

Spinósa Bearing spines.

'Spiralis' Spiral.

spléndens Splendid.

spontánea Spontaneous, in the sense of not being planted; growing wild.

squamáta Scaly, with small scale-like leaves.

'Squarrósa' Spreading or curved.

standíshii In honour of John Standish (1809–75), a Surrey nurseryman who raised the plants introduced from China and Japan by Robert Fortune.

stelláta Starry.

stenóptera With narrow wings.

Stewártia (*Stuartia* of some botanists) In honour of John Stuart (1713–92), 3rd Earl of Bute (and Prime Minister 1762–63), a keen patron of botany and horticulture.

'Stricta' Upright.

stróbus The old Latin name for an incense-bearing tree.

styraciflúa Flowing with gum.

Stýrax A Greek name derived from the original Semitic name for these plants.

suaveólens Fragrant.

súber Cork.

subhirtélla Somewhat hairy.

'Suécica' Swedish.

sylvática, sylvéstris Forest-loving, growing in woods.

T

taéda The old Latin name for resinous trees, the wood of which was used for torches—*taeda*, a torch.

Taiwánia From Taiwan, formerly Formosa.

tatáricum From Tartary, a region in central Asia.

Taxódium The name for the swamp cypress; from the Latin *Taxus*, the yew, and the Greek *eidios*, resemblance, the leaves of the swamp cypress and yew are somewhat similar in shape.

Táxus The old Latin name for the yew tree.

Tetraclínis From the Greek *tetra*, four and *kline*, bed; referring to the leaves which are in fours.

'Tetragona Aurea' From the Greek *tetra*, four, *gonus*, angled, and the Latin *aurum*, gold.

tetraptera From the Greek *tetra*, four, and *terus*, winged. Four wing-like appendages or projections.

thomsonii In honour of Thomas Thompson (1817–78), Scottish physician and Superintendent of Calcutta Botanic Garden.

Thúja From the Greek name *thuia* (*thya* or *thyia*) for a resin-bearing tree, almost certainly a kind of juniper.

Thujópsis Resembling *Thuja*, q.v.

thunbérgii In honour of Carl Peter Thunberg (1743–1828), a student of Linnaeus and later professor of botany at Uppsala, Sweden, who collected in Japan and Batavia.

thuringiáca From Thuringia, central Germany.

thyoídes Resembling *Thuja* (in turn derived from *thya*, *thyia* or *thuia*, Greek names for a resin-bearing tree, probably a juniper).

tibética Of Tibet.

Tília The Latin name for the lime or linden tree.

tobira Local name.

tomentósa Covered with short woolly or matted hairs.

toríngoides Like toringo.

torminális Used to alleviate (or capable of giving) a stomach-ache.

Torréya In honour of Dr. John Torrey (1796–1873), one of the most famous of America's botanists who described many thousands of plants brought back by explorers and collectors. Also co-author with Asa Gray of *The Flora of North America*.

torreyana After Dr. John Torrey (see *Torreya*).

'Tortuósa' Twisted as contorted.

tótara The native Maori name (New Zealand).

Trachycárpus From the Greek *trachys*, rough, and *karpos*, a fruit.

trémula Trembling.

trémuloides Like *Populus tremula* (aspen) in general appearance.

triacánthos Three-thorned.

triándra Each flower having three anthers.

trichocárpa With hairy fruits.

tríchotomum Having all divisions in threes.

triflórum *Tri* means three, and *flora*, a flower; the flowers are borne in groups of three.

trifoliáta Having leaves composed of three leaflets.

trilóba Three lobes.

'Triomf van Boskoop' From the nursery area of this name in Holland.

'Trístis' Dull or sad.

tschonoskii In honour of Tschonoski (Chonosuke Sukawa) (1841–1925), who collected for Maximowicz in Japan.

Tsúga The Japanese name for hemlock.

tulipifera Tulip-bearing.

turbináta Shaped like a spinning top.

typhína Resembling reed-mace (*Typha*).

U

'Ukon' From the Japanese for yellow or yellowish.

ulmoídes Like *Ulmus* (elm).

Ulmus The Latin name for the elm.

Umbellulária Bearing umbels; the floral clusters are of this form.

'Umbraculífera' Umbrella-bearing.

undulátum Undulating.

úneco The Latin name for the strawberry tree and its fruit.

ussuriénsis From the vicinity of the Ussuri River in eastern Asia.

V

variábilis Variable.

variegáta, -um Variegated.

végeta Vigorous.

véitchii In honour of the Veitch family, nurserymen of Exeter, Devon, and Chelsea, London. The original nursery was founded in 1808 at Exeter, dividing in 1854, the Chelsea firm finishing on Sir Harry James Veitch's retirement in 1914.

velutína Velvety.

véra True to type.

verniciflua Yielding varnish.

verticilláta Whorled.

vestíta Covered.

Vibúrnum The Latin name of one species of the wayfaring tree.

vilmoriniana, -ii In honour of the French nurseryman Vilmorin-Andrieux.

viminális With long slender shoots like the willow or osier.

'Violacea' Blue-red colour.

virginiána From the states of East or West Virginia, U.S.A.

virgínicus From Virginia, U.S.A.

víridis Green.

viscósa Sticky.

'Vitellína' The colour of an egg-yolk.

'Vitifólium' With leaves like *Vitis* (grapevine).

vomitória Emetic.

vossii In honour of Andreas Voss (1857–1924), German nurseryman.

'Vranja' Named after Vranje in Yugoslavia.

W

wallichiána In honour of Nathaniel Wallich (1786–1854), a Danish doctor and botanist who became Superintendent of the Calcutta Botanic Garden in India from 1814 to 1841.

Washingtónia In honour of George Washington (1732–99), first President of the United States.

wátereri For the nursery firm of John Waterer Sons & Crisp Ltd, Twyford, Berkshire (in the case of *Laburnum anagyroides x watereri*). In honour of the nurseryman Waterer of Surrey (in the case of *Cotoneaster frigidus x watereri*).

wilsónii In honour of Ernest Henry Wilson (1876–1930), the famous plant collector who travelled widely in China and later became curator of the Arnold Arboretum.

'Wissellii' In honour of the Dutch nurseryman Wissel.

X

'Xanthocárpa' Yellow-fruited.

Y

yedoénsis From Tokyo (formerly Yedo), Japan.

'Youngii' In honour of the Young family, nurserymen at Epsom, Surrey, during the first half of the 19th century.

Yucca From the Carib name for cassava, a member of the *Euphorbia* family.

yunnanénsis From Yunnan, western China.

Z

'Zebrína' Zebra-striped.

Zelkóva From the Caucasian native name.

General Index

A

Abel, Ur. Clarke 49
Aberconway, Lord 50
Abscission layer 13
Acacia, Common See *Robinia pseudoacacia*
    True See *Acacia*
Aceraceae 25, 226–33
Acid in soil 22
Acid rain 36–7
Acorn 16, 17, 148, 155–7, 160–1
Aiton, William 43
Alabama 88
Alaska 46, 85, 100
Alder, Common See *Alnus glutinosa*
    European See *Alnus glutinosa*
    Grey See *Alnus incana, A. rugosa*
    Japanese See *Alnus japonica*
    Italian See *Alnus cordata*
    Red See *Alnus rubra*
    Speckled See *Alnus incana*
Alerce See *Tetraclinis articulata*
Aleurites fordii 235
Almonds See *Prunus dulcis*
Alps, the 28, 29, 38, 76
America See North and South America
Amherst, Lady 49
Anacardiaceae 234–5
Angelica Tree, Japanese See *Aralia*
Angelica, Wild 23
Angiosperm 25, 125
Annual growth rings 10, 18, 20, 21
Anthracnose 320, 321
Aphids 320, 321
    on larch 93
    on lime 175
    on willow 179
Apple See *Malus domestica*
Apple brandy 195
Apple, Crab See *Malus*
Apricot See *Prunus armeniaca*
Apricot, Japanese See *Prunus mume*
Apricots 200, 202, 203
Aquifoliaceae 220–3
Aralia, Castor See *Kalopanax pictus*
Ararat, Mount 80, 133
Araucariaceae 116–17
Arborvitae, American See *Thuja occidentalis*
    False See *Thujopsis dolabrata*
    Giant See *Thuja plicata*
    Japanese See *Thuja standishii*
Argyll, Duke of 43
Aristotle 24
Arizona, University of 21, 96
Arnold Arboretum 27, 30, 49, 50, 56, 102, 113, 147, 201, 206
Ash See *Fraxinus excelsior*
    American See *Fraxinus americana*
    American mountain See *Sorbus americana*
    Black See *Fraxinus nigra*
    Blue See *Fraxinus quadrangulata*
    Chinese See *Fraxinus chinensis*
    Common European See *Fraxinus excelsior*
    Green See *Fraxinus pensylvanica lanceolata*
    Manna See *Fraxinus ornus*
    Mountain See *Sorbus aucuparia*
    Narrow-leaved See *Fraxinus angustifolia, F. oxycarpa*
    Oregon See *Fraxinus latifolia*
    Red See *Fraxinus pensylvanica*
    Velvet See *Fraxinus arizonica*
    Wafer See *Ptelea trifoliata*
    Weeping See *Fraxinus excelsior* 'Pendula'
    White See *Fraxinus americana*

Asia
    climate of 31, 38
    plant collecting in 44–5, 48–9
    tree species of 68, 74–5, 80–1, 156–7, 318–19
Aspen, American quaking See *Populus tremuloides*
    Bigtooth See *Populus grandidentata*
    European See *Populus tremula*
    Weeping See *Populus tremula, P. tremuloides*
Athens 31, 55
Atholl, Dukes of 43, 83, 92, 93
Atlanta 30, 55
'Atlantic' period 39
Australia 68, 96, 208, 318–19
Austria 33
Auxin 10

B

Balm of Gilead See *Populus x candicans*
Bacteria 22, 23, 320, 321
Badminton 43
Balsam, 180
Balsams (Firs) See *ABIES*
Baltics, the 76, 86, 238
Banks, Sir Joseph 45, 49
Bannister, John 42, 46
Baranof Island 85
Barcelona 31
Bark
    function of 19
    -patterns 19, 70, 76, 80
    regrowth of 62
    resin in 78
    structure of 11, 18
Barres, les 50
Bartram, John 42–3, 46, 131, 173
Basswood, American See *Tilia americana*
Basswoods See *TILIA*
Baton Rouge 28
Bauhin, Jean 41
Bavaria 37
Bay, Bull See *Magnolia grandiflora*
    Golden See *Laurus nobilis* 'Aurea'
    Loblolly See *Gordonia lasianthus*
    Swamp See *Magnolia virginiana*
    Sweet See *Laurus nobilis*. See also *Magnolia virginiana*
Bay tree See *Laurus nobilis*
Bead tree See *Melia azedarach*
Bean, W. J. 50–1, 176, 246
Beaufort, Duchess of 43
Beckett, Ken 9
Bedford, Duke of 43, 178
Bedgebury Pinetum 50, 103
Beech, American See *Fagus grandifolia*
    Antarctic See *Nothofagus antarctica*
    Black See *Nothofagus solandri*
    Common See *Fagus sylvatica*
    Copper See *Fagus sylvatica*
    Dawyck See *Fagus sylvatica* 'Dawyck'
    European See *Fagus sylvatica*
    Fern-leafed See *Fagus sylvatica heterophylla*
    Mountain See *Nothofagus cliffortioides*
    New Zealand black See *Nothofagus solandri*
    Purple See *Fagus sylvatica*
    Red See *Fagus sylvatica*
    Roblé See *Nothofagus obliqua*
    Upright See *Fagus sylvatica* 'Dawyck'
    Weeping See *Fagus sylvatica*
Beeches, Southern See *Nothofagus*
Bell heather 23
Benelux 33

Betulaceae 164–9
Bigbud See *Carya tomentosa*
'Big tree' See *Sequoiadendron giganteum*
Bignoniaceae 244–5
Bilberry 22, 23
Binomial system 25
Birch, Black See *Betula nigra*
    Canoe See *Betula papyrifera*
    Cherry See *Betula lenta*
    Chinese paper See *Betula albo-sinensis*
    Common See *Betula pubescens*
    European See *Betula pendula*
    Forrest's See *Betula forrestii*
    Gray See *Betula populifolia*
    Himalayan See *Betula jaquemontii*
    Japanese silver See *Betula platyphylla japonica*
    Monarch See *Betula maximowicziana*
    Paper See *Betula papyrifera*
    Polish hybrid See *Betula x fetisowii*
    Poplar-leaved See *Betula populifolia*
    Purple leaf See *Betula pendula*
    River See *Betula nigra*
    Russian rock See *Betula ermanii*
    Common silver See *Betula pendula*
    Southern white Chinese See *Betula albo-sinensis septentrionalis*
    Swedish 'Dalecarlica', 'Tristis' See *Betula pendula*
    Yellow See *Betula lutea*
    Young's weeping See *Betula pendula* 'Youngii'
Bitternut See *Carya cordiformis*
Birkenhead Park 47
Black Forest, the 36–7
Black-gum See *Nyssa sylvatica*
Blackhaw See *Viburnum prunifolium*
Blackthorn See *Prunus spinosa*
Black Wood of Rannoch 76
Bodnant 50
Boletus badius 23
Boletus granulatus 23
Boletus luteus 23
Boletus pulverulentus 22
Bonsai 64–5, 118
Bordeaux 31, 321
'Boreal' period 39
Boston 26, 27, 30, 50, 55
Botanical names 328–31
Box 65 See also *Buxus*
Breeding 52–3 See also Reproduction
Bremontier, M. 77
Bridgeman 43
Britain
    Roman planting in 40, 41
    tree species of 26, 40, 41, 99 (See also England)
British National Arboretum (Westonbirt) 85
Broom, Moroccan See *Cytisus battandieri*
    Mount Etna See *Genista aetnensis*
Brown, Capability 42, 43, 56–7, 91
Brown, Zimmermann and 18
Brussels 31
Buckeye American See *Aesculus neglecta*
    California See *Aesculus californica*
    Ohio See *Aesculus glabra*
    Red See *Aesculus pavia*
    Sweet See *Aesculus flava*
    Yellow See *Aesculus flava*
Budapest 31
Bud
    function of the 9, 20
    scars 11
    sticky 11
    terminal 11
    varieties of 28, 79, 83, 113
Bull bay See *Magnolia grandiflora*

Bunge, Alexander von 49
Burghley, Lord 154
Burma 48, 318–19
Bute, Earl of 43, 45, 173
Butternut See *Juglans cinerea*
Buttonwood See *Platanus occidentalis*
Buxaceae 223

C

Calcium 13, 22
Calcutta Botanic Garden 48
Caledonian Forest 41, 76
Calgary 21
California
    climate of 21, 120
    discoveries in 47
    exports from 99
    heathland of 184
    mountains of 27, 71, 104
    pollution of 37
    tree species of 75, 79, 96, 120, 130, 159, 215, 240
Calvados 195
Cambium 18, 19
Cambridge University Library 9
Camphor 130
Camphor tree See *Cinnamomum camphora*
Canada 26, 33, 37, 79, 83
Canary Islands 107
Candelabra tree See *Araucaria angustifolia*
Canker See Disease
Caprifoliaceae 246
Carbon dioxide 12, 38
    -14 method 21
Caribbean, the 123
Carob tree See *Ceratonia siliqua*
Carpinaceae 170–71
Cascades, the 26
Catkins 15, 28
Caucasus, the 40, 80, 87, 318–19
Cedar, Alaska See *Chamaecyparis nootkatensis*
    Atlantic See *Cedrus atlantica*
    Atlantic white See *Chamaecyparis thyoides*
    Chinese See *Cedrela sinensis*
    Deodar See *Cedrus deodara*
    Eastern red See *Juniperus virginiana*
    Incense See *Calocedrus decurrens*
    Japanese See *Cryptomeria japonica*
    of Goa See *Cupressus lusitanica*
    of Lebanon See *Cedrus libani*
    Northern white See *Thuja occidentalis*
    Pencil See *Juniperus virginiana*
    Port Orford See *Chamaecyparis lawsoniana*
    Spanish See *Cedrela odorata*
    Western red See *Thuja plicata*
    White See *Thuja occidentalis*
    Yellow See *Chamaecyparis nootkatensis*
Cedars See *Cedrus*
Cephalotaxaceae 110–11
Chalk See Soil
Charles I 40, 42
Charles II 41
Charleston 43
Chaucer, Tree catalogue by 40
Chelsea Physick Garden 43, 52, 147
Cherry Autumn Bird See *Prunus subhirtella* 'Autumnalis'
    Bird See *Prunus padus*
    Black See *Prunus serotina*
    Choke See *Prunus virginiana*
    Cornelian See *Cornus mas*
    Flowering 195, 198–202 See also *Prunus x yedoensis*
    Gean See *Prunus avium*
    Great mountain See *Prunus sargentii*
    Great white See *Prunus* 'Tai Haku'
    Hiu See *Prunus serrulata spontanea*

    Japanese See *Prunus serrulata*
    Manchurian See *Prunus maackii*
    Morello See *Prunus cerasus*
    'Pin' See *Prunus pensylvanica*
    Rum See *Prunus serotina*
    Sargent's See *Prunus sargentii*
    'Shimidsu'
    Sour See *Prunus cerasus*
    Spring See *Prunus subhirtella*
    Sweet See *Prunus avium*
    Village See *Prunus serrulata*
    Waterer's Bird See *Prunus padus* 'Watereri'
    White See *Prunus* 'Tai Haku'
    Wild See *Prunus avium*
    Wild red See *Prunus pensylvanica*
    Yoshino See *Prunus x yedoensis*
Cherry-worship 198–9
Chestnut, American See *Castanea dentata*
    Chinese See *Castanea mollissima*
    Golden See *Chrysolepis chrysophylla*
    Common horse See *Aesculus hippocastanum*
    Indian horse See *Aesculus indica*
    Japanese See *Castanea crenata*
    Japanese horse See *Aesculus turbinata*
    Red horse See *Aesculus x carnea*
    Spanish See *Castanea sativa*
    Sweet See *Castanea sativa*
Chicago 30, 55
Chichester, Roman garden at 40
Childrey 91
Chile 44, 48, 116
China
    forests of 68, 152, 176
    gardens of 44–5, 126
    tree species of 38, 39, 48, 50, 83, 86, 113, 189, 218
    Wilson's discoveries in 219
Chinaberry See *Melia azedarach*
Chinese wood-oil tree See *Aleurites fordii*
Chinkapin, Golden See *Chrysolepis chrysophylla*
Chlorophyll 12
Choosing trees 54, 326–7
Christmas tree See *Picea abies*
Chusan 44
Cider 195
Cincinnati 30
Citrange See *Poncirus trifoliata x Citrus sinensis*
Citrangequat See *Poncirus trifoliata x Citrus sinensis x Fortunella sp.*
Citrus 97, 236–7, 321
Clark, Captain 46, 47
Classification 24–5
Climate
    effects of 26–31, 38, 39, 87, 101, 110, 150, 314–15
    sun, angles of 55
    for the conifer 67
    for transplanting 61
    in garden design 58
'Clones' 52
Clusius 25, 41
Cobbett, William 209
Cobnut See *Corylus avellana*
Coffee tree, Kentucky See *Gymnocladus dioica*
Coimbra 29
Colbert 154
Coleridge 166
Collinson, Peter 42–3, 44
Colorado 55
Columbia, British 27, 83
Columbia River 46, 47
Compositae 24–5
Compton, Henry 42
Conder, Josiah 50, 51
Cones 15, 17, 67
Conifer Conference 1972 77
Conker 224
Connecticut 57, 167, 220

Constable, John 136
Cook, Captain James 45
Coppicing 64, 162
Cordon 64
Cork cambium 19, 156, 237
Cork tree, Amur See
    Phellodendron amurense
Cornaceae 216–17
Cortex See Bark
Corylaceae 170–1
Cotoneaster, Tree See
    Cotoneaster frigidus
Cottonwood See Populus
    Black See Populus trichocarpa
Cotyledons 16, 17
    Dicotyledon class 25
    Monocotyledon class 16
    See also Seed
Cox, Euan 49, 106
Crab-apples See MALUS
Crab, Bechtel's See Malus
    ioensis 'Plena'
    'Cherry' See Malus x robusta
    Cutleaf See Malus toringoides
    English wild See Malus
    sylvestris
    Hupeh See Malus hupehensis
    Japanese See Malus
    floribunda
    Manchurian See Malus
    baccata 'Mandshurica'
    Prairie See Malus ioensis
    Rivers' See Malus spectabilis
    'Riversii'
    Sargent's See Malus sargentii
    Siberian See Malus baccata
    Tea See Malus hupehensis
Crabs See MALUS
Cronquist, Arthur 25, 125
Crossing 15 See also Breeding
Crowe, Dame Sylvia 9, 58
Cucumber tree See Magnolia
    acuminata
    Yellow See Magnolia cordata
Cultivars 52, 85, 86, 98, 118, 222
    See also Breeding
Cunningham, James 44, 49, 116
Cupressaceae 24, 94–107
Cuttings 52–3
Cyatheaceae 24
Czechoslovakia 37
Cypress, Arizona See Cupressus
    glabra
    Bald See Taxodium distichum
    Classic See Cupressus
    sempervirens
    Hinoki See Chamaecyparis
    obtusa
    Japanese Sawara See
    Chamaecyparis pisifera
    Kashmir See Cupressus
    cashmeriana
    Lawson See Chamaecyparis
    lawsoniana
    Leyland See Cupressocyparis
    leylandii
    Mediterranean See Cupressus
    sempervirens
    Mexican See Cupressus
    lusitanica
    Monterey See Cupressus
    macrocarpa
    Montezuma See Taxodium
    mucronatum
    Nootka (false) See
    Chamaecyparis nootkatensis
    Pond See Taxodium
    ascendens
    Smooth Arizona See
    Cupressus glabra
    Southern See Taxodium
    distichum
    Swamp See Taxodium
    distichum
    White See Chamaecyparis
    thyoides

D

Dalles, The 46
Darwin, Charles 9, 24
Date palm See Phoenix
    dactylifera
    Canary Island See Phoenix
    canariensis

Egyptian See Phoenix
    dactylifera
David, Father Armand 48, 218
Davidiaceae 218–19
Dawyck 93, 151
Day-length 10, 28 See also
    Climate
Deal 86
Delavay, Father Jean Marie 48,
    81, 187
Denmark 33, 151
Denver 30
Deodar See Cedrus deodara
Des Moines 30
Disease 139
    canker 179, 320, 321
    chestnut blight 320, 321
    Dutch elm 19, 136, 139, 321
Distribution 40
Dodoens 41
Dogwood See CORNUS
    American See Cornus
    alternifolia
    Flowering See Cornus florida
    Giant See Cornus controversa
    Japanese See Cornus kousa
    Pacific See Cornus nuttallii
Dogwood shrubs See CORNUS
Dormancy 10, 16
Douglas, David 46–7, 72, 78, 83,
    85, 239
Dovaston 108
Dove tree See Davidia
    involucrata
Downing, A. J. 47
Drought 10 See also Climate
Dryden 238
Dublin 31
Duck's-foot tree See Ginkgo
    biloba
Dunkeld 92
Dutch East India Company 45
Dutch East Indies, the 120
Dutch Elm disease 136 See also
    Pests
'Dwarfing' See Roots

E

'Early Wood' 18
Fast Germany 37
East India Company 44, 48
East Malling Research Station 23
East River, Manhattan 312
Ebenaceae 188–9
Ebony See Diospyros ebenum
Edinburgh 29, 31
Edinburgh Botanic Garden 49
Edmonton 30, 55
El Paso 30
Elaeagnaceae 215
Elder, Blueberry See Sambucus
    coerulea
    Box See Acer negundo
    Common See Sambucus nigra
Elderberry See Sambucus
    canadensis
Elm, American See Ulmus
    americana
    Belgian See Ulmus x
    hollandica 'Belgica'
    Chinese See Ulmus parvifolia
    Cornish See Ulmus
    angustifolia cornubiensis
    Dutch See Ulmus x hollandica
    'Major'
    English See Ulmus procera
    Goodyer See Ulmus
    angustifolia
    Huntingdon See Ulmus x
    vegeta
    Jersey See Ulmus x sarniensis
    Rock See Ulmus thomasii
    Siberian See Ulmus pumila
    Slippery See Ulmus rubra
    Smooth-leaved See Ulmus
    carpinifolia
    Tabletop See Ulmus glabra
    Weeping wych See Ulmus
    glabra 'Pendula'
    Wheatley See Ulmus x
    sarniensis
    White See Ulmus americana
    Wych See Ulmus glabra
Elwes, Henry John 48, 50, 51

Empress tree See Paulownia
    tomentosa
England
    gardens of 45, 50, 52, 58–9,
    90
    tree species in 21, 108, 114, 217
Enniskillen, Earl of 108
Epaulette tree See Pterostyrax
    hispida
Epidermis See Leaves, structure
    of
Epping Forest 192
Ericaceae 184–7
Espalier 64
Eucalypts See EUCALYPTUS
Eucalyptus, oil of 212
Europe
    climate of 27, 28, 38
    gardens of 45, 50, 52, 58–9,
    90
    pollution of 36–7
    rarities in 131
    tree species of 26, 76–7, 80–1,
    86–7, 126, 156–7, 232–3,
    318–19
    vegetation zones of 314–15
Evelyn, John 41, 42, 91, 92, 153,
    154, 220, 246
Evolution 24, 25, 38–9, 40, 67
    tree grouping by 164, 240

F

Fagaceae 24, 148–63
Fairbrother, Nan 57
Falling Water, 56
False cypress See
    CHAMAECYPARIS
Families of trees 24–5
Farges, Father Paul Guillaume 48,
    218, 219
Fargo 30
Farrer, Reginald 49
Felling 62–3
Fertilisers 63
Fertilization 15, 32–3
Fescue 23
Fig-tree See Ficus carica
Filberts See CORYLUS
Finland 33
Fir, Alpine See Abies lasiocarpa
    Balsam See Abies balsamea
    Caucasian See Abies
    nordmanniana
    Chinese See Cunninghamia
    lanceolata
    Colorado white See Abies
    concolor
    Common silver See Abies alba
    East Himalayan See Abies
    spectabilis
    Forrest's See Abies delavayi
    forrestii
    Fraser's See Abies fraseri
    Grand See Abies grandis
    Greek See Abies cephalonica
    Grey Douglas See
    Pseudotsuga menziesii
    Korean See Abies koreana
    Low's See Abies lowiana
    Maries' See Abies mariesii
    Nikko See Abies homolepis
    Noble See Abies procera
    Oregon Douglas See
    Pseudotsuga menziesii
    Red See Abies magnifica
    Red Silver See Abies amabilis
    Santa Lucia See Abies
    bracteata
    Shasta See Abies magnifica
    Spanish See Abies pinsapo
    Veitch See Abies veitchii
    West Himalayan See Abies
    pindrow
    White See Abies concolor
Firebush See Embothrium
    lanceolatum
    Chilean See Embothrium
    coccineum
Firs, Silver See ABIES
Fitzherbert 41
Flanders 25
Florida 28, 120, 244
Flowers 14–15, 16, 24–5,
    316–17, 326

Foliage 25, 85, 86, 97
    beech 13
    conifer 13
    cypress 24
    fir See also Needles
    pollution of 36–7
Fontainebleau 206
Forest vegetation 314–15
Forestry 32–3, 62–3, 91
Forestry Commission, the 9, 50
Forêt de Tronçais 154
Formosa 318–19
Forrest, George 49, 81
Fort Alexandria 46
Fort Edmonton 46
Fort Ross 46
Fort St. George 46
Fort St. James 46
Fort Vancouver 46
Fortune, Robert 49, 172
Fossils 24, 39
France
    forests of 33, 180
    gardens of 41
    tree species of 26, 40, 151
Frankfurt 31, 55
Franklin, Benjamin 173
Fraser, John 45
Frederick, Prince of Wales 43
Fremont, Colonel 104
French National Arboretum 75
Fribourg 29
Fringe-tree See Chionanthus
    virginicus
    American See Chionanthus
    Chinese See Chionanthus
Frost See Climate
Fruit
    as reproductive organ 16
    edible 142–3, 148, 188, 195,
    204–5, 210, 234–5
    varieties of 110, 116, 224
Fulham Palace Garden 42
Fungi
    destruction of 62–3
    infection by 13, 18, 19
    value of 23
    varieties of 22–3, 320–1

G

Galls 320–1
Gardener's Chronicle, the 9
Gardens 25, 44, 45, 47, 96
    of China 44–5
    of England 45, 50, 52
    of France 41–2
    of North America 56
Gean See Prunus avium
'General Grant' 114
Genus 24
George III 43
Georgia 42, 123, 133
Gerrard, John 40, 41
Germany, West 33, 36–7, 76
Germination 16, 17 See also
    Seed
Ghost tree See Davidia
    involucrata
Gibbons, Grinling 174
Gibbs, Hon. Vicary 109
Gibraltar 31
Gilpin, William 136, 177, 178
Gin See Fruit, edible
Ginkgo See Ginkgo biloba
Ginkgoaceae 24, 68–9
Girdling 18
Glasgow 46
Gley 23
Glossary 247
Golden chinkapin See
    Chrysolepis chrysophylla
Golden rain tree See Koelreuteria
    paniculata
Gordon, James 173
Grafting 32, 52, 54
Grapefruit See Citrus paradisi
Gravity 10–11, 20, 22
Great Falls 30
Great Lakes, the 42, 84, 126
Great Smoky Mountains 78, 84
Greece 33, 40, 80, 107
Growth rings See Annual
    growth rings

Guelder rose See Viburnum
    opulus
Gulf of Mexico 30, 126
Gulf Stream, the 31
Gum, Black See Nyssa sylvatica
    Blue See Eucalyptus globulus
    Cider See Eucalyptus gunnii
    Ghost See Eucalyptus
    papuana
    River red See Eucalyptus
    camaldulensis
    Snow See Eucalyptus
    niphophila
    Spinning See Eucalyptus
    perriniana
    Tasmanian cider See
    Eucalyptus gunnii
    Tasmanian snow See
    Eucalyptus coccifera
Gunz See Ice Ages
Gwillimia See MAGNOLIA
Gymnosperms 125

H

Hackberry, American See Celtis
    occidentalis
    Chinese See Celtis sinensis
    Common See Celtis
    occidentalis
    Mississippi See Celtis laevigata
    Southern European See Celtis
    australis
Hadfield, Miles 174
Hamamelidaceae 132–3
Hamburg 31, 55
Handkerchief tree See Davidia
    involucrata
Hartweg, Theodor 47
Harvard Botanic Garden 47
    University 50
Hawaii 47
Hawthorn, Common See
    Crataegus monogyna
    Downy See Crataegus mollis
    English See Crataegus
    oxyacantha
    single-seed See Crataegus
    monogyna
    Variegated See Crataegus
    monogyna
Hazel, Californian See Corylus
    californica
    European See Corylus avellana
    Purple See Corylus maxima
    purpurea
    Turkish See Corylus colurna
Heartwood 19
Heather 23, 184–7
Hedges 64, 148, 170, 220, 223
Hedge-thorn See Crataegus
    monogyna
Hedging techniques 64–5, 109
Helsinki 31
Hemiptera 321
Hemlock, Carolina See Tsuga
    caroliniana
    Eastern See Tsuga canadensis
    Japanese See Tsuga
    diversifolia and T. sieboldii
    Mountain See Tsuga
    mertensiana
    Western See Tsuga
    heterophylla
Henry IV 208
Henry, Augustine 49, 50, 51,
    218–19
Herb Robert 23, 48–9
Herbals 23–4, 40–1
Hercules' club See ARALIA
Hergest Croft 185
Hers 231
Hesse 37
Hiba See Thujopsis dolabrata
Hickories See CARYA
Hickory, Shag-bark See Carya
    ovata
Hillier's arboretum 9, 52–3, 97,
    133, 201
Himalayas 48, 86, 91, 106
Hippocastanaceae 224–5
Hoey Smith, Dick van 9
Hokkaido 26, 80
Holford family 50
Holland 37

GENERAL INDEX

Hollies See *ILEX*
Holly, American See *Ilex opaca*
  Camellia-leaved See *Ilex x altaclerensis* 'Camelliifolia'
  Dahoon See *Ilex cassine*
  English See *Ilex aquifolium*
  Perny's See *Ilex pernyi*
  Hedgehog See *Ilex aquifolium* 'Ferox'
  Highclere hybrids See *Ilex x altaclerensis*
  Japanese broadleaf See *Ilex latifolia*
  Weeping silver-variegated See *Ilex aquifolium* 'Argenteomarginata Pendula'
  Yaupon See *Ilex vomitoria*
  Yellow-berried, English See *Ilex aquifolium*
Holmes, Oliver Wendell 154
Honeydew 175, 321
Honey-locust See *Gleditsia triacanthos*
Hooker, Sir Joseph 48, 90–1, 187
Hooker, William Jackson 46
Hop-hornbeam See *OSTRYA*
Hop-tree See *Ptelea trifoliata*
Hormones 10
Hornbeam See *Carpinus betulus*
  American See *Carpinus caroliniana*
  European See *Carpinus betulus*
  Hop See *OSTRYA*
  Japanese See *Carpinus cordata, C. japonica*
  Japanese hop See *Ostrya japonica*
Horse chestnut, Indian See *Aesculus indica*
  Japanese See *Aesculus turbinata*
  Red-flowered See *Aesculus x carnea*
Horticultural Society (London) 46, 47, 49, 83
Hounslow 43
Houston 30
Hudson Bay Company 46–7, 83
Humboldt, Alexander von 44
Hybrids 15, 52, 92–3
Hydrogen 13

I

Ice Ages 38–40, 68, 76, 86, 114, 120, 218
Idaho 106
d'Incarville, Father Pierre 44, 49
Incense 104
India 188, 318–19
Indian bean tree See *Catalpa*
Indiana Dunes National Park 34–5
Ingatestone 43
Ingram, Captain Collingwood 49, 198, 199, 200, 202
Inkcap 22
Insecticides 53, 136, 321
Insects
  as pests 320–1
  in pollination 15, 125
  bark- 320–1
  forest- 22, 209
  wax- 241
Institute of Landscape Architects 9
International Paper Company 9
Iron 13 See also Roots
Iron-wood See *Ostrya virginiana*
  Persian See *Parrotia persica*
Italy 33
Ivy 22, 108, 234

J

Jacaranda See *Jacaranda acutifolia*
Jackson 30
Jacksonville 30
Jacquemont, Victor 48
Japan 26, 37, 48, 50, 83, 86, 116

European botanists in 45
  forests of 68, 74
  garden design in 58–9, 74, 126
  tree discoveries in 318–19
Jardin des Plantes 42, 44, 45
Jekyll, Gertrude 50, 51, 105
Jefferson, Thomas 46
Jeffrey, John 47
Joseph of Arimathea 193
Judas tree See *Cercis siliquastrum*
Juglandaceae 144–7
Julibrissin See *Albizia julibrissin*
Juneberry See *AMELANCHIER*
Juniper See *JUNIPERUS*
  'Alligator' See *Juniperus deppeana pachyphlaea*
  Cherrystone See *Juniperus monosperma*
  Chinese See *Juniperus chinensis*
  Common See *Juniperus communis*
  Greek See *Juniperus chinensis* 'Pyramidalis'
  Himalayan See *Juniperus squamata*
  Hollywood See *Juniperus chinensis* 'Kaizuka'
  Irish See *Juniperus communis* 'Hibernica'
  Pencil See *Juniperus virginiana*
  Phoenician See *Juniperus phoenicea*
  Prickly See *Juniperus oxycedrus*
  Rocky Mountain See *Juniperus scopulorum*
  'Swedish' See *Juniperus communis*
  Syrian See *Juniperus drupacea*
  Temple See *Juniperus rigida*
  Utah See *Juniperus osteosperma*
  Western See *Juniperus occidentalis*
Jussieu, Bernard de 44, 45

K

Kaempfer, Engelbert 45, 48, 69
Kansas City 30
Katsura, Japanese See *Cercidiphyllum japonicum*
Kawamoto and Kurihara 64
Kent, William 23, 43
Kerr, William 49
Kew House 42
Kew, Royal Botanical Gardens 9, 43, 45, 46, 48, 50, 69, 77, 97, 177, 234
Keys 17, 226, 239
Killarney See *Arbutus unedo*
Kip's engravings 41
Kirsch 200
'Knees' 112
Korea 318–19
Kowhai, New Zealand See *Sophora tetraptera*
Kumquat See *Fortunella margarita*
Kyoto 117

L

Laburnum, Common See *Laburnum anagyroides*
  Scotch See *Laburnum alpinum*
  Waterer's See *Laburnum watereri*
Lacquered furniture 235
Lake Michigan 34–5
Lambeth 40, 42
Lammas shoots 155
Lancaster, Roy 9, 133
Landes, the 77
Landscaping 41, 42, 54–9 See also Planting
Laramie 30
Larch, Dunkeld hybrid See *Larix x eurolepis*
  Eastern See *Larix laricina*
  European See *Larix decidua*

False See *Pseudolarix amabilis*
  Himalayan See *Larix griffithiana*
  Japanese See *Larix kaempferi*
  Water See *Metasequoia glyptostroboides*
  Western See *Larix occidentalis*
Larches See *LARIX*
'Late wood' 18
Lauraceae 130–1
Laurel See *Cinnamomum camphora, Laurus nobilis, Prunus laurocerasus, P. lusitanica, Umbellularia californica*
  Bay See *Laurus nobilis*
  California See *Umbellularia californica*
  Camphor See *Cinnamomum camphora*
  Cherry See *Prunus laurocerasus*
  Chilean See *Laurelia serrata*
  Common See *Laurus nobilis*
  Portugal See *Prunus lusitanica*
  True See *Laurus nobilis*
Lawson 98
Leasowes 56
Leaves 10
  cell structure of 13
  colour and design of 12, 89, 91, 98, 140, 178–9, 327
  evergreen- 12, 13
  function of 12, 18
  varieties of 327
Lebanon, Mount 90
Lecluse, Charles de 25
Leguminosae 25, 208–11
Leiden 25
Lemon See *Citrus limon*
Le Nôtre, André 41
Lenticels 11
Lewis, Captain 46, 47
Leyden Botanic Garden 25, 40
Leyland, C. J. 101
Light 11, 12, 55
Lily-of-the-valley tree See *Clethra arborea*
Lime See Soil
Lime See *Citrus aurantifolia*
  Big-leafed See *Tilia platyphyllos*
  Common See *Tilia x europaea*
  Crimean See *Tilia x euchlora*
  Silver See *Tilia tomentosa*
  Small-leafed See *Tilia cordata*
  Weeping silver See *Tilia petiolaris*
Limes See *Citrus aurantifolia*
  Pendant silver linden See *Tilia petiolaris*
Linnaeus 24, 25, 43, 45
Linné, Carl 25
Lisbon 31
Little Rock 30
Lindens See *TILIA*
Lloyd Wright, Frank 56
Lobb, Thomas 48
Lobb, William 44, 47
Loch Rannoch 76
Locust See *Ceratonia siliqua*
  Black See *Robinia pseudoacacia*
  Caspian See *Gleditsia caspica*
  Clammy See *Robinia viscosa*
  Honey See *Gleditsia triacanthos*
London
  Horticultural Society of 83
  tree growing in 28, 29, 54, 134–5
London, Bishop of 42
Longleat 43, 71
Los Angeles 30, 55
Louisville 30, 55
Loudon, John Claudius 47, 183
Louis XV 45
Lucombe and Pince 52, 155
Lucombe of Exeter See Lucombe and Pince
Ludlow, Frank 48
Luxembourg 31
Lyon 31, 41, 55

M

Macao 48
Madrid 31
Magdalen College, Oxford 22
Magnesium 13, 22 See also Roots
Magnolia, Bigleaf See *Magnolia macrophylla*
  Chinese See *Magnolia sinensis*
  Japanese See *Magnolia kobus*
  Japanese 'whiteleaf' See *Magnolia obovata*
  Japanese willowleaf See *Magnolia salicifolia*
  Laurel See *Magnolia grandiflora*
  Lily See *Magnolia liliiflora*
  Oyama See *Magnolia sieboldii*
  Saucer See *Magnolia soulangiana*
  Southern See *Magnolia grandiflora*
  Star See *Magnolia stellata*
  Wilson's See *Magnolia wilsonii*
Magnoliaceae 24, 126–9
Magnus, Albertus 40
Maidenhair tree See *Ginkgo biloba*
Maintenance 62–3
Malathion 321
Mallee See *EUCALYPTUS*
Mammals See Wildlife
Manchuria 318–19
Mangoes 234
Manitoba 30
Maple, Aconite-leaved Japanese See *Acer japonicum* 'Aconitifolium'
  Amur See *Acer ginnala*
  Bigleaf See *Acer macrophyllum*
  Black See *Acer nigrum*
  Cappadocian See *Acer cappadocicum*
  Chinese See *Acer forrestii, Acer henryi*
  David's See *Acer davidii*
  Eagle's-claw See *Acer platanoides*
  Field See *Acer campestre*
  Full-moon See *Acer japonicum*
  Hedge See *Acer campestre*
  Hers's Chinese See *Acer hersii*
  Hornbeam See *Acer carpinifolium*
  Italian See *Acer opalus*
  Japanese See *Acer micranthum*
  Japanese horned See *Acer diabolicum*
  Montpellier See *Acer monspessulanum*
  Nikko See *Acer nikoense*
  Norway See *Acer platanoides*
  Oregon See *Acer macrophyllum*
  Paper-bark See *Acer griseum*
  Purple horned See *Acer diabolicum purpurascens*
  Red See *Acer rubrum*
  Silver See *Acer saccharinum*
  Sugar See *Acer saccharum*
  Swamp See *Acer rubrum*
  Sycamore See *Acer pseudoplatanus*
  Trident See *Acer buergeranum*
  Turkish See *Acer cappadocicum*
  Vine See *Acer circinatum*
  Vine-leaved Japanese See *Acer japonicum* 'Vitifolium'
Marco Polo 44
Maries, Charles 49
Maritime areas 327
Marram grass 34
Marseilles 31
Massachusetts 109
Masson, Francis 45
Mastic (gum) 234
Mathiolus, Petrus Andreas 16
Maximowicz, Carl 49
May (May Tree) See *Crataegus monogyna*
Mayten tree See *Maytenus boaria*
Mazzard See *Prunus avium*

Meadow-grass 22
Mediterranean 38, 76, 107, 122, 155
  tree discoveries in lands 318–19
Medlar, Bronvaux See *Crataegomespilus dardarii*
Melbourne, Botanic Gardens in 96
Meliaceae 242–3
Menzies, Archibald 46, 47, 83, 100
Mespilus, Snowy See *AMELANCHIER*
Messel, Leonard 50
Mexico 44, 73, 83, 123, 318–19
Meyer, Frank 49
Miami 30, 55
Michaux, André 43, 127
Microclimates 27
Milan 69
Mildews 321
Miller, Philip 43, 147
Milton, John 142
Milwaukee 30
Mimosa See *Acacia dealbata*
Mindel See Ice Ages
Minerals 13, 22 See also Soil
Minneapolis 30
Mist house 52
Mitchell, Alan 9, 61, 81, 106, 175, 318–19
Mockernut See *Carya tomentosa*
Monceau, Duhamel du 44
Monkey puzzle tree See *Araucaria araucana*
Monte Carlo 130
Monterey 46, 47, 72–3, 96
Montpellier 29
Montreal 30, 55
Moosewood See *Acer pensylvanicum*
Moraceae 142–3
Morris, William 192
Mountain ashes See *SORBUS*
Mulberry, Black See *Morus nigra*
  Paper See *BROUSSONETIA*
  White See *Morus alba*
Mulching 62
Multistemmed trees 327
Munich 31
Mycorrhizae 23, 184
Myrobalan See *Prunus cerasifera*
Myrtaceae 25, 212–14
Myrtle, Oregon See *Umbellularia californica*
  Crape See *Lagerstroemia indica*

N

Naesmith 151
Nagasaki 45
Names, Botanical 328–31
Nannyberry See *Viburnum lentago*
Naples 28, 77
Napoleon 177
Nashville 30
National Arboretum, France 50
National Arboretum, U.S.A. 75
National Pinetum, Britain 50
Nectar 125
Nectarines See *Prunus persica* 'Laevis'
Needles 12–13, 70, 73, 74, 78, 84, 113
Nettle-tree See *Celtis occidentalis*
New England 9
  forests of 71, 87
  tree species of 24, 26
New Orleans 30
New World, the 42–3
New York 30
New York Botanic Garden 25
  Central Park 47
New Zealand 104, 111, 153
Nitrogen 13, 18, 22, 63
Nomenclature, International rules of 25
Norfolk, Duke of 43
North Africa 120, 122
North America 26, 27, 36–7, 42, 43, 47
  climate of 28, 30, 58
  forests of 33, 69, 73, 159
  soil of 38

334

tree discoveries in 318–19
tree species of 70–3, 78–9,
84–5, 138–9, 158–61, 226–9
vegetation zones in 314–15
Norway 33, 36, 77, 87
Nova Scotia 88
Nurseries 43, 44, 97, 115, 118
Japanese 198
modern 52–3
Nutmeg, California See *Torreya californica*
Nuttall, Thomas 47
Nymans 50

O

Oak, Algerian See *Quercus canariensis*
Basket See *Quercus prinus*
Black See *Quercus velutina*
Blackjack See *Quercus marilandica*
Blue See *Quercus douglasii*
Burr See *Quercus macrocarpa*
California black See *Quercus kelloggii*
California blue See *Quercus douglasii*
California white See *Quercus lobata*
Cambridge See *Quercus warburgii*
Canyon live See *Quercus chrysolepis*
Caucasian See *Quercus macranthera*
Chestnut See *Quercus prinus*
Chestnut-leafed See *Quercus castaneifolia*
Chinese cork See *Quercus variabilis*
Chinkapin See *Quercus muehlenbergii*
Coast live See *Quercus agrifolia*
Common See *Quercus robur*
Cork See *Quercus suber*
Daimyo See *Quercus dentata*
Durmast See *Quercus petraea*
English See *Quercus robur*
Fulham See *Quercus x hispanica* 'Fulhamensis'
Holly-leaved See *Quercus ilex*
Holm See *Quercus ilex*
Hungarian See *Quercus frainetto*
Kew See *Quercus x kewensis*
Laurel See *Quercus laurifolia*
Lebanon See *Quercus libani*
Live See *Quercus virginiana*
Lucombe See *Quercus x hispanica* 'Lucombeana'
Mossy-cup See *Quercus macrocarpa*
Nuttall See *Quercus nuttallii*
Oregon white See *Quercus garryana*
Overcup See *Quercus lyrata*
Pedunculate See *Quercus robur*
Pin See *Quercus palustris*
Portuguese See *Quercus lusitanica*
Post See *Quercus stellata*
Red See *Quercus rubra*
Sadler See *Quercus sadlerana*
Sawtooth See *Quercus acutissima*
Scarlet See *Quercus coccinea*
Sessile See *Quercus petraea*
She- See *Casuarina*
Shingle See *Quercus imbricaria*
Shumard See *Quercus shumardii*
Silk See *Grevillea robusta*
Southern red See *Quercus falcata*
Spanish See *Quercus falcata*
Swamp white See *Quercus bicolor*
Tanbark See *Lithocarpus densiflorus*
Turkey See *Quercus cerris*
Turner's See *Quercus x turneri*

Water See *Quercus nigra*
White See *Quercus alba*
Willow See *Quercus phellos*
Oakwood 22, 23
Odèn, Svante 36
Ohio 26, 126
Oklahoma City 30
Olantigh 312
Oldham, Richard 49
Oleaceae 25, 238–41
Oleaster See *Elaeagnus angustifolia*
Olive See *Olea europaea*
Russian See *Elaeagnus angustifolia*
Olmsted, Frederick Law 47, 50
Omaha 30
Orange, Japanese bitter See *Poncirus trifoliata*
Sweet See *Citrus sinensis*
Orangequat 237
Oranges See *Citrus*
Orangery 236, 237
Oregon 72, 85, 102, 104, 106, 130, 161
Association of 47
forests of 38
timber trees of 168
Ornamental flowers 316–17
Osage orange See *Maclura pomifera*
Osier See *Salix viminalis*
Osier beds 178
Oslo 29, 31
Ovary 16, 125
Ovule 16 See also Reproduction, organs of
Oxford 22
Oxygen 38 See also Roots

P

Pagoda tree See *Sophora japonica*
Paleozoic era 68
Palm, California fan See *Washingtonia filifera*
Caribbean cabbage See *Sabal palmetto*
Chilean wine See *Jubaea chilensis*
Chusan See *Trachycarpus fortunei*
Coconut See *Cocos nucifera*
King See *Archontophoenix alexandrae*
Petticoat See *Washingtonia filifera*
Queen See *Arecastrum romanzoffianum*
Royal See *Roystonea regia*
Windmill See *Trachycarpus fortunei*
Palmae 25, 120–3
Palms 120–3
Palm Springs 234
Paper from trees 67, 84, 143
Paris 31, 42, 44, 45, 52
Parkinson, John 40, 41
Parnis, Mount 81
Parrot 133
Pawpaw See *Asimina triloba*
Paxton, Sir Joseph 47
Peaches See *Prunus persica*
Pear, Common See *Pyrus communis*
Ussurian See *Pyrus ussuriensis*
Willow-leaf See *Pyrus salicifolia*
Pears See *PYRUS*
Peawood See *Halesia monticola*
Pecan See *Carya illinoensis*
Peking 49
Pennsylvania 56
Pepper tree See *Schinus molle*
Perny, Father Paul 48
Perry, Commodore 48
Persia 40
Persimmon, Common See *Diospyros virginiana*
Chinese See *Diospyros kaki*
Kaki See *Diospyros kaki*
Persimmons 188–9
Perthshire 43, 46, 92
Peru 44

Pests 320–1
Peter the Great 220
Petre, Lord 43
Philadelphia 42, 69, 75, 244
Phloem 18, 19
Phosphorus 13, 22, 63
Photoperiod 28
Photosynthesis 12–13, 18, 38, 125
Phylogeny 24
Pigmy trees 118–19
Pignut 22
Pignut See *Carya glabra*
Pincushion tree See *Hakea laurina*
Pine, Arolla See *Pinus cembra*
Austrian black See *Pinus nigra nigra*
Bhutan See *Pinus wallichiana*
Bigcone See *Pinus coulteri*
Bishop See *Pinus muricata*
Black See *Podocarpus*
Bosnian See *Pinus leucodermis*
Bristlecone See *Pinus aristata*
Brown See *Podocarpus*
Calabrian/Corsican See *Pinus nigra maritima*
Canary Island See *Pinus canariensis*
Coulter pine See *Pinus coulteri*
Crimean black See *Pinus nigra caramanica*
Digger See *Pinus sabiniana*
Eastern white See *Pinus strobus*
Gerard's See *Pinus gerardiana*
Himalayan white See *Pinus wallichiana*
Japanese black See *Pinus thunbergii*
Japanese red See *Pinus densiflora*
Japanese umbrella See *Sciadopitys*
Japanese white See *Pinus parviflora*
Jeffrey's See *Pinus jeffreyi*
Jelecote See *Pinus patula*
King William See *Athrotaxis selaginoides*
Knob-cone See *Pinus attenuata*
Korean See *Pinus koraiensis*
Lacebark See *Pinus bungeana*
Loblolly See *Pinus taeda*
Lodgepole See *Pinus contorta latifolia*
Longleaf See *Pinus palustris*
Macedonian See *Pinus peuce*
Mexican white See *Pinus ayacahuite*
Monterey See *Pinus radiata*
Montezuma See *Pinus montezumae*
Mountain See *Pinus mugo*
Nepalese See *Pinus wallichiana*
Norfolk Island See *Araucaria excelsa*
Pinaster See *Pinus pinaster*
Piñon See *Pinus cembroides*
Pitch See *Pinus rigida*
Ponderosa See *Pinus ponderosa*
Red See *Pinus resinosa*
Scots See *Pinus sylvestris*
Scrub (Alps) See *Pinus mugo*
Shore See *Pinus contorta*
Shortleaf See *Pinus echinata*
Siberian See *Pinus cembra*
Slash See *Pinus elliottii*
Spreading-leaf See *Pinus patula*
Stone See *Pinus pinea*
Sugar See *Pinus lambertiana*
Tasmanian huon See *Dacrydium franklinii*
Torrey See *Pinus torreyana*
Umbrella See *Pinus pinea*
Western white See *Pinus monticola*
Weymouth See *Pinus strobus*
White See *Pinus strobus*

Whitebark See *Pinus albicaulis*
Pistachio See *Pistacia chinensis, P. vera*
Pittosporum See *Pittosporum tenuifolium*
'Plane' (Sycamore) See *Acer pseudoplatanus*
Plane American See *Platanus occidentalis*
California See *Platanus racemosa*
Eastern See *Platanus orientalis*
London See *Platanus x hispanica*
Oriental See *Platanus orientalis*
Spanish cross See *Platanus x hispanica*
Western See *Platanus occidentalis*
Planting and landscaping 32, 54–9, 91
See also Transplanting
Platanaceae 134–5
Pliocene period See Evolution
Plum, Cherry See *Prunus cerasifera*
Purple-leaved See *Prunus cerasifera* 'Pissardii'
Plums, Plum-trees See *Prunus cerasifera, P. spinosa*
Podocarp, Willow-leaf See *Podocarpus salignus*
Podocarps See *PODOCARPUS*
Pocock, Dr. 91
Poland 80
Pollarding See Hedging techniques
Pollination 14, 39, 89, 109
agencies of 15
selective 33
Poplar, Balsam See *Populus balsamifera*
Black See *Populus nigra*
Chinese See *Populus simonii*
Golden See *Populus serotina* 'Aurea'
Grey See *Populus x canescens*
Lombardy See *Populus nigra* 'Italica'
Richard's See *Populus alba*
Tacamahac See *Populus balsamifera*
Virginia See *Liriodendron tulipifera*
White See *Populus alba*
Yellow See *Liriodendron tulipifera*
Portugal 33, 194
Potanin, Grigori, Nicolaevitch 49
Pride of India See *Koelreuteria paniculata*
Privet, Glossy See *Ligustrum lucidum*
Proteaceae 215
Pruning 63
Pyrenees 38, 86

Q

Quebec 78
Quick See *Crataegus monogyna*
Quince See *Cydonia oblonga*

R

Rainfall See Climate
Ravello 77
Ray, John 41
Red-bud, Eastern See *Cercis canadensis*
North American See *Cercis canadensis*
Redwood See *Sequoia sempervirens*
Coast/Californian See *Sequoia sempervirens*
Dawn See *Metasequoia glyptostroboides*
Reed, J. L. 180
Rehder, Dr. Alfred 41
Reproduction 14–15, 86, 99
organs of 14, 15, 16, 24
Repton, Humphrey 43, 50, 54, 56, 57, 61
Resin See Bark

Retinospora moss See *Chamaecyparis pisifera* 'Squarrosa'
Rhus, Chinese See *Rhus verniciflua*
Ribbonwood See *HOHERIA*
Richmond, Duke of 43, 91
Rimu, New Zealand See *Dacrydium cupressinum*
Riss See Ice Ages
Rivers, Thomas 150
Robin, Jean 42
Robinson, William 50–1, 57, 116
Rockefeller Forest 115
Rocky Mountains 83
Roots
'dwarfing' 23
functions of 22
growth of 22, 53
minerals in 13
oxygen intake of 22
suckers from 14
transplanting of 62
Rosaceae 25, 190–207
Rose, Himalayan musk See *Rosa brunonii*
Rosebay See *Rhododendron maximum*
Rothschild, Lionel de 9
Rowan See *Sorbus aucuparia*
Roxburgh, William 45
Royal Horticultural Society 9, 46, 109
Rubber plant 141
Russia 42, 80
Rutaceae 236–7

S

Sahara 30, 38
St. Petersburg 47
-Botanic Garden 49
Salicaceae 25, 176–183
Saling 58–9, 138
Sallow, Grey See *Salix cinerea*
Sallows See *Salix caprea, Salix cinerea*
San Francisco 28
Sap 18, 19
Sargent, Charles Sprague 49, 50, 102
Sassafras See *Sassafras albidum*
Sato Zakura See *Prunus serrulata*
Savill, Sir Eric 50
Savin See *Juniperus sabina*
Scandinavia 76
Schuylkill River 42
Scone 46
Scotland 76, 80, 108
Sea-buckthorn See *Hippophae rhamnoides*
Seattle 28, 29, 75
Seed
for breeding 52
sowing of 32, 50
'stratifying' of 16
Sequoia, Giant See *Sequoiadendron giganteum*
Serviceberry See *AMELANCHIER*
Allegheny See *Amelanchier laevis*
Service tree, Wild See *Sorbus torminalis*
Shadblow See *AMELANCHIER*
Shadbush See *AMELANCHIER*
Shasta, Mount 79
She-oak See *CASUARINA*
Sheepberry See *Viburnum lentago*
Sheffield Park 69
Sherriff, George 48
Siberia 26
Siebold, Philip 48, 49
Sierras, the 26, 79, 115
Sikkim 48
Silk tree See *Albizia julibrissin*
Silverbell, Carolina See *Halesia carolina*
Mountain See *Halesia monticola*
Silverbell tree See *HALESIA*
Simaroubaceae 242–3
Smoke-bush See *COTINUS*
Japanese See *Styrax japonica*

GENERAL INDEX

Snowball tree See *Viburnum opulus* 'Sterile'
Snowbell, Japanese See *Styrax japonica*
  fragrant See *Styrax obassia*
Snowdrop tree See *HALESIA*
Soil
  enrichment of 34, 85
  for transplanting 60–1
  minerals in 23
  pollution of 36–7
  types 22–3
Sorrel tree See *Oxydendrum arboreum*
Soulié, Jean André 48
South Africa 38
South America 38
Southern beeches See *NOTHOFAGUS*
Spain 33, 80
Späth 52
Sprengel, C. C. 15
Spruce, Black See *Picea mariana*
  Blue See *Picea pungens*
  Brewer's See *Picea brewerana*
  Colorado See *Picea pungens*
  Colorado blue See *Picea pungens*
  Dragon See *Picea asperata*
  Engelmann See *Picea engelmannii*
  Himalayan weeping See *Picea smithiana*
  Japanese tiger-tail See *Picea polita*
  Likiang See *Picea likiangensis*
  Norway See *Picea abies*
  Oriental See *Picea orientalis*
  Red See *Picea rubens*
  Sargent See *Picea brachytyla*
  Serbian See *Picea omorika*
  Shrenk's See *Picea schrenkiana*
  Sitka See *Picea sitchensis*
  Weeping See *Picea brewerana*
  White See *Picea glauca*
Spruces See *PICEA*
Stewartia, Japanese See *Stewartia pseudocamellia*
  Korean See *Stewartia koreana*
Stinkhorn 22
Stourhead 312
Strawberry tree See *Arbutus unedo*
Strobili See Reproduction,
  organs of
Stuart, John 3rd Earl of Bute 43
Styracaceae 188 9
Sugarberry See *Celtis occidentalis*
Sulphur 13, 22, 36–7
Sumach, Staghorn See *Rhus typhina*
Sweden 33, 45
Sweetgum See *LIQUIDAMBAR*
Switzerland 33
Sycamore See *Platanus occidentalis*
  American See *Platanus occidentalis*
  Golden See *Acer pseudoplatanus* 'Worleei'
  Purple See *Acer pseudoplatanus* 'Purpureum' or 'Spaethii'
Sycamore-maple See *Acer pseudoplatanus*

T

Tamarack See *Larix laricina*
Tangerine See *Citrus reticulata*
Tangor 237
Tasmania 80
Taurus Mountains 90
Taxaceae 24, 108–10
Taxodiaceae 24, 112–15
Taylor, Sir George 9
Tea-tree See *Camellia sinensis*
'Tebbuland' 49
Tertiary period See *Evolution*
Theaceae 172–3
Theophrastus 24
Thorn, Cockspur See *Crataegus crus-galli*
  English See *Crataegus oxyacantha*
  Glossy-leaved See *Crataegus nitida*
  Washington See *Crataegus phaenopyrum*
Thuja, Chinese See *Thuja orientalis*
  Japanese See *Thuja standishii*
Thunberg, Carl Peter 45, 49
Tibet 48
Tiliaceae 174–5
Tilleuls See *TILIA*
Timber 67, 112, 116, 169
Time magazine 9
Tokyo 64, 198
Toon See *Cedrela sinensis*
Topographical Engineers, U.S. Corps of 104

Traczewitz, Oscar 9
Tradescant, John 42
Transplanting 60–1, 96
Tree of heaven See *Ailanthus altissima*
Tree of life See *Thuja occidentalis*
Treseder 52
Trianon, the 45
Trompenburg Arboretum 9, 103
Trunk See Wood, structure of
Truro 52
Tulip tree See *LIRIODENDRON*
Tung tree See *Aleurites fordii*
Tunnel houses 52
Tupelo See *Nyssa sylvatica*
Turkey 41, 90, 163
Turner, William 41
Twigs 11, 12, 13, 18

U

Ulmaceae 136–141
United Kingdom, forests of 33
Uppsala 45
Utrecht 69

V

Valentine tree See *Cercidiphyllum japonicum*
Vanburgh 41
Vancouver 47, 78, 83, 100
Vancouver, Captain 46
Varnish tree See *Rhus verniciflua*
Vaux-le-Vicomte 41, 57
Veitch, John Gould 44, 49, 52, 93
Verjus 195
Versailles 45, 57
Vignola 40
Villa Lante 40
Vilmorin, Maurice de 50, 52
Virginia 42

W

Wafer-ash See *Ptelea trifoliata*
Wales, Frederick Prince of 43
  Princess of 43
Wallich, Nathaniel 48
Walnut, American See *Juglans nigra*
  Black See *Juglans nigra*
  Circassian See *Juglans regia*
  English See *Juglans regia*
  Persian See *Juglans regia*
Walnuts See *JUGLANS*
Ward, Frank Kingdon 48
Washington D.C. 28, 29, 75, 78, 82, 102

'Washingtonia' See *Sequoiadendron giganteum*
Water-larch See *Metasequoia glyptostroboides*
Wattle, Cootamundra See *Acacia baileyana*
  Silver See *Acacia dealbata*
  Sydney See *Acacia longifolia*
Wayfaring tree See *Viburnum lantana*
Wellingtonia, Weeping See *Sequoiadendron giganteum, S. g.* 'Pendulum'
Weymouth, Lord 43
White Mountains 21
Whitebeam, Japanese See *Sorbus alnifolia*
  Swedish See *Sorbus intermedia*
Whitebeams See *SORBUS*
Wildlife
  birds 16–17, 155, 193, 321
  forest 34–5
  mammals 34, 183
Willow, Almond-leafed See *Salix triandra*
  Bat See *Salix x caerulea*
  Bay See *Salix pentandra*
  Corkscrew See *Salix matsudana* 'Tortuosa'
  Coyote See *Salix exigua*
  Crack See *Salix fragilis*
  European pussy See *Salix caprea*
  Goat See *Salix caprea*
  Golden-stemmed See *Salix alba* 'Vitellina'
  Peach-leafed See *Salix amygdaloides*
  Purple See *Salix daphnoides*
  Pussy See *Salix discolor, Salix caprea*
  Scarlet See *Salix alba* 'Chermesina'
  Silver See *Salix alba* 'Sericea'
  Thurlow weeping See *Salix x elegantissima*
  Weeping See *Salix x chrysocoma*
  White See *Salix alba*
  Wisconsin weeping See *Salix x blanda*
  Woolly See *Salix lanata*
Wilson, E. H. 22, 49, 50, 81, 128, 197
  discoveries in China 219
  on the wax insect 241
Wilton House 90
Winchester 52

Windsor Great Park 50
Wingnut See *PTEROCARYA*
  Ash-leaved See *Pterocarya fraxinifolia*
  Caucasian See *Pterocarya fraxinifolia*
  Chinese See *Pterocarya stenoptera*
Wintergreen 23
Witch Hazel See *HAMAMELIS*
  Chinese See *Hamamelis mollis*
Woburn Abbey 178
Wood
  dating of 21
  structure of 18–19
  uses for 67, 102, 144–5, 183, 237
Wood meadow-grass 22
Woodsorrel 22
Wright, Frank Lloyd 56
Würm See Ice Ages
Wyman, Donald 50, 75

Y

Yellow-wood See *Cladrastis lutea, Podocarpus latifolius*
  American See *Cladrastis lutea*
  Chinese See *Maackia sinensis*
Yew See *TAXUS*
  Chile See *Podocarpus andinus*
  Chinese plum See *Cephalotaxus fortunei*
  Common See *Taxus baccata*
  English See *Taxus baccata*
  European See *Taxus baccata*
  Golden upright See *Taxus baccata* 'Fastigiata Aurea'
  Irish See *Taxus baccata* 'Fastigiata'
  Japanese See *Taxus cuspidata*
  Japanese plum See *Cephalotaxus harringtonia drupacea*
  Plum-fruited See *Podocarpus andinus*
  Prince Albert's See *Saxegothaea conspicua*
Yin-Kuo See *Ginkgo biloba*
Yugoslavia 76, 86
Yulan, Chinese See *Magnolia denudata*

Z

Zelkova, Caucasian See *Zelkova carpinifolia*
  Japan See *Zelkova serrata*
Zimmermann and Brown 18

Acknowledgments

The publishers wish to extend their thanks to the following artists, photographers and studios:

Photographers
A–Z Botanical Collections Ltd. Abbott/Rapho-Guillumette. Christer Ågren. Malcolm Aird. Bernard Alfieri. Allen/NHPA. Michael Andrews. Heather Angel. Johannes Apel. The Arnold Arboretum. N. Asche/Institut für Bodenkunde und Waldernährung der Universität Göttingen. The Ashmolean Museum. Auvin/Top. Barnaby's Picture Library. Kenneth A. Beckett. Bennett/Colorific. The Bettmann Archive. Christian Bonington. Michael Boys. Stanley Breeden. Pat Brindley. F. Brockman. Brosselin/Jacana. John E. Bryan, Strybing Arboretum. Jock Brydon/Strybing Arboretum Society. René Burri/Magnum. Burton/Bruce Coleman Ltd. Camera Press Ltd. Coleman/Bruce Coleman Ltd. Robert J. Corbin. Crown Copyright Her Majesty's Stationery Office and the Royal Botanic Gardens, Kew. Dalton/NHPA. W. F. Davidson. Anthony Denney. Douglas Dickins. Patrick Eagar/

Report. Edouard/Explorer. Robert Estall. Mary Evans Picture Library. Fenaux/Jacana. Graham Finlayson. Fletcher/Natural Science Photos. Foord/NHPA. The Forestry Commission. Fox-Davies/Bruce Coleman Ltd. R. Freeman & Co. Ltd. Hatton Gardner. Georg Gerster/John Hillelson Agency. W. A. T. Gilmour. Burt Glinn/Magnum. Greenhill/Transworld. George Haling. Sonia Halliday. Robert Harding Associates. George H. Harrison/Grant Heilman. Erich Hartmann/Magnum. John Hedgecoe. Hedrich-Blessing. Henri/Jacana. F. Hepper. J. R. P. van Hoey Smith. The Hunt Botanical Library. David Hurn/Magnum. Anthony Huxley. Hyde/NHPA. Japan Society of London Library. P. Roland Johanson. Hugh Johnson. Kasterine/Daily Telegraph Colour Library. Kinne/Bruce Coleman Ltd. Kraulis/Canada Wide. Gerd Krüssmann. Kuusik/Colorific. Roy Lancaster. Lanceau/Jacana. Harold Langford. Erich Leach. Lecourt/Jacana. Leutscher/National Science Photos. The Linnaean Society. William MacQuitty. The Mansell Collection. Fosco Maraini. John Marmaras. André Martin.

Matthews/National Science Photos. Pat Matthews. Elsa Megson. Paul Miles. Alan Mitchell/NHPA. Inge Morath/Magnum. M. Morcombe. Jean Mounicq/Fotogram. Margaret Mulligan. Myers/Bruce Coleman Ltd. Nardin/Jacana. The National Gallery of Scotland. The Natural History Museum. Natural Science Photos. The National Trust. Naturfotograferna. N.Z. Forest Service. Paf. Peters/Transworld. Photo Researchers. Pictor. Picturepoint. Plessey/Explorer. President and Fellows of Trinity College, Oxford. M. C. F. Proctor. Radio Times Hulton Picture Library. Reichel/Top. Simon Relph. Ricard/Top. John Richardson/John Hillelson Agency. Roger-Viollet. James P. Rowan/Click/Chicago. The Royal Horticultural Society. Ruffier-Lanche/Jacana. Savonius/NHPA. Schmitz/Bruce Coleman Ltd. Schneiders/Bruce Coleman Ltd. SchwarzWeissVerlag Köln. Roger Settimo. Simon/Bruce Coleman Ltd. Marcel Sire. Edwin Smith. Harry Smith. Sommer/Explorer. Spectrum Colour Library. Ted Spiegel/John Hillelson Agency. John Massey Stewart. Tony Stone Associates Ltd. Svenska Porträttarkivet. Teurtroy/Jacana. G. S. Thomas. Patrick

Thurston. Topham Picture Library. Ann Usborne. U.S. National Park Service. Vala/Jacana. The Victoria & Albert Museum. Christopher Walker. Michael Warren. H. J. Welch. Gerald Wilkinson. David Williamson. Myron Wood/Photo Researchers. Dennis Woodland. Adam Woolfitt.

Artists
Arka Graphics. Ken Astrop. S. R. Badmin. Olivia Beasley. Stephen Bishop. Broadway Arts. Jim Bulman. John Collings. Roy Coombes. Terry Dalley. John Davis. John Michael Davis. Barry Evans. Sherine Fairclough. Freelance Presentations. Ian Garrard. Gilchrist Studios. Vana Haggerty. Garry Hincks. Allan Hood. Tony Jenkins. Tony Joyce. Patrick Leeson. Linden Artists. Annabel Milne and Peter Stebbing. Ben Minichip. David Moore. Brian Morris. Tilley Northage. Richard Orr. Elizabeth Rankin. Charles Raymond. Harry Sida. Gwen Simpson. Joyce Tuhill. Eddie Wade. David Watson. John Wilson. Julia Wright. Paul Wrigley.